6/04

COLONIALISM

An International Social, Cultural,
and Political Encyclopedia

EDITORIAL BOARD

COLONIALISM

An International Social, Cultural,
and Political Encyclopedia

VOLUME THREE: DOCUMENTS

Melvin E. Page
General Editor

Penny M. Sonnenburg
Assistant Editor

A B C ☰ C L I O

Santa Barbara, California   Denver, Colorado   Oxford, England

Library of Congress Cataloging-in-Publication Data
Colonialism : an international social, cultural, and political
encyclopedia / Melvin E. Page, Penny M. Sonnenburg.
    p. cm.
  Includes index.
  ISBN 1-57607-335-1 (hardcover : alk. paper) ISBN 1-57607-762-4 (e-book)
  1. Colonies—History—Encyclopedias. 2. Imperialism—History—Encyclopedias.
3. Colonies—History—Sources. 4. Imperialism—History—Sources. I. Page, Melvin E.
(Melvin Eugene), 1944– II. Sonnenburg, Penny M.

HV22.C59 2003
325'.3'03—dc21

                                                        2003014643
07 06 05 04 03   10 9 8 7 6 5 4 3 2 1

This book is also available on the World Wide Web as an eBook. Visit abc-clio.com for details.

ABC-CLIO, Inc.
130 Cremona Drive, P.O. Box 1911
Santa Barbara, California 93116–1911
This book is printed on acid-free paper.

Manufactured in the United States of America

CONTENTS

Colonialism: An International Social, Cultural, and Political Encyclopedia

VOLUME ONE

VOLUME TWO

x   **Contents**

VOLUME THREE: DOCUMENTS

MAPS

AUSTRO-HUNGARIAN EMPIRE

Declaration Relative to the Separation of Hungary from Austria (Hungarian Declaration of Independence) (April 1849)

As revolutions against conservative regimes broke out across the face of Europe, rebellions against Austro-Hungarian imperial rule convulsed Budapest, capital of Hungary. In March 1848, the Hungarian national parliament passed laws virtually making the country independent of the imperial capital of Vienna. By the autumn, however, Austrian troops had defeated the Hungarian rebels in Budapest, forcing them to the provincial town of Debrecen. There, inspired by the words of the Hungarian nationalist leader Louis Kossuth, the exiled assembly passed this declaration of separation from Austria, a kind of Hungarian declaration of independence. However, with the help of Russian troops, Austrian troops had crushed all signs of the rebellion.

WE, the legally constituted representatives of the Hungarian nation, assembled in Diet, do by these presents solemnly proclaim, in maintenance of the inalienable natural rights of Hungary, with all its dependencies, to occupy the position of an independent European State—that the house of Hapsburg-Lorraine, as perjured in the sight of God and man, has forfeited its right to the Hungarian throne. At the same time we feel ourselves bound in duty to make known the motives and reasons which have impelled us to this decision, that the civilized world may learn we have taken this step not out of overweening confidence in our own wisdom, or out of revolutionary excitement, but that it is an act of the last necessity, adopted to preserve from utter destruction a nation persecuted to the limit of the most enduring patience.

Three hundred years have passed since the Hungarian nation, by free election, placed the house of Austria upon its throne, in accordance with stipulations made on both sides, and ratified by treaty. These three hundred years have been, for the country, a period of uninterrupted suffering.

The Creator has blessed this country with all the elements of wealth and happiness. Its area of 100,000 square miles presents in varied profusion innumerable sources of prosperity. Its population, numbering nearly fifteen millions, feels the glow of youthful strength within its veins, and has shown temper and docility which warrant its proving at once the main organ of civilization in eastern Europe, and the guardian of that civilization when attacked. Never was a more grateful task appointed to a reigning dynasty by the dispensation of Providence, than that which devolved upon the house of Hapsburg-Lorraine. It would have sufficed to do nothing that could impede the development of the country. Had this been the rule observed Hungary would now rank among the most prosperous nations. It was only necessary that it should not envy the Hungarians the moderate share of constitution liberty which they timidly maintained during the difficulties of a thousand years with rare fidelity to their sovereigns, and the house of Hapsburg might long have counted this nation among the most faithful adherents of the throne.

This dynasty, however, which can at no epoch point to a ruler who based his power on the freedom of the people, adopted a course toward this nation from father to son, which deserves the appellation of perjury.

The house of Austria has publicly used every effort to deprive the country of its legitimate independence and constitution, designing to reduce it to a level with the other provinces long since deprived of all freedom, and to unite all in a common link of slavery. Foiled in this effort by the untiring vigilance of the people, it directed its endeavor to lame the power, to check the progress of Hungary, causing it to minister to the gain of the provinces of Austria, but only to the extent which enabled those provinces to bear the load of taxation with which the prodigality of the imperial house weighed them down; having first deprived those provinces of all constitutional means of remonstrating against a policy which was not based upon the welfare of the subject, but solely tended to maintain despotism and crush liberty in every country of Europe.

It has frequently happened that the Hungarian nation, in spite of this systemized [*sic*] tyranny, has been obliged to take up arms in self-defense. Although constantly victorious in these constitutional struggles, yet so moderate has the nation ever been in its use of the victory, so strongly has it confided in the plighted word of the king, that it has ever laid down arms as soon as the king by new compact and fresh oaths has guaranteed the duration of its rights and liberty. But every new compact was as futile as those which preceded. Each oath which fell from the royal lips was but a renewal of previous perjuries. The policy of the house of Austria, which aimed at destroying the independence of Hungary as a state, has been pursued without alteration for three hundred years.

It was in vain that the Hungarian nation shed its blood for the deliverance of Austria whenever it was in danger; in vain were all the sacrifices which it made to serve the interests of the reigning house; in vain did it, on the renewal of the royal promises, forget the wounds which the past had inflicted; vain was the fidelity cherished by the Hungarians for their king, and which, in moments of danger, assumed a character of devotion;—they were in vain, because the history of the government of that dynasty in Hungary presents but an unbroken series of perjured acts from generation to generation.

In spite of such treatment, the Hungarian nation has all along respected the tie by which it was united to this dynasty; and in now decreeing its expulsion from the throne, it acts under the natural law of self-preservation, being driven to pronounce this sentence by the full conviction that the house of Hapsburg-Lorraine is compassing the destruction of Hungary as an independent state; so that this dynasty has been the first to tear the bands by which it was united to the Hungarian nation, and to confess that it had torn them in the face of Europe. For many causes a nation is justified, before God and man, in expelling a reigning dynasty. Among such are the following:

When it forms alliances with the enemies of the country, with robbers, or partisan chieftains, to oppress the nation; when it attempts to annihilate the independence of the country and its constitution, solemnly sanctioned by oaths, attacking with an armed force the people who have committed no act of revolt; when the integrity of a country, which the sovereign has sworn to maintain, is violated, and its power diminished; when foreign armies are employed to murder the people, and to oppress their liberties.

Each of the grounds here enumerated would justify the exclusion of a dynasty from the throne. But the House of Lorraine-Hapsburg is unexampled in the compass of its perjuries, and has committed every one of these crimes against the nation; and its determination to extinguish the independence of Hungary has been accompanied with a succession of criminal acts, comprising robbery, destruction of property by fire, murder, maiming, and personal ill-treatment of all kinds, besides setting the laws of the country at defiance, so that humanity will shudder when reading this disgraceful page of history.

The main impulse to this recent unjustifiable course was the passing of the laws adopted in the spring of 1848, for the better protection of the constitution of the country. These laws provided reforms in the internal government of the country, by which the commutation of servile services and of the tithe were decreed; a fair representation guaranteed to the people in the Diet, the constitution of which was, before that, exclusively aristocratical; equality before the law proclaimed; the privilege of exemption from taxation abolished; freedom of the press pronounced; and, to stem the torrent of abuses, trial by jury established, with other improvements. Notwithstanding that troubles broke out in every province of the Austrian empire, as a consequence of the French February Revolution, and the reigning dynasty was left without support, the Hungarian nation was too generous at such a moment to demand more privileges, and contented itself with enforcing the administration of its old rights upon a system of ministerial responsibility, and with maintaining them and the independence of the country against the often renewed and perjured attempts of the crown. These rights, and the independence sought to be maintained, were, however, no new acquisition, but were what the king, by his oath, and according to law, was bound to keep up, and which had not in the slightest degree been affected by the relation in which Hungary stood to the provinces of the empire.

In point of fact, Hungary and Transylvania, with all their possessions and dependencies, never were incorporated into the Austrian empire, but formed a separate, independent kingdom, even after the adoption of the pragmatic sanction by which the same law of succession was adopted for Hungary which obtained in the other countries and provinces.

The clearest proof of this legal fact is furnished by the law incorporated into the act of the pragmatic sanction, and which stipulates that the territory of Hungary and its dependencies, as well as its independence, self-government, constitution, and privileges, shall remain inviolate and specially guaranteed.

Another proof is contained in the stipulation of the pragmatic sanction, according to which the heir of the crown only becomes legally king of Hungary upon the conclusion of a coronation treaty with the nation, and upon his swearing to maintain the constitution and the laws of the country, whereupon he is to be crowned with the crown of St. Stephen. The act signed at the coronation contains the stipulation that all laws, privileges, and the entire constitution, shall be observed, together with the order of succession. Only one sovereign since the adoption of the pragmatic sanction refused to enter into the coronation compact, and swear to the constitution. This was Joseph II, who died without being crowned, but for that reason his name is not recorded among the kings of Hungary, and all his acts are considered illegal, null and void. His successor, Leopold II., was obliged, before ascending the Hungarian throne, to enter into the coronation compact, to take the oath, and to let himself be crowned. On this occasion it was distinctly declared in Art. IC, 1790, sanctioned upon oath by the king, that Hungary was a free and independent country with regard to its government, and not subordinate to any other state or people whatever, consequently that it was to be governed by its own customs and laws.

The same oath was taken by Francis I., who came to the throne in the year 1792. On the extinction of the imperial dignity in Germany, and the foundation of the Austrian empire, this emperor, who allowed himself to violate the law in innumerable instances, had still sufficient respect for his oath, publicly to avow that Hungary formed no portion of the Austrian empire. For this reason Hungary was separated from the rest of the Austrian states by a chain of custom guards along the whole frontier, which still continues.

The same oath was taken on his accession to the throne by Ferdinand V., who, at the Diet held at Pressburg last year, of his own free-will, sanctioned the laws that were passed, but who, soon after, breaking that oath, entered into a conspiracy with the other members of his family with the intent of erasing Hungary from the list of independent nations.

Still the Hungarian nation preserved with useless piety its loyalty to its perjured sovereign, and during March last year, while the empire was on the brink of destruction, while its armies in Italy suffered one defeat after another, and he in his imperial palace had to fear at any moment that he, might be driven from it; Hungary did not take advantage of so favorable a moment to make increased demands; it only asked that its constitution might be guaranteed, and abuses rectified—a constitution, to maintain which fourteen kings of the Austrian dynasty had sworn a solemn oath, which every one of them had broken.

When the king undertook to guarantee those ancient rights, and gave his sanction to the establishment of a responsible ministry, the Hungarian nation flew enthusiastically to his support, and rallied its might around his tottering throne. At that eventful crisis, as at so many others, the house of Austria was saved by the fidelity of the Hungarians.

Scarcely, however, had this oath fallen from his lips when he conspired anew with his family, the accomplices of his crime, to compass the destruction of the Hungarian nation. This conspiracy did not take place on the ground that any new privileges were conceded by the recent laws which diminished the royal authority. From what has been said, it is clear that no such demands were made. The conspiracy was founded to get rid of the responsible ministry, which made it impossible for the Vienna cabinet to treat the Hungarian constitution any longer as a nullity.

In former times a governing council, under the name of the Royal Hungarian Stadtholdership, (Consilium Locumtenentiale Hungaricum,) the president of which was the Palatine, held its seat at Buda, whose sacred duty it was to watch over the integrity of the state, the inviolability of the constitution, and the sanctity of the laws; but this collegiate authority not presenting any element of personal responsibility, the Vienna cabinet gradually degraded this council to the position of an administrative organ of court absolutism. In this manner, while Hungary had ostensibly an independent government, the despotic Vienna cabinet disposed at will of the money and blood of the people for foreign purposes, postponing its trading interests to the success of courtly cabals, injurious to the welfare of the people, so that we were excluded from all connection with the other countries of the world, and were degraded to the position of a colony. The mode of governing by a ministry was intended to put a stop to these proceedings, which caused the rights of the country to molder uselessly in its parchments; by the change, these rights and the royal oath were both to become a reality. It was the apprehension of this, and especially the fear of losing its control over the money and blood of the country, which caused the house of Austria to determine to involve Hungary, by the foulest intrigues, in the horrors of fire and slaughter, that, having plunged the country in a civil war, it might seize the opportunity to dismember the lands, and blot out the name of Hungary from the list of independent nations, and unite its plundered and bleeding limbs with the Austrian monarchy.

The beginning of this course was by issuing orders during the existence of the ministry, directing an Austrian general to rise in rebellion against the laws of the country, and by nominating the same general Ban of Croatia, a kingdom belonging to the kingdom of Hungary. Croatia and Slavonia were chosen as the seat of military operations in this rebellion, because the military organization of a portion of these countries promised to present the greatest number of disposable troops; it was also thought, that since a portion of those countries had for centuries been excluded from the enjoyment of constitutional rights, and subjected to a military organization in the name of the emperor, they would easily be induced to rise at his bidding.

Croatia and Slavonia were chosen to begin this rebellion, because, in those countries, the inhuman policy of Prince Metternich had, with a view to the weakening of all parties, for years cherished hatred against the Hungarian nation. By exciting, in every possible manner, the most unfounded national jealousies, and by employing the most disgraceful means, he had succeeded in inflaming a party with rage, although the Hungarians, far from desiring to oppress the Croatians, allowed the most unrestrained development to the provincial institutions of Croatia, and shared with their Croatian and Slavonian brethren their political rights; even going the length of sacrificing some of their own rights, by acknowledging special privileges and immunities in those dependencies.

The ban revolted, therefore, in the name of the emperor. and rebelled, openly, against the king of Hungary, who is, however, one and the same person; and he went so far as to decree the separation of Croatia and Slavonia from Hungary, with which they had been united for eight hundred years, as well as to incorporate them with the Austrian empire. Public opinion, and undoubted facts threw the blame of these proceedings on the Archduke Louis, uncle to the emperor; on his brother, the Archduke Francis Charles, and especially on the consort of the last-named prince, the Archduchess Sophia; and, since the ban, in this act of rebellion, openly alleged [sic] that he acted as a faithful subject of the emperor, the ministry of Hungary requested their sovereign, by a public declaration, to wipe off the stigma which these proceedings threw upon the family. At that moment affairs were not prosperous for Austria in Italy; the emperor, therefore, did proclaim that the ban and his associates were guilty of high treason, and of exciting to rebellion. But, at the same time that this edict was published, the ban and his accomplices were covered with favors at court, and supplied, for their enterprise, with money, arms, and ammunition. The Hungarians, confiding in the royal proclamation, and not wishing to provoke a civil conflict, did not hunt out those proscribed traitors in their lair, and only adopted measures for checking any extension of the rebellion. But soon afterward, the inhabitants of South Hungary, of Servian race, were excited to rebellion by precisely the same means.

These were also declared, by the king, to be rebels, but were, nevertheless, like the others, supplied with money, arms, and ammunition. The king's commissioned officers and civil servants enlisted bands of robbers, in the principality of Serbia, to strengthen the rebels, and aid them in massacring the peaceable Hungarian and German inhabitants of the Banat. The command of these rebellious bodies was farther entrusted to the rebel leaders of the Croatians. During this rebellion of the Hungarian Serbians, scenes of cruelty were witnessed at which the heart shudders. Whole towns and villages, once flourishing, were laid waste; Hungarians, fleeing before these murderers, were reduced to the condition of vagrants and beggars in their own country; the most lovely districts were converted into a wilderness.

Thus were the Hungarians driven to self-defense; but the Austrian cabinet had dispatched, some time previously, the bravest portion of the national troops to Italy, to oppress the kingdoms of Lombardy and Venice; notwithstanding that our country was, at home, bleeding from a thousand wounds, still she had allowed them to leave for the defense of Austria. The greater part of the Hungarian regiments were, according to the old system of government, scattered through the other provinces of the empire. In Hungary itself the troops quartered were mostly Austrian, and they afforded more protection to the rebels than to the laws, or to the internal peace of the country.

The withdrawal of these troops, and the return of the national militia was demanded of the government, but was either refused or its fulfillment delayed; and when our brave comrades, on hearing the distress of the country, returned in masses, they were persecuted, and such as were obliged to

yield to superior force were disarmed and sentenced to death, for having defended their country against rebels.

The Hungarian ministry begged the king earnestly to issue orders to all troops and commanders of fortresses in Hungary, enjoining fidelity to the constitution, and obedience to the ministers of Hungary. Such a proclamation was sent to the Palatine, the Viceroy of Hungary, Archduke Stephen, at Buda. The necessary letters were written and sent to the post-office. But this nephew of the king, the Archduke Palatine, shamelessly caused the letters to be smuggled back from the post-office, although they had been countersigned by the responsible ministers, and they were afterward found among his papers, when he treacherously departed from the country.

The rebel band menaced the Hungarian coast with an attack, and the government, with the king's consent, ordered an armed corps to march through Styria for the defense of Fiume; but this whole force received orders to march into Italy. Yet such glaring treachery was not disavowed by the Vienna cabinet.

The rebel force occupied Fiume, and disunited it from the kingdom of Hungary, and this irruption was disavowed by the Vienna cabinet, as having been a misunderstanding. The furnishing of arms, ammunition, and money to the rebels of Croatia was also declared to have been a misunderstanding. Instructions were issued to the effect that, unless special orders were given, the army and commanders of fortresses were not to follow the orders of the Hungarian ministers, but were to execute the orders of the Austrian cabinet.

Finally, to reap the fruit of so much perfidy, the Emperor Francis Joseph dared to call himself King of Hungary in the manifesto of 9th March, wherein he openly declares that he erases the Hungarian nation from the list of the independent nations of Europe, and that he divided its territory into five parts, dividing Transylvania, Croatia, Slavonia, and Fiume from Hungary, creating at the same time a principality for the Serbian rebels (the Voivodina,) and having paralyzed the political existence of the country, declared it incorporated into the Austrian monarchy.

Never was so disgraceful a line of policy followed toward a nation. Hungary, unprepared with money, arms and troops, and not expecting to be called on to make resistance, was entangled in a net of treachery, and was obliged to defend itself against the threatened annihilation with the aid of volunteers, national guards, and an undisciplined unarmed levy, "en masse," aided by the few regular troops which remained in the country. In open battles the Hungarians have, however, been successful, but they could not rapidly enough put down the Serbian rebels, and those of the military frontier, who were led by officers devoted to Austria, and were enabled to take refuge behind entrenched positions.

It was necessary to provide a new armed force. The king, still pretending to yield to the undeniably lawful demands of the nation, had summoned a new Diet for the 2d of July, 1848, and had called upon the representatives of the nation to provide soldiers and money for the suppression of the Serbian and Croatian rebellion, and the re-establishment of public peace. He at the same time issued a solemn proclamation in his own name, and in that of his family, condemning and denouncing the Croatian, and Serbian rebellion. The necessary steps were taken by the Diet. A levy of 200,000 men, and a subsidy of 40,000,000 of florins were voted as the necessary force, and the bills were laid before the king for the royal sanction. At the same moment the Hungarians gave an unexampled proof of their loyalty, by inviting the king, who had fled to Innsbruck, to go to Pest, and by his presence tranquilize the people, trusting to the loyalty of the Hungarians, who had shown themselves at all times the best supports of the throne.

This request was proffered in vain, for Radetzky had in the mean time been victorious in Italy. The house of Hapsburg-Lorraine, restored to confidence by that victory, thought the time come to take off the mask and to involve Hungary, still bleeding from previous wounds, in the horrors of a flesh war of oppression. The king from that moment began to address the man whom he himself had branded as a rebel, as dear and loyal, he praised him for having revolted, and encouraged him to proceed in the path he had entered upon.

He expressed a like sympathy for the Serbian rebels, whose hands yet reeked from the massacres they had perpetrated. It was under this command that the ban of Croatia, after being proclaimed as a rebel, assembled an army, and announced his commission from the king to carry fire and sword into Hungary, upon which the Austrian troops stationed in the country united with him. The commanders of the fortresses, Temeswar Esseg and Karlsburg, and the commanders of the forces in the Banat and in Transylvania, breaking their oaths taken to the country, treacherously surrendered their trusts; a Slovak clergyman, with the commission of colonel, who had fraternized at Vienna with the revolted Czechs, broke into Hungary, and the rebel Croat leader advanced with confidence, through an unprepared country, to occupy its capital, expecting that the army in Hungary would not oppose him.

Even the Diet did not give up all confidence in the power of the royal oath, and the king was once more requested to order the rebels to quit the country. The answer given was a reference to a manifesto of the Austrian ministry, declaring it to be their determination to deprive the Hungarian nation of the independent management of their financial, commercial and war affairs. The king at the same time refused his as sent to the laws submitted for approval respecting the troops and the subsidy for covering the expenditure.

Upon this the Hungarian ministers resigned, but the names submitted by the president of the council, at the demand of the king, were not approved of for successors. The Diet then, bound by its duty to secure the interests of the country, voted the supplies, and ordered the troops to be levied. The nation obeyed the summons with readiness.

The representatives of the people then summoned the nephew of the emperor to join the camp, and as palatine, to lead the troops against the rebels. He not only obeyed the summons, but made public professions of his devotion to the cause. As soon, however, as an engagement threatened, he fled secretly from the camp and the country, like a coward traitor. Among his papers a plan formed by him some time previously was found, according to which Hungary was to be simultaneously attacked on nine sides at once from Austria, Moravia, Silesia, Gallicia, Transylvania and Styria. From a correspondence with the minister of war, seized at the same time, it was discovered that the commanding generals in the military frontier and the Austrian provinces adjoining Hungary, had received orders to enter Hungary and support the rebels with their united forces.

The attack from nine points at once really began. The most painful aggression took place in Transylvania, for the traitorous commander in that district did not content himself with the practices considered lawful in war by disciplined troops. He stirred up the Wallachian peasants to take up arms against their own constitutional rights, and, aided by the rebellious Serbian hordes, commenced a course of Vandalism and extraction, sparing neither women, children, nor aged men; murdering and torturing the defenseless Hungarian inhabitants; burning the most flourishing villages and towns, among which Nagy-Enyed, the seat of learning for Transylvania, was reduced to a heap of ruins.

But the Hungarian nation, although taken by surprise, unarmed and unprepared, did not abandon its future prospects in any agony of despair.

Measures were immediately taken to increase the small standing army by volunteers and the levy of the people. These troops, supplying the want of experience by the enthusiasm arising from the feeling that they had right on their side, defeated the Croatian armies and drove them out of the country.

The defeated army fled toward Vienna.

One of their leaders appealed, after an unsuccessful flight, to the generosity of the Hungarians for a truce, which he used to escape by night and surreptitiously, with his beaten troops; the other corps, of more than ten thousand men, was surrounded and taken prisoners, from the general to the last private.

The defeated army fled in the direction of Vienna, where the emperor continued his demoralizing policy, and nominated the beaten and flying rebel as his plenipotentiary and substitute in Hungary, suspending by this act the constitution and institutions of the country, all its authorities, courts of justice and tribunals, laying the kingdom under martial law, and placing in the hand and under the unlimited authority of a rebel, the honor, the property, and the lives of the people in the hand of a man who, with armed bands, had braved the laws, and attacked the constitution of the country.

But the house of Austria was not contented with this unjustifiable violation of oaths taken by its head.

The rebellious ban was placed under the protection of the troops stationed near Vienna, and commanded by Prince Windischgratz. These troops, after taking Vienna by storm, were led as an Imperial Austrian army to conquer Hungary. But the Hungarian nation, persisting in its loyalty, sent an envoy to the advancing enemy. This envoy, coming under a flag of truce, was treated as a prisoner and thrown into prison. No heed was paid to the remonstrances and the demands of the Hungarian nation for justice. The threat of the gallows was, on the contrary, thundered against all who had taken arms in defense of a wretched and oppressed country. But before the army had time to enter Hungary, a family revolution in the tyrannical reigning house was perpetrated at Olmutz. Ferdinand V was forced to resign a throne which had been polluted with so much blood and perjury, and the son of Francis Charles, who also abdicated his claim to the inheritance, the youthful Archduke Francis Joseph, caused himself to be proclaimed Emperor of Austria and King of Hungary. But no one but the Hungarian nation can, by compacts, dispose of the constitutional throne of Hungary.

At this critical moment the Hungarian nation demanded nothing more than the maintenance of its laws and institutions, and peace guaranteed by their integrity. Had the assent of the nation to this change in the occupant of the throne been asked in a legal manner, and the young Prince offered to take the customary oath that he would preserve the Constitution, the Hungarian nation would not have refused to elect him King, in accordance with the treaties extant, and to crown him with St. Stephen's crown before he had dipped his hand in the blood of his people.

He, however, refusing to perform an act so sacred in the eyes of God and man, and in strange contrast to innocence natural to youthful breasts, declared in his first words, his intention of conquering Hungary, which he dared to call a rebellious country, although he himself had raised rebellion there, and of depriving it of that independence which it had maintained for a thousand years, to incorporate it into the Austrian monarchy.

And he has but too well labored to keep his word. He ordered the army under Windischgratz to enter Hungary, and at the same time, directed several corps of troops to attack this country from Gallicia and Styria. Hungary resisted the projected invasion, but being unable to make head against so many armies at once, on account of the devastation carried on in several parts of the interior by the excited rebels, and being thus prevented from displaying its whole power of defense, the troops were at first obliged to retire. To save the capital from the horrors of a storm like that to which Prague and Vienna had mercilessly been exposed, and not to stake the fortunes of a nation—which deserved a better fate—on the chances of a pitched battle, for which there had not been sufficient preparation, the capital was abandoned, and the Parliament and national government removed, in January last, to Debreczin, trusting to the help of a just God, and to the energies of the nation, to prevent the cause from being lost, even when it should be seen that the capital was given up. Thanks be to Heaven, the cause was not lost!

But even then an attempt was made to bring about a peaceful arrangement, and a deputation was sent to the generals of the perjured dynasty. That dynasty, in its blind self-confidence, refused to enter into any negotiation, and dared to demand an unconditional submission from the nation. The deputation was detained, and one of the number, the former president of the ministry, was thrown into prison. The deserted capital was occupied, and turned into a place of execution; a part of the prisoners of war were there consigned to the scaffold, another part were thrown into dungeons, while the remainder were forced to enter the ranks of the army in Italy.

The measure of the crimes of the Austrian house was, however, filled up, when—after its defeat—it applied for help to the Emperor of Russia; and, in spite of the remonstrances and protestations of the [Ottoman] porte, and of the consuls of the European powers at Bucharest, in defiance of international rights, and with signal danger to the balance of power in Europe, caused the Russian troops stationed in Wallachia to be led into Transylvania, for the destruction of the Hungarian nation.

Three months ago we were driven back upon the Theiss; our arms have already recovered all Transylvania; Clausenburg, Hermanstadt, and Kronstadt are taken; one portion of the troops of Austria is driven into the Bukovina; another, together with the Russian force sent to aid them, is totally defeated, and to the last man obliged to evacuate Transylvania, and to fly into Wallachia. Upper Hungary is cleared of foes.

The Serbian rebellion is suppressed; the forts of St. Tama's and the Roman entrenchment have been taken by storm, and the whole country between the Danube and the Theiss, including the county of Bacs, has been recovered for the nation. The general of the perjured house of Austria has been defeated in five battles, and with his whole army he has been driven back upon and even across the Danube. Framing our conduct according to these events, and confiding in the justice of Eternal God, we, before the world, and relying on the natural rights of the Hungarian nation, and on the power it has developed to maintain them, further impelled by that sense of duty which urges every nation to defend its existence, do hereby declare and proclaim in the name of the nation legally represented by us, the following:

1st. Hungary, with Transylvania, as legally united with it, and its dependencies, are hereby declared to constitute a free, independent, sovereign state. The territorial unity of this state is declared to be inviolable, and its territory to be indivisible.

2d. The house of Hapsburg-Lorraine—having, by treachery, perjury, and levying of war against the Hungarian nation, as well as by its outrageous violation of all compacts, in breaking up the integral territory of the kingdom, in the separation of Transylvania, Croatia, Slavonia, Fiume, and its districts from Hungary—further, by compassing the destruction of the independence of the country by arms, and by calling in the disciplined army of a foreign power, for the purpose of annihilating its nationality, by violation both of the Pragmatic Sanction and of treaties concluded between Austria and Hungary, on which the alliance between the two countries depended—is, as treacherous and perjured, forever excluded from the throne of the united states of Hungary and Transylvania, and all their possessions and dependencies, and is hereby deprived of the style and title, as well as of the armorial bearings belonging to the crown of Hungary, and declared to be banished forever from the united countries and their dependencies and possessions. They are therefore declared to be deposed, degraded, and banished from the Hungarian territory.

3d. The Hungarian nation, in the exercise of its rights and sovereign will, being determined to assume the position of a free and independent state among the nations of Europe, declares it to be its intention to establish and maintain friendly and neighborly relations with those states with which it was formerly united under the same sovereign, as well as to contract alliances with all other nations.

4th. The form of government to be adopted for the future will be fixed by the Diet of the nation.

But until this shall be decided, on the basis of the ancient and received principles which have been recognized for ages, the government of the united countries, their possessions and dependencies, shall be conducted on personal responsibility, and under the obligation to render an account of all acts, by Louis Kossuth, who has by acclamation, and with the unanimous approbation of the Diet of the nation, been named Governing President, (Gubernator,) and the ministers whom he shall appoint.

And this resolution of oars we shall proclaim and make known to all the nations of the civilized world, with the conviction that the Hungarian nation will be received by them among the free and independent nations of the world, with the same friendship and free acknowledgment of its rights which the Hungarians proffer to other countries.

We also hereby proclaim and make known to all the inhabitants of the united states of Hungary and Transylvania, and their dependencies, that all authorities, communes, towns, and the civil officers both in the counties and cities, are completely set free and released from all the obligations under which they stood, by oath or otherwise, to the said house of Hapsburg-Lorraine, and that any individual daring to contravene this decree, and by word or deed in any way to aid or abet any one violating it, shall be treated and punished as guilty of high treason. And by the publication of this decree, we hereby bind and oblige all the inhabitants of these countries to obedience to the government now instituted formally, and endowed with all necessary legal powers.

DEBRECZIN, April 14, 1849.

Source: De Puy, Henry M. *Kossuth and His Generals.* Buffalo: Phinney & Co., 1852, 202–225.

Law Altering the Fundamental Law of February 26, 1861, Concerning Imperial Representation (1867)

Under the so-called February Patent of 1861, excerpts from which are reproduced here, the Austro-Hungarian Empire centralized administrative control over Hungary with the bureaucracy in Vienna, Austria's capital. As part of the generalized reforms of 1867, which included a newly liberalized constitution, the Austro-Hungarian government overturned the February Patent, effectively creating a dual monarchy of Austria and Hungary.

Section 1. The Reichsrat is the common representative body of the kingdoms of Bohemia, Dalmatia, Galicia and Lodomeria with the Grand Duchy of Cracow, of the Archduchies of Lower and Upper Austria, of the Duchies of Salzburg, Styria, Carinthia, Carniola, and Bukovina, of the Margravate of Moravia, of the Duchy of Upper and Lower Silesia, of the Princely County of Tyrol and the territory of Voralberg, of the Margravate of Istria, of the Princely County of Gorz and Gradizia, and of the City of Trieste with its territory. The Reichsrat is composed of a House of Lords and a House of Representatives . . . Section 7. Every male person who has attained the age of twenty-four years, possesses Austrian citizenship, is not excluded from the right to vote by the provisions of the election law of the Reichsrat, and who at the time of the election is ordered has resided for at least one year in the Austrian commune in which the right to vote is to be exercised, is qualified to vote for representatives . . . Section 10. The Reichsrat shall be convened annually by the Emperor . . .

Section 11. The competence of the Reichsrat extends to all matters which relate to the rights, obligations, and interests common to the countries represented therein, in so far as these matters are not to be handled in common, in consequence of the agreement of the countries of the Hungarian crown with the other countries of the monarchy. Thus, the competence of the Reichsrat extends to: a) The examination and approval of commercial treaties and of those political treaties which place a financial burden upon the empire or upon any part thereof . . . b) All matters which relate to the form as well as to the regulation and term of military service . . . c) The establishment of the budget, and particularly the annual grant of taxes and duties to be levied . . . d) The regulation of the monetary system and of banks of issue, of customs and commercial affairs . . . e) Legislation concerning credit, banks, patents of inventions, industry . . . weights and measures, the protection of trade marks and of industrial goods . . . g) Legislation concerning citizenship and domicile . . . h) Concerning confessional relations, the rights of assembly and association [and] the press . . . i) The establishment of the principles of the educational system in the primary and secondary schools, and legislation concerning the universities . . . k) Legislation concerning criminal justice and police penalties [and] the civil law . . . l) Legislation concerning the principles of the judicial and administrative organization . . . o) Legislation concerning the manner of handling matters which, through the agreement with Hungary, are recognized as common to the two parts of the empire . . . Section 19. The adjournment of the Reichsrat or the dissolution of the House of Representatives shall take place by decree of the Emperor. In case of dissolution a new election shall be held in conformity with Section 7.

Source: Dodd, Walter Farleigh, ed. *Modern Constitutions: A Collection of the Fundamental Laws of Twenty-two of the Most Important Countries of the World, With Historical and Bibliographical Notes.* Chicago: University of Chicago Press, 1909.

Fundamental Law Concerning the General Rights of Citizens (Austrian Constitution of 1867)

The Austrian constitution of 1867 represented a substantial liberalization and modernization in the governance and administration of the Austro-Hungarian Empire. It attempted to streamline the bureaucracy in Vienna and effectively eliminated numerous medieval legacies. Most important, the constitution bestowed virtually equal citizenship on all the constituent nationalities within the empire.

Article 1. For all natives of the various kingdoms and countries represented in the Reichsrat there exists a common right of Austrian citizenship. The law shall determine under what conditions Austrian citizenship is gained, exercised, and lost.

Article 2. All citizens are equal before the law.

Article 3. Public offices shall be equally open to all citizens. The admission of foreigners to public office is dependent upon their acquisition of Austrian citizenship.

Article 4. The freedom of passage of persons and property, within the territories of the state, shall be subject to no restrictions.

All citizens who live within a commune and pay therein a tax on real property, business, or income, shall have the right to vote for members of the communal assembly and shall be eligible to that body, under the same conditions as natives of the commune.

Freedom of emigration is limited by the state only by the obligation to serve in the army.

Taxes on emigration shall be levied only as a measure of retaliation.

Article 5. Property is inviolable. Forced expropriation shall take place only in the cases and according to the forms determined by law.

Article 6. Every citizen may dwell temporarily or establish his residence in any part of the territory of the state, acquire real property of any kind and freely dispose of the same, and may also engage in any form of business, under legal conditions.

In the matter of mortmain the law may, for reasons of public policy, restrict the right of acquiring and of disposing of real property.

Article 7. Every relation of vassalage or dependence is forever abolished. Every burden or charge resting upon the title of real property is redeemable, and in future no land shall be burdened with an irredeemable charge.

Article 8. Liberty of person is guaranteed. The law of October 27, 1862, on the protection of individual liberty is hereby declared to be an integral part of the present fundamental law. Every arrest ordered or prolonged in violation of law imposes an obligation upon the state to indemnify the injured party.

Article 9. The domicile is inviolable. The law of October 27, 1862, for the protection of the domicile is hereby declared an integral part of this fundamental law.

Article 10. The secrecy of letters shall not be violated; the seizure of letters, except in case of a legal arrest or search, shall take place only in time of war, or by virtue of a judicial order issued in conformity with the law.

Article 11. The right of petition is free to everyone. Petitions under a collective name should emanate only from legally recognized corporations or associations.

Article 12. Austrian citizens shall have the right to assemble together, and to form associations. The exercise of these rights is regulated by special laws.

Article 13. Everyone shall have the right, within legal limits, freely to express his thoughts orally, in writing, through the press, or by pictorial representation.

The press shall not be placed under censorship, nor restrained by the system of licenses. Administrative prohibitions of the use of the mail are not applicable to matter printed within the country.

Article 14. Full freedom of religion and of conscience is guaranteed to all. The enjoyment of civil and political rights is independent of religious belief; however, religious belief shall in no way interfere with the performance of civil duties.

No one shall be forced to perform any religious rite or to participate in any religious ceremony except in so far as he is subject to another who has legal authority in this matter.

Article 15. Every legally recognized church and religious society has the right publicly to exercise its religious worship; it regulates and administers its internal affairs independently, remains in possession and enjoyment of its establishments, institutions, and property held for religious, educational, and charitable purposes; but is subject, as other societies, to the general laws of the state.

Article 16. Adherents of a religious confession not legally recognized are permitted to worship privately, in so far as their religious services are not illegal or contrary to public morals.

Article 17. Science and its teaching shall be free. Every citizen, whose capacity has been established in conformity with law, shall have the right to establish institutions of instruction and education, and to give instruction therein. Private instruction shall be subject to no such restriction. Religious instruction in the schools shall be left to the church or religious society to which the school is attached. The state shall have the right to superior direction and superintendence over the entire system of education and instruction.

Article 18. Everyone shall be free to choose his occupation and to prepare himself for it in such places and in such manner as he may wish.

Article 19. All the races of the state shall have equal rights, and each race shall have the inviolable right of maintaining and cultivating its nationality and language.

The state recognizes the equality of the various languages in the schools, public offices, and in public life.

In the countries populated by several races, the institutions of public instruction shall be so organized that each race may receive the necessary instruction in its own language, without being obliged to learn a second language.

Article 20. A special law shall determine the right of the responsible governing power to suspend temporarily and in certain places the rights mentioned in Articles 8, 9, 10, 12, and 13.

Source: Dodd, Walter Farleigh, ed. *Modern Constitutions: A Collection of the Fundamental Laws of Twenty-two of the Most Important Countries of the World, With Historical and Bibliographical Notes.* Chicago: University of Chicago Press, 1909.

BELGIAN EMPIRE

Leopold II: Communiqué to Agents of the Congo Free State (1897)

Beginning in the 1870s, King Leopold II laid claim to the vast Congo River basin of Central Africa, which was eventually incorporated into his own personal colony, the Congo Free State. Leopold made fabulous profits through the extraction of the colony's enormous natural rubber deposits. But to tap this resource, Leopold instituted a murderous policy whereby local people were forced to look ever deeper into the jungle for untapped rubber trees. When they failed to meet their quotas, they were tortured, mutilated, and killed. The brutality of Leopold's regime caused an international outcry. In this 1897 communiqué, written to his agents in the Congo, Leopold defends his rule as a "civilizing" force for Africa.

Brussels, June 16, 1897

Sir,

The agents of the Congo Free State have been much tried in recent years. Their ranks have been thinned by cruel and repeated attacks. Associating myself with the unanimous expressions of regret aroused by these painful losses, I desire to pay my tribute of acknowledgement to all those who have so bravely sacrificed their lives in the performance of their duties.

As every great cause, that which we serve in the Congo has had many martyrs.

The task which the State agents have had to accomplish in the Congo is noble and elevated. They have had to carry on the work of civilization in Equatorial Africa, guided by the principles set forth in the Berlin and Brussels resolutions.

Face to face with primitive barbarity, struggling against dreadful customs, thousands of years old, their duty has been to modify gradually those customs.

Civilized society attaches to human life a value unknown among savage peoples. When our guiding will is implanted among the latter, it must aim at overcoming all obstacles. The result cannot be reached by mere speeches, however philanthropic may be their tenor. . . .

The soldiers of the State must be recruited among the natives. They do not easily abandon their sanguinary customs transmitted from generation to generation. The example of white officers and military discipline will make them hate the human trophies of which they are now proud. . . .

I am glad to think that our agents, nearly all of whom are volunteers from the ranks of the Belgian army, always bear in mind the rules of the honorable career in which they are engaged. Animated with a pure sentiment of patriotism . . .they will care all the more for the natives who will find in them the powerful protectors of life and property, the kindly guardians they need so much.

The aim of all of us—I desire to repeat it here with you—is to regenerate, materially and morally, races whose degradation and misfortune it is hard to realize. The fearful scourges of which, in the eyes of our humanity, these races seemed the victims, are already lessening, little by little, through our intervention. Each step forward made by our people should mark an improvement in the condition of the natives.

In those vast tracts, mostly uncultivated and many unproductive, where the natives hardly knew how to get their daily food, European experience, knowledge, resource and enterprise, have brought to light unthought-of wealth. If wants are created they are satisfied even more liberally. Exploration of virgin land goes on, communications are established, highways are opened, the soil yields produce in exchange for our varied manufactured articles. Legitimate trade and industry are established. As the economic state is formed, property assumes an intrinsic character; private and public ownership, the basis of all social development, is founded and respected instead of being left to the law of change and of the strongest.

Upon this material prosperity, in which whites and blacks have evidently a common interest, will follow a desire on the part of the blacks to elevate themselves. Their primitive nature will not always resist the efforts of Christian culture. Their education, once begun, will no more be interrupted. In its success I see crowning of the task undertaken by our people and so ably seconded by religious missionaries of both sexes. The most urgent part of the program we wished to realize was to set up direct communication with the natives all over the Congo Basin. And this was done in the course of fifteen years, without the help of any State . . . The establishment of a whole, compact series of stations gradually substitutes for savage warfare, carried on incessantly between tribes and villages, a regime of peace.

From a geographical entity, physically determined, the Congo State has become a country with distinct frontiers, occupied and guarded at every point—a result almost without precedent in the history of colonization but which is explained by the concentration of our united efforts on a single field of activity.

Our own difficulties will be considerably lessened in a short time when the railway between the Lower Congo and Stanley Pool is completed.

I here make a renewed appeal to the devotion, of which our agents have already given such abundant proof, that the establishment of this means of communication may bear fruit as soon as possible. It will closely connect the Congo with the mother country, it will afford all Europe, which is so interested in our work, an opportunity to take an intelligent and kindly interest in our work. It will, finally, give a decided fillip to our progress, and it will speedily introduce into the vast regions of the Congo all the benefits of our Christian civilization.

I thank our agents for their efforts and I reiterate to them the expression of my royal regard.

Source: La Belgique Coloniale, August 14, 1898.

Report of British Consul Roger Casement on the Administration of the Congo Free State (1903)

Beginning in the 1870s, King Leopold II of Belgium began to assume administrative control over the Congo, a move ratified by the Berlin Congress of 1885. Over the next two decades, Leopold and various companies he chartered exploited the population of the territory to extract and process natural rubber. To do so, they instituted a regime of terror and torture that increasingly raised human rights concerns throughout Europe and the United States. Following reports by a British-based journalist named E. D. Morel, the British Foreign Office dispatched its consul in the Congo, Roger Casement, on a fact-finding mission. The following is his report. Along with other exposés, the Casement report led Britain and other powers to pressure Leopold to give up control of the Congo and turn it over to the Belgian government, an act he reluctantly acceded to in 1908.

The colonial regime of the Belgian King Leopold II—the Congo Free State—became one of the more infamous international scandals of the turn of the century. Leopold had acquired the vast Congo region through considerable investment of his own fortune in setting up his administration there and by cajoling the great powers at the Berlin Conference of 1884–5 to award his International Congo Association title to what was to become the Congo Free State. By the mid-1890s the Congo Basin and its products became a source of great wealth to Leopold who used his riches to beautify his Belgian capital Brussels while using his agents in Africa to establish a brutal exploitative regime for the extraction of rubber in the interior forest regions of the Free State

Leopold's ability to administer the Congo government coupled with his gift for self-promotion and dissimulation, kept knowledge of what was taking place there to a minimum. Inevitably the truth leaked out as it became known through missionary reports and the like that the natives were being willfully exploited and brutally treated in the interests of amassing revenue for the King and his agents. Foremost in the campaign to expose the regime—based on forced labor and various forms of terror—was E. D. Morel whose ceaseless pursuit of Leopold's regime resulted in questions being raised in the British House of Commons, for Britain, after all, had been a signatory to the Berlin Act which bound the Congo Government "to bind themselves to watch over the preservation of the native tribes and to care for their moral and material welfare." The Report (below) of the British consul sent to investigate the accumulating reports of torture, murder and virtual enslavement was published to the world in 1904 and from that point on the pressure for reform mounted until, finally, Leopold was forced to yield up his private African preserve to the Belgian government which formally took over the 'Belgian Congo' by an act of annexation in August 1908.

Leopold II has not fared well by historians. As one English historian has bitterly commented: "(Leopold) was an Attila in modern dress, and it would have been better for the world if he had never been born."

I have the honor to submit my Report on my recent journey on the Upper Congo...the region visited was one of the most central in the Congo State...Moreover, I was enabled, by visiting this district, to contrast its present state with the condition in which I had known it some sixteen years ago...and I was thus able to institute a comparison between a state of affairs I had myself seen when the natives loved their own savage lives in anarchic and disorderly communities, uncontrolled by Europeans, and that created by more than a decade of very energetic European intervention by Belgian officials in introducing their methods of rule over one of the most savage regions of Africa...

A fleet of steamers...navigate the main river and its principal effluents at fixed intervals. Regular means of communication are thus afforded to some of the most inaccessible parts of Central Africa.

A railway, excellently constructed in view of the difficulties to be encountered, now connects the ocean ports with Stanley Pool, over a tract of difficult country, which formerly offered to the weary traveler on foot many obstacles to be overcome and many days of great bodily fatigue...The cataract region, through which the railway passes...is...the home, or birthplace of the sleeping sickness—a terrible disease, which is, all too rapidly, eating its way into the heart of Africa...The population of the Lower Congo has been gradually reduced by the unchecked ravages of this, as yet undiagnosed and incurable disease, and as one cause of the seemingly wholesale diminution of human life which I everywhere observed in the regions revisited, a prominent place must be assigned to this malady...Communities I had formerly known as large and flourishing centers of population are to-day entirely gone...

On the whole the Government workmen (Congolese natives)...struck me as being well cared for...

The chief difficulty in dealing with so large a staff arises from the want of a sufficiency of food supply in the surrounding country...The natives of the districts are forced to provide a fixed quantity each week...which is levied by requisitions on all the surrounding villages...This, however necessary, is not a welcome task to the native suppliers who complain that their numbers are yearly decreasing, while the demands made upon them remain fixed, or tend even to increase...The (official in charge)is forced to exercise continuous pressure on the local population, and within recent times that pressure has not always taken the form of mere requisition. Armed expeditions have been necessary and a more forcible method of levying supplies [e.g., goats, fowl, etc.] adopted than the law either contemplated or justifies.

The result of an expedition, which took place towards the end of 1900, was that in fourteen small villages traversed seventeen persons disappeared. Sixteen of these whose names were given to me were killed by the soldiers, and their bodies recovered by their friends...Ten persons were tied up and taken away as prisoners, but were released on payment of sixteen goats by their friends...

A hospital for Europeans and an establishment designed as a native hospital are in charge of a European doctor...When I visited the three mud huts which serve (as the native hospital), all of them dilapidated . . . I found seventeen sleeping sickness patients, male and female, lying about in the utmost dirt. The structures I had visited . . . had endured for many years as the only form of hospital accommodation for the numerous native staff of the district . . .

The people have not easily accommodated themselves to the altered condition of life brought about by European government in their midst. Where formerly they were accustomed to take long voyages down to Stanley Pool to sell slaves, ivory, dried fish, or other local products. they find themselves today debarred from all such activity . . . The open selling of slaves and the canoe convoys, which navigated the Upper Congo (River), have everywhere disappeared. . . . (but) much that was not reprehensible in native life has disappeared along with it. The trade in ivory has today entirely passed from the hands of the natives of the Upper Congo . . .

Complaints as to the manner of exacting service are . . . frequent . . . If the local official has to go on a sudden journey men are summoned on the instant to paddle his canoe, and a refusal entails imprisonment or a beating. If the Government plantation or the kitchen garden require weeding, a soldier will be sent to call in the women from some of the neighboring towns . . . ; to the women suddenly forced to leave their household tasks and to tramp off, hoe in hand, baby on back, with possibly a hungry and angry husband at home, the task is not a welcome one.

I visited two large villages in the interior . . . wherein I found that fully half the population now consisted of refugees . . . I saw and questioned several groups of these people . . . They went on to declare, when asked why they had fled (their district), that they had endured such ill-treatment at the hands of the government soldiers in their own (district) that life had become intolerable; that nothing had remained for them at home but to be killed for failure to bring in a certain amount of rubber or to die from starvation or exposure in their attempts to satisfy the demands made upon them . . . I subsequently found other (members of the tribe) who confirmed the truth of the statements made to me . . .

On the 25th of July (1903) we reached Lukolela, where I spent two days. This district had, when I visited it in 1887, numbered fully 5,000 people;

today the population is given, after a careful enumeration, at less than 600. The reasons given me for their decline in numbers were similar to those furnished elsewhere, namely, sleeping-sickness, general ill-health, insufficiency of food, and the methods employed to obtain labor from them by local officials and the exactions levied on them.

At other villages which I visited, I found the tax to consist of baskets, which the inhabitants had to make and deliver weekly as well as, always, a certain amount of foodstuffs. (The natives) were frequently flogged for delay or inability to complete the tally of these baskets, or the weekly supply of food. Several men, including a Chief of one town, showed broad weals across their buttocks, which were evidently recent. One, a lad of 15 or so, removing his cloth, showed several scars across his thighs, which he and others around him said had formed part of a weekly payment for a recent shortage in their supply of food . . .

A careful investigation of the conditions of native life around (Lake Mantumba) confirmed the truth of the statements made to me—that the great decrease in population, the dirty and ill-kept towns, and the complete absence of goats, sheep, or fowls—once very plentiful in this country— were to be attributed above all else to the continued effort made during many years to compel the natives to work India-rubber. Large bodies of native troops had formerly been quartered in the district, and the punitive measures undertaken to this end had endured for a considerable period. During the course of these operations there had been much loss of life, accompanied, I fear, by a somewhat general mutilation of the dead, as proof that the soldiers had done their duty . . .

Two cases (of mutilation) came to my actual notice while I was in the lake district. One, a young man, both of whose hands had been beaten off with the butt ends of rifles against a tree; the other a young lad of 11 or 12 years of age, whose right hand was cut off at the wrist. . . . In both these cases the Government soldiers had been accompanied by white officers whose names were given to me. Of six natives (one a girl, three little boys, one youth, and one old woman) who had been mutilated in this way during the rubber regime, all except one were dead at the date of my visit.

[A sentry in the employ of one of the concessionary private companies] said he had caught and was detaining as prisoners (eleven women) to compel their husbands to bring in the right amount of rubber required of them on the next market day ...When I asked what would become of these women if their husbands failed to bring in the right quantity of rubber, he said at once that then they would be kept there until their husbands had redeemed them] ...

R. Casement.

Source: Great Britain. *Parliamentary Papers,* 1904. Volume LXII, Cd. 1933.

Arthur Conan Doyle: *The Crime of the Congo* (1909)

King Leopold's regime in the Congo was based on the exploitation of natural rubber. To obtain the rubber, the regime established a brutal police to force the local people to find and process this resource. When they failed to do so, they were tortured, mutilated, and killed. The brutal regime produced a horrified reaction among many intellectuals in Europe and North America, including Arthur Conan Doyle, creator of the Sherlock Holmes novels. The following is the introduction to his 1909 book The Crime of the Congo.

I am convinced that the reason why public opinion has not been more sensitive upon the question of the Congo Free State is that the terrible story has not been brought thoroughly home to the people. Mr. E. D. Morel has done the work of ten men, and the Congo Reform Association has struggled hard with very scanty means; but their time and energies have, for the most part, been absorbed in dealing with each fresh phase of the situation as it arose. There is room, therefore, as it seemed to me, for a general account which would cover the whole field and bring the matter up to date. This account must necessarily be a superficial one, if it is to be produced at such a size and such a price, as will ensure its getting at that general public for which it has been prepared. Yet it contains the essential facts, and will enable the reader to form his own opinion upon the situation.

It may be objected that some of this is ancient history, and that the greater part of it refers to a period before the Congo State was annexed to Belgium on August 10th, 1908. But responsibility can-

not be so easily shaken off. The Congo State was founded by the Belgian King, and exploited by Belgian capital, Belgian soldiers and Belgian concessionnaires. It was defended and upheld by successive Belgian Governments, who did all they could to discourage the Reformers. In spite of legal quibbles, it is an insult to common sense to suppose that the responsibility for the Congo has not always rested with Belgium. The Belgian machinery was always ready to help and defend the State, but never to hold it in control and restrain it from crime.

One chance the Belgians had. If immediately upon taking over the State they had formed a Judicial Commission for the rigid inspection of the whole matter, with power to punish for all past offences, and to examine all the scandals of recent years, then they would have done something to clear the past. If on the top of that they had freed the land, given up the system of forced labour entirely, and cancelled the charters of all the concessionnaire companies, for the obvious reason that they have notoriously abused their powers, then Belgium could go forward in its colonizing enterprise on the same terms as other States, with her sins expiated so far as expiation is now possible.

She did none of these things. For a year now she has herself persevered in the evil ways of her predecessor. Her colony is a scandal before the whole world. The era of murders and mutilations has, as we hope, passed by, but the country is sunk into a state of cowed and hopeless slavery. It is not a new story, but merely another stage of the same. When Belgium took over the Congo State, she took over its history and its responsibilities also. What a load that was is indicated in these pages.

The record of the dates is the measure of our patience. Can anyone say that we are precipitate if we now brush aside vain words and say definitely that the matter has to be set right by a certain near date, or that we will appeal to each and all of the Powers, with the evidence before them, to assist us in setting it right? If the Powers refuse to do so, then it is our duty to honour the guarantees which we made as to the safety of these poor people, and to turn to the task of setting it right ourselves. If the Powers join in, or give us a mandate, all the better. But we have a mandate from something higher than the Powers which obliges us to act.

Sir Edward Grey has told us in his speech of July 22nd, 1909, that a danger to European peace lies in the matter. Let us look this danger squarely in the face. Whence does it come? Is it from Germany, with her traditions of kindly home life—is this the power which would raise a hand to help the butchers of the Mongalla and of the Domaine de la Couronne? Is it likely that those who so justly admire the splendid private and public example of William II would draw the sword for Leopold? Both in the name of trade rights and in that of humanity Germany has a long score to settle on the Congo. Or is it the United States which would stand in the way, when her citizens have vied with our own in withstanding and exposing these iniquities? Or, lastly, is France the danger? There are those who think that because France has capital invested in these enterprises, because the French Congo has itself degenerated under the influence and example of its neighbor, and because France holds some vague right of pre-emption, that therefore our trouble lies across the Channel. For my own part, I cannot believe it. I know too well the generous, chivalrous instincts of the French people. I know, also, that their colonial record during centuries has been hardly inferior to our own. Such traditions are not lightly set aside, and all will soon be right again when a strong Colonial Minister turns his attention to the concessionnaires in the French Congo. He will remember de Brazza's dying words: "Our Congo must not be turned into a Mongalla." It is an impossibility that France could ally herself with King Leopold, and certainly if such were, indeed, to be the case, the *entente cordiale* would be strained to breaking. Surely, then, if these three Powers, the ones most directly involved, have such obvious reasons for helping, rather than hindering, we may go forward without fear. But if it were not so, if all Europe frowned upon our enterprise, we should not be worthy to be the sons of our fathers if we did not go forward on the plain path of national duty.

Arthur Conan Doyle.

Source: Doyle, Arthur Conan, Sir. 1909. *The Crime of the Congo.* New York: Doubleday, Page.

A Belgian Defense of Its Rule in the Congo (1954)

In 1908, King Leopold II—facing international protest against the brutal regime he had established in the Congo Free State—surrendered control of the territory to the Belgian government. Over the next half century, Belgium ruled its Congolese territory with a not-so-benign neglect, failing to educate the population or prepare it for self-rule. In a 1954 report excerpted below, the Belgian government tried to justify its rule in condescending and even racist tones, by arguing that the pre-existing society there was brutal and chaotic.

Primitive Congolese society consisted of the rulers, the elders of the tribe and the anonymous hoi-polloi. The basic principles of the social and political structure was a kind of paternalism, that all too often degenerated into brutal tyranny. In fact, the people had little voice in their own affairs and the very idea of democracy would have been considered by those in power as an heresy. White paternalism has been decried nearly as much as colonialism itself. It has been represented as an attack on the dignity of man. It certainly is objectionable when one deals with people who socially and intellectually are full grown. It is not when one has to educate to modern ways a population that is supposed to have covered in 50 years the road the western world took more than two thousand years to travel.

The mental inferiority of the Congolese has never been an axiom of Belgian colonial action. On the contrary, the educators, administrators and missionaries have always contended that the possibilities of the Congolese were those of any man anywhere else. Consequently, the idea of discrimination and racial superiority was absent from their policy. However, a de facto distinction was made between those Congolese who already have achieved a degree of civilization, mental as well as technical, and those who have not yet done so. In western society, we discriminate against people who do not wash, or whose way of speech is objectionable; we discriminate all the time in order to preserve our civilization . . . and to educate the boor and the country-bumpkin. That kind of discrimination exists and will continue to exist until the majority of the Congolese have attained a certain degree of evolution.

To prepare the way, the Belgians have improved the housing of the Congolese, they have taught him the elements of hygiene, they have taught him to dress decently and practically, they have shown him the advantage of membership in clubs and societies. They have put into his hands the great means of communication of our day, the radio, the press, the film. . . . Human contact on the social level between whites and Congolese remains the cornerstone of a harmonious society. This is achieved in clubs and circles where both groups mingle and discuss freely and on equal terms. It is also obtained in the schools where, after careful selection, both races are admitted without discrimination. . . ..

The desire for freedom may be innate in the human heart, it is practically realized only after a long struggle and it is a task of everybody to preserve it. Ancient Congolese society ignored democracy. It was based on power. The dynastic history of the royal house of Ruanda-Urundi is a tale of horror. . . . Murder, poisoning, extreme cruel disfiguration, were the political weapons. With all that the Belgians have done away. They respected within certain limits the established order: the local chiefs are confirmed in their power, as democratic methods could not have been introduced overnight, but the chiefs are no longer absolute rulers. They are expected to live up

to a code of rulership and as soon as they transgress it, they are removed and replaced. . . .

To what extent do the Congolese participate in the government of their own affairs? This question, often asked, is as much a leading question as the classic: Have you stopped beating your wife? Because the premise of the discussion should be that nobody, white or colored, has the franchise in the Congo, and that in their present stage, the majority of the population does not have an idea what effective government is all about. . . .

Without false modesty, the Belgians can say to the world, to the ignorant sentimentalists who deplore the disappearance of the picturesque old ways of primitive society, as well as to the hypocritical critics who treat them as exploiters of the natives: "Look at the Belgian Congo today, look at what we have done in scarcely half a century, look at the roads, the cities, the industries, the churches and the schools, above all, look at the millions of primitive, miserable beings we are making into citizens of the world."

Source: Belgian Congo: American Survey. New York: Belgian Embassy, 1954.

BRITISH EMPIRE

Francis Pretty: Sir Francis Drake's Famous Voyage round the World (1580)

In 1577, Francis Drake, an English seaman notorious throughout the Spanish empire for his buccaneering attacks on shipping and coastal towns in the Americas, embarked on one of the most ambitious voyages in British seafaring history. Drake attacked a number of Spanish seaports along the coast of the Americas before making his way homeward across the Pacific in a round-the-globe voyage. While Drake's journey did not directly lead to British settlement overseas, it demonstrated the island nation's growing stature as a naval power. In these excerpts from his journal, Francis Petty, one of Drake's Gentlemen at Arms, recounts the many novelties and adventures Drake and his crew experienced in their three-year journey.

The Famous Voyage of Sir Francis Drake into the South Sea, and therehence about the whole Globe of the Earth, begun in the year of our Lord 1577.

The 15. day of November, in the year of our Lord 1577, Master Francis Drake, with a fleet of five ships and barks, and to the number of 164 men, gentlemen and sailors, departed from Plymouth, giving out his pretended voyage for Alexandria. But the wind falling contrary, he was forced the next morning to put into Falmouth Haven, in Cornwall, where such and so terrible a tempest took us, as few men have seen the like, and was indeed so vehement that all our ships were like to have gone to wrack. But it pleased God to preserve us from that extremity, and to afflict us only for that present with these two particu-

lars: the mast of our Admiral, which was the Pelican, was cut overboard for the safeguard of the ship, and the Marigold was driven ashore, and somewhat bruised. For the repairing of which damages we returned again to Plymouth; and having recovered those harms, and brought the ships again to good state, we set forth the second time from Plymouth, and set sail the 13. day of December following.

The 25. day of the same month we fell with the Cape Cantin, upon the coast of Barbary; and coasting along, the 27. day we found an island called Mogador, lying one mile distant from the main. Between which island and the main we found a very good and safe harbour for our ships to ride in, as also very good entrance, and void of any danger. On this island our General erected a pinnace, whereof he brought out of England with him four already framed. While these things were in doing, there came to the water's side some of the inhabitants of the country, shewing forth their flags of truce; which being seen of our General, he sent his ship's boat to the shore to know what they would. They being willing to come aboard, our men left there one man of our company for a pledge, and brought two of theirs aboard our ship; which by signs shewed our General that the next day they would bring some provision, as sheep, capons, and hens, and such like. Whereupon our General bestowed amongst them some linen cloth and shoes, and a javelin, which they very joyfully received, and departed for that time. The next morning they failed not to come again to the water's side. And our General again setting out our boat, one of our men leaping over-rashly ashore, and offering friendly to embrace them, they set violent hands on him, offering a dagger to his throat if he had made any resistance; and so laying him on a horse carried him away. So that a man cannot be too circumspect and wary of himself among such miscreants. Our pinnace being finished, we departed from this place the 30. and last day of December, and coasting along the shore we did descry, not contrary to our expectation, certain canters' which were Spanish fishermen, to whom we gave chase and took three of them. And proceeding further we met with three carvels, and took them also.

The 17. day of January we arrived at Cape Blanco, where we found a ship riding at anchor, within the Cape, and but two simple mariners in her. Which ship we took and carried her further into the harbour, where we remained four days; and in that space our General mustered and trained his men on land in warlike manner, to make them fit for all occasions. In this place we took of the fishermen such necessaries as we wanted, and they could yield us; and leaving here one of our little barks, called the Benedict, we took with us one of theirs which they called canters, being of the burden of 40 tons or thereabouts. All these things being finished we departed this harbour the 22. of January, carrying along with us one of the Portugal carvels [caravels], which was bound to the islands of Cape Verde for salt, whereof good store is made in one of those islands. The master or pilot of that carvel did advertise our General that upon one of those islands, called Mayo, there was a great store of dried cabritos [goats], which a few inhabitants there dwelling did yearly make ready for such of the king's ships as did there touch, being bound for his country of Brazil or elsewhere. We fell with this island the 27. of January, but the inhabitants would in no case traffic with us, being thereof forbidden by the king's edict. Yet the next day our General sent to view the island, and the likelihoods that might be there of provision of victuals, about threescore and two men under the conduct and government of Master Winter and Master Doughty. And marching towards the chief place of habitation in this island (as by the Portugal we were informed), having travelled to the mountains the space of three miles, and arriving there somewhat before the daybreak, we arrested ourselves, to see day before

us. Which appearing, we found the inhabitants to be fled; but the place, by reason that it was manured, we found to be more fruitful than the other part, especially the valleys among the hills.

Here we gave ourselves a little refreshing, as by very ripe and sweet grapes, which the fruitfulness of the earth at that season of the year yielded us; and that season being with us the depth of winter, it may seem strange that those fruits were then there growing. But the reason thereof is this, because they being between the tropic and the equinoctial, the sun passeth twice in the year through their zenith over their heads, by means whereof they have two summers; and being so near the heat of the line they never lose the heat of the sun so much, but the fruits have their increase and continuance in the midst of winter. The island is wonderfully stored with goats and wild hens; and it hath salt also, without labour, save only that the people gather it into heaps; which continually in greater quantity is increased upon the sands by the flowing of the sea, and the receiving heat of the sun kerning the same. So that of the increase thereof they keep a continual traffic with their neighbours.

Amongst other things we found here a kind of fruit called cocos, which because it is not commonly known with us in England, I thought good to make some description of it. The tree beareth no leaves nor branches, but at the very top the fruit groweth in clusters, hard at the top of the stem of the tree, as big every several fruit as a man's head; but having taken off the uttermost bark, which you shall find to be very full of strings or sinews, as I may term them, you shall come to a hard shell, which may hold in quantity of liquor a pint commonly, or some a quart, and some less. Within that shell, of the thickness of half-an-inch good, you shall have a kind of hard substance and very white, no less good and sweet than almonds; within that again, a certain clear liquor, which being drunk, you shall not only find it very delicate and sweet, but most comfortable and cordial.

After we had satisfied ourselves with some of these fruits, we marched further into the island, and saw great store of cabritos alive, which were so chased by the inhabitants that we could do no good towards our provision; but they had laid out, as it were to stop our mouths withal, certain old dried cabritos, which being but ill, and small and few, we made no account of. Being returned to our ships, our General departed hence the 31. of this month, and sailed by the island of Santiago, but far enough from the danger of the inhabitants, who shot and discharged at us three pieces; but they all fell short of us, and did us no harm. The island is fair and large, and, as it seemeth, rich and fruitful, and inhabited by the Portugals; but the mountains and high places of the island are said to be possessed by the Moors, who having been slaves to the Portugals, to ease themselves, made escape to the desert places of the island, where they abide with great strength. Being before this island, we espied two ships under sail, to the one of which we gave chase, and in the end boarded her with a ship-boat without resistance; which we found to be a good prize, and she yielded unto us good store of wine. Which prize our General committed to the custody of Master Doughty; and retaining the pilot, sent the rest away with his pinnace, giving them a butt of wine and some victuals, and their wearing clothes, and so they departed. The same night we came with the island called by the Portugals Ilha do Fogo, that is, the burning island; in the north side whereof is a consuming fire. The matter is said to be of sulphur, but, notwithstanding, it is like to be a commodious island, because the Portugals have built, and do inhabit there. Upon the south side thereof lieth a most pleasant and sweet island, the trees whereof are always green and fair to look upon; in respect whereof they call it Ilha Brava, that is, the brave island. From the banks thereof into the sea do run in many places reasonable streams of fresh water easy to come by, but there was no convenient road for our ships; for such was the depth that no ground could be had for anchoring. And it is reported that ground was never found in that place; so that the tops of Fogo burn not so high in the air, but the roots of Brava are quenched as low in the sea.

Being departed from these islands, we drew towards the line, where we were becalmed the space of three weeks, but yet subject to divers great storms, terrible lightnings and much thunder. But with this misery we had the commodity of great store of fish, as dolphins, bonitos, and flying-fishes, whereof some fell into our ships; wherehence they could not rise again for want of moisture, for when their wings are dry they cannot fly.

From the first day of our departure from the islands of Cape Verde, we sailed 54 days without sight of land. And the first land that we fell with was the coast of Brazil, which we saw the fifth of April, in the height of 33 degrees towards the pole Antarctic. And being discovered at sea by the inhabitants of the country, they made upon the coast great fires for a sacrifice (as we learned) to the devils; about which they use conjurations, making heaps of sand, and other ceremonies, that when any ship shall go about to stay upon their coast, not only sands may be gathered together in shoals in every place, but also that storms and tempests may arise, to the casting away of ships and men, whereof, as it is reported, there have been divers experiments.

The 7. day in a mighty great storm, both of lightning, rain, and thunder, we lost the canter, which we called the Christopher. But the eleventh day after, by our General's great care in dispersing his ships, we found her again; and the place where we met our General called the Cape of Joy, where every ship took in some water. Here we found a good temperature and sweet air, a very fair and pleasant country with an exceeding fruitful soil, where were great store of large and mighty deer, but we came not to the sight of any people; but travelling further into the country we perceived the footing of people in the clay ground, shewing that they were men of great stature. Being returned to our ships we weighed anchor, and ran somewhat further, and harboured ourselves between the rock and the main; where by means of the rock that brake the force of the sea, we rid very safe. And upon this rock we killed for our provision certain sea-wolves, commonly called with us seals. From hence we went our course to 36 degrees, and entered the great river of Plate, and ran into 54 and 53 1-2 fathoms of fresh water, where we filled our water by the ship's side; but our General finding here no good harbour, as he thought he should, bare out again to sea the 27. of April, and in bearing out we lost sight of our fly-boat wherein Master Doughty was. But we, sailing along, found a fair and reasonable good bay, wherein were many and the same profitable islands; one whereof had so many seals as would at the least have laden all our ships, and the rest of the islands are, as it were, laden with fowls, which is wonderful to see, and they of divers sorts. It is a place very plentiful of victuals, and hath in it no want of fresh water. Our General, after certain days of his abode in this place, being on shore in an island, the people of the country shewed themselves unto him, leaping and dancing, and entered into traffic with him; but they would not receive anything at any man's hands, but the same must be cast upon the ground. They are of clean, comely, and strong bodies, swift on foot, and seem to be very active.

The 18. day of May, our General thought it needful to have a care of such ships as were absent; and therefore endeavouring to seek the fly-boat wherein Master Doughty was, we espied her again the next day. And whereas certain of our ships were sent to discover the coast and to search an harbour, the Marigold and the canter being employed in that business, came unto us and gave us understanding of a safe harbour that they had found. Wherewith all our ships bare, and entered it; where we watered and made new provision of victuals, as by seals, whereof we slew to the number of 200 or 300 in the space of an hour. Here our General in the Admiral rid close aboard the fly-boat, and took out of her all the provision of victuals and what else was in her, and hauling her to the land, set fire to her, and so burnt her to save the iron work. Which being a-doing, there came down of the country certain of the people naked, saving only about their waist the skin of some beast, with the fur or hair on, and something also wreathed on their heads. Their faces were painted with divers colours, and some of them had on their heads the similitude of horns, every man his bow, which was an ell in length, and a couple of arrows. They were very agile people and quick to deliver, and seemed not to be ignorant in the feats of wars, as by their order of ranging a few men might appear. These people would not of a long time receive anything at our hands; yet at length our General being ashore, and they dancing after their accustomed manner about him, and he once turning his back towards them, one leaped suddenly to him, and took his cap with his gold band off his head, and ran a little distance from him, and shared it with his fellow, the cap to the one, and the band to the other. Having despatched all our business in this place, we departed and set sail. And immediately upon our setting forth we lost our canter, which was absent three of four days; but when our General had her again, he took out the necessaries, and so gave her over, near to the Cape of Good Hope. The next day after, being the 20. of June, we harboured ourselves again in a very good harbour, called by Magellan, Port St. Julian, where we found a gibbet standing upon the main; which we supposed to be the place where Magellan did execution upon some of his disobedient and rebellious company.

The two and twentieth day our General went ashore to the main, and in his company John Thomas, and Robert Winterhie, Oliver the master-gunner, John Brewer, Thomas Hood, and Thomas Drake. And entering on land, they presently met with two or three of the country people. And Robert Winterhie having in his hands a bow and arrows, went about to make a shoot of pleasure, and, in his draught, his bowstring brake; which the rude savages taking as a token of war, began to bend the force of their bows against our company, and drove them to their shifts very narrowly.

In this port our General began to enquire diligently of the actions of Master Thomas Doughty, and found them not to be such as he looked for, but tending rather of contention or mutiny, or some other disorder, whereby, without redress, the success of the voyage might greatly have been hazarded. Whereupon the company was called together and made acquainted with the particulars of the cause, which were found, partly by Master Doughty's own confession, and partly by the evidence of the fact, to be true. Which when our General saw, although his private affection to Master Doughty, as he then in the presence of us all sacredly protested, was great, yet the care he had of the state of the voyage, of the expectation of her Majesty, and of the honour of his country did more touch him, as indeed it ought, than the private respect of one man. So that the cause being thoroughly heard, and all things done in good order as near as might be to the course of our laws in England, it was concluded that Master Doughty should receive punishment according to the quality of the offence. And he, seeing no remedy but patience for himself, desired before his death to receive the communion, which he did at the hands of Master Fletcher, our minister, and our General himself accompanied him in that holy action. Which being done, and the place of execution made ready, he having embraced our General, and taken his leave of all the company, with prayers for the Queen's Majesty and our realm, in quiet sort laid his head to the block, where he ended his life. This being done, our General made divers speeches to the whole company, persuading us to unity, obedience, love, and regard of our voyage; and for the better confirmation thereof, willed every man the next Sunday following to prepare himself the communion, as Christian brethren and friends, ought to do. Which was done in very reverent sort; and so with good contentment every man went about his business.

The 17. day of August we departed the port of St. Julian, and the 20. day we fell with the Strait of Magellan, going into the South Sea; at the cape or headland whereof we found the body of a dead man, whose flesh was clean consumed. The 21. day we entered the Strait, which we found to have many turnings, and as it were shuttings-up, as if there were no passage at all. By means whereof we had the wind often against us; so that some of the fleet recovering a cape or point of land, others should be forced to turn back again, and to come to an anchor where they could. In this Strait there be many fair harbours, with store of fresh water. But yet they lack their best commodity, for the water there is of such depth, that no man shall find ground to anchor in, except it be in some narrow river or corner, or between some rocks; so that if any extreme blasts or contrary winds do come, whereunto the place is much subject, it carrieth with it no small danger. The land on both sides is very huge and mountainous; the lower mountains whereof, although they be monstrous and wonderful to look upon for their height, yet there are others which in height exceed them in a strange manner, reaching themselves above their fellows so high, that between them did appear three regions of clouds. These mountains are covered with snow. At both the southerly and easterly parts of the Strait there are island, among which the sea hath his indraught into the Straits, even as it hath in the main entrance of the frete. This Strait is extreme cold, with frost and snow continually; the trees seem to stoop with the burden of the weather, and yet are green continually, and many good and sweet herbs do very plentifully grow and increase under them. The breadth of the Strait is in some places a league, in some other places two leagues and three leagues, and in some

other four leagues; but the narrowest place hath a league over.

The 24. of August we arrived at an island in the Straits, where we found great store of fowl which could not fly, of the bigness of geese; whereof we killed in less than one day 3,000, and victualled ourselves thoroughly therewith. The 6. day of September we entered the South Sea at the cape or head shore. The 7. day we were driven by a great storm from the entering into the South Sea, 200 leagues and odd in longitude, and one degree to the southward of the Strait; in which height, and so many leagues to the westward, the 15. day of September, fell out the eclipse of the moon at the hour of six of the clock at night. But neither did the ecliptical conflict of the moon impair our state, nor her clearing again amend us a whit; but the accustomed eclipse of the sea continued in his force, we being darkened more than the moon sevenfold.

From the bay which we called the Bay of Severing of Friends, we were driven back to the southward of the Straits in 57 degrees and a tierce; in which height we came to an anchor among the islands, having there fresh and very good water, with herbs of singular virtue. Not far from hence we entered another bay, where we found people, both men and women, in their canoes naked, and ranging from one island to another seek their meat; who entered traffic with us for such things as they had. We returning hence northward again, found the third of October three islands, in one of which was such plenty of birds as is scant credible to report. The 8. day of October we lost sight of one of our consorts, wherein Master Winter was; who, as then we supposed, was put by a storm into the Straits again. Which at our return home we found to be true, and he not perished, as some of our company feared. Thus being come in to the height of the Straits again, we ran, supposing the coast of Chili to lie as the general maps have described it, namely north-west; which we found to lie and trend to the north-east and eastwards. Whereby it appeareth that this part of Chili hath not been truly hitherto discovered, or at the least not truly reported, for the space of twelve degrees at the least; being set down either of purpose to deceive, or of ignorant conjecture.

We continuing our course, fell the 29. of November with an island called La Mocha, where we cast anchor; and our General, hoisting out our boat, went with ten of our company to shore. Where we found people, whom the cruel and extreme dealings of the Spaniards have forced, for their own safety and liberty, to flee from the main, and to fortify themselves in this island. We being on land, the people came down to us to the water side with show of great courtesy, bringing to us potatoes, roots, and two very fat sheep; which our General received, and gave them other things for them, and had promised to have water there. But the next day repairing again to the shore, and sending two men a-land with barrels to fill water, the people taking them for Spaniards (to whom they use to show no favour if they take them) laid violent hands on them, and, as we think, slew them. Our General seeing this, stayed here no longer, but weighed anchor, and set sail towards the coast of Chili. And drawing towards it, we met near to the shore an Indian in a canoa, who thinking us to have been Spaniards, came to us and told us, that at a place called Santiago, there was a great Spanish ship laden from the kingdom of Peru; for which good news our General gave him divers trifles. Whereof he was glad, and went along with us and brought us to the place, which is called the port of Valparaiso. When we came thither we found, indeed, the ship riding at anchor, having in her eight Spaniards and three negroes; who, thinking us to have been Spaniards, and their friends, welcomed us with a drum, and made ready a botija of wine of Chili to drink to us. But as soon as we were entered, one of our company called Thomas Moon began to lay about him, and struck one of the Spaniards, and said unto him, Abaxo, perro! that is in English. 'Go down, dog!' One of these Spaniards, seeing persons of that quality in those seas, all to crossed and blessed himself. But, to be short, we stowed them under hatches, all save one Spaniard, who suddenly and desperately leapt overboard into the sea, and swam ashore to the town of Santiago, to give them warning of our arrival.

They of the town, being not above nine households, presently fled away and abandoned the town. Our General manned his boat and the Spanish ship's boat, and went to the town; and, being come to it, we rifled it, and came to a small chapel, which we entered, and found therein a silver chalice, two cruets, and one altar-cloth, the spoil whereof our General gave to Master Fletcher, his

minister. We found also in this town a warehouse stored with wine of Chili and many boards of cedar-wood; all which wine we brought away with us, and certain of the boards to burn for firewood. And so, being come aboard, we departed the haven, having first set all the Spaniards on land, saving one John Griego, a Greek born, whom our General carried with him as pilot to bring him into the haven of Lima.

When we were at sea our General rifled the ship, and found in her good store of the wine of Chili, and 25,000 pesos of very pure and fine gold of Valdivia, amounting in value to 37,000 ducats of Spanish money, and above. So, going on our course, we arrived next at a place called Coquimbo, where our General sent fourteen of his men on land to fetch water. But they were espied by the Spaniards, who came with 300 horsemen and 200 footmen, and slew one of our men with a piece. The rest came aboard in safety, and the Spaniards departed. We went on shore again and buried our man, and the Spaniards came down again with a flag of truce; but we set sail, and would not trust them. From hence we went to a certain port called Tarapaca; where, being landed, we found by the sea side a Spaniard lying asleep, who had lying by him thirteen bars of silver, which weighed 4,000 ducats Spanish. We took the silver and left the man. Not far from hence, going on land for fresh water, we met with a Spaniard and an Indian boy driving eight llamas or sheep of Peru, which are as big as asses; every of which sheep had on his back two bags of leather, each bag containing 50 lb. weight of fine silver. So that, bringing both the sheep and their burthen to the ships, we found in all the bags eight hundred weight of silver.

Herehence we sailed to a place called Arica; and, being entered the port, we found there three small barks, which we rifled, and found in one of them fifty-seven wedges of silver, each of them weighing about 20 lb. weight, and every of these wedges were of the fashion and bigness of a brickbat. In all these three barks, we found not one person. For they, mistrusting no strangers, were all gone a-land to the town, which consisteth of about twenty houses; which we would have ransacked if our company had been better and more in number. But our General, contented with the spoil of the ships, left the town and put off again to sea, and set sail for Lima, and, by the way, met with a small bark, which he boarded, and found in her good store of linen cloth. Whereof taking some quantity, he let her go.

To Lima we came the 13. of February; and, being entered the haven, we found there about twelve sail of ships lying fast moored at an anchor, having all their sails carried on shore; for the masters and merchants were here most secure, having never been assaulted by enemies, and at this time feared the approach of none such as we were. Our General rifled these ships, and found in one of them as chest full of reals of plate, and good store of silks and linen cloth; and took the chest into his own ship, and good store of the silks and linen. In which ship he had news of another ship called the Cacafuego, which was gone towards Payta, and that the same ship was laden with treasure. Whereupon we stayed no longer here, but, cutting all the cables of the ships in the haven, we let them drive whither they would, either to sea or to the shore; and with all speed we followed the Cacafuego toward Payta, thinking there to have found her. But before we arrived there she was gone from thence towards Panama; whom our General still pursued, and by the way met with a bark laden with ropes and tackle for ships, which he boarded and searched, and found in her 80 lb. weight of gold, and a crucifix of gold with goodly great emeralds set in it, which he took, and some of the cordage also for his own ship. From hence we departed, still following the Cacafuego; and our General promised our company that whosoever should first descry her should have his chain of gold for his good news. It fortuned that John Drake, going up into the top, descried her about three of the clock. And about six of the clock we came to her and boarded her, and shot at her three pieces of ordnance, and strake down her mizen; and, being entered, we found in her great riches, as jewels and precious stones, thirteen chests full of reals of plate, fourscore pound weight of gold, and six-and-twenty ton of silver. The place where we took this prize was called Cape de San Francisco, about 150 leagues [south] from Panama. The pilot's name of this ship was Francisco; and amongst other plate that our General found in this ship he found two very fair gilt bowls of silver, which were the pilot's. To whom our General said, Senor Pilot, you have here two silver cups, but I must needs have one of them; which the pilot, because he could not otherwise choose, yielded unto, and gave the other to the steward of our General's ships. When this pilot departed from us, his boy said thus unto our General: Captain, our ship shall be called no more the Cacafuego, but the Cacaplata, and your ship shall be called the Cacafuego. Which pretty speech of the pilot's boy ministered matter of laughter to us, both then and long after. When our General had done what he would with this Cacafuego, he cast her off, and we went on our course still towards the west; and not long after met with a ship laden with linen cloth and fine China dishes of white earth, and great store of China silks, of all which things we took as we listed. The owner himself of this ship was in her, who was a Spanish gentleman, from whom our General took a falcon of gold, with a great emerald in the breast thereof; and the pilot of the ship he took also with him, and so cast the ship off.

This pilot brought us to the haven of Guatulco, the town whereof, as he told us, had but 17 Spaniards in it. As soon as we were entered this haven, we landed, and went presently to the town and to the town-house; where we found a judge sitting in judgment, being associated with three other officers, upon three negroes that had conspired the burning of the town. Both which judges and prisoners we took, and brought them a-shipboard, and caused the chief judge to write his letter to the town to command all the townsmen to avoid, that we might safely water there. Which being done, and they departed, we ransacked the town; and in one house we found a pot, of the quantity of a bushel, full of reals of plate, which we brought to our ship. And here one Thomas Moon, one of our company, took a Spanish gentleman as he was flying out of the town; and, searching him, he found a chain of gold about him, and other jewels, which he took, and so let him go. At this place our General, among other Spaniards, set ashore his Portugal pilot which he took at the islands of Cape Verde out of a ship of St. Mary port, of Portugal. And having set them ashore we departed hence, and sailed to the island of Canno; where our General landed, and brought to shore his own ship, and discharged her, mended and graved her, and furnished our ship with water and wood sufficiently.

And while we were here we espied a ship and set sail after her, and took her, and found in her two pilots and a Spanish governor, going for the islands of the Philippines. We searched the ship, and took some of her merchandises, and so let her go. Our General at this place and time, thinking himself, both in respect of his private injuries received from the Spaniards, as also of their contempts and indignities offered to our country and prince in general, sufficiently satisfied and revenged; and supposing that her Majesty at his return would rest contented with this service, purposed to continue no longer upon the Spanish coast, but began to consider and to consult of the best way for his country.

He thought it not good to return by the Straits, for two special causes; the one, lest the Spaniards should there wait and attend for him in great number and strength, whose hands, he, being left but one ship, could not possibly escape. The other cause was the dangerous situation of the mouth of the Straits in the South Sea; where continual storms reigning and blustering, as he found by experience, besides the shoals and sands upon the coast, he thought it not a good course to adventure that way. He resolved, therefore, to avoid these hazards, to go forward to the Islands of the Malucos, and therehence to sail the course of the Portugals by the Cape of Buena Esperanza. Upon this resolution he began to think of his best way to the Malucos, and finding himself, where he now was, becalmed, he saw that of necessity he must be forced to take a Spanish course; namely, to sail somewhat northerly to get a wind. We therefore set sail, and sailed 600 leagues at the least for a good wind; and thus much we sailed from the 16. of April till the third of June.

The fifth of June, being in 43 degrees towards the pole Arctic, we found the air so cold, that our men being grievously pinched with the same, complained of the extremity thereof; and the further we went, the more the cold increased upon us. Whereupon we thought it best for that time to seek the land, and did so; finding it not mountainous, but low plain land, till we came within 38 degrees towards the line. In which height it pleased God to send us into a fair and good bay, with a good wind to enter the same. In this bay we anchored; and the people of the country, having their houses close by the water's side, shewed themselves unto us, and sent a present to our General. When they came unto us, they greatly wondered at the things that we brought. But our General, according to his natural and accustomed humanity, courteously intreated them, and liberally bestowed on them necessary things to cover their nakedness; whereupon they supposed us to be gods, and would not be persuaded to the contrary. The presents which they sent to our General, were feathers, and cauls of network. Their houses are digged round about with earth, and have from the uttermost brims of the circle, clifts of wood set upon them, joining close together at the top like a spire steeple, which by reason of that closeness are very warm. Their bed is the ground with rushes strowed on it; and lying about the house, [they] have the fire in the midst. The men go naked; the women take bulrushes, and kemb them after the manner of hemp, and thereof make their loose garments, which being knit about their middles, hang down about their hips, having also about their shoulders a skin of deer, with the hair upon it. These women are very obedient and serviceable to their husbands.

After they were departed from us, they came and visited us the second time, and brought with them feathers and bags of tabacco for presents. And when they came to the top of the hill, at the bottom whereof we had pitched our tents, they stayed themselves; where one appointed for speaker wearied himself with making a long oration; which done, they left their bows upon the hill, and came down with their presents. In the meantime the women, remaining upon the hill, tormented themselves lamentably, tearing their flesh from their cheeks, whereby we perceived that they were about a sacrifice. In the meantime our General with his company went to prayer, and to reading of the Scriptures, at which exercise they were attentive, and seemed greatly to be affected with it; but when they were come unto us, they restored again unto us those things which before we bestowed upon them. The news of our being there being spread through the country, the people that inhabited round about came down, and amongst them the king himself, a man of goodly stature, and comely personage, with many other tall and warlike men; before whose coming were sent two ambassadors to our General, to signify that their king was coming, in doing of which message, their speech was continued about half an hour. This ended, they by signs requested our General to send something by their hand to their king, as a token that his coming might be in peace. Wherein our General having satisfied them, they returned with glad tidings to their king, who marched to us with a princely majesty, the people crying continually after their manner; and as they drew near unto us, so did they strive to behave themselves in their actions with comeliness. In the fore-front was a man of a goodly personage, who bare the sceptre or mace before the king; whereupon hanged two crowns, less and a bigger, with three chains of marvellous length. The crowns were made of knit work, wrought artificially with feathers of divers colours. The chains were made of a bony substance, and few be the persons among them that are admitted to wear them; and of that number also the persons are stinted, as some ten, some twelve, &c. Next unto him which bare the sceptre, was the king himself, with his guard about his person, clad with coney skins, and other skins. After them followed the naked common sort of people, every one having his face painted, some with white, some with black, and other colours, and having in their hands one thing or another for a present. Not so much as their children, but they also brought their presents.

In the meantime our General gathered his men together, and marched within his fenced place, making, against their approaching, a very warlike show. They being trooped together in their order, and a general salutation being made, there was presently a general silence. Then he that bare the sceptre before the king, being informed by another, whom they assigned to that office, with a manly and lofty voice proclaimed that which the other spake to him in secret, continuing half an hour. Which ended, and a general Amen, as it were, given, the king with the whole number of men and women, the children excepted, came down without any weapon; who, descending to the foot of the hill, set themselves in order. In coming towards our bulwarks and tents, the sceptre-bearer began a song, observing his measures in a dance, and that with a stately countenance; whom the king with his guard, and every degree of persons following, did in like manner sing and dance, saving only the women, which danced and kept silence. The General permitted them to enter within our bulwark, where they continued their song and dance a reasonable time. When they had satisfied themselves, they made signs to our General to sit down; to whom the king and divers others made several orations, or rather supplications, that he would take their province and kingdom into his hand, and become their king, making signs that they would resign unto him their right and title of the whole land, and become his subjects. In which, to persuade us the better, the king and the rest, with one consent, and with great reverence, joyfully singing a song, did set the crown upon his head, enriched his neck with all their chains, and offered him many other things, honouring him by the name of Hioh, adding thereunto, as it seemed, a sign of triumph; which thing our General thought not meet to reject, because he knew not what honour and profit it might be to our country. Wherefore in the name, and to the use of her Majesty, he took the sceptre, crown, and dignity of the said country into his hands, wishing that the richest and treasure thereof might so conveniently be transported to the enriching of her kingdom at home, as it aboundeth in the same.

The common sort of people, leaving the king and his guard with our General, scattered themselves together with their sacrifices among our people, taking a diligent view of every person: and such as pleased their fancy (which were the youngest), they enclosing them about offered their sacrifices unto them with lamentable weeping, scratching and tearing their flesh from their faces with their nails, whereof issued abundance of blood. But we used signs to them of disliking this, and stayed their hands from force, and directed them upwards to the living God, whom only they ought to worship. They shewed unto us their wounds, and craved help of them at our hands; whereupon we gave them lotions, plaisters, and ointments agreeing to the state of their griefs, beseeching God to cure their diseases. Every third day they brought their sacrifices unto us, until they understood our meaning, that we had no pleasure in them; yet they could not be long absent from us, but daily frequented our company to the hour of our departure, which departure seemed so grievous unto them, that their joy was turned into sorrow. They entreated us, that being absent we would remember them, and by stealth provided a sacrifice, which we misliked.

Our necessary business being ended, our General with his company travelled up into the country to their villages, where we found herds of deer by a thousand in a company, being most large, and fat of body. We found the whole country to be a warren of a strange kind of coneys; their bodies in bigness as be the Barbary coneys, their heads as the heads of ours, the feet of a want, and the tail of a rat, being of great length. Under her chin is on either side a bag, into the which she gathereth her meat, when she hath filled her belly abroad. The people eat their bodies, and make great account of their skins, for their king's coat was made of them. Our General called this country Nova Albion, and that for two causes; the one in respect of the white banks and cliffs, which lie towards the sea, and the other, because it might have some affinity with our country in name, which sometime was so called. There is no part of earth here to be taken up, wherein there is not some probable show of gold or silver.

At our departure hence our General set up a monument of our being there, as also of her Majesty's right and title to the same; namely a plate, nailed upon a fair great post, whereupon was engraved her Majesty's name, the day and year of our arrival there, with the free giving up of the province and people into her Majesty's hands, together with her Highness' picture and arms, in a piece of six pence of current English money, under the plate, whereunder was also written the name of our General.

It seemeth that the Spaniards hitherto had never been in this part of the country, neither did ever discover the land by many degrees to the southwards of this place.

Source: *Voyages and Travels: Ancient and Modern, with Introductions, Notes and Illustrations.* New York: P. F. Collier, 1910.

Charter to Sir Walter Raleigh (1584)

Soldier, explorer, and courtier of Elizabeth I, Sir Walter Raleigh was granted the right to establish colonies in North America by this charter of 1584. Despite the backing of the crown, which was more political than economic, Raleigh's three attempts to create settlements on the coast of what is now North Carolina failed. Most notorious of these was the colony of Roanoke. Established in 1587, its entire contingent of 100-plus colonists disappeared almost *without a trace, victims, many historians believe, of hostile inhabitants.*

Elizabeth by the Grace of God of England, Fraunce and Ireland Queene, defender of the faith, &c. To all people to whome these presents shall come, greeting.

Knowe yee that of our especial grace, certaine science, and meere motion, we have given and graunted, and by these presents for us, our heires and successors, we give and graunt to our trustie and welbeloved servant *Walter Ralegh,* Esquire, and to his heires assignee for ever, free libertie and licence from time to time, and at all times for ever hereafter, to discover, search, finde out, and view such remote, heathen and barbarous lands, countries, and territories, not actually possessed of any Christian Prince, nor inhabited by Christian People, as to him, his heires and assignee, and to every or any of them shall seeme good, and the same to have, horde, occupie and enjoy to him, his heires and assignee for euer, with all prerogatives, commodities, jurisdictions, royalties, privileges, franchises, and preheminences, thereto or thereabouts both by sea and land, whatsoever we by our letters patents may graunt, and as we or any of our noble progenitors have heretofore graunted to any person or persons, bodies politique.or corporate: and the said *Walter Ralegh,* his heires and assignee, and all such as from time to time, by licence of us, our heires and successors, shall goe or travaile thither to inhabite or remaine, there to build and fortifie, at the discretion of the said *Walter Ralegh,* his heires and assignee, the statutes or acte of Parliament made against fugitives, or against such as shall depart, romaine or continue out of our Realme of England without licence, or any other statute, acte, lawe, or any ordinance whatsoever to the contrary in anywise notwithstanding.

And we do likewise by these presents, of our especial grace, meere motion, and certain knowledge, for us, our heires and successors, give and graunt full authoritie, libertie and power to the said Walter Salem, his heires and assignee, and every of them, that he and they, and every or any of them, shall and may at all and every time, and times hereafter, have, take, and leade in the saide voyage, and travaile thitherward, or to inhabit there with him, or them, and every or any of them, such and so many of our subjects as shall willingly accompanie him or them, and every or any of them to whom also we doe by these presents, give full libertie and authority in that behalfe, and also to have, take, and employ, and use sufficient shipping and furniture for the Transportations and Navigations in that behalfe, so that none of the same persons or any of them, be such as hereafter shall be restrained by us, our heires, or successors.

And further that the said *Walter Ralegh,* his heires and assignee, and every of them, shall have holde, occupie, and enioye to him, his heires and assignee, and every of them for ever, all the soile of all such lands, territories, and Countreis, so to bee discovered and possessed as aforesaide, and of all such Cities, castles, townes, villages, and places in the same, with the right, royalties, franchises, and iurisdictions, as well marine as other within the saide lands, or Countreis, or the seas thereunto adioyning, to be had, or used, with full power to dispose thereof, and of every part in fee-simple or otherwise, according to the order of the lawes of England, as neere as the same conveniently may bee, at his, and their will and pleasure, to any persons then being, or that shall romaine within the allegiance of us, our heires, and successors: reserving always to us our heires, and successors, for all services, duties, and demaundes, the first part of all the oare of golde and silver, that from time to time, and at all times after such discoverie, subduing and possessing, shal be there gotten and obtained: All which lands, Countreis, and territories, shall for ever be holden of the said *Walter Ralegh,* his heires and assignee, of us, our heirs and successors, by homage, and by the said paiment of the said first part, reserved onely for all services.

And moreover, we doe by these presents, for us, our heires and. successors, give and graunt licence to the said *Walter Ralegh,* his heirs, and assignee, and every of them, that he, and they, and every or any of them, shall and may from time to time, and at all times for ever hereafter, for his and their defence, encounter and expulse, repell and resist as well by sea as by land, and by all other wayes whatsoever, all, and every such person and persons whatsoever, as without the especiall liking and licence of the saide *Walter Ralegh,* and of his heires and assignee, shall attempt to inhabite within the said Countreis, or any of them, or within the space of two hundreth leagues neere to the place or places within such Countreis as aforesaide (if they shall not bee before planted or inhabited within the limits as aforesaide with the subjects of any Christian Prince being in amitie with us) where the saide *Walter Ralegh,* his heires, or assignee, or any of them, or his, or their or any of their associates or company, shall within sine yeeres (next ensuing) make their dwellings or abidings, or that shall enterprise or attempt at any time hereafter unlawfully to annoy, either by sea or land, the saide *Walter Ralegh,* his heirs or assignee, or any of them, or his or their, or any of his or their companies giving, and graunting by these presents further power and authoritie, to the said *Walter Ralegh,* his heirs and assignee, and every of them from time to time, and at all times for ever hereafter, to take and surprise by all maner of meanes whatsoever, all and every those person or persons, with their shipper, vessels, and other goods and furniture, which without the licence of the saide *Walter Ralegh,* or his heires, or assignee, as aforesaide, shal be founde trafiquing into any harbour or harbors, creeke, or creekes, within the limits aforesaide, (the subjects of our Realms and Dominions, and all other persons in amitie with us, trading to the Newfound land for fishing as heretofore they have commonly used, or being driven by force of a tempest, or shipwracke onely excepted:) and those persons, and every of them, with their shippes, vessels, goods and furniture to deteine and possesse as of good and lawfull prize, according to the discretion of him the saide *Walter Ralegh,* his heires, and assignee, and every, or any of them. And for uniting in more perfect league and amitie, of such Countreis, lands, and territories so to bee possessed and inhabited as aforesaide with our Realmes of Englande, and Ireland, and the better incouragement of men to these enterprises: we do by these presents, graunt and declare that all such Countreis, so hereafter to be possessed and inhabited as is aforesaide, from thencefoorth shall bee of the allegiance of us, our heires and successours. And wee doe graunt to the saide *Walter Ralegh,* his heires, and assignee, and to all, and every of them, and to all and every other person, and persons being of our allegiance, whose names shall be noted or entred in some of our Courtes of recorde within our Realme of Englande, that with the assent of the saide *Walter Ralegh,* his heires or assignes, shall in his journeis for discoverie, or in the journeis for conquest, hereafter travelle to such lands, countreis and territories, as aforesaide, and to their, and to every of their heires, that they, and every or any of them, being either borne within our saide Realmes of Englande, or Irelande or in any other place within our allegiance, and which hereafter shall be inhabiting within any the lands, Countreis, and territories, with such licence (as aforesaide) shall and may have all the priviledges of free Denizens, and persons native of England, and within our allegiance in such like ample manor and fourme, as if they were borne and personally resident within our saide Realme of England, any lawe, custome, or usage to the contrary notwithstanding

And for asmuch as upon the finding out, discovering, or inhabiting of such remote lands, countreis, and territories as aforesaid, it shal be necessary for the safetie of al men, that shal adventure them selves in those murnies or voyages, to determine to live together in Christian peace, and civil quietnes ech with other, whereby every one may with more pleasure and profit enjoy that whereunto they shall attaine with great Paine and perill, we for us, our heires and successors, are likewise pleased and contented, and by these presents do give and graunt to the said *Walter Ralegh,* his heires and assignee for ever, that he and they, and every or any of them, shall and may from time to time for ever hereafter, within the said mentioned remote lands and Countreis in the way by the seas thither, and from thence, inane full and meere power and authoritie to correct, punish, pardon, governe, and rule by their and every or any of their good discretions and pollicies, as well in causes capital, or criminal, as civil, both marine and other all such our subjects as shall from time to time adventure themselves in the said journies or voyages, or that shall at any time hereafter inhabite any such lands, countreis, or territories as aforesaide, or shall abide within 200. leagues of any of the saide place or places, where the saide Walter Ralegh, his heires or assignee, or any of them, or any of his or their associates or companies, shall inhabits within 6. yeeres next ensuing the date hereof, according to such statutes, lawes and ordinances, as shall bee by him the saide Walter Ralegh his heires and assignee, and every or any of them devised, or established, for the better government of the said people as aforesaid. So always as the said statutes, lawes, and ordinances

may be as neere as conveniently may be, agreeable to the forme of the lawes, statutes, governement, or pollicie of England, and also so as they be not against the true Christian faith, nowe professed in the Church of England, nor in any wise to withdraws any of the subjects or people of those lances or places from the allegiance of us. our heires and successours, as their immediate Soueraigne under God.

And further, wee doe by these presents for us, our heires and successors, give and graunt full power and authoritie to our trustie and welbeloved counsailer sir *William Cicill* knight, Lorde *Burghley,* our high Treasourer of England, and to the Lorde Treasourer of England, for us, our heires and successours for the time being, and to the privie Counsell, of us, our heirs and successours, or any foure or more of them for the time being, that hee, they, or any fours or more of them, shall and may from time to time, and at all times hereafter, under his or their handes or scales by vertue of these presents, authorise and licence the saide *Walter Ralegh,* his heires and assignee. and every or any of them by him, and by themselves, or by their, of any of their sufficient Atturnies, deputies, officers, ministers, factors, and servants, to imbarke and transport out of our Realme of England and Ireland, and the Dominions thereof all, or any of his, or their goods, and all or any the goods of his and their associate and companies, and every or any of them, with such other necessaries and commodities of any our Realmes, as to the saide Lorde Treasourer, or foure or more of the privie Counsaile, of us, our heires and successors for the time being (as aforesaide) shalbe from time to time by his or their wisdomes, or discretions thought meete and convenient, for the better reliefe and supportation of him the saide *Walter Ralegh,* his heires, and assignee, and every or any of them, and of his or their or any of their associate and companies, any acte, statute, lawe, or other thing to the contrary in any wise notwithstanding.

Provided alwayes, and our will and pleasure is, and wee do hereby declare to all Christian kings, princes and states, that if the saide *Walter Ralegh,* his heires or assignee, or any of them, or any other by their licence or appointment, shall at any time or times hereafter, robbe or spoile by sea or by land, or do any acte of unjust or unlawful hostilitie, to any of the subjects of us, our heires or successors, or to any of the subjects of any the kings, princes, rulers, governors, or estates, being then in perfect league and amitie with us, our heires and successors, and that upon such injury, or upon just complaint of any such prince, ruler, governoir, or estate, or their subjects, wee, our heires and successours, shall make open proclamation within any the Fortes of our Realme of England, that the saide *Walter Ralegh,* his heires and assignee, and adherents, or any to whome these our letters patents may extende, shall within the termes to be Emitted, by such proclamation, make full restitution, and satisfaction of all such injuries done, so as both we and the said princes, or other so complayning, may horde us and themselves fully contented. And that if the saide *Walter Ralegh,* his heires and assignee, shall not make or cause to be made satisfaction accordingly, within such time so to be limitted, that then it shall be lawfull to us our heires and successors, to put the saide *Walter Ralegh,* his heires and assignee and adherents, and all the inhabitants of the said places to be discovered (as is aforesaide) or any of them out of our allegiance and protection, and that from and after such time of putting out of protection the said Walter Ralegh, his heires, assignee and adherents, and others so to be put out, and the said places within their habitation, possession and rule, shal be out of our allegeance and protection, and free for all princes and others, to pursue with hostilitie, as being not our subjects, nor by us any way to be avouched, maintained or defended, nor to be holden as any of ours, nor to our protection or dominion, or allegiance any way belonging, for that expresse mention of the cleer yeerely value of the certaintie of the premisses, or any part thereof, or of any other gift, or grant by us, or any our progenitors, or predecessors to the said Walter Ralegh, before this time made in these presents be not expressed, or any other grant, ordinance, provision, proclamation, or restraint to the contrarye thereof, before this time given, ordained, or provided, or any other thing, cause, or matter whatsoever, in any wise notwithstanding. In witness whereof, we have caused these our letters to be made patents. Witnesse our selves, at *Westminster,* the 25. day of March, in the sixe and twentieth yeere of our Raigne.

Source: Thorpe, Francis Newton, ed. *The Federal and State Constitutions, Colonial Charters, and Other Organic Laws of the States, Territories, and Colonies Now or Heretofore Forming the United States of America.* Washington, DC: Government Printing Office, 1909.

Elizabeth I on the Spanish Armada (1588)

For several decades leading up to 1588 and the launch of the Spanish Armada against England, the latter country had been engaging in barely disguised official piracy against Spanish shipping to, from, and within New Spain and other Spanish possessions in the Americas. To put a stop to these depredations, Spain launched its great armada in preparation of an invasion of the English home islands. Here, Elizabeth I, queen of England, speaks to her troops preparing for battle. Ultimately, bad weather and England's smaller but more maneuverable fleet would defeat the armada and end the threat of invasion by Spain. Most historians agree that the defeat of the armada is a milestone in England's emergence as a great power and colonizer.

My loving people, we have been persuaded by some, that are careful of our safety, to take heed how we commit ourselves to armed multitudes, for fear of treachery; but I assure you, I do not desire to live to distrust my faithful and loving people. Let tyrants fear; I have always so behaved myself that, under God, I have placed my chiefest strength and safeguard in the loyal hearts and good will of my subjects. And therefore I am come amongst you at this time, not as for my recreation or sport, but being resolved, in the midst and heat of the battle, to live or die amongst you all; to lay down, for my God, and for my kingdom, and for my people, my honor and my blood, even the dust. I know I have but the body of a weak and feeble woman; but I have the heart of a king, and of a king of England, too; and think foul scorn that Parma or Spain, or any prince of Europe, should dare to invade the borders of my realms: to which, rather than any dishonor should grow by me, I myself will take up arms; I myself will be your general, judge, and rewarder of every one of your virtues in the field. I know already, by your forwardness, that you have deserved rewards and crowns; and we do assure you, on the word of a prince, they shall be duly paid you. In the mean my lieutenant general shall be in my stead, than whom never prince commanded a more noble and worthy subject; not doubting by your obedience to my general, by your concord in the camp, and by your valor in the field, we shall shortly have a famous victory over the enemies of my God, of my kingdom, and of my people.

Elizabeth I of England—1588

Source: "Spanish Armada," in *The Catholic Encyclopedia*, ed. J. H. Pollen. New York: Robert Appleton, 1907.

Instructions for the Virginia Colony (1606)

In 1606, a number of merchants who had organized the Virginia Company were issued a charter by James I for the settlement of a colony in North America. Wishing to emulate the Spanish, the stockholders of the Virginia Company hoped that the colonists would find precious metals and entice the people of the region to work for them. Given the following instructions, three small ships set forth for the Chesapeake Bay in 1607. Finding no precious metals and a native population most definitely unwilling to work for them, the colonists barely survived the starvation and disease that faced them in the new land during their first decade there.

As we doubt not but you will have especial care to observe the ordinances set down by the King's Majesty and delivered unto you under the Privy Seal; so for your better directions upon your first landing we have thought good to recommend unto your care these instructions and articles following.

When it shall please God to send you on the coast of Virginia, you shall do your best endeavour to find out a safe port in the entrance of some navigable river, making choice of such a one as runneth farthest into the land, and if you happen to discover divers portable rivers, and amongst them any one that hath two main branches, if the difference be not great, make choice of that which bendeth most toward the North-West for that way you shall soonest find the other sea.

When you have made choice of the river on which you mean to settle, be not hasty in landing your victuals and munitions; but first let Captain Newport discover how far that river may be found navigable, that you make election of the strongest, most wholesome and fertile place; for if you make many removes, besides the loss of time, you shall greatly spoil your victuals and your caske, and with great pain transport it in small boats.

But if you choose your place so far up as a bark of fifty tuns will float, then you may lay all your provisions ashore with ease, and the better receive the trade of all the countries about you in the land; and such a place you may perchance find a hundred miles from the river's mouth, and the further up the better. For if you sit down near the entrance, except it be in some island that is strong by nature, an enemy that may approach you on even ground, may easily pull you out; and if he be driven to seek you a hundred miles [in] the land in boats, you shall from both sides of the river where it is narrowest, so beat them with your muskets as they shall never be able to prevail against you.

And to the end that you be not surprised as the French were in Florida by Melindus, and the Spaniard in the same place by the French, you shall do well to make this double provision. First, erect a little stoure [store] at the mouth of the river that may lodge some ten men; with whom you shall leave a light boat, that when any fleet shall be in sight, they may come with speed to give you warning. Secondly, you must in no case suffer any of the native people of the country to inhabit between you and the sea coast; for you cannot carry yourselves so towards them, but they will grow discontented with your habitation, and be ready to guide and assist any nation that shall come to invade you; and if you neglect this, you neglect your safety.

When you have discovered as far up the river as you mean to plant yourselves, and landed your victuals and munitions; to the end that every man may know his charge, you shall do well to divide your six score men into three parts; whereof one party of them you may appoint to fortifie and build, of which your first work must be your storehouse for victuals; the other you may imploy in preparing your ground and sowing your corn and roots; the other ten of these forty you must leave as centinel at the haven's mouth. The other forty you may imploy for two months in discovery of the river above you, and on the country about you; which charge Captain Newport and Captain Gosnold may undertake of these forty discoverers. When they do espie any high lands or hills, Captain Gosnold may take twenty of the company to cross over the lands, and carrying a half dozen pickaxes to try if they can find any minerals. The other twenty may go on by river, and pitch up boughs upon the bank's side, by which the other boats shall follow them by the same turnings. You may also take with them a wherry, such as is used here in the Thames; by which you may send back to the President for supply of munition or any other want, that you may not be driven to return for every small defect.

You must observe if you can, whether the river on which you plant doth spring out of mountains or out of lakes. If it be out of any lake, the passage to the other sea will be more easy, and [it] is like enough, that out of the same lake you shall find some spring which run[s] the contrary way towards the East India Sea; for the great and famous rivers of Volga, Tan[a]is and Dwina have three heads near joynd; and yet the one falleth into the Caspian Sea, the other into the Euxine Sea, and the third into the Paelonian Sea.

In all your passages you must have great care not to offend the naturals [natives], if you can eschew it; and imploy some few of your company to trade with them forcorn and all other . . . victuals if you have any; and this you must do before that they perceive you mean to plant among them; for not being sure how your own seed corn will prosper the first year, to avoid the danger of famine, use and endeavour to store yourselves of the country corn.

Your discoverers that pass over land with hired guides, must look well to them that they slip not from them: and for more assurance, let them take a compass with them, and write down how far they go upon every point of the compass; for that country having no way nor path, if that your guides run from you in the great woods or desert, you shall hardly ever find a passage back.

And how weary soever your soldiers be, let them never trust the country people with the carriage of their weapons; for if they run from you with your shott, which they only fear, they will easily kill them all with their arrows. And whensoever any of yours shoots before them, be sure they may be chosen out of your best marksmen; for if they see your learners miss what they aim at, they will think the weapon not so terrible, and thereby will be bould to assault you.

Above all things, do not advertize the killing of any of your men, that the country people may know it; if they perceive that they are but common men, and that with the loss of many of theirs they diminish any part of yours, they will make many adventures upon you. If the country be populous, you shall do well also, not to let them see or know of your sick men, if you have any; which may also encourage them to many enterprizes.

You must take especial care that you choose a seat for habitation that shall not be over burthened with woods near your town; for all the men you have, shall not he able to cleanse twenty acres a year; besides that it may serve for a covert for your enemies round about.

Neither must you plant in a low or moist place, because it will prove unhealthfull. You shall judge of the good air by the people; for some part of that coast where the lands are low, have their people blear eyed, and with swollen bellies and legs; but if the naturals he strong and clean made, it is a true sign of a wholesome soil.

You must take order to draw up the pinnace that is left with you, under the fort: and take her sails and anchors ashore, all but a small kedge to ride by; least some ill-dispositioned persons slip away with her.

You must take care that your marriners that go for wages, do not mar your trade; for those that mind not to inhabite, for a little gain will debase the estimation of exchange, and hinder the trade for ever after; and therefore you shall not admit or suffer any person whatsoever, other than such as shall be appointed by the President and Counsel there, to buy any merchandizes or other things whatsoever.

It were necessary that all your carpenters and other such like workmen about building do first build your storehouse and those other rooms of publick and necessary use before any house be set up for any private person: and though the workman may belong to any private persons yet let them all work together first for the company and then for private men.

And seeing order is at the same price with confusion, it shall be adviseably done to set your houses even and by a line, that your street may have a good breadth, and be carried square about your market place and every street's end opening into it; that from thence, with a few field pieces, you may command every street throughout; which market place you may also fortify if you think it needfull.

You shall do well to send a perfect relation by Captaine Newport of all that is done, what height you are seated, how far into the land, what commodities you find, what soil, woods and their several kinds, and so of all other things else to advertise particularly; and to suffer no man to return but by pasport from the President and Counsel, nor to write any letter of anything that may discourage others.

Lastly and chiefly the way to prosper and achieve good success is to make yourselves all of one mind for the good of your country and your own, and to serve and fear God the Giver of all Goodness, for every plantation which our Heavenly Father hath not planted shall be rooted out.

Source: Avalon Project of the Yale Law School: www.yale.edu/lawweb/avalon/avalon.htm.

Charter of Massachusetts Bay (1629)

Under Charles I, the English government became increasingly hostile to dissenters from the Church of England, most notably a group disparagingly called the Puritans. Believing themselves a "saving remnant" of England and hoping that their colony would prove to be an ideal "City upon a Hill," which others in the home country would look to for inspiration, some 900 Puritans set sail for New England, where they established a colony on Massachusetts Bay in 1630. Under the charter, excerpted here, they set up a system of self-governance. The Charter of Massachusetts Bay, while hardly democratic in nature, remains a milestone in the establishment of the modern American state.

That the said Governour and Companye, and their Successors, maie have forever one comon Seale, to be used in all Causes and Occasions of the said Company, and the same Seale may alter, chaunge, breake, and newe make, from tyme to tyme, at their pleasures. And our Will and Pleasure is, and Wee doe hereby for Us, our Heires and Successors, ordeyne and graunte, That from henceforth for ever, there shalbe one Governor, one Deputy Governor, and eighteene Assistants of the same Company, to be from tyme to tyme consti-

tuted, elected and chosen out of the Freemen of the saide Company, for the twyme being, in such Manner and Forme as hereafter in theis Presents is expressed, which said Officers shall applie themselves to take Care for the best disposeing and ordering of the generall buysines and Affaires of, for, and concerning the said Landes and Premisses hereby mentioned, to be graunted, and the Plantation thereof, and the Government of the People there. And for the better Execution of our Royall Pleasure and Graunte in this Behalf, Wee doe, by theis presents, for Us, our Heires and Successors, nominate, ordeyne, make, and constitute; our welbeloved the saide Mathewe Cradocke, to be the first and present Governor of the said Company, and the saide Thomas Goffe, to be Deputy Governor of the saide Company, and the saide Sir Richard Saltonstall, Isaack Johnson, Samuell Aldersey, John Ven, John Humfrey, John Endecott, Simon Whetcombe, Increase Noell, Richard Pery, Nathaniell Wright, Samuell Vassall, Theophilus Eaton, Thomas Adams, Thomas Hutchins, John Browne, George Foxcrofte, William Vassall, and William Pinchion, to be the present Assistants of the saide Company, to continue in the saide several Offices respectivelie for such tyme, and in such manner, as in and by theis Presents is hereafter declared and appointed.

And further, Wee will, and by theis Presents, for Us, our Heires and Successors, doe ordeyne and graunte, That the Governor of the saide Company for the tyme being, or in his Absence by Occasion of Sicknes or otherwise, the Deputie Governor for the tyme being, shall have Authoritie from tyme to tyme upon all Occasions, to give order for the assembling of the saide Company, and calling them together to consult and advise of the Bussinesses and Affaires of the saide Company, and that the said Governor, Deputie Governor, and Assistants of the saide Company, for the tyme being, shall or maie once every Moneth, or oftener at their Pleasures, assemble and houlde and keepe a Courte or Assemblie of themselves, for the better ordering and directing of their Affaires, and that any seaven or more persons of the Assistants, togither with the Governor, or Deputie Governor soe assembled, shalbe saide, taken, held, and reputed to be, and shalbe a full and sufficient Courte or Assemblie of the said Company, for the handling, ordering, and dispatching of all such Buysinesses and Occurrents as shall from tyme to tyme happen, touching or concerning the said Company or Plantation; and that there shall or maie be held and kept by the Governor, or Deputie Governor of the said Company, and seaven or more of the said Assistants for the tyme being, upon every last Wednesday in Hillary, Easter, Trinity, and Michas Termes respectivelie forever, one greate generall and solemne assemblie, which foure generall assemblies shalbe stiled and called the foure great and generall Courts of the saide Company.

In all and every, or any of which saide greate and generall Courts soe assembled, Wee doe for Us, our Heires and Successors, give and graunte to the said Governor and Company, and their Successors, That the Governor, or in his absence, the Deputie Governor of the saide Company for the tyme being, and such of the Assistants and Freeman of the saide Company as shalbe present, or the greater nomber of them so assembled, whereof the Governor or Deputie Governor and six of the Assistants at the least to be seaven, shall have full Power and authoritie to choose, nominate, and appointe, such and soe many others as they shall thinke fitt, and that shall be willing to accept the same, to be free of the said Company and Body, and them into the same to admitt; and to elect and constitute such officers as they shall thinke fill and requisite, for the ordering, mannaging, and dispatching of the Affaires of the saide Governor and Company, and their Successors; And to make Lawes and Ordinances for the Good and Welfare of the saide Company, and for the Government and ordering of the saide Landes and Plantation, and the People inhabiting and to inhabite the same, as to them from tyme to tyme shalbe thought meete, soe as such Lawes and Ordinances be not contrarie or repugnant to the Lawes and Statuts of this our Realme of England.

And, our Will and Pleasure is, and Wee doe hereby for Us, our Heires and Successors, establish and ordeyne, That yearely once in the yeare, for ever hereafter, namely, the last Wednesday in Easter Tearme, yearely, the Governor, Deputy-Governor, and Assistants of the saide Company and all other officers of the saide Company shalbe in the Generall Court or Assembly to be held for that Day or Tyme, newly chosen for the Yeare ensueing by such greater parte of the said Company, for the Tyme being, then and there present, as is afore-

saide. And, if it shall happen the present governor, Deputy Governor, and assistants, by theis presents appointed, or such as shall hereafter be newly chosen into their Roomes, or any of them, or any other of the officers to be appointed for the said Company, to dye, or to be removed from his or their severall Offices or Places before the saide generall Day of Election (whome Wee doe hereby declare for any Misdemeanor or Defect to be removeable by the Governor, Deputie Governor, Assistants, and Company, or such greater Parte of them in any of the publique Courts to be assembled as is aforesaid) That then, and in every such Case, it shall and maie be lawfull, to and for the Governor, Deputie Governor, Assistants, and Company aforesaide, or such greater Parte of them soe to be assembled as is aforesaide, in any of their Assemblies, to proceade to a new Election of one or more others of their Company in the Roome or Place, Roomes or Places of such Officer or Officers soe dyeing or removed according to their Discretions, And, immediately upon and after such Election and Elections made of such Governor, Deputie Governor, Assistant or Assistants, or any other officer of the saide Company, in Manner and Forme aforesaid, the Authoritie, Office, and Power, before given to the former Governor, Deputie Governor, or other Officer and Officers soe removed, in whose Steade and Place newe shalbe soe chosen, shall as to him and them, and everie of them, cease and determine

Provided alsoe, and our Will and Pleasure is, That aswell such as are by theis Presents appointed to be the present Governor, Deputie Governor, and Assistants of the said Company, as those that shall succeed them, and all other Officers to be appointed and chosen as aforesaid, shall, before they undertake the Execution of their saide Offices and Places respectivelie, take their Corporal Oathes for the due and faithfull Performance of their Duties in their severall Offices and Places, before such Person or Persons as are by theis Presents hereunder appointed to take and receive the same. . . .

And, further our Will and Pleasure is, and Wee doe hereby for Us, our Heires and Successors, ordeyne and declare, and graunte to the saide Governor and Company and their Successors, That all and every the Subjects of Us, our Heires or Successors, which shall goe to and inhabite within the saide Landes and Premisses hereby mentioned to be graunted, and every of their Children which shall happen to be borne there, or on the Seas in goeing thither, or retorning from thence, shall have and enjoy all liberties and Immunities of free and naturall Subjects within any of the Domynions of Us, our Heires or Successors, to all Intents, Constructions, and Purposes whatsoever, as if they and everie of them were borne within the Realme of England. And that the Governor and Deputie Governor of the said Company for the Tyme being, or either of them, and any two or more of such of the saide Assistants as shalbe thereunto appointed by the saide Governor and Company at any of their Courts or Assemblies to be held as aforesaide, shall and maie at all Tymes, and from tyme to tyme hereafter, have full Power and Authoritie to minister and give the Oathe and Oathes of Supremacie and Allegiance, or either of them, to all and everie Person and Persons, which shall at any Tyme or Tymes hereafter goe or passe to the Landes and Premisses hereby mentioned to be graunted to inhabite in the same.

And, Wee doe of our further Grace, certen Knowledg and meere Motion, give and graunte to the saide Governor and Company, and their Successors, That it shall and maie be lawfull, to and for the Governor or Deputie Governor, and such of the Assistants and Freemen of the said Company for the Tyme being as shalbe assembled in any of their generall Courts aforesaide, or in any other Courtes to be specially sumoned and assembled for that Purpose, or the greater Parte of them (whereof the Governor or Deputie Governor, and six of the Assistants to be alwaies seaven) from tyme to tyme, to make, ordeine, and establishe all Manner of wholesome and reasonable Orders, Lawes, Statutes, and Ordinances, Directions, and Instructions, not contrairie to the Lawes of this our Realme of England, aswell for setling of the Formes and Ceremonies of Government and Magistracy, fitt and necessary for the said Plantation, and the Inhabitants there, and for nameing and setting of all sorts of Officers, both superior and inferior, which they shall finde needefull for that Governement and Plantation, and the distinguishing and setting forth of the severall duties, Powers, and Lymytts of every such Office and Place, and the Formes of such Oathes warrantable by the Lawes and Statutes of this our Realme of England, as shalbe respectivelie ministred unto them for the Execution of the said severall Offices and Places; as also, for the disposing and ordering of the Elections of such of the said Officers as shalbe annuall, and of such others as shalbe to succeede in Case of Death or Removeall, and ministring the said Oathes to the newe elected Officers, and for Impositions of lawfull Fynes, Mulcts, Imprisonment, or other lawfull Correction, according to the Course of other Corporations in this our Realme of England, and for the directing, ruling, and disposeing of all other Matters and Thinges, whereby our said People, Inhabitants there, may be soe religiously, peaceablie, and civilly governed, as their good Life and orderlie Conversation, maie wynn and incite the Natives of Country, to the Knowledg and Obedience of the onlie true God and Savior of Mankinde, and the Christian Fayth, which in our Royall Intention, and the Adventurers free Profession, is the principall Ende of this Plantation.

Willing, commaunding, and requiring, and by theis Presents for Us, our Heires, and Successors, ordeyning and appointing, that all such Orders, Lawes, Statuts and Ordinances, Instructions and Directions, as shalbe soe made by the Governor, or Deputie Governor of the said Company, and such of the Assistants and Freemen as aforesaide, and published in Writing, under their common Seale, shalbe carefullie and dulie observed, kept, performed, and putt in Execution, according to the true Intent and Meaning of the same; and theis our Letters- patents, or the Duplicate or exemplification thereof, shalbe to all and everie such Officers, superior and inferior, from Tyme to Tyme, for the putting of the same Orders, Lawes, Statutes, and Ordinances, Instructions, and Directions, in due Execution against Us, our Heires and Successors, a sufficient Warrant and Discharge.

And Wee doe further, for Us, our Heires and Successors, give and graunt to the said Governor and Company, and their Successors by theis Presents, that all and everie such Chiefe Comaunders, Captaines, Governors, and other Officers and Ministers, as by the said Orders, Lawes, Statuts, Ordinances, Instructions, or Directions of the said Governor and Company for the Tyme being, shalbe from Tyme to Tyme hereafter imploied either in the Government of the saide Inhabitants and Plantation, or in the Waye by Sea thither, or from thence, according to the Natures and Lymitts of their Offices and Places respectively, shall from Tyme to Tyme hereafter for ever, within the Precincts and Partes of Newe England hereby mentioned to be graunted and confirmed, or in the Waie by Sea thither, or from thence, have full and Absolute Power and Authoritie to correct, punishe, pardon, governe, and rule all such the Subjects of Us, our Heires and Successors, as shall from Tyme to Tyme adventure themselves in any Voyadge thither or from thence, or that shall at any Tyme hereafter, inhabite within the Precincts and Partes of Newe England aforasaid, according to the Orders, Lawes, Ordinances, Instructions, and Directions aforesaid, not being repugnant to the Lawes and Statutes of our Realme of England as aforesaid. . . .

Source: Avalon Project of the Yale Law School: www.yale.edu/lawweb/avalon/avalon.htm.

Bacon's Declaration in the Name of the People (July 30, 1676)

For most of its first seventy years of existence, the Virginia colony was dominated by large landholders, many of whom ruthlessly exploited indentured servants from Britain for labor. Under standard indentured contracts, servants served seven years before being released and given small plots of land on the frontier. Confronting a hostile native population and paying an unfair share of the colony's taxes, many of these freed indentured servants were angry with the landholders of Virginia. Under the leadership of a recently arrived land-poor noble named Nathaniel Bacon, they rose up against large landholder rule in 1676. Briefly successful, the rebellion was crushed by the timely arrival of a British warship and the death of Bacon from malaria.

The Declaracon of the People.

1. For haveing upon specious pretences of publiqe works raised great unjust taxes upon the Comonality for the advancement of private favorites and other sinister ends, but noe visible effects in any measure adequate, For not haveing dureing this long time of his Gouvernement in any measure advanced this hopefull Colony either by fortificacons Townes or Trade.

2. For haveing abused and rendred contemptable the Magistrates of Justice, by advanceing to places of Judicature, scandalous and Ignorant favorites.

3. For haveing wronged his Majesties prerogative and interest, by assumeing Monopoly of the Beaver trade, and for haveing in that unjust gaine betrayed and sold his Majesties Country and the lives of his loyall subjects, to the barbarous heathen.

4. For haveing, protected, favoured, and Imboldned the Indians against his Majesties loyall subjects, never contriveing, requireing, or appointing any due or proper meanes of sattisfaction for theire many Invasions, robbories, and murthers comitted upon us.

5. For haveing when the Army of English, was just upon the track of those Indians, who now in all places burne, spoyle, murther and when we might with ease have distroyed them: who then were in open hostillity, for then haveing expressly countermanded, and sent back our Army, by passing his word for the peaceable demeanour of the said Indians, who imediately prosecuted theire evill intentions, comitting horred murthers and robberies in all places, being protected by the said ingagement and word past of him the said Sir William Berkeley, haveing ruined and laid desolate a greate part of his Majesties Country, and have now drawne themselves into such obscure and remote places, and are by theire success soe imboldned and confirmed, by theire confederacy soe strengthned that the cryes of blood are in all places, and the terror, and constimation of the people soe greate, are now become, not onely a difficult, but a very formidable enimy, who might att first with ease have beene distroyed.

6. And lately when upon the loud outcryes of blood the Assembly had with all care raised and framed an Army for the preventing of further mischeife and safeguard of this his Majesties Colony.

7. For haveing with onely the privacy of some few favorites, without acquainting the people, onely by the alteracon of a figure, forged a Comission, by we know not what hand, not onely without, but even against the consent of the people, for the raiseing and effecting civill warr and distruction, which being happily and without blood shed prevented, for haveing the second time attempted the same, thereby calling downe our forces from the defence of the fronteeres and most weekely expoased places.

8. For the prevencon of civill mischeife and ruin amongst ourselves, whilst the barbarous enimy in

all places did invade, murther and spoyle us, his majesties most faithfull subjects.

Of this and the aforesaid Articles we accuse Sir William Berkeley as guilty of each and every one of the same, and as one who hath traiterously attempted, violated and Injured his Majesties interest here, by a loss of a greate part of this his Colony and many of his faithfull loyall subjects, by him betrayed and in a barbarous and shamefull manner exposed to the Incursions and murther of the heathen, And we doe further declare these the ensueing persons in this list, to have beene his wicked and pernicious councellours Confederates, aiders, and assisters against the Comonality in these our Civill comotions.

Sir Henry Chichley
William Claiburne Junior
Lieut. Coll. Christopher
Thomas Hawkins Wormeley
William Sherwood
Phillip Ludwell
John Page Clerke
Robert Beverley
John Cluffe Clerke
Richard Lee
John West
Thomas Ballard
Hubert Farrell
William Cole
Thomas Reade
Richard Whitacre
Matthew Kempe
Nicholas Spencer
Joseph Bridger

And we doe further demand that the said Sir William Berkeley with all the persons in this list be forthwith delivered up or surrender themselves within fower days after the notice hereof, Or otherwise we declare as followeth.

That in whatsoever place, howse, or ship, any of the said persons shall reside, be hidd, or protected, we declaire the owners, Masters or Inhabitants of the said places, to be confederates and trayters to the people and the estates of them is alsoe of all the aforesaid persons to be confiscated, and this we the Comons of Virginia doe declare, desiering a firme union amongst our selves that we may joyntly and with one accord defend our selves against the common Enimy, and lett not the faults of the guilty be the reproach of the inocent, or the faults or crimes of the oppressours devide and separate us who have suffered by theire oppressions.

These are therefore in his majesties name to command you forthwith to seize the persons above mentioned as Trayters to the King and Country and them to bring to Midle plantacon, and there to secure them untill further order, and in case of opposition, if you want any further assistance you are forthwith to demand itt in the name of the people in all the Counties of Virginia.

Nathaniel Bacon
Generall by Consent of the people.

Source: Avalon Project of the Yale Law School: www.yale.edu/lawweb/avalon/avalon.htm.

"Rule Britannia" (1740)

"Rule Britannia" was written by composer Thomas Arne for his masque Alfred *in 1740 and first performed in public for the Prince of Wales in 1745. The tune became an immediate favorite of the public and came to be an unofficial anthem of the country's sea-borne empire for two centuries.*

When Britain first, at heaven's command,
Arose from out the azure main,
Arose, arose, arose from out the azure main.
This was the charter, the charter of the land,
And guardian angels sang the strain.

Rule Britannia! Britannia rule the waves.
Britons never, never, never shall be slaves.

The nations not so blest as thee,
Must in their turn to tyrants fall,
Must in their turn, must in their turn,
To tyrants fall,
While thou shall flourish,
Shall flourish great and free,
The dread and envy of them all.

Chorus.

Still more majestic shalt thou rise,
More dreadful from each foreign stroke.
More dreadful, more dreadful
From each foreign stroke.

As the loud blast that tears the skies,
Serves but to root thy native oak.

Chorus.

Thee haughty tyrants ne'er shall tame,
All their attempts to bend thee down,
All their attempts, all their attempts
To bend thee down,
Will but arouse thy generous flame.
But work their woe and thy renown.

Chorus.

To thee belongs the rural reign,
Thy cities shall with commerce shine,
Thy cities shall, thy cities shall
With commerce shine.
All thine shall be the subject main,
And every shore it circles thine.

Chorus.

The muses still, with freedom found,
Shall to thy happy coast repair,
Shall to thy happy coast,
Thy happy coasts repair,
Best isle of beauty,
With matchless beauty crowned,
And manly hearts to guard the fair.

Chorus.

Source: Arne, Thomas Augustine (composer). 1740. "Rule
   Britannia!" http://www.expage.com/guardsman19.

Proclamation of 1763 (Indian Provisions)

*Following their victory in the Seven Years' War
(known in the United States as the French and Indian War), the British took possession of vast territories in Canada, the trans-Appalachian west, and
Florida. Formerly administered by France, these
territories were largely inhabited by Native Americans of many different tribes. In order to maintain
peace in these regions, and to promote trade with
the native peoples, the British issued the Proclamation of 1763. Among its provisions was a mandate
to prevent white colonial encroachment west of the
Appalachians. The Proclamation of 1763 was
highly resented by the inhabitants of the thirteen
American colonies and was one of the eventual
causes of the American Revolution a dozen years
later.*

And whereas it is just and reasonable, and essential to our Interest, and the Security of our
Colonies, that the several Nations or Tribes of Indians with whom We are connected, and who live
under our Protection, should not be molested or
disturbed in the Possession of such Parts of Our
Dominions and Territories as, not having been
ceded to or purchased by Us, are reserved to them,
or any of them, as their Hunting Grounds—We do
therefore, with the Advice of our Privy Council, declare it to be our Royal Will and Pleasure, that no
Governor or Commander in Chief in any of our
Colonies of Quebec, East Florida. or West Florida,
do presume, upon any Pretence whatever, to grant
Warrants of Survey, or pass any Patents for Lands
beyond the Bounds of their respective Governments as described in their Commissions: as also
that no Governor or Commander in Chief in any of
our other Colonies or Plantations in America do
presume for the present, and until our further
Pleasure be known, to grant Warrants of Survey, or
pass Patents for any Lands beyond the Heads or
Sources of any of the Rivers which fall into the Atlantic Ocean from the West and North West, or
upon any Lands whatever, which, not having been
ceded to or purchased by Us as aforesaid, are reserved to the said Indians, or any of them.

And We do further declare it to be Our Royal
Will and Pleasure, for the present as aforesaid, to
reserve under our Sovereignty, Protection, and Dominion, for the use of the said Indians, all the
Lands and Territories not included within the
Limits of Our said Three new Governments, or
within the Limits of the Territory granted to the
Hudson's Bay Company, as also all the Lands and
Territories lying to the Westward of the Sources of
the Rivers which fall into the Sea from the West
and North West as aforesaid.

And We do hereby strictly forbid, on Pain of our
Displeasure, all our loving Subjects from making
any Purchases or Settlements whatever, or taking
Possession of any of the Lands above reserved,
without our especial leave and Licence for that
Purpose first obtained.

And We do further strictly enjoin and require
all Persons whatever who have either wilfully or
inadvertently seated themselves upon any Lands

within the Countries above described. or upon any other Lands which, not having been ceded to or purchased by Us, are still reserved to the said Indians as aforesaid, forthwith to remove themselves from such Settlements.

And whereas great Frauds and Abuses have been committed in purchasing Lands of the Indians, to the great Prejudice of our Interests, and to the great Dissatisfaction of the said Indians: In order, therefore, to prevent such Irregularities for the future, and to the end that the Indians may be convinced of our Justice and determined Resolution to remove all reasonable Cause of Discontent, We do, with the Advice of our Privy Council strictly enjoin and require, that no private Person do presume to make any purchase from the said Indians of any Lands reserved to the said Indians, within those parts of our Colonies where We have thought proper to allow Settlement: but that, if at any Time any of the Said Indians should be inclined to dispose of the said Lands, the same shall be Purchased only for Us, in our Name, at some public Meeting or Assembly of the said Indians, to be held for that Purpose by the Governor or Commander in Chief of our Colony respectively within which they shall lie: and in case they shall lie within the limits of any Proprietary Government, they shall be purchased only for the Use and in the name of such Proprietaries, conformable to such Directions and Instructions as We or they shall think proper to give for that Purpose: And we do, by the Advice of our Privy Council, declare and enjoin, that the Trade with the said Indians shall be free and open to all our Subjects whatever, provided that every Person who may incline to Trade with the said Indians do take out a Licence for carrying on such Trade from the Governor or Commander in Chief of any of our Colonies respectively where such Person shall reside, and also give Security to observe such Regulations as We shall at any Time think fit, by ourselves or by our Commissaries to be appointed for this Purpose, to direct and appoint for the Benefit of the said Trade:

And we do hereby authorize, enjoin, and require the Governors and Commanders in Chief of all our Colonies respectively, as well those under Our immediate Government as those under the Government and Direction of Proprietaries, to grant such Licences without Fee or Reward, taking

especial Care to insert therein a Condition, that such Licence shall be void, and the Security forfeited in case the Person to whom the same is granted shall refuse or neglect to observe such Regulations as We shall think proper to prescribe as aforesaid.

And we do further expressly conjoin and require all Officers whatever, as well Military as those Employed in the Management and Direction of Indian Affairs, within the Territories reserved as aforesaid for the use of the said Indians, to seize and apprehend all Persons whatever, who standing charged with Treason, Misprisions of Treason, Murders, or other Felonies or Misdemeanors, shall fly from Justice and take Refuge in the said Territory, and to send them under a proper guard to the Colony where the Crime was committed, of which they stand accused, in order to take their Trial for the same.

Given at our Court at St. James's the 7th Day of October 1763, in the Third Year of our Reign.

God Save the King.

Source: Government of Nova Scotia website: www.gov.ns.ca/abor/pubs/1763proc.PDF.

India: Regulating Act (1773)

With the East India Company experiencing one of its periodic financial crises, the British government passed the Regulating Act for India in 1773. Under this act, the governor-general of British India and a council would be nominated both by the East India Company and the government. The Regulating Act was yet another milestone in the gradual shift of colonial authority from chartered company to crown, a process that would culminate with the shift to full crown rule in 1857, following the great Indian Mutiny.

An Act for Establishing Certain Regulations for the Better Management of the Affairs of the East India Company, as Well in India as in Europe

Whereas the several powers and authorities granted by charters to the united company of merchants in England trading to the East Indies have been found, by experience, not to have sufficient force and efficacy to prevent various abuses which have prevailed in the government and administration of the affairs of the said united company, as well at home as in India, to the manifest injury of the public credit, and of the commercial interests of the said company; and it is therefore become highly expedient that certain further regulations, better adapted to their present circumstances and condition, should be provided and established: ...

... And, for the better management of the said united company's affairs in India, be it further enacted by the authority aforesaid, That, for the government of the presidency of Fort William in Bengal, there shall be appointed a governor-general, and four counsellors; and that the whole civil and military government of the said presidency, and also the ordering, management and government of all the territorial acquisitions and revenues in the kingdoms of *Bengal, Bahar,* and *Orissa,* shall, during such time as the territorial acquisitions and revenues shall remain in the possession of the said united company, be, and are hereby vested in the said governor-general and council of the said presidency of Fort William in Bengal, in like manner, to all intents and purposes whatsoever; as the same now are, or at any time heretofore might have been exercised by the president and council, or select committee, in the said kingdoms.

And be it enacted by the authority aforesaid, That in all cases whatsoever wherein any difference of opinion shall arise upon any question proposed in any consultation, the said governor-general and council shall be bound and concluded by the opinion and decision of the major part of those present: and if it shall happen that, by the death or removal, or by the absence, of any of the members of the said council, such governor-general and council shall happen to be equally divided; then, and in every such case, the said governor-general, or in his absence, the eldest counsellor present, shall have a casting voice, and his opinion shall be decisive and conclusive.

And be it further enacted by the authority aforesaid, That the said governor-general and council, or the major part of them, shall have, and they are hereby authorised to have, power of superintending and countroling the government and management of the presidencies of *Madras, Bombay,* and *Bencoolen* respectively.

Source: Horn, D. B., and Mary Ransome, eds. *English Historical Documents, 1714–1783.* London: Eyre and Spottiswoode, 1957.

Quebec Act (1774)

Britain's victory over France in the Seven Years' War—known in the United States as the French and Indian War—presented London with a number of problems. Among these was how to govern a population of 60,000 French-speaking Catholics. To assure their loyalty to the crown, the British government protected the Catholic faith in all territories once owned by France, including Quebec and much of the Mississippi Valley. To the largely Protestant settlers of the thirteen colonies, the Quebec Act was considered an outrage. To them, it assured Catholic domination over a hinterland they themselves hoped one day to settle. Thus, the Quebec Act became yet another instigating factor in the rebellion that would result, in the succeeding years, in an American declaration of independence from the British Empire.

Whereas his Majesty, by his Royal Proclamation bearing Date the seventh Day of October, in the third Year of his Reign, thought fit to declare the Provisions which had been made in respect to certain Countries, Territories, and Islands in America, ceded to his Majesty by the definitive Treaty of Peace, concluded at Paris on the tenth day of February, one thousand seven hundred and sixty-three:

And whereas, by the Arrangements made by the said Royal Proclamation a very large Extent of Country, within which there were several Colonies and Settlements of the Subjects of France who claimed to remain therein under the Faith of the said Treaty, was left, without any Provision being made for the Administration of Civil Government therein; and certain Parts of the Territory of Canada, where sedentary Fisheries had been established and carried on by the Subjects of France, Inhabitants of the said Province of Canada under Grants and Concessions from the Government thereof, were annexed to the Government of Newfoundland.

"II. Provided always that nothing herein contained, relative to the Boundary of the Province of Quebec shall in anywise affect the Boundaries of any other Colony.

"III. Provided always, and be it enacted, That nothing in this Act contained shall extend, or be construed to extend to make void, or to vary or alter any Right, Title, or Possession, derived under any Grant, Conveyance, or otherwise howsoever, of or to any Lands within the said Province, or the Provinces thereto adjoining; but that the same shall remain and be in Force, and have Effect, as if this Act had never been made.

"IV. And whereas the Provisions, made by the said Proclamation, in respect to the Civil Government of the said Province of Quebec, and the Powers and Authorities given to the Governor and other Civil Officers of the said Province, by the Grants and Commissions issued in consequence thereof, have been found, upon Experience, to be inapplicable to the State and Circumstances of the said Province, the Inhabitants whereof amounted, at the Conquest, to above sixty-five thousand Persons professing the Religion of the Church of Rome, and enjoying an established Form of Constitution and System of Laws, by which their Persons and Property had been protected, governed, and ordered, for a long Series of Years, from the first Establishment of the said Province of Canada;" be it therefore further enacted by the Authority aforesaid. That the said Proclamation, so far as the same relates to the said Province of Quebec, and the Commission under the Authority whereof the Government of the said Province is at present administered.

V. And, for the more perfect Security and Ease of the Minds of the Inhabitants of the said Province, it is hereby declared, That his Majesty's Subjects, professing the Religion of the Church of Rome of and in the said Province of Quebec. may have, hold, and enjoy, the free Exercise of the Religion of the Church of Rome, subject to the King's Supremacy, declared and established by an Act, made in the first Year of the Reign of Queen Elizabeth, over all the Dominions and Countries which then did, or thereafter should belong, to the Imperial Crown of this Realm; and that the Clergy of the said Church may hold, receive, and enjoy, their accustomed Dues and Rights, with respect to such Persons only as shall profess the said Religion.

VI. Provided nevertheless, That it shall be lawful for his Majesty, his Heirs, or Successors, to make such Provision out of the rest of the said accustomed Dues and Rights, for the Encouragement of the Protestant Religion, and for the Maintenance and Support of a Protestant Clergy within the said Province, as he or they shall from Time to Time think necessary and expedient.

"Vll Provided always and be it enacted, That no Person professing the Religion of the Church of Rome, and residing in the said Province, shall be obliged to take the Oath required by the said Statute passed in the first Year of the Reign of Queen Elizabeth, or any other Oaths substituted by any other Act in the Place thereof; but that every such Person who, by the said Statute, is required to take the Oath therein mentioned, shall be obliged, and is hereby required, to take and subscribe the following Oath before the Governor, or such other Person in such Court of Record as his Majesty shall appoint, who are hereby authorized to administer the same;

"I A. B. do sincerely promise and swear, That I will be faithful, and bear true Allegiance to his Majesty King George, and him will defend to the utmost of my Power, against all traitorous Conspiracies, and Attempts whatsoever, which shall be made against his Person. Crown, and Dignity; and I will do my utmost Endeavor to disclose and make known to his Majesty, his Heirs and Successors, all Treasons, and traitorous Conspiracies, and Attempts, which I shall know to be against him, or any of them; and all this I do swear without any Equivocation, mental Evasion, or secret Reservation, and renouncing all Pardons and Dispensations from any Power or Person whomsoever to the contrary. So help me GOD."

And every such Person, who shall neglect or refuse to take the said Oath before mentioned, shall incur and be liable to the same Penalties, Forfeitures, Disabilities, and Incapacities, as he would have incurred and been liable to for neglecting or refusing to take the Oath required by the said Statute passed in the first Year of the Reign of Queen Elizabeth.

"VIII. And be it further enacted by the Authority aforesaid, That all his Majesty's Canadian Subjects within the Province of Quebec. the religious orders and Communities only excepted, may also hold and enjoy their Property and Possessions, together with all Customs and Usages relative thereto, and all other their Civil Rights . . .

Source: American Historical Documents, 1000–1904.
Cambridge, MA: Harvard Classics, 1909.

Proclamation of Rebellion (August 23, 1775)

In April 1775, colonists in Massachusetts opened fire on British troops at Lexington and Concord, initiating the armed conflict stage of the American Revo-

lution. The slow pace of trans-Atlantic communications in the eighteenth century meant that the news took several months to reach London. In this document, issued some four months after the fighting began, King George III expresses his outrage at the rebellion and the stern measures he plans to take to crush it. In fact, the American Revolution would continue for six years, taking the lives of more than 25,000 colonists.

GEORGE R. [King George III]

Whereas many of our subjects in divers parts of our Colonies and Plantations in *North America,* misled by dangerous and ill designing men, and forgetting the allegiance which they owe to the power that has protected and supported them; after various disorderly acts committed in disturbance of the publick peace, to the obstruction of lawful commerce, and to the oppression of our loyal subjects carrying on the same; have at length proceeded to open and avowed rebellion, by arraying themselves in a hostile manner, to withstand the execution of the law, and traitorously preparing, ordering and levying war against us: And whereas, there is reason to apprehend that such rebellion hath been much promoted and encouraged by the traitorous correspondence, counsels and comfort of divers wicked and desperate persons within this realm: To the end therefore, that none of our subjects may neglect or violate their duty through ignorance thereof, or through any doubt of the protection which the law will afford to their loyalty and zeal, we have thought fit, by and with the advice of our Privy Council, to issue our Royal Proclamation, hereby declaring, that not only all our Officers, civil and military, are obliged to exert their utmost endeavours to suppress such rebellion, and to bring the traitors to justice, but that all our subjects of this Realm, and the dominions thereunto belonging, are bound by law to be aiding and assisting in the suppression of such rebellion, and to disclose and make known all traitorous conspiracies and attempts against us our crown and dignity; and we do accordingly strictly charge and command all our Officers, as well civil as military, and all others our obedient and loyal subjects, to use their utmost endeavours to withstand and suppress such rebellion, and to disclose and make known all treasons and traitorous conspiracies which they shall know to be against us, our crown and dignity; and for that purpose, that they transmit to one of our principal Secretaries of State, or other proper officer, due and full information of all persons who shall be found carrying on correspondence with, or in any manner or degree aiding or abetting the persons now in open arms and rebellion against our Government, within any of our Colonies and Plantations in *North America,* in order to bring to condign punishment the authors, perpetrators, and abetters of such traitorous designs.

Given at our Court at St. James's the twenty-third day of *August,* one thousand seven hundred and seventy-five, in the fifteenth year of our reign.

GOD save the KING.

Source: MacDonald, William. *Documentary Source Book of American History.* New York: Macmillan, 1909.

U.S. Declaration of Independence (July 4, 1776)

In the wake of Britain's imperial war with France of the 1750s and 1760s, the government in London began imposing new taxes and restrictions on its thirteen colonies on the North American mainland. Feeling unrepresented in Parliament, many colonists gradually came to the conclusion that their interests would best be served in an independent nation. A young Virginia planter and intellectual, Thomas Jefferson, drafted the colonies' declaration of independence, which was passed at the Second Continental Congress in Philadelphia in the summer of 1776. While a powerful expression of humanity's right to liberty, its provenance is laced with irony, as the document's author was himself a slaveholder and the declaration itself said nothing about the nearly half million African slaves in the thirteen colonies.

The Declaration of Independence of the Thirteen Colonies

In CONGRESS, July 4, 1776

The unanimous Declaration of the thirteen united States of America,

When in the Course of human events, it becomes necessary for one people to dissolve the political bands which have connected them with another, and to assume among the powers of the earth, the separate and equal station to which the Laws of Nature and of Nature's God entitle them, a decent respect to the opinions of mankind requires that they should declare the causes which impel them to the separation.

We hold these truths to be self-evident, that all men are created equal, that they are endowed by their Creator with certain unalienable Rights, that among these are Life, Liberty and the pursuit of Happiness.—That to secure these rights, Governments are instituted among Men, deriving their just powers from the consent of the governed,—That whenever any Form of Government becomes destructive of these ends, it is the Right of the People to alter or to abolish it, and to institute new Government, laying its foundation on such principles and organizing its powers in such form, as to them shall seem most likely to effect their Safety and Happiness. Prudence, indeed, will dictate that Governments long established should not be changed for light and transient causes; and accordingly all experience hath shewn, that mankind are more disposed to suffer, while evils are sufferable, than to right themselves by abolishing the forms to which they are accustomed. But when a long train of abuses and usurpations, pursuing invariably the same Object evinces a design to reduce them under absolute Despotism, it is their right, it is their duty, to throw off such Government, and to provide new Guards for their future security.—Such has been the patient sufferance of these Colonies; and such is now the necessity which constrains them to alter their former Systems of Government. The history of the present King of Great Britain [George III] is a history of repeated injuries and usurpations, all having in direct object the establishment of an absolute Tyranny over these States. To prove this, let Facts be submitted to a candid world.

He has refused his Assent to Laws, the most wholesome and necessary for the public good.

He has forbidden his Governors to pass Laws of immediate and pressing importance, unless suspended in their operation till his Assent should be obtained; and when so suspended, he has utterly neglected to attend to them.

He has refused to pass other Laws for the accommodation of large districts of people, unless those people would relinquish the right of Representation in the Legislature, a right inestimable to them and formidable to tyrants only.

He has called together legislative bodies at places unusual, uncomfortable, and distant from the depository of their public Records, for the sole purpose of fatiguing them into compliance with his measures.

He has dissolved Representative Houses repeatedly, for opposing with manly firmness his invasions on the rights of the people.

He has refused for a long time, after such dissolutions, to cause others to be elected; whereby the Legislative powers, incapable of Annihilation, have returned to the People at large for their exercise; the State remaining in the mean time exposed to all the dangers of invasion from without, and convulsions within.

He has endeavoured to prevent the population of these States; for that purpose obstructing the Laws for Naturalization of Foreigners; refusing to pass others to encourage their migrations hither, and raising the conditions of new Appropriations of Lands.

He has obstructed the Administration of Justice, by refusing his Assent to Laws for establishing Judiciary powers.

He has made Judges dependent on his Will alone, for the tenure of their offices, and the amount and payment of their salaries.

He has erected a multitude of New Offices, and sent hither swarms of Officers to harass our people, and eat out their substance.

He has kept among us, in times of peace, Standing Armies without the consent of our legislatures.

He has affected to render the Military independent of and superior to the Civil power.

He has combined with others to subject us to a jurisdiction foreign to our constitution and unacknowledged by our laws; giving his Assent to their Acts of pretended Legislation:

For Quartering large bodies of armed troops among us:

For protecting them, by a mock Trial, from punishment for any Murders which they should commit on the Inhabitants of these States:

For cutting off our Trade with all parts of the world:

For imposing Taxes on us without our Consent:

For depriving us, in many cases, of the benefits of Trial by Jury:

For transporting us beyond Seas to be tried for pretended offences:

For abolishing the free System of English Laws in a neighbouring Province, establishing therein an Arbitrary government, and enlarging its

Boundaries so as to render it at once an example and fit instrument for introducing the same absolute rule into these Colonies:

For taking away our Charters, abolishing our most valuable Laws, and altering fundamentally the Forms of our Governments:

For suspending our own Legislatures, and declaring themselves invested with power to legislate for us in all cases whatsoever.

He has abdicated Government here, by declaring us out of his Protection and waging War against us.

He has plundered our seas, ravaged our Coasts, burnt our towns, and destroyed the lives of our people.

He is at this time transporting large Armies of foreign Mercenaries to compleat the works of death, desolation and tyranny, already begun with circumstances of Cruelty and perfidy scarcely paralleled in the most barbarous ages, and totally unworthy the Head of a civilized nation.

He has constrained our fellow Citizens taken Captive on the high Seas to bear Arms against their Country, to become the executioners of their friends and Brethren, or to fall themselves by their Hands.

He has excited domestic insurrections amongst us, and has endeavoured to bring on the inhabitants of our frontiers, the merciless Indian Savages, whose known rule of warfare, is an undistinguished destruction of all ages, sexes and conditions.

In every stage of these Oppressions We have Petitioned for Redress in the most humble terms: Our repeated Petitions have been answered only by repeated injury. A Prince whose character is thus marked by every act which may define a Tyrant, is unfit to be the ruler of a free people.

Nor have We been wanting in attentions to our British brethren. We have warned them from time to time of attempts by their legislature to extend an unwarrantable jurisdiction over us. We have reminded them of the circumstances of our emigration and settlement here. We have appealed to their native justice and magnanimity, and we have conjured them by the ties of our common kindred to disavow these usurpations, which, would inevitably interrupt our connections and correspondence. They too have been deaf to the voice of justice and of consanguinity. We must, therefore, acquiesce in the necessity, which denounces our

Separation, and hold them, as we hold the rest of mankind, Enemies in War, in Peace Friends.

We, therefore, the Representatives of the united States of America, in General Congress, Assembled, appealing to the Supreme Judge of the world for the rectitude of our intentions, do, in the Name, and by the Authority of the good People of these Colonies, solemnly publish and declare, That these United Colonies are, and of Right ought to be Free and Independent States; that they are Absolved from all Allegiance to the British Crown, and that all political connection between them and the State of Great Britain, is and ought to be totally dissolved; and that as Free and Independent States, they have full Power to levy War, conclude Peace, contract Alliances, establish Commerce, and to do all other Acts and Things which Independent States may of right do. And for the support of this Declaration, with a firm reliance on the protection of divine Providence, we mutually pledge to each other our Lives, our Fortunes and our sacred Honor.

The signers of the Declaration represented the new states as follows:

New Hampshire:
Josiah Bartlett, William Whipple, Matthew Thornton

Massachusetts:
John Hancock, Samual Adams, John Adams, Robert Treat Paine, Elbridge Gerry

Rhode Island:
Stephen Hopkins, William Ellery

Connecticut:
Roger Sherman, Samuel Huntington, William Williams, Oliver Wolcott

New York:
William Floyd, Philip Livingston, Francis Lewis, Lewis Morris

New Jersey:
Richard Stockton, John Witherspoon, Francis Hopkinson, John Hart, Abraham Clark

Pennsylvania:
Robert Morris, Benjamin Rush, Benjamin Franklin, John Morton, George Clymer, James Smith, George Taylor, James Wilson, George Ross

Delaware:
Caesar Rodney, George Read, Thomas McKean

Maryland:
Samuel Chase, William Paca, Thomas Stone, Charles Carroll of Carrollton

Virginia:

George Wythe, Richard Henry Lee, Thomas Jefferson, Benjamin Harrison, Thomas Nelson, Jr., Francis Lightfoot Lee, Carter Braxton

North Carolina:

William Hooper, Joseph Hewes, John Penn

South Carolina:

Edward Rutledge, Thomas Heyward, Jr., Thomas Lynch, Jr., Arthur Middleton

Georgia:

Button Gwinnett, Lyman Hall, George Walton

Instructions for Arthur Phillip, Governor of New South Wales (April 25, 1787)

For much of the eighteenth century, Britain transported its criminals to the colony of Georgia. Following the American Revolution, this was no longer possible. In 1779, Joseph Banks, a botanist traveling with explorer James Cook, suggested Australia's Botany Bay as a new penal colony. The following are instructions from King George III to Arthur Phillip of the Royal Navy, who commanded the first shipment of penal colonists to Botany Bay and served as the latter's first governor general. Notable amid the instructions for managing the convicts, cultivating the land, and exploring Australia is an order to protect the Aborigines and establish friendly relations with them. Still, the presumption was that Australia was land that belonged to no one and could thus be settled freely by the British. The full title of the document is "Instructions for our well beloved Arthur Phillip Esq. Our Captain General and Governor in Chief, in and over Our Territory of New South Wales and its Dependencies, or to the Lieutenant Governor or Commander in Chief of the said Territory for the time being. Given at Our Court at St. James the 25th day of April 1787."

With these Our Instructions you will receive Our Commission under Our Great seal constituting and appointing you to be Our Captain General and Governor in Chief of Our Territory called New South Wales extending from the Northern Cape or Extremity of the Coast called Cape York in the Latitude of Ten Degrees thirty seven Minutes south, to the Southern Extremity of the said Territory of New South Wales, or South Cape, in the Latitude of Forty three Degrees Thirty nine Minutes south,

and of all the Country Inland to the Westward as far as the One hundred and Thirty fifth Degree of East Longitude, reckoning from the Meridian of Greenwich including all the Islands adjacent in the Pacific-Ocean within the Latitudes aforesaid of 10° 37_ South, and 43° 39_ South, and of all Towns, Garrisons, Castles, Forts, and all other Fortifications, or other Military Works which may be hereafter erected upon the said Territory, or any of the said Islands, with directions to obey such Orders and Instructions as shall from time to time be given to you under Our Signet and Sign Manual, or by Our Order in our Privy Council; You are therefore to fit Yourself with all convenient speed, and to hold yourself in readiness to repair to Your said Command, and being arrived, to take, upon the execution of the trust We have reposed in You, and as soon as conveniently may be with all due solemnity to cause our said Commission under our Great Seal of Great Britain constituting you Our Governor and Commander in chief as aforesaid, to be read and published. And whereas we have ordered that about 600 Male, and 180 Female Convicts now under sentence or order of Transportation whose names are contained in the List hereunto annexed, should be removed out the Gaols and other places of Confinement in this Our Kingdom, and be put on board of the several Transport Ships which have been taken up for their reception. It is our Royal Will and Pleasure that as soon as the said Convicts, the several persons composing the Civic Establishments, and the Stores, Provisions etc. provided for their use shall be embarked on board the Supply Tender, and the Transport Ships named in the Margin, and be in readiness to depart, that you do take them under your protection and proceed in the Sirius with the said Tender and Transports to the Port on the Coast of New South Wales, situated in the Latitude of 33°41_ called by the name of Botany Bay, agreeably to the Instructions with which you will be furnished by the Commissioner of Our Admiralty, in pursuance of our Royal Commands already signified to them.

And Whereas it may happen upon your Passage to New South Wales that you may find it necessary and expedient to call with the Ships and Vessels under your Convoy, at the Island of Teneriffe, at the Rio di Janeiro, and also at the Cape of Good Hope, for Supplies of Water, and other Refreshments for the Voyage; It is Our further Will and Pleasure, that you do, upon your arrival at the former of, those places, take on board any of the ships of the Convoy which you may think proper, such quantities of Wine as may be requisite for the supply of the said settlement, according to the Instructions with which the Commissary of Stores and Provisions will be furnished by the Commissioners of Our Treasury, taking care that the Quantities purchased do not exceed the proportions to be issued to the several Persons composing the said settlements entitled thereto, agreeably to the said Instructions, for the time to which they have confined the Supply of that article; and for the Amount of such purchases, You will direct the Commissary to draw Bills of Exchange upon them properly certified by you, or Our Lieut: Governor of the said intended settlement, with the other usual attestations, that the same has been obtained at the most reasonable Rates, transmitting at the same time an account thereof to them in order that You may be released from any Imprest which such purchases might occasion. Notwithstanding there is already a considerable quantity of Corn and other seed Grain put onboard the Ships of the Convoy, probably more than may be immediately necessary for raising supplies for the settlement; We are disposed to guard as much as possible against accidents which may happen, or Injuries which these articles might sustain during the Passage; It is therefore Our further Will and Pleasure, that you do upon your arrival at any of the Places you may have occasion to touch at, endeavour to obtain such further Quantities of Seed Grain as You may think requisite for the Tillage of the Land, at the place of your Destination; And also that You do take onboard any number of Black Cattle, Sheep, Goats or Hogs which you can procure, and the Ships of the Convoy can contain, in order to propagate the Breed of these Animals for the general Benefit of the intended settlement, causing the Commissary of Stores and Provisions to draw Bills for the same as in before directed for such Supplies, as well as for any Fresh Provisions which it may be requisite to procure for the use of the Marines or Convicts, at those places, and transmitting information to the Commissioners of Our Treasury such proceedings.

And Whereas it is intended that several of the Transport Ships and Victuallers which are to ac-company you to New South Wales, should be employed in bringing home Cargoes of Tea, and other Merchandise, from China, for the use of our the East India Company; provided they can arrive at Canton in due time whereby a very considerable saving would arise to the Public in the Freight of these Vessels; It is Our Royal Will and Pleasure, that upon your arrival at Botany Bay, on the said Coast of New South Wales, You do cause every possible exertion to be made use of for disembarking the Officers and Men composing the Civil and Military Establishments, together with the Convicts, Stores, Provisions etc. and having so done you are to discharge all the said Transports or Victuallers, in order that such of them as may be engaged by the East India Company may proceed to China, and that the rest may return home; You will however take care, before the said Transport Ships are discharged, to obtain an assignment to You or the Governor in chief for the time being, from the Masters of them, of the servitude of the several Convicts, for the remainder of the Times or Terms specified in their several sentences or Orders of Transportation.

According to the best Information which We have obtained, Botany Bay appears to be the most eligible situation upon the said Coast for the first Establishment, possessing a commodious Harbour and other Advantages which no part of the Coast hitherto discovered affords. It is therefore Our Will and Pleasure that you do immediately upon your landing after taking Measures for securing Yourself and the people who accompany you, as much as possible from any attacks or Interruptions of the Natives of that Country, as well as for the preservation and safety of the Public Stores, proceed to the Cultivation of the Land, distributing the Convicts for that purpose in such manner, and under such Inspectors or Overseers and under such Regulations as may appear to You to be necessary and best calculated for procuring Supplies of Grain and Ground Provisions. The Assortment of Tools and Utensils which have been provided for the use of the Convicts and other Persons who are to compose the intended settlement, are to be distributed according to Your discretion, and according to the employment, assigned to the several persons. In the Distribution however, you will use every proper degree of economy, be careful that the Commissary do transmit an Account of the Issues from time to time to the Commissioners of Our Treasury, to enable them to judge of the propriety or expediency of granting farther supplies. The Clothing of the Convicts and the Provisions issued to them, and the Civil and Military Establishments must be accounted for in the same manner. And Whereas the Commissioners of Our Admiralty have appointed Capt. Hunter to repair on board the Sirius to assist you in the execution of Your Duty, and to take the Command of the Ship whenever you may see occasion to detach her from the Settlement, and also to station the supply Tender under Your Orders, and to be assisting to You upon occasional services after your arrival. And whereas it is Our Royal Intention that Measures should be taken in addition to those which are specified in the Article of these Our Instructions, for obtaining Supplies of Live Stock, and having in consequence of such Intention, caused a Quantity of Arms and other Articles of Merchandise to be provided, and sent out in the Ships under your Convoy, in order to barter with the Natives either on the Territory of New South Wales, or the Islands adjacent in those Seas; It is our Will and Pleasure that as soon as either of these Vessels can be spared with safety from the Settlements that you do detach one or both of them for that purpose, confining their Intercourse as much as possible to such parts as are not in the possession or under the Jurisdiction of other European Powers; The Increase of the Stock of Animals, must depend entirely upon the measures you may adopt on the outset for their preservation, and as the settlement with be amply supplied with vegetable production and most likely with Fish, Fresh Provisions, excepting for the Sick and Convalescents, may in a great degree be dispensed with; For these Reasons it will become you to be extremely cautious in permitting any Cattle, Sheep Hogs etc. intended for propagating the Breed of such animals being to be slaughtered, until a competent stock may be acquired to admit of Your supplying the settlement from it with animal Food without having further recourse to the places from whence such stock may have originally been obtained. It is our Will and Pleasure that the Productions of all Descriptions acquired by the Labour of the Convicts shall be considered as a Public Stock and which we so far leave to your disposal, that such parts there of as may be requisite for the subsistence of the said Convicts and their Families, or the Subsistence of the Civil and Military Establishments of the Settlement may be applied by you to that use. The remainder of such Productions you will reserve as a provision for a further number of Convicts which you may expect will shortly follow you from hence, to be employed under your direction in the manner pointed out in these our Instructions to you. From the natural Increase of Corn and other vegetable food from a common Industry after the Ground has been once cultivated, as well as of Animals; It cannot be expedient that all the Convicts which accompany you, should be employed in attending only to the object of Provisions. And as it has been humbly represented unto us that advantages may be derived from the Flax Plant which is found in the Islands not far distant from the intended Settlement, not only as a means of acquiring Clothing for the Convicts and other persons who may become settlers, but from its superior excellence for a variety of maritime purposes and as it may ultimately may become an Article of Export.

It is therefore Our Will and Pleasure that you do particularly attend to its Cultivation, and that you do send home by every opportunity which may offer, Samples of that Article, in order that a Judgement may be formed whether it may not be necessary to instruct you further upon this Subject.

And Whereas We are desirous that some further Information should be obtained of the several Ports or Harbours upon the Coast and the Islands contiguous thereto within the Limits of Your Government; you are, whenever the Sirius or the Supply Tender, can conveniently be spared, to send one, or both of them, upon that service. Norfolk Island situated in the Lat: and Long: East from Greenwich about being represented as a spot which may hereafter become useful; you are, as soon as circumstances will admit of it, to send a small Establishment thither to secure the same to us, and prevent its being occupied by the subjects of any other European Power, and you will cause any Remarks or Observations which you obtain in consequence of this Instruction to be transmitted to Our Principal Secretary of State for Plantation affairs for Our Information.

And Whereas it may happen, when the Settlement shall be brought into some state of Regulation, that the service of the Sirius may not be necessary at the said settlement; and as we are desirous to diminish as much as possible the Expences which the intended Establishment occasions; You will, whenever the service of the said ship can be dispensed with, and or Capt. Hunter to return with to England; And as from such an arrangement, the Emoluments of your station will be diminished, It is our Royal Intention, that the same shall be made good to you by Bills to be drawn by you upon the Commissioners of Our Treasury.

You are to endeavour by every possible means to open an Intercourse with the Natives and to conciliate their affections, enjoining all Our Subjects to live in amity and kindness with them. And if any of Our Subjects shall wantonly destroy them, or give them any unnecessary Interruption in the exercise of their several occupations. It is our Will and Pleasure that you do cause such offenders to be brought to punishment according to the degree of the Offence. You will endeavour to procure an account of the Numbers inhabiting the Neighbourhood of the intended settlement and report your opinion to one of our Secretaries of State in what manner Our Intercourse with these people may be turned to the advantage of this country.

And whereas from the great disproportion of Female Convicts, those of the Males, who are put under your Superintendance, it, appears advisable that a further number of the latter should be introduced into the new intended Settlements; You are, whenever the Sirius or the Tender shall touch at any of the Islands in the Seas, to instruct their Commanders to take on board any of the women who may be disposed to accompany them to the said settlements; you will however take special care, that the Officers who may happen to be employed upon this Service, do not upon any account, exercise any compulsive measures, or make use of fallacious pretences for bringing away any of the said Woman from the places of their present Residence.

Whereas We have by our Commission bearing date given and granted unto you other acknowledgements whatsoever full power and authority to emancipate and discharge from their Servitude, any of the Convicts under your superindendance, who shall from their good conduct and a disposition to Industry, be deserving of favor; It is our Will and Pleasure that in every such case you do

issue your Warrant to the Surveyor of Lands to make surveys of, and mark out in Lots such Lands upon the said Territory as may be necessary for their use; and when that shall be done, that you do pass Grants thereof with all convenient speed to any of the said Convicts so emancipated, in such proportions, and under such conditions and acknowledgements, as shall hereafter be specified viz. To every Male shall be granted, 30 Acres of land, and in case he shall be married, 20 Acres more, and for every child who may be with them at the Settlement, at the time of making the said Grant, a further quantity of 10 Acres, free of all Fees, Taxes, Quit Rents, or, for the space of Ten years, provided that the person to whom the said Land shall be been granted, shall reside within the same, and proceed to the cultivation and improvement thereof. Reserving only to us such Timber as may be growing, or to grow hereafter, upon the said Land, which may be fit for Naval purposes, and an annual Quit Rent after the expiration of the term or time before mentioned. You will cause Copies of such Grants as may be passed to be preserved, and make a regular return of the said Grants to the Commissioners of Our Treasury and the Lords of the Committee of Our Privy Council for Trade and Plantations.

And Whereas it is likely to happen that the Convicts, who may, after their Emancipation, in consequence of this Instruction, be put in possession of Lands, will not have the means of proceedings to their Cultivation without the Public Aid; it is Our Will and Pleasure that you do cause every such person you may so emancipate, to be supplied with such a Quantity of Provisions as may be sufficient, for the subsistence of himself and also of this family for twelve months, together with an assortment of Tools and Utensils, and such a proportion of Seed Grain, Cattle, Sheep, Hogs etc. as may be proper, and can be spared from the general stock of the Settlement.

And Whereas many of Our subjects, employed upon Military service, at the said Settlement, and others who may resort thither upon their private occupations, may hereafter be desirous of proceedings to the cultivation and Improvement of the Land, and as we are dispersed to afford them every reasonable Encouragement in such an undertaking; It is Our Will and Pleasure that you do with all convenient speed transmit a report of the actual state and Quality of the Soil at and near the said intended Settlement, the probable and most effectual means of Improving and Cultivating the same and of the mode and upon what terms and conditions according to the best of your Judgements the said Lands should be granted, that proper Instructions and authorities may be given to you for that purpose.

And Whereas It is Our Royal Intention that every sort of Intercourse between the intended settlement at Botany Bay, or other places which may be hereafter-established on the coast of New South Wales, and its Dependencies, and the settlements of Our East India Company, as well as the Coasts of China, and the Islands situated in that part of the World, to which any Intercourse has been established by any European Nation, should be prevented by every possible means; It is Our Royal Will and Pleasure that you do not upon any account allow Craft of any sort to be built for the use of private Individuals, which might enable them to effect such Intercourse, and that you do prevent any Vessels which may at any time hereafter arrived the said settlement from any of the Ports before mentioned, from having communication with any of the Inhabitants residing within your Government, without first receiving especial permission from you for that purpose.

Source: Commonwealth of Australia. *Documenting a Democracy: Australia's Story,* 2000. www.foundingdocs.gov.au/places/transcripts/nsw/nsw_pdf/nsw2_doc_1787.pdf.

William Bentinck: On Ritual Murder in India (1829)

The practice of sati *(anglicized as suttee), whereby widows were burned on the funeral pyres of their husbands, had persisted, if rarely practiced, among the Hindu population of India for centuries before the British East India Company began assuming administrative control over parts of the subcontinent in the eighteenth century. Authorities of the East India Company, including Governor-General William Bentinck, who served in that post after 1828, found the practice appalling. In this 1829 report, Bentinck explains why the company should outlaw the practice and why such a ban would not result in major unrest.*

Whether the question be to continue or to discontinue the practice of *sati,* the decision is equally surrounded by an awful responsibility. To consent to the consignment year after year of hundreds of innocent victims to a cruel and untimely end, when the power exists of preventing it, is a predicament which no conscience can contemplate without horror. But, on the other hand, if heretofore received opinions are to be considered of any value, to put to hazard by a contrary course the very safety of the British Empire in India, and to extinguish at once all hopes of those great improvements—affecting the condition not of hundreds and thousands but of millions—which can only be expected from the continuance of our supremacy, is an alternative which even in the light of humanity itself may be considered as a still greater evil. It is upon this first and highest consideration alone, the good of mankind, that the tolerance of this inhuman and impious rite can in my opinion be justified on the part of the government of a civilized nation. While the solution of this question is appalling from the unparalleled magnitude of its possible results, the considerations belonging to it are such as to make even the stoutest mind distrust its decision. On the one side, Religion, Humanity, under the most appalling form, as well as vanity and ambition—in short, all the most powerful influences over the human heart—are arrayed to bias and mislead the judgment. On the other side, the sanction of countless ages, the example of all the Mussulman [Muslim] conquerors, the unanimous concurrence in the same policy of our own most able rulers, together with the universal veneration of the people, seem authoritatively to forbid, both to feeling and to reason, any interference in the exercise of their natural prerogative. In venturing to be the first to deviate from this practice it becomes me to show that nothing has been yielded to feeling, but that reason, and reason alone, has governed the decision.

. . . So far from being chargeable with political rashness, as this departure from an established policy might infer, I hope to be able so completely to prove the safety of the measures as even to render unnecessary any calculation of the degree of risk which for the attainment of so great a benefit might wisely and justly be incurred. . . . With the firm undoubting conviction entertained upon this question, I should be guilty of little short of the crime of multiplied murder if I could hesitate in the performance of this solemn obligation. I have been already stung with this feeling. Every day's delay adds a victim to the dreadful list, which might perhaps have been prevented by a more early submission of the present question . . .

. . .When we had powerful neighbours and had greater reason to doubt our own security, expediency might recommend an indirect and more cautious proceeding, but now that we are supreme my opinion is decidedly in favour of an open, avowed, and general prohibition, resting altogether upon the moral goodness of the act and our power to enforce it; and so decided is my feeling against any half measure that, were I not convinced of the safety of total abolition, I certainly should have advised the cessation of all interference.

Of all those who have given their advice against the abolition of the rite, and have described the ill effects likely to ensue from it, there is no one to whom I am disposed to pay greater deference than Mr. Horace Wilson. I purposely select his opinion because, independently of his vast knowledge of Oriental literature, it has fallen to his lot, as secretary to the Hindu College, and possessing the general esteem both of the parents and of the youths, to have more confidential intercourse with natives of all classes than any man in India. While his opportunity of obtaining information has been great beyond all others, his talents and judgement enable him to form a just estimate of its value. I shall state the most forcible of his reasons, and how far I do and do not agree with him.

1st. Mr. Wilson considers it to be a dangerous evasion of the real difficulties to attempt to prove that *satis* are not "essentially a part of the Hindu religion." I entirely agree in this opinion. The question is not what the rite is but what it is supposed to be, and I have no doubt that the conscientious belief of every order of Hindus, with few exceptions, regards it as sacred.

2nd. Mr. Wilson thinks that the attempt to put down the practice will inspire extensive dissatisfaction. I agree also in this opinion. He thinks that success will only be partial, which I doubt. He does not imagine that the promulgated prohibition will lead to any immediate and overt act of insubordination, but that affrays and much agitation of the public mind must ensue. But he conceives that, if once they suspect that it is the intention of the

British Government to abandon this hitherto inviolate principle of allowing the most complete toleration in matters of religion, there will arise in the minds of all so deep a distrust of our ulterior designs that they will no longer be tractable to any arrangement intended for their improvement, and that principle of a purer morality, as well as of a more virtuous and exalted rule of action, now actively inculcated by European education and knowledge, will receive a fatal check. I must acknowledge that a similar opinion as the probable excitation of a deep distrust of our future intentions was mentioned to me in conversation by that enlightened native, Ram Mohun Roy, a warm advocate for the abolition of *sati* and of all other superstitions and corruptions engrafted on the Hindu religion, which he considers originally to have been a pure Deism. It was his opinion that the practice might be suppressed quietly and unobservedly by increasing the difficulties and by the indirect agency of the police. He apprehended that any public enactment would give rise to general apprehension, that the reasoning would be, "While the English were contending for power, they deemed it politic to allow universal toleration and to respect our religion, but having obtained the supremacy their first act is a violation of their profession, and the next will probably be, like the Muhammadan conquerors, to force upon us their own religion."

Admitting, as I am always disposed to do, that much truth is contained in these remarks, but not at all assenting to the conclusions which, though not described, bear the most unfavourable import, I shall now inquire into the evil and the extent of danger which may practically result from this measure.

It must be first observed that of the 463 *satis* occurring in the whole of the Presidency of Fort William, 420 took place in Bengal, Behar, and Orissa, or what is termed the Lower Provinces, and of these latter 287 in the Calcutta Division alone.

It might be very difficult to make a stranger to India understand, much less believe, that in a population of so many millions of people as the Calcutta Division includes, and the same may be said of all the Lower Provinces, so great is the want of courage and of vigour of character, and such the habitual submission of centuries, that insurrection or hostile opposition to the will of the ruling power may be affirmed to be an impossible danger. . . .

Were the scene of this sad destruction of human life laid in the Upper instead of the Lower Provinces, in the midst of a bold and manly people, I might speak with less confidence upon the question of safety. In these Provinces the *satis* amount to forty-three only upon a population of nearly twenty millions. It cannot be expected that any general feeling, where combination of any kind is so unusual, could be excited in defense of a rite in which so few participate, a rite also notoriously made too often subservient to views of personal interest on the part of the other members of the family. . . .

But I have taken up too much time in giving my own opinion when those of the greatest experience and highest official authority are upon our records. In the report of the Nizamat Adalat for 1828, four out of five of the Judges recommended to the Governor-General in Council the immediate abolition of the practice, and attest its safety . . . No documents exist to show the opinions of the public functionaries in the interior, but I am informed that nine-tenths are in favour of the abolition. . . .

Having made inquiries, also, how far *satis* are permitted in the European foreign settlements, I find from Dr. Carey that at Chinsurah no such sacrifices had ever been permitted by the Dutch Government. That within the limits of Chandarnagar itself they were also prevented, but allowed to be performed in the British territories. The Danish Government of Serampur has not forbidden the rite, in conformity to the example of the British Government. . . . Mr. Wilson also is of opinion that no immediate overt act of insubordination would follow the publication of the edict. The Regulation of Government may be evaded, the police may be corrupted, but even here the price paid as hush money will operate as a penalty, indirectly forwarding the object of Government.

I venture, then, to think it completely proved that from the native population nothing of extensive combination, or even of partial opposition, may be expected from the abolition. . . .

I have now to submit for the consideration of Council the draft of a regulation enacting the abolition of *satis*. . . . It is only in the previous processes, or during the actual performance of the

rite, when the feelings of all may be more or less roused to a high degree of excitement, that I apprehend the possibility of affray or of acts of violence through an indiscreet and injudicious exercise of authority. It seemed to me prudent, therefore, that the police, in the first instance, should warn and advise, but not forcibly prohibit, and if the *sati,* in defiance of this notice, were performed, that a report should be made to the magistrate, who would summon the parties and proceed as in any other case of crime. . . .

The first and primary object of my heart is the benefit of the Hindus. I know nothing so important to the improvement of their future condition as the establishment of a purer morality, whatever their belief, and a more just conception of the will of God. The first step to this better understanding will be dissociation of religious belief and practice from blood and murder. They will then, when no longer under this brutalizing excitement, view with more calmness acknowledged truths. They will see that there can be no inconsistency in the ways of Providence, that to the command received as divine by all races of men, "No innocent blood shall be spilt," there can be no exception; and when they shall have been convinced of the error of this first and most criminal of their customs, may it not be hoped that others, which stand in the way of their improvement, may likewise pass away, and that, thus emancipated from those chains and shackles upon their minds and actions, they may no longer continue, as they have done, the slaves of every foreign conqueror, but that they may assume their first places among the great families of mankind? I disown in these remarks, or in this measure, any view whatever to conversion to our own faith. I write and feel as a legislator for the Hindus, and as I believe many enlightened Hindus think and feel.

Source: "Lord William Bentinck on the Suppression of *Sati,* 8 November 1829," in *Speeches and Documents on Indian Policy, 1750–1921,* ed. Arthur Keith. Oxford: Oxford University Press, 1922.

Daniel O'Connell: Justice for Ireland (February 4, 1836)

Daniel O'Connell, known as the "liberator" in Ireland, was first elected to the British Parliament from Ire-

land in 1828, forcing the British government to pass the Catholic Emancipation Act, allowing Catholics to serve in Parliament, the following year. O'Connell, however, was far from satisfied with this token gesture and demanded full equality for Catholic Irish citizens within the British system. Eventually, O'Connell would be supplanted by younger radicals who sought an independent Ireland. At the time of this speech, however, O'Connell was at the peak of his popularity and his oratorical powers, pointing out the gross inequities of British rule in Ireland, arguably England's first overseas colony.

It appears to me impossible to suppose that the House will consider me presumptuous in wishing to be heard for a short time on this question, especially after the distinct manner in which I have been alluded to in the course of the debate. If I had no other excuse, that would be sufficient; but I do not want it; I have another and a better—the question is one in the highest degree interesting to the people of Ireland. It is, whether we mean to do justice to that country—whether we mean to continue the injustice which has been already done to it, or to hold out the hope that it will be treated in the same manner as England and Scotland. That is the question. We know what "lip service" is; we do not want that. There are some men who will even declare that they are willing to refuse justice to Ireland; while there are others who, though they are ashamed to say so, are ready to consummate the iniquity, and they do so.

England never did do justice to Ireland—she never did. What we have got of it we have extorted from men opposed to us on principle—against which principle they have made us such concessions as we have obtained from them. The right honorable baronet opposite [Sir Robert Peel] says he does not distinctly understand what is meant by a principle. I believe him. He advocated religious exclusion on religious motives; he yielded that point at length, when we were strong enough to make it prudent for him to do so.

Here am I calling for justice to Ireland; but there is a coalition tonight—not a base unprincipled one—God forbid!—it is an extremely natural one; I mean that between the right honorable baronet and the noble lord the member for North Lancashire [Lord Stanley]. It is a natural coalition, and it is impromptu; for the noble lord informs us he

had not even a notion of taking the part he has until the moment at which he seated himself where he now is. I know his candor; he told us it was a sudden inspiration which induced him to take part against Ireland. I believe it with the most potent faith, because I know that he requires no preparation for voting against the interests of the Irish people. [Groans.] I thank you for that groan—it is just of a piece with the rest. I regret much that I have been thrown upon arguing this particular question, because I should have liked to have dwelt upon the speech which has been so graciously delivered from the throne today—to have gone into its details, and to have pointed out the many great and beneficial alterations and amendments in our existing institutions which it hints at and recommends to the House. The speech of last year was full of reforms in words, and in words only; but this speech contains the great leading features of all the salutary reforms the country wants; and if they are worked out fairly and honestly in detail, I am convinced the country will require no further amelioration of its institutions, and that it will become the envy and admiration of the world. I, therefore, hail the speech with great satisfaction.

It has been observed that the object of a king's speech is to say as little in as many words as possible; but this speech contains more things than words—it contains those great principles which, adopted in practice, will be most salutary not only to the British Empire, but to the world. When speaking of our foreign policy, it rejoices in the cooperation between France and this country; but it abstains from conveying any ministerial approbation of alterations in the domestic laws of that country which aim at the suppression of public liberty, and the checking of public discussion, such as call for individual reprobation, and which I reprobate as much as any one. I should like to know whether there is a statesman in the country who will get up in this House and avow his approval of such proceedings on the part of the French government. I know it may be done out of the House amid the cheers of an assembly of friends; but the government have, in my opinion, wisely abstained from reprobating such measures in the speech, while they have properly exulted in such a union of the two countries as will contribute to the national independence and the public liberty of Europe.

Years are coming over me, but my heart is as young and as ready as ever in the service of my country, of which I glory in being the pensionary and the hired advocate. I stand in a situation in which no man ever stood yet—the faithful friend of my country—its servant—its slave, if you will—I speak its sentiments by turns to you and to itself. I require no £20,000,000 on behalf of Ireland—I ask you only for justice: will you—can you—I will not say dare you refuse, because that would make you turn the other way. I implore you, as English gentlemen, to take this matter into consideration now, because you never had such an opportunity of conciliating. Experience makes fools wise; you are not fools, but you have yet to be convinced. I cannot forget the year 1825. We begged then as we would for a beggar's boon; we asked for emancipation by all that is sacred amongst us, and I remember how my speech and person were treated on the Treasury Bench, when I had no opportunity of reply. The other place turned us out and sent us back again, but we showed that justice was with us. The noble lord says the other place has declared the same sentiments with himself; but he could not use a worse argument. It is the very reason why we should acquiesce in the measure of reform, for we have no hope from that House—all our hopes are centered in this; and I am the living representative of those hopes. I have no other reason for adhering to the ministry than because they, the chosen representatives of the people of England, are anxiously determined to give the same measure of reform to Ireland as that which England has received. I have not fatigued myself, but the House, in coming forward upon this occasion. I may be laughed and sneered at by those who talk of my power; but what has created it but the injustice that has been done in Ireland? That is the end and the means of the magic, if you please—the groundwork of my influence in Ireland. If you refuse justice to that country, it is a melancholy consideration to me to think that you are adding substantially to that power and influence, while you are wounding my country to its very heart's core; weakening that throne, the monarch who sits upon which, you say you respect; severing that union which, you say, is bound together by the tightest links, and withholding that justice from Ireland which she will not cease to seek till it is obtained; every man must admit that the course I am taking is the legitimate and proper course—I defy any man to say it is not. Condemn me elsewhere as much as you please, but this you must admit. You may taunt the ministry with having coalesced me, you may raise the vulgar cry of "Irishman and Papist" against me, you may send out men called ministers of God to slander and calumniate me; they may assume whatever garb they please, but the question comes into this narrow compass. I demand, I respectfully insist: on equal justice for Ireland, on the same principle by which it has been administered to Scotland and England. I will not take less. Refuse me that if you can.

Source: Modern History Sourcebook (on-line): www.fordham.edu/halsall/mod/modsbook.html.

Treaty of Waitangi (1840)

In 1840, the British and the leaders of the Maori, the native people of New Zealand, signed the Treaty of Waitangi, granting Britain sovereignty over the islands. The treaty was intended to prevent violent disputes between British settlers and Maoris by creating a mechanism for the peaceful purchase of lands. But misunderstandings and violence continued between the British and the Maori, most notably in the Maori War of the 1860s.

Signed at Waitangi, February 1840, and afterwards by over 500 chiefs.

Victoria, the Queen of England, in her kind (gracious) thoughtfulness to the Chiefs and Hapū of New Zealand, and her desire to preserve to them their chieftainship and their land, and that peace and quietness may be kept with them, because a great number of the people of her tribe have settled in this country, and (more) will come, has thought it right to send a chief (an officer) as one who will make a statement to (negotiate with) Māori people of New Zealand. Let the Māori chiefs accept the governorship (Kawanatanga) of the Queen over all parts of this country and the Islands. Now, the Queen desires to arrange the governorship lest evils should come to the Māori people and the Europeans who are living here without law. Now, the Queen has been pleased to send me, William Hobson, a Captain in the Royal Navy to be Governor for all places of New Zealand which are now given up or which shall be given up to the

Queen. And she says to the Chiefs of the Confederation of the Hapū of New Zealand and the other chiefs, these are the laws spoken of.

This is the First
The Chiefs of the Confederation, and all these chiefs who have not joined in that Confederation give up to the Queen of England for ever all the Governorship (Kawanatanga) of their lands.

This is the Second
The Queen of England agrees and consents to the Chiefs, hapū, and all the people of New Zealand the full chieftainship (rangatiratanga) of their lands, their villages and all their possessions (taonga: everything that is held precious) but the Chiefs give to the Queen the purchasing of those pieces of land which the owner is willing to sell, subject to the arranging of payment which will be agreed to by them and the purchaser who will be appointed by the Queen for the purpose of buying for her.

This is the Third
This is the arrangement for the consent to the governorship of the Queen. The Queen will protect all the Māori people of New Zealand, and give them all the same rights as those of the people of England.

William Hobson, Consul and Lieutenant-Governor

Now, we the Chiefs of the Confederation of the Hapū of New Zealand, here assembled at Waitangi, and we, the chiefs of New Zealand, see the meaning of these words and accept them, and we agree to all of them. Here we put our names and our marks.

This was done at Waitangi on the 6th day of February in the year of our Lord 1840.

At a meeting before any of the Chiefs had signed the Treaty, Hobson agreed under questioning from the Catholic Bishop Pompallier to read the following statement which was a record of discussion on religious freedom and customary law, which the Bishop Pompallier had had with the Anglican Missionary William Colenso.

E mea ana te Kawana ko ngā wakapono katoa o Ingarani, o ngā Weteriana, o Roma, me te ritenga Māori hoki e tiakina ngātahitia e ia.

Translation:

The Governor says that the several faiths (beliefs) of England, of the Wesleyans, of Rome, and also Māori custom shall alike be protected by him.

This is sometimes referred to as the fourth article or protocol.

Source: Government of New Zealand website. http://www.govt.nz/en/aboutnz/?id=a32f7d70e71e96 32aad1016cb343f900.

British Admiralty: Negotiating with African Chiefs (1844)

While Britain profited from the international trade in African slaves for centuries, the country outlawed the practice in 1807 and made its suppression a central part of its foreign and naval policy for much of the nineteenth century. Indeed, the suppression of the slave trade became one of the justifications for British intervention in Africa during the mid- to late nineteenth century. The following document is a set of British Admiralty instructions to officers outlining the methods for getting coastal African chiefs to suppress the slave trade.

1. The suppression of the Slave Trade may be materially assisted by obtaining the co-operation of the Native Chiefs of Africa in the object; you are therefore authorized to conclude engagements for this purpose with the African Chiefs; but you must strictly adhere to the regulations herein laid down on the subject.

2. You will procure the fullest and most correct information as to the state of those parts of the coast in which Slave Trade is carried on, so as to enable you to determine, with what Chiefs it may be expedient to enter into negotiations for the conclusion of Engagements. With this in view, you will endeavor to ascertain the power and influence of the several Chiefs; their personal character, and the habits of the people; the extent and force of the country; the sources, amount, and description of the legitimate trade carried on. You will endeavor to obtain the most accurate information as to the Slave Trade; its present extent, and whether it has recently increased or diminished: . . . You will investigate the means whereby the Slave Trade may most effectually and speedily be extinguished, and you will enquire into the inclination and the power of the Chief to carry into effect an Engagement for

that purpose, and the means which Great Britain may have for enforcing it. . . .

4. When you shall desire to open negotiations with any African Chief, you will, after taking every proper precaution for the safety of yourself and your people, at the same time avoiding giving offence to the Natives, obtain a personal interview with the Chiefs, and endeavor to induce them to conclude an Engagement . . .

6. Every opportunity is to be taken of impressing the minds of the Native Chiefs and their people with a conviction of the efforts Great Britain has made for their benefit, and of her earnest desire to raise them in the scale of nations. It is most desirable to excite in them an emulation of the habits of the Christian world, and to enable them to make the first practical step towards civilization by the abandonment of the Slave Trade.

7. Special care must be taken not to offend the prejudices of the Natives; and every respect must be paid to their peculiar usages, so far as the same are not of an inhuman character; and allowance must be made for any jealousy or distrust that may be shown by them. . . .

9. Threats or intimidation are never to be used to induce the Native Chiefs to conclude the Engagement: on the contrary, forbearance and conciliation must be in all cases the rule of conduct; and if the Native Chiefs refuse the Engagement, every means must be taken to encourage in them feelings of confidence, and to leave a favorable impression that may facilitate the renewal of negotiations at a future period. . . .

11. Immediately after the conclusion of the Engagement, you will require the Chiefs to proclaim a law to their people by which its stipulations shall be publicly made known.

12. In case the Slave Trade is actually carried on within the jurisdiction of the Chief at the time the Engagement is concluded, . . . you will then require that all the Slaves held for exportation shall be delivered up to you to be made free at a British colony. You will also demand that all implements of the Slave Trade, such as shackles, bolts, and handcuffs, chains, whips, branding irons, etc., or articles of Slave equipment for fitting up vessels to carry Slaves, shall be given up to you, or destroyed in your presence. You will also insist on the immediate destruction of the barracoons, or buildings exclusively devoted to the re-

ception of Slaves, and, if necessary, you will enforce all these demands. . . .

14. You are not, without the signed consent in writing of a Native Chief, to take any step upon his territory for putting down the Slave Trade by force, excepting when, by Engagement, Great Britain is entitled to adopt coercive measures on shore for that purpose.

15. . . . You will cause a vigilant watch to be kept over the proceedings of the Chiefs, until you are satisfied of their fidelity to their Engagements. After which, you will visit the Chiefs in person, or send a Commander of one of Her Majesty's Ships, at least once in six months, to see to the due execution of the Engagements on the part of the Chiefs.

16. In the event, however, of ultimate failure of the negotiations you will finally state to the Chief that every civilized Naval Power in the world has declared that it has abandoned the Slave Trade; that most nations have united with Great Britain in endeavors to put it down; that Great Britain will not allow the subjects of the Chief . . . to carry Slaves for sale to or from any places beyond the limits of his own territory, and that Her Majesty's Officers have orders to liberate Slaves when found embarked in boats of his subjects for that purpose. . . .

Source: http://home.planet.nl/~pbdavis/Slave_1.htm#First.

Treaty of Amritsar (March 16, 1846)

As was the case in many areas of the Indian subcontinent, the British preferred to rule the northern provinces of Jammu and Kashmir indirectly, through compliant local nobles, or rajahs. In this case, the British turned over a predominantly Muslim regime to a Hindu rajah. Upon independence 100 years later, the descendants of the rajah decided to affiliate with Hindu India rather than Muslim Pakistan. An unhappy Muslim population, supported by Pakistan, has been in revolt ever since.

The treaty between the British Government on the one part and Maharajah Gulab Singh of Jammu on the other concluded on the part of the British Government by Frederick Currie, Esq. and Brevet-Major Henry Montgomery Lawrence, acting under the orders of the Rt. Hon. Sir Henry Hardinge, G.C.B., one of her Britannic Majesty's most Honorable Privy Council, Governor-General of the possessions of the East India Company, to direct and control all the affairs in the East Indies and by Maharajah Gulab Singh in person—1846.

Article 1

The British Government transfers and makes over for ever in independent possession to Maharajah Gulab Singh and the heirs male of his body all the hilly or mountainous country with its dependencies situated to the eastward of the River Indus and the westward of the River Ravi including Chamba and excluding Lahul, being part of the territories ceded to the British Government by the Lahore State according to the provisions of Article IV of the Treaty of Lahore, dated 9th March, 1846.

Article 2

The eastern boundary of the tract transferred by the foregoing article to Maharajah Gulab Singh shall be laid down by the Commissioners appointed by the British Government and Maharajah Gulab Singh respectively for that purpose and shall be defined in a separate engagement after survey.

Article 3

In consideration of the transfer made to him and his heirs by the provisions of the foregoing article Maharajah Gulab Singh will pay to the British Government the sum of seventy-five lakhs of rupees (Nanukshahee), fifty lakhs to be paid on or before the 1st October of the current year, A.D., 1846.

Article 4

The limits of territories of Maharajah Gulab Singh shall not be at any time changed without concurrence of the British Government.

Article 5

Maharajah Gulab Singh will refer to the arbitration of the British Government any disputes or question that may arise between himself and the Government of Lahore or any other neighboring State, and will abide by the decision of the British Government.

Article 6

Maharajah Gulab Singh engages for himself and heirs to join, with the whole of his Military Forces, the British troops when employed within the hills or in the territories adjoining his possessions.

Article 7

Maharajah Gulab Singh engages never to take to retain in his service any British subject nor the subject of any European or American State without the consent of the British Government.

Article 8

Maharajah Gulab Singh engages to respect in regard to the territory transferred to him, the provisions of Articles V, VI and VII of the separate Engagement between the British Government and the Lahore Durbar, dated 11th March, 1846.

Article 9

The British Government will give its aid to Maharajah Gulab Singh in protecting his territories from external enemies.

Article 10

Maharajah Gulab Singh acknowledges the supremacy of the British Government and will in token of such supremacy present annually to the British Government one horse, twelve shawl goats of approved breed (six male and six female) and three pairs of Cashmere shawls.

This Treaty of ten articles has been this day settled by Frederick Currie, Esq. and Brever-Major Henry Montgomery Lawrence, acting under directions of the Rt. Hon. Sir Henry Hardinge, Governor-General, on the part of the British Government and by Maharajah Gulab Singh in person, and the said Treaty has been this day ratified by the seal of the Rt. Hon. Sir Henry Hardinge, Governor-General. Done at Amritsar the sixteenth day of March, in the year of our Lord one thousand eight hundred and forty-six, corresponding with the seventeenth day of Rubee-ul-Awal (1262 Hijree).

(Signed) H. Hardinge (Seal)
(Signed) F. Currie
(Signed) H. M. Lawrence

Source: www.kashmir.no/treaty_of_amritsar.htm.

John Stuart Mill: "On Colonies and Colonization" (1848)

John Stuart Mill (1806–1873) was a British economist and proponent of a then-radical philosophical school known as utilitarianism, which argued that all right beliefs and actions should promote the greatest happiness to the greatest number of people. In his 1848 work, "On Colonies and Colonization," Mill argued that the establishment and settling of colonies would lead to the greatest good for the greatest number, in that it promoted economic effi-

ciency adding "to the joint wealth of the old and the new country." Mill also argued that only government had the capacity to effectively promote this kind of colonization and settlement.

If it is desirable, as no one will deny it to be, that the planting of colonies should be conducted, not with an exclusive view to the private interests of the first founders, but with a deliberate regard to the permanent welfare of the nations afterwards to arise from these small beginnings; such regard can only be secured by placing the enterprise, from its commencement, under regulations constructed with the foresight and enlarged views of philosophical legislators; and the government alone has power either to frame such regulations, or to enforce their observance.

The question of government intervention in the work of Colonization involves the future and permanent interests of civilization itself, and far outstretches the comparatively narrow limits of purely economical considerations. But even with a view to those considerations alone, the removal of population from the overcrowded to the unoccupied parts of the earth's surface is one of those works of eminent social usefulness, which most require, and which at the same time best repay, the intervention of government. To appreciate the benefits of colonization, it should be considered in its relation, not to a single country, but to the collective economical interests of the human race. The question is in general treated too exclusively as one of distribution; of relieving one labor market and supplying another. It is this, but it is also a question of production, and of the most efficient employment of the productive resources of the world.

Much has been said of the good economy of importing commodities from the place where they can be bought cheapest; while the good economy of producing them where they can be produced cheapest, is comparatively little thought of. If to carry consumable goods from the places where they are superabundant to those where they are scarce, is a good pecuniary speculation, is it not an equally good speculation to do the same thing with regard to labor and instruments? The exportation of laborers and capital from old to new countries, from a place where their productive power is less, to a place where it is greater, in-

creases by so much the aggregate produce of the labor and capital of the world. It adds to the joint wealth of the old and the new country, what amounts in a short period to many times the mere cost of effecting the transport. There needs be no hesitation in affirming that Colonization, in the present state of the world, is the best affair of business, in which the capital of an old and wealthy country can engage.

It is equally obvious, however, that Colonization on a great scale can be undertaken, as an affair of business, only by the government, or by some combination of individuals in complete understanding with the government; except under such very peculiar circumstances as those which succeeded the Irish famine. Emigration on the voluntary principle rarely has any material influence in lightening the pressure of population in the old country, though as far as it goes it is doubtless a benefit to the colony. Those laboring persons who voluntarily emigrate are seldom the very poor; they are small farmers with some little capital, or laborers who have saved something, and who, in removing only their own labor from the crowded labor market, withdraw from the capital of the country a fund which maintained and employed more laborers than themselves. Besides, this portion of the community is so limited in number, that it might be removed entirely, without making any sensible impression upon the numbers of the population, or even upon the annual increase. Any considerable emigration of labor is only practicable, when its cost is defrayed, or at least advanced, by others than the emigrants themselves.

Who then is to advance it? Naturally, it may be said, the capitalists of the colony, who require the labor, and who intend to employ it. But to this there is the obstacle, that a capitalist, after going to the expense of carrying out laborers, has no security that he shall be the person to derive any benefit from them. If all the capitalists of the colony were to combine, and bear the expense by subscription, they would still have no security that the laborers, when there, would continue to work for them. After working for a short time and earning a few pounds, they always, unless prevented by the government, squat on unoccupied land, and work only for themselves. The experiment has been repeatedly tried whether it was possible to enforce contracts for labor, or the repayment of the passage money of emigrants to those who advanced it, and the trouble and expense have always exceeded the advantage. The only other resource is the voluntary contributions of parishes or individuals, to rid themselves of surplus laborers who are already, or who are likely to become, locally chargeable on the poor rate. Were this speculation to become general, it might produce a sufficient amount of emigration to clear off the existing unemployed population, but not to raise the wages of the employed; and the same thing would require to be done over again in less than another generation.

One of the principal reasons why Colonization should be a national undertaking, is that in this manner alone, save in highly exceptional cases, can emigration be self-supporting. The exportation of capital and labor to a new country being, as before observed, one of the best of all affairs of business, it is absurd that it should not, like other affairs of business, repay its own expenses. Of the great addition which it makes to the produce of the world, there can be no reason why a sufficient portion should not be intercepted, and employed in reimbursing the outlay incurred in effecting it. For reasons already given, no individual, or body of individuals, can reimburse themselves for the expense; the government, however, can. It can take from the annual increase of wealth, caused by the emigration, the fraction which suffices to repay with interest what the emigration has cost. The expenses of emigration to a colony ought to be borne by the colony; and this, in general, is only possible when they are borne by the colonial government.

Of the modes in which a fund for the support of colonization can be raised in the colony, none is comparable in advantage to that which was first suggested, and so ably and perseveringly advocated, by Mr Wakefield: the plan of putting a price on all unoccupied land, and devoting the proceeds to emigration. The unfounded and pedantic objections to this plan have been answered in a former part of this chapter: we have now to speak of its advantages. First, it avoids the difficulties and discontents incident to raising a large annual amount by taxation; a thing which is almost useless to attempt with a scattered population of settlers in the wilderness, who, as experience proves, can seldom be compelled to pay direct taxes, except at a cost exceeding their amount; while in an infant community indirect taxation soon reaches its limit. The sale of lands is thus by far the easiest mode of raising the requisite funds. But it has other and still greater recommendations. It is a beneficial check upon the tendency of a population of colonists to adopt the tastes and inclinations of savage life, and to disperse so widely as to lose all the advantages of commerce, of markets, of separation of employments, and combination of labor. By making it necessary for those who emigrate at the expense of the fund, to earn a considerable sum before they can become landed proprietors, it keeps up a perpetual succession of laborers for hire, who in every country are a most important auxiliary even to peasant proprietors: and by diminishing the eagerness of agricultural speculators to add to their domain, it keeps the settlers within reach of each other for purposes of co-operation, arranges a numerous body of them within easy distance of each center of foreign commerce and non-agricultural industry, and insures the formation and rapid growth of towns and town products. This concentration, compared with the dispersion which uniformly occurs when unoccupied land can be had for nothing, greatly accelerates the attainment of prosperity, and enlarges the fund which may be drawn upon for further emigration. Before the adoption of the Wakefield system, the early years of all new colonies were full of hardship and difficulty: the last colony founded on the old principle, the Swan River settlement, being one of the most characteristic instances. In all subsequent colonization, the Wakefield principle has been acted upon, though imperfectly, a part only of the proceeds of the sale of land being devoted to emigration: yet wherever it has been introduced at all, as in South Australia, Victoria, and New Zealand, the restraint put upon the dispersion of the settlers, and the influx of capital caused by the assurance of being able to obtain hired labor, has, in spite of many difficulties and much mismanagement, produced a suddenness and rapidity of prosperity more like fable than reality.

The self-supporting system of Colonization, once established, would increase in efficiency every year; its effect would tend to increase in geometrical progression: for since every able-bodied emigrant, until the country is fully peopled, adds in a very short time to its wealth, over and above his own consumption, as much as would defray the expense of bringing out another emigrant, it follows that the greater the number already sent, the greater number might continue to be sent, each emigrant laying the foundation of a succession of other emigrants at short intervals without fresh expense, until the colony is filled up. It would therefore be worth while, to the mother country, to accelerate the early stages of this progression, by loans to the colonies for the purpose of emigration, repayable from the fund formed by the sales of land. In thus advancing the means of accomplishing a large immediate emigration, it would be investing that amount of capital in the mode, of all others, most beneficial to the colony; and the labor and savings of these emigrants would hasten the period at which a large sum would be available from sales of land. It would be necessary, in order not to overstock the labor market, to act in concert with the persons disposed to remove their own capital to the colony. The knowledge that a large amount of hired labor would be available, in so productive a field of employment, would insure a large emigration of capital from a country, like England, of low profits and rapid accumulation: and it would only be necessary not to send out a greater number of laborers at one time, than this capital could absorb and employ at high wages.

Inasmuch as, on this system, any given amount of expenditure, once incurred, would provide not merely a single emigration, but a perpetually flowing stream of emigrants, which would increase in breadth and depth as it flowed on; this mode of relieving overpopulation has a recommendation, not possessed by any other plan ever proposed for making head against the consequences of increase without restraining the increase itself: there is an element of indefiniteness in it; no one can perfectly foresee how far its influence, as a vent for surplus population, might possibly reach. There is hence the strongest obligation on the government of a country like our own, with a crowded population, and unoccupied continents under its command, to build, as it were, and keep open, in concert with the colonial governments, a bridge from the mother country to those continents, by establishing the self-supporting system of colonization on such a scale,

that as great an amount of emigration as the colonies can at the time accommodate, may at all times be able to take place without cost to the emigrants themselves.

The importance of these considerations, as regards the British islands, has been of late considerably diminished by the unparalleled amount of spontaneous emigration from Ireland; an emigration not solely of small farmers, but of the poorest class of agricultural laborers, and which is at once voluntary and self-supporting, the succession of emigrants being kept up by funds contributed from the earnings of their relatives and connections who had gone before. To this has been added a large amount of voluntary emigration to the seats of the gold discoveries, which has partly supplied the wants of our most distant colonies, where, both for local and national interests, it was most of all required. But the stream of both these emigrations has already considerably slackened, and though that from Ireland has since partially revived, it is not certain that the aid of government in a systematic form, and on the self-supporting principle, will not again become necessary to keep the communication open between the hands needing work in England, and the work which needs hands elsewhere.

Source: Mill, John Stuart. *Principles of Political Economy,*
ed. Arthur T. Hadley. New York: P. F. Collier, 1900.

Sample Native Treaty, Royal Niger Company (1880s)

During the late nineteenth century, the various European powers began to acquire vast holdings in the interior of Africa. The "great scramble" involved Britain, France, and Germany in a headlong rush to claim as much territory as possible. In order to expedite the process, European powers and the European trading companies that spearheaded the colonizing effort coerced or tricked indigenous leaders into signing treaties that offered goods in exchange for lands. The following is a sample treaty used by the Royal Niger Company with blanks to be filled in by agents negotiating with local leaders.

We, the undersigned Chiefs of. . . . . . , with the view of bettering the condition of our country and people, do this day cede to the Royal Niger Company

(Chartered and Limited), for ever, the whole of our territory extending from. . . . .

We also give to the said Royal Niger Company (Chartered and Limited) full power to settle all native disputes arising from any cause whatever, and we pledge ourselves not to enter into any war with other tribes without the sanction of the said Royal Niger Company (Chartered and Limited).

We understand that the said Royal Niger Company (Chartered and Limited) have full power to mine, farm, and build in any portion of our country.

We bind ourselves not to have any intercourse [i.e., transactions or communications] with any strangers or foreigners except through the said Royal Niger Company (Chartered and Limited).

In consideration of the foregoing, the said Royal Niger Company (Chartered and Limited) bind themselves not to interfere with any of the native laws or customs of the country, consistently with the maintenance of order and good government

The said Royal Niger Company (Chartered and Limited) agree to pay native owners of land a reasonable amount for any portion they may require.

The said Royal Niger Company (Chartered and Limited) bind themselves to protect the said Chiefs from the attacks of any neighbouring aggressive tribes.

The said Royal Niger Company (Chartered and Limited) also agree to pay the said Chiefs . . . . native value.

We, the undersigned witnesses, do hereby solemnly declare that the. Chiefs whose names are placed opposite their respective crosses have in our presence affixed their crosses of their own free will and consent, and that the said. has in our presence affixed his signature.

Done in triplicate at. this. . . . . .day of. . . . ., 188.

Declaration by Interpreter.

I,. . . . . .of . . . ., do hereby solemnly declare that I am well acquainted with the language of the . . . . country, and that of the. . . . . day of. . . . ., 188., I truly and faithfully explained the above Agreement to all the Chiefs present, and that they understood its meaning.

Source: web.jjay.cuny.edu/~jobrien/reference/ob43.html.

Major-General Charles Gordon: The Siege of Khartoum (1884)

British interest in the Sudan dates back to London's administrative takeover in the 1870s of Egypt and the Suez Canal, the latter a waterway critical to imperial trade with India. Working with the local ruler, Ismail Pasha, an experienced British officer named Charles Gordon was appointed governor of the Sudan and established trading posts along the Nile River. Ill health forced him to resign and return to England in 1880. In 1884, London recalled Gordon to the Sudan to help evacuate British-led Egyptian forces threatened by an anti-British uprising in the Sudan, led by the mystical Islamic leader Muhammed Ahmad al-Mahdi (al-Mahdi meaning "messiah" in Arabic). Gordon, however, was besieged in Khartoum, the Sudanese capital, and eventually killed, along with his forces, by the rebels. His tenacious defense, recorded in his journal, and his death gave Gordon a martyr's status among the British people.

December 3—This morning Arabs fired eight rounds at us, and we replied; one of our shells struck their casemate. Numbers of Arabs left Mahdi's camp for the north. Arabs fired nine rounds into the town at night from the south lines. One shell fell into the garden of the Palace; this from the south lines. A shell from Arabs at Goba fell in the garden, so it will be seen the attention which is being paid to the Palace.

Twenty shells fell in town yesterday, but none did any harm.

I think this is the programme, and though it is of doubtful morality, perhaps it is the shortest route out of a mess. "British Expedition comes up to relieve British subjects in distress, nothing else; it finds one of its subjects acting as ruler; it takes him away, and he, on going away, appoints Zubair ruler, subject to approval of Towfik, Zubair having been allowed to come up to Kartoum, as a private individual, to look after his family."

Now who can say anything to the British Government? It has had nothing to do with the appointment of Zubair, or with the Government of Towfik; it came up to relieve its subjects, and "Gordon is entirely responsible for the appointment of Zubair;" "even Towfik is not responsible, for Gordon did it on his own responsibility." This will be a splendid dodge; it first clears Her Majesty's Government of any blame, it puts the blame on me, and in the storm that is caused, I shall have been so effectually blackened that every one will forget the—well! we did not say it in direct words (count the months), we will call the DELAY; in fact, I expect the public will rather blame the Government for having sent any Expedition at all for such a style of British subject; the Government will chuckle over it all, and will preserve the fiction that they have nought to do with the Soudan or Egypt.

The Opposition will be perfectly wild at seeing the Ministry get out of the mess, with what one may call really credit, while the Anti-Slavery Society and Europe at large will empty their vials of wrath on me. Towfik and his pashas will wring their hands openly over such an act. . . . will get such kudos! For my part I shall get out of any of those wretched honours, for the Ministry will be only too glad to say, "We could not, you know, confer any honours on him after such very disreputable conduct," knowing well enough I would not take them if offered; and as I am not going to England again, and shall not see the papers, I shall not much mind the abuse. I think it is a splendid programme. Zubair must be given either £200,000 or £300,000 a year for two years, replenished magazines, and stores of all sorts, all the Expedition's boats and steamers, &c., and must be aided for two months in small expeditions; besides the £200,000 or £300,000 for two years, he must have down on the nail £150,000 to £200,000.

I must clear, in disgrace, out of the country, to prevent any appearance of any connivance on the part of . . . in this arrangement, which he will or ought officially to deplore. I do not think Zubair will care for the Equator Province; he will agree to give that up; he will agree to uphold the Treaty of 1877 Slave Convention, and laugh as he does so. As for the Bahr Gazelle, I expect the Mahdi has it, and if so, his people will move up there, when Zubair by his politics recaptures Obeyed.

What a fearful row there will be. I know one man who will write: "Better, my dear Gordon, far better! to have died, than have so very far departed from the right path; nothing, no nothing can explain it away. A happy Christmas to you." . . . "This news from the Soudan is very satisfactory; I call it a great triumph, for it not only delivers us out of a dilemma, but it effectually settles our friends, and vitiates anything he may say as to the Delay." Any military operations undertaken after the proclamation of Zubair will be put down "as measures necessary to be undertaken to secure the return, unmolested, of the expeditionary force." 5 P.M. Artillery duel going on between our two guns and the Arab gun; our practice is very bad. The shells the Arabs fire from their Krupp gun reach the Palace Garden, but the report of their gun is not to be heard. The Arab shells from Goba fall just about 200 yards short of the Palace; but in its line there is just the second of suspense (after seeing them fire), while one hears the soft sighing of their shells coming nearer and nearer, till they strike. 7 P.M. Another battle! (the third to-day). The Arabs came down to the river and fired on the Palace; we could not stand that. 7.10 P.M. Battle over; we are as we were, minus some cartridges. 7.20 P.M. Battle begun again, because the buglers played "Salaam Effendina," the Arabs wasting ammunition. 8 P.M. The Arabs are firing from the south at the Krupps on the Palace; they (i.e., the Arabs) are at least 4000 yards distant; one hears the shells burst, but not the report of their gun; they reached the river close to the Palace.

December 4—Omdurman Fort all right. They had a man wounded yesterday. There was a small battle at Bourré this morning. The Arabs at Goba are quiet after the exertions of yesterday. Firing was heard (on north) towards Shoboloha last night. Report in town says the steamers are near there.

Should the Zubair arrangement be accepted, then comes the question of the military action during two months, at end of which time the expeditionary force should be wending its way back. The driving away of the Arabs from the Dem at the north of the Palace will be immediate on the arrival of the troops; the Arabs will then hold on to El foun and to Giraffe. They will vacate the vicinity of Omdurman Fort; 1000 men will deal with El foun and Giraffe, supported by our tag-rag. First Giraffe, then El foun; but at the same time as this takes place, the retreat of Arabs ought to be cut off at Gitana from Kordofan by the steamers and another 1000 men; the Mahdi will return to Schatt, and the town will be free, and all the troops defending the lines will be available. Then comes the question of going inland and attacking the family of the Sheikh el Obeyed's son, two and a half hours inland, or else going on and attacking Mesalamieh. I think Sheikh el Obeyed's family will give in as soon as the Arabs are driven from El foun (an affair of an hour, D.V.). I tried to entice the Arabs at Goba into a fight this evening, but they would not be drawn, and only replied by two shells, which fell in the river. We played on them with the mitrailleuse, and made them move their gun, and then they fired two more shells, one which fell near the Palace in the river. With a good mitrailleuse, and a sharp operator, with telescope sight, no gun could be served with impunity at 2000 yards range, though it could be served against artillery fire, for at that range there is plenty of time to dodge under cover after seeing the flash ere the shell arrives. The band, principally of small boys, the men being on the lines, went on to the roof of the Palace to play (they always come on the eve of their Sabbath, the Friday). The Arabs heard them, and fired a volley at them; they, furious, threw down their instruments, and flew to arms, and a regular fusillade went on for some moments, the other places supporting the fire. The buglers are bugling now "Come to us, come to us," to the Arabs. (The Egyptian Government have the French calls, and can converse by bugle; I do not think we have.) Last night a renegade Dervish bugler in the Arab ranks replied, "Come to us, come to us."

December 5—Small church parades. Three caravans of some size came in from the north to Mahomet Achmet's camp this morning. Two deserters came in from the Arabs Fort at Omdurman all right. In store 737 ardebs of dhoora, 121,300 okes of biscuit.

We are going to make an attempt to relieve Omdurman Fort (really things are looking very black). The men who came in say the Mahdi is short of ammunition. The Arabs fired three shells at the palace this afternoon, which fell in the river. A soldier deserted to-day to the Arabs. 5 P.M. The Arabs fired two shells at the palace, which fell into the water (if they only knew! that if they sank the trail they would touch us up! their line is quite correct). 6.30 P.M. Since 3 P.M. we have been firing on them, and they on us, only wasting ammunition, for though our bullets reach them, few of theirs reach us. According to the men who came in from the Arabs, it is the pet detachment of the Mahdi

who are opposite the Palace; they do not number more than one hundred, and are principally our Soudan soldiers. I have almost given up all idea of saving the town; it is a last resource, this attempt we make to open the route to the Omdurman Fort.

December 6—(Certainly every fortified place ought to be provided with a hundred good telescopes.) The steamers went down and fired on the Arabs at Omdurman. We have £150 in cash in the treasury. In the affair to-day we had three killed and thirty-six wounded in the steamers, and Ferratch Ullah Bey reports he had five wounded at Omdurman Fort. The Arabs came down in good force, and must have lost.

I have given up all idea of landing at Omdurman: we have not the force to do it. The Arabs fired forty-five rounds from their guns at Mogrim and the steamers. We had two men wounded at Mogrim, and one killed. This is most distressing to have these poor fellows wounded and killed. To-morrow it will be 270 days 9 months that we have endured one continuous misery and anxiety. The Greeks who were at Mogrim say at least 300 or 400 Arabs were killed and wounded in to-day's engagement. The Ismailia was struck by four, and the Bordeen by two shells, but not in vital parts. I visited the steamers, and had weariness of heart at hearing the complaint of the men as to the robbery of their rations by the officers.

December 7—The 270th day of our imprisonment. The Arabs fired from their guns at Boga 8 shells, one of which fell in the town near Palace, but did no harm. Omdurman reports the fort all right, one more man wounded there. A great force of Arabs strayed down near Omdurman last night, and left at dawn. The cock turkey has killed one of his companions, reason not known. (Supposed to be correspondence with Mahdi, or some harem infidelity.) Report in town that Berber surrendered, "sans coup férir." I hope so. We are going to send the steamers down again to attack the Arabs at Omdurman at noon to-morrow. The Arabs fired nine shells at Bourré, and begun again their practice on the Palace, firing five shells, one of which came close to the roof of Palace.

A soldier escaped from the Arabs and came in; he says the Expeditionary Force has captured Berber. Two soldiers deserted to the Arabs to-day! The Arabs at Goba fired three shells this evening at the Palace; two fell close to it, one fell in the water. One shell from the Arabs at Bourré fell in the hospital. One of the shells of the Arabs this evening struck the building next the Palace, and stuck in the wall, about 9 feet from the ground. A man came in from the Arabs, who says the Expeditionary Force is approaching. I saw a body of horsemen going north to-day, very fast, from El foun. In the Ismailia were eighty bullet holes on the water line of her hull; in the Bordeen there were seventy-five bullet holes, ditto in the last engagement!!! These holes were stopped by screws made for the purpose. As for the bullet marks elsewhere they are not to be counted.

My belief is that the Mahdi business will be the end of slavery in the Soudan. The Arabs have invariably put their slaves in the front and armed them; and the slaves have seen that they were plucky, while their masters shirked: is it likely that those slaves will ever yield obedience to those masters as heretofore?

December 8—The Arabs this morning fired twelve rounds from guns at Bourré, and five rounds at the North Fort and Palace. Two men came in from the Arabs; they say no Arabs have gone down towards Berber; that the report in the Arab camp was that Berber was captured; this report was four days old. 10 A.M. The steamers are going down to attack. Omdurman Fort reports "All right." 10.30 A.M. The steamers are engaged; the Arabs have two nasty wasp batteries with regular embrasures, quite à l'Europe. (Query Slatin Bey's design.) Though we have protected the steam-chests of the steamers, one cannot help being very anxious. The Arabs at Goba are silent. Another soldier from the Arabs came in and states report of advance of the Expeditionary Force, who are coming by land. Every time I hear the guns fire I have a twitch of the heart of gnawing anxiety for my penny steamers. 11.30 A.M. The battle is over, and my penny boats are safe, thank God! (not in words only, but from my heart). We had two wounded on board the Bordeen, none on board the Ismailia. We are meditating an attack with 500 men on the 50 Arabs, who with their gun, are at Goba. The Bordeen was struck by four shells, the Ismailia by two shells, one of which destroyed a cabin: they had not much musketry fire, but the Arabs fired a great number of rounds; they had six guns playing on the steamers. At noon Arabs fired five shells at

Bourré. In the evening they fired three shells against the Palace from Goba which fell in the town. Had we not cased the steam-chest of the Ismailia with wood she would have had her boiler blown up by one of the shells. The Arab rifle force of Goba is completely innocuous; we do not even hear their bullets, yet our bullets reach them, for they cannot stay in the open, and we can see the dust the bullets throw up that we fire. Wadji Barra, an Ameer of the Mahdi, on the north side, sent me a letter (in Appendix AB) asking me to surrender, and saying it is all lies about the Expedition, the Mahdi is evidently (like H.M.G.) offended with my curt answer to his last, and so his holiness will not write direct. Whenever we have what we call a victory we fire some fireworks at the main posts of our lines, which infuriates the Arabs, and puzzle them as to the reason. They were very angry to-night, and came down in a good number, and fired on the Palace several volleys. I ordered up the three buglers, who put them to flight. The letter Wadji Barra sent me was sent by a woman who came to the North Fort. I telegraphed the officer "Open the letter and tell me contents." He did so, and I answered, "Send the woman back to the Ameer and tell him to go, &c." I expect this irritated the Ameer, who ordered the advance of his men, and consequent expenditure of his ammunition.

December 9—A party of sixty men, with ammunition, camels, and some horsemen, left the Dem of the Mahdi, and went north this morning. The Arabs on the right bank of the White Nile came over to the left bank of the Blue Nile, and went through some antics, so we suppose something is up. A man was wounded yesterday at Omdurman, which fort reports all right. Letter sent by Wadji Barra in Appendix AB. The Arabs fired yesterday not rifled shell, but round shell, which they must have got at Obeyed, which shows they are out of ammunition of the regulation sort. What called forth the letter from Wadji Barra (Appendix AB) was a paper I issued (Appendix CD) to the town, when I received Towfik's telegram saying he would hold the Soudan, and which I gave to a man to send to the Arabs. If Lord Palmerston was alive (or Forster was Premier) he would never leave the Soudan, without proclaiming the emancipation of the slaves. On 18th December, 1862, Lincoln proclaimed abolition of slavery in the United States; this would be a good day to issue such a proclamation in the Soudan. Wadji Barra's letter calls me Pasha of Kartoum, and says I have been deaf to all their entreaties. Stewart left this place three months ago! to-day. A man was wounded by the Arab fire at Bourré: they fired twelve rounds from these guns at the fort. I feel sure that the cause of the Mahdi's coming here is, that he got hold of Herbin's 'French Consul's' journal, written in a hostile critical spirit, and thinking it true, he advanced from Schatt. I expect Hansall, the Austrian Consul, also wrote in the style of Lamentations, for he also sent down a journal by the Abbas. It is remarkable that the very effort which I made to obtain the ear of Europe should have thus recoiled on us. I have for the present abandoned the attack on the Arabs at Goba, as Omdurman is more important, and as I expect the Arabs there have taken away their gun; it has not (up to 2 P.M.) fired to-day. I would like to ask the Mahdi—allowing pro formá that he is the Mahdi—what will be his ultimate work? Certainly his present work is not exhilarating, firing on his fellow-creatures night and day. The siege of Sevastopol lasted 326 days. We are at our 271st day. In their case they had always their communication open, and they dealt with an enemy who would recognise the rights of war; whereas we are not so placed. They, the Russians, were united, and had no civil population to deal with; yet I cannot say I think we are over great heroes (the fact is, that, if one analyses human glory, it is composed of nine-tenths twaddle, perhaps ninety-nine hundredths twaddle). We are only short of the duration of siege of Sevastopol 57 days, and we have had no respite, like the Russians had, during the winter of 1854–55; and neither Nicholas nor Alexander speculated on (well, we will not say what, but we will put it) "counting the months." Of course it will be looked on as very absurd to compare the two blockades, that of Sevastopol and Kartoum; but if properly weighted, one was just as good as the other. The Russians had money, we had none; they had skilled officers, we had none; they had no civil population, we had forty thousand; they had their route open and had news, we had neither.

December 10—A slave came in to-day, he had been with Slatin. He says Slatin is still in chains, that there are two insurrections in Kordofan, and rumour is rife that the Expeditionary force is near. Fort Omdurman is all right. The slave says the Arabs have not much ammunition. The Arabs fired thirty-one rounds at Bourré to-day, and wounded four men (one an officer, a Major Souleiman Effi, fatally). The Arabs have been firing stones to-day. Goba is quiet, they did not fire their gun to-day, or yesterday. I expect it has gone down to the riverbank. The slave who came in says the Mahdi's return to Kordofan is cut off by the insurrection in his rear; so we and he are like two rats in a box. (I wish he was out of the box!) I have ordered the two steamers to stay up at Bourré, towards which place the Arabs seem to be directing an unpleasant degree of attention. (Truly I am worn to a shadow with the food question; it is one continual demand.) Five men deserted to-day. The Arabs shape the stones they fire, like to the shells of their guns; they will soon spoil the rifling of their guns if they continue this.

December 11—The Arabs fired their gun from Goba three times; one shell fell into the water before the Palace—two passed over it. I put down more mines at Bourré. I have given the whole garrison an extra month's pay in addition to the three months they had before received—I will not hesitate to give them £100,000, if I think it will keep the town.

Three soldiers came in from the Arabs who report advance of the Expedition towards Berber. The Arabs fired fourteen rounds from their guns at Bourré. The officers say that there is a European directing the Arab guns there. (I wonder if it is that Frenchman who came from Dongola, and who, I thought, might have been Renan.) Sennaar is holding out and in great force (so say the three soldiers), so is Kassala. The Dem of the Mahdi is altered in appearance. They say he has sent off the families of his adherents into the interior.

3.30 P.M.—The Arabs fired three shells at the Palace from Goba; two went into the water, one passed over the Palace. This always irritates me, for it is so personal, and from one's own soldiers too! It is not very pleasant also to feel at any moment you may have a shell in your room, for the creatures fire at all hours. The steamers fired on the Arabs at Bourré this morning, and one of the Arab shells struck one steamer, and another struck a santal which we have there to defend the flank; but neither did any harm. Two soldiers deserted to the Arabs to-day—these men are generally those who have before been with the Arabs, and had deserted to us. The Arabs fired another shell at the Palace this evening, which burst in the air.

December 12—Small Church Parade. I sincerely hope this will be the last we shall have to witness. We have in hand 1,796,000 rounds Remingtons ammunition; 540 rounds Krupp; 6000 rounds mountain gun ammunition; £140 in specie; £18,000 in paper in treasury!! £60,000 in town in paper; 110,000 okes of biscuits; 700 ardebs of dhoora. This morning I was told a long story of report concerning the expeditionary force being at El Damer, near the Atbara river; of how Berber had surrendered, &c. On tracing it, I found it was a fib put in circulation by one of the chief Ulemas, to encourage the people.

3.30 P.M.—The Arabs fired two shells at the Palace; one burst in the air, the other fell in the water in a direct line with the window I was sitting at, distant about a hundred yards.

3.40 P.M.—They fired another shell, which fell only fifty yards short of the Palace; another burst in the air. I have sent the buglers up to stop this target practice. All these shells are in good line for the west wing, in which the Arabs know I stop. They fired seven shells in all in this affair; though the Arabs have fired over two thousand shells at us, I do not think we have lost by artillery fire more than three men.

December 13—The steamers went up and attacked the Arabs at Bourré (certainly this day-after-day delay has a most disheartening effect on every one. To-day is the 276th day of our anxiety). The Arabs appear, by all accounts, to have suffered to-day heavily at Bourré. We had none wounded by the Arabs; but one man, by the discharge of a bad cartridge, got a cut in neck: this was owing to the same cause as nearly blew out my eyes the other day. We are going to send down the Bordeen the day after to-morrow, and with her I shall send this journal. If some effort is not made before ten days' time the town will fall. It is inexplicable, this delay. If the Expeditionary Forces have reached the river and met my steamers, one hundred men are all that we require, just to show themselves.

I send this journal, for I have little hopes of saving it if the town falls. I put in the sort of arrangement I would make with Zubair Pasha for the future government of the Soudan. Ferratch Pasha is really showing an amount of vigour I did not give him credit for. Even if the town falls under the nose of the Expeditionary Force, it will not, in my opinion, justify the abandonment of Senaar and Kassala, or of the Equatorial Province, by Her Majesty's Government. All that is absolutely necessary is, for fifty of the Expeditionary Force to get on board a steamer and come up to Halfeyeh, and thus let their presence be felt; this is not asking much, but it must happen at once; or it will (as usual) be too late. A soldier deserted to the Arabs to-day from the North Fort. The buglers on the roof, being short of stature, are put on boxes to enable them to fire over the parapet; one with the recoil of rifle was knocked right over, and caused considerable excitement. We thought he was killed, by the noise he made in his fall. The Arabs fired their Krupps continually into town from the south front, but no one takes any notice of it. The Arabs at Goba only fired one shell at the Palace to-day, which burst in the air.

December 14—Arabs fired two shells at the Palace this morning; 546 ardebs dhoora! in store; also 83,525 okes of biscuit! 10.30 A.M. The steamers are down at Omdurman, engaging the Arabs, consequently I am on tenterhooks! 11.30 A.M. Steamers returned; the Bordeen was struck by a shell in her battery; we had only one man wounded. We are going to send down the Bordeen to-morrow with this journal. If I was in command of the two hundred men of the Expeditionary Force, which are all that are necessary for the movement, I should stop just below Halfeyeh, and attack the Arabs at that place before I came on here to Kartoum. I should then communicate with the North Fort, and act according to circumstances. Now mark this, if the Expeditionary Force, and I ask for no more than two hundred men, does not come in ten days, the town may fall; and I have done my best for the honour of our country. Good bye.

C. G. Gordon

Gordon, Major-General Charles George. *The Journals of Major-General C. G. Gordon, C. B., at Kartoum.* London, 1885, 378–395.

Rudyard Kipling: "The White Man's Burden" (1899)

Born in British India in 1865 and educated in the United Kingdom, Rudyard Kipling was, in effect, the unofficial poet laureate of the British Empire at its height in the late nineteenth and early twentieth centuries. Presenting British imperialism as an essen-

tially benevolent enterprise, Kipling wrote this—arguably his most famous poem—as a plea to Americans to take up the role of Anglo-Saxon governance of the non-European world. The poem was written shortly after the Spanish-American War, during a time of great debate about whether the United States should hold onto the Philippines as a colony.

Take up the White Man's burden—
Send forth the best ye breed—
Go bind your sons to exile
To serve your captives' need;
To wait in heavy harness,
On fluttered folk and wild—
Your new-caught, sullen peoples,
Half-devil and half-child.

Take up the White Man's burden—
In patience to abide,
To veil the threat of terror
And check the show of pride;
By open speech and simple,
An hundred times made plain
To seek another's profit,
And work another's gain.

Take up the White Man's burden—
The savage wars of peace—
Fill full the mouth of Famine
And bid the sickness cease;
And when your goal is nearest
The end for others sought,
Watch sloth and heathen Folly
Bring all your hopes to nought.

Take up the White Man's burden—
No tawdry rule of kings,
But toil of serf and sweeper—
The tale of common things.
The ports ye shall not enter,
The roads ye shall not tread,
Go mark them with your living,
And mark them with your dead.

Take up the White Man's burden—
And reap his old reward:
The blame of those ye better,
The hate of those ye guard—
The cry of hosts ye humour (Ah, slowly!) toward the
    light:—
"Why brought he us from bondage,
Our loved Egyptian night?"

Take up the White Man's burden—
Ye dare not stoop to less—
Nor call too loud on Freedom
To cloke your weariness;
By all ye cry or whisper,
By all ye leave or do,
The silent, sullen peoples
Shall weigh your gods and you.

Take up the White Man's burden—
Have done with childish days—
The lightly proferred laurel,
The easy, ungrudged praise.
Comes now, to search your manhood
Through all the thankless years
Cold, edged with dear-bought wisdom,
The judgment of your peers!

Source: Kipling, Rudyard. *The Works of Rudyard Kipling.* London: Edinburgh Society, 1909.

A Proclamation to the Orange Free State Burghers (1900)

As the descendents of the Dutch settlers in South Africa, the Boers, or Afrikaners, fled British rule in the Cape of Good Hope in the mid-nineteenth century, establishing an independent republic known as the Orange Free State in 1854. But the discovery of gold and diamonds in the nearby Transvaal precipitated British expansion into the interior of South Africa, resulting in an uprising of the Afrikaners known as the Boer War. Britain's victory resulted in a half-century of Boer exclusion from the government in South Africa. In this declaration, Orange Free State President M. T. Stein outlines the Boer grievances against the British imperialists. Little mention, however, is made of the African population, which the Boer settlers themselves had displaced.

Burghers of the Orange Free State: The time which we had so much desired to avoid, the moment when we as a nation are compelled with arms to oppose injustice and shameless violence, is at hand. Our sister Republic to the north of the Vaal River is about to be attacked by an unscrupulous enemy, who for many years has prepared himself, and sought pretexts for the violence of which he is now guilty, whose purpose it is to destroy the existence of the Afrikander race.

With our sister Republic we are not only bound by ties of blood, of sympathy and of common interest, but also by formal treaty, which has been necessitated by circumstances. This treaty demands of us that we assist her if she should be unjustly attacked, which we, unfortunately, for a long time have had too much reason to expect. We, therefore, cannot passively look on while injustice is done her, and while also our own dearly bought freedom is endangered, but are called as men to resist, trusting the Almighty, firmly believing that He will never permit injustice and unrighteousness to triumph.

Now that we thus resist a powerful enemy, with whom it has always been our honest desire to live in friendship, notwithstanding injustice and wrong done by him to us in the past, we solemnly declare, in the presence of the Almighty God, that we are compelled thereto by the injustice done to our kinsmen, and by the consciousness that the end of their independence will make our existence as an independent State of no significance, and that their fate, should they be obliged to bend under an overwhelming power, will also soon after be our own fate.

Solemn treaties have not protected our sister Republic against annexation; against conspiracy; against the claim of an abolished suzerainty; against the continuous oppression and interference, and now against a renewed attack, which aims only at her downfall.

Our own unfortunate experiences in the past have also made it sufficiently clear to us that we cannot rely on the most solemn promises and agreements of Great Britain, when she has at her helm a Government prepared to trample on treaties, to look for feigned pretexts for every violation of good faith by her committed. This is proved among other things by the unjust and unlawful British intervention, after we had overcome an armed and barbarous black tribe on our eastern frontier, as also by the forcible appropriation of the dominion over part of our territory where the discovery of diamonds had caused the desire for this appropriation, although contrary to existing treaties.

The desire and intention to trample on our rights as an independent and sovereign nation, notwithstanding a solemn convention existing between this State and Great Britain, have also been more than once, and are now again, shown by the present Government by giving expression in public documents to an unfounded claim of paramountcy over the whole of South Africa, and, therefore, also over this State.

With regard to the South Africa Republic, Great Britain has, moreover, refused until the present to allow her to regain her original position in respect to foreign affairs, a position which she had lost in no sense by her own faults. The original intention of conventions, to which the Republic has consented under pressure of circumstances, has been perverted and continually been used by the present British administration as a means for the practice of tyranny and of injustice, and, among other things, for the support of a revolutionary propaganda within the Republic in favor of Great Britain.

And while no redress has been offered, as justice demands, for injustice done to the South Africa Republic on the part of the British Government, and while no gratitude is exhibited for the magnanimity shown at the request of the British Government to British subjects who had forfeited under the laws of the Republic their lives and property, yet no feeling of shame has prevented the British Government, now that the gold mines of immense value have been discovered in the country, to make claims of the Republic, the consequence of which, if allowed, will be that those who, or whose forefathers have saved the country from barbarism and have won it for civilization with their blood and their tears, will lose their control over the interests of the country, to which they are justly entitled according to divine and human laws. The consequence of these claims would be, moreover, that the greater part of the power will be placed in the hands of those who, foreigners by birth, enjoy the privilege of depriving the country of its chief treasure, while they have never shown any loyalty to a foreign government.

Besides, the inevitable consequence of the acceptance of these claims would be that the independence of the country as a self-governing, independent sovereign republic would be irreparably lost. For years past British troops in great numbers have been placed on the frontiers of our sister republic in order to compel her by fear to accede to the demand which would be pressed upon her, and in order to encourage revolutionary disturbances and the cunning plans of those whose greed for gold is the cause of their shameless undertakings.

Those plans have now reached their climax in the open violence to which the present British Government now resorts. While we readily acknowledge the honorable character of thousands of Englishmen, who loathe such deeds of robbery and wrong, we cannot but abhor the shameless breaking of treaties, the feigned pretexts for the transgression of law, the violation of international law and of justice, and the numerous right-rending deeds of the British statesmen, who will now force a war upon the South African Republic. On their heads be the guilt of blood, and may a just Providence reward all as they deserve.

Burghers of the Orange Free State, rise as one man against the oppressor and the violator of right.

In the strife, to which we are now driven, have a care to commit no act unworthy of a Christian and of a Burgher of the Orange Free State. Let us look forward with confidence to a fortunate end of this conflict, trusting to that Higher Power, without whose help human weapons are of no avail.

May He bless our arms. Under His banner we advance to battle for liberty and for Fatherland.

M. T. STEIN, *State President.*

Source: Gordon, Ruth E., and Clive J. Talbot, eds. *From Dias to Vorster: Source Material on South African History.* Cape Town: Nasou, 1977.

An Act to Constitute the Commonwealth of Australia/ Constitution of the Commonwealth of Australia (July 9, 1900)

In its administration of empire and its attitudes toward colonial lands, the British government distinguished sharply between colonies dominated by native, non-European peoples and the so-called settler colonies where colonists from Europe or their descendants were sufficient in numbers and/or power to effectively rule over whatever indigenous population existed. Thus, settler colonies like Australia were set on the road to independence, or Commonwealth membership, far earlier than nonsettler colonies in Asia and Africa.

An Act to constitute the Commonwealth of Australia.

WHEREAS the people of New South Wales, Victoria, South Australia, Queensland, and Tasmania, humbly relying on the blessing of Almighty God, have agreed to unite in one indissoluble Federal Commonwealth under the Crown of the United Kingdom of Great Britain and Ireland, and under the Constitution hereby established:

And whereas it is expedient to provide for the admission into the Commonwealth of other Australasian Colonies and possessions of the Queen:

Be it therefore enacted by the Queen's most Excellent Majesty, by and with the advice and consent of the Lords Spiritual and Temporal, and Commons, in this present Parliament assembled, and by the authority of the same, as follows:—

1. This Act may be cited as the Commonwealth of Australia Constitution Act.

2. The provisions of this Act referring to the Queen shall extend to Her Majesty's heirs and successors in the sovereignty of the United Kingdom.

3. It shall be lawful for the Queen, with the advice of the Privy Council, to declare by proclamation that, on and after a day therein appointed, not being later than one year after the passing of this Act, the people of New South Wales, Victoria, South Australia, Queensland, and Tasmania, and also, if Her Majesty is satisfied that the people of Western Australia have agreed thereto, of Western Australia, shall be united in a Federal Commonwealth under the name of the Commonwealth of Australia. But the Queen may, at any time after the proclamation, appoint a Governor-General for the Commonwealth.

4. The Commonwealth shall be established, and the Constitution of the Commonwealth shall take effect, on and after the day so appointed. But the Parliaments of the several colonies may at any time after the passing of this Act make any such laws, to come into operation on the day so appointed, as they might have made if the Constitution had taken effect at the passing of this Act.

5. This Act, and all laws made by the Parliament of the Commonwealth under the Constitution, shall be binding on the courts, judges, and people of every State and of every part of the Commonwealth, notwithstanding anything in the laws of any State; and the laws of the Commonwealth shall be in force on all British ships, the

Queen's ships of war excepted, whose first port of clearance and whose port of destination are in the Commonwealth.

6. "The Commonwealth" shall mean the Commonwealth of Australia as established under this Act.

"The States" shall mean such of the colonies of New South Wales, New Zealand, Queensland, Tasmania, Victoria, Western Australia, and South Australia, including the northern territory of South Australia, as for the time being are parts of the Commonwealth, and such colonies or territories as may be admitted into or established by the Commonwealth as States; and each of such parts of the Commonwealth shall be called "a State."

"Original States" shall mean such States as are parts of the Commonwealth at its establishment.

7. The Federal Council of Australasia Act, 1885, is hereby repealed, but so as not to affect any laws passed by the Federal Council of Australasia and in force at the establishment of the Commonwealth.

Any such law may be repealed as to any State by the Parliament of the Commonwealth, or as to any colony not being a State by the Parliament thereof.

After the passing of this Act the Colonial Boundaries Act, 1895, shall not apply to any colony which becomes a State of the Commonwealth; but the Commonwealth shall be taken to be a self-governing colony for the purposes of that Act . . .

Source: Commonwealth of Australia. *Documenting a Democracy: Australia's Story,* 2000. www.foundingdocs.gov.au/places/cth/cth1.htm.

Mohandas K. Gandhi: Indian Home Rule (1909)

Even while living in South Africa, Mohandas K. Gandhi held strong views on the independence of his homeland India from British colonial rule. In this imaginary interview from 1909, Gandhi, as the "editor" addresses a hypothetical "reader" about the "extremists" demanding full independence for India. Gandhi makes it clear that he sides with the "extremists" and moreover sees their position as nonextremist, but quite rational and justified.

EDITOR:

I would say to the extremists: "I know that you want Home Rule (1) for India; it is not to be had

for your asking. Everyone will have to take it for himself. What others get for me is not Home Rule but foreign rule; therefore, it would not be proper for you to say that you have obtained Home Rule if you have merely expelled the English. I have already described the true nature of Home Rule. This you would never obtain by force of arms. Brute-force is not natural to Indian soil. You will have, therefore, to rely wholly on soul-force. You must not consider that violence is necessary at any stage for reaching our goal." I would say to the moderates: "Mere petitioning is derogatory; we thereby confess inferiority. To say that British rule is indispensable, is almost a denial of the Godhead. We cannot say that anybody or anything is indispensable except God. Moreover, common sense should tell us that to state that, for the time being, the presence of the English in India is a necessity, is to make them conceited.

"If the English vacated India, bag and baggage, it must not be supposed that she would be widowed. It is possible that those who are forced to observe peace under their pressure would fight after their withdrawal. There can be no advantage in suppressing an eruption; it must have its vent. If, therefore, before we can remain at peace, we must fight amongst ourselves, it is better that we do so. (2) There is no occasion for a third party to protect the weak. It is this so-called protection which has unnerved us. Such protection can only make the weak weaker. Unless we realize this, we cannot have Home Rule. I would paraphrase the thought of an English divine (3) and say that anarchy under Home Rule were better than orderly foreign rule. Only, the meaning that the learned divine attached to Home Rule is different from Indian Home Rule according to my conception. We have to learn, and to teach others, that we do not want the tyranny of either English rule or Indian rule."

If this idea were carried out, both the extremists and the moderates could join hands. There is no occasion to fear or distrust one another.

READER:

What then, would you say to the English?

EDITOR:

To them I would respectfully say: "I admit you are my rulers. It is not necessary to debate the question whether you hold India by the sword or by my consent. I have no objection to your remaining in my country, but although you are the rulers;

you will have to remain as servants of the people. It is not we who have to do as you wish, but it is you who have to do as we wish. You may keep the riches that you have drained away from this land, but you may not drain riches henceforth. Your function will be, if you so wish, to police India; you must abandon the idea of deriving any commercial benefit from us. We hold the civilization that you support to be the reverse of civilization. We consider our civilization to be far superior to yours. If you realize this truth, it will be to your advantage and, if you do not, according to your own proverb, (4) you should only live in our country in the same manner as we do. You must not do anything that is contrary to our religions. It is your duty as rulers that for the sake of the Hindus you should eschew beef, and for the sake of Mahomedans (5) you should avoid bacon and ham. We have hitherto said nothing because we have been cowed down, but you need not consider that you have not hurt our feelings by your conduct. We are not expressing our sentiments either through base selfishness or fear, but because it is our duty now to speak out boldly. We consider your schools and courts to be useless. We want our own ancient schools and courts to be restored. The common language of India is not English but Hindi. You should, therefore, learn it. We can hold communication with you only in our national language.

"We cannot tolerate the idea of your spending money on railways and the military. We see no occasion for either. You may fear Russia; we do not. When she comes we shall look after her. If you are with us, we may then receive her jointly. We do not need any European cloth. We shall manage with articles produced and manufactured at home. You may not keep one eye on Manchester (6) and the other on India. We can work together only if our interests are identical.

(1) Independence, self-government.

(2) Gandhi thus foresees the possibility of something like the divisive violence that occurred at Independence, even though it was to break his heart and take his life.

(3) Clergyman.

(4) "When in Rome, do as the Romans do."

(5) An old English term for "Muslim." Note that Gandhi is already trying to be sensitive to both religions. This was the issue that in the end defeated him.

(6) The center of the English cotton-weaving trade. One of Gandhi's most important campaigns was to persuade Indians to wear only traditional Indian homespun garments, boycotting English imports.

Source: Gandhi, Mohandas. *Indian Home Rule*. Phoenix, Natal, South Africa: International Printing Press, 1910.

McMahon-Hussein Correspondence (1915–1916)

In his hopes of gaining Arab support in the fight against the Ottoman Empire in the Middle East during World War I, British High Commissioner for Egypt Sir Henry McMahon corresponded with the Sharif Hussein of Mecca, the scion of the Hashemite dynasty. In this critical exchange of letters, McMahon promised Hussein that Britain would support independent Arab states after the war. Even as McMahon was making this promise, however, the British and the French were secretly negotiating, in the contemporary Sykes-Picot Treaty, to divide former Ottoman domains in the Middle East between them. This betrayal bedeviled relations between the European powers and the Arabs for decades.

Letter from Sharif Hussein, 14 July 1915

Whereas the whole of the Arab nation without any exception have decided in these last years to accomplish their freedom, and grasp the reins of their administration both in theory and practice; and whereas they have found and felt that it is in the interest of the Government of Great Britain to support them and aid them in the attainment of their firm and lawful intentions (which are based upon the maintenance of the honour and dignity of their life) without any ulterior motives whatsoever unconnected with this object;

And whereas it is to their (the Arabs') interest also to prefer the assistance of the Government of Great Britain in consideration of their geographic position and economic interests, and also of the attitude of the above-mentioned Government, which is known to both nations and therefore need not be emphasized;

For these reasons the Arab nation sees fit to limit themselves, as time is short, to asking the Government of Great Britain, if it should think fit, for the approval, through her deputy or representative, of the following fundamental propositions, leaving out all things considered secondary in comparison with these, so that it may prepare all means necessary for attaining this noble purpose, until such time as it finds occasion for making the actual negotiations:—

Firstly.- England will acknowledge the independence of the Arab countries, bounded on the north by Mersina and Adana up to the 37th degree of latitude, on which degree fall Birijik, Urfa, Mardin, Midiat, Jezirat (Ibn 'Umar), Amadia, up to the border of Persia; on the east by the borders of Persia up to the Gulf of Basra; on the south by the Indian Ocean, with the exception of the position of Aden to remain as it is; on the west by the Red Sea, the Mediterranean Sea up to Mersina. England to approve the proclamation of an Arab Khalifate of Islam.

Secondly.- The Arab Government of the Sherif will acknowledge that England shall have the preference in all economic enterprises in the Arab countries whenever conditions of enterprises are otherwise equal.

Thirdly.- For the security of this Arab independence and the certainty of such preference of economic enterprises, both high contracting parties will offer mutual assistance, to the best ability of their military and naval forces, to face any foreign Power which may attack either party. Peace not to be decided without agreement of both parties.

Fourthly.- If one of the parties enters into an aggressive conflict, the other party will assume a neutral attitude, and in case of such party wishing the other to join forces, both to meet and discuss the conditions.

Fifthly.- England will acknowledge the abolition of foreign privileges in the Arab countries, and will assist the Government of the Sherif in an International Convention for confirming such abolition.

Sixthly.- Articles 3 and 4 of this treaty will remain in vigour for fifteen years, and, if either wishes it to be renewed, one year's notice before lapse of treaty is to be given.

Consequently, and as the whole of the Arab nation have (praise be to God) agreed and united for the attainment, at all costs and finally, of this noble object, they beg the Government of Great Britain to answer them positively or negatively in a period of thirty days after receiving this intimation; and if this period should lapse before they receive an answer, they reserve to themselves complete freedom of action. Moreover, we (the Sherif's family) will consider ourselves free in work and deed from the bonds of our previous declaration which we made through Ali Effendi.

Letter from Sir Henry McMahon, 24 October 1915

I have received your letter of the 29th Shawal, 1333, with much pleasure and your expressions of friendliness and sincerity have given me the greatest satisfaction.

I regret that you should have received from my last letter the impression that I regarded the question of the limits and boundaries with coldness and hesitation; such was not the case, but it appeared to me that the time had not yet come when that question could be discussed in a conclusive manner.

I have realised, however, from your last letter that you regard this question as one of vital and urgent importance. I have, therefore, lost no time in informing the Government of Great Britain of the contents of your letter, and it is with great pleasure that I communicate to you on their behalf the following statement, which I am confident you will receive with satisfaction:—

The two districts of Mersina and Alexandretta and portions of Syria lying to the west of the districts of Damascus, Homs, Hama and Aleppo cannot be said to be purely Arab, and should be excluded from the limits demanded.

With the above modification, and without prejudice of our existing treaties with Arab chiefs, we accept those limits.

As for those regions lying within those frontiers wherein Great Britain is free to act without detriment to the interest of her ally, France, I am empowered in the name of the Government of Great Britain to give the following assurances and make the following reply to your letter:—

1. Subject to the above modifications, Great Britain is prepared to recognize and support the independence of the Arabs in all the regions within the limits demanded by the Sherif of Mecca.

2. Great Britain will guarantee the Holy Places against all external aggression and will recognise their inviolability.

3. When the situation admits, Great Britain will give to the Arabs her advice and will assist them to establish what may appear to be the most suitable forms of government in those various territories.

4. On the other hand, it is understood that the Arabs have decided to seek the advice and guidance of Great Britain only, and that such European advisers and officials as may be required for the formation of a sound form of administration will be British.

5. With regard to the vilayets of Bagdad and Basra, the Arabs will recognise that the established position and interests of Great Britain necessitate special administrative arrangements in order to secure these territories from foreign aggression, to promote the welfare of the local populations and to safeguard our mutual economic interests.

I am convinced that this declaration will assure you beyond all possible doubt of the sympathy of Great Britain towards the aspirations of her friends the Arabs and will result in a firm and lasting alliance, the immediate results of which will be the expulsion of the Turks from the Arab countries and the freeing of the Arab peoples from the Turkish yoke, which for so many years has pressed heavily upon them.

I have confined myself in this letter to the more vital and important questions, and if there are any other matters dealt with in your letter which I have omitted to mention, we may discuss them at some convenient date in the future.

It was with very great relief and satisfaction that I heard of the safe arrival of the Holy Carpet and the accompanying offerings which, thanks to the clearness of your directions and the excellence of your arrangements, were landed without trouble or mishap in spite of the dangers and difficulties occasioned by the present sad war. May God soon bring a lasting peace and freedom to all peoples!

I am sending this letter by the hand of your trusted and excellent messenger, Sheikh Mohammed Ibn Arif Ibn Uraifan, and he will inform you of the various matters of interest, but of less vital importance, which I have not mentioned in this letter.

Source: World Zionist Organization website: www.wzo.org.il/home/politic/d148a.htm.

Balfour Declaration (November 2, 1917)

Since the late nineteenth century, Jewish leaders in Europe, including Lord Rothschild, had been encouraging emigration to Palestine. During World War I, the British army took Palestine from the Ottoman Empire. While the majority Arab inhabitants of the region received British promises that the land would become an independent state after the war, British Foreign Secretary Arthur Balfour issued this declaration to Rothschild, promising a "national home" for the Jewish people. The declaration's promise, along with its dismissal of the Arab majority in Palestine as merely "non-Jewish communities," angered many Arabs, setting the stage for future conflicts between Arabs and the British and between Arabs and Jews.

Foreign Office
November 2nd, 1917
Dear Lord Rothschild,

I have much pleasure in conveying to you, on behalf of His Majesty's Government, the following declaration of sympathy with Jewish Zionist aspirations which has been submitted to, and approved by, the Cabinet.

"His Majesty's Government view with favour the establishment in Palestine of a national home for the Jewish people, and will use their best endeavours to facilitate the achievement of this object, it being clearly understood that nothing shall be done which may prejudice the civil and religious rights of existing non-Jewish communities in Palestine, or the rights and political status enjoyed by Jews in any other country."

I should be grateful if you would bring this declaration to the knowledge of the Zionist Federation.

Yours sincerely, Arthur James Balfour

Source: http://www.yale.edu/lawweb/avalon/mideast/ balfour.htm.

League of Nations: Palestine Mandate (1922)

For several centuries before World War I, Palestine had been a province of the Ottoman Empire. To enlist Arab support against the Ottomans in that war, Britain promised the former independence. At the same time, the British also made promises to the new Jewish immigrants in Palestine that they would be given a "national home" in Palestine. In the wake of World War I, however, Britain reneged on its promises to the Arabs, while hedging on the meaning of a "national home" for the Jews. Ultimately, the western-dominated League of Nations made the province a British mandate. In this document establishing the mandate, the League of Nations sets the rules by which Britain will try to reconcile the two increasingly hostile populations, a mandate that the British would wholly fail to fulfill.

Whereas the Principal Allied Powers have agreed, for the purpose of giving effect to the provisions of Article 22 of the Covenant of the League of Nations, to entrust to a Mandatory selected by the said Powers the administration of the territory of Palestine, which formerly belonged to the Turkish Empire, within such boundaries as may be fixed by them; and

Whereas the Principal Allied Powers have also agreed that the Mandatory should be responsible for putting into effect the declaration originally made on November 2nd, 1917, by the Government of His Britannic Majesty, and adopted by the said Powers, in favor of the establishment in Palestine of a national home for the Jewish people, it being clearly understood that nothing should be done which might prejudice the civil and religious rights of existing non-Jewish communities in Palestine, or the rights and political status enjoyed by Jews in any other country; and

Whereas recognition has thereby been given to the historical connection of the Jewish people with Palestine and to the grounds for reconstituting their national home in that country; and

Whereas the Principal Allied Powers have selected His Britannic Majesty as the Mandatory for Palestine; and

Whereas the mandate in respect of Palestine has been formulated in the following terms and submitted to the Council of the League for approval; and

Whereas His Britannic Majesty has accepted the mandate in respect of Palestine and undertaken to exercise it on behalf of the League of Nations in conformity with the following provisions; and

Whereas by the afore-mentioned Article 22 (paragraph 8), it is provided that the degree of authority, control or administration to be exercised by the Mandatory, not having been previously agreed upon by the Members of the League, shall be explicitly defined by the Council of the League of Nations; confirming the said Mandate, defines its terms as follows:

ARTICLE 1. The Mandatory shall have full powers of legislation and of administration, save as they may be limited by the terms of this mandate.

ART. 2. The Mandatory shall be responsible for placing the country under such political, administrative and economic conditions as will secure the establishment of the Jewish national home, as laid down in the preamble, and the development of self-governing institutions, and also for safeguarding the civil and religious rights of all the inhabitants of Palestine, irrespective of race and religion.

ART. 3. The Mandatory shall, so far as circumstances permit, encourage local autonomy.

ART. 4. An appropriate Jewish agency shall be recognised as a public body for the purpose of advising and co-operating with the Administration of Palestine in such economic, social and other matters as may affect the establishment of the Jewish national home and the interests of the Jewish population in Palestine, and, subject always to the control of the Administration to assist and take part in the development of the country.

The Zionist organization, so long as its organization and constitution are in the opinion of the Mandatory appropriate, shall be recognised as such agency. It shall take steps in consultation with His Britannic Majesty's Government to secure the co-operation of all Jews who are willing to assist in the establishment of the Jewish national home.

ART. 5. The Mandatory shall be responsible for seeing that no Palestine territory shall be ceded or leased to, or in any way placed under the control of the Government of any foreign Power.

ART. 6. The Administration of Palestine, while ensuring that the rights and position of other sections of the population are not prejudiced, shall facilitate Jewish immigration under suitable conditions and shall encourage, in co-operation with the Jewish agency referred to in Article 4, close settlement by Jews on the land, including State lands and waste lands not required for public purposes.

ART. 7. The Administration of Palestine shall be responsible for enacting a nationality law. There shall be included in this law provisions framed so as to facilitate the acquisition of Palestinian citizenship by Jews who take up their permanent residence in Palestine.

ART. 8. The privileges and immunities of foreigners, including the benefits of consular jurisdiction and protection as formerly enjoyed by Capitulation or usage in the Ottoman Empire, shall not be applicable in Palestine.

Unless the Powers whose nationals enjoyed the afore-mentioned privileges and immunities on August 1st, 1914, shall have previously renounced the right to their re-establishment, or shall have agreed to their non-application for a specified period, these privileges and immunities shall, at the expiration of the mandate, be immediately reestablished in their entirety or with such modifications as may have been agreed upon between the Powers concerned.

ART. 9. The Mandatory shall be responsible for seeing that the judicial system established in Palestine shall assure to foreigners, as well as to natives, a complete guarantee of their rights.

Respect for the personal status of the various peoples and communities and for their religious interests shall be fully guaranteed. In particular, the control and administration of Wakfs shall be exercised in accordance with religious law and the dispositions of the founders.

ART. 10. Pending the making of special extradition agreements relating to Palestine, the extradition treaties in force between the Mandatory and other foreign Powers shall apply to Palestine.

ART. 11. The Administration of Palestine shall take all necessary measures to safeguard the interests of the community in connection with the development of the country, and, subject to any international obligations accepted by the Mandatory, shall have full power to provide for public ownership or control of any of the natural resources of the country or of the public works, services and utilities established or to be established therein. It shall introduce a land system appropriate to the needs of the country, having regard, among other things, to the desirability of promoting the close settlement and intensive cultivation of the land.

The Administration may arrange with the Jewish agency mentioned in Article 4 to construct or operate, upon fair and equitable terms, any public works, services and utilities, and to develop any of the natural resources of the country, in so far as these matters are not directly undertaken by the Administration. Any such arrangements shall provide that no profits distributed by such agency, directly or indirectly, shall exceed a reasonable rate of interest on the capital, and any further profits shall be utilised by it for the benefit of the country in a manner approved by the Administration.

ART. 12. The Mandatory shall be entrusted with the control of the foreign relations of Palestine and the right to issue exequaturs to consuls appointed by foreign Powers. He shall also be entitled to afford diplomatic and consular protection to citizens of Palestine when outside its territorial limits.

ART. 13. All responsibility in connection with the Holy Places and religious buildings or sites in Palestine, including that of preserving existing rights and of securing free access to the Holy Places, religious buildings and sites and the free exercise of worship, while ensuring the requirements of public order and decorum, is assumed by the Mandatory, who shall be responsible solely to the League of Nations in all matters connected herewith, provided that nothing in this article shall prevent the Mandatory from entering into such arrangements as he may deem reasonable with the Administration for the purpose of carrying the provisions of this article into effect; and provided also that nothing in this mandate shall be construed as conferring upon the Mandatory authority to interfere with the fabric or the management of purely Moslem sacred shrines, the immunities of which are guaranteed.

ART. 14. A special commission shall be appointed by the Mandatory to study, define and determine the rights and claims in connection with the Holy Places and the rights and claims relating to the different religious communities in Palestine. The method of nomination, the composition and the functions of this Commission shall be submitted to the Council of the League for its approval, and the Commission shall not be appointed or enter upon its functions without the approval of the Council.

ART. 15. The Mandatory shall see that complete freedom of conscience and the free exercise of all forms of worship, subject only to the maintenance of public order and morals, are ensured to all. No discrimination of any kind shall be made between the inhabitants of Palestine on the ground of race, religion or language. No person shall be excluded from Palestine on the sole ground of his religious belief.

The right of each community to maintain its own schools for the education of its own members in its own language, while conforming to such educational requirements of a general nature as the Administration may impose, shall not be denied or impaired.

ART. 16. The Mandatory shall be responsible for exercising such supervision over religious or eleemosynary bodies of all faiths in Palestine as may be required for the maintenance of public order and good government. Subject to such supervision, no measures shall be taken in Palestine to obstruct or interfere with the enterprise of such bodies or to discriminate against any representative or member of them on the ground of his religion or nationality.

ART. 17. The Administration of Palestine may organise on a voluntary basis the forces necessary for the preservation of peace and order, and also for the defence of the country, subject, however, to the supervision of the Mandatory, but shall not use them for purposes other than those above specified save with the consent of the Mandatory. Except for such purposes, no military, naval or air forces shall be raised or maintained by the Administration of Palestine.

Nothing in this article shall preclude the Administration of Palestine from contributing to the cost of the maintenance of the forces of the Mandatory in Palestine.

The Mandatory shall be entitled at all times to use the roads, railways and ports of Palestine for the movement of armed forces and the carriage of fuel and supplies.

ART. 18. The Mandatory shall see that there is no discrimination in Palestine against the nationals of any State Member of the League of Nations (including companies incorporated under its laws) as compared with those of the Mandatory or of any foreign State in matters concerning taxation, commerce or navigation, the exercise of industries or professions, or in the treatment of merchant vessels or civil aircraft. Similarly, there shall be no discrimination in Palestine against goods originating in or destined for any of the said States, and there shall be freedom of transit under equitable conditions across the mandated area.

Subject as aforesaid and to the other provisions of this mandate, the Administration of Palestine may, on the advice of the Mandatory, impose such taxes and customs duties as it may consider necessary, and take such steps as it may think best to promote the development of the natural resources of the country and to safeguard the interests of the population. It may also, on the advice of the Mandatory, conclude a special customs agreement with any State the territory of which in 1914 was wholly included in Asiatic Turkey or Arabia.

ART. 19. The Mandatory shall adhere on behalf of the Administration of Palestine to any general international conventions already existing, or which may be concluded hereafter with the approval of the League of Nations, respecting the slave traffic, the traffic in arms and ammunition, or the traffic in drugs, or relating to commercial equality, freedom of transit and navigation, aerial navigation and postal, telegraphic and wireless communication or literary, artistic or industrial property.

ART. 20. The Mandatory shall co-operate on behalf of the Administration of Palestine, so far as religious, social and other conditions may permit, in the execution of any common policy adopted by the League of Nations for preventing and combating disease, including diseases of plants and animals.

ART. 21. The Mandatory shall secure the enactment within twelve months from this date, and shall ensure the execution of a Law of Antiquities based on the following rules. This law shall ensure equality of treatment in the matter of excavations and archaeological research to the nationals of all States Members of the League of Nations.

(1) "Antiquity" means any construction or any product of human activity earlier than the year 1700 A. D.

(2) The law for the protection of antiquities shall proceed by encouragement rather than by threat.

Any person who, having discovered an antiquity without being furnished with the authorization referred to in paragraph 5, reports the same to an official of the competent Department, shall be rewarded according to the value of the discovery.

(3) No antiquity may be disposed of except to the competent Department, unless this Department renounces the acquisition of any such antiquity.

No antiquity may leave the country without an export licence from the said Department.

(4) Any person who maliciously or negligently destroys or damages an antiquity shall be liable to a penalty to be fixed.

(5) No clearing of ground or digging with the object of finding antiquities shall be permitted, under penalty of fine, except to persons authorised by the competent Department.

(6) Equitable terms shall be fixed for expropriation, temporary or permanent, of lands which might be of historical or archaeological interest.

(7) Authorization to excavate shall only be granted to persons who show sufficient guarantees of archaeological experience. The Administration of Palestine shall not, in granting these authorizations, act in such a way as to exclude scholars of any nation without good grounds.

(8) The proceeds of excavations may be divided between the excavator and the competent Department in a proportion fixed by that Department. If division seems impossible for scientific reasons, the excavator shall receive a fair indemnity in lieu of a part of the find.

ART. 22. English, Arabic and Hebrew shall be the official languages of Palestine. Any statement or inscription in Arabic on stamps or money in Palestine shall be repeated in Hebrew and any statement or inscription in Hebrew shall be repeated in Arabic.

ART. 23. The Administration of Palestine shall recognise the holy days of the respective communities in Palestine as legal days of rest for the members of such communities.

ART. 24. The Mandatory shall make to the Council of the League of Nations an annual report to the satisfaction of the Council as to the measures taken during the year to carry out the provisions of the mandate. Copies of all laws and regulations promulgated or issued during the year shall be communicated with the report.

ART. 25. In the territories lying between the Jordan and the eastern boundary of Palestine as ultimately determined, the Mandatory shall be entitled, with the consent of the Council of the League of Nations, to postpone or withhold application of such provisions of this mandate as he may consider inapplicable to the existing local conditions, and to make such provision for the administration of the territories as he may consider suitable to those conditions, provided that no action shall be taken which is inconsistent with the provisions of Articles 15, 16 and 18.

ART. 26. The Mandatory agrees that, if any dispute whatever should arise between the Mandatory and another member of the League of Nations relating to the interpretation or the application of the provisions of the mandate, such dispute, if it cannot be settled by negotiation, shall be submitted to the Permanent Court of International Justice provided for by Article 14 of the Covenant of the League of Nations.

ART. 27. The consent of the Council of the League of Nations is required for any modification of the terms of this mandate.

ART. 28. In the event of the termination of the mandate hereby conferred upon the Mandatory, the Council of the League of Nations shall make such arrangements as may be deemed necessary for safeguarding in perpetuity, under guarantee of the League, the rights secured by Articles 13 and 14, and shall use its influence for securing, under the guarantee of the League, that the Government of Palestine will fully honour the financial obligations legitimately incurred by the Administration of Palestine during the period of the mandate, including the rights of public servants to pensions or gratuities.

The present instrument shall be deposited in original in the archives of the League of Nations and certified copies shall be forwarded by the Secretary-General of the League of Nations to all members of the League.

Done at London the twenty-fourth day of July, one thousand nine hundred and twenty-two.

Source: Israel Ministry of Foreign Affairs website: www.mfa.gov.il/mfa/go.asp?MFAH00pr0.

British White Paper on Palestine (June 1922)

Shortly before issuing this official government White Paper, the League of Nations had granted Britain a mandate over Palestine. Under the mandate system, the mandatory power was supposed to prepare the mandated territory for eventual independence. In Palestine, there were complications, however. In 1917, Britain had declared its intent— with the Balfour Declaration—to create a Jewish

"national home" in the territory, thereby antagoniz-
ing Arab inhabitants. To placate the latter, Britain
issued the following White Paper, dividing the man-
date into two territories: Palestine proper (later Is-
rael, the West Bank, and Gaza) and Trans-Jordan
(later the nation of Jordan), with Jews forbidden to
emigrate to the latter. This, however, did little to re-
solve the situation in Palestine, which continued to
be plagued by Jewish-Arab strife.

The Secretary of State for the Colonies has
given renewed consideration to the existing political situation in Palestine, with a very earnest
desire to arrive at a settlement of the outstanding questions which have given rise to uncertainty and unrest among certain sections of the
population. After consultation with the High
Commissioner for Palestine [Sir Herbert
Samuel] the following statement has been drawn
up. It summarizes the essential parts of the correspondence that has already taken place between the Secretary of State and a delegation
from the Moslem Christian Society of Palestine,
which has been for some time in England, and it
states the further conclusions which have since
been reached.

The tension which has prevailed from time to
time in Palestine is mainly due to apprehensions,
which are entertained both by sections of the Arab
and by sections of the Jewish population. These
apprehensions, so far as the Arabs are concerned
are partly based upon exaggerated interpretations
of the meaning of the *[Balfour] Declaration*
favouring the establishment of a Jewish National
Home in Palestine, made on behalf of His
Majesty's Government on 2nd November, 1917.

Unauthorized statements have been made to
the effect that the purpose in view is to create a
wholly Jewish Palestine. Phrases have been used
such as that Palestine is to become "as Jewish as
England is English." His Majesty's Government regard any such expectation as impracticable and
have no such aim in view. Nor have they at any
time contemplated, as appears to be feared by the
Arab delegation, the disappearance or the subordination of the Arabic population, language, or
culture in Palestine. They would draw attention to
the fact that the terms of the Declaration referred
to do not contemplate that Palestine as a whole
should be converted into a Jewish National Home,

but that such a Home should be founded "in Palestine." In this connection it has been observed with
satisfaction that at a meeting of the Zionist Congress, the supreme governing body of the Zionist
Organization, held at Carlsbad in September, 1921,
a resolution was passed expressing as the official
statement of Zionist aims "the determination of
the Jewish people to live with the Arab people on
terms of unity and mutual respect, and together
with them to make the common home into a flourishing community, the upbuilding of which may
assure to each of its peoples an undisturbed national development."

It is also necessary to point out that the Zionist
Commission in Palestine, now termed the Palestine Zionist Executive, has not desired to possess,
and does not possess, any share in the general administration of the country. Nor does the special
position assigned to the Zionist Organization in
Article IV of the Draft Mandate for Palestine imply
any such functions. That special position relates to
the measures to be taken in Palestine affecting the
Jewish population, and contemplates that the organization may assist in the general development
of the country, but does not entitle it to share in
any degree in its government.

Further, it is contemplated that the status of all
citizens of Palestine in the eyes of the law shall be
Palestinian, and it has never been intended that
they, or any section of them, should possess any
other juridical status. So far as the Jewish population of Palestine are concerned it appears that
some among them are apprehensive that His
Majesty's Government may depart from the policy
embodied in the *Declaration of 1917*. It is necessary, therefore, once more to affirm that these fears
are unfounded, and that that Declaration, re affirmed by the Conference of the Principle Allied
Powers at San Remo and again in the Treaty of
Sevres, is not susceptible of change.

During the last two or three generations the
Jews have recreated in Palestine a community, now
numbering 80,000, of whom about one fourth are
farmers or workers upon the land. This community has its own political organs; an elected assembly for the direction of its domestic concerns;
elected councils in the towns; and an organization
for the control of its schools. It has its elected Chief
Rabbinate and Rabbinical Council for the direction of its religious affairs. Its business is con-

ducted in Hebrew as a vernacular language, and a Hebrew Press serves its needs. It has its distinctive intellectual life and displays considerable economic activity. This community, then, with its town and country population, its political, religious, and social organizations, its own language, its own customs, its own life, has in fact "national" characteristics. When it is asked what is meant by the development of the Jewish National Home in Palestine, it may be answered that it is not the imposition of a Jewish nationality upon the inhabitants of Palestine as a whole, but the further development of the existing Jewish community, with the assistance of Jews in other parts of the world, in order that it may become a centre in which the Jewish people as a whole may take, on grounds of religion and race, an interest and a pride. But in order that this community should have the best prospect of free development and provide a full opportunity for the Jewish people to display its capacities, it is essential that it should know that it is in Palestine as of right and not on the sufferance. That is the reason why it is necessary that the existence of a Jewish National Home in Palestine should be internationally guaranteed, and that it should be formally recognized to rest upon ancient historic connection.

This, then, is the interpretation which His Majesty's Government place upon the *Declaration of 1917,* and, so understood, the Secretary of State is of opinion that it does not contain or imply anything which need cause either alarm to the Arab population of Palestine or disappointment to the Jews.

For the fulfillment of this policy it is necessary that the Jewish community in Palestine should be able to increase its numbers by immigration. This immigration cannot be so great in volume as to exceed whatever may be the economic capacity of the country at the time to absorb new arrivals. It is essential to ensure that the immigrants should not be a burden upon the people of Palestine as a whole, and that they should not deprive any section of the present population of their employment. Hitherto the immigration has fulfilled these conditions. The number of immigrants since the British occupation has been about 25,000.

It is necessary also to ensure that persons who are politically undesirable be excluded from Palestine, and every precaution has been and will be taken by the Administration to that end.

It is intended that a special committee should be established in Palestine, consisting entirely of members of the new Legislative Council elected by the people, to confer with the administration upon matters relating to the regulation of immigration. Should any difference of opinion arise between this committee and the Administration, the matter will be referred to His Majesty's Government, who will give it special consideration. In addition, under Article 81 of the draft Palestine Order in Council, any religious community or considerable section of the population of Palestine will have a general right to appeal, through the High Commissioner and the Secretary of State, to the League of Nations on any matter on which they may consider that the terms of the Mandate are not being fulfilled by the Government of Palestine.

With reference to the Constitution which it is now intended to establish in Palestine, the draft of which has already been published, it is desirable to make certain points clear. In the first place, it is not the case, as has been represented by the Arab Delegation, that during the war His Majesty's Government gave an undertaking that an independent national government should be at once established in Palestine. This representation mainly rests upon a letter dated the 24th October, 1915, from Sir Henry McMahon, then His Majesty's High Commissioner in Egypt, to the Sharif of Mecca, now King Hussein of the Kingdom of the Hejaz. That letter is quoted as conveying the promise to the Sherif of Mecca to recognise and support the independence of the Arabs within the territories proposed by him. But this promise was given subject to a reservation made in the same letter, which excluded from its scope, among other territories, the portions of Syria lying to the west of the District of Damascus. This reservation has always been regarded by His Majesty's Government as covering the vilayet of Beirut and the independent Sanjak of Jerusalem. The whole of Palestine west of the Jordan was thus excluded from Sir. Henry McMahon's pledge.

Nevertheless, it is the intention of His Majesty's government to foster the establishment of a full measure of self government in Palestine. But they are of the opinion that, in the special circumstances of that country, this should be accomplished by gradual stages and not suddenly. The first step was taken when, on the institution of a

Civil Administration, the nominated Advisory Council, which now exists, was established. It was stated at the time by the High Commissioner that this was the first step in the development of self governing institutions, and it is now proposed to take a second step by the establishment of a Legislative Council containing a large proportion of members elected on a wide franchise. It was proposed in the published draft that three of the members of this Council should be non official persons nominated by the High Commissioner, but representations having been made in opposition to this provision, based on cogent considerations, the Secretary of State is prepared to omit it. The legislative Council would then consist of the High Commissioner as President and twelve elected and ten official members. The Secretary of State is of the opinion that before a further measure of self government is extended to Palestine and the Assembly placed in control over the Executive, it would be wise to allow some time to elapse. During this period the institutions of the country will have become well established; its financial credit will be based on firm foundations, and the Palestinian officials will have been enabled to gain experience of sound methods of government. After a few years the situation will be again reviewed, and if the experience of the working of the constitution now to be established so warranted, a larger share of authority would then be extended to the elected representatives of the people.

The Secretary of State would point out that already the present administration has transferred to a Supreme Council elected by the Moslem community of Palestine the entire control of Moslem Religious endowments (Waqfs), and of the Moslem religious Courts. To this Council the Administration has also voluntarily restored considerable revenues derived from ancient endowments which have been sequestrated by the Turkish Government. The Education Department is also advised by a committee representative of all sections of the population, and the Department of Commerce and Industry has the benefit of the co-operation of the Chambers of Commerce which have been established in the principal centres. It is the intention of the Administration to associate in an increased degree similar representative committees with the various Departments of the Government.

The Secretary of State believes that a policy upon these lines, coupled with the maintenance of the fullest religious liberty in Palestine and with scrupulous regard for the rights of each community with reference to its Holy Places, cannot but commend itself to the various sections of the population, and that upon this basis may be built up that a spirit of cooperation upon which the future progress and prosperity of the Holy Land must largely depend.

Source: Winer, Joel H. *Great Britain: Foreign Policy and the Span of Empire, 1689–1971, A Documentary History,* vol. 4. New York: Chelsea House, 1972.

Statute of Westminster (1931)

The 1931 Statute of Westminster was a major milestone in Britain's long march from empire. Under the law, Britain recognized that the various dominions established in the late nineteenth and early twentieth centuries—most notably Canada, Australia, and South Africa—were autonomous and that the British Parliament had no right to pass laws for them. In effect, the statute was the founding document of the British Commonwealth and, while it affected only white-settler-dominated former colonies, it would be extended after World War II to most of Britain's former colonies in Africa, Asia, the Pacific, and the Caribbean.

Preamble. Whereas the delegates to His Majesty's Governments in the United Kingdom, the Dominion of Canada, the Commonwealth of Australia, the Dominion of New Zealand, the Union of South Africa, the Irish Free State and Newfoundland, at Imperial Conferences . . . at Westminster in the years of our Lord nineteen hundred and twenty-six and nineteen hundred and thirty did concur in making the declarations and resolutions set forth in the Reports of the said Conference: And whereas it is meet and proper to set out by way of preamble to this Act that, inasmuch as the Crown is the symbol to the free association of the members of the British Commonwealth of Nations, and as they are united by a common allegiance to the Crown, it would be in accord with the established constitutional position of all the members of the Commonwealth in relation to one another that any alteration in the law touching the Succession to the Throne or the Royal Style and Titles shall hereafter require the assent as well of the Parliaments of all the Dominions as of the Parliament of the United Kingdom: And whereas it is in accord with the established constitutional position that no law hereafter made by the Parliament of the United Kingdom shall extend to any of the said Dominions as part of the law of that Dominion otherwise than at the request and with the consent of that Dominion. And whereas it is necessary for the ratifying, confirming and establishing of certain of the said declarations and resolutions of the said Conferences that a law be made and enacted in due form by authority of the Parliament of the United Kingdom: And whereas the Dominion of Canada, the Commonwealth of Australia, the Dominion of New Zealand, the Union of South Africa, the Irish Free State and Newfoundland have severally requested and consented to the submission of a measure to the Parliament of the United Kingdom for making such provision with regard to the matters aforesaid as is hereafter in this Act contained: Now, therefore, be it enacted by the King's Most Excellent Majesty by and with the advice and consent of the Lords Spiritual and Temporal, and Commons, in this present Parliament assembled, and by the authority of the same, as follows:

Section 1 In this Act the expression "Dominion" means any of the following Dominions, that is to say, the Dominion of Canada, the Commonwealth of Australia, the Dominion of New Zealand, the Union of South Africa, the Irish Free State and Newfoundland.

Section 2 (1) The Colonial Laws Validity Act, 1865, shall not apply to any law made after the commencement of this Act by the Parliament of a Dominion. (2) No law and no provision of any law made after the commencement of this Act by the Parliament of a Dominion shall be void or inoperative on the ground that it is repugnant to the law of England, or to the provisions of any existing or future Act of Parliament of the United Kingdom, or to any order, rule, or regulation made under any such Act, and the powers of the Parliament of a Dominion shall include the power to repeal or amend any such Act, order, rule or regulation in so far as the same is part of the law of the Dominion.

Section 3 It is hereby declared and enacted that the Parliament of a Dominion has full power to make laws having extra-territorial operation.

Section 4 No Act of Parliament of the United Kingdom passed after the commencement of this Act shall extend or be deemed to extend, to a Dominion as part of the law of that Dominion, unless it is expressly declared in that Act that that Dominion has requested, and consented to, the enactment thereof.

Section 5 Without prejudice to the generality of the foregoing provisions of this Act, sections seven hundred and thirty-five and seven hundred and thirty-six of the Merchant Shipping Act, 1894, shall be construed as though reference therein to the Legislature of a British possession did not include reference to the Parliament of a Dominion.

Section 6 Without prejudice to a generality of the foregoing provisions of this Act, section four of the Colonial Courts of Admiralty Act, 1890 (which requires certain laws to be reserved for the signification of His Majesty's pleasure or to contain a suspending clause), and so much of section seven of that Act as requires the approval of His Majesty in Council to any rules of Court for regulating the practice and procedure of a Colonial Court of Admiralty, shall cease to have effect in any Dominion as from the commencement of this Act.

Section 7 (1) Nothing in this Act shall be deemed to apply to the repeal, amendment or alteration of the British North America Acts, 1867 to 1930, or any order, rule or regulation made thereunder. (2) The provisions of section two of this Act shall extend to laws made by any of the Provinces of Canada and to the powers of the legislatures of such Provinces. (3) The powers conferred by this Act upon the Parliament of Canada or upon the legislatures of the Provinces shall be restricted to the enactment of laws in the relation to matters within the competence of the Parliament of Canada or of any of the legislatures of the Provinces respectively.

Section 8 Nothing in this Act shall be deemed to confer any power to repeal or alter the Constitution or the Constitution Act of the Commonwealth of Australia or the Constitution Act of the Dominion of New Zealand otherwise than in accordance with the law existing before the commencement of this Act.

Section 9 (1) Nothing in this Act shall be deemed to authorize the Parliament of the Commonwealth of Australia to make laws on any matter within the authority of the States of Australia, not being a matter within the authority of the Parliament or Government of the Commonwealth of Australia. (2) Nothing in this Act shall be deemed to require the concurrence of the Parliament or Government of the Commonwealth of Australia, in any law made by the Parliament of the United Kingdom with respect to any matter within the authority of the States of Australia, not being a matter within the authority of the Parliament or Government of the Commonwealth of Australia, in any case where it would have been in accordance with the constitutional practice existing before the commencement of this Act that the Parliament of the United Kingdom should make that law without such concurrence. (3) In the application of this Act to the Commonwealth of Australia the request and consent referred to in section four shall mean the request and consent of the Parliament and Government of the Commonwealth.

Section 10 (1) None of the following sections of this Act, that is to say, sections two, three, four, five and six, shall extend to a Dominion to which this section applies as part of the law of that Dominion unless that section is adopted by the Parliament of the Dominion, and any Act of that Parliament adopting any section of this Act may provide that the adoption shall have effect either from the commencement of this Act or from such later date as is specified in the adopting Act. (2) The Parliament of any such Dominion as aforesaid may at any time revoke the adoption of any section referred to in subsection (1) of this section. (3) The Dominions to which this section applies are the Commonwealth of Australia, the Dominion of New Zealand and Newfoundland.

Section 11 Notwithstanding anything in the Interpretation Act, 1889, the expression "Colony" shall not, in any Act of the Parliament of the United Kingdom passed after the commencement of this Act, include a Dominion or any Province or State forming a part of a Dominion.

Section 12 This Act may be cited as the Statute of Westminster, 1931.

Source: 22 George V, Chapter 4; 11th December, 1931. Solon Law Archive website. http://www.solon.org/ Constitutions/Canada/English/StatuteofWestminster. html.

British White Paper for Palestine (1939)

Ever since it received a mandate over Palestine in 1922, Britain had faced the problem of reconciling two distinctly hostile populations in the territory: incoming Jews and native Arabs. Over the course of two decades, the British had tried to placate both parties but only succeeded in antagonizing them. In this official White Paper, issued in 1938 and following a major Arab uprising, the British decided to create a single Palestinian state, governed by Jews and Arabs, within ten years. But the mutual hostility of the two groups resulted in a separate Jewish state and Palestinian areas governed by Jordan and Egypt.

In the statement on Palestine, issued on 9 November, 1938, His Majesty's Government announced their intention to invite representatives of the Arabs of Palestine, of certain neighboring countries and of the Jewish Agency to confer with them in London regarding future policy. It was their sincere hope that, as a result of full, free and frank discussions, some understanding might be reached. Conferences recently took place with Arab and Jewish delegations, lasting for a period of several weeks, and served the purpose of a complete exchange of views between British Ministers and the Arab and Jewish representatives. In the light of the discussions as well as of the situation in Palestine and of the Reports of the Royal Commission and the Partition Commission, certain proposals were formulated by His Majesty's Government and were laid before the Arab and Jewish Delegations as the basis of an agreed settlement. Neither the Arab nor the Jewish delegation felt able to accept these proposals, and the conferences therefore did not result in an agreement. Accordingly His Majesty's Government are free to formulate their own policy, and after careful consideration they have decided to adhere generally to the proposals which were finally submitted to and discussed with the Arab and Jewish delegations.

The *Mandate for Palestine*, the terms of which were confirmed by the Council of the League of

Nations in 1922, has governed the policy of successive British Governments for nearly 20 years. It embodies the *Balfour Declaration* and imposes on the Mandatory four main obligations. These obligations are set out in *Article 2, 6* and *13* of the Mandate. There is no dispute regarding the interpretation of one of these obligations, that touching the protection of and access to the Holy Places and religious building or sites. The other three main obligations are generally as follows:

To place the country under such political, administrative and economic conditions as will secure the establishment in Palestine of a national home for the Jewish People. To facilitate Jewish immigration under suitable conditions, and to encourage, in cooperation with the Jewish Agency, close settlement by Jews on the Land.

To safeguard the civil and religious rights of all inhabitants of Palestine irrespective of race and religion, and, whilst facilitating Jewish immigration and settlement, to ensure that the rights and position of other sections of the population are not prejudiced.

To place the country under such political, administrative and economic conditions as will secure the development of self governing institutions.

The Royal Commission and previous commissions of Enquiry have drawn attention to the ambiguity of certain expressions in the Mandate, such as the expression "a national home for the Jewish people," and they have found in this ambiguity and the resulting uncertainty as to the objectives of policy a fundamental cause of unrest and hostility between Arabs and Jews. His Majesty's Government are convinced that in the interests of the peace and well being of the whole people of Palestine a clear definition of policy and objectives is essential. The proposal of partition recommended by the Royal Commission would have afforded such clarity, but the establishment of self supporting independent Arab and Jewish States within Palestine has been found to be impracticable. It has therefore been necessary for His Majesty's Government to devise an alternative policy which will, consistent with their obligations to Arabs and Jews, meet the needs of the situation in Palestine. Their views and proposals are set forth below under three heads, Section I, "The Constitution," Section II. Immigration and Section III. Land.

Section I. "The Constitution"

It has been urged that the expression "a national home for the Jewish people" offered a prospect that Palestine might in due course become a Jewish State or Commonwealth. His Majesty's Government do not wish to contest the view, which was expressed by the Royal Commission, that the Zionist leaders at the time of the issue of the Balfour Declaration recognised that an ultimate Jewish State was not precluded by the terms of the Declaration. But, with the Royal Commission, His Majesty's Government believe that the framers of the *Mandate* in which the *Balfour Declaration* was embodied could not have intended that Palestine should be converted into a Jewish State against the will of the Arab population of the country. That Palestine was not to be converted into a Jewish State might be held to be implied in the passage from the *Command Paper of 1922* which reads as follows

"Unauthorized statements have been made to the effect that the purpose in view is to create a wholly Jewish Palestine. Phrases have been used such as that 'Palestine is to become as Jewish as England is English.' His Majesty's Government regard any such expectation as impracticable and have no such aim in view. Nor have they at any time contemplated. . . . the disappearance or the subordination of the Arabic population, language or culture in Palestine. They would draw attention to the fact that the terms of the (Balfour) Declaration referred to do not contemplate that Palestine as a whole should be converted into a Jewish National Home, but that such a Home should be founded *in Palestine.*"

But this statement has not removed doubts, and His Majesty's Government therefore now declare unequivocally that it is not part of their policy that Palestine should become a Jewish State. They would indeed regard it as contrary to their obligations to the Arabs under the Mandate, as well as to the assurances which have been given to the Arab people in the past, that the Arab population of Palestine should be made the subjects of a Jewish State against their will.

The nature of the Jewish National Home in Palestine was further described in the *Command Paper of 1922* as follows

"During the last two or three generations the Jews have recreated in Palestine a community now numbering 80,000, of whom about one fourth are farmers or workers upon the land. This community has its own political organs; an elected assembly for the direction of its domestic concerns; elected councils in the towns; and an organisation for the control of its schools. It has its elected Chief Rabbinate and Rabbinical Council for the direction of its religious affairs. Its business is conducted in Hebrew as a vernacular language, and a Hebrew press serves its needs. It has its distinctive intellectual life and displays considerable economic activity. This community, then, with its town and country population, its political, religious and social organisations, its own language, its own customs, its own life, has in fact 'national' characteristics. When it is asked what is meant by the development of the Jewish National Home in Palestine, it may be answered that it is not the imposition of a Jewish nationality upon the inhabitants of Palestine as a whole, but the further development of the existing Jewish community, with the assistance of Jews in other parts of the world, in order that it may become a centre in which the Jewish people as a whole may take, on grounds of religion and race, an interest and pride. But in order that this community should have the best prospect of free development and provide a full opportunity for the Jewish people to display its capacities, it is essential that it should know that it is in Palestine as of right and not on sufferance. That is the reason why it is necessary that the existence of a Jewish National Home in Palestine should be internationally guaranteed, and that it should be formally recognised to rest upon ancient historic connection."

His Majesty's Government adhere to this interpretation of the *(Balfour) Declaration of 1917* and regard it as an authoritative and comprehensive description of the character of the Jewish National Home in Palestine. It envisaged the further development of the existing Jewish community with the assistance of Jews in other parts of the world. Evidence that His Majesty's Government have been carrying out their obligation in this respect is to be found in the facts that, since the statement of 1922 was published, more than 300,000 Jews have immigrated to Palestine, and that the population of the National Home has risen to some 450,000, or approaching a third of the entire population of the country. Nor has the Jewish community failed to

take full advantage of the opportunities given to it. The growth of the Jewish National Home and its achievements in many fields are a remarkable constructive effort which must command the admiration of the world and must be, in particular, a source of pride to the Jewish people.

In the recent discussions the Arab delegations have repeated the contention that Palestine was included within the area in which Sir Henry McMahon, on behalf of the British Government, in October, 1915, undertook to recognise and support Arab independence. The validity of this claim, based on the terms of the correspondence which passed between Sir Henry McMahon and the Sharif of Mecca, was thoroughly and carefully investigated by the British and Arab representatives during the recent conferences in London. Their report, which has been published, states that both the Arab and the British representatives endeavoured to understand the point of view of the other party but that they were unable to reach agreement upon an interpretation of the correspondence. There is no need to summarize here the arguments presented by each side. His Majesty's Government regret the misunderstandings which have arisen as regards some of the phrases used. For their part they can only adhere, for the reasons given by their representatives in the Report, to the view that the whole of Palestine west of Jordan was excluded from Sir Henry McMahon's pledge, and they therefore cannot agree that the McMahon correspondence forms a just basis for the claim that Palestine should be converted into an Arab State.

His Majesty's Government are charged as the Mandatory authority "to secure the development of self governing institutions" in Palestine. Apart from this specific obligation, they would regard it as contrary to the whole spirit of the Mandate system that the population of Palestine should remain forever under Mandatory tutelage. It is proper that the people of the country should as early as possible enjoy the rights of self-government which are exercised by the people of neighbouring countries. His Majesty's Government are unable at present to foresee the exact constitutional forms which government in Palestine will eventually take, but their objective is self government, and they desire to see established ultimately an independent Palestine State. It should be a State in which the two peoples in Palestine, Arabs and

Jews, share authority in government in such a way that the essential interests of each are shared.

The establishment of an independent State and the complete relinquishment of Mandatory control in Palestine would require such relations between the Arabs and the Jews as would make good government possible. Moreover, the growth of self governing institutions in Palestine, as in other countries, must be an evolutionary process. A transitional period will be required before independence is achieved, throughout which ultimate responsibility for the Government of the country will be retained by His Majesty's Government as the Mandatory authority, while the people of the country are taking an increasing share in the Government, and understanding and cooperation amongst them are growing. It will be the constant endeavour of His Majesty's Government to promote good relations between the Arabs and the Jews.

In the light of these considerations His Majesty's Government make the following declaration of their intentions regarding the future government of Palestine:

The objective of His Majesty's Government is the establishment within 10 years of an independent Palestine State in such treaty relations with the United Kingdom as will provide satisfactorily for the commercial and strategic requirements of both countries in the future. The proposal for the establishment of the independent State would involve consultation with the Council of the League of Nations with a view to the termination of the *Mandate.*

The independent State should be one in which Arabs and Jews share government in such a way as to ensure that the essential interests of each community are safeguarded.

The establishment of the independent State will be preceded by a transitional period throughout which His Majesty's Government will retain responsibility for the country. During the transitional period the people of Palestine will be given an increasing part in the government of their country. Both sections of the population will have an opportunity to participate in the machinery of government, and the process will be carried on whether or not they both avail themselves of it.

As soon as peace and order have been sufficiently restored in Palestine steps will be taken to carry out this policy of giving the people of Palestine an increasing part in the government of their country, the objective being to place Palestinians in charge of all the Departments of Government, with the assistance of British advisers and subject to the control of the High Commissioner. Arab and Jewish representatives will be invited to serve as heads of Departments approximately in proportion to their respective populations. The number of Palestinians in charge of Departments will be increased as circumstances permit until all heads of Departments are Palestinians, exercising the administrative and advisory functions which are presently performed by British officials. When that stage is reached consideration will be given to the question of converting the Executive Council into a Council of Ministers with a consequential change in the status and functions of the Palestinian heads of Departments.

His Majesty's Government make no proposals at this stage regarding the establishment of an elective legislature. Nevertheless they would regard this as an appropriate constitutional development, and, should public opinion in Palestine hereafter show itself in favour of such a development, they will be prepared, provided that local conditions permit, to establish the necessary machinery.

At the end of five years from the restoration of peace and order, an appropriate body representative of the people of Palestine and of His Majesty's Government will be set up to review the working of the constitutional arrangements during the transitional period and to consider and make recommendations regarding the constitution of the independent Palestine State.

His Majesty's Government will require to be satisfied that in the treaty contemplated by sub-paragraph (6) adequate provision has been made for:

the security of, and freedom of access to the Holy Places, and protection of the interests and property of the various religious bodies.

the protection of the different communities in Palestine in accordance with the obligations of His Majesty's Government to both Arabs and Jews and for the special position in Palestine of the Jewish National Home.

such requirements to meet the strategic situation as may be regarded as necessary by

His Majesty's Government in the light of the circumstances then existing. His Majesty's Government will also require to be satisfied that the interests of certain foreign countries in Palestine, for the preservation of which they are at present responsible, are adequately safeguarded.

His Majesty's Government will do everything in their power to create conditions which will enable the independent Palestine State to come into being within 10 years. If, at the end of 10 years, it appears to His Majesty's Government that, contrary to their hope, circumstances require the postponement of the establishment of the independent State, they will consult with representatives of the people of Palestine, the Council of the League of Nations and the neighbouring Arab States before deciding on such a postponement. If His Majesty's Government come to the conclusion that postponement is unavoidable, they will invite the co-operation of these parties in framing plans for the future with a view to achieving the desired objective at the earliest possible date.

During the transitional period steps will be taken to increase the powers and responsibilities of municipal corporations and local councils.

Section II. Immigration

Under *Article 6 of the Mandate,* the Administration of Palestine, "while ensuring that the rights and position of other sections of the population are not prejudiced," is required to "facilitate Jewish immigration under suitable conditions." Beyond this, the extent to which Jewish immigration into Palestine is to be permitted is nowhere defined in the Mandate. But in the *Command Paper of 1922* it was laid down that for the fulfilment of the policy of establishing a Jewish National Home:

"It is necessary that the Jewish community in Palestine should be able to increase its numbers by immigration. This immigration cannot be so great in volume as to exceed whatever may be the economic capacity of the country at the time to absorb new arrivals. It is essential to ensure that the immigrants should not be a burden upon the people of Palestine as a whole, and that they should not deprive any section of the present population of their employment."

In practice, from that date onwards until recent times, the economic absorptive capacity of the country has been treated as the sole limiting factor, and in the letter which Mr. Ramsay MacDonald, as Prime Minister, sent to Dr. Weizmann in February 1931 it was laid down as a matter of policy that economic absorptive capacity was the sole criterion. This interpretation has been supported by resolutions of the Permanent Mandates Commissioner. But His Majesty's Government do not read either the Statement of Policy of 1922 or the letter of 1931 as implying that the *Mandate* requires them, for all time and in all circumstances, to facilitate the immigration of Jews into Palestine subject only to consideration of the country's economic absorptive capacity. Nor do they find anything in the Mandate or in subsequent Statements of Policy to support the view that the establishment of a Jewish National Home in Palestine cannot be effected unless immigration is allowed to continue indefinitely. If immigration has an adverse effect on the economic position in the country, it should clearly be restricted; and equally, if it has a seriously damaging effect on the political position in the country, that is a factor that should not be ignored. Although it is not difficult to contend that the large number of Jewish immigrants who have been admitted so far have been absorbed economically, the fear of the Arabs that this influx will continue indefinitely until the Jewish population is in a position to dominate them has produced consequences which are extremely grave for Jews and Arabs alike and for the peace and prosperity of Palestine. The lamentable disturbances of the past three years are only the latest and most sustained manifestation of this intense Arab apprehension. The methods employed by Arab terrorists against fellow Arabs and Jews alike must receive unqualified condemnation. But it cannot be denied that fear of indefinite Jewish immigration is widespread amongst the Arab population and that this fear has made possible disturbances which have given a serious setback to economic progress, depleted the Palestine exchequer, rendered life and property insecure, and produced a bitterness between the Arab and Jewish populations which is deplorable between citizens of the same country. If in these circumstances immigration is continued up to the economic absorptive capacity of the country, regardless of all other considerations, a fatal enmity between the two peoples will be perpetuated, and the situation in Palestine may become a permanent source of friction amongst all peoples in the Near and Middle East. His Majesty's Government cannot take the view that either their obligations under the Mandate, or considerations of common sense and justice, require that they should ignore these circumstances in framing immigration policy.

In the view of the Royal Commission the association of the policy of the Balfour Declaration with the Mandate system implied the belief that Arab hostility to the former would sooner or later be overcome. It has been the hope of British Governments ever since the *Balfour Declaration* was issued that in time the Arab population, recognizing the advantages to be derived from Jewish settlement and development in Palestine, would become reconciled to the further growth of the Jewish National Home. This hope has not been fulfilled. The alternatives before His Majesty's Government are either (i) to seek to expand the Jewish National Home indefinitely by immigration, against the strongly expressed will of the Arab people of the country; or (ii) to permit further expansion of the Jewish National Home by immigration only if the Arabs are prepared to acquiesce in it. The former policy means rule by force. Apart from other considerations, such a policy seems to His Majesty's Government to be contrary to the whole spirit of *Article 22 of the Covenant of the League of Nations,* as well as to their specific obligations to the Arabs in the Palestine Mandate. Moreover, the relations between the Arabs and the Jews in Palestine must be based sooner or later on mutual tolerance and goodwill; the peace, security and progress of the Jewish National Home itself requires this. Therefore His Majesty's Government, after earnest consideration, and taking into account the extent to which the growth of the Jewish National Home has been facilitated over the last twenty years, have decided that the time has come to adopt in principle the second of the alternatives referred to above.

It has been urged that all further Jewish immigration into Palestine should be stopped forthwith. His Majesty's Government cannot accept such a proposal. It would damage the whole of the financial and economic system of Palestine and thus effect adversely the interests of Arabs and Jews alike. Moreover, in the view of His Majesty's Government, abruptly to stop further immigration would be unjust to the Jewish National Home. But,

above all, His Majesty's Government are conscious of the present unhappy plight of large numbers of Jews who seek refuge from certain European countries, and they believe that Palestine can and should make a further contribution to the solution of this pressing world problem. In all these circumstances, they believe that they will be acting consistently with their Mandatory obligations to both Arabs and Jews, and in the manner best calculated to serve the interests of the whole people of Palestine, by adopting the following proposals regarding immigration:

Jewish immigration during the next five years will be at a rate which, if economic absorptive capacity permits, will bring the Jewish population up to approximately one third of the total population of the country. Taking into account the expected natural increase of the Arab and Jewish populations, and the number of illegal Jewish immigrants now in the country, this would allow of the admission, as from the beginning of April this year, of some 75,000 immigrants over the next five years. These immigrants would, subject to the criterion of economic absorptive capacity, be admitted as follows:

For each of the next five years a quota of 10,000 Jewish immigrants will be allowed on the understanding that a shortage one year may be added to the quotas for subsequent years, within the five year period, if economic absorptive capacity permits.

In addition, as a contribution towards the solution of the Jewish refugee problem, 25,000 refugees will be admitted as soon as the High Commissioner is satisfied that adequate provision for their maintenance is ensured, special consideration being given to refugee children and dependents.

The existing machinery for ascertaining economic absorptive capacity will be retained, and the High Commissioner will have the ultimate responsibility for deciding the limits of economic capacity. Before each periodic decision is taken, Jewish and Arab representatives will be consulted.

After the period of five years, no further Jewish immigration will be permitted unless the Arabs of Palestine are prepared to acquiesce in it.

His Majesty's Government are determined to check illegal immigration, and further preventive measures are being adopted. The numbers of any Jewish illegal immigrants who, despite these measures, may succeed in coming into the country and cannot be deported will be deducted from the yearly quotas.

His Majesty's Government are satisfied that, when the immigration over five years which is now contemplated has taken place, they will not be justified in facilitating, nor will they be under any obligation to facilitate, the further development of the Jewish National Home by immigration regardless of the wishes of the Arab population.

Section III. Land

The Administration of Palestine is required, under *Article 6 of the Mandate,* "while ensuring that the rights and position of other sections of the population are not prejudiced," to encourage "close settlement by Jews on the land," and no restriction has been imposed hitherto on the transfer of land from Arabs to Jews. The Reports of several expert Commissions have indicated that, owing to the natural growth of the Arab population and the steady sale in recent years of Arab land to Jews, there is now in certain areas no room for further transfers of Arab land, whilst in some other areas such transfers of land must be restricted if Arab cultivators are to maintain their existing standard of life and a considerable landless Arab population is not soon to be created. In these circumstances, the High Commissioner will be given general powers to prohibit and regulate transfers of land. These powers will date from the publication of this statement of policy and the High Commissioner will retain them throughout the transitional period.

The policy of the Government will be directed towards the development of the land and the improvement, where possible, of methods of cultivation. In the light of such development it will be open to the High Commissioner, should he be satisfied that the "rights and position" of the Arab population will be duly preserved, to review and modify any orders passed relating to the prohibition or restriction of the transfer of land.

In framing these proposals His Majesty's Government have sincerely endeavoured to act in strict accordance with their obligations under the Mandate to both the Arabs and the Jews. The vagueness of the phrases employed in some instances to describe these obligations has led to controversy and has made the task of interpretation difficult. His Majesty's Government cannot hope to satisfy the partisans of one party or the other in such controversy as the Mandate has aroused. Their purpose is to be just as between the two people in Palestine whose destinies in that country have been affected by the great events of recent years, and who, since they live side by side, must learn to practice mutual tolerance, goodwill and co-operation. In looking to the future, His Majesty's Government are not blind to the fact that some events of the past make the task of creating these relations difficult; but they are encouraged by the knowledge that as many times and in many places in Palestine during recent years the Arab and Jewish inhabitants have lived in friendship together. Each community has much to contribute to the welfare of their common land, and each must earnestly desire peace in which to assist in increasing the well being of the whole people of the country. The responsibility which falls on them, no less than upon His Majesty's Government, to co-operate together to ensure peace is all the more solemn because their country is revered by many millions of Moslems, Jews and Christians throughout the world who pray for peace in Palestine and for the happiness of her people.

Source: The Jerusalem Fund for Education and Community Development website. www.palestine-center.org/cpap/documents/british.html.

British Government Statement: Policy in India (1946)

Britain's decision to grant its colony in India independence shortly after World War II was complicated by many factors, most notably the insistence by the Muslim minority that they be given a separate nation of their own, the future Pakistan. The resulting partition of India into Hindu-majority and Muslim-majority states led to one of the bloodiest episodes in post–World War II history, as hundreds of thousands of people were slain and millions forced to flee their homes. Historians differ significantly on the responsibility of the British for this carnage. The following is an official statement by the British government announcing its hope that India, once independent, will elect to stay within the newly formed British Commonwealth. As it turns out, India, although becoming a republic and eschewing the queen as official head of state, chose to remain inside the Commonwealth.

1. On the 15th March last, just before the dispatch of the Cabinet Mission to India, Mr. Attlee, the British Prime Minister, used these words:

My colleagues are going to India with the intention of using their utmost endeavours to help her to attain her freedom as speedily and fully as possible. What form of Government is to replace the present regime is for India to decide; but our desire is to help her to set up forthwith the machinery for making that decision . . .

I hope that the Indian people may elect to remain within the British Commonwealth. I am certain that she will find great advantages in doing so . . .

But if she does so elect, it must be by her own free will. The British Commonwealth and Empire is not bound together by chains of external compulsion. It is a free association of free peoples. If, on the other hand, she elects for independence, in our view she has a right to do so. It will be for us to help to make the transition as smooth and easy as possible.

2. Charged in these historic words, we—the Cabinet Ministers and the Viceroy—have done our utmost to assist the two main political parties to reach agreement upon the fundamental issue of the unity or division of India. After prolonged discussions in New Delhi we succeeded in bringing the Congress and the Muslim League together in conference at Simla. There was a full exchange of views and both parties were prepared to make considerable concessions in order to try to reach a settlement, but it ultimately proved impossible to close the remainder of the gap between the parties and so no agreement could be concluded. Since no agreement has been reached, we feel that it is our duty to put forward what we consider are the best arrangements possible to ensure a speedy setting up of the new constitution. This statement is made with the full approval of His Majesty's Government in the United Kingdom.

3. We have accordingly decided that immediate arrangements should be made whereby Indians may decide the future constitution of India, and an interim Government may be set up at once to carry on the administration of British India until such time as a new constitution can be brought into being. We have endeavoured to be just to the smaller as well as to the larger sections of the people; and to recommend a solution which will lead to a practicable way of governing the India of the future, and will give a sound basis for defence and a good opportunity for progress in the social, political and economic field.

4. It is not intended in this statement to review the voluminous evidence which has been submitted to the Mission; but it is right that we should state that it has shown an almost universal desire, outside the supporters of the Muslim League, for the unity of India.

5. This consideration did not, however, deter us from examining closely and impartially the possibility of a partition of India; since we were greatly impressed by the very, genuine and acute anxiety of the Muslims lest they should find themselves subjected to a perpetual Hindu-majority rule. This feeling has become so strong and widespread amongst the Muslims that it cannot be allayed by mere paper safeguards. If there is to be internal peace in India it must be secured by measures which will assure to the Muslims a control in all matters vital to their culture, religion, and economic or other interests.

6. We therefore examined in the first instance the question of a separate and fully independent sovereign state of Pakistan as claimed by the Muslim League. Such a Pakistan would comprise two areas: one in the North-West consisting of the provinces of the Punjab, Sind, North-West Frontier, and British Baluchistan; the other in the North-East consisting of the provinces of Bengal and Assam. The League were prepared to consider adjustment of boundaries at a later stage, but insisted that the principle of Pakistan should first be acknowledged. The argument for a separate state of Pakistan was based, first, upon the right of the Muslim majority to decide their method of government according to their wishes, and, secondly, upon the necessity to include substantial areas in which Muslims are in a minority in order to make Pakistan administratively and economically workable.

The setting up of a separate sovereign state of Pakistan on the lines claimed by the Muslim League would not solve the communal minority problem; nor can we see any justification for including within a sovereign Pakistan those districts of the Punjab and of Bengal and Assam in which the population is predominantly non-Muslim. Every argument that can be used in favour of

Pakistan can equally, in our view, be used in favour of the exclusion of the non-Muslim areas from Pakistan. This point would particularly affect the position of the Sikhs.

7. We, therefore, considered whether a smaller sovereign Pakistan confined to the Muslim majority areas alone might be a possible basis of compromise. Such a Pakistan is regarded by the Muslim League as quite impracticable because it would entail the exclusion from Pakistan of (a) the whole of the Ambala and Jullundur divisions in the Punjab; (b) the whole of Assam except the district of Sylhet; and (c) a large part of Western Bengal, including Calcutta, in which city the percentage of the Muslim population is 23.6 per cent. We ourselves are also convinced that any solution which involves a radical partition of the Punjab and Bengal, as this would do, would be contrary to the wishes and interests of a very large proportion of the inhabitants of these provinces. Bengal and the Punjab each has its own common language and a long history and tradition. Moreover, any division of the Punjab would of necessity divide the Sikhs, leaving substantial bodies of Sikhs on both sides of the boundary. We have therefore been forced to the conclusion that neither a larger nor a smaller sovereign state of Pakistan would provide all acceptable solution for the communal problem.

8. Apart from the great force of the foregoing arguments there are weighty administrative, economic and military, considerations . . .

10. Finally, there is the geographical fact that the two halves of the proposed Pakistan state are separated by some seven hundred miles and the communications between them both in war and peace would be dependent on the goodwill of Hindustan.

11. We are therefore unable to advise the British Government that the power which at present resides in British hands should be handed over to two entirely separate sovereign states.

12. This decision does not, however, blind us to the very real Muslim apprehensions that their culture and political and social life might become submerged in a purely unitary India, in which the Hindus with their greatly superior numbers must be a dominating element. To meet this the Congress have put forward a scheme under which provinces would have full autonomy subject only to a minimum of central subjects, such as foreign affairs, defence and communications.

Under this scheme provinces, if they wished to take part in economic and administrative planning on a large scale, could cede to the centre optional subjects in addition to the compulsory ones mentioned above.

13. Such a scheme would, in our view, present considerable constitutional disadvantages and anomalies. It would be very difficult to work a central executive and legislature in which some ministers, who dealt with compulsory subjects, were responsible to the whole of India while other ministers, who dealt with optional subjects, would be responsible only to those provinces who had elected to act together in respect of such subjects. This difficulty would be accentuated in the central legislature, where it would be necessary to exclude certain members from speaking and voting when subjects with which their provinces were not concerned were under discussion. Apart from the difficulty of working such a scheme, we do not consider that it would be fair to deny to other provinces, which did not desire to take the optional subjects at the centre, the right to form themselves into a group for a similar purpose. This would indeed be no more than the exercise of their autonomous powers in a particular way . . .

14. Before putting forward our recommendations we turn to deal with the relationship of the Indian States to British India. It is quite clear that with the attainment of independence by British India, whether inside or outside the British Commonwealth, the relationship which has hitherto existed between the Rulers of the States and the British Crown will no longer be possible. Paramountcy can neither be retained by the British Crown nor transferred to the new government. This fact has been fully recognised by those whom we interviewed from the States. They have at the same time assured us that the States are ready and willing to co-operate in the new development of India. The precise form which their co-operation will take must be a matter for negotiation during the building up of the new constitutional structure and it by no means follows that it will be identical for all the States . . .

15. We now indicate the nature of a solution which in our view would be just to the essential claims of all parties and would at the same time be

most likely to bring about a stable and practicable form of constitution for All-India.

We recommend that the constitution should take the following basic form:

(1) There should be a Union of India, embracing both British India and the States, which should deal with the following subjects: foreign affairs, defence, and communications; and should have the powers necessary to raise the finances required for the above subjects.

(2) The Union should have an executive and a legislature constituted from British Indian and States representatives. Any question raising a major communal issue in the legislature should require for its decision a majority of the representatives present and voting of each of the two major communities as well as a majority of all the members present and voting.

(3) All subjects other than the Union subjects and all residuary powers should vest in the provinces.

(4) The States will retain all subjects and powers other than those ceded to the Union.

(5) Provinces should be free to form groups with executives and legislatures, and each group could determine the provincial subjects to be taken in common.

(6) The constitutions of the Union and of the groups should contain a provision whereby any province could by a majority vote of its legislative assembly call for a reconsideration of the terms of the constitution after an initial period of ten years and at ten-yearly intervals thereafter....

23. While the constitution-making proceeds the administration of India has to be carried on. We attach the greatest importance therefore to the setting up at once of an interim Government having the support of the major political parties. It is essential during the interim period that there should be the maximum of co-operation in carrying through the difficult tasks that face the Government of India. Besides the heavy tasks of day-to-day administration, there is the grave danger of famine to be countered, there are decisions to be taken in many matters of post-war development which will have a far-reaching effect on India's future and there are important international conferences in which India has to be represented. For all these purposes a government having popular support is necessary. The Viceroy has already started

discussions to this end and hopes soon to form an interim government in which all the portfolios, including that of War Member, will be held by Indian leaders having the full confidence of the people. The British Government, recognising the significance of the changes, will give the fullest measure of co-operation to the Government so formed in the accomplishment of its tasks of administration and in bringing about as rapid and smooth a transition as possible ...

We hope that the new independent India may choose to be a member of the British Commonwealth. We hope, in any event, that you will remain in close and friendly association with our people. But these are matters for your own free choice. Whatever that choice may be, we look forward with you to your ever-increasing prosperity among the greatest nations of the world and to a future even more glorious than your past.

Source: India: *Statement by the Cabinet Mission and His Excellency the Viceroy,* Cmd 6821. London: HMSO, 1946.

Treaty between the Government of the United Kingdom and the Provisional Government of Burma/Burma Independence Act (1947)

As in many countries in Southeast Asia, the World War II occupation by Japanese forces broke the back of European colonial rule in Burma (now Myanmar). The anti-Japanese struggle of the Anti-Fascist People's Freedom League metamorphosed into an anti-British campaign after the war, one that included communist elements. Recognizing their own stretched resources and fearful of a communist takeover, the British agreed to Burmese independence in 1947, drawing up a treaty for independence that guaranteed British defense rights in the new country as well as protection of British and foreign property holdings. The treaty and independence act are followed by correspondence between British and Burmese officials.

Treaty between the Government of the United Kingdom and the Provisional Government of Burma
London, 17th October, 1947

The Government of the United Kingdom of Great Britain and Northern Ireland, and the Provisional Government of Burma;

Considering that it is the intention of the Government of the United Kingdom of Great Britain and Northern Ireland to invite Parliament to pass legislation at an early date providing that Burma shall become an independent State; Desiring to define their future relations as the Governments of independent States on the terms of complete freedom, equality and independence and to consolidate and perpetuate the cordial friendship and good understanding which subsist between them; and Desiring also to provide for certain matters arising from the forthcoming change in the relations between them, Have decided to conclude a treaty for this purpose and have appointed as their plenipotentiaries:- The Government of the United Kingdom of Great Britain and Northern Ireland: The Right Hon. Clement Richard Attlee, C.H., M.P., Prime Minister and First Lord of the Treasury. The Provisional Government of Burma: The Hon'ble Thakin Nu, Prime Minister Who have agreed as follows:—

Article 1

The Government of the United Kingdom recognize the Republic of the Union of Burma as a fully Independent Sovereign State. The contracting Governments agree to the exchange of diplomatic representatives duly accredited.

Article 2

All obligations and responsibilities heretofore devolving on the Government of the United Kingdom which arise from any valid international instrument shall henceforth, in so far as such instrument may be held to have application to Burma, devolve upon the Provisional Government of Burma. The rights and benefits heretofore enjoyed by the Government of the United Kingdom in virtue of the application of any such international instrument to Burma shall henceforth be enjoyed by the Provisional Government of Burma.

Article 3

Any person who at the date of the coming into force of the present Treaty is, by virtue of the Constitution of the Union of Burma, a citizen thereof and who is, or by virtue of a subsequent election is deemed to be, also a British subject, may make a declaration of alienage in the manner prescribed by the law of the Union, and thereupon shall cease to be a citizen of the Union. The Provisional Government of Burma undertake to introduce in the Parliament of the Union as early as possible, and in any case within a period of one year from the coming into force of the present Treaty, legislation for the purpose of implementing the provisions of this Article.

Article 4

The relations of the contracting Governments in the sphere of Defence shall be regulated by the Agreement concluded between them on 29th August, 1947, the provisions of which are set out in the Annex hereto and which shall have force and effect as integral parts of the present Treaty.

Article 5

The Provisional Government of Burma reaffirm their obligation to pay to British subjects domiciled on the date of the coming into force of the present Treaty in any country other than India and Pakistan all pensions, proportionate pensions, gratuities, family pension fund and provident fund payments and contributions, leave salaries and other sums payable to them from the revenues of Burma or other funds under the control of the executive authority of Burma, in virtue of all periods of service prior to that date under the rules applicable immediately prior thereto.

Article 6

The contracting Governments agree that the following provisions shall constitute a final settlement of the financial questions dealt with in this Article:—

1. The Provisional Government of Burma reaffirm their agreement to pay over in full proceeds of the sale of Army stores. The Government of the United Kingdom agree to make no claim on the Provisional Government of Burma for repayment of the cost of the Civil Affairs Administration prior to the restoration of civil government.

2. The Government of the United Kingdom agree to cancel 15 million of the sums advanced towards the deficits on the Ordinary Budget and the Frontier Areas Budget. The balance of the sums will be repaid by Burma in twenty equal yearly instalments beginning not later than 1st April, 1952, no interest being chargeable. The cancellation of this amount of Burma's indebtedness is accepted by the Provisional Government of Burma as a further contribution by the Government of the United Kingdom towards the restora-

tion of Burma's financial position and as a final liquidation of their claim in respect of the cost of supplies and services furnished to the British Military Administration in Burma.

3. The Provisional Government of Burma agree to repay in full the sums advanced by the Government of the United Kingdom towards expenditure on Projects (including Public Utilities, etc.). In accordance with existing agreements, repayment will continue to be made from current receipts in excess of necessary outgoings and working capital and from the proceeds of liquidation, and the balance of advances outstanding will be repaid by the Provisional Government of Burma in twenty equal yearly instalments beginning not later than 1st April, 1952, no interest being chargeable.

4. The Government of the United Kingdom agree to continue to reimburse the Provisional Government of Burma for expenditure in respect of claims for supplies and services rendered to the Burma Army in the Burma campaign of 1942; and release benefits payable on demobilisation to Burma Army personnel for war service.

5. Except in so far as they are specifically modified or superseded by the terms of this Agreement and of the Defence Agreement of 29th August, 1947, the provisions of the Financial Agreement of 30th April, 1947 [Hansard, 22nd May, 1947, Columns 276–7.] between the Government of the United Kingdom and the Government of Burma remain in force.

Article 7

(a) All contracts other than contracts for personal service made in the exercise of the executive authority of Burma before the coming into force of the Constitution of the Union of Burma to which any person being a British subject domiciled in the United Kingdom or any Company, wherever registered, which is mainly owned, or which is managed and controlled by British subjects so domiciled, was a party, or under which any such person or company was entitled to any right or benefit, shall as from that date, have effect as if made by the Provisional Government of Burma as constituted on and from that date; and all obligations that were binding on the Provisional Government of Burma immediately prior to the said date, and all liabilities, contractual or otherwise, to which that Government was then subject, shall, in so far as any such person or company as aforesaid is in-

terested, devolve on the Provisional Government of Burma as so constituted.

(b) In so far as any property, or any interest in any property vested in any person or authority in Burma before the coming into force of the Constitution of the Union of Burma, or the benefit of any contract entered into by any such person or authority before that date, is thereafter transferred to, or vested in the Provisional or any successor Government of Burma, it shall be so transferred or vested subject to such rights as may previously have been created and still subsist therein, or in respect thereof, in favour of any person or company of the status or character described in the preceding sub-article.

Article 8

The contracting Governments being resolved to conclude at the earliest possible date a mutually satisfactory Treaty of Commerce and Navigation have agreed for a period of two years from the date of the coming into force of the present Treaty or until the conclusion of such a Treaty of Commerce and Navigation to conduct their commercial relations in the spirit of Nos. 1–3 of the Exchange of Notes annexed hereto, provided that, at any time after six months from the date of the coming into force of the present Treaty, either party may give three months' notice to terminate the undertaking set out therein.

Article 9

The contracting Governments agree to maintain postal services, including Air Mail services and Money Order services, on the existing basis, subject to any alteration in matters of detail which may be arranged between their respective Postal Administrations as occasion may arise.

Article 10

The Provisional Government of Burma agree to negotiate Treaty arrangements in respect of the care and upkeep of war cemeteries and/or war graves of the British Commonwealth and Empire in Burma with the Governments represented on the Imperial War Graves Commission and, pending negotiation of such arrangements, to recognize the Imperial War Graves Commission as the sole authority responsible for dealing with such war cemeteries and/or war graves and to accord to the Commission the privileges set out in Nos. 4 and 5 of the Exchange of Notes annexed to the present Treaty.

Article 11

The contracting Governments will accord to each other the same treatment in civil aviation matters as heretofore, pending the conclusion of an Agreement in regard to them, provided that this arrangement may be terminated on six months' notice given by either side.

Article 12

The contracting Governments agree to conclude at the earliest possible date an agreement for the avoidance of double taxation.

Article 13

Nothing in the present Treaty is intended to or shall in any way prejudice the rights and obligations which devolve or may devolve upon either of the contracting parties under the Charter of the United Nations or from any special agreements concluded in virtue of Article 43 of the Chapter.

Article 14

Should any difference arise relative to the application or the interpretation of the present Treaty, and should the contracting parties fail to settle such difference by direct negotiations, the difference shall be deferred to the International Court of Justice unless the parties agree to another mode of settlement.

Article 15

The present Treaty shall be ratified and shall come into force immediately upon the exchange of Instruments of Ratification, which shall take place on the day on which Burma becomes independent in accordance with the appropriate legislation to be introduced in the United Kingdom for that purpose.

In witness whereof the above-named plenipotentiaries have signed the present Treaty and have affixed thereto their Seals. Done in duplicate in London this 17th day of October, 1947.

Clement Richard Attlee.

Thakin Nu.

Burma Independence Act
17th October, 1947.

Burma Independence (A.D. 1947) a bill to Provide for the independence of Burma as a country not within His Majesty's dominions and not entitled to His Majesty's protection, and for consequential and connected matters. Be it enacted by the King's Most Excellent Majesty, by and with the advice and consent of the Lords Spiritual and Temporal, and Commons, in this present Parliament assembled, and by the authority of the same, as follows:—

Independence of Burma 1. —

(1) On the appointed day, Burma shall become an independent country, neither forming part of His Majesty's dominions nor entitled to His Majesty's protection.

(2) In this Act, the expression "the appointed day" means the fourth day of January, nineteen hundred and forty-eight.

(3) The suzerainty of His Majesty over the part of Burma known as the Karenni States shall lapse as from the appointed day, and with it all treaties and agreements in force between His Majesty and the rulers of the Karenni States, all functions exercisable by His Majesty with respect to the Karenni States, all obligations of His Majesty towards the Karenni States or the rulers thereof, and all powers, rights, authority or jurisdiction exercisable by His Majesty in or in relation to the Karenni States by treaty, grant, usage, sufferance or otherwise.

Certain persons to cease to be British Subjects 2. —

(1) Subject to the provisions of this section, the persons specified in the First Schedule to this Act, being British subjects immediately before the appointed day, shall on that day cease to be British subjects: Provided that a woman who immediately before the appointed day is the wife of a British subject shall not cease by virtue of this sub-section to be a British subject unless her husband ceases by virtue of this sub-section to be a British subject.

(2) A person who by virtue of sub-section (1) of this section ceases to be a British subject on the appointed day and is immediately before that day domiciled or ordinarily resident in either —

(a) any part of the United Kingdom;
(b) any of the Channel Islands;
(c) the Isle of Man;
(d) Newfoundland;
(e) any colony;
(f) any territory in respect of which a mandate from the League of Nations was accepted by His Majesty, being a territory under the sole administration of His Majesty's Government in the United Kingdom;
(g) any territory administered under the trusteeship system of the United Nations, being

a territory under the sole administration of His Majesty's Government in the United Kingdom;

(h) any British protectorate;

(i) any British protected state outside Burma; or

(j) any other place outside Burma in which, by treaty, capitulation, grant, usage, sufferance or other lawful means, His Majesty has jurisdiction over British subjects.

may, by a declaration made before the expiration of the two years beginning with the appointed day to such person and in such manner as may be prescribed, elect to remain a British subject, and if he so elects, the provisions of sub-section (1) of this section (including the proviso thereto) shall be deemed never to have applied to or in relation to him or, except so far as the declaration otherwise provides, any child of his who is under the age of eighteen years at the date of the declaration: Provided that a declaration under this sub-section shall be of no effect unless it is registered in the prescribed manner in pursuance of an application made within, or within the prescribed period after the expiration of, the said two years. In this sub-section, the expression "prescribed" means prescribed by regulations of the Secretary of State or of such Government, authority or person as may be authorized in that behalf by the Secretary of State, and different provision may be made under this sub-section for different classes of cases.

(3) A person who by virtue of sub-section (1) of this section ceases to be a British subject on the appointed day, not being such a person as is mentioned in sub-section (2) of this section, shall, if on that day he neither becomes, nor becomes qualified to become, a citizen of the independent country of Burma for which provision is made by section one of this Act, have the like right of election as is provided for by sub-section (2) of this section, and the said sub-section (2) shall have effect accordingly.

(4) If provision is made by the law of any part of His Majesty's dominions not mentioned in sub-section (2) of this section for the exercise by any persons, being persons domiciled or ordinarily resident in that part of His Majesty's dominions or in any territory administered by the Government thereof, of a right to elect not to cease to be British

subjects on the appointed day by reason of Burma becoming an independent country on that day, then, so far as is necessary to give effect under the law of the United Kingdom to the results flowing under the law of that part of His Majesty's dominions from the exercise of the right of election, the provisions of sub-section (1) of this section shall be deemed never to have applied to or in relation to, or to or in relation to the children of, the persons who duly exercise that right.

(5) Save as provided in this section, no person who is a British subject immediately before the appointed day shall cease to be a British subject by reason of Burma ceasing on that day to be part of His Majesty's dominions.

(6) The exercise by a person of any such right of election as is referred to in sub-section (2), sub-section (3) and sub-section (4) of this section shall not render unlawful anything done before the date of the election which would have been lawful if the election had not been made.

Temporary continuation of customs preferences 3. —

(1) Notwithstanding any of the provisions of this Act, the enactments relating to customs (including the enactments relating to customs in the Isle of Man) shall, on and after the appointed day, have effect, until such date as may be specified by His Majesty by Order in Council, as if Burma were part of His Majesty's dominions: Provided that His Majesty may by Order in Council direct that as from a specified date all goods or goods of specified classes or descriptions shall be charged under said enactments either as if preceding provisions of this section had not passed or at such rates as may be specified in Order not being rates higher than would have been chargeable if said provision had not passed.

(2) Any Order in Council made under this sub-section may be revoked or varied by a subsequent Order in Council made thereunder.

(3) Any Order in Council made under this section shall be laid before both Houses of Parliament after it is made and if, within a period of forty days beginning with the day on which any such Order is so laid before it, either House of Parliament presents an Address to His Majesty praying that the Order may be revoked, His Majesty may revoke the Order accordingly, but without prejudice to the making of a new Order.

(4) In reckoning the said period of forty days, no account shall be taken of any time during which Parliament is dissolved or prorogued, or during which both Houses are adjourned for more than four days.

(5) Section one of the Rules Publication Act, 1893 (which requires notice to be given of a proposal to make statutory rules) shall not apply to any Order in Council made under this section.

Legal proceedings 4. —

(1) Any appeal to His Majesty in Council from any court in Burma which is pending on the appointed day shall abate on that day.

(2) No proceedings shall be brought in any court on or after the appointed day against the Secretary of State in any such case as is mentioned in section one hundred and thirty-three of the Government of Burma Act, 1935, and any proceedings brought by or against the Secretary of State by virtue of that section which are pending immediately before the appointed day shall abate on that day so far as the Secretary of State is concerned.

(3) Nothing in this Act shall affect the jurisdiction of the High Court in England or the Court of Session in Scotland under the Indian and Colonial Divorce Jurisdiction Acts, 1926 and 1940, as respects decrees or orders made in Burma which, before the appointed day, have been registered in those Courts respectively under those Acts: Provided that —

(a) notwithstanding anything in those Acts, the said Courts may entertain applications for the modification or discharge of orders notwithstanding that the person on whose petition the decree for dissolution was pronounced is resident in Burma; and
(b) no regard shall be had to any order made in Burma on or after the appointed day modifying or discharging any decree or order made before the appointed day.

Short Title, interpretation, repeals and construction of existing Orders in Council and other instruments 5. —

(1) This Act may be cited as the Burma Independence Act, 1947.

(2) Any reference in this Act to any other enactment shall be construed as a reference to that enactment as amended by any subsequent Act or by an order or other instrument made under any subsequent Act, including, without prejudice to the generality of the preceding words, the Government of India (Adaptation of Acts of Parliament) Order, 1937 and any subsequent Orders in Council made under sub-section (5) of section three hundred and eleven of the Government of India Act, 1935.

(3) The enactments specified in the Second Schedule [Not reproduced.] to this Act are hereby repealed as from the appointed day to the extent specified in that Schedule; Provided that if, by the law of Burma, any such enactment is continued on or after the appointed day as part of the law of Burma, nothing in this repeal shall be taken to prevent the recognition outside Burma of that enactment as part of the law of Burma.

(4) It is hereby declared that references (however worded) to Burma or British Burma in Orders in Council and other instruments made before the passing of this Act under any enactments not repealed by this Act do not include references to, or to any part of, the independent country of Burma for which provision is made by section one of this Act, but nothing in this sub-section shall be construed as affecting any power to make a new Order in Council or other instrument under any such enactment in relation to the said independent country.

Persons who cease to be British Subjects

1. The persons who, being British subjects immediately before the appointed day, are, subject to the provisions of section two of this Act, to cease on that day to be British subjects are the following persons, that is to say —

(a) persons who were born in Burma or whose father or paternal grandfather was born in Burma, not being persons excepted by paragraph 2 of this Schedule from the operations of this sub-paragraph; and
(b) women who were aliens at birth and became British subjects by reason only of their marriage to any such person as is specified in sub-paragraph (a) of this paragraph.

2. (1) A person shall be deemed to be excepted from the operation of sub-paragraph (a) of paragraph 1 of this Schedule if he or his father or his paternal grandfather was born outside Burma in a place which, at the time of the birth, —

(a) was within His Majesty's dominions, was a British protectorate, was a British protected state, was a territory in respect of which a mandate from the League of Nations had been accepted by His Majesty and which was under the administration of the Government of any part of His Majesty's dominions or was a territory under the trusteeship system of the United Nations which was under the administration of the Government of any part of His Majesty's dominions; or

(b) was a place where, by treaty, capitulation, grant, usage, sufferance or other lawful means, His Majesty had jurisdiction over British subjects: Provided that a person shall not be excepted under this sub-paragraph from the operation of the said sub-paragraph (a) by virtue of the place of birth of his father or paternal grandfather unless his father or, as the case may be, his paternal grandfather, was at some time before the appointed day a British subject.

(2) A person shall also be deemed to be excepted from the operation of the said sub-paragraph (a) if he or his father or his paternal grandfather became a British subject by naturalization or by annexation of any territory which is outside Burma.

(3) Where, in pursuance of the British Nationality and Status of Aliens Act, 1914, the name of a child has been included in a certificate of naturalization granted to his parent, or where, in pursuance of any Act repealed by that Act, any child has been deemed to be a naturalized British subject by reason of residence with his parent, that child shall, for the purposes of this paragraph, be deemed to have become a British subject by naturalization.

3. For the purposes of this Schedule, a person born in a ship, other than an unregistered ship, shall be deemed to have been born in the country in which the ship was registered.

4. In this Schedule the expression "Burma" means the territories which, immediately before the appointed day, were included in Burma.

Defence Agreement signed on 29th August, 1947, in Rangoon General

This Defence Agreement between the Government of Burma and the United Kingdom Government has been freely concluded between the two countries and is without prejudice to any Military alliance which may be made in the future between the Government of Burma and the United Kingdom Government. It has been negotiated in relation to the treaty of transfer, the provisions of which in regard to the international obligations of either party, the settlement of disputes and to similar matters will apply in respect of this Agreement subject to the provisions of the treaty.

Evacuation of British Troops 2. Subject to the provisions of this Agreement, the United Kingdom Government will move all United Kingdom troops out of Burma as soon as possible after the date of transfer of power. The margin of time necessary to effect this movement will be a matter for adjustment between the two Governments. The Government of Burma agree to afford all possible help and protection to His Majesty's Forces in the course of this evacuation.

Financial Concessions by the United Kingdom Government 3. The United Kingdom Government agree —

(a) to forego the financial claims made upon the Government of Burma in the letter to the Finance and Revenue Department of 22nd February, 1947, in respect of Defence charges in Burma subsequent to 1st April 1947;

(b) to make no charge in respect of the transfer of initial equipment for the Burma Army up to the scales agreed;

(c) to make no charge in respect of the transfer of initial maintenance reserves for the Burma Army up to the agreed scales;

(d) to transfer to the Government of Burma free of cost fixed assets of the Army and the Royal Air Force remaining in Burma at the date of the transfer of power: provided that the transfers agreed to in clauses (b), (c) and (d) above shall explicitly exclude all Lend/Lease material.

United Kingdom Service Mission 4. In accordance with the wishes of the Government of Burma the United Kingdom Government agree —

(i) to provide a Naval, Military and Air Force Mission to Burma;

(ii) that the Mission will, provided volunteers are available, include instructional and other staff for service with the Burma Forces;

(iii) to provide training facilities in His Majesty's establishment for personnel of the

Burma forces. The functions and composition of the Mission and of instructional and other staff, the terms and conditions of service of United Kingdom personnel and particulars of training facilities to be provided will fall to be negotiated separately between the two Governments. As a special arrangement to meet the circumstances giving rise to this Agreement, the United Kingdom Government are prepared to waive the cost of the Mission, excluding instructional and other staff under (ii) above, and the cost of training facilities in His Majesty's establishments for a period of three years from the transfer of power. The cost, other than Home effective and non-effective charges, of instructional and other staff for service with the Burma forces will be borne by the Burma Government.

Naval 5. The United Kingdom Government agree to transfer to the Government of Burma free of cost the Naval vessels set out in the Appendix to this Agreement.

Air Provisions 6. Subject to the provisions of this Agreement the United Kingdom Government agree —

(a) to contribute such portion of the cost of the maintenance of Mingaladon Airfield including the cost of technical personnel as may be agreed between the two Governments;

(b) to provide necessary technical personnel for the maintenance and operation of this airfield at appropriate standards to be agreed between the two Governments for such period, not exceeding one year, as will enable the Government of Burma to assume this responsibility;

(c) to contribute for a period of three years a sum not exceeding 40,000 annually to the maintenance at standards to be agreed between the two Governments of the landing grounds at Akyab and Mergui.

Supply of War Material 7. Having regard to the friendly relations signified by the conclusion of this Agreement, the United Kingdom Government agree to give all reasonable facilities for purchase by the Government of Burma of War Material.

Undertaking of the Government of Burma 8. The Government of Burma agree —

(a) to receive a Naval, Military and Air Force Mission from the United Kingdom Government and not from any Government outside the British Commonwealth;

(b) that, in view of the close association between His Majesty's Navy and the Burma Naval Forces and in accordance with customary peace-time practice with other friendly Powers, ships of either navy shall have the right of entry into the ports of the other party upon notification direct between their respective naval authorities on the spot;

(c) that, in view of the friendly association between the air forces of the two parties, military aircraft of either party shall have the right in accordance with customary peace-time practice upon notification direct between the respective air authorities, to fly over the territories of the other, and to enjoy staging facilities at airfields to be prescribed from time to time by agreement between the two Governments, including those referred to in Article 6;

(d) that His Majesty's forces bringing help and support to Burma by agreement with the Government of Burma or to any part of the Commonwealth by agreement with the Government of Burma and with the Government of that part of the Commonwealth shall be afforded all reasonable assistance including facilities of access and entry into Burma by air, land and sea.

Further Negotiations 9. Nothing in this Agreement shall preclude either party from opening fresh negotiations with the other on any matter within the defence sphere, but such negotiations shall not, except by agreement, affect the obligations of either party under this Agreement.

Duration 10. The provisions of this Agreement shall remain in operation in the first instance for three years from the transfer of power and thereafter subject to twelve months' notice on either side.

Bo Let Ya, John W. Freeman, 29th August, 1947

Appendix (Article 5) Vessels now on loan which His Majesty's Government agree to transfer free of cost to the Government of Burma:- One Ocean-going Vessel (His Majesty's Government require the frigate F.A.L. now on loan but will consider the offer of a corvette in substitution). Thirteen Harbour Defence Motor Launches. Three 90-ft. Motor Fishing Vessels. o 61+-ft. Motor Fishing Vessels. One 45-ft. Motor Fishing Vessel. Five Harbour Launches, Petrol. Six Fast Motor Boats. Four Cargo

Lighters (viz., two R.C.L., two "Z" craft). Two Motor Minesweepers.

Demi-official letter from the Hon'ble Bo Let Ya, Counsellor for Defence, Government of Burma, to J. Freeman, Esq., M.B.E., M.P., Chairman, British Defence Mission to Burma, dated Rangoon, the 29th August, 1947.

In connexion with Articles 4 (i) and 8 (a) of our Agreement about the provision of a British Naval, Military and Air Force Mission for Burma, I would like, if you agree, to place on record our expectation that as Burma has agreed to receive no Mission from outside the Commonwealth the United Kingdom Government will do their best to provide qualified advisers and other staff for the Mission in sufficient numbers, but that if this should prove impossible through lack of volunteers or other causes, it may become necessary for the two Governments to take advantage of Article 9 to terminate the provisions relating to the Mission.

Demi-official letter from J. Freeman, Esq., M.B.E., M.P., Chairman, British Defence Mission to Burma, to the Hon'ble Bo Let Ya, Counsellor for Defence, Government of Burma,—No. B.D.M.–6, dated Rangoon, the 29th August, 1947.

Thank you for your letter of 29th August. It is, of course, the intention of the United Kingdom Government, in concluding the Defence Agreement under reference, that it shall be made to work effectively. In the event of the United Kingdom Government being unable to provide a mission capable of carrying out its task effectively, I agree with you that a new situation would arise and both parties could properly re-examine the matter in the light of Clause 9.

Demi-official letter from J. Freeman, Esq., M.B.E., M.P., Chairman, British Defence Mission to Burma, to the Hon'ble Bo Let Ya, Counsellor for Defence, Government of Burma, dated Rangoon, the 29th August, 1947.

I think it somewhat below the dignity of our two Governments to include in a formal agreement between them the latter part of Article 5 relating to naval vessels in the latest draft of our Defence Agreement. On the other hand, the point relating to the use and disposal of the vessels is of some importance, and I suggest that instead of writing it into the agreement you should let me have an acknowledgment of this present letter, and in it place on record the fact that your Government has agreed that the naval vessels referred to in the Appendix to Clause 5 of the Defence Agreement shall only be employed for Government purposes and shall not be sold for commercial or other uses.

Demi-official letter from the Hon'ble Bo Let Ya, Counsellor for Defence, Government of Burma, to J. Freeman, Esq., M.B.E., M.P., Chairman, British Defence Mission to Burma, dated Rangoon, the 29th August, 1947.

I acknowledge with thanks your note of today's date. The Government of Burma have agreed that the naval vessels referred to in the Appendix to Clause 5 of the Defence Agreement shall only be employed for Government purposes and shall not be sold for commercial or other uses.

Exchange of notes

From the Rt. Hon. C. R. Attlee, C.H., M.P., Prime Minister of the United Kingdom of Great Britain and Northern Ireland, to the Hon'ble Thakin Nu, Prime Minister of the Provisional Government of Burma, dated London, the 17th October, 1947: With a view to the most friendly commercial relations with the new independent State of Burma, the Government of the United Kingdom are desirous to conclude a Commercial Treaty with the least possible delay, but realize that the complex nature of such a Treaty makes it impossible to hope to complete negotiations before the coming into force of the Constitution of the Union of Burma. At the same time the Government of the United Kingdom are sure that the Provisional Government of Burma share their view that the commercial relations of the two countries should not be left entirely unregulated in the meantime and that suitable transitional arrangements cannot but help the conclusion of a mutually satisfactory Treaty at as early a date as possible. 2. I have therefore to express the hope that the Provisional Government of Burma will not during this interim period take action which would prejudicially affect existing United Kingdom interests in Burma in the legitimate conduct of the businesses or professions in which they are now engaged, and that if the Provisional Government of Burma, in the formulation of national policy, are convinced that such action must be taken in any particular case they will consult with the Government of the United Kingdom in advance with a view to reaching a mutually satisfactory settlement. For their part the Government of the United Kingdom will be glad to observe the same principles in regard to the treatment of Burma interests in the United Kingdom. 3. If the Provisional Government of Burma agree with the foregoing proposals, I suggest that this letter and your reply should constitute an understanding between our two Governments to that effect.

From the Hon'ble Thakin Nu, Prime Minister of the Provisional Government of Burma, to the Rt. Hon. C. R. Attlee, C.H., M.P., Prime Minister of the United Kingdom of Great Britain and Northern Ireland, dated London, the 17th October, 1947: I have the honour on behalf of the Provisional Government of Burma, to acknowledge receipt of your letter of today's date. The Provisional Government of Burma share the view of the Government of the United Kingdom that the commercial relations of the two countries should not be left entirely unregulated during the period which will elapse between the coming into force of the constitution of the Union of Burma and the conclusion of a mutually satisfactory Treaty of Commerce and Navigation. The Provisional Government of Burma therefore agree, subject to paragraph 2 below, that they will not take action which would prejudicially affect existing United Kingdom interests in Burma in the legitimate conduct of the businesses or professions in which they are now engaged. The Provisional Government of Burma also agree that if convinced of the necessity of such action in any particular case they will consult with the Government of the United Kingdom in advance with a view to reaching a mutually satisfactory settlement, although there may be occasional cases of emergency in which full prior consultation is impracticable and only short notice can be give to the United Kingdom Ambassador. The Provisional Government of Burma note with satisfaction that the Government of the United Kingdom will observe the same principles in regard to the treatment of Burma interests in the United Kingdom. 2. I have however to explain that the undertaking given in the preceding paragraph must be read as subject to the provisions of the Constitution of the Union of Burma as now adopted, and in particular to the policy of State socialism therein contained to which my Government is committed. If however the implementation of the provisions of Articles 23 (4) and (5), 30, 218, or 219 of the Constitution should involve the expropriation or acquisition in whole or in part of existing United Kingdom interests in Burma, the Provisional Government of Burma will provide equitable compensation to the parties affected. 3. Finally I suggest that, in so far as questions arise which, in the opinion of either Government, do not appropriately fall within the scope of the preceding paragraphs of this letter, these should be discussed by representatives of our two Governments, and decided in accordance with the generally accepted principles of international law and with modern international practice.

From the Rt. Hon. C. R. Attlee, C.H., M.P., Prime Minister of the United Kingdom of Great Britain and Northern Ireland, to the Hon'ble Thakin Nu, Prime Minister of the Provisional Government of Burma, dated London, the 17th October, 1947: I have the honour, on behalf of the Government of the United Kingdom, to acknowledge receipt of your letter of today's date. The Government of the United Kingdom welcome both the Provisional Government of Burma's acceptance of the suggestion contained in my previous letter and their assurance of equitable compensation to United Kingdom interests in the circumstances set out in paragraph 2 of your letter. The Government of the United Kingdom readily accept the suggestion contained in paragraph 3 of your letter.

From the Hon'ble Thakin Nu, Prime Minister of the Provisional Government of Burma, to the Rt. Hon. C. R. Attlee, C.H., M.P., Prime Minister of the United Kingdom of Great Britain and Northern Ireland, dated London, the 17th October, 1947: In connexion with Article 10 of the Treaty signed by us to-day, I have the honour to inform you that, pending the conclusion of a formal Agreement with the Governments represented on the Commission, the Provisional Government of Burma agree to permit the Imperial War Graves Commission—(1) to lay out, construct and maintain the war cemeteries and/or war graves in accordance with their usual practice; (2) to enjoy the use, free of cost, of the sites of such war cemeteries and/or war graves for so long as they are used solely as cemeteries and/or graves; (3) to appoint and maintain staff to carry out their work and occupy the accommodation required for the purpose of their operations; (4) to import free of duty such materials and implements as may be required for the carrying out of their work.

From the Rt. Hon. C. R. Attlee, C.H., M.P., Prime Minister of the United Kingdom of Great Britain and Northern Ireland, to the Hon'ble Thakin Nu, Prime Minister of the Provisional Government of Burma, dated London, the 17th October, 1947: I have the honour to acknowledge the receipt of your note of today's date regarding the treatment which the Provisional Government of Burma propose to accord to the Imperial War Graves Commission pending the conclusion of a formal Agreement on the subject, and to state that the arrangement therein recorded have been noted with satisfaction by the Government of the United Kingdom.

Protocol of signature

On the signature this day of the Treaty between the Government of the United Kingdom of Great Britain and Northern Ireland and the Provisional Government of Burma the undersigned plenipotentiaries declare as follows:- Having regard to the close administrative relations which have hitherto existed between them, and the fact that it may not in every appropriate case have proved possible by the appointed date to complete such alternative arrangements as may be needed, the Government of the United Kingdom and the Provisional Government of Burma affirm their intention to co-operate to ensure that, pending the completion of such arrangements, the minimum of administrative inconvenience and disturbance shall be caused to one another.

Clement Richard Attlee. Thakin Nu.

Source: www.ibiblio.org/freeburma/docs/burma_ independence_docs.html.

Jomo Kenyatta: "The Kenya Africa Union Is Not the *Mau Mau*" (July 26, 1952)

Among the many African liberation movements of the 1950s and 1960s, Kenya's Mau Mau (pronounced "mumu") were among the most militant, calling for the expulsion of all white settlers from the country and, beginning in 1952, attacking white farmers who were occupying the traditional lands of the majority Kikuyu people. The British colonial authorities retaliated. Other nonviolent independence leaders, notably Jomo Kenyatta of the Kenya African Union, were jailed by the British. In this speech to the Kenya African Union meeting at Nyeri, given early in the history of the uprising, Kenyatta tried to dissuade KAU members from joining the Mau Mau and to encourage them to achieve self-determination by peaceful means.

. . . I want you to know the purpose of K.A.U. It is the biggest purpose the African has. It involves every African in Kenya and it is their mouthpiece which asks for freedom. K.A.U. is you and you are the K.A.U. If we unite now, each and every one of us, and each tribe to another, we will cause the implementation in this country of that which the European calls democracy. True democracy has no colour distinction. It does not choose between black and white. We are here in this tremendous gathering under the K.A.U. flag to find which road leads us from darkness into democracy. In order to find it we Africans must first achieve the right to elect our own representatives. That is surely the first principle of democracy. We are the only race in Kenya which does not elect its own representatives in the Legislature and we are going to set about to rectify this situation. We feel we are dominated by a handful of others who refuse to be just. God said this is our land. Land in which we are to flourish as a people. We are not worried that other races are here with us in our country, but we insist that we are the leaders here, and what we want we insist we get. We want our cattle to get fat on our land so that our children grow up in prosperity; we do not want that fat removed to feed others. He who has ears should now hear that K.A.U. claims this land as its own gift from God and I wish those who are black, white or brown at this meeting to know this. K.A.U. speaks in daylight. He who calls us the *Mau Mau* is not truthful. We do not know this thing *Mau Mau*. We want to prosper as a nation, and as a nation we demand equality, that is equal pay for equal work. Whether it is a chief, headman or labourer be needs in these days increased salary. He needs a salary that compares with a salary of a European who does equal work.

We will never get our freedom unless we succeed in this issue. We do not want equal pay for equal work tomorrow—we want it right now. Those who profess to be just must realize that this is the foundation of justice. It has never been known in history that a country prospers without equality. We despise bribery and corruption, those two words that the European repeatedly refers to. Bribery and corruption is prevalent in this country, but I am not surprised. As long as a people are held down, corruption is sure to rise and the only answer to this is a policy of equality. If we work together as one, we must succeed.

Our country today is in a bad state for its land is full of fools—and fools in a country delay the independence of its people. K.A.U. seeks to remedy this situation and I tell you now it despises thieving, robbery and murder for these practices ruin our country. I say this because if one man steals, or two men steal, there are people sitting close by lapping up information, who say the whole tribe is bad because a theft has been committed. Those people are wrecking our chances of advancement. They will prevent us getting freedom. If I have my own way, let me tell you I would butcher the criminal, and there are more criminals than one in more senses than one. The policeman must arrest an offender, a man who is purely an offender, but he must not go about picking up people with a small horn of liquor in their hands and march them in procession with his fellow policemen to Government and say he has got a *Mau Mau* amongst the Kikuyu people. The plain clothes man who hides in the hedges must, I demand, get the truth of our words before be flies to Government to present them with false information. I ask this of them who are in the meeting to take heed of my words and do their work properly and justly. . . .

. . . K.A.U. is not a fighting union that uses fists and weapons. If any of you here think that force is good, I do not agree with you: remember the old saying that he who is hit with a rungu returns, but he who is hit with justice never comes back. I do not want people to accuse us falsely—that we steal and that we are *Mau Mau*. I pray to you that we join hands for freedom and freedom means abolishing criminality. Beer harms us and those who drink it do us harm and they may be the so-called *Mau Mau*. Whatever grievances we have, let us air them here in the open. The criminal does not want freedom and land—he wants to line his own pocket. Let us therefore demand our rights justly. The British Government has discussed the land problem in Kenya and we hope to have a Royal Commission to this country to look into the land problem very shortly. When this Royal Commission comes, let us show it that we are a good peaceful people and not thieves and robbers.

Source: Kenya African Union. Sessional Paper No. 5 of 1959–1960. Nairobi, 1960.

Rhodesia's Unilateral Declaration of Independence (November 11, 1965)

As Britain divested itself of its territories across Africa in the late 1950s and early 1960s, two of its colonies in the southern part of the continent presented special problems. With significant white minorities, South Africa and Rhodesia refused to accept majority black rule. In 1965, white Rhodesians preempted British efforts to turn over power to a multiracial government by issuing the Unilateral Declaration of Independence, asserting white control over an independent Rhodesia. After fifteen years of guerrilla warfare against two black liberation armies, white Rhodesians were eventually forced to cede power to a black majority government, which changed the name of the country to Zimbabwe.

Whereas in the course of human affairs history has shown that it may become necessary for a people to resolve the political affiliations which have connected them with another people and to assume amongst other nations the separate and equal status to which they are entitled:

And whereas in such event a respect for the opinions of mankind requires them to declare to other nations the causes which impel them to assume full responsibility for their own affairs:

Now therefore, we, the Government of Rhodesia, do hereby declare:

That it is an indisputable and accepted historic fact that since 1923 the Government of Rhodesia have exercised the powers of self-government and have been responsible for the progress, development and welfare of their people;

That the people of Rhodesia having demonstrated their loyalty to the Crown and to their kith and kin in the United Kingdom and elsewhere through two world wars, and having been prepared to shed their blood and give of their substance in what they believed to be the mutual interests of freedom-loving people, now see all that they have cherished about to be shattered on the rocks of expediency;

That the people of Rhodesia have witnessed a process which is destructive of those very precepts upon which civilization in a primitive country has been built, they have seen the principles of Western democracy, responsible government and moral standards crumble elsewhere, nevertheless they have remained steadfast;

That the people of Rhodesia fully support the requests of their government for sovereign independence but have witnessed the consistent refusal of the Government of the United Kingdom to accede to their entreaties;

That the government of the United Kingdom have thus demonstrated that they are not prepared to grant sovereign independence to Rhodesia on terms acceptable to the people of Rhodesia, thereby persisting in maintaining an unwarrantable jurisdiction over Rhodesia, obstructing laws and treaties with other states and the conduct of affairs with other nations and refusing assent to laws necessary for the public good, all this to the detriment of the future peace, prosperity and good government of Rhodesia;

That the Government of Rhodesia have for a long period patiently and in good faith negotiated with the Government of the United Kingdom for the removal of the remaining limitations placed upon them and for the grant of sovereign independence;

That in the belief that procrastination and delay strike at and injure the very life of the nation, the Government of Rhodesia consider it essential that Rhodesia should attain, without delay, sovereign independence, the justice of which is beyond question;

Now therefore, we the Government of Rhodesia, in humble submission to Almighty God who controls the destinies of nations, conscious that the people of Rhodesia have always shown unswerving loyalty and devotion to Her Majesty the Queen and earnestly praying that we and the people of Rhodesia will not be hindered in our determination to continue exercising our undoubted right to demonstrate the same loyalty and devotion, and seeking to promote the common good so that the dignity and freedom of all men may be assured, do, by this proclamation, adopt, enact and give to the people of Rhodesia the constitution annexed hereto;

God Save The Queen

Given under Our Hand at Salisbury this eleventh day of November in the Year of Our Lord one thousand nine hundred and sixty five.

Source: Akers, Mary, ed. Encyclopedia Rhodesia. Salisbury, Rhodesia (now Harare, Zimbabwe): College Press, 1973.

Hong Kong Constitution (1990)

Between its seizure during the Opium War of 1840 and its return to China in 1997, Hong Kong was a colony of the British. Particularly in the years following World War II, Hong Kong flourished economically, a capitalist bastion on the coast of communist mainland China. As the end of the treaty granting Hong Kong to Britain approached, London and Beijing engaged in lengthy negotiations about the colony's future as part of China. Led by negotiator Chris Patten, the British insisted on basic western civil rights for Hong Kong's citizens. In the end, China agreed. Many experts believe that China was willing to grant these freedoms in order to preserve Hong Kong's economic freedom and vitality. Indeed, in the years since China began to adopt a market economy in the late 1970s, Hong Kong has served a critical role as China's liaison to the capitalist outside world.

Preamble

Hong Kong has been part of the territory of China since ancient times; it was occupied by Britain after the Opium War in 1840. On 19 December 1984, the Chinese and British Governments signed the Joint Declaration on the Question of Hong Kong, affirming that the Government of the People's Republic of China will resume the exercise of sovereignty over Hong Kong with effect from 1 July 1997, thus fulfilling the long-cherished common aspiration of the Chinese people for the recovery of Hong Kong.

Upholding national unity and territorial integrity, maintaining the prosperity and stability of Hong Kong, and taking account of its history and realities, the People's Republic of China has decided that upon China's resumption of the exercise of sovereignty over Hong Kong, a Hong Kong Special Administrative Region will be established in accordance with the provisions of Article 31 of the Constitution of the People's Republic of China, and that under the principle of "one country, two systems," the socialist system and policies will not be practised in Hong Kong. The basic policies of the People's Republic of China regarding Hong Kong have been elaborated by the Chinese Government in the Sino-British Joint Declaration.

In accordance with the Constitution of the People's Republic of China, the National People's Congress hereby enacts the Basic Law of the Hong Kong Special Administrative Region of the People's Republic of China, prescribing the systems to be practised in the Hong Kong Special Administrative Region, in order to ensure the implementation of the basic policies of the People's Republic of China regarding Hong Kong.

Chapter I General Principles

Article 1 The Hong Kong Special Administrative Region is an inalienable part of the People's Republic of China.

Article 2 The National People's Congress authorizes the Hong Kong Special Administrative Region to exercise a high degree of autonomy and enjoy executive, legislative and independent judicial power, including that of final adjudication, in accordance with the provisions of this Law.

Article 3 The executive authorities and legislature of the Hong Kong Special Administrative Region shall be composed of permanent residents of Hong Kong in accordance with the relevant provisions of this Law.

Article 4 The Hong Kong Special Administrative Region shall safeguard the rights and freedoms of the residents of the Hong Kong Special Administrative Region and of other persons in the Region in accordance with law.

Article 5 The socialist system and policies shall not be practised in the Hong Kong Special Administrative Region, and the previous capitalist system and way of life shall remain unchanged for 50 years.

Article 6 The Hong Kong Special Administrative Region shall protect the right of private ownership of property in accordance with law.

Article 7 The land and natural resources within the Hong Kong Special Administrative Region shall be State property. The Government of the Hong Kong Special Administrative Region shall be responsible for their management, use and development and for their lease or grant to individuals, legal persons or organizations for use or development. The revenues derived therefrom shall be exclusively at the disposal of the government of the Region.

Article 8 The laws previously in force in Hong Kong, that is, the common law, rules of equity, ordinances, subordinate legislation and customary law shall be maintained, except for any that contravene this Law, and subject to any amendment by the legislature of the Hong Kong Special Administrative Region.

Article 9 In addition to the Chinese language, English may also be used as an official language by the executive authorities, legislature and judiciary of the Hong Kong Special Administrative Region . . .

Article 11

(1) In accordance with Article 31 of the Constitution of the People's Republic of China, the systems and policies practised in the Hong Kong Special Administrative Region, including the social and economic systems, the system for safeguarding the fundamental rights and freedoms of its residents, the executive, legislative and judicial systems, and the relevant policies, shall be based on the provisions of this Law. (2) No law enacted by the legislature of the Hong Kong Special Administrative Region shall contravene this Law.

Source: www.oefre.unibe.ch/law/icl/hk00000_.html.

DUTCH EMPIRE

Charter of the Dutch West India Company (June 3, 1621)

Much exploration, colonization, and trade by Europeans in the early years of the continent's expansion into the rest of the world was financed and organized by chartered companies. Begun by the English and adopted by the Dutch and other colonizing countries, these companies were put together by investors, usually wealthy merchants or landowners well connected with the political authorities. They then received a royal charter that allowed them a monopoly over trade with a given region; in the case of the Dutch West India Company, this included West Africa and all of the Western Hemisphere. Perhaps the best-known accomplishment of the Dutch West India Company was the founding of New Amsterdam, a colony that later came to be known as New York under the English.

The States-General of the United Netherlands, to all who shall see these Presents, or hear them read, Greeting.

Be it known, that we knowing the prosperity of these countries, and the welfare of their inhabitants depends principally on navigation and trade, which in all former times by the said Countries were carried on happily, and with a great blessing to all countries and kingdoms; and desiring that the aforesaid inhabitants should not only be preserved in their former navigation, traffic, and trade, but also that their trade may be encreased as much as possible in special conformity to the treaties, alliances, leagues and covenants for traffic and navigation formerly made with other princes, republics and people, which we give them to understand must be in all parts punctually kept and adhered to: And we find by experience, that without the common help, assistance, and interposition of a General Company, the people designed from hence for those parts cannot be profitably protected and maintained in their great risque from pirates, extortion and otherwise, which will happen in so very long a voyage. We have, therefore, and for several other important reasons and considerations as thereunto moving, with mature deliberation of counsel, and for highly necessary causes, found it good, that the navigation, trade, and commerce, in the parts of the West-Indies, and Africa, and other places hereafter described, should not henceforth be carried on any otherwise than by the common united strength of the merchants and inhabitants of these countries; and for that end there shall be erected one General Company, which we out of special regard to their common well-being, and to keep and preserve the inhabitants of those places in good trade and welfare, will maintain and strengthen with our Help, Favour and assistance as far as the present state and condition of this Country will admit: and moreover furnish them with a proper Charter, and with the following Priveleges and Exemptions, to wit, That for the Term of four and twenty Years, none of the Natives or Inhabitants of these countries shall be permitted to sail to or from the said lands, or to traffic on the coast and countries of *Africa* from the *Tropic of Cancer* to the *Cape of Good Hope,* nor in the countries of *America,* or the West-Indies, beginning at the fourth end of *Terra Nova,* by the streights of *Magellan, La Maire,* or any other streights and passages situated thereabouts to the straights of *Anian,* as well on the north sea as the south sea, nor on any islands situated on the one side or the other, or between both; nor in the western or southern countries reaching, lying, and between both the meridians, from the Cape of Good Hope, in the East, to the east end of New Guinea, in the West, inclusive, but in the Name of this United Company of these United Netherlands. And whoever shall presume without the consent of this Company, to sail or to traffic in any of the Places within the aforesaid Limits granted to this Company, he shall forfeit the ships and the goods which shall be found for sale upon the aforesaid coasts and lands; the which being actually seized by the aforesaid Company, shall be by them kept for their own Benefit and Behoof. And in case such ships or goods shall be sold either in other countries or havens they may touch at, the owners and partners must be fined for the value of those ships and goods: Except only, that they who before the date of this charter, shall have sailed or been sent out of these or any other countries, to any of the aforesaid coasts, shall be able to continue their trade for the sale of their goods, and cosine back again, or otherwise, until the expiration of this charter, if they have had any before, and not longer: Provided, that after the first of July sixteen hundred and twenty one, the day and time of this charters commencing, no person shall be able to send any ships or goods to the places comprehended in this charter, although that before the date hereof, this Company was not finally incorporated: But shall provide therein as is becoming, against those who knowingly by fraud endeavour to frustrate our intention herein for the public good: Provided that the salt trade at *Ponte del Re* may be continued according to the conditions and instructions by us already given, or that may be given respecting it, any thing in this charter to the contrary notwithstanding.

II. That, moreover, the aforesaid Company may, in our name and authority, within the limits herein before prescribed, make contracts, engagements and alliances with the limits herein before prescribed, make contracts, engagements and alliances with the princes and natives of the countries comprehended therein, and also build any forts and fortifications there, to appoint and dis-

charge Governors, people for war, and officers of justice, and other public officers, for the preservation of the places, keeping good order, police and justice, and in like manner for the promoting of trade; and again, others in their place to put, as they from the situation of their affairs shall see fit: Moreover, they must advance the peopling of those fruitful and unsettled parts, and do all that the service of those countries, and the profit and increase of trade shall require: and the Company shall successively communicate and transmit to us such contracts and alliances as they shall have made with the aforesaid princes and nations; and likewise the situation of the fortresses, fortifications, and settlements by them taken.

III. Saving, that they having chosen a governor in chief, and prepared instructions for him, they shall be approved, and a commission given by us, And that further, such governor in chief, as well as other deputy governors, commanders, and officers, shall be held to take an oath of allegiance to us and also to the Company.

IV. And if the aforesaid Company in and of the aforesaid places shall be cheated under the appearance of friendship, or badly treated, or shall suffer loss in trusting their money or Goods, without having restitution, or receiving payment for them, they may use the best methods in their power, according to the situation of their affairs, to obtain satisfaction.

V. And if it should be necessary for the establishment, security and defence of this trade, to take any troops with them, we will, according to the constitution of this country, and the situation of affairs furnish the said Company with such troops, provided they be paid and supported by the Company.

VI. Which troops, besides the oath already taken to us and to his excellency, shall swear to obey the commands of the said Company, and to endeavour to promote their interest to the utmost of their ability.

VII. That the provosts of the Company on shore may apprehend any of the military, that have inlisted in the service of the aforesaid company, and may confine them on board the ships in whatever city, place, or jurisdiction they may be found; provided, the provosts first inform the officers and magistrates of the cities and places where this happens.

VIII. That we will not take any ships, ordnance, or ammunition belonging to the company, for the use of this country, without the consent of the said company.

IX. We have moreover incorporated this company, and favoured them with privileges, and we give them a charter besides this, that they may pass freely with all their ships and goods without paying any toll to the United Provinces; and that they themselves may use their liberty in the same manner as the free inhabitants of the cities of this country enjoy their freedom, notwithstanding any person who is not free may be a member of this company.

X. That all the goods of this company during the eight next ensuing years, be carried out of this country to the parts of the West Indies and Africa, and other places comprehended within the aforesaid limits, and those which they shall bring into this country, shall be from outward and home convoys; provided, that if at the expiration of the aforesaid eight years, the state and situation of these Countries will not admit of this Freedom's continuing for a longer time, the said goods, and the merchandises coming from the places mentioned in this Charter, and exported again out of these countries, and the outward convoys and licenses, during the whole time of this Charter, shall not be rated higher by us than they have formerly been rated, unless we should be again engaged in a war, in which case, all the aforesaid goods and merchandises will not be rated higher by us than they were in the last list in time of war.

XI. And that this company may be strengthened by a good government, to the greatest profit and satisfaction of all concerned, we have ordained, that the said government shall be vested in five chambers of managers; one at Amsterdam, this shall have the management of four-ninths parts; one chamber in Zealand, for two-ninth parts; one chamber at the Maeze, for one-ninth part; one chamber in North Holland, for one-ninth-part; and the fifth chamber in Friesland, with the city and country, for one-ninth part; upon the condition entered in the record of our resolutions, and the Act past respecting it. And the Provinces in which there are no chambers shall be accommodated with so many managers, divided among the respective chambers, as their hundred thousand guilders in this company shall entitle them to.

XII. That the chamber of Amsterdam shall consist of twenty managers; the chamber of Zealand of twelve; the chambers of Maeze and of the North Part, each of fourteen, and the chamber of Friesland, with the city and country, also of fourteen managers; if it shall hereafter appear, that this work cannot be carried on without a greater number of persons; in that case, more may be added, with the knowledge of nineteen, and our approbation, but not otherwise

XIII. And the States of the respective United Provinces are authorized, to lay before their High Mightinesses' ordinary deputies, or before the magistrates of the cities of these Provinces, any order for registering the members, together with the election of managers, if they find they can do it according to the constitution of their Provinces. Moreover, that no person in the chamber of Amsterdam shall be chosen a manager who has not of his own in the fields of the company, the sum of five thousand guilders; and the Chamber of Zealand four thousand Guilders, and the chamber of Maeze, of the North Part, and of Friesland, with the city and country, the like sum of four thousand guilders.

XIV. That the first managers shall serve for the term of six years, and then one-third part of the number of managers shall be changed by lot; and two years after a like third part, and the two next following years, the last third part; and so on successively the oldest in the service shall be dismissed; and in the place of those who go off, or of any that shall die, or for any other reason be dismissed, three others shall be nominated by the managers, both remaining and going off, together with the principal adventures in person, and at their cost, from which the aforesaid Provinces, the deputies, or the magistrates, shall make a new election of a manager, and successively supply the vacant places; and it shall be held before the principal adventurers, who have as great a concern as the respective managers.

XV. That the accounts of the furniture and outfit of the vessels, with their dependencies, shall be made up three months after the departure of the vessels, and one month after, copies shall be sent to us, and to the respective chambers: and the state of the returns, and their sales, shall the chambers (as often as we see good, or they are required thereto by the chambers) send to us and to one another.

XVI. That every six years they shall make a general account of all outfits and returns, together with all the gains and losses of the company; to wit, one of their business, and one of the war, each separate; which accounts shall be made public by an advertisement, to the end that every one who is interested may, upon hearing of it, attend; and if by the expiration of the seventh year, the accounts are not made out in manner aforesaid, the managers shall forfeit their commissions, which shall be appropriated to the use of the poor, and they themselves be held to render their account as before, till such time and under such penalty as shall be fixed by us respecting offenders. And notwithstanding there shall be a dividend made of the profits of the business, so long as we find that term per Cent shall have been gained.

XVII. No one shall, during the continuance of this charter, withdraw his capital, or sum advanced, from this company; nor shall any new members be admitted. If at the expiration of four and twenty years it shall be found good to continue this company, or to erect a new one, a final account and estimate shall be made by the nineteen, with our knowledge, of all that belongs to the company, and also of all their expences, and any one, after the aforesaid settlement and estimate, may withdraw his money, or continue it in the new company, in whole or in part, in the same proportion as in this; And the new company shall in such case take the remainder, and pay the members which do not think fit to continue in the company their share, at such times as the nineteen, with our knowledge and approbation, shall think proper.

XVIII. That so often as it shall be necessary to have a general meeting of the aforesaid chambers, it shall be by nineteen persons, of whom eight shall come from the chamber of Amsterdam; from Zealand, four; from the Maeze, two; from North Holland, two; from Friesland, and the city and country, two, provided, that the nineteen persons, or so many more as we shall at any time think fit, shall be deputed by US for the purpose of helping to direct the aforesaid meeting of the company.

XIX. By which general meeting of the aforesaid chambers, all the business of this Company which shall come before them shall be managed and finally settled, provided, that in case of resolving upon a war, our approbation shall be asked.

XX. The aforesaid general meeting being summoned, it shall meet to resolve when they shall fit out, and how many vessels they will send to each place, the company in general observing that no particular chamber shall undertake any thing in opposition to the foregoing resolution, but shall be held to carry the same effectually into execution. And if any chamber shall be found not following the common resolution, or contravening it, we have authorized, and by these presents do authorize, the said meeting, immediately to cause reparation to be made of every defect or contravention, wherein we, being desired, will assist them.

XXI. The said general meeting shall be held the first six years in the city of Amsterdam, and two years thereafter in Zealand. and so on from time to time in the aforesaid two places.

XXII. The managers to whom the affairs of the company shall be committed, who shall go from home to attend the aforesaid meeting or otherwise, shall have for their expences and wages, four guilders a day, besides boat and carriage hire; Provided, that those who go from one city to another, to the chambers as managers and governors, shall receive no wages or travelling charges, at the cost of the company.

XXIII. And if it should happen that in the aforesaid general meeting, any weighty matter should come before them wherein they cannot agree, or in case the vote are equally divided, the same shall be left to our decision; and whatever shall be determined upon shall be carried into execution.

XXIV. And all the inhabitants of these countries, and also of other countries, shall be notified by public advertisements within one month after the date hereof, that they may be admitted into this Company, during five months from the first of July this year, sixteen hundred and twenty one, and that they must pay the money they put into the Stock in three payments; to wit, one third part at the expiration of the aforesaid five months, and the other two-thirds parts within three next succeeding years. In case the aforesaid general meeting shall find it necessary to prolong the time the members shall be notified by an advertisement.

XXV. The ships returning from a voyage shall come to the place they sailed from; and if by stress of weather the vessels which sailed out from one part shall arrive in another; as those from Amsterdam, or North Holland, in Zealand, or in the Maeze; or from Zealand, in Holland; or those from Friesland, with the city and country, in another part; each chamber shall nevertheless have the direction and management of the vessels and goods it sent out, and shall send and transport the goods to the places from whence the vessels sailed, either in the same or other vessels: Provided, that the managers of that chamber shall be held in person to find the place where the vessels and goods are arrived, and not appoint factors to do this business; but in case they shall not be in a situation for travelling, they shall commit this business to the chamber of the place where the vessels arrived.

XXVI. If any chamber has got any goods or returns from the places included within the Limits of this charter, with which another is not provided, it shall be held to send such goods to the chamber which is unprovided, on its request, according to the situation of the case, and if they have sold them, to send to another chamber for more. And in like manner, if the managers of the respective chambers have need of any persons for fitting out the vessels, or otherwise, from the cities where there are chambers or managers, they shall require and employ the managers, of this company, without making use of a factor.

XXVII. And if any of the Provinces think fit to appoint an agent to collect the money from the inhabitants, and to make a fund in any chamber, and for paying dividends, the chamber shall be obliged to give such agent access, that he may obtain information of the state of the disbursements and receipts, and of the debts; provided, that the money brought in by such agent amount to fifty thousand guilders or upwards.

XXVIII. The managers shall have for commissions one per cent. On the outfits and returns, besides the Prince's; and an half per cent. On gold and silver: which commission shall be divided; to the Chamber of Amsterdam, four-ninth parts; the Chamber of Zealand, two-ninth parts; the Maeze, one-ninth part; North Holland, one-ninth part, and Friesland, with the city and country, a like ninth part.

XXIX. Provided that they shall not receive commissions on the ordnance and the ships more than once. They shall, moreover, have no commissions on the ships, ordnance, and other things with which we shall strengthen the Company; nor on the money which they shall collect for the Company, nor on the profits they receive from the goods, nor shall they charge the Company with any expenses of traveling or provisions for those to whom they shall commits the providing a cargo, and purchasing goods necessary for it.

XXX. The book-keepers and cashiers shall have a salary paid them by the managers out of their commissions.

XXXI. The manager shall not deliver or sell to the Company, in whole or in part, any of their own ships, merchandise or goods; nor buy or cause to be bought, of the said Company, directly or indirectly, any goods or merchandize nor have any portion or part therein on forfeiture of one year's commissions for the use of the poor, and the loss of Office.

XXXII. The managers shall give notice by advertisement, as often as they have a fresh importation of goods and merchandize, to the end that every one may have seasonable knowledge of it, before they proceed to a final sale.

XXXIII. And if it happens that in either Chamber, any of the managers shall get into such a situation, that he cannot make good what was entrusted to him during his administration, and in consequence thereof any loss shall happen, such Chamber shall be liable for the damage, and shall also be specially bound for their administration, which shall also be the case with all the members, who, on account of goods purchased, or otherwise, shall become debtors to the Company, and so shall be reckoned all cases relating to their stock and what may be due to the Company.

XXXIV. The managers of the respective chambers shall be responsible for their respective cashiers and book-keepers.

XXXV. That all the goods of this Company which shall be sold by weight shall be sold by one weight, to wit, that of Amsterdam; and that all such goods shall be put on board ship, or in store without paving any excise, import or weigh-money; provided that they being sold; shall not be delivered in any other way than by weight; and provided that the impost and weigh-money shall be paid as often as they are alienated, in the same manner as other goods subject to weigh-money.

XXXVI. That the persons or goods of the managers shall not be arrested, attached or encumbered, in order to obtain from them an account of the administration of the Company, nor for the payment of the wages of those who are in the service of the Company, but those who shall pretend to take the same upon them, shall be bound to refer the matter to their ordinary judges.

XXXVII. So when any ship shall return from a voyage, the generals or commanders of the fleets, shall be obliged to come and report to us the success of the voyage of such ship or ships, within ten days after their arrival, and shall deliver and leave with us a report in writing, if the case requires it.

XXXVIII. And if it happens (which we by no means expect) that any person will, in any manner, hurt or hinder the navigation, business, trade, or traffic of this Company, contrary to the common right, and the contents of the aforesaid treaties, leagues, and covenants, they shall defend it against them, and regulate it by the instructions we have given concerning it.

XXXIX. We have moreover promised and do promise, that we will defend this Company against every person in free navigation and traffic, and assist them with a million of guilders, to be paid in five years, whereof the first two hundred thousand guilders shall be paid them when the first payment shall be made by the members; Provided that we, with half the aforesaid million of guilders, shall receive and bear profit and risque in the same manner as the other members of this Company shall.

XL. And if by a violent and continued interruption of the aforesaid navigation and traffic, the business within the limits of their Company shall be brought to an open war, we will, if the situation of this country will in any wise admit of it, give them for their assistance sixteen ships of war, the least one hundred and fifty lasts burthen; with four good well sailing yachts, the least, forty lasts burthen, which shall be properly mounted and provided in all respects, both with brass and other cannon, and a proper quantity of ammunition, together with double suits of running and standing rigging, sails, cables, anchors, and other things thereto belonging, such as are proper to be provided and used in all great expeditions; upon condition, that they shall be manned, victualled, and supported at the expense of the Company, and that the Company shall be obliged to add thereto sixteen like ships of war, and four yachts, mounted and provided as above, to be used in like manner for the defence of trade and all exploits of war: Provided that all the ships of war and merchantmen (that shall be with those provided and manned as aforesaid) shall be under an admiral appointed by us according to the previous advise of the aforesaid General Company, and shall obey our commands, together with the resolutions of the Company, if it shall be necessary, in the same manner as in time of war; so notwithstanding that the merchantmen shall not unnecessarily hazard their lading.

XLI. And if it should happen that this country should be remarkably eased of its burthens, and that this Company should be laid under the grievous burthen of a war, we have further promised, and do promise, to encrease the aforesaid subsidy in such a manner as the situation of these countries will admit, and the affairs of the Company shall require.

XLII. We have moreover ordained, that in case of a war, all the prizes which shall be taken from enemies and pirates within the aforesaid limits, by the Company or their assistants; also the goods which shall be seized by virtue of our proclamation, after deducting all expenses and the damage which the Company shall suffer in taking each prize, together with the just part of his excellency the admiral, agreeable to our resolution of the first of April sixteen hundred and two; and the tenth part for the officers, sailors and soldiers, who have taken the prize, shall await the disposal of the managers of the aforesaid Company; Provided that the account of them shall be kept separate and apart from the account of trade and commerce; and that the nett proceeds of the said prizes shall be employed in fitting our ships, paying the troops, fortifications, garrisons, and like matters of war and defence by sea and land; but there shall be no distribution unless the said nett proceeds shall amount to so much that a notable share may be distributed without weakening the said defence, and after paying the expenses of the war, which shall be done separate and apart from the distributions on account of Trade: And the distribution shall be made one-tenth part for the use of the United Netherlands, and the remainder for the members of this Company, in exact proportion to the capital they have advanced.

XLIII. Provided nevertheless, that all the prizes and goods, taken by virtue of our proclamation, shall be brought in, and the right laid before the judicature of the counsellors of the admirality for the part to which they are brought, that they may take cognizance of them, and determine the legality or illegality of the said prizes: the process of the administration of the goods brought in by the Company remaining nevertheless pending, and that under a proper inventory; and saving a revision of what may be done by the sentence of the admirality, agreeable to the instruction given the admiralty in that behalf. Provided that the venduemasters and other officers of the Admiralty shall not have or pretend to any right to the prizes taken by this Company, and shall not be employed respecting them.

XLIV. The managers of this Company shall solemnly promise and swear, that they will act well and faithfully in their administration, and make good and just accounts of their trade: That they in all things will consult the greatest profit of the Company, and as much as possible prevent their meeting with losses: That they will not give the principal members any greater advantage in the payments or distribution of money than the least: That they, in getting in and receiving outstanding debts, will not favour one more than another: that they for their own account will take, and, during the continuance of their administration, will continue to take such sum of money as by their charter is allotted to them; and moreover, that they will, as far as concerns them, to the utmost of their power, observe and keep, and cause to be observed and kept, all and every the particulars and articles herein contained.

XLV. All which privileges, freedoms and exemptions, together with the assistance herein before mentioned, in all their particulars and articles, we have, with full knowledge of the business, given, granted, promised and agreed to the-aforesaid Company; giving, granting, agreeing and promising moreover that they shall enjoy them peaceably and freely; ordaining that the same shall be observed and kept by all the magistrates, officers and subjects of the United Netherlands, without doing anything contrary thereto directly or indirectly, either within or out of these Netherlands, on penalty of being punished both in life and goods as obstacles to the common welfare of this country, and transgressors of our ordinance: promising moreover that we will maintain and establish the Company in the things contained in this charter, in all treaties of peace, alliances and agreements with the neighboring princes, kingdoms and countries, without doing anything, or suffering any thing to be done which will weaken their establishment. Charging and expressly commanding all governors, justices, officers, magistrates and inhabitants of the aforesaid United Netherlands, that they permit the aforesaid Company and managers peaceably and freely to enjoy the full effect of this charter, agreement, and privilege, without any contradiction or impeachment to the contrary. And that none may pretend ignorance hereof, we command that the contents of this charter shall be notified by publication, or an advertisement, where, and in such manner, as is proper; for we have found it necessary for the service of this country.

Given under our Great Seal, and the Signature and Seal of our Recorder, at the Hague, on the third day of the month of June, in the year sixteen hundred and twenty one.

Was countersigned

J. MAGNUS, Secr.

Underneath was written,

The ordinance of the High and Mighty Lords the States General.

It was subscribed,

C. AERSSEN.

And has a Seal pendant, of red Wax, and a string of white silk.

Source: Thorpe, Francis Newton. *The Federal and State Constitutions, Colonial Charters, and Other Organic Laws of the States, Territories, and Colonies Now or Heretofore Forming the United States of America.* Washington, DC: Government Printing Office, 1909.

Cape Slave Code (1754)

The following is a set of codes meant to regulate the public behavior of slaves in the Cape Colony, a settlement founded and governed by the Dutch East India Company in what is now Cape Town, South Africa, to supply the company's trade ships to the East Indies with food, water, and other necessities for the long voyage. The slave code below was compiled by Governor Rijk Tulbagh; its emphasis on control of the colony's slave population is self-evident.

Slaves are to be in-doors after 10 pm or carry a lantern at night. Thus Slaves are not permitted to be on the street at night after 10 pm without a torch;

Slaves are not to ride horses nor wagons in the streets;

Slaves are not to sing, whistle or make any other sound at night. Thus Slaves are not allowed to whistle loudly, and thereby entice other slaves from their master's homes;

Slaves are not to meet in bars, buy alcohol, or form groups on public holidays;

Slaves are not to gather near entrances of a church during the time of religious services being conducted;

Slaves are not to stop in the street to talk to other slaves;

Slaves who insulted or falsely accused a freeman, would be flogged. Thus Slaves are not permitted to be cheeky with any slaveowner in public;

Slaves who struck a slaveholder were to be put to death;

Slaves are not permitted to own guns or to carry dangerous weapons;

Free Blacks aren't equal to white Free Burghers;

Freed slave women are not to wear coloured silk or hoop skirts, fine lace, or any decoration on their hats, or earrings made of gems or imitation gems;

Slaves are banned from public assemblies in groups of 3, 4 or more in the streets or anywhere else. VOC [Dutch East India Company] law enforcement officials had standing instructions to disperse any crowd of slaves of 3 or more;

Slaves nor any-one else are permitted to walk-about with a burning tobacco pipe in public in order to prevent fires; . . .

Source: batavia.rug.ac.be/slavery/code1754.htm.

FRENCH EMPIRE

Samuel de Champlain:
The Foundation of Quebec (1608)

This report by Samuel de Champlain, founder of Quebec, reveals the varying motives that compelled the French to explore and settle Quebec and Canada in the early seventeenth century. There was the hope that the St. Lawrence River might provide the much-sought-after passage to the western sea and China. And there was the interest in establishing trading relations with the inhabitants, specifically for the prolific fur pelts of the region, a trade pioneered by St. Malo merchant Pont Gravé, Sieur de Monts. Indeed, the trade would become the basis of the economy of France's colonies on the North American mainland in the seventeenth and eighteenth centuries.

Having returned to France after a stay of three years in New France, I proceeded to Sieur de Monts, and related to him the principal events of which I had been a witness since his departure, and gave him the map and plan of the most remarkable coasts and harbors there. Some time afterward Sieur de Monts determined to continue his undertaking, and complete the exploration of the interior along the great river St. Lawrence, where I had been by order of the late King Henry the Great in the year 1603, for a distance of some hundred and eighty leagues, commencing in latitude 48E 40', that is, at Gaspé, at the entrance of the river, as far as the great fall, which is in latitude 45E and some minutes, where our exploration ended, and where boats could not pass as we then thought, since we had not made a careful examination of it as we have since done.

Now, after Sieur de Monts had conferred with me several times in regard to his purposes concerning the exploration, he resolved to continue so noble and meritorious an undertaking, notwithstanding the hardships and labors of the past. He honored me with his lieutenancy for the voyage; and, in order to carry out his purpose, he had two vessels equipped, one commanded by Pont Gravé, who was commissioned to trade with the savages of the country and bring back the vessels, while I was to winter in the country.

Sieur de Monts, for the purpose of defraying the expenses of the expedition, obtained letters from his majesty for one year, by which all persons were forbidden to traffic in pelts with the savages, on penalties stated in the following commission:

Henry by the Grace of God King of France and Navarre, to our beloved and faithful counselors, the officers of our admiralty in Normandy, Brittany, and Guienne, bailiffs, marshals, provosts, judges, or their lieutenants, and to each one of them, according to his authority, throughout the extent of their powers, jurisdictions, and precincts, greeting:

Acting upon the information which has been given us by those who have returned from New France, respecting the good quality and fertility of the lands of that country, and the disposition of the people to accept the knowledge of God, We have resolved to continue the settlement previously undertaken there, in order that our subjects may go there to trade without hindrance. And in view of the proposition to us of Sieur de Monts, gentleman in ordinary of our chamber, and our lieutenant-general in that country, to make a settlement, on condition of our giving him means and supplies for sustaining the expense of it, it has pleased us to promise and assure him that none of our subjects but himself shall be permitted to trade in pelts and other merchandise, for the period of one year only, in the lands, regions, harbors, rivers, and highways throughout the extent of his jurisdiction: this we desire to have fulfilled. For these causes and other considerations impelling us thereto, we command and decree that each one of you, throughout the extent of your powers, jurisdictions, and precincts, shall act in our stead and carry out our will in distinctly prohibiting and forbidding all merchants, masters, and captains of vessels, also sailors and others of our subjects, of whatever rank and profession, to fit out any vessels in which to go themselves or send others in order to engage in trade or barter in pelts and other things with the savages of New France, to visit, trade, or communicate with them during the space of one year, within the jurisdiction of Sieur de Monts, on penalty of disobedience, and the entire confiscation of their vessels, supplies, arms, and merchandise for the benefit of Sieur de Monts; and, in order that the punishment of their disobedience may be assured, you will allow, as we have and do allow, the aforesaid Sieur de Monts or his lieutenants to seize, apprehend, and arrest all violators of our present prohibition and order, also their vessels, merchandise, arms, supplies, and victuals, in order to take and deliver them up to the hands of justice, so that action may be taken not only against the persons, but also the property of the offenders, as the case shall require.

This is our will, and we bid you to have it at once read and published in all localities and public places within your authority and jurisdiction, as you may deem necessary, by the first one of our officers or sergeants in accordance with this requisition by virtue of these presents, or a copy of the same, properly attested once only by one of our well-beloved and faithful counselors, notaries, and secretaries, to which it is our will that credence should be given as to the present original, in order that none of our subjects may claim ground for ignorance, but that all may obey and act in accordance with our will in this matter. We order, moreover, all captains of vessels, mates, and second

mates, and sailors of the same, and others on board of vessels or ships in the ports and harbors of the aforesaid country, to permit, as we have done, Sieur de Monts, and others possessing power and authority from him, to search the aforesaid vessels which shall have engaged in the fur trade after the present prohibition shall have been made known to them. It is our will that, upon the requisition of the aforesaid Sieur de Monts, his lieutenants, and others having authority, you should proceed against the disobedient and offenders, as the case may require: to this end, we give you power, authority, commission, and special mandate, notwithstanding the act of our council of the 17th day of July last, any hue and cry, Norman charter, accusation, objection, or appeals of whatsoever kind; on account of which and for fear of disregarding which, it is our will that there should be no delay, and, if any of these occur, we have withheld and reserved cognizance of the same to ourselves and our council, apart from all other judges, and have forbidden and prohibited the same to all our courts and judges: for this is our pleasure.

Given at Paris the seventh day of January, in the year of grace sixteen hundred and eight, and the nineteenth of our reign. Signed, HENRY. And lower down, by the king, Delomenie. And sealed with the single label of the great seal of yellow wax. Collated with the original by me, counselor, notary, and secretary of the king.

I proceeded to Honfleur for embarkation, where I found the vessel of Pont Gravé in readiness. He left port on the 5th of April. I did so on the 13th, arriving at the Grand Bank on the 15th of May, in latitude 45E 15'. On the 26th we sighted Cape St. Mary, in latitude 46E 45', on the Island of Newfoundland. On the 27th of the month we sighted Cape St. Lawrence, on Cape Breton, and also the Island of St. Paul, distant eighty-three leagues from Cape St. Mary. On the 30th we sighted Isle Percée, and Gaspé, in latitude 48E 40', distant from seventy to seventy-five leagues.

On the 3d of June we arrived before Tadoussac, distant from Gaspé from eighty to ninety leagues; and we anchored in the roadstead of Tadoussac, a league distant from the harbor, which latter is a kind of cove at the mouth of the River Saguenay, and where there are sometimes violent winds, bringing severe cold. It is maintained that from the harbor of Tadoussac it is some forty-five or fifty leagues to the first fall on this river, which comes from the north-northwest. The harbor is small, and can accommodate only about twenty vessels. It has water enough, and is under shelter of the River Saguenay and a little rocky island, which is almost cut by the river. Elsewhere there are very high mountains, with little soil and only rocks and sand, thickly covered with such wood as fir and birch. There is a small pond near the harbor, shut in by mountains covered with wood. There are two points at the mouth: one on the southwest side, extending out nearly a league into the sea, called Point St. Matthew, or otherwise Point aux Allouettes; and another on the north-west side, extending out one-eighth of a league, and called Point of all Devils, from the dangerous nature of the place. The winds from the south-south-east strike the harbor, which are not to be feared; but those, however, from the Saguenay are. The two points above mentioned are dry at low tide.

Our vessel was unable to enter the harbor, as the wind and tide were unfavorable. I at once had the boat lowered, in order to go to the port and ascertain whether Pont Gravé had arrived. While on the way, I met a shallop with the pilot of Pont Gravé and a Basque, who came to inform me of what had happened to them because they attempted to hinder the Basque vessels from trading, according to the commission obtained by Sieur de Monts from his Majesty, that no vessels should trade without permission of Sieur de Monts, as well as expressed in it; and that, notwithstanding the notifications which Pont Gravé made in behalf of his Majesty, they did not desist from forcibly carrying on their traffic; and that they have used their arms and maintained themselves so well in their vessels that, discharging all their cannon upon that of Pont Gravé, and letting off many musket-shots, he was severely wounded, together with three of his men, one of whom died, Pont Gravé meanwhile making no resistance, for at the first shower of musketry he was struck down. The Basques came on board of the vessel and took away all the cannon and arms, declaring that they would trade, notwithstanding the prohibition of the King, and that when they were ready to set out from France they would restore to him his cannon and ammunition, and that they were keeping them in order to be in a state of security. Upon hearing all these particulars I was greatly annoyed at such a beginning, which we might have easily avoided.

Now, after hearing from the pilot all these things, I asked him why the Basque had come on board of our vessel. He told me that he came in behalf of their master, named Darache, and his companions to obtain assurance from me that I would do them no harm, when our vessel entered the harbor. I replied that I could not give any until I had seen Pont Gravé. The Basque said that, if I had need of anything in their power, they would assist me accordingly. What led them to use this language was simply their recognition of having done wrong, as they confessed, and the fear that they would not be permitted to engage in the whale-fishery. After talking at length, I went ashore to see Pont Gravé, in order to deliberate as to what was to be done. I found him very ill. He related to me in detail all that had happened. We concluded that we could only enter the harbor by force, and that the settlement must not be given up for this year, so that we considered it best, in order not to make a bad cause out of a just one, and thus work our ruin, to give them assurances on my part so long as I should remain there, and that Pont Gravé should undertake nothing against them, but that justice should be done in France, and their differences should be settled there. Darache, master of the vessel, begged me to go on board, where he gave me a cordial reception. After a long conference, I secured an agreement between Pont Gravé and him, and required him to promise that he would undertake nothing against Pont Gravé, or what would be prejudicial to the King and Sieur de Monts; that, if he did the contrary, I should regard my promise as null and void. This was agreed to, and signed by each.

In this place were a number of savages who had come for traffic in furs, several of whom came to our vessels with their canoes, which are from eight to nine paces long, and about a pace or pace and a half broad in their middle, growing narrower toward the two ends. They are very apt to turn over, in case one does not understand managing them, and are made of birch bark, strengthened on the inside by little ribs of white cedar, very neatly arranged. They are so light that a man can easily carry one. Each can carry a weight equal to that of a pipe. When they want to go overland to a river where they have business, they carry them with them. From Chouacoet along the coast as far as the harbor of Tadoussac, they are all alike. After this agreement, I had some carpenters set to work to fit up a little barque of twelve or fourteen tons, for carrying all that was needed for our settlement, which, however, could not be got ready before the last of June.

Meanwhile I managed to visit some parts of the river Saguenay, a fine river, which has the incredible depth of one hundred and fifty to two hundred fathoms. About fifty leagues from the mouth of the harbor there is, as is said, a great waterfall, descending from a very high elevation with great impetuosity. There are some islands in this river, very barren, being only rocks covered with small furs and heathers. It is half a league broad in places, and a quarter of a league at its mouth, where the current is so strong that at three-quarters flood-tide in the river it is still running out. All the land that I have seen consists only of mountains and rocky promontories, for the most part covered with fir and birch, a very unattractive country on both sides of the river. In a word, it is mere wastes, uninhabited by either animals or birds; for, going out hunting in places which seemed to me the most pleasant, I found only some very small birds, such as swallows and river birds, which go there in summer. At other times there are none whatever, in consequence of the excessive cold. The river flows from the north-west.

The savages told me that after passing the first fall, they meet with eight others, when they go to a day's journey without finding any. Then they pass ten others, and enter a lake, which they are three days in crossing, and they are easily able to make ten leagues a day upstream. At the end of the lake there dwells a migratory people. Of the three rivers which flow into this lake, one comes from the north, very near the sea, where they consider it much colder than in their own country; and the other two from other directions in the interior, where are migratory savages, living only from hunting, and where our savages carry the merchandise we give them for their furs, such as beaver, marten, lynx, and otter, which are found there in large numbers, and which they then carry to our vessels. These people of the north report to our savages that they see the salt sea; and, if that is true, as I think it certainly is, it can be nothing but a gulf entering the interior on the north. The savages say that the distance from the north sea to the port of Tadoussac is perhaps forty-five or fifty days' journey, in consequence of the difficulties presented by the roads, rivers and country, which is very mountainous, and where there is snow for the most part of the year. This is what I have definitely ascertained in regard to this river. I have often wished to explore it, but could not do so without the savages, who were unwilling that I or any of our party should accompany them. Nevertheless, they have promised that I shall do so. This exploration would be desirable, in order to remove the doubts of many persons in regard to the existence of this sea on the north, where it is maintained that the English have gone in these latter years to find a way to China.

I set out from Tadoussac the last day of the month to go to Quebec. We passed near the island called Hare Island, distant six leagues from the above named port; it is two leagues from the northern, and nearly four leagues from the southern shore. From Hare Island we proceeded to a little river, dry at low tide, up which some seven hundred or eight hundred paces there are two falls. We named it Salmon River, since we caught some of these fish in it. Coasting along the north shore, we came to a point extending into the river, which we called Cape Dauphin, distant three leagues from Salmon River. Thence we proceeded to another, which we named Eagle Cape, distant eight leagues from Cape Dauphin. Between the two there is a large bay, at the extremity of which there is a little river dry at low tide. From Eagle Cape we proceeded to Isle aux Coudres, a good league distant, which is about a league and a half long. It is nearly level, and grows narrower towards the two ends. On the western side there are meadows, and rocky points extending some distance out into the river On the south-west side it is very reefy, yet very pleasant in consequence of the woods surrounding it. It is distant about half a league from the northern shore, where is a little river extending some distance into the interior. We named it Riviere du Gouffre, since abreast of it the tide runs with extraordinary rapidity; and, although it has a calm appearance, it is always much agitated, the depth there being great: but the river itself is shallow, and there are many rocks at and about its mouth.

Coasting along from Isle aux Coudres, we reached a cape which we named Cap de Tourmente, five leagues distant; and we gave it this name because, however little wind there may be, the water rises there as if it were full tide. At this point the water begins to be fresh. Thence we proceeded to the Isle d'Orleans, a distance of two leagues, on the south side of which are numerous islands, low, covered with trees and very pleasant, with large meadows, having plenty of game, some being, so far as I could judge, two leagues in length, others a trifle more or less. About these islands are many rocks, also very dangerous shallows, some two leagues distant from the main land on the south. All this shore, both north and south, from Tadoussac to the Isle d'Orleans, is mountainous, and the soil very poor. The wood is pine, fir, and birch only, with very ugly rocks, so that in most places one could not make his way.

Now we passed along south of the Isle d'Orleans, which is a league and a half distant from the main land and a half a league on the north side, being six leagues in length, and one in breadth, or in some places a league and a half. On the north side, it is very pleasant, on account of the great extent of woods and meadows there; but it is very dangerous sailing, in consequence of the numerous points and rocks between the main land and the island, on which are numerous fine oaks and in some places nut-trees, and on the borders of the woods wines and other trees such as we have in France. This place is the commencement of the fine and fertile country of the great river, and is distant one hundred and twenty leagues from its mouth. Off the end of the island is a torrent of water on the north shore, proceeding from a lake ten leagues in the interior: it comes down from a height nearly twenty-five fathoms, above which the land is level and pleasant, although further inland are seen high mountains appearing to be from fifteen to twenty leagues distant.

From the Isle d'Orleans to Quebec the distance is a league. I arrived there on the 3rd of July, when I searched for a place suitable for our settlement; but I could find none more convenient or better suited than the point of Quebec, so called by the savages, which was covered with nut-trees. I at once employed a portion of our workmen in cutting them down, that we might construct our habitations there: one I set to sawing boards, another

to making a cellar and digging ditches, another I sent to Tadoussac with the barque to get supplies, which was promptly accomplished through the zeal of all, and my attention to the work.

Some days after my arrival at Quebec a locksmith conspired against the service of the king. His plan was to put me to death, and, getting possession of our fort, to put into the hands of the Basques or Spaniards, then at Tadoussac, beyond which vessels cannot go, from not having a knowledge of the route, nor of the banks and rocks on the way. In order to execute his wretched plan, by which he hoped to make his fortune, he suborned four of the worst characters, as he supposed, telling them a thousand falsehoods, and presenting to them prospects of acquiring riches. These four men, having been won over, all promised to act in such a manner as to gain the rest over to their side, so that, for the time being, I had no one with me in whom I could put confidence, which gave them still more hope of making their plan succeed; for four or five of my companions, in whom they knew that I put confidence, were on board of the barques, for the purpose of protecting the provisions and supplies necessary for our settlement. In a word, they were so skillful in carrying out their intrigues with those who remained that they were on the point of gaining all over to their cause, even my lackey, promising them many things which they could not have fulfilled.

Being now all agreed, they made daily different plans as to how they should put me to death, so as not to be accused of it, which they found to be a difficult thing. But the devil, blindfolding them all and taking away their reason and every possible difficulty, they determined to take me while unarmed, and strangle me, or to give a false alarm at night, and shoot me as I went out, in which manner they judged that they would accomplish their work sooner than otherwise. They made a mutual promise not to betray each other, on penalty that the first one who opened his mouth should be poniarded. They were to execute their plan in four days, before the arrival of our barques, otherwise they would have been unable to carry out their scheme.

On this very day one of our barques arrived, with our pilot, Captain Testu, a very discreet man. After the barque was unloaded, and ready to return to Tadoussac, there came to him a locksmith, named Natel, an associate of Jean du Val, the head of the conspiracy, who told him that he had promised the rest to do just as they did, but that he did not in fact desire the execution of the plot, yet did not dare to make a disclosure in regard to it from fear of being poniarded. Antoine Natel made the pilot promise that he would make no disclosure in regard to what he should say, since, if his companions should discover it, they would put him to death. The pilot gave him his assurance in all particulars, and asked him to state the character of the plot which they wished to carry out. This Natel did at length, when the pilot said to him: "My friend you have done well to disclose such a malicious design, and you show that you are an upright man, and under the guidance of the Holy Spirit. But these things cannot be passed by without bringing them to the knowledge of Sieur de Champlain, that he may make provision against them, and I promise you that I will prevail upon him to pardon you and the rest. And I will at once," said the pilot, "go to him without exciting any suspicion; and do you go about your business, listening to all they may say, and not troubling yourself about the rest."

The pilot came at once to me, in a garden which I was having prepared, and said that he wished to speak to me in a private place, where we could be alone. I readily assented, and we went into the wood, where he related to me the whole affair. I asked who had told it to him. He begged me to pardon him who had made the disclosure, which I consented to do, although he ought to have addressed himself to me. He was afraid, he replied, that you would become angry, and harm him. I told him that I was able to govern myself better than that in such a matter, and desired him to have the man come to me, that I might hear the statement. He went, and brought him all trembling with fear lest I should do him harm. I reassured him, telling him not to be afraid, that he was in a place of safety, and that I should pardon him for all that he had done, together with the others, provided he would tell me in full the truth in regard to the whole matter, and the motive which had impelled them to it. "Nothing," he said, "had impelled them, except that they had imagined that, by giving up the place into the hands of the Basques or Spaniards, they might all become rich, and that they did not want to go back to France." He also re-

lated to me the remaining particulars in regard to their conspiracy.

After having heard and questioned him, I directed him to go about his work. Meanwhile I ordered the pilot to bring up his shallop, which he did. Then I gave two bottles of wine to a young man, directing him to say to these four worthies, the leaders of the conspiracy, that it was a present of wine, which his friends at Tadoussac had given him, and that he wished to share it with them. This they did not decline, and at evening were on board the barque where he was to give them the entertainment. I lost no time in going there shortly after, and caused them to be seized and held until the next day. Then were my worthies astonished indeed. I at once had all get up, for it was about ten o'clock in the evening, and pardoned them all on condition that they would disclose to me the truth in regard to all that had occurred, which they did, when I had them retire.

The next day I took the depositions of all, one after the other, in the presence of the pilot and sailors of the vessel, which I had put down in writing; and they were well pleased, as they said, since they had lived only in fear of each other, especially of the four knaves who had ensnared them. But now they lived in peace, satisfied, as they declared, with the treatment which they had received. The same day I had six pairs of handcuffs made for the authors of the conspiracy: one for our surgeon, named Bonnerme, one for another, named La Taille, whom the four conspirators had accused, which, however, proved false, and consequently they were given their liberty.

This being done, I took my worthies to Tadoussac, begging Pont Gravé to do me the favor of guarding them, since I had as yet no secure place for keeping them, and as we were occupied in constructing our places of abode. Another object was to consult with him, and others on the ship, as to what should be done in the premises. We suggested that, after he had finished his work at Tadoussac, he should come to Quebec with the prisoners, where we should have them confronted with their witnesses, and, after giving them a hearing, order justice to be done according to the offense which they had committed.

I went back the next day to Quebec, to hasten the completion of our storehouse, so as to secure our provisions, which had been misused by all those scoundrels, who spared nothing, without re-flecting how they could find more when these failed; for I could not obviate the difficulty until the storehouse should be completed and shut up. Pont Gravé arrived some time after me, with the prisoners, which caused uneasiness to the work-men who remained, since they feared that I should pardon them, and that they would avenge them-selves upon them for revealing their wicked de-sign. We had them brought face to face, and they affirmed before them all which they had stated in their depositions, the prisoners not denying it, but admitting that they had acted in a wicked manner, and should be punished, unless mercy might be exercised towards them; accusing, above all, Jean du Val, who had been trying to lead them into such a conspiracy from the time of their departure from France. Du Val knew not what to say, except that he deserved death, that all stated in the depositions was true, and that he begged for mercy upon him-self and the others, who had given in their adher-ence to his pernicious purposes.

After Pont Gravé and I, the captain of the ves-sel, surgeon, mate, second mate, and other sailors had heard their depositions and face to face state-ments, we adjudged that it would be enough to put to death Du Val, as the instigator of the conspiracy; and that he might serve as an example to those who remained, leading them to deport themselves correctly in future, in the discharge of their duty; and that the Spaniards and Basques, of whom there were large numbers in the country, might not glory in the event. We adjudged that the three oth-ers be condemned to be hung, but that they should be taken to France and put into the hands of Sieur de Monts, that such ample justice might be done them as he should recommend; that they should be sent with all the evidence of their sentence, as well as that of Jean du Val, who was strangled and hung at Quebec, and his head was put on the end of a pike, to be set up in the most conspicuous place on our fort. After all these occurrences, Pont Gravé set out from Quebec, on the 18th of Septem-ber, to return to France with the three prisoners. After he had gone, all who remained conducted themselves correctly in the discharge of their duty.

I had the work of our quarters continued, which was composed of three buildings of two stories. Each one was three fathoms long, and two and a half wide, with a fine cellar six feet deep. I had a gallery made all around our buildings, on the outside, at the second story, which proved very convenient. There were also ditches, fifteen feet wide and six deep. On the other side of the ditches I constructed several spurs, which en-closed a part of the dwelling, at the points where we placed our cannon. Before the habitation there is a place four fathoms wide and six or seven long, looking out upon the riverbank. Surround-ing the habitation are very good gardens, and a place on the north side some hundred or hundred and twenty paces long and fifty or sixty wide. Moreover, near Quebec, there is a little river, com-ing from a lake in the interior, distant six or seven leagues from our settlement. I am of the opinion that this river, which is north a quarter north-west from our settlement, is the place where Jacques Cartier wintered, since there are still, a league up the river, remains of what seems to have been a chimney, the foundation of which has been found, and indications of there having been ditches surrounding their dwelling, which was small. We found, also, large pieces of hewn, worm-eaten timber, and some three or four can-non-balls. All these things show clearly that there was a settlement there founded by Christians; and what leads me to say and believe that it was that of Jacques Cartier is the fact that there is no evidence whatever that any one wintered and built a house in these places except Jacques Cartier, at the time of his discoveries.

This place, as I think, must have been called St. Croix, as he named it, which name has since been transferred to another place fifteen leagues west of our settlement. But there is no evidence of his hav-ing wintered in the place now called St. Croix, nor in any other there, since in this direction there is no river or other place large enough for vessels ex-cept the main river or that of which I spoke above; here there is a half a fathom of water at low tide, many rocks, and a bank at the mouth, for vessels, if kept in the main river, where there are strong cur-rents and tides, and ice in the winter, drifting along, would run the risk of being lost; especially as there is a sandy point extending out into the river, and filled with rocks, between which we have found, within the last three years, a passage not before discovered; but one must go through cau-tiously, in consequence of the dangerous points there. This place is exposed to the north-west winds; and the river runs as if it were a fall, the tide ebbing two and a half fathoms. There are no signs of buildings here, nor any indications that a man of judgment would settle in this place, there being many other better ones, in case one were obliged to make a permanent stay. I have been desirous of speaking at length on this point, since many believe that the abode of Jacques Cartier was here, which I do not believe, for the reasons here given; for Cartier would have left to posterity a narrative of the matter, as he did in the case of all he saw and discovered; and I maintain that my opinion is the true one, as can be shown by the history which he has left in writing.

Source: Thatcher, Oliver J., ed., *The Library of Original Sources,* vol. 5. Milwaukee: University Research Extension Company, 1907.

Note to the Memoir on the English Aggression (October 1750)

The British and the French fought a series of imperial wars in the seventeenth and eighteenth centuries, including King George's War between 1744 and 1748 (known as the War of Austrian Succession in Europe). As in previous conflicts, King George's War failed to decide which country would dominate North America. The British feared that the French would try to seal off the English coastal colonies by establishing control over a wide swath of territory between Quebec and Louisiana. The French, as this note by an anonymous French official makes clear, believed that the British had designs on Quebec and Louisiana. Ultimately, the British-French conflict would be decided, in the former's favor, in the Seven Years' War (known in North America as the French and Indian War) of 1756–1763.

The restoration of peace has in no wise diverted the English from their constant design to get possession of all the commerce of America. It is only necessary to consider their actual conduct to be convinced of this truth.

No doubt Spain has good proof on its side. France's is but too certain, both from the publicly professed plans of the English and from the difficulties their commissaries are daily making in the settlement of the disputes of the two nations in America.

England, not content with having already encroached on the lands of France on the side of Hudson Bay, and with pushing its settlements in Acadia on the mainland of New France at the Bay of Fundy, despite the boundaries assigned that country by the Treaty of Utrecht, now plans the invasion of Florida and Louisiana.

It is true the English have already encroached on those provinces, but they have not hitherto pushed their claims to the extravagant extent revealed by the map just published at London, on which, under pretence of correcting one of our recent geographers, they extend their boundaries into Spanish Florida in such fashion as to seat themselves on waters flowing into the Gulf of Mexico.

As to Louisiana, they claim to extend their boundaries over all the lands of the Indians friendly to France as far as the Alabamas; they partially recompense Spain for what they took from Florida at the expense of Louisiana. Although this map is not made by express order of the government, it is well known to be by authority.

However there is no doubt that the English have no justification for such enterprises which have long been no secret. They wish to be in a position to invade Florida, and by that conquest, along with their possession of the Isle of Providence in the Bahamas, to make themselves masters of the outlet of the Bahama Channel, and as a result of the treasure of Europe.

To carry out this plan more easily they seek to put it out of the power of the French of Louisiana to give aid to the Spanish as formerly, and as they will never fail to do in all attempts of the English to work their hurt. In this they can best succeed by seeking to cut the communication of the French of Louisiana with New France and Florida; but is not the common danger resulting to France and Spain a warning to the two powers to concert measures as soon as possible that will insure the failure of this pernicious design? The king on his side is ready to enter into all the measures His Catholic Majesty may think most proper to protect himself from the ambitious projects of a nation with no other aim than to subjugate all the others by seizing on their colonies and their commerce, and which terms that the "balance of Europe."

Source: Canadahistory.com: www.canadahistory.com/ sections/documents/memoir_on_english_agression. htm.

Proposal for the Establishment of a Native Army in Algeria (1830)

Like many other colonial powers, the French attempted to save imperial administrative costs by getting the native population to police itself, under the command of European officers. Often, colonizers would use minority populations within the colony to govern the majority. In the case of Algeria, which was first colonized in 1830, the French would eventually come to use Berbers to police the larger Arab population, causing antagonisms between the populations that would linger beyond independence. The following is a letter from an unidentified army officer to the French navy minister.

Dear Minister,

At a moment when the government is considering abandoning one of its colonies, I think it is my duty, in the interests of the nation and in particular of the French army, to lay before Your Excellency my proposal for speeding up the pacification of the Regency of Algiers and ensuring that it will continue to be held.

Experience has shown that French soldiers are little suited to endure the fatigue of warfare under the burning African sun. It is not that they lack courage, but the climate is so much against them that they quickly succumb and in far too great numbers for war to be waged for any long period in this continent.

I believe, M. le Ministre, that the considerable losses we have suffered in Algeria, Madagascar and Senegal may be attributed to two causes: firstly, to the intemperate climate and secondly to the lack of those foodstuffs to which a Frenchman's body is accustomed. In France there is never a shortage of water, and it is usually fit to drink: it is what the soldiers do normally drink. In Africa, it is difficult to find and often unfit for consumption. Soldiers cannot always drink wine: there often is none, it is very expensive, and under a burning sky wine does not quench the thirst and is injurious to health. Some of the fruits found in Africa are also unhealthy, and a young soldier, unthinking of the harm he may be doing to himself, may eat them without taking proper precautions, sometime before they are properly ripe, and this can lead to death.

Let me return to my proposal:

After the colony of Ste Marie was founded in Madagascar, the government set up several companies of black soldiers, Wollofs from Senegal. These African soldiers have demonstrated that they are quite the equal of French soldiers in courage. They are intelligent and inured to fatigue. Military discipline is easily imposed upon them and they can be turned into excellent auxiliary troops, especially when they are employed in their own climates. With a few corps of these black soldiers, it would be easy to drive back the Kabyles into their mountains; we could then force into submission those Arabs who have so far not recognised the authority of the King of France. This would avoid the immense drain on the population of the mother country, and the soldiers whom we are presently sending to Algeria where they sicken and die in huge numbers, could be used to reinforce the active forces to carry out the important task of fighting our enemies in Europe. Lt General Count Clauzel has come to the firm conclusion that it will be impossible to hold onto the Regency of Algiers, and bring it under our control in order to turn it into a dynamic colony which would pay back all France's sacrifices, without using African soldiers, and he too has set up some detachments of Zouaves, which have already shown much promise.

However, it is important not to let these forces become too big, and so place in the hands of the Arabs an armed force which would be superior to our own. The slightest change in circumstances could be enough to make them change sides. Then they would be against us, and we would regret having strengthened our enemies.

If we employed detachments of Wollofs and others from the centre of Africa, the soldiers, who would not be slaves, would find it was in their interest to support us and to serve us well. But we would have to give them some advantages, and allow them to use the title of Soldiers of France, one which they would be proud to use.

This, then, is what I have the honour of proposing to Your Excellency.

We should set up in France, at l'Orient or Port Louis, for example, where sea transport is easy and where there are plenty of barracks available, a single regiment (as an experiment) made up of four battalions of Senegalese blacks. It would be a simple matter to set up an officer corps for this regiment. The Corps of Naval Artillery would be a valuable source, and officers in the Naval Infantry corps, who are distributed around the different ports and in ships of the line, would, I think, be generally quite happy to join the ranks of the active army by this means. The French African Regiment would, therefore, be composed of four battalions, one of which would be the garrison battalion. The ordinary soldiers would be recruited in Senegal or from among the blacks that the Government already employs in every colony, provided that they were in good enough physical shape for at least ten years' service.

The two companies at present in Madagascar and the two which would be set up in Senegal would form the nucleus. We could also allow to enlist those free men of colour from our other colonies who wish to join up.

The pay of these soldiers would be the same as the foot soldiers in the light infantry. Their clothing would also be the same, because we should make no distinctions between free men, whatever their colour. The soldiers should, moreover, be dressed like the officers.

When they are first set up, the officer corps should be made up of French officers, the senior n.c.o.s and corporals could be either Frenchmen or French Africans. But once the corps has been trained, we should allow a third, or even half of the personnel at every rank—except that of colonel—to be men of colour.

It would perhaps be a good idea to create a special military decoration for the men of colour employed in the Regency of Algiers, which could be called "the Order of Fidelity and Bravery" or the "Order of Military Merit." This decoration would consist of three classes and could also be awarded to Frenchmen employed in the auxiliary corps. It should attract a bonus payment, and the amount of the bonus would be paid with the regular salary. It may, of course, not be necessary to create an entirely new decoration: the Order of Military Merit or even the Legion of Honour could fulfil the function which I propose, and which I believe to be necessary to encourage the loyalty and courage of these soldiers.

The soldiers in this corps should spend six months in the garrison, in order to learn a little of the French language and to be trained. At the end of this period, they could be sent to Algiers, marching them across France, in order to give them an idea of the advantages of civilisation, and to get them used to the rigours of marching.

The African soldiers would be enrolled for ten years, but at the end of their terminal leave, they would be allowed to stay on by signing on again. Those who did so would be given a bonus in their salary. Those who, having finished their term of service, wanted to stay in Algeria would be given land, and those who wished to return to their native land would be transported there by French government ships sent for the purpose. This would have the happy effect of spreading civilisation in central Africa, and to implant there, so to speak, the mores of France, which would be of great advantage to our trade.

The soldiers of the auxiliary units should be pensioned-off on the same basis as Frenchmen.

I have the honour to lay these ideas before your excellency, and I earnestly desire, in the interest of my country, that they should be considered and found acceptable.

Kindly deign to accept, M. le Ministre, this token of the most profound respect of your humble and most obedient servant.

L'Orient, 23 December 1830

Source: National Archives (Paris). ANF Marine BB/4 1016 Dossier: 1830, Algerian Expedition, Various Documents.

Anatole France: "The Colonial Folly" (1904)

Anatole France was one of France's premier novelists and intellectuals at the turn of the twentieth century. A socialist and an anti-imperialist, France shared with other critics of empire—such as Mark Twain in the United States and Joseph Conrad in the United Kingdom—the belief that, far from civilizing the non-European peoples of the world, European empires were in fact making barbaric the Europeans who participated in the imperial mission.

Imperialism is the most recent form of barbarism, the end of the line for civilization. I do not distinguish between the two terms—imperialism and barbarism—for they mean the same thing.

We Frenchmen, a thrifty people, who see to it that we have no more children than we are able to support easily, careful of adventuring into foreign lands, we Frenchmen, who hardly ever leave our own gardens, for what in the world do we need colonies? What can we do with them? What are the benefits for us? It has cost France much in lives and money so that the Congo, Cochin China, Annam, Tonkin, Guinea, and Madagascar may be able to buy cotton from Manchester, liquors from Danzig, and wine from Hamburg. For the last seventy years France has attacked and persecuted the Arabs so that Algeria might be inhabited by Italians and Spaniards!

The French people get nothing from the colonial lands of Africa and Asia. But their government finds it profitable. Through colonial conquest the military people get promotions, pensions, and awards, in addition to the glory gained by quelling the natives. Ship owners, army contractors, and shady politicians prosper. The ignorant mob is flattered because it believes that an overseas empire will make the British and Germans green with envy.

Will this colonial madness never end? I know well that nations are not reasonable. Considering their composition, it would be strange, indeed, if they were. But sometimes they know instinctively what is bad for them. Through long and bitter experience they will come to see the mistakes they have made. And, one day, they will realize that colonies bring only danger and ruin.

Source: France, Anatole. "La Folie coloniale." *Neue Freie Presse,* April 18, 1904.

Brazzaville Conference (February 1944)

The future of the French Empire in Africa was left in doubt by Nazi Germany's conquest of France and the establishment of the collaborationist Vichy regime in 1940. By 1944, however, Vichy had lost what little say it had over France's African colonies. In February 1944, the anti-Vichy French Committee of National Liberation called a conference in the French Congolese capital of Brazzaville to lay out the postwar future of French Africa. While the conference led to agreements for significant political and economic reforms, there was no serious discussion of independence or even autonomy within the empire, as this official statement makes clear.

First Part: Political Organization

Political Organization of the French Colonies.—In view of the complex problems involved, the representation of the colonies in a new French Constitution can be studied adequately only by a commission of experts, designated by the Government.

It appears, however, that these experts should take into consideration the following principles to guide and inspire their work:

1. It is desirable and even indispensable that the colonies be represented in the future Assembly whose task will be to draw up the new Constitution of France.

2. It is indispensable to ensure that the colonies be represented in the central government in Metropolitan France in a much more comprehensive and much more effective manner than in the past.

3. Any project of reform which would aim merely at an amelioration of the system of representation existing on September 1, 1939 (colonial Deputies and Senators in the French Parliament, Supreme Council of France Overseas) appears a priori to be inadequate and sterile. . . .

4. In any case, the new body to be created, Colonial Parliament or, preferably Federal Assembly, must fulfill the following purposes: Proclaim and guarantee the indissoluble unity of the French world—respect the regional life and freedom of each of the territories members of the bloc, composed of France and her colonies (or "French Federation," if this term is accepted . . .). With this in view it will be necessary to define, with great accuracy and precision, the power reserved to the central authority or federating body on the one hand and those allotted to the colonies, on the other hand.

5. The legislative regime of the colonies or, to use a more specific terminology, the respective fields of the laws, decrees and regulations, will be adequately determined only after the adoption of the decisions which will establish on a new basis the powers of the central authority or federating body, and those of the various territories. Special emphasis will be laid on the fact that the colonies should gradually advance on the way leading from administrative decentralization to a status of political personality.

Internal Political Organization of the Colonies.—The chiefs of the colonies must exercise as much initiative as possible in their internal administration. With this in view, bodies of political expression must be created which will provide them with a perfectly balanced and legitimate system toward the European administration as well as toward the native population

It is consequently suggested that the existing consultative bodies be abolished and replaced:

In the first place, by Councils of subdivision and Regional Councils, composed of native notables and availing themselves, whenever possible, of the framework provided by existing traditional institutions.

Secondly, by representative Assemblies, composed partly of Europeans, partly of natives.

The members of these bodies would be elected by universal suffrage wherever and whenever this would be practicable. . . .

The powers of the Councils of subdivision and the Regional Councils would be consultative; those of the Assemblies would be deliberative. . . .

Second Part: Social Problems

The Constitutive Elements of the Colonial Society: the Respective Place of the Europeans and of the Natives in Colonization.—Our entire colonial policy will be based upon the respect and the progress of the native society, and we shall have to accept fully and absolutely the demands and consequences implied by this principle. The natives may not be treated as devoid of human dignity, they can be subjected neither to eviction nor to exploitation. However, the colonies are destined, by their very nature, to be inhabited jointly by both Europeans and natives. Although our policy must be subordinated to the full development of the local races, we must also give European activity the place to which it is entitled.

1. The prerequisite for the progress of the African continent is the development of the native populations. The activity of the Europeans and other non-Africans in the colonial territories of Africa must conform to this condition.

2. On the other hand, this progress of the African continent, as it is being contemplated, cannot be achieved without the collaboration of non-African persons and enterprises to a much greater extent and in greater proportion than at the present time. Consequently, all necessary talent, ability and services will be duly enlisted and utilized. . . .

4. All the various trades must gradually be taken over by the natives. The Governors-General and the Governors of the territories shall establish,

within a brief period, an inventory of the enterprises which will be progressively opened to the natives. . . .

5. The education of the natives will be directed towards this progressive accession to public office. Proper selection and adequate training will be the dominant tendency in this field.

6. The necessity for training replacement personnel, as well as the realization of the reforms recommended in all domains by the French African Conference at Brazzaville, make it imperative to launch . . . large-scale recruitment in order to meet the needs of the administrative personnel as well as of the new colonial economy. . . .

Third Part: Economic Questions

The aim of our colonial economic policy must be to develop production and to bring prosperity to the territories overseas, with a view to ensuring a better life for the Africans by increasing their purchasing power and by raising their standard of living. . . .

The industrialization of colonial territories is to be encouraged. Industrialization should proceed methodically . . . within the strict limits imposed by the application of the plan for general production. With this in view, it will be subjected to the regime of prior authorization and of the control of its production by the public authorities. Subject to these reservations, industrialization will be effected by private enterprise. . . .

It is recommended that the quality of [agricultural] products be improved by imposing high standards . . . and by conducting scientific research work . . .

It is recommended that the colonies submit within four months a tentative estimate of the personnel, equipment, materials and supplies which will be necessary to ensure, after the conclusion of hostilities, the functioning of public services. . . .

Source: "French Colonial Policy in Africa." In Service de Presse et d'Information, *Free France*. New York: French Embassy, September 1944.

Abdication of Bao Dai, Emperor of Annam (August 1945)

To lend legitimacy to their rule in Vietnam, the French installed Bao Dai, son of the Vietnamese emperor, on the throne of the country in 1932. Con-

sidered a puppet by the Vietnamese people, Bao Dai collaborated with the Japanese and the Nazi-installed French Vichy regime during World War II. Upon the collapse of the Japanese Empire in August 1945, Vietnamese nationalist leader Ho Chi Minh demanded and won Bao Dai's abdication. Four years later, however, the French installed him as head of the new state of Vietnam, which remained largely under French control. Upon France's defeat by Ho Chi Minh's forces in 1954, and the division of Vietnam into two countries, Bao Dai was forced to resign again. Bao Dai abdicated in 1955 and eventually lived out his life in a modest Paris apartment, dying in 1997.

The happiness of the people of Vietnam!

The Independence of Vietnam!

To achieve these ends, we have declared ourself ready for any sacrifice and we desire that our sacrifice be useful to the people.

Considering that the unity of all our compatriots is at this time our country's need, we recalled to our people on August 22: "In this decisive hour of our national history, union means life and division means death."

In view of the powerful democratic spirit growing in the north of our kingdom, we feared that conflict between north and south could be inevitable if we were to wait for a National Congress to decide us, and we know that this conflict, if it occurred, would plunge our people into suffering and would play the game of the invaders.

We cannot but have a certain feeling of melancholy upon thinking of our glorious ancestors who fought without respite for 400 years to aggrandise our country from Thuan Hoa to Hatien.

Despite this, and strong in our convictions, we have decided to abdicate and we transfer power to the democratic Republican Government.

Upon leaving our throne, we have only three wishes to express:

1. We request that the new Government take care of the dynastic temples and royal tombs.

2. We request the new Government to deal fraternally with all the parties and groups which have fought for the independence of our country even though they have not closely followed the popular movement; to do this in order to give them the opportunity to participate in the reconstruction of the country and to demonstrate that the new regime is built upon the absolute union of the entire population.

3. We invite all parties and groups, all classes of society, as well as the royal family, to solidarize in unreserved support of the democratic Government with a view to consolidating the national independence.

As for us, during twenty years' reign, we have known much bitterness. Henceforth, we shall be happy to be a free citizen in an independent country. We shall allow no one to abuse our name or the name of the royal family in order to sow dissent among our compatriots.

Long live the independence of Vietnam!

Long live our Democratic Republic!

Source: La Republique (Hanoi) 1, 1 (October 1, 1945).

Ho Chi Minh: Independence Speech (September 2, 1945)

Following the collapse of the Japanese Empire in August–September 1945, Vietnamese nationalist leader Ho Chi Minh declared the independence of the Vietnamese state on September 2, 1945. Ironically, Ho Chi Minh, in appealing to the principles of the French Revolution and America's Declaration of Independence, was borrowing from the political traditions of the two countries he would have to fight against for the rest of his life, as he struggled to establish a unified, socialist Vietnam.

"All men are created equal. They are endowed by their Creator with certain inalienable rights, among these are Life, Liberty, and the pursuit of Happiness"

This immortal statement was made in the Declaration of Independence of the United States of America in 1776. In a broader sense, this means: All the peoples on the earth are equal from birth, all the peoples have a right to live, to be happy and free.

The Declaration of the French Revolution made in 1791 on the Rights of Man and the Citizen also states: "All men are born free and with equal rights, and must always remain free and have equal rights." Those are undeniable truths.

Nevertheless, for more than eighty years, the French imperialists, abusing the standard of Liberty,

Equality, and Fraternity, have violated our Fatherland and oppressed our fellow-citizens. They have acted contrary to the ideals of humanity and justice. In the field of politics, they have deprived our people of every democratic liberty.

They have enforced inhuman laws; they have set up three distinct political regimes in the North, the Center and the South of Vietnam in order to wreck our national unity and prevent our people from being united.

They have built more prisons than schools. They have mercilessly slain our patriots—they have drowned our uprisings in rivers of blood. They have fettered public opinion; they have practised obscurantism against our people. To weaken our race they have forced us to use opium and alcohol.

In the fields of economics, they have fleeced us to the backbone, impoverished our people, and devastated our land.

They have robbed us of our rice fields, our mines, our forests, and our raw materials. They have monopolised the issuing of bank-notes and the export trade.

They have invented numerous unjustifiable taxes and reduced our people, especially our peasantry, to a state of extreme poverty.

They have hampered the prospering of our national bourgeoisie; they have mercilessly exploited our workers.

In the autumn of 1940, when the Japanese Fascists violated Indochina's territory to establish new bases in their fight against the Allies, the French imperialists went down on their bended knees and handed over our country to them.

Thus, from that date, our people were subjected to the double yoke of the French and the Japanese. Their sufferings and miseries increased. The result was that from the end of last year to the beginning of this year, from Quang Tri province to the North of Vietnam, more than two million of our fellow-citizens died from starvation. On March 9, the French troops were disarmed by the Japanese. The French colonialists either fled or surrendered, showing that not only were they incapable of "protecting" us, but that, in the span of five years, they had twice sold our country to the Japanese.

On several occasions before March 9, the Vietminh League urged the French to ally themselves with it against the Japanese. Instead of agreeing to this proposal, the French colonialists so intensified their terrorist activities against the Vietminh members that before fleeing they massacred a great number of our political prisoners detained at Yen Bay and Cao Bang.

Not withstanding all this, our fellow-citizens have always manifested toward the French a tolerant and humane attitude. Even after the Japanese putsch of March 1945, the Vietminh League helped many Frenchmen to cross the frontier, rescued some of them from Japanese jails, and protected French lives and property.

From the autumn of 1940, our country had in fact ceased to be a French colony and had become a Japanese possession.

After the Japanese had surrendered to the Allies, our whole people rose to regain our national sovereignty and to found the Democratic Republic of Vietnam.

The truth is that we have wrested our independence from the Japanese and not from the French

The French have fled, the Japanese have capitulated, Emperor Bao Dai has abdicated. Our people have broken the chains which for nearly a century have fettered them and have won independence for the Fatherland. Our people at the same time have overthrown the monarchic regime that has reigned supreme for dozens of centuries. In its place has been established the present Democratic Republic.

For these reasons, we, members of the Provisional Government, representing the whole Vietnamese people, declare that from now on we break off all relations of a colonial character with France; we repeal all the international obligation that France has so far subscribed to on behalf of Vietnam and we abolish all the special rights the French have unlawfully acquired in our Fatherland.

The whole Vietnamese people, animated by a common purpose, are determined to fight to the bitter end against any attempt by the French colonialists to reconquer their country.

We are convinced that the Allied nations which at Tehran and San Francisco have acknowledged the principles of self-determination and equality of nations, will not refuse to acknowledge the independence of Vietnam.

A people who have courageously opposed French domination for more than eighty years, a people who have fought side by side with the Allies against the Fascists during these last years, such a people must be free and independent.

For these reasons, we, members of the Provisional Government of the Democratic Republic of Vietnam, solemnly declare to the world that Vietnam has the right to be a free and independent country—and in fact it is so already. The entire Vietnamese people are determined to mobilise all their physical and mental strength, to sacrifice their lives and property in order to safeguard their independence and liberty.

Source: Ho Chi Minh, Selected Works. Hanoi: Foreign Languages Publishing House, 1977.

The French Union (1946)

It was often said that while the British believed their colonial subjects never should—or, indeed, could— become Englishmen, the French insisted theirs must become Frenchmen. While Britain in the immediate postwar years began preparing itself for the dissolution of its empire, France redoubled its efforts to maintain the integrity of its empire. The French Union—established under the Fourth Republic's constitution in 1946—attempted to do this, by offering limited local self-government within a global French state.

Preamble

France shall form with the people of her Overseas Territories a Union based upon equality of rights and privileges, without distinction as to race or religion.

The French Union shall be composed of nations and peoples who shall place in common or coordinate their resources and their efforts in order to develop their respective civilizations, further their well-being, and ensure their security.

Faithful to her traditional mission, France shall guide the peoples for whom she has assumed responsibility, toward freedom to govern themselves and toward the democratic administration of their own affairs; rejecting any system of colonization based upon arbitrary power, she shall guarantee to all equal access to public office and the individual or collective exercise of the rights and liberties . . .

THE FRENCH UNION
Section I—Principles

ARTICLE 60. The French Union shall be composed, on the one hand, of the French Republic which comprises Metropolitan France and the Overseas Departments and Territories, and, on the other hand, of the Associated Territories and States.

ARTICLE 61. The position of the Associated States within the French Union shall, in the case of each individual State, depend upon the Act that defines its relationship to France.

ARTICLE 62. The members of the French Union shall place all their resources so as to guarantee the defense of the whole Union. The Government of the Republic shall coordinate these resources and direct such policies as will prepare and ensure this defense.

Section II—Organization

ARTICLE 63. The central organs of the French Union shall be: the President, the High Council and the Assembly.

ARTICLE 64. The President of the French Republic shall be the President of the French Union; he shall represent its permanent interests.

ARTICLE 65. The High Council of the French Union, under the chairmanship of the President of the Union, shall be composed of a delegation of the French Government and of the representatives that each Associated State shall accredit to the President of the Union. . . .

ARTICLE 66. The Assembly of the French Union shall be composed half of members representing Metropolitan France and half of members representing the Overseas Departments and Territories and the Associated States. An organic law shall determine the mode of representation of the different sections of the population.

ARTICLE 67. The members of the Assembly of the Union shall be elected by the Territorial Assemblies for the Overseas Departments and Territories; for Metropolitan France, two thirds shall be elected by the National Assembly representing Metropolitan France and one third by the Council of the Republic also representing Metropolitan France.

ARTICLE 68. The Associated States may appoint delegates to the Assembly of the French Union within the limitations and conditions determined by a law and by an act individual to each State.

ARTICLE 69. The President of the French Union shall convoke the Assembly of the French Union and shall close its sessions. He must convene it upon the request of half of its members. The Assembly of the Union may not sit during recesses of Parliament. . . .

ARTICLE 71. The Assembly of the French Union shall examine the bills or proposals submitted to it by the National Assembly or the Government of the French Republic or the Governments of the Associated States, in order that it may give its opinion thereof. The Assembly shall be empowered to express its opinion on resolutions proposed by one of its members and, if these resolutions are accepted for deliberation, to instruct its Secretariat to send them to the National Assembly. It may submit proposals to the French Government and to the High Council of the French Union. . . .

ARTICLE 72. Legislative powers with regard to penal law, civil liberties, and political and administrative organization in the Overseas Territories, shall rest with Parliament. In all other matters, the French law shall be applicable in the Overseas Territories only by an express provision to that effect, or if it has been extended to the Overseas Territories by decree, after consultation with the Assembly of the Union . . . Special provisions for each Territory may be enacted by the President of the Republic in the Council of Ministers, after preliminary consultation with the Assembly of the Union.

Section III—The Overseas Departments and Territories

ARTICLE 73. The legislative regime of the Overseas Departments shall be the same as that of the Departments of Metropolitan France, save for exceptions determined by law.

ARTICLE 74. The Overseas Territories shall be granted a special statute which takes into account their particular interests with relation to the general interests of the Republic. This statute and the internal organization of each Overseas Territory or group of Territories shall be determined by law after the Assembly of the French Union has expressed its opinion thereon, and after consultation with the Territorial Assemblies.

ARTICLE 75. The status of the respective members of the French Republic and of the French Union shall be subject to change. Modifications of status and passage from one category to another within the framework established in Article 60 may take place only as the result of a law passed by Parliament, after consultation with the Territorial Assemblies and the Assembly of the Union.

ARTICLE 76. The representative of the Government in each Territory or group of Territories shall be vested with the powers of the Republic. He shall be the administrative head of the Territory. He shall be responsible to the Government for his actions.

ARTICLE 77. An elective Assembly shall be instituted in each Territory. The electoral regime, composition and powers of this Assembly shall be determined by law.

ARTICLE 78. In the groups of territories, the management of matters of common interest shall be entrusted to an Assembly composed of members elected by the Territorial Assemblies.

ARTICLE 79. The Overseas Territories shall elect representatives to the National Assembly and to the Council of the Republic under condition determined by law.

ARTICLE 80. All subjects of the Overseas Territories shall be citizens with the same status as French nationals of Metropolitan France or of the Overseas Territories. Special laws shall determine the conditions under which they may exercise their rights as citizens.

ARTICLE 81. All French nationals and subjects of the French Union shall have the status of citizens of the French Union, and thereby they shall be ensured the enjoyment of the rights and liberties guaranteed by the Preamble of the present Constitution.

Source: Constitution of the French (Fourth) Republic. Paris, 1946.

Gaston C. F. Monnerville Presents Point of View of French Colonials (1946)

A new constitution—laying out France's relationship with its colonies—was submitted to and eventually passed by voters shortly after the end of World War II. Part of this constitutional process included an extensive debate. In this speech to the French National Assembly, a French colonist in New Guinea, Gaston C. F. Monnerville, offers the perspective of overseas Frenchmen. Monnerville defends his fellow colonialists against charges that they are secession-minded. Instead, he says they want to be treated as equals within the French Community of nations.

We representatives of the native populations have had anxiety and a desire. . . . We have thought that it was our duty to warn the Assembly against decisions that might appear to run counter to the secular traditions of France, to the thinking of the French masses, and to the aspirations of the peoples overseas.

Many times we have taken the responsibility of examining the problem. Fears were immediately aroused. We have been described in terms that were not always courteous—especially by the press—in terms even injurious to us, because it is an insult for a Frenchman to be treated as a disgraceful separatist.

We are accused of encouraging secession because we think daily about certain difficult problems, many times unhappy and often tragic problems.

Those who have spoken to us have shown that this problem is a particularly complex one, that it is exceedingly difficult to resolve, and that it is perhaps unwise and unreasonable to wish to treat it uniformly by a text that sets up no differentiations. . . .

Much too often we hear it said here or outside these walls: What do these colonials finally want? They set up perpetual demands. What do they wish? If they make demands it is perhaps because we have promised them too much and have given them too much. . . .

We have the right to say with a completely free spirit that obviously all is not perfect and that all has not been done. This is human. Above all do not consider us to be inconsistent, a class of infants who talk irresponsibly about these matters. Too often one has the attitude when speaking of overseas natives of considering them a little emotional, but also as a bit infantile in their thinking. The speeches that we make from this podium are not solely the expression of an elite among us. Believe me, they are the expression of the thinking of our peoples. . . .

I had the very great honor in January 1946 of being among the delegates of France to the Assembly of the United Nations. In the name of France and in accord with her government I made similar speeches before 51 nations. The government approved those speeches. When there was a question of defining the situation of the overseas peoples in the French family, in the French community, when certain foreign nations intimated that the peoples of the overseas territories wish to leave that community because the French Republic apparently did not wish to promote their political and social evolution, I replied in the name of France: "No! The tradition of France has always been one of not distinguishing among men according to their race, creed, or color." She makes no distinction among men according to the latitude in which they were born. She distinguishes among them solely according to their merits and according to what they are able to contribute to human progress!

We know full well that there are men, even Frenchmen, in the overseas territory who do not remain faithful to that French tradition. But we would be the last to say that all France is like them. . . .

Instead of thinking of leaving France, of separating from her, [the overseas French] have no other desire than to enter more quickly into the French community, to be full citizens, because they know that the more quickly they do this the more they are working for humanity.

Colonization . . . may be considered from a certain angle as work which has grandeur in the sense that certain nations having the sense of colonization are permitted to give a fraternal hand to other peoples. . . . It also has from another angle what one may call the burden of the colonizer, that is to say obligations.

We do not speak here solely of rights but also of duties. All the preceding speakers have noted . . . that the overseas peoples never escape from their duties, whatever they might be. . . .

Do the examples offered you by the territories represented by natives seem so bad that you fear for the future? Is the example given us by Africa and the old colonies such that you fear that the future representatives of these territories may chase out the French and European who live there? . . .

The process of colonization is ended. No one supports colonization any longer . . . Make something new. Do not patch up. To make a French Union means to show the overseas population that you want to act with courage and loyalty.

The democrats of 1848 showed that they had faith in the men they liberated. They were not deceived. Let the democrats of 1946 show the same faith in the perfectibility of man . . .

Source: Monnerville, Gaston C. F. Speech in the National Constituent Assembly, 2d Session, September 18, 1946, *Journal Officiel des Débats de l'Assemblée Constituante* (1946).

Proclamation of the Algerian National Front, National Liberation Front (November 1954)

From 1830 through 1962, the French ruled over Algeria. The colony's proximity to France and the Mediterranean climate of its coastal regions enticed colonists from France and other southern European countries. By the early 1950s, these colons represented about one-tenth of Algeria's 10-million-strong population. Although a small minority, they owned most of the fertile land and industry and utterly dominated the colonial government. Native Algerians were treated as second-class citizens in their own land. After years of political agitation, Algerian nationalists formed the National Liberation Front (FLN, its French acronym) and launched military operations against the French in 1954. This initial proclamation makes clear the central demand of the FLN: total independence for Algeria.

After decades of struggle, the National Movement has reached its final phase of fulfilment. At home, the people are united behind the watchwords of independence and action. Abroad, the atmosphere is favourable, especially with the diplomatic support of our Arab and Moslem brothers. Our National Movement, prostrated by years of immobility and routine, badly directed was disintegrating little by little. Faced with this situation, a youthful group, gathering about it the majority of wholesome and resolute elements, judged that the moment had come to take the National Movement out of the impasse into which it had been forced by the conflicts of persons and of influence and to launch it into the true revolutionary struggle at the side of the Moroccan and Tunisian brothers. We are independent of the two factions that are vying for power Our movement gives to compatriots of every social position, to all the purely Algerian parties and movements, the possibility of joining in the liberation struggle.

GOAL. National independence through:

1) the restoration of the Algerian state, sovereign, democratic, and social, within the framework of the principles of Islam;

2) the preservation of a fundamental freedoms, without distinction of race or religion.

INTERNAL Objective Political house-cleaning through the destruction of the last vestiges of corruption and reformism

EXTERNAL Objectives:

1) The internationalization of the Algerian problem;

2) The pursuit of North African unity in its national Arabo-Islamic context;

3) The assertion, through United Nations channels, of our active sympathy toward all nations that may support our liberating action.

MEANS OF STRUGGLE: Struggle by every means until our goal is attained. Exertion at home and abroad through political and direct action, with a view to making the Algerian problem a reality for the entire world. The struggle will be long, but the outcome is certain. To limit the bloodshed, we propose an honourable platform for discussion with the French authorities:

1. The opening of negotiations with the authorized spokesmen the Algerian people, on the basis of a recognition of Algerian sovereignty, one and indivisible.

2. The inception of an atmosphere of confidence brought about freeing all those who are detained, by annulling all measures exception, and by ending all legal action against the combatant forces.

3. The recognition of Algerian nationhood by an official declaration abrogating all edicts, decrees, and laws by virtue of which Algeria was "French soil."

In return for which:

1. French cultural and economic interests will be respected, as well as persons and families.

2. All French citizens desiring to remain in Algeria will be allowed to opt for their original nationality, in which case they will be considered as foreigners, or for Algerian nationality, in which case they will be considered as Algerians, equal both as to rights and as to duties.

3. The ties between France and Algeria will be the object of agreement between the two Powers on the basis of equality and mutual respect.

Algerians: The F.L.N. is your front; its victory is your victory. For our part, strong in your support, we shall give the best of ourselves to the Fatherland.

Loi-Cadre (June 23, 1956)

The 1956 Loi-Cadre laid the foundation for the French Community. Like the British, with their Commonwealth, the French hoped to retain a say in the affairs of their former colonies in Asia and Africa after independence. Even more than the Commonwealth, the French Community, which replaced the French Union of 1946, was a more centralized association. While the colonies would govern themselves, Paris would retain control over collective foreign policy, defense, economic and financial policy, policy on strategic raw materials, supervision of courts, higher education, and communications. As it was seen by former colonies as a continuation of imperial rule in another guise, the French Community has become largely defunct, though it has never been formally abolished.

Authorizing the French Government to Carry out the Reforms and Take the Measures Calculated to Ensure the Development of the Territories under the Jurisdiction of the Ministry of France Overseas

Article First. Without prejudice to the expected reform of Title VIII of the Constitution, in order to give the overseas peoples a more direct share in the management of their own interests, measures of administrative decentralization and devolution shall be introduced within the territories, groups of territories and central services under the jurisdiction of the Ministry of France Overseas.

To this end, decrees taken . . . on the basis of the report given by the Minister of France Overseas and, on occasion, by the Ministers concerned, may:

1) Modify the role and powers of administration and management of the general governments with a view to transforming them into coordinating bodies, and modify the composition and attributes of the grand councils and of the representative assembly of Madagascar;

2) Institute government councils in all the territories and in addition, in Madagascar, provincial councils charged, in particular, with administering the territorial services;

3) Grant broadened deliberative powers, notably for the organization and management of the territorial services, to the assemblies of the territories as well as to the representative assembly and provincial assemblies of Madagascar, regarding the exercise of their attributes, which shall be defined in tile decrees to be introduced, and when the decrees taken in pursuance of the present article shall authorize them to do so, the assemblies may abrogate or modify any regulatory text governing matters which fall under said attributes;

4) Determine the conditions of the institution and functioning, as well as the attributes of the councils in the administrative circumscriptions and rural communities, and the modalities of granting legal status to these circumscriptions, without this impeding in any way the establishment of new municipalities.

The decrees taken in pursuance of the present article may modify, abrogate or revive in the form of regulations existing legislative provisions . . .

Article 3. The Government may, by decree taken in the Council of Ministers on the basis of the report given by the Minister of France Overseas and, on occasion, by the Ministers concerned, and after consultation with the Council of State, inaugurate a reform of the public services charged with managing the interests of the State and, on the other hand, the territorial services charged with managing the interests of the territories, as well as the division of attributes between those services. The purpose of this reform shall be:

On the one hand, to facilitate the access of native-born civil servants to all ranks in the administration;

On the other hand, to institute independent regulations pertaining to the civil service overseas, as far as the territorial services are concerned. . . .

Article 4. The Government may, in the manner stipulated in Article 3 above, without interfering in any way with Law No. 46—860 of April 30, 1946 and the legislative provisions referring to it, take all measures intended to raise the standard of living in the territories under the jurisdiction of the Ministry of France Overseas, to promote economic development and social progress and to facilitate economic and financial cooperation between Metropolitan France and those territories, especially:

By generalizing and standardizing education;

By organizing and supporting the production of goods necessary to the economic equilibrium of the territories and to the needs of the franc area;

By inaugurating modern methods of rural development and establishing a cadastral plan in which the customary rights of the autochthones will be respected;

By setting up and enforcing the registration of births, marriages and deaths;

By setting up suitable structures in the field of credit and savings;

By effecting all modifications, in matters of financial law and regulations, calculated to promote private investment overseas, without derogating in any way from the prerogatives of the territorial assemblies;

By taking all measures calculated to ensure a successful social program,

The Government must make all useful arrangements to ensure on a permanent basis and at the level of the presidency of the council the coordination of economic and financial measures concerning the Metropolitan Overseas complex . . .

Article 10. In the territories under the jurisdiction of the Ministry of France Overseas, elections to the National Assembly, to the territorial assemblies, to the provincial assemblies of Madagascar, to the circumscription councils and to the municipal assemblies shall be held on the basis of universal suffrage of citizens of both sexes, without regard to their personal status, who are twenty-one years of age or over, who are regularly inscribed on the election rolls and who are not disqualified for any reason stipulated by law . . .

Article 12. The election of members of the National Assembly, members of the Council of the Republic, members of the territorial assemblies, members of the representative assembly and the provincial assemblies of Madagascar, of the circumscription councils, and also members of the municipal assemblies of the fully organized communes, the semi-organized communes and the mixed communes shall be by a single electoral college.

Source: Loi-Cadre, 1956, English translation provided by the French Press and Information Service, New York.

Charles de Gaulle: Speech at Constantine, Algeria (October 3, 1958)

In 1954, the National Liberation Front (FLN, its French acronym) of Algeria launched its eight-year war for national independence. Four years later, the Fourth Republic of France collapsed over its inability to end the war and reconcile the interests of French colonists, or colons, *and native Algerians, bringing World War II leader Charles de Gaulle to the helm of the French state with a mandate to end the war. Within a few months, de Gaulle made his landmark speech at Constantine, French Algeria, offering self-determination to Algerians. But the unwillingness of the* colons *to share power prolonged the war another four years, resulting in the victory of the FLN and the flight of the nearly one million* colons.

Last Sunday, three and a half million men and women of Algeria, without distinction of community, in complete equality, gave France and myself their vote of confidence. They did this quite simply without any constraint and in spite of the threats that certain fanatics brought to bear against them, their families and their property. This is a fact, as clear as the bright light of day. And this fact is fundamental not only because it mutually and forever pledges, one to the other, Algeria and France, but also because it ties in with what happened that same day in Metropolitan France, in the Overseas Departments, in the Territories of the Community.

The least that can be said of this great demonstration is that the French people proved to themselves and to the entire world their determination for renovation, and that, at the same time, a hundred million men decided to build their future together in Liberty, Equality and Fraternity.

With regard to Algeria, what is the future to which France is calling her? Women and men of Algeria, I have come here to tell you what it is.

What must be achieved is the basic transformation of this country, so brave, so alive, but also so full of difficulties and suffering. This means that it is necessary for the living conditions of each man and woman to improve from day to day. This means that, for the benefit of the inhabitants, the resources of the earth and the ability of the elites must be brought to light and developed. This means that children must be taught. This means that all Algeria must have her share in what modern civilization can and must bring to men in terms of well-being and dignity.

But the loftiest plans call for practical measures. Here are the measures that my Government intends to take in the near future covering the next five years by virtue of the full powers that the new Constitution has just conferred upon it.

During these five years, of the young people in Metropolitan France—yes, I say in Metropolitan France—that enter the service of the State, in the Administration, in the Army, in education and in the public services, at least a tenth of these young people must be recruited from the Arab, the Kabyle and Mozabite communities, and that without prejudice to an increased proportion of Algerians serving in Algeria.

In the course of these five years, salaries and wages in Algeria will be raised to a level comparable to what they are in Metropolitan France.

Before the end of these five years, 250,000 hectares [617,500 acres] of new land will be allotted to Moslem farmers.

Before the end of these five years, the first phase of the plan for the agricultural and industrial development of Algeria will be brought to its conclusion. This phase includes, in particular, the delivery and the distribution of the oil and gas of the Sahara, the setting up, on this soil, of great metallurgical and chemical complexes, the construction of housing for a million people, the corresponding development of health services, of roads, ports, means of communication—in short, the regular employment of 400,000 new workers.

Gradually in the course of these five years, two-thirds of the girls and boys will be enrolled in school and, during the three years after that, complete school enrollment of all Algerian youth will be achieved.

During these five years, the human contact that has been made especially by the French Army—by its career officers, its reserve officers, its fighting men, its young conscripts—will be continued and developed and, in Metropolitan France, the same must be true, in Paris and in our provinces.

What will be the political consequences of this evolution which calls for very extensive and prolonged efforts? I believe it is quite useless to freeze in advance, in words, that which, in any event, is going to take shape, little by little, as it is under-

taken. But, in any case, two things are certain as of now: the first concerns the present.

In two months, Algeria will elect her representatives under the same conditions as will Metropolitan France. But at least two thirds of her representatives will have to be Moslem citizens.

The other refers to the future. The future of Algeria will in any event—because that is the nature of things—be built on a double foundation: her personality and her close solidarity with Metropolitan France.

In any case, it is absolutely essential that this fruitful transformation be accomplished. This is necessary for the good of the men of Algeria, for the good of the women, for the good of the children who live here; but it is also necessary for the honor of mankind. It is necessary for the peace of the world. For no one has any interest in the stagnation of a people, except the kind of people, who, to serve their ambitions, gamble on the spirit of revolt and the poverty of others.

This transformation, this immense political, economic, social and cultural task—who could effect this transformation, if not France?

Now it happens that France has the will and the means to do so. It also happens that the vote of the Algerians has just proved that they desire this transformation and that it should be carried out with France.

Therefore, turning toward those who are prolonging a fratricidal conflict, who are organizing lamentable attacks in Metropolitan France, or who are spreading through the chancelleries, through underground dens, by means of the radios and the newspapers of certain foreign capitals—vilifications of France, to those I say: Why kill? We must enable people to live. Why destroy? Our duty is to build. Why hate? We must cooperate.

Stop this absurd fighting and you will at once see a new blossoming of hope over all the land of Algeria. You will see the prisons emptying; you will see the opening up of a future big enough for everybody, and for you yourselves in particular. And then, speaking to those States which are throwing oil on the fire here while their unhappy peoples writhe under dictatorships, I say: Could you do what France is in a position to do here, what only France is capable of doing? Could you people do it? No. Then let France carry on, unless you deliberately decide to envenom the conflict in order to distract attention from your own difficulties. But in the present state of the world, where can these bitter incitements lead if not to a universal cataclysm? Only two paths lie open to the human race today: war or brotherhood. In Algeria as everywhere, France, for her part, has chosen brotherhood.

Long live the Republic! Long live Algeria and long live France!

Source: De Gaulle, Charles. Speech at Constantine, October 3, 1958. Information Service of the French Embassy, New York.

Ferhat Abbas Proclaims the Historical Phenomenon of Decolonization While Demanding Algerian Independence (1960)

On November 1, 1954, the National Liberation Front of Algeria (FLN) launched its military campaign for national independence from French colonizers. But the FLN was also engaged in a war of ideas and words. While Paris claimed that it had built a modern economy in Algeria, Ferhat Abbas, premier of the provisional government of the Algerian Republic established by the FLN in neighboring Tunisia, claimed that few of its benefits filtered down to native Algerian Muslims, who represented 90 percent of the colony's population. The other 10 percent consisted of French and European settlers, or colons, whose presence was a major reason the French proved unwilling to give in to Algerian demands for independence.

People of Algeria,

Tomorrow, November 1, 1960, the war in Algeria will enter its seventh year. The fight for liberty and independence will continue with its inevitable wake of suffering and sacrifice.

A great deal has been said and written about the war in Algeria. Never will its unjust nature, its horrors, its crimes be sufficiently denounced. With this war of colonial reconquest, designed to perpetuate French domination over an Arab and African country, imperialism has plundered, wrought terror and famine its principal arms in the attempt to bring our people to their knees.

When history takes stock of the atrocities committed by the French army during the six years of war, the French people and the civilized world will be astounded. They will know the exact nature and the monstrous price of "pacification."

The truth of the matter is that beginning with the slaughter of the El-Ouafia tribe by General de Rovigo in 1832, from the smoking-out operations in the Dahra, ordered by Bugeaud and executed by Pelissier, until the use of torture, "crimes of escape," "wood-chopping details," the napalm bombardments commanded by the Massu's and the Salan's, colonialism has maintained the same face. Its language may vary. Neither its methods nor its aspect change.

The colonial regime is the very negation of justice and law. It is useless to think that what was usurped by force can be restored other than by force. Imperialism has never given liberty to its victims as a gift. As I have said, independence is not offered, it is obtained by force.

The Algerian problem was only imposed upon the colonialists the day the Army of National Liberation imposed itself on the adversary. Who would dare deny this?

The single electoral body, the alleged equality of Algerians before the law, the supposed advancement of Arab mayors and "elected officials," the formal recognition of the right of the Algerian people to self-determination were all envisaged only because our people took up arms, and also with the ulterior motive of diverting us from our primary objective which is independence.

I spoke of self-determination. There is need to reiterate that the declaration of September 16, 1959 could have constituted the basis for a peaceful solution of the conflict. 1960 could have been the year of peace.

In this respect, it is fitting to sum up the situation and to establish the responsibilities.

As concerns the Provisional Government of the Algerian Republic, no efforts have been spared to reach a just and peaceful solution. Following our reply to the September 16th speech, I went to see His Majesty Mohammed V. We had occasion to make it known that we were ready to send a delegation to Paris provided that the meeting was prepared through diplomatic channels and not by public statements subject to varying interpretations. This mission failed.

On November 20, 1959 we publicly named our negotiators to discuss the guarantees and conditions of the implementation of self-determination. Our imprisoned brothers were not found acceptable on the pretext that they were in prison and out of the fight. But the entire Algerian people is imprisoned. No one is free in Algeria. It is precisely in order to free our people that negotiation is called for. And what better negotiators could we have named than those who were among the first to enter the fight?

Once again, after the uprising of the ultras on January 24, we had a request put to the President of the French Republic, in February, to determine whether he was prepared to receive one of our emissaries carrying a personal message which I proposed to send to him.

We met with a third refusal, even more meaningful than its predecessors, because in reply to our offers of a secret meeting we were answered by the bellicose speeches to the French army in the field (*discours des popotes*) of March, 1960.

A fourth refusal awaited us:

Following General de Gaulle's declaration of June 14, we felt that the tone of the French Chief of State had changed and that there was something more serious to his invitation. So despite all that separated his position from ours, we decided to embark on a "goodwill operation," in the belief that the human contact would produce better results than public statements.

But at Melun, the French Government made it clear to our emissaries that, for it, negotiation meant out and out surrender. It therefore put an end, once and for all, to a negotiated settlement of the conflict.

The capitulation which the French Government attempts in vain to obtain through alleged negotiations on a cease-fire is madness. We only took up arms as a last resort, when all peaceful means were found to be unworkable. We are not going to lay them down on the basis of vague promises of a self-determination whose implementation is entrusted to an army, an administration and a police which condemns the very principle of self-determination. That would be to betray our dead, our martyrs and our flag. It would mean condemning our country to a neo-colonialism as pernicious as the former.

Those who are counting on our defeat and those who speculate on our lassitude are making a mistake. To be or not to be, to live as an African people, free and independent, or to remain a multitude of slaves—confronted with this alternative, our choice is clear.

The juridical quibbling of the imperialists and the threat of genocide, which a French army in search of prestige hangs over the heads of our people, will not win out over our will, our obstinate will to assert ourselves as Algerians, as people of the Maghreb and to make Algeria a free and independent country like the other countries of Africa.

During the period when Robert Lacoste became the spokesman for the fascist generals and the ultras, he said in Oran that he only needed to reinstate the "scorched earth" strategy used by his compatriot from Perigord, Bugeaud, in order to triumph over our revolution.

There is no doubt that such methods are criminal and inhuman because they strike the innocent civilian population primarily. But colonial criminality is no longer sufficient for its own survival. It finished by triumphing over our ancestors because they were isolated. From 1830 to 1871 they fought ceaselessly, but they momentarily succumbed because they were alone for forty years against a rich nation and one of the biggest armies in the world.

Today, the circumstances of our struggle have changed. While French imperialism is increasingly disapproved of and isolated, we receive messages of sympathy and tangible proofs of active solidarity from all over the world.

As dawn breaks on the seventh year of war, the international juncture is not unfavorable to us. At the United Nations, the Algerian question is posed in clearer terms this year. We hope that this international body will finally assume its responsibilities.

The various trips of governmental delegations to China, to the Soviet Union have been crowned with success. Our Government has been recognized by the great Union of Soviet Socialist Republics. This recognition will have wide repercussions. The support of the socialist camp is henceforth behind us. This is a source of satisfaction to us and we willingly leave to certain Westerners the hypocritical waving of the banner of anti-communism.

Our Arab brothers stand beside us and assure us of their support.

The era of colonization is over. This year, rightly called the African Year, has seen 15 brother countries make their entry into the family of nations.

This historical phenomenon of de-colonization and of the achievement of an authentic national life is irresistible. It is the result of a long battle to which the Algerian people is conscious of having greatly contributed.

Our African brothers know that in the Algerian war, French imperialism wants to impose a myth, while the Algerian people are defending a reality. The Algerian people, which is an African people, is fighting for its freedom and its independence. We are convinced that whatever happens, the African peoples who have waged the same battle will continue to show their solidarity for our cause.

Public opinion in Europe and in South America is more and more sensitive to the struggle of the Algerian people. All those who have fought for freedom identify our struggle with theirs. Even in France, the French people, more and more conscious of their responsibilities, denounce the war of colonial reconquest and vigorously demand peace in Algeria. We salute that French youth, those workers, intellectuals and all those fighting against the continuation of the war in our country.

Everywhere in the world the forces of peace are regrouping themselves.

These are comforting realities. But more than anything else, the unity and the vigilance of our people and the combativeness and the valor of our Army of National Liberation remain the unflinching armor against which the colonialist conspiracies and the hate of certain French soldiers will be shattered.

The Algerian combatants have well merited their home and country. Their courage, their heroism, their abnegation have become legendary. They call forth the world's admiration.

People of Algeria,

Despite all these favorable and encouraging factors, our task still remains difficult. Our responsibilities are heavy. Our adversary has not exhausted his reserve of ruses and manoeuvres. Equivocations and ambiguities are, in his hands, formidable weapons. To the weight of an army of more than 800,000 men which does not recoil before any means to attempt to humiliate and destroy us, must be added the promises that the French Government knows full well it cannot keep.

Let us speak frankly. Self-determination presupposes a free referendum. This freedom would be illusory if the French army controlled and organized the consultation by terrorizing the population.

Free choice signifies the freedom to determine one's own destiny and not the limitation of that choice to the furthering of a chopped-up Algerian State, deprived of most of its essential attributes, partitioned into several groupings, with its Saharan sector amputated, as General de Gaulle's "Algerian Algeria" would have it.

The Algeria for which the people are fighting is an independent and fully sovereign Algeria. This means an Algeria where all the inhabitants will enjoy fully and completely their rights as citizens without regard to their origins.

Have those who, by puerile camouflages, still attempt to have prevail the false solution of an imposed status learned nothing then? Have they already forgotten the smarting failure of the Bao Dai experience, when they wanted to impose an executive against the Vietnamese people?

The war in Algeria is a fight for freedom. The Algerian people which has suffered colonial domination for more than 130 years, which has shed its blood generously for the last six years, is conscious of the price of its struggle. It is aware of the occult forces which lust after the riches of its soil. The policy of the lie and of dupery will no longer affect it. All the Algerian people, men and women, children and old people, are aware of colonial realities.

And so the people will continue their struggle until victory, that is, until the liberation of Algeria and the construction of the Arab Maghreb.

LONG LIVE THE ALGERIAN REPUBLIC,
LONG LIVE ALGERIAN INDEPENDENCE.

Source: National Liberation Front, Algerian Office, New York, 1960.

GERMAN EMPIRE

Otto von Bismarck: Speech to the Reichstag on German Colonial Policy (June 26, 1884)

More than any other individual, Otto von Bismarck was responsible for the unification of the German Reich in the 1870s. Unlike many of his fellow German nationalists, Bismarck was highly skeptical of the colonial enterprise, seeing it as a waste of resources. By the 1880s, however, the "iron chancellor" had come around to support the idea of a German Empire, as this official summary of his June 26, 1884, speech to the Reichstag, or German parliament, indicates.

On the question of the relationship between the steamship proposals and overseas policies, the Reich Chancellor had the following to say:

He has himself expressed earlier, and still retains, the view that it would not be right for us to occupy tracts of land where we have no interests, merely to stimulate artificially German emigration, have the area controlled by German officials, and erect garrisons there. We do not possess properly trained officials for this purpose; that would be too expensive for us and would tax our navy too much. Moreover, our navy has been limited through our small expansion and a resultant weak seagoing population, whose low wages have impelled many of them to seek service with the English and Americans. It is something else again to place under the protection of the German Reich the free settlements of citizens of the Reich in areas which are not under the recognized sovereignty of other nations. The Chancellor holds it to be a duty of the Reich to place under her protection such settlements overseas by citizens of the Reich, not only their factories but also the territory acquired by them. Even here the usefulness of the procedure cannot be predicted on the theoretical basis, but one can await the experiences of other nations in this respect.

Source: *Norddeutsche Allgemeine Zeitung* 43 (1884).

Charter of Protection Granted by William II to the German Colonization Society (February 17, 1885)

Often, in the course of imperial expansion, it was private interests that led the way, forcing governments to respond. Such was the case with Carl Peters and his German East African Company. In 1884, Peters and the company signed numerous treaties with chiefs in East Africa. Chancellor Otto von Bismarck, at first opposed to the venture, was soon forced to advise Kaiser William II to provide a Charter of Protection, thereby setting Germany on course toward its colonial empire in what is now Tanzania, Rwanda, Burundi, Southwest Africa (now Namibia), and a number of Pacific islands.

His Majesty the Emperor has been graciously pleased to address the following Imperial "Charter of Protection" to the Society for German Colonization for their territorial acquisitions in East Africa:—

"We, William, by the Grace of God, German Emperor, King of Prussia, make known and ordain as follows:—

The present Presidents of the Society for German Colonization, Dr. Carl Peters, and our Chamberlain Felix, Count Behr-Bandelin, having sought our protection for the territorial acquisitions of the Society in East Africa, west of the Empire of the Sultan of Zanzibar, and outside of the suzerainty of other Powers, and the Treaties lately concluded by the said Dr. Carl Peters with the Rulers of Usagara, Nguru, Useguha, and Ukami in November and December last, by which these territories have been ceded to him for the German Colonial Society with sovereign rights over the same, having been laid before us, with the Petition to place these territories under our suzerainty, we hereby declare that we have accepted the suzerainty, and have placed under our Imperial protection the territories in question, reserving to ourselves a right of deciding hereafter respecting any further acquisitions in the same district which may be proved to have been obtained by legal contract by the Society or by their legitimate successors.

We grant unto the said Society, on the condition that it remains German, and that the members of the Board of Directors or other persons entrusted with its management are subjects of the German Empire, as well as to the legitimate successors of this Society under the same conditions, the authority to exercise all rights arising from the Treaties submitted to us, including that of jurisdiction over both the natives and the subjects of Germany and of other nations established in those territories, or sojourning there for commercial or other purposes, under the superintendence of our Government, subject to further regulations to be issued by us, and supplementary additions to this, our Charter of Protection.

In witness whereof we have with our Royal hand executed this Charter of Protection, and have caused it to be sealed with our Imperial seal.

Given at Berlin the 17th February, 1885.

v. Bismarck

Hertslet, Edward. *Map of Africa by Treaty.* 3d ed. London, 1909, 2: 303–304.

Program of the Pan-German League (1890–1898)

The Pan-German philosophy had several components, including the call for the unification of all German-speaking peoples of Europe within a single German state and the establishment of colonies outside of Europe for the settlement of German peoples overseas. In this series of documents of the Pan-German League—the main organization promoting this philosophy—the writers argue that Germany must become more aggressive vis-à-vis other European states—most notably, England—or lose out in the European scramble for empire.

Germany Awake!

(Newspaper Advertisement), June 24, 1890:

The diplomacy of the English works swiftly and secretly. What they created burst in the face of the astonished world on June 18th like a bomb—the German-English African Treaty. With one stroke of the pen—the hope of a great German colonial empire was ruined! Shall this treaty really be? No, no and again no! The German people must arise as one and declare that this treaty is unacceptable! ... The treaty with England harms our interests and wounds our honor; this time it *dares* not become a reality! We are ready at the call of our Kaiser to step into the ranks and allow ourselves dumbly and obediently to be led against the enemy's shots, but we may also demand in exchange that the reward come to us which is worth the sacrifice, and this reward is: that we shall be a conquering people which takes its portion of the world itself! Deutschland wach auf!

Letter of Dr. Hugenberg, August 1, 1890

There are also still larger territories—one need only think of Central Sudan, the natural hinterland of the Cameroons, the fate of which has not as yet been settled by any treaty. He who seizes these territories quickest and holds fast the most tenaciously will possess them. Does not *everything,* and especially the slowness with which the German government moves to assert itself in colonial affairs, point to the fact that our fatherland, be it from one side or the other, will not be spared a new war if it wishes only to maintain the position which it won in 1870? The official memoir which has just appeared concerning the motives of the Anglo-German treaty, leaves no doubt but that a certain indifference to colonial expansion exists in official places. In a tone of contempt it has been said that "the period of hissing the flag and shooting at the treaty must now be ended!" Similar reverses can be prevented in the future only if foreign countries deal with a sensitive German nationalism!

Policies of the Pan-German League, 1898:

2. Laying of a cable from Kiachow [China] to Port Arthur [Dairen, in Manchuria], with connection with the Russian-Siberian cable.

3. Strengthening of the German foothold in Kiaochow.

4. German coaling and cable stations in the Red Sea, the West Indies, and near Singapore.

5. Complete possession of Samoa.

6. More subsidized German steamship lines to Kiaochow and Korea.

7. Understanding with France, Spain, Portugal, and the Netherlands about the laying of an independent cable from West Africa through the Congo to German East Africa, Madagascar, Batavia, and Tongkin to Kiaochow.

8. Development of harbor of Swakopmund [in German Southwest Africa] and railroads to Windhoek [the capital of the territory].

9. Securing of concessions for commerce and industry in Asia Minor . . .

22. Increase in the number of German consulates in the Levant, Far East, South Africa, Central & South America . . .

Source: Mildred S. Wertheimer, ed. *The Pan-German League.* New York: Columbia University Press, 1923.

Chancellor von Hohenlohe Advises William II to Take His Share of China (1895)

During the latter years of the nineteenth century, various European powers and Japan began partitioning China into "spheres of influence," areas of the Asian nation where they would enjoy special commercial and legal privileges. In this 1895 communiqué, Chancellor Prince von Hohenlohe lays out German interests in China to Kaiser William II. In the original version of the note, the Kaiser offers comments that indicate his overall agreement with his chancellor's opinions.

Berlin, March 19, 1895

. . .Conformable to the previous decision of Your Majesty, our attitude hitherto was one of strict neutrality. Even before it came to real hostilities Your Majesty's representatives in Peking and Tokyo were empowered to join in the common efforts of the other Great Powers for the peaceful settlement of differences, and later after the outbreak of hostilities we declared ourselves ready to cooperate in common measures of the Powers insofar as these were restricted to the protection of persons and property.

On the other hand, the repeated requests from England and also from China that we participate in intervention were rejected on the ground that such a step seemed premature.

The following were the essential considerations: England and Russia are especially interested in the development of things in the Far East to the extent that the former would like to see China maintained as far as possible unweakened as a buffer state to protect India against the advance of Russia and the latter does not wish to see its possible claims upon Korea, or at least upon portions of that country, prejudiced by further Japanese progress. But Germany, for the present at any rate, has not at stake any interests of like importance in Eastern Asia. German commerce especially has not suffered noticeably under war conditions. On the contrary, our manufacturers, merchants, and ship owners have had a good opportunity to make profit by supplying and transporting war materials. With our participation in the intervention undertaken by England and Russia merely for the restoration of peace, we would serve the interests of those States and indeed probably with considerable sacrifice for us, for it is obvious that against a victorious Japan only an armed intervention or at least the display of preponderant forces upon the theater of war would offer prospect of success.

It already follows from these considerations that our attitude would be altered if there were a prospect of special advantages as compensation for the sacrifices on our part. And indeed the gaining of several places on the Chinese coast might be considered as such an advantage of first rate importance, which could serve as points of support for the navy and for our commerce, a need which has already been felt for some decades.

Naturally it cannot be the affair of Germany, relatively the least directly interested, to come forward with claims of this sort and thereby give a signal to a certain extent for the first partition of the Chinese Empire. Rather we should have to wait until other powers set about to realize similar purposes.

Whether or not it comes to this will depend on the peace negotiations. Japan holds back for the time being the conditions which it will set up and appears to be willing to reveal its final demands only gradually. There are in the meantime indications that these will be very hard for China. The Japanese Ambassador here spoke a few days ago in strictest confidence and with the request for secrecy of an exchange of views between the Russians and his Government at the end of last month whereby Japan would acquiesce in the Russian demand for the complete independence of Korea and in return Russia will accord its benevolent support in the peace negotiations in the sense of procuring war indemnity, surrender of territory, and new regulations of commercial relations between Japan and China. In harmony with this is the fact that according to the announcement of Your Majesty's Ambassador in London, Russia and England have agreed that the independence of Korea is to be maintained.

Mr. Aoki added the confidential communication that Japanese military men consider the cession of Port Arthur with a part of the hinterland as indispensable while in their eyes the surrender of an island, for example Formosa, would be only of lesser significance.

Now, in my opinion, Port Arthur in Japanese hands would signify the domination of the Gulf of Chili and hence a standing menace to the Chinese capital. It may be assumed therefore that the Chinese will resist such a cession to the utmost.

To be sure, China's position in a military way is almost hopeless. Your Majesty's minister in Peking answered to questions sent by telegraph to the effect that he did not believe that the Chinese forces could hold the enemy back from Peking; that the capture of the capital would not necessarily result in the dissolution of the existing political order; but that nevertheless Le-Hung-Chang considers the withdrawal of the Court from Peking as no longer possible. On the other hand, Baron von Gutschmid telegraphs from Tokyo that Japan can continue the war till next winter without fearing exhaustion of man power, financial means or materials of war. Moreover, that the war enthusiasm of the Japanese nation was undiminished.

Likewise, it seems not impossible that the disposition which has thus far prevailed among Chinese statesmen to deceive themselves regarding the true situation reaches even to the extent of renewing the unequal struggle if Japan will not let drop its demand regarding Port Arthur and be satisfied possibly with Formosa.

In this case it might indeed come to an intervention of the powers in spite of existing differences of interests among them and so precipitate for us as well the Chinese question.

In this situation it follows in my humble opinion as a criterion of our policy that on the one hand we must avoid allowing ourselves to be drawn prematurely into action to serve primarily foreign interests, but on the other hand we must hold open to ourselves the participation in such undertakings as could lead to dislocations in the relative strength of the great European powers in Eastern Asia.

I ask Your Majesty, accordingly, to authorize me to direct the Imperial Ambassador in London, who is for the time being generally informed regarding the above-mentioned viewpoint, to give the Government there to understand at this time orally and without committing ourselves that Your Majesty's Government is not essentially opposed to the idea of a common intervention, and indeed would not hesitate, in the face of essential alterations in the situation in Eastern Asia, to take an emphatic stand for German interests.

England seems urgently to desire our participation to have at least a counterweight against France and Russia, judging from the utterances thus far of the statesmen there, and will undoubtedly meet our wishes to a certain extent at any rate.

What and how much we shall ask for our cooperation can scarcely at this time be determined and will depend among other things upon what the other powers claim. In this connection there is the statement of the English Ambassador, Sir F. Lascelles, at Petersburg, and reported by Your Majesty's Ambassador there, indicating that England would have no objections to Russia's annexing a part of Northern China on account of her railway and perhaps a harbor in Korea. What England would take for herself is not known. Past experience suggests among other possibilities the Island of Chusan opposite Ningpo, which was once occupied by her.

In the meantime I have asked the Secretary of State for the Imperial Navy for a statement as to which points in Eastern Asia might perhaps be desirable for Germany in the interest of her Navy. I still await this statement.

In this connection, the Island of Formosa could hardly be considered. Among other things, Baron von Richthofen, the Professor at the University here and a distinguished authority on China, warns against the acquisition of this place. So far as is known, it has no harbors suitable for large vessels; on account of its relatively dense and wild population it is unsuited for colonization; and on account of its extent it is hard to defend. An effort to secure Formosa would bring us into conflict not only with Japan but probably also with France who has herself asserted claims to it since 1885. On the other hand, it would not be disadvantageous to us if Japan with England's and Russia's support would make claims to Formosa because in that way France would be brought into a certain opposition to Russia.

Finally, as regards the Chinese Emperor's telegram mentioned at the beginning, I humbly ask permission to say to the Chinese envoy that Your Majesty has taken cognizance thereof and authorized him to report to his Imperial Master that Your Majesty has the most complete sympathy with his and his Empire's hard lot and also that Your Majesty's most fervent wishes are directed to the early success of the approaching peace negotiations. Your Majesty is ready and glad to have renewed expression of these wishes given to the Japanese Government.

Prince v. Hohenlohe

Source: *German Diplomatic Documents, 1871–1914*, selected and translated by E. T. S. Dugdale, vol. 3, *The Growing Antagonism, 1898–1910*. New York: Harper and Brothers, 1920.

Kaiser Wilhelm II on the Boxer Rebellion (July 2, 1900)

While mainland China was never formally colonized by Europeans, it was increasingly divided into "spheres of influence" by various European powers and Japan in the late nineteenth century. In these spheres, including that controlled by Germany in northeast China, centered on the Shandong province, European colonizers enjoyed special economic privileges and virtual immunity from Chinese laws. This created great resentment among many Chinese. In 1900, a secret organization, the Society of Righteous Fists (called Boxers in the West), rose up in violent protest, killing many westerners and besieging many more in their colonial enclaves. A multinational force was sent to lift the siege. The following are excerpts from three different speeches given by Kaiser Wilhelm II to German troops leaving for China.

Into the midst of the deepest peace—alas, not surprising to me—the torch of war has been hurled. A crime unprecedented in its brazenness, horrifying in its cruelty, has struck my trusted representative and carried him off. The ambassadors of the other powers are in danger of their lives and along with them your comrades who were dispatched for their protection. Perhaps, they have today fought their last battle. The German flag has been insulted, and the German Empire held up to scorn. This demands an exemplary punishment and revenge.

With fearful speed the conditions have become extremely serious. Since I have summoned you to arms, [the situation has become] still more serious. What I had hoped to restore with the help of the marines will now require the united contingents of troops from all the civilized nations. Today the chief of the cruiser squadron has implored me to consider sending an [entire] division.

You will oppose an enemy no less resolute in the face of death than yourselves. Trained by European officers, the Chinese have learned the use of European weapons. Thank God your comrades in the marines and in my navy, with whom you will join, have asserted and maintained the old German repute in combat; they have defended themselves with glory and victory and eased your task.

Thus I send you now to avenge injustice, and I shall not rest until the German flag, united with those of the other powers, waves victoriously over the Chinese, planted on the walls of Peking, and dictating peace to the Chinese.

Maintain a good comradeship with all the troops whom you will join with there. Russians, Englishmen, Frenchmen, and whoever else—they all fight for one cause, for civilization.

Yet we also bear in mind something higher, our religion, and the defense and protection of our brothers overseas, some of whom have stood up for their Savior with their life.

Think also of our military honor, of those who have fought for you, and depart with the old motto of the flag of Brandenburg: "Trust God, defend yourself bravely. In that lies all your honor! For whoever ventures on God with a full heart will never be routed."

The flags that wave above you here go into fire for the first time. Bring them back to me pure, unblemished, and without stain!

My thanks and my concern, my prayers and my solicitude will not leave you. With these I accompany you.

Great overseas tasks have fallen to the newly arisen German Empire, tasks far greater than many of my countrymen expected. It is in character for the German Empire to meet the obligation of defending its citizens who are being oppressed in foreign lands. These tasks that the old Holy Roman Empire was not up to, the new German Empire is in position to perform. The means that makes this possible is our army. During thirty years of peaceful labor it has been built up according to the principles of my late grandfather [Wilhelm I, 1861–88]. You, too, have received your training according to these principles and shall now test them before the enemy. Your comrades in the navy have already undergone this test and have demonstrated that the principles of our training are sound. I am proud of the praise from foreign leaders which your comrades have earned over there. It is for you to do the same.

A great task awaits you: You must see to it that a serious injustice is expiated. The Chinese have overturned the law of nations. Never before in world history have the sanctity of diplomats and the obligations of hospitality been subjected to such contempt. It is all the more outrageous that these crimes have been committed by a nation which prides itself on its ancient culture.

Maintain the old Prussian virtue. Show yourselves Christians in the joyful bearing of sorrow. May honor and fame follow your banners and your arms. Give all the world an example of manliness and discipline. Well you know that you shall be fighting against a sly, brave, well-armed, and cruel foe.

When you come upon him, know this: *Pardon will not be given.* Prisoners will not be taken. Bear your weapons so that for a thousand years *no Chinaman will dare even to squint at a German.*

Carry yourselves like men, and the blessing of God go with you. The prayers of the entire nation and my good wishes go with you, each and everyone. *Open the way for civilization once and for all!* Now you can depart! Adieu, comrades!

The task which I am sending you out to do is a great one. You must see that a serious injustice is expiated. In this case the Chinese have dared to overturn a thousand year old international law and to make a mockery of the sanctity of the diplomat and the right of hospitality. The case is unprecedented in world history—and this from a people proud of its ancient culture!

But you can see from this what a culture not based on Christianity comes to. *Every heathen culture, no matter how beautiful or august, will come to nought at the first catastrophe!*

. . . When you come upon the enemy, smite him. Pardon will not be given. Prisoners will not be taken. Whoever falls into your hands is forfeit. Once, a thousand years ago, the Huns under their King Attila made a name for themselves, one still potent in legend and tradition. May you in this way make the name German remembered in China for a thousand years so that no Chinaman will ever again dare to *even squint at a German!*

You will have to fight a force superior in numbers. But, as our military history demonstrates, we are accustomed to this. . . . Gather new laurels for your [regimental] flags. The blessings of the Lord go with you and your prayers. An entire nation accompanies you on all your paths. My best wishes to you for the fortune of your arms. . . . And may God's blessing attach itself to your banner and bring a blessing upon this war so that Christianity may survive in that land and such sad events never reoccur. To this end stand by your oath. And now, a prosperous voyage! Adieu, comrades!

Source: Schroeder, Wilhelm, ed. *Das persönliche Regiment: Reden und sonstige öffentliche Äusserungen Wilhelms II.* Munich, 1912.

Proclamation of General von Trotha to the Hottentot People (April 22, 1905)

Namibia, an arid and semi-arid region on the southwest coast of Africa, was first settled by Ger-

man settlers in the late nineteenth century and formally claimed by the German Reich following the Berlin Congress of 1884–1885, in which virtually all of Africa was apportioned among various European colonial powers. The Herero, pejoratively referred to at the time as Hottentot, were evicted from their lands to make way for German colonists. When they rose up in rebellion in the early 1900s, their revolt was ruthlessly suppressed. In spite of the conciliatory tone of this proclamation by the German commander in charge of the colony, more than 60,000 Herero were massacred by the Germans in what has been called the first genocide of the twentieth century.

To the Rebellious Hottentots:

The powerful, great German Kaiser wants to grant clemency to those of the Hottentot people who surrender themselves voluntarily, they will be presented with life. Only those who at the beginning of the rebellion have committed murder against Whites or who have commanded that Whites be murdered have by law forfeited their lives. This I declare publicly and state further that of the few who have not been defeated, it will fare with them just as it has fared with the Hereros, who in their blindness also believed that they could make successful war against the powerful German Kaiser and the great German people. I ask you, where are the Hereros today, where are their chiefs? Samuel Maherero, who at one time styled himself the ruler of thousands of children, has, hunted like a wild animal, fled across the English border; he has become as poor as the poorest field Herero and now owns nothing. Just so has it fared with the other Herero people, most of whom have lost their lives—some having died of hunger and thirst in the *Sandfeld*, some having been killed by German *Reiters*, some having been murdered by the Owambos. No harm will befall the Hottentot people as soon as they voluntarily appear and turn over their weapons. You should come with a white cloth on a stick along with your entire household and nothing shall happen to you. You will be given work and will receive food until after the conclusion of the war when the great German Kaiser will present new rules governing the affairs of the Protectorate. He who after this chooses not to make an application for mercy must emigrate, because where he allows himself to be seen in the German

area, he will be shot until all are exterminated. For the surrender of the murderous culprits, whether dead or alive, I offer the following rewards: for Hendrik Witboi 5,000 Marks, Stürmann 3,000 Marks, Cornelius 3,000 Marks, and for the remaining guilty leaders 1,000 Marks.

signed
Trotha.

Source: Kriegsgeschichtlichen Abteilung I des Grossen Generalstabes. *Die Kämpfe der deutschen Truppen in Südwestafrika.* Berlin: Ernst Siegfried Mittler, 1907.

Maherero on the Uprising in German South-West Africa (1905)

In what some historians consider to be the first genocide of the twentieth century, the German army massacred roughly one-third of the Herero population of Southwest Africa (now Namibia), a German settler colony, between 1901 and 1906. The genocide followed an uprising by the Hereros, who had been witnessing their herds slaughtered and lands confiscated by German settlers. In this brief statement to the German colonial authorities in Southwest Africa, Herero chief Maherero proclaims the innocence of his people.

I and my headmen reply to you as follows: I did not commence the war this year; it has been started by the white people; for as you know how many Hereros have been killed by the white people, particularly traders, with rifles and in the prisons. And always when I brought these cases to Windhoek the blood of the people was valued at no more than a few head of small stock, namely, from fifty to fifteen. The traders increased the troubles also in this way, that they voluntarily gave credit to my people. After doing so they robbed us; they went so far as to pay themselves by, for instance, taking away by force two or three head of cattle to cover a debt of one pound sterling. It is these things which have caused the war in this land. And in these times the white people said to us you who were peacefully disposed and liked us, were no longer here. They said to us, the Governor who loves you has gone to a difficult war; he is dead, and as he is dead you also [the Hereros] must die.

Source: Morel, E. D. *The Black Man's Burden.* London, 1920.

German Conservative Party Proclamation on Imperialism (1906)

As in other European colonial powers, German politics included a powerful anti-imperialist strain. Again, as in other countries, this was usually associated with the left, in Germany's case, the Social Democrats. Not so concerned with the fate of indigenous peoples, the left in Germany believed that the maintenance of empire increased the power of the conservative military and siphoned off government revenues that could be used for social welfare at home. The Conservative Party's response, as in this manifesto issued before the 1907 national elections—in which the question of imperialism loomed large—was that the Social Democrats were unpatriotic in their opposition to the expansion of German power globally.

The Reichstag has been dissolved because it did not grant the government the troops and supplies demanded for the energetic and complete suppression of the uprisings in German Southwest Africa. For the first time the Reichstag has been dissolved for reasons which belong to the sphere of foreign policy, and which spring from the necessity of defending our rapidly growing interests beyond the seas. With just indignation at the triumphant vote of the opposition, the Chancellor exclaims: "Shall the German nation show itself weaker than other nations, and acknowledge itself weaker?" That is the great question which the German people must answer at the polls on January 25. For the German nation, which for thirty years has been restricted to its position of a great power in Europe, has to-clay to direct its attention not only to its colonial possessions but also to its overseas trade, mounting upward into the billions.

We Conservatives, for our part, cannot and will not leave the government in the lurch in its task of guarding and maintaining the honor, power, and national dignity of our country, whether it be to protect the German Empire itself or the colonies dearly bought and boldly defended by the life blood of thousands of German soldiers; for their economic development and settlement are attainable only under this preliminary condition. Only thus can we expect a conscious, well-directed, and orderly administration conformable to the conditions of each colony; and only thus can we hope that the government, taking into account our financial resources, will guard and advance the development of our colonies in the interests of the German nation, and yet with due regard for the principle of constitutional responsibility.

In the conflict for our national possessions and ideals as well as for our social and political institutions, sorely threatened by Social Democracy, we expect from the imperial authority energetic and effective measures which will oppose more vigorously than ever before the endeavors of those unpatriotic socialists who are in open opposition to the Christian culture of the German Empire.

And now to the election campaign for German honor, courage, and reputation against all enemies.

The Committee of the German Conservative Party, Berlin, December 18, 1906

Source: Schulthess, H., ed. *European History Calendar.* Munich, 1906.

Versailles Treaty (1919)

At the Versailles conference of 1919, the victorious Allied powers attempted to establish a new order for Europe in the wake of World War I. High on the agenda of some of the delegates, particularly those of France and Britain, was the punishment of Germany for its alleged role in starting the conflict. Along with heavy reparations payments, the Allies punished Germany by stripping it of its colonies in Africa and the Pacific, as well as its legal, political, and economic privileges in other parts of the non-European world.

PART IV

GERMAN RIGHTS AND INTERESTS OUTSIDE GERMANY.

ARTICLE 118.

In territory outside her European frontiers as fixed by the present Treaty, Germany renounces all rights, titles and privileges whatever in or over territory which belonged to her or to her allies, and all rights, titles and privileges whatever their origin which she held as against the Allied and Associated Powers.

Germany hereby undertakes to recognise and to conform to the measures which may be taken now or in the future by the Principal Allied and

Associated Powers, in agreement where necessary with third Powers, in order to carry the above stipulation into effect.

In particular Germany declares her acceptance of the following Articles relating to certain special subjects.

SECTION I.

GERMAN COLONIES.

ARTICLE 119.

Germany renounces in favour of the Principal Allied and Associated Powers all her rights and titles over her oversea possessions.

ARTICLE 120.

All movable and immovable property in such territories belonging to the German Empire or to any German State shall pass to the Government exercising authority over such territories, on the terms laid down in Article 257 of Part IX (Financial Clauses) of the present Treaty. The decision of the local courts in any dispute as to the nature of such property shall be final.

ARTICLE 121.

The provisions of Sections I and IV of Part X (Economic Clauses) of the present Treaty shall apply in the case of these territories whatever be the form of Government adopted for them.

ARTICLE 122.

The Government exercising authority over such territories may make such provisions as it thinks fit with reference to the repatriation from them of German nationals and to the conditions upon which German subjects of European origin shall, or shall not, be allowed to reside, hold property, trade or exercise a profession in them.

ARTICLE 123.

The provisions of Article 260 of Part IX (Financial Clauses) of the present Treaty shall apply in the case of all agreements concluded with German nationals for the construction or exploitation of public works in the German oversea possessions, as well as any sub-concessions or contracts resulting therefrom which may have been made to or with such nationals.

ARTICLE 124.

Germany hereby undertakes to pay, in accordance with the estimate to be presented by the French Government and approved by the Reparation Commission, reparation for damage suffered by French nationals in the Cameroons or the frontier zone by reason of the acts of the German civil and military authorities and of German private individuals during the period from January 1, 1900, to August 1, 1914.

ARTICLE 125.

Germany renounces all rights under the Conventions and Agreements with France of November 4, 1911, and September 28, 1912, relating to Equatorial Africa. She undertakes to pay to the French Government, in accordance with the estimate to be presented by that Government and approved by the Reparation Commission, all the deposits, credits, advances, etc., effected by virtue of these instruments in favour of Germany.

ARTICLE 126.

Germany undertakes to accept and observe the agreements made or to be made by the Allied and Associated Powers or some of them with any other Power with regard to the trade in arms and spirits, and to the matters dealt with in the General Act of Berlin of February 26, 1885, the General Act of Brussels of July 2, 1890, and the conventions completing or modifying the same.

ARTICLE 127.

The native inhabitants of the former German oversea possessions shall be entitled to the diplomatic protection of the Governments exercising authority over those territories.

SECTION II.

CHINA.

ARTICLE 128.

Germany renounces in favour of China all benefits and privileges resulting from the provisions of the final Protocol signed at Peking on September 7, 1901, and from all annexes, notes and documents supplementary thereto. She likewise renounces in favour of China any claim to indemnities accruing thereunder subsequent to March 14, 1917.

ARTICLE 129.

From the coming into force of the present Treaty the High Contracting Parties shall apply, in so far as concerns them respectively:

(1) The Arrangement of August 29, 1902, regarding the new Chinese customs tariff;

(2) The Arrangement of September 27, 1905, regarding Whang-Poo, and the provisional supplementary Arrangement of April 4, 1912.

China, however, will no longer be bound to grant to Germany the advantages or privileges which she allowed Germany under these Arrangements.

ARTICLE 130.

Subject to the provisions of Section VIII of this Part, Germany cedes to China all the buildings, wharves and pontoons, barracks, forts, arms and munitions of war, vessels of all kinds, wireless telegraphy installations and other public property belonging to the German Government, which are situated or may be in the German Concessions at Tientsin and Hankow or elsewhere in Chinese territory.

It is understood, however, that premises used as diplomatic or consular residences or offices are not included in the above cession, and, furthermore, that no steps shall be taken by the Chinese Government to dispose of the German public and private property situated within the so-called Legation Quarter at Peking without the consent of the Diplomatic Representatives of the Powers which, on the coming into force of the present Treaty, remain Parties to the Final Protocol of September 7, 1901.

ARTICLE 131.

Germany undertakes to restore to China within twelve months from the coming into force of the present Treaty all the astronomical instruments which her troops in 1900–1901 carried away from China, and to defray all expenses which may be incurred in effecting such restoration, including the expenses of dismounting, packing, transporting, insurance and installation in Peking.

ARTICLE 132.

Germany agrees to the abrogation of the leases from the Chinese Government under which the German Concessions at Hankow and Tientsin are now held.

China, restored to the full exercise of her sovereign rights in the above areas, declares her intention of opening them to international residence and trade. She further declares that the abrogation of the leases under which these concessions are now held shall not affect the property rights of nationals of Allied and Associated Powers who are holders of lots in these concessions.

ARTICLE 133.

Germany waives all claims against the Chinese Government or against any Allied or Associated Government arising out of the internment of German nationals in China and their repatriation. She equally renounces all claims arising out of the capture and condemnation of German ships in China,

or the liquidation, sequestration or control of German properties, rights and interests in that country since August 14, 1917. This provision, however, shall not affect the rights of the parties interested in the proceeds of any such liquidation, which shall be governed by the provisions of Part X (Economic Clauses) of the present Treaty.

ARTICLE 134.

Germany renounces in favour of the Government of His Britannic Majesty the German State property in the British Concession at Shameen at Canton. She renounces in favour of the French and Chinese Governments conjointly the property of the German school situated in the French Concession at Shanghai.

SECTION III.

SIAM.

ARTICLE 135.

Germany recognises that all treaties, conventions and agreements between her and Siam, and all rights, title and privileges derived therefrom, including all rights of extraterritorial jurisdiction, terminated as from July 22, 1917.

ARTICLE 136.

All goods and property in Siam belonging to the German Empire or to any German State, with the exception of premises used as diplomatic or consular residences or offices, pass ipso facto and without compensation to the Siamese Government.

The goods, property and private rights of German nationals in Siam shall be dealt with in accordance with the provisions of Part X (Economic Clauses) of the present Treaty.

ARTICLE 137.

Germany waives all claims against the Siamese Government on behalf of herself or her nationals arising out of the seizure or condemnation of German ships, the liquidation of German property, or the internment of German nationals in Siam. This provision shall not affect the rights of the parties interested in the proceeds of any such liquidation, which shall be governed by the provisions of Part X (Economic Clauses) of the present Treaty.

SECTION IV.

LIBERIA.

ARTICLE 138.

Germany renounces all rights and privileges arising from the arrangements of 1911 and 1912 regarding Liberia, and particularly the right to nominate a German Receiver of Customs in Liberia.

She further renounces all claim to participate in any measures whatsoever which may be adopted for the rehabilitation of Liberia.

ARTICLE 139.

Germany recognises that all treaties and arrangements between her and Liberia terminated as from August 4, 1917.

ARTICLE 140.

The property, rights and interests of Germans in Liberia shall be dealt with in accordance with Part X (Economic Clauses) of the present Treaty.

SECTION V.

MOROCCO.

ARTICLE 141.

Germany renounces all rights, titles and privileges conferred on her by the General Act of Algeciras of April 7, 1906, and by the Franco-German Agreements of February 9, 1909, and November 4, 1911. All treaties, agreements, arrangements and contracts concluded by her with the Sherifian Empire are regarded as abrogated as from August 3, 1914

In no case can Germany take advantage of these instruments and she undertakes not to intervene in any way in negotiations relating to Morocco which may take place between France and the other Powers.

ARTICLE 142.

Germany having recognised the French Protectorate in Morocco, hereby accepts all the consequences of its establishment, and she renounces the regime of the capitulations therein.

This renunciation shall take effect as from August 3, 1914.

ARTICLE 143.

The Sherifian Government shall have complete liberty of action in regulating the status of German nationals in Morocco and the conditions in which they may establish themselves there.

German protected persons, semsars and "associes agricoles," shall be considered as having ceased, as from August 3, 1914, to enjoy the privileges attached to their status and shall be subject to the ordinary law.

ARTICLE 144.

All property and possessions in the Sherifian Empire of the German Empire and the German States pass to the Maghzen without payment.

For this purpose, the property and possessions of the German Empire and States shall be deemed to include all the property of the Crown, the Empire or the States, and the private property of the former German Emperor and other Royal personages.

All movable and immovable property in the Sherifian Empire belonging to German nationals shall be dealt with in accordance with Sections III and IV of Part X (Economic Clauses) of the present Treaty.

Mining rights which may be recognised as belonging to German nationals by the Court of Arbitration set up under the Moroccan Mining Regulations shall form the subject of a valuation, which the arbitrators shall be requested to make, and these rights shall then be treated in the same way as property in Morocco belonging to German nationals.

ARTICLE 145.

The German Government shall ensure the transfer to a person nominated by the French Government of the shares representing Germany's portion of the capital of the State Bank of Morocco. The value of these shares, as assessed by the Reparation Commission, shall be paid to the Reparation Commission for the credit of Germany on account of the sums due for reparation. The German Government shall be responsible for indemnifying its nationals so dispossessed.

This transfer will take place without prejudice to the repayment of debts which German nationals may have contracted towards the State Bank of Morocco.

ARTICLE 146.

Moroccan goods entering Germany shall enjoy the treatment accorded to French goods

SECTION VI.

EGYPT.

ARTICLE 147.

Germany declares that she recognises the Protectorate proclaimed over Egypt by Great Britain on December 18, 1914, and that she renounces the regime of the Capitulations in Egypt.

This renunciation shall take effect as from August 4, 1914.

ARTICLE 148.

All treaties, agreements, arrangements and contracts concluded by Germany with Egypt are regarded as abrogated as from August 4, 1914.

In no case can Germany avail herself of these instruments and she undertakes not to intervene in any way in negotiations relating to Egypt which may take place between Great Britain and the other Powers.

ARTICLE 149.

Until an Egyptian law of judicial organization establishing courts with universal jurisdiction comes into force, provision shall be made, by means of decrees issued by His Highness the Sultan, for the exercise of jurisdiction over German nationals and property by the British Consular Tribunals.

ARTICLE 150.

The Egyptian Government shall have complete liberty of action in regulating the status of German nationals and the conditions under which they may establish themselves in Egypt.

ARTICLE 151.

Germany consents to the abrogation of the decree issued by His Highness the Khedive on November 28, 1914, relating to the Commission of the Egyptian Public Debt, or to such changes as the Egyptian Government may think it desirable to make therein.

ARTICLE 152.

Germany consents, in so far as she is concerned, to the transfer to His Britannic Majesty's Government of the powers conferred on His Imperial Majesty the Sultan by the Convention signed at Constantinople on October 29, 1888, relating to the free navigation of the Suez Canal.

She renounces all participation in the Sanitary, Maritime, and Quarantine Board of Egypt and consents, in so far as she is concerned, to the transfer to the Egyptian Authorities of the powers of that Board.

ARTICLE 153.

All property and possessions in Egypt of the German Empire and the German States pass to the Egyptian Government without payment.

For this purpose, the property and possessions of the German Empire and States shall be deemed to include all the property of the Crown, the Empire or the States, and the private property of the former German Emperor and other Royal personages.

All movable and immovable property in Egypt belonging to German nationals shall be dealt with in accordance with Sections III and IV of Part X (Economic Clauses) of the present Treaty.

ARTICLE 154.

Egyptian goods entering Germany shall enjoy the treatment accorded to British goods.

SECTION VII

TURKEY AND BULGARIA.

ARTICLE 155.

Germany undertakes to recognise and accept all arrangements which the Allied and Associated Powers may make with Turkey and Bulgaria with reference to any rights, interests and privileges whatever which might be claimed by Germany or her nationals in Turkey and Bulgaria and which are not dealt with in the provisions of the present Treaty.

SECTION VIII

SHANTUNG.

ARTICLE 156.

Germany renounces, in favour of Japan, all her rights, title and privileges particularly those concerning the territory of Kiaochow, railways, mines and submarine cables which she acquired in virtue of the Treaty concluded by her with China on March 6 1898, and of all other arrangements relative to the Province of Shantung.

All German rights in the Tsingtao-Tsinanfu Railway, including its branch lines together with its subsidiary property of all kinds, stations, shops, fixed and rolling stock, mines, plant and material for the exploitation of the mines, are and remain acquired by Japan, together with all rights and privileges attaching thereto.

The German State submarine cables from Tsingtao to Shanghai and from Tsingtao to Chefoo, with all the rights, privileges and properties attaching thereto, are similarly acquired by Japan, free and clear of all charges and encumbrances.

ARTICLE 157.

The movable and immovable property owned by the German State in the territory of Kiaochow, as well as all the rights which Germany might claim in consequence of the works or improvements made or of the expenses incurred by her, directly or indirectly, in connection with this territory, are and remain acquired by Japan, free and clear of all charges and encumbrances.

ARTICLE 158.

Germany shall hand over to Japan within three months from the coming into force of the present Treaty the archives, registers, plans, title-deeds and documents of every kind, wherever they may be, relating to the administration, whether civil, military, financial, judicial or other, of the territory of Kiaochow.

Within the same period Germany shall give particulars to Japan of all treaties, arrangements or agreements relating to the rights, title or privileges referred to in the two preceding Articles.

Source: The Treaty of Versailles and After: Annotations of the Text of the Treaty. Washington, DC: Government Printing Office, 1944.

INTERNATIONAL

The Interesting Narrative of the Life of Olaudah Equiano or Gustavus Vassa the African (1789)

Other than a few settlements along the coasts and in southern Africa, Europeans largely stayed away from Africa until the mid-nineteenth century. While much of the Americas and Asia was colonized, Africa remained ruled by Africans. At the same time, Africa was crucial to the colonial order in that its people—as slaves—provided the labor force for the plantation and mining economies of European colonies in the Americas. In this famous eighteenth-century memoir, a former slave describes the terror and brutality by which slaves were brought to the Western Hemisphere.

Their [the Europeans] complexions, differing so much from ours, their long hair and the language they spoke, which was different from any I had ever heard, united to confirm me in this belief. Indeed, such were the horrors of my views and fears at the moment, that if ten thousand worlds had been my own, I would have freely parted with them all to have exchanged my condition with that of the meanest slave of my own country. When I looked around the ship and saw a large furnace of copper boiling, and a multitude of black people of every description chained together, every one of their countenances expressing dejection and sorrow, I no longer doubted my fate. Quite overpowered with horror and anguish, I fell motionless on the deck and fainted. When I recovered a little, I found some black people about me, and I believe some were those who had brought me on board

and had been receiving their pay. They talked to me in order to cheer me up, but all in vain. I asked them if we were not to be eaten by those white men with horrible looks, red faces and long hair. They told me I was not.

I took a little down my palate, which, instead of reviving me as they thought it would, threw me into the greatest consternation at the strange feeling it produced, having never tasted such liquor before. Soon after this, the blacks who had brought me on board went off and left me abandoned to despair.

I now saw myself deprived of all chance of returning to my native country or even the least glimpse of hope of gaining the shore, which I now considered as friendly. I even wished for my former slavery in preference to my present situation, which was filled with horrors of every kind.

There I received such a salutation in my nostrils as I had never experienced in my life. With the loathesomeness of the stench and the crying together, I became so sick and low that I was not able to eat, nor had I the least desire to taste anything. I now wished for the last friend, Death, to relieve me.

Soon, to my grief, two of the white men offered me eatables and on my refusing to eat, one of them held me fast by the hands and laid me across the windlass and tied my feet while the other flogged me severely. I had never experienced anything of this kind before. If I could have gotten over the nettings, I would have jumped over the side, but I could not. The crew used to watch very closely those of us who were not chained down to the decks, lest we should leap into the water. I have seen some of these poor African prisoners most severely cut for attempting to do so, and hourly whipped for not eating. This indeed was often the case with myself.

I inquired of these what was to be done with us. They gave me to understand we were to be carried to these white people's country to work for them. I then was a little revived, and thought if it were no worse than working, my situation was not so desperate. But still I feared that I should be put to death, the white people looked and acted in so savage a manner. I have never seen among my people such instances of brutal cruelty, and this not only shown towards us blacks, but also to some of the whites themselves.

One white man in particular I saw, when we were permitted to be on deck, flogged so unmercifully with a large rope near the foremast that he died in consequence of it, and they tossed him over the side as they would have done a brute. This made me fear these people the more, and I expected nothing less than to be treated in the same manner.

I asked them if these people had no country, but lived in this hollow place? They told me they did not but came from a distant land. "Then," said I, "how comes it that in all our country we never heard of them?"

They told me because they lived so far off. I then asked where were their women? Had they any like themselves? I was told they had.

"And why do we not see them" I asked. They answered, "Because they were left behind."

I asked how the vessel would go? They told me they could not tell, but there was cloth put upon the masts by the help of the ropes I saw, and then vessels went on, and the white men had some spell or magic they put in the water when they liked in order to stop the vessel when they liked.

I was exceedingly amazed at this account, and really thought they were spirits. I therefore wished much to be from amongst them, for I expected they would sacrifice me. But my wishes were in vain—for we were so quartered that it was impossible for us to make our escape.

At last, when the ship we were in had got in all her cargo, they made ready with many fearful noises, and we were all put under deck, so that we could not see how they managed the vessel.

The stench of the hold while we were on the coast was so intolerably loathsome, that it was dangerous to remain there for any time . . . some of us had been permitted to stay on the deck for the fresh air. But now that the whole ship's cargo were confined together, it became absolutely pestilential. The closeness of the place and the heat of the climate, added to the number of the ship, which was so crowded that each had scarcely room to turn himself, almost suffocated us.

This produced copious perspirations so that the air became unfit for respiration from a variety of loathsome smells, and brought on a sickness among the slaves, of which many died—thus falling victims of the improvident avarice, as I may call it, of their purchasers. This wretched situation was again aggravated by the galling of the chains, which now became insupportable, and the filth of the necessary tubs [toilets] into which the children often fell and were almost suffocated. The shrieks of the women and the groans of the dying rendered the whole a scene of horror almost inconceivable.

Happily perhaps for myself, I was soon reduced so low that it was necessary to keep me almost always on deck and from my extreme youth I was not put into fetters. In this situation I expected every hour to share the fate of my companions, some of whom were almost daily brought upon the deck at the point of death, which I began to hope would soon put an end to my miseries. Often did I think many of the inhabitants of the deep much more happy than myself. I envied them the freedom they enjoyed, and as often wished I could change my condition for theirs. Every circumstance I met with, served only to render my state more painful and heightened my apprehensions and my opinion of the cruelty of the whites.

One day, when we had a smooth sea and moderate wind, two of my wearied countrymen who were chained together (I was near them at the time), preferring death to such a life of misery, somehow made through the nettings and jumped into the sea. Immediately another quite dejected fellow, who on account of his illness was suffered to be out of irons, followed their example. I believe many more would very soon have done the same if they had not been prevented by the ship's crew, who were instantly alarmed. Those of us that were the most active were in a moment put down under the deck, and there was such a noise and confusion among the people of the ship as I never heard before to stop her and get the boat out to go after the slaves. However, two of the wretches were drowned, but they got the other and afterwards flogged him unmercifully for thus attempting to prefer death to slavery.

I can now relate hardships which are inseparable from this accursed trade. Many a time we were near suffocation from the want of fresh air, which we were often without for whole days together. This, and the stench of the necessary tubs, carried off many.

Source: Equiano, Olaudah. *The Interesting Narrative of the Life of Olaudah Equiano or Gustavus Vassa the African.* London, 1789.

Treaty between France and the Ottoman Empire (June 25, 1802)

To many partisans, the principles of democracy inherent in the French Revolution of 1789 should not be confined to France. With the rise of an expansionist state under Napoleon in the late 1790s that belief was acted upon as France and French agents spread the revolutionary message throughout Europe, including the Balkan territories controlled by the autocratic Ottoman Empire. This led to a break between the two countries, especially after Napoleon invaded Egypt. With Napoleon's defeat there, a rapprochement between France and the Ottoman sultan was achieved in this 1802 treaty. Still, the seeds of liberty planted by the French in the late eighteenth century would bear fruit in the nineteenth, as numerous subject nationalities of the Ottoman Empire in the Balkans rebelled, starting with the Greeks.

A. Definitive Treaty of Peace between the French Republic and the Sublime Ottoman Porte

The first consul of the French Republic, in the name of the French people, and the sublime Ottoman emperor, being desirous to restore the relations of peace and amity which have of old subsisted between France and the sublime Porte, have for that purpose appointed ministers plenipotentiaries, viz. the first consul, in the name of the French people, citizen C. M. Talleyrand, minister for foreign affairs to the French republic; and the

sublime Ottoman Porte, Esseid Mahomed Said Ghalib Effendi, private secretary and director of foreign affairs; who, after exchanging their full powers, have agreed to the following articles:

1. There shall hereafter be peace and friendship between the French republic and the sublime Ottoman Porte: hostilities shall for the future, and for ever, cease between the two states.

2. The treaties or capitulations which, before the war, defined the respective relations of every kind, existing between the two powers, shall be renewed in all their particulars.

In consequence of this renewal, and in fulfillment of the ancient capitulation, according to which the French have a right to enjoy, in the states of the sublime Porte, all the advantages granted to other nations, the sublime Porte consents that the French merchant ships bearing the French flag, shall for the future possess the undisputed right to navigate and pass freely in the Black sea. The sublime Porte likewise consents, that the said French merchant ships, on their passage into and out of this sea, shall, with respect to every thing that can favor the free navigation of it, be placed precisely on the same footing with the merchant ships of those nations which now navigate it.

The sublime Porte and the government of the French republic will with common consent take vigorous measures to cleanse the seas, which the ships of both states navigate, from all kinds of pirates.

The sublime Porte promises to protect the French trading ships in the Black Sea against all kinds of pirates.

It is hereby understood, that the advantages secured by the present article to the French in the Ottoman empire, shall in like manner extend to the subjects and flag of the sublime Porte in the seas and territory of the French republic.

3. The French republic shall, in the Ottoman countries which lie on, or in the vicinity of, the Black Sea, both with respect to their trade and the agents and commissars which that trade may render it necessary to appoint in such places, enjoy the same rights and privileges which France, before the war, enjoyed by virtue of the old capitulations, in any other parts of the states of the sublime Porte.

4. The sublime Porte assents to all that was stipulated with respect to it in the treaty concluded at Amiens between France and England, on the 4th

Germinal of the year ten (25th of March 1801), or the 22d of Zillides, of the year of the Hegira 1216. All the articles of this treaty, which have relation to the sublime Porte, are by the present treaty formally renewed.

5. The French republic and the sublime Porte mutually guaranty the integrity of the possessions.

6. The restorations and indemnifications which are due to the agents of the two powers, or to their citizens and subjects, whose effects have been confiscated or sequestrated during the war, shall be regulated in an equitable manner, by a particular agreement to be concluded between the two governments at Constantinople.

7. Until by common consent new regulations shall be agreed on, with respect to the tolls or customs on which disputes may have arisen, these shall in both countries continue to be regulated by the old capitulations.

8. Should any prisoners be found in the two countries, who are detained in consequence of the war, they shall immediately be set at liberty, without ransom.

9. As the French republic and the sublime Porte, by the present treaty, wish to place their states reciprocally in the situation of the most favoured powers, it is expressly understood that each state grants to the other, all the advantages which have been or shall be granted to any other powers, in the same manner as if they were expressly stipulated in the present treaty.

10. The ratifications of the present treaty shall be exchanged within eighty days, or sooner, if possible, at Paris.

Done at Paris, the 6th of Messidor, of the year ten (June 25, 1802), or the 24th of Safernair, the year of the Hegira 1217.

Ch. Mau. Talleyrand. Esseid Mahomed Said Ghalib Effendi.

Source: *The Annual Register,* or, *A View of the History, Politics, and Literature for the Year 1802.* London: Printed by R. Wilks for W. Otridge and Sons, et al. (Publisher varies by year.) Published for the years 1758–1837 in 80 volumes.

Alaska Purchase Treaty (1867)

From the late Middle Ages through the nineteenth century, the Russian Empire gradually expanded eastward across Siberia to the Bering Strait. Beginning with the founding of the Russian American Company in 1799 and the first settlement at Sitka in 1802, Russian traders and settlers moved into Alaska. Eventually, the Russian presence was felt as far south as northern California. Indeed, President Monroe's issuing of his doctrine in 1823, insisting that European powers stay out of the Americas, came about in part because of Russian encroachment. But by the middle of the nineteenth century, the Russians were eager to shed the costly colony, especially since they believed that much of its wealth—specifically, sea mammals for their hides—had been depleted. Americans, at the same time, believed that their secretary of state, William Seward, had been sold a worthless piece of real estate. For years, the new territory was referred to as "Seward's folly."

CONVENTION between the United States of America and His Majesty the Emperor of Russia, for the Cession of the Russian Possessions in North America to the United States, Concluded at Washington, March 30, 1867; Ratification Advised by Senate, April 9, 1867; Ratified by President, May 28, 1867; Ratification Exchanged at Washington, June 20, 1867; Proclaimed, June 20, 1867.

The United States of America and His Majesty the Emperor of all the Russias, being desirous of strengthening, if possible, the good understanding which exists between them, have, for that purpose, appointed as their Plenipotentiaries, the President of the United States, William H. Seward, Secretary of State; and His Majesty the Emperor of all the Russias, the Privy Counsellor Edward de Stoeckl, his Envoy Extraordinary and Minister Plenipotentiary to the United States;

And the said Plenipotentiaries, having exchanged their full powers, which were found to be in due form, have agreed upon and signed the following articles:

Article I His Majesty the Emperor of all the Russias, agrees to cede to the United States, by this convention, immediately upon the exchange of the ratifications thereof, all the territory and dominion now possessed by his said Majesty on the continent of America and in adjacent islands, the same being contained within the geographical limits herein set forth, to wit: The eastern limit is the line of demarcation between the Russian and the British possessions in North America, as established by the convention between Russia and Great Britain, of February 28-16, 1825, and described in Articles III and IV of said convention, in the following terms:

"III Commencing from the southernmost point of the island called Prince of Wales Island, which point lies in the parallel of 54 degrees 40 minutes north latitude, and between the 131st and 133d degree of west longitude (meridian of Greenwich), the said line shall ascend to the north along the channel called Portland Channel, as far as the point of the continent where it strikes the 56th degree of north latitude; from this last-mentioned point, the line of demarcation shall follow the summit of the mountains situated parallel to the coast, as far as the point of intersection of the 141st degree of west longitude (of the same meridian); and finally, from the said point of intersection, the said meridian line of the 141st degree, in its prolongation as far as the Frozen Ocean.

"IV With reference to the line of demarcation laid down in the preceding article, it is understood—"1st That the island called Prince of Wales Island shall belong wholly to Russia" (now, by this cession to the United States).

"2d That whenever the summit of the mountains which extend in a direction parallel to the coast, from the 56th degree of north latitude to the point of intersection of the 141st degree of west longitude, shall prove to be at the distance of more than ten marine leagues from the ocean, the limit between the British possessions and the line of coast which is to belong to Russia as above mentioned (that is to say, the limit to the possessions ceded by this convention), shall be formed by a line parallel to the winding of the coast, and which shall never exceed the distance of ten marine leagues therefrom." The western limit within which the territories and dominion conveyed are contained passes through a point in Behring's Straits on the parallel of sixty-five degrees thirty minutes north latitude, at its intersection by the meridian which passes midway between the islands of Krusenstern of Ignalook, and the island of Ratmanoff, or Noonarbook, and proceeds due north without limitation, into the same Frozen Ocean. The same western limit, beginning at the same initial point, proceeds thence in a course nearly southwest, through Behring's Straits and

Behring's Sea, so as to pass midway between the northwest point of the island of St. Lawrence and the southeast point of Cape Choukotski, to the meridian of one hundred and seventy-two west longitude; thence, from the intersection of that meridian, in a southwesterly direction, so as to pass midway between the island of Attou and the Copper Island of the Kormandorski couplet or group, in the North Pacific Ocean, to the meridian of one hundred and ninety-three degrees west longitude, so as to include in the territory conveyed the whole of the Aleutian Islands east of that meridian.

Article II In the cession of territory and dominion made by the preceding article, are included the right of property in all public lots and squares, vacant lands, and all public buildings, fortifications, barracks, and other edifies which are not private individual property. It is, however, understood and agreed, that the churches which have been built in the ceded territory by the Russian Government, shall remain the property of such members of the Greek Oriental Church resident in the territory as may choose to worship therein. Any Government archives, papers, and documents relative to the territory and dominion aforesaid, which may now be existing there, will be left in the possession of the agent of the United States; but an authenticated copy of such of them as may be required, will be, at all times, given by the United States to the Russian Government, or to such Russian officers or subjects as they may apply for.

Article III The inhabitants of the ceded territory, according to their choice, reserving their natural allegiance, may return to Russia within three years; but if they should prefer to remain in the ceded territory, they, with the exception of uncivilized native tribes, shall be admitted to the enjoyment of all the rights, advantages, and immunities of citizens of the United States, and shall be maintained and protected in the free enjoyment of their liberty, property, and religion. The uncivilized tribes will be subject to such laws and regulations as the United States may from time to time adopt in regard to aboriginal tribes of that country.

Article IV His Majesty, the Emperor of all the Russias, shall appoint, with convenient despatch, an agent or agents for the purpose of formally delivering to a similar agent or agents, appointed on

behalf of the United States, the territory, dominion, property, dependencies, and appurtenances
which are ceded as above, and for doing any other
act which may be necessary in regard thereto. But
the cession, with the right of immediate possession, is nevertheless to be deemed complete and
absolute on the exchange of ratifications, without
waiting for such formal delivery.

Article V Immediately after the exchange of the
ratifications of this convention, any fortifications
or military posts which may be in the ceded territory shall be delivered to the agent of the United
States, and any Russian troops which may be in
the territory shall be withdrawn as soon as may be
reasonably and conveniently practicable.

Article VI In consideration of the cession aforesaid, the United States agree to pay at the Treasury
in Washington, within ten months after the exchange of the ratifications of this convention, to
the diplomatic representative or other agent of His
Majesty the Emperor of all the Russias, duly authorized to receive the same, seven million two
hundred thousand dollars in gold. The cession of
territory and dominion herein made is hereby declared to be free and unincumbered by any reservations, privileges, franchises, grants, or possessions, by any associated companies, whether
corporate or incorporate, Russian or any other; or
by any parties, except merely private individual
property-holders; and the cession hereby made
conveys all the rights, franchises, and privileges
now belonging to Russia in the said territory or
dominion, and appurtenances thereto.

Article VII When this convention shall have
been duly ratified by the President, of the United
States, by and with the advice and consent of the
Senate, on the one part, and, on the other, by His
Majesty the Emperor of all the Russias, the ratifications shall be exchanged at Washington within
three months from the date thereof, or sooner if
possible.

In faith whereof the respective Plenipotentiaries have signed this convention, and thereto affixed the seals of their arms.

Done at Washington, the thirtieth day of
March, in the year of our Lord one thousand eight
hundred and sixty-seven.

William H. Seward   Edward de Stoeckl

Source: American Historical Documents, 1000–1904.
Cambridge, MA: Harvard Classics, 1909–1914.

Official Summary of Anglo-Portuguese Treaty (February 26, 1884)

*Since the 1870s, King Leopold II had attempted to
colonize the Congo River basin as his own personal fiefdom. By the early 1800s, he had come
close to achieving his end, which the British considered detrimental to their own interests in the
region. Lacking claims to the basin itself, Britain
signed a treaty with the geriatric Portuguese empire, giving it control over the mouth of the Congo
River. In doing so, the British cut off Leopold's access to the Atlantic, while gaining navigation
rights on the lower part of the river themselves.
The Anglo-Portuguese Treaty of 1884 was part of
the multilateral maneuvering by European imperial powers that came to be called the "scramble
for Africa."*

Treaty between Her Majesty and His Majesty
the King of Portugal respecting the Rivers Congo
and Zambesi, and the Territory on the West Coast
of Africa between the 8° and 5° 12′ of South Latitude. Signed at London, 26th February, 1884.

Her Majesty the Queen of the United Kingdom
of Great Britain and Ireland, Empress of India,
&c., &c., &c., and His Most Faithful Majesty the
King of Portugal and the Algarves, etc., etc., etc.,
being animated with the desire to draw closer the
ties of friendship which unite the two nations; to
put an end to all difficulties relative to the rights
of sovereignty over the districts at the mouth of
the Congo on the West Coast of Africa, situated
between 8° and 5° 12′ of south latitude; to provide for the complete extinction of the Slave
Trade; and to promote the development of commerce and civilization in the African Continent;
have resolved to conclude a Treaty for this purpose, and have named as their Plenipotentiaries,
that is to say:

Her Majesty the Queen of the United Kingdom
of Great Britain and Ireland, Empress of India, the
Right Honourable Granville George, Earl Granville,
K.G., Her Majesty's Principal Secretary of State for
Foreign Affairs, &c., &c.;

And His Most Faithful Majesty the King of Portugal and the Algarves, Senhor Miguel Martins
d'Antas, Envoy Extraordinary and Minister
Plenipotentiary of His Most Faithful Majesty at the
Court of Her Britannic Majesty, &c., &c.;

Who, after having communicated to each other their respective full powers, found in good and due form, have agreed upon the following Articles:—

Article I. Subject to the conditions of the present Treaty, Her Britannic Majesty agrees to recognize the sovereignty of His Most Faithful Majesty the King of Portugal and the Algarves over that part of the West Coast of Africa situated between 8° and 5° 12′ of south latitude: and inland as far as follows:—

On the River Congo the limit shall be Nokki.

On the coast situated between 8° and 5° 12′ of south latitude the inland eastern frontier shall co-incide with the boundaries of the present posses-sions of the coast and riparian tribes. This frontier shall be defined, and the definition shall be com-municated with the least possible delay by His Most Faithful Majesty to Her Britannic Majesty.

The definition, when approved by the High Contracting Parties, shall be recorded in a Protocol to be annexed to the present Treaty.

Article II.—Right of Access of Subjects of all Nations to the above Territory.

Article III.—Freedom of Navigation of the Rivers Congo and Zambesi and their affluents. Claims of Portugal on the Shiré not to extend be-yond the confluence of the River Ruo with that river.

Article IV.—Freedom of Trade and Navigation, &c.

Article V.—No Transit or other Duties to be levied.

Article VI.—Open Roads.

Article VII.—Protection of Missionaries. Reli-gious Liberty.

Article VIII.—Treaties with Native Chiefs to be communicated by either Power to the other.

Article IX.—Customs Tariff.

Article X.—Confirmation of Privileges to British Subjects and their Commerce Most-favoured-nation Treatment.

Article XI.—Wrecks.

Article XII.—Slavery and the Slave Trade. Per-mission to British Ships of War to enter Territorial Waters of Portuguese Eastern African Colonies for Suppression of the Slave Trade. Similar powers to be given, if required, to Portuguese Vessels in British South African Possessions.

Article XIII.—Stipulations of Art. I. to apply to all Territories hereafter brought under Portuguese Sovereignty.

Article XIV.—British right of pre-emption in event of abandonment by Portugal of Fort of St. John the Baptist of Ajudá, on the Coast of Mina, or of any rights claimed by Portugal between 5° East and 5° West Longitude on the same coast.

Source: Hertslet, Sir Edward. *Map of Africa by Treaty,* 3d ed. London, 1909.

Berlin Act of 1885, Berlin Imperialist Conference (1885)

Beginning in the 1870s, King Leopold II had at-tempted to take control of the central African re-gion drained by the Congo River (modern-day Democratic Republic of Congo). This land-grab an-tagonized the great colonial powers of Europe, in-cluding Britain, France, Germany, and Portugal. In order to prevent a general conflict over the Congo and other disputed regions of Africa, the great pow-ers met in Berlin in the winter of 1884–1885 to di-vide up the continent and set forth collective poli-cies for its administration. The United States, attending as an observer, agreed to the final proto-cols. No Africans, however, were invited. The arbi-trary borders created at the conference—lumping certain antagonistic ethnic groups into the same ju-risdiction, while dividing other ethnic groups into different jurisdictions—were maintained after the colonies achieved nationhood in the mid-twentieth century, leading to numerous internal postindepen-dence conflicts.

Chap. I [relating to the Congo River Basin and adjacent territories]

I. The trade of all nations shall enjoy complete freedom

II. All flags, without distinction of nationality, shall have free access to the whole of the coast-line of the territories . . .

III. Wares of whatever origin, imported into these regions, under whatsoever flag, by sea or river, or overland, shall be subject to no other taxes than such as may be levied as fair compensation for expenditure in the interests of trade . . .

IV. Merchandise imported into these regions shall remain free from import and transit duties [subject to review after 20 years]

V. No power which exercises or shall exercise sovereign rights in the regions shall be allowed to grant therein a monopoly or favor of any kind in matters of trade . . .

VI. All the powers exercising sovereign rights or influence in the aforesaid territories bind themselves to watch over the preservation of the native tribes, and to care for the improvement of the conditions of their moral and material well-being and to help in suppressing slavery, and especially the Slave Trade. They shall, without distinction of creed or nation, protect and favor all religious, scientific, or charitable institutions and undertakings created and organized for the above ends, or which aim at instructing the natives and bringing home to them the blessings of civilization. Christian missionaries, scientists, and explorers, with their followers, property, and collections, shall likewise be the objects of especial protection. Freedom of conscience and religious toleration are expressly guaranteed to the natives, no less than to subjects and to foreigners . . .

Chap. II Documents relative to the Slave Trade

IX. . . . . the Powers which do or shall exercise sovereign rights or influence in the territories forming the basin of the Congo declare that these territories may not serve as a market or means of transit for the trade in slaves, of whatever race they may be. Each of the Powers binds itself to employ all the means at its disposal for putting an end to this trade and for punishing those who engage in it.

Chap. IV Act of Navigation for the Congo

XIII. The navigation of the Congo, without excepting any of its branches or outlets, is, and shall remain, free for the merchant ships of all nations equally . . . the subjects and flags of all nations shall in all respects be treated on a footing of perfect equality . . . no exclusive privilege of navigation will be conceded to Companies, Corporations, or private persons whatsoever . . .

Chap. V Act of Navigation for the Niger.

XXVI. The navigation of the (River) Niger, without excepting any of its branches and outlets, is and shall remain entirely free for the merchant ships of all nations equally . . .

Chap. VI [Regarding new occupations on the coasts of Africa]

XXXIV. Any power which henceforth takes possession of a tract of land on the coasts of the African Continent outside of its present possessions, or which, being hitherto without such pos-

sessions, shall acquire them . . . shall accompany the respective act with a notification thereof, addressed to the other Signatory Powers of the present Act, in order to enable them, if need be, to make good any claims of their own.

XXXV. The Signatory Powers of the present Act recognize the obligation to insure the establishment of authority in the regions occupied by them on the coasts of the African Continent sufficient to protect existing rights, and, as the case may be, freedom of trade and of transit under the conditions agreed upon.

XXXVII. The Powers signatory to the present general Act reserve to themselves the right of eventually, by mutual agreement, introducing therein modifications or improvements the utility of which has been shown by experience . . .

Done at Berlin, the 26th day of February, 1885.

Source: web.jjay.cuny.edu/~jobrien/reference/ob45.html.

U.S. Recognition of Cuban Independence (1898)

Beginning as early as the 1870s and culminating in the late 1890s, the people of Cuba rose up in rebellion against the rule of Spain. By the latter part of this period, the American press—particularly the major urban dailies controlled by William Randolph Hearst and other media moguls—had taken up the cause of Cuban freedom. When the U.S. battleship Maine *blew up in Havana harbor, Americans jumped to the conclusion that the deed had been committed by agents of Spain. The outcome was an increased bellicosity in the United States toward Spain and, on April 11, a congressional joint resolution recognizing the independence of the Cuban people, a stance that inevitably led to war with Spain. In that war, the United States would seize a number of Spanish colonies in the Caribbean and Pacific, although Cuba, ironically, would be given its independence within a couple of years, while other territories would be held for decades or, in the case of Puerto Rico, through the present day.*

Whereas, the abhorrent conditions which have existed for more than three years in the Island of Cuba, so near our own borders, have shocked the moral sense of the people of the United States, have been a disgrace to Christian civilization, culminating, as they have, in the destruction of a United States battleship, with two hundred and sixty-six of its officers and crew, while on a friendly visit in the harbor of Havana, and can not longer be endured, as has been set forth by the President of the United States in his message to Congress of April eleventh, eighteen hundred and ninety-eight, upon which the action of Congress was invited: Therefore,

Resolved, by the Senate and House of Representatives of the United States of America in Congress assembled, First. That the people of the Island of Cuba are, and of right ought to be, free and independent.

Second. That it is the duty of the United States to demand, and the Government of the United States does hereby demand, that the Government of Spain at once relinquish its authority and government in the Island of Cuba, and withdraw its land and naval forces from Cuba and Cuban waters.

Third. That the President of the United States be, and he hereby is, directed and empowered to use the entire land and naval forces of the United States, and to call into the actual service of the United States, the militia of the several States, to such extent as may be necessary to carry these resolutions into effect.

Fourth. That the United States hereby disclaims any disposition or intention to exercise sovereignty, jurisdiction, or control over said Islands except for the pacification thereof, and asserts its determination, when that is accomplished, to leave the government and control of the Island to its people.

Approved, April 20, 1898.

Source: American Historical Documents, 1000–1904.
Cambridge, MA: Harvard Classics, 1909–1914.

Boxer Protocol (September 7, 1901)

Following China's defeat in the Sino-Japanese war of 1895, European powers moved in to divide the country up into "spheres of influence." Not fully colonies, these spheres nevertheless offered commercial privileges and judicial immunity to various European colonizers. While the imperial government had little power to confront the Europeans directly, it did sponsor secret societies to fight back, including the Society of Righteous and Harmonious Fists, known in the West as the Boxers. In 1900, the Boxers rose up in rebellion and besieged thousands of Europeans in their urban enclaves in Beijing, until they were defeated by a multinational force. The resulting Boxer Protocol (excerpted here), which called for a western military presence in the capital of Beijing and the paying of indemnities to the West, was a further humiliation for China, but it did set in motion reforms that would modernize the Chinese state.

Peace Agreement between the Great Powers and China.

THE PLENIPOTENTIARIES of . . . [Germany, Austria-Hungary, Belgium, Spain, United States, France, Great Britain, Italy, Japan, Netherlands, Russia, China] have met for the purpose of declaring that China has complied with the conditions laid down in the note of the 22nd December, 1900, and which were accepted in their entirety by His Majesty the Emperor of China in a Decree dated the 27th December, 1900.

ARTICLE 1.

1) By an Imperial Edict of the 9th June last, Prince of the First Rank, Chun, was appointed Ambassador of His Majesty the Emperor of China, and directed in that capacity to convey to His Majesty the German Emperor the expression of the regrets of His Majesty the Emperor of China and of the Chinese Government at the assassination of his Excellency the late Baron von Ketteler, German Minister. Prince Chun left Peking on the 12th July last to carry out the orders which had been given him. 2) The Chinese Government has stated that it will erect on the spot of the assassination of his Excellency the late Baron von Ketteler, commemorative monument worthy of the rank of the deceased, and bearing an inscription in the Latin, German, and Chinese languages which shall express the regrets of His Majesty the Emperor of China for the murder committed. The Chinese Plenipotentiaries have informed his Excellency the German Plenipotentiary, in a letter dated the 22nd July last, that an arch of the whole width of the street would be erected on the said spot, and that work on it was begun on the 25th June last.

ARTICLE II.

1) Imperial Edicts of the 13th and 21st February, 1901, inflicted the following punishments on

the principal authors of the attempts and of the crimes committed against the foreign Governments and their nationals:—Tsa-Ii, Prince Tuan, and Tsai-Lan, Duke Fu-kuo, were sentenced to be brought before the Autumnal Court of Assize for execution, and it was agreed that if the Emperor saw fit to grant them their lives, they should be exiled to Turkestan, and there imprisoned for life, without the possibility of commutation of these punishments. Tsai Hsun, Prince Chuang, Ying-Nien, President of the Court of Censors, and Chao Shu-chiao, President of the Board of Punishments, were condemned to commit suicide. Yu Hsun, Governor of Shansi, Chi Hsiu, President of the Board of Rites, and Hsu Cheng-yu, formerly Senior Vice-President of the Board of Punishments, were condemned to death. Posthumous degradation was inflicted on Kang Yi, Assistant Grand Secretary, President of the Board of Works, Hsu Tung, Grand Secretary, and Li Ping-heng, former Governor-General of Szu-chuan. Imperial Edict of the 13th February last rehabilitated the memories of Hsu Yung-yi, President of the Board of War; Li Shan, President of the Board of Works; Hsu Ching Cheng, Senior Vice-President of the Board of Civil Office; Lien Yuan, Vice-Chancellor of the Grand Council; and Yuan Chang, Vice-President of the Court of Sacrifices, who had been put to death for having protested against the outrageous breaches of international law of last year. Prince Chuang committed suicide on the 21st February last; Ying Nien and Chao Shu-chiao on the 24th February; Yu Hsien was executed on the 22nd February; Chi Hsiu and Hsu Cheng-yu on the 26th February; Tung Fu-hsiang, General in Kan-su, has been deprived of his office by Imperial Edict of the 13th February last, pending the determination of the final punishment to be inflicted on him. Imperial Edicts, dated the 29th April and 19th August, 1901, have inflicted various punishments on the provincial officials convicted of the crimes and outrages of last summer. 2) An Imperial Edict, promulgated the 19th August, 1901, ordered the suspension of official examinations for five years in all cities where foreigners were massacred or submitted to cruel treatment.

ARTICLE III.

So as to make honourable reparation for the assassination of Mr. Sugiyama, Chancellor of the Japanese Legation, His Majesty the Emperor of China, by an Imperial Edict of the 18th June, 1901, appointed Na T'ung, Vice-President of the Board of Finances, to be his Envoy Extraordinary, and specially directed him to convey to His Majesty the Emperor of Japan the expression of the regrets of His Majesty the Emperor of China and of his Government at the assassination of Mr. Sugiyama.

ARTICLE IV.

The Chinese Government has agreed to erect an expiatory monument in each of the foreign or international cemeteries which were desecrated, and in which the tombs were destroyed. It has been agreed with the Representatives of the Powers that the Legations interested shall settle the details for the erection of these monuments, China bearing all the expenses thereof, estimated at 10,000 taels, for the cemeteries at Peking and in its neighbourhood, and at 5,000 taels for the cemeteries in the provinces. The amounts have been paid, and the list of these cemeteries is inclosed herewith.

ARTICLE V.

China has agreed to prohibit the importation into its territory of arms and ammunition, as well as of materials exclusively used for the manufacture of arms and ammunition. An Imperial Edict has been issued on the 25th August, forbidding said importation for a term of two years. New Edicts may be issued subsequently extending this by other successive terms of two years in case of necessity recognized by the Powers.

ARTICLE VI.

By an Imperial Edict dated the 29th May, 1901, His Majesty the Emperor of China agreed to pay the Powers an indemnity of 450,000,000 of Haikwan taels. This sum represents the total amount of the indemnities for States, Companies, or Societies, private individuals and Chinese, referred to in Article 6 of the note of the 22nd December, 1900. 1) These 450,000,000 constitute a gold debt calculated at the rate of the Haikwan tael to the gold currency of each country [335 million gold dollars, etc.] . . .

This sum in gold shall bear interest at 4 per cent. per annum, and the capital shall be reimbursed by China in thirty-nine years in the manner indicated in the annexed plan of amortization. Capital and interest shall be payable in gold or at the rates of exchange corresponding to the dates at which the different payments fall due. The amortization shall commence the 1st January, 1902, and shall finish at the end of the year 1940. The amortizations are payable annually, the first payment being fixed on the 1st January, 1903. Interest shall run from the 1st July, 1901, but the Chinese Government shall have the right to pay off within a term of three years, beginning January 1902, the arrears of the first six months ending the 31st December, 1901, on condition, however, that it pays compound interest at the rate of 4 per cent. a year on the sums the payment of which shall have been thus deferred. Interest shall be payable semi-annually, the first payment being fixed on the 1st July, 1902.

2) The service of the debt shall take place in Shanghai in the following manner:—Each Power shall be represented by a Delegate on a Commission of bankers authorized to receive the amount of interest and amortization which shall be paid to it by the Chinese authorities designated for that purpose, to divide it among the interested parties, and to give a receipt for the same.

3) The Chinese Government shall deliver to the Doyen [i.e., the senior member] of the Diplomatic Corps at Peking a bond for the lump sum, which shall subsequently be converted into fractional bonds bearing the signature of the Delegates of the Chinese Government designated for that purpose. This operation and all those relating to issuing of the bonds shall be performed by the above-mentioned Commission, in accordance with the instructions which the Powers shall send their Delegates.

4) The proceeds of the revenues assigned to the payment of the bonds shall be paid monthly to the Commission.

5) The seven assigned as security for the bonds are the following: a) The balance of the revenues of the Imperial Maritime Customs, after payment of the interest and amortization of preceding loans secured on these revenues, plus the proceeds of the raising to 5 per cent. effective of the present tariff of maritime imports, including articles until now on the free list, but exempting rice, foreign cereals, and flour, gold and silver bullion and coin. b) The revenues of the native Customs, administered in the open ports by the Imperial Maritime Customs. c) The total revenues of the salt gabelle, exclusive of the fraction previously set aside for other foreign loans.

6) The raising of the present tariff on imports to 5 per cent. effective is agreed to on the conditions mentioned below. It shall be put in force two months after the signing of the present Protocol, and no exceptions shall be made except for merchandize in transit not more than ten days after the said signing. . . . . b) The beds of the Rivers Whangpoo and Peiho shall be improved with the financial participation of China.

ARTICLE VII.

The Chinese Government has agreed that the quarter occupied by the Legations shall be considered as one specially reserved for their use and placed under their exclusive control, in which Chinese shall not have the right to reside, and which may be made defensible. . . . . In the Protocol annexed to the letter of the 16th January, 1901, China recognized the right of each Power to maintain a permanent guard in the said quarter for the defence of its Legation.

ARTICLE VIII.

The Chinese Government has consented to raze the forts of Taku, and those which might impede free communication between Peking and the sea. Steps have been taken for carrying this out.

ARTICLE IX.

The Chinese Government conceded the right to the Powers in the Protocol annexed to the letter of the 16th January, 1901, to occupy certain points, to be determined by an Agreement between them for the maintenance of open communication between the capital and the sea. The points occupied by the Powers are:- Huang-tsun, Lang-fang, Yang-tsun, Tien-tsin, Chun-liang-Cheng, Tong-ku, Lu-tai, Tong-shan, Lan-chou, Chang-li, Chin-wang Tao, Shan-hai Kuan.

ARTICLE X.

The Chinese Government has agreed to post and to have published during two years in all district cities the following Imperial Edicts: 1) Edict of the 1st February, 1901, prohibiting for ever under pain of death, membership in any anti-foreign society. 2) Edicts of the 13th and 21st February, 29th April and 19th August, 1901, enumerating the punishments inflicted on the guilty. 3) Edict of the 19th August, 1901, prohibiting examinations in all cities where foreigners were massacred or subjected to cruel treatment. 4) Edicts of the 1st February, 1901, declaring all Governors General, Governors, and provincial or local officials responsible for order in their respective districts, and that in case of new anti-foreign troubles or other infractions of the Treaties which shall not be immediately repressed and the authors of which shall not have been punished, these officials shall be immediately dismissed without possibility of being given new functions or new honours. The posting of these Edicts is being carried on throughout the Empire.

ARTICLE XI.

The Chinese Government has agreed to negotiate the amendments deemed necessary by the foreign Governments to the Treaties of Commerce and Navigation and the other subjects concerning commercial relations with the object of facilitating them. At present, and as a result of the stipulation contained in Article 6 concerning the indemnity, the Chinese Government agrees to assist in the improvement of the courses of the Rivers Peiho and Whangpoo, as stated below.- 1) The works for the improvement of the navigability of the Peiho, begun in 1898 with the co-operation of the Chinese Government, have been resumed under the direction of an International Commission. As soon as the Administration of Tien-tsin shall have been handed back to the Chinese Government it will be in a position to be represented on this Commission, and will pay each year a sum of 60,000 Haikwan taels for maintaining the works.

2) A Conservancy Board, charged with the management and control of the works for straightening the Whangpoo and the improvement of the course of that river, is hereby created. The Board shall consist of members representing the interests of the Chinese Government and those of foreigners in the shipping trade of Shanghai. The expenses incurred for the works and the general management of the undertaking are estimated at the annual sum of 460,000 Haikwan taels for the first twenty years. This sum shall be supplied in equal portions by the Chinese Government and the foreign interests concerned.

ARTICLE XII.

An Imperial Edict of the 24th July, 1901, reformed the Office of Foreign Affairs, Tsung-li Yamen, on the lines indicated by the Powers, that is to say, transformed it into a Ministry of Foreign Affairs, Wai Wu Pu, which takes precedence over the six other Ministries of State; the same Edict

appointed the principal Members of this Ministry. An agreement has also been reached concerning the modification of Court ceremonial as regards the reception of foreign Representatives, and has been the subject of several notes from the Chinese Plenipotentiaries, the substance of which is embodied in a Memorandum herewith annexed. Finally, it is expressly understood that as regards the declarations specified above and the annexed documents originating with the foreign Plenipotentiaries, the French text only is authoritative. The Chinese Government having thus complied to the satisfaction of the Powers with the conditions laid down in the above-mentioned note of the 22nd December, 1900, the Powers have agreed to accede to the wish of China to terminate the situation created by the disorders of the summer of 1900. In consequence thereof, the foreign Plenipotentiaries are authorized to declare in the names of their Governments that, with the exception of the Legation guards mentioned in Article VII, the international troops will completely evacuate the city of Peking on the 7th September, 1901, and, with the exception of the localities mentioned in Article IX, will withdraw from the Province of Chihli on the 22nd September, 1901. The present final Protocol has been drawn up in twelve identical copies, and signed by all the Plenipotentiaries of the contracting countries.

Source: Fox, Charles James. *The Protocol of 1901, Charter of Peking's Diplomatocracy.* Tientsin: North China Star, 1926.

John Hobson: *Imperialism* (1902)

John Hobson, a British economist and journalist, was one of the first theorists to dispense with self-glorifying explanations for empire and examine its economic underpinnings. In his classic Imperialism: A Study *(1902), Hobson argued that Europe's imperialist expansion was a product of its economy, specifically its excess of capital in search of investment markets. While Hobson was not against empire per se, his writings inspired such ardent anti-imperialists as the Bolshevik Vladimir Lenin.*

Amid the welter of vague political abstractions to lay one's finger accurately upon any "ism" so as to pin it down and mark it out by definition seems impossible. Where meanings shift so quickly and so subtly, not only following changes of thought, but often manipulated artificially by political practitioners so as to obscure, expand, or distort, it is idle to demand the same rigour as is expected in the exact sciences. A certain broad consistency in its relations to other kindred terms is the nearest approach to definition which such a term as Imperialism admits. Nationalism, internationalism, colonialism, its three closest congeners, are equally elusive, equally shifty, and the changeful overlapping of all four demands the closest vigilance of students of modern politics.

During the nineteenth century the struggle towards nationalism, or establishment of political union on a basis of nationality, was a dominant factor alike in dynastic movements and as an inner motive in the life of masses of population. That struggle, in external politics, sometimes took a disruptive form, as in the case of Greece, Servia, Roumania, and Bulgaria breaking from Ottoman rule, and the detachment of North Italy from her unnatural alliance with the Austrian Empire. In other cases it was a unifying or a centralising force, enlarging the area of nationality, as in the case of Italy and the Pan-Slavist movement in Russia. Sometimes nationality was taken as a basis of federation of States, as in United Germany and in North America.

It is true that the forces making for political union sometimes went further, making for federal union of diverse nationalities, as in the cases of Austria-Hungary, Norway and Sweden, and the Swiss Federation. But the general tendency was towards welding into large strong national unities the loosely related States and provinces with shifting attachments and alliances which covered large areas of Europe since the break-up of the Empire. This was the most definite achievement of the nineteenth century. The force of nationality, operating in this work, is quite as visible in the failures to achieve political freedom as in the successes; and the struggles of Irish, Poles, Finns, Hungarians, and Czechs to resist the forcible subjection to or alliance with stronger neighbours brought out in its full vigour the powerful sentiment of nationality.

The middle of the century was especially distinguished by a series of definitely "nationalist" revivals, some of which found important interpreta-tion in dynastic changes, while others were crushed or collapsed. Holland, Poland, Belgium, Norway, the Balkans, formed a vast arena for these struggles of national forces.

The close of the third quarter of the century saw Europe fairly settled into large national States or federations of States, though in the nature of the case there can be no finality, and Italy continued to look to Trieste, as Germany still looks to Austria, for the fulfillment of her manifest destiny.

This passion and the dynastic forms it helped to mould and animate are largely attributable to the fierce prolonged resistance which peoples, both great and small, were called on to maintain against the imperial designs of Napoleon. The national spirit of England was roused by the tenseness of the struggle to a self-consciousness it had never experienced since "the spacious days of great Elizabeth." Jena made Prussia into a great nation; the Moscow campaign brought Russia into the field of European nationalities as a factor in politics, opening her for the first time to the full tide of Western ideas and influences.

Turning from this territorial and dynastic nationalism to the spirit of racial, linguistic, and economic solidarity which has been the underlying motive, we find a still more remarkable movement. Local particularism on the one hand, vague cosmopolitanism upon the other, yielded to a ferment of nationalist sentiment, manifesting itself among the weaker peoples not merely in a sturdy and heroic resistance against political absorption or territorial nationalism, but in a passionate revival of decaying customs, language, literature and art; while it bred in more dominant peoples strange ambitions of national "destiny" and an attendant spirit of Chauvinism.

No mere array of facts and figures adduced to illustrate the economic nature of the new Imperialism will suffice to dispel the popular delusion that the use of national force to secure new markets by annexing fresh tracts of territory is a sound and a necessary policy for an advanced industrial country like Great Britain. . . .

But these arguments are not conclusive. It is open to Imperialists to argue thus: "We must have markets for our growing manufactures, we must have new outlets for the investment of our surplus capital and for the energies of the adventurous surplus of our population: such expansion is a necessity of life to a nation with our great and growing powers of production. An ever larger share of our population is devoted to the manufactures and commerce of towns, and is thus dependent for life and work upon food and raw materials from foreign lands. In order to buy and pay for these things we must sell our goods abroad. During the first three-quarters of the nineteenth century we could do so without difficulty by a natural expansion of commerce with continental nations and our colonies, all of which were far behind us in the main arts of manufacture and the carrying trades. So long as England held a virtual monopoly of the world markets for certain important classes of manufactured goods, Imperialism was unnecessary.

After 1870 this manufacturing and trading supremacy was greatly impaired: other nations, especially Germany, the United States, and Belgium, advanced with great rapidity, and while they have not crushed or even stayed the increase of our external trade, their competition made it more and more difficult to dispose of the full surplus of our manufactures at a profit. The encroachments made by these nations upon our old markets, even in our own possessions, made it most urgent that we should take energetic means to secure new markets. These new markets had to lie in hitherto undeveloped countries, chiefly in the tropics, where vast populations lived capable of growing economic needs which our manufacturers and merchants could supply. Our rivals were seizing and annexing territories for similar purposes, and when they had annexed them closed them to our trade. The diplomacy and the arms of Great Britain had to be used in order to compel the owners of the new markets to deal with us: and experience showed that the safest means of securing and developing such markets is by establishing 'protectorates' or by annexation. . . .

It was this sudden demand for foreign markets for manufactures and for investments which was avowedly responsible for the adoption of Imperialism as a political policy. . . . They needed Imperialism because they desired to use the public resources of their country to find profitable employment for their capital which otherwise would be superfluous. . . .

Every improvement of methods of production, every concentration of ownership and control, seems to accentuate the tendency. As one nation after another enters the machine economy and adopts advanced industrial methods, it becomes more difficult for its manufacturers, merchants, and financiers to dispose profitably of their economic resources, and they are tempted more and more to use their Governments in order to secure for their particular use some distant undeveloped country by annexation and protection.

The process, we may be told, is inevitable, and so it seems upon a superficial inspection. Everywhere appear excessive powers of production, excessive capital in search of investment. It is admitted by all business men that the growth of the powers of production in their country exceeds the growth in consumption, that more goods can be produced than can be sold at a profit, and that more capital exists than can find remunerative investment.

It is this economic condition of affairs that forms the taproot of Imperialism. If the consuming public in this country raised its standard of consumption to keep pace with every rise of productive powers, there could be no excess of goods or capital clamorous to use Imperialism in order to find markets: foreign trade would indeed exist. . . .

Everywhere the issue of quantitative versus qualitative growth comes up. This is the entire issue of empire. A people limited in number and energy and in the land they occupy have the choice of improving to the utmost the political and economic management of their own land, confining themselves to such accessions of territory as are justified by the most economical disposition of a growing population; or they may proceed, like the slovenly farmer, to spread their power and energy over the whole earth, tempted by the speculative value or the quick profits of some new market, or else by mere greed of territorial acquisition, and ignoring the political and economic wastes and risks involved by this imperial career. It must be clearly understood that this is essentially a choice of alternatives; a full simultaneous application of intensive and extensive cultivation is impossible. A nation may either, following the example of Denmark or Switzerland, put brains into agriculture, develop a finely varied system of public education, general and technical, apply the ripest science to its special manufacturing industries, and so support in progressive comfort and character a considerable population upon a strictly limited area; or it may, like Great Britain, neglect its agriculture, allowing its lands to go out of cultivation and its population to grow up in towns, fall behind other nations in its methods of education and in the capacity of adapting to its uses the latest scientific knowledge, in order that it may squander its pecuniary and military resources in forcing bad markets and finding speculative fields of investment in distant corners of the earth, adding millions of square miles and of unassimilable population to the area of the Empire.

The driving forces of class interest which stimulate and support this false economy we have explained. No remedy will serve which permits the future operation of these forces. It is idle to attack Imperialism or Militarism as political expedients or policies unless the axe is laid at the economic root of the tree, and the classes for whose interest Imperialism works are shorn of the surplus revenues which seek this outlet.

Source: Hobson, John A. *Imperialism: A Study.* New York: J. Pott, 1902.

Entente Cordiale between Britain and France (April 8, 1904)

In 1898, British and French forces—rapidly moving to consolidate their control over African territories—met at Fashoda, in modern-day Sudan. The Fashoda incident nearly led to general war between the two colonial powers. But cooler heads prevailed. Six years later, the two countries signed the Entente Cordiale, laying out their respective interests in Morocco, a disputed territory. But the agreement, which included secret protocols, angered the Germans, who called for yet another conference two years later, which gave Germany certain commercial rights in Morocco as well.

Formally titled, the 'Declaration between the United Kingdom and France Respecting Egypt and Morocco, Together with the Secret Articles Signed at the Same Time.'

The Franco-British Declaration, 1904

ARTICLE 1.

His Britannic Majesty's Government declare that they have no intention of altering the political status of Egypt.

The Government of the French Republic, for their part, declare that they will not obstruct the action of Great Britain in that country. . . .

It is agreed that the post of Director-General of Antiquities in Egypt shall continue, as in the past, to be entrusted to a French *savant.*

The French schools in Egypt shall continue to enjoy the same liberty as in the past.

ARTICLE 2.

The Government of the French Republic declare that they have no intention of altering the political status of Morocco.

His Britannic Majesty's Government, for their part, recognise that it appertains to France, more particularly as a Power whose dominions are conterminous for a great distance with those of Morocco, to preserve order in that country, and to provide assistance for the purpose of all administrative, economic, financial, and military reforms which it may require.

They declare that they will not obstruct the action taken by France for this purpose, provided that such action shall leave intact the rights which Great Britain, in virtue of treaties, conventions, and usage, enjoys in Morocco, including the right of coasting trade between the ports of Morocco, enjoyed by British vessels since 1901.

ARTICLE 3.

His Britannic Majesty's Government for their part, will respect the rights which France, in virtue of treaties, conventions, and usage, enjoys in Egypt, including the right of coasting trade between Egyptian ports accorded to French vessels.

ARTICLE 4.

The two Governments, being equally attached to the principle of commercial liberty both in Egypt and Morocco, declare that they will not, in those countries, countenance any inequality either in the imposition of customs duties or other taxes, or of railway transport charges. The trade of both nations with Morocco and with Egypt shall enjoy the same treatment in transit through the French and British possessions in Africa. An agreement between the two Governments shall settle the conditions of such transit and shall determine the points of entry.

This mutual engagement shall be binding for a period of thirty years. Unless this stipulation is expressly denounced at least one year in advance, the period shall be extended for five years at a time.

Nevertheless the Government of the French Republic reserve to themselves in Morocco, and His Britannic Majesty's Government reserve to themselves in Egypt, the right to see that the concessions for roads, railways, ports, etc., are only granted on such conditions as will maintain intact the authority of the State over these great undertakings of public interest.

ARTICLE 5.

His Britannic Majesty's Government declare that they will use their influence in order that the French officials now in the Egyptian service may not be placed under conditions less advantageous than those applying to the British officials in the service.

The Government of the French Republic, for their part, would make no objection to the application of analogous conditions to British officials now in the Moorish service.

ARTICLE 6.

In order to ensure the free passage of the Suez Canal, His Britannic Majesty's Government declare that they adhere to the treaty of the 29th October, 1888, and that they agree to their being put in force. The free passage of the Canal being thus guaranteed, the execution of the last sentence of paragraph 1 as well as of paragraph 2 of Article of that treaty will remain in abeyance.

ARTICLE 7.

In order to secure the free passage of the Straits of Gibraltar, the two Governments agree not to permit the erection of any fortifications or strategic works on that portion of the coast of Morocco comprised between, but not including, Melilla and the heights which command the right bank of the River Sebou.

This condition does not, however, apply to the places at present in the occupation of Spain on the Moorish coast of the Mediterranean.

ARTICLE 8.

The two Governments, inspired by their feeling of sincere friendship for Spain, take into special consideration the interests which that country derives from her geographical position and from her territorial possessions on the Moorish coast of the Mediterranean. In regard to these interests the French Government will come to an understanding with the Spanish Government. The agreement which may be come to on the subject between France and Spain shall be communicated to His Britannic Majesty's Government.

ARTICLE 9.

The two Governments agree to afford to one another their diplomatic support, in order to obtain the execution of the clauses of the present Declaration regarding Egypt and Morocco.

In witness whereof his Excellency the Ambassador of the French Republic at the Court of His Majesty the King of the United Kingdom of Great Britain and Ireland and of the British Dominions beyond the Seas, Emperor of India, and His Majesty's Principal Secretary of State for Foreign Affairs, duly authorised for that purpose, have signed the present Declaration and have affixed thereto their seals.

Done at London, in duplicate, the 8th day of April, 1904.

[Henry Charles Keith Petty-Fitzmaurice] LANSDOWNE

PAUL CAMBON

Secret Articles

ARTICLE 1.

In the event of either Government finding themselves constrained, by the force of circumstances, to modify their policy in respect to Egypt or Morocco, the engagements which they have undertaken towards each other by Articles 4, 6, and 7 of the Declaration of today's date would remain intact.

ARTICLE 2.

His Britannic Majesty's Government have no present intention of proposing to the Powers any changes in the system of the Capitulations, or in the judicial organisation of Egypt.

In the event of their considering it desirable to introduce in Egypt reforms tending to assimilate the Egyptian legislative system to that in force in other civilised Countries, the Government of the French Republic will not refuse to entertain any such proposals, on the understanding that His Britannic Majesty's Government will agree to entertain the suggestions that the Government of the French Republic may have to make to them with a view of introducing similar reforms in Morocco.

ARTICLE 3.

The two Governments agree that a certain extent of Moorish territory adjacent to Melilla, Ceuta, and other *presides* should, whenever the Sultan ceases to exercise authority over it, come within the sphere of influence of Spain, and that the administration of the coast from Melilla as far as, but not including, the heights on the right bank of the Sebou shall be entrusted to Spain.

Nevertheless, Spain would previously have to give her formal assent to the provisions of Articles 4 and 7 of the Declaration of today's date, and undertake to carry them out.

She would also have to undertake not to alienate the whole, or a part, of the territories placed under her authority or in her sphere of influence.

ARTICLE 4.

If Spain, when invited to assent to the provisions of the preceding article, should think proper to decline, the arrangement between France and Great Britain, as embodied in the Declaration of today's date, would be none the less at once applicable.

ARTICLE 5.

Should the consent of the other Powers to the draft Decree mentioned in Article I of the Declaration of today's date not be obtained, the Government of the French Republic will not oppose the repayment at par of the Guaranteed, Privileged, and Unified Debts after the 15th July, 1910.

Done at London, in duplicate, the 8th day of April, 1904.

LANSDOWNE   PAUL CAMBON

Source: Great Britain, *Parliamentary Papers.* Vol. CIII, Cmd. 5969. London, 1911.

Treaty of Portsmouth (September 5, 1905)

In February 1904, the Japanese launched a surprise attack against the Russian warships at Port Arthur, China, setting off the Russo-Japanese War. The two powers were fighting over influence in the Port Arthur region of northeast China. Japan, worried that the completion of a Russian railway would secure Moscow's control of the strategic port, decided to make their move before the track was finished. Japan's victory over the Russians, confirmed in the Treaty of Portsmouth, which ended the war, was more than just another imperialist tussle—it was the first defeat of a European power by a non-European power in modern times. In addition, the treaty—negotiated by U.S. President Theodore Roosevelt—signaled America's growing emergence as a force in international politics.

The Emperor of Japan on the one part, and the Emperor of all the Russias, on the other part, animated by a desire to restore the blessings of peace, have resolved to conclude a treaty of peace, and have for this purpose named their plenipotentiaries, that is to say, for his Majesty the Emperor of Japan, Baron Komura Jutaro, Jusami, Grand Cordon of the Imperial Order of the Rising Sun, his Minister for Foreign Affairs, and his Excellency Takahira Kogoro, Imperial Order of the Sacred Treasure, his Minister to the United States, and his Majesty the Emperor of all the Russias, his Excellency Sergius Witte, his Secretary of State and President of the Committee of Ministers of the Empire of Russia, and his Excellency Baron Roman Rosen, Master of the Imperial Court of Russia, his Majesty's Ambassador to the United States, who, after having exchanged their full powers, which were found to be in good and due form, and concluded the following articles:

ARTICLE I. There shall henceforth be peace and amity between their Majesties the Emperor of Japan and the Emperor of all the Russias, and between their respective States and subjects.

ARTICLE II. The Imperial Russian Government, acknowledging that Japan possesses in Korea paramount political, military and economical interests engages neither to obstruct nor interfere with measures for guidance, protection and control which the Imperial Government of Japan may find necessary to take in Korea. It is understood that Russian subjects in Korea shall be treated in exactly the same manner as the subjects and citizens of other foreign Powers; that is to say, they shall be placed on the same footing as the subjects and citizens of the most favored nation. It is also agreed that, in order to avoid causes of misunderstanding, the two high contracting parties will abstain on the Russian-Korean frontier from taking any military measure which may menace the security of Russian or Korean territory.

ARTICLE III. Japan and Russia mutually engage:

First.—To evacuate completely and simultaneously Manchuria, except the territory affected by the lease of the Liaotung Peninsula, in conformity with the provisions of the additional article I annexed to this treaty, and,

Second.—To restore entirely and completely to the exclusive administration of China all portions of Manchuria now in occupation, or under the control of the Japanese or Russian troops, with the exception of the territory above mentioned.

The Imperial Government of Russia declares that it has not in Manchuria any territorial advantages or preferential or exclusive concessions in the impairment of Chinese sovereignty, or inconsistent with the principle of equal opportunity.

ARTICLE IV. Japan and Russia reciprocally engage not to obstruct any general measures common to all countries which China may take for the development of the commerce or industry of Manchuria.

ARTICLE V. The Imperial Russian Government transfers and assigns to the Imperial Government of Japan, with the consent of the Government of China, the lease of Port Arthur, Talien and the adjacent territorial waters, and all rights, privileges and concessions connected with or forming part of such lease, and it also transfers and assigns to the Imperial government of Japan all public works and properties in the territory affected by the above-mentioned lease.

The two contracting parties mutually engage to obtain the consent of the Chinese Government mentioned in the foregoing stipulation.

The Imperial Government of Japan, on its part, undertakes that the proprietary rights of Russian subjects in the territory above referred to shall be perfectly respected.

ARTICLE VI. The Imperial Russian Government engages to transfer and assign to the Imperial Government of Japan, without compensation and with the consent of the Chinese Government, the railway between Chang-chunfu and Kuanchangtsu and Port Arthur, and all the branches, together with all the rights, privileges and properties appertaining thereto in that region, as well as all the coal mines in said region belonging to or worked for the benefit of the railway. The two high contracting parties mutually engage to obtain the consent of the Government of China mentioned in the foregoing stipulation.

ARTICLE VII. Japan and Russia engage to exploit their respective railways in Manchuria exclusively for commercial and industrial purposes and nowise for strategic purposes. It is understood that this restriction does not apply to the railway in the territory affected by the lease of the Liaotung Peninsula.

ARTICLE VIII. The imperial Governments of Japan and Russia with the view to promote and fa-

cilitate intercourse and traffic will as soon as possible conclude a separate convention for the regulation of their connecting railway services in Manchuria.

ARTICLE IX. The Imperial Russian Government cedes to the Imperial Government of Japan in perpetuity and full sovereignty the southern portion of the Island of Saghalin and all the islands adjacent thereto and the public works and properties thereon. The fiftieth degree of north latitude is adopted as the northern boundary of the ceded territory. The exact alignment of such territory shall be determined in accordance with the provisions of the additional article II annexed to this treaty.

Japan and Russia mutually agree not to construct in their respective possessions on the Island of Saghalin or the adjacent islands any fortification or other similar military works. They also respectively engage not to take any military measures which may impede the free navigation of the Strait of La Perouse and the Strait of Tartary.

ARTICLE X. It is reserved to Russian subjects, inhabitants of the territory ceded to Japan, to sell their real property and retire to their country, but if they prefer to remain in the ceded territory they will be maintained protected in the full exercise of their industries and rights of property on condition of submitting to the Japanese laws and jurisdiction. Japan shall have full liberty to withdraw the right of residence in or to deport from such territory of any inhabitants who labor under political or administrative disability. She engages, however, that the proprietary rights of such inhabitants shall be fully respected.

ARTICLE XI. Russia engages to arrange with Japan for granting to Japanese subjects rights of fishery along the coasts of the Russian possession in the Japan, Okhotsk and Bering Seas.

It is agreed that the foregoing engagement shall not affect rights already belonging to Russian or foreign subjects in those regions.

ARTICLE XII. The treaty of commerce and navigation between Japan and Russia having been annulled by the war the Imperial Governments of Japan and Russia engage to adopt as a basis for their commercial relations pending the conclusion of a new treaty of commerce and navigation the basis of the treaty which was in force previous to the present war, the system of reciprocal treatment on the footing of the most favored nation, in which are included import and export duties, customs formalities, transit and tonnage dues and the admission and treatment of agents, subjects and vessels of one country in the territories of the other.

ARTICLE XIII. As soon as possible after the present treaty comes in force all prisoners of war shall be reciprocally restored. The Imperial Governments of Japan and Russia shall each appoint a special commissioner to take charge of the prisoners. All prisoners in the hands of one Government shall be delivered to and be received by the commissioner of the other Government or by his duly authorized representative in such convenient numbers and at such convenient ports of the delivering State as such delivering State shall notify in advance to the commissioner of the receiving State.

The Governments of Japan and Russia shall present each other as soon as possible after the delivery of the prisoners is completed with a statement of the direct expenditures respectively incurred by them for the care and maintenance of the prisoners from the date of capture or surrender and up to the time of death or delivery. Russia engages to repay as soon as possible after the exchange of statement as above provided the difference between the actual amount so expended by Japan and the actual amount similarly disbursed by Russia.

ARTICLE XIV. The present treaty shall be ratified by their Majesties the Emperor of Japan and the Emperor of all the Russias. Such ratification shall be with as little delay as possible, and in any case no later than fifty days from the date of the signature of the treaty, to be announced to the Imperial Governments of Japan and Russia respectively through the French Minister at Tokio and the Ambassador of the United States at St. Petersburg, and from the date of the latter of such announcements shall in all its parts come into full force. The formal exchange of ratifications shall take place at Washington as soon as possible.

ARTICLE XV. The present treaty shall be signed in duplicate in both the English and French languages. The texts are in absolute conformity, but in case of a discrepancy in the interpretation the French text shall prevail.

SUB-ARTICLES In conformity with the provisions of articles 3 and 9 of the treaty of the peace between Japan and Russia of this date the undersigned plenipotentiaries have concluded the following additional articles:

SUB-ARTICLE TO ARTICLE III. The Imperial Governments of Japan and Russia mutually engage to commence the withdrawal of their military forces from the territory of Manchuria simultaneously and immediately after the treaty of peace comes into operation, and within a period of eighteen months after that date the armies of the two countries shall be completely withdrawn from Manchuria, except from the leased territory of the Liaotung Peninsula. The forces of the two countries occupying the front positions shall first be withdrawn.

The high contracting parties reserve to themselves the right to maintain guards to protect their respective railway lines in Manchuria. The number of such guards shall not exceed fifteen per kilometre and within that maximum number the commanders of the Japanese and Russian armies shall by common accord fix the number of such guards to be employed as small as possible while having in view the actual requirements.

The commanders of the Japanese and Russian forces in Manchuria shall agree upon the details of the evacuation in conformity with the above principles and shall take by common accord the measures necessary to carry out the evacuation as soon as possible, and in any case not later than the period of eighteen months.

SUB-ARTICLE TO ARTICLE IX. As soon as possible after the present treaty comes into force a committee of delimitation composed of an equal number of members is to be appointed by the two high contracting parties which shall on the spot mark in a permanent manner the exact boundary between the Japanese and Russian possessions on the Island of Saghalin. The commission shall be bound so far as topographical considerations permit to follow the fiftieth parallel of north latitude as the boundary line, and in case any deflections from that line at any points are found to be necessary compensation will be made by correlative deflections at other points. It shall also be the duty of the said commission to prepare a list and a description of the adjacent islands included in the cession, and finally the commission shall prepare and sign maps showing the boundaries of the ceded territory. The work of the commission shall be subject to the approval of the high contracting parties.

The foregoing additional articles are to be considered ratified with the ratification of the treaty of peace to which they are annexed.

In witness whereof the respective plenipotentiaries have signed and affixed seals to the present treaty of peace.

Done at Portsmouth, New Hampshire, this fifth day of the ninth month of the thirty-eighth year of the Meijei, corresponding to the twenty-third day of August, one thousand nine hundred and five (September 5, 1905).

Source: Tyler, Sydney. *The Japan-Russia War.* Harrisburg, PA: Minter Company, 1905.

Anglo-Russian Agreement Concerning Persia (1907)

While much of Asia was absorbed into European (and Japanese) empires in the late nineteenth and early twentieth centuries, several states were spared this fate, usually because they served as useful buffers between competing empires. One such state was the Persian empire (modern-day Iran). Situated between the expanding Russian empire looking for access to warm water ports and British possessions on the subcontinent of India, Persia was eventually divided into Russian and British spheres of influence by the Anglo-Russian Treaty of 1907, reprinted in part here.

The Governments of Great Britain and Russia having mutually engaged to respect the integrity and independence of Persia, and sincerely desiring the preservation of order throughout that country and its peaceful development, as well as the permanent establishment of equal advantages for the trade and industry of all other nations;

Considering that each of them has, for geographical and economic reasons, a special interest in the maintenance of peace and order in certain provinces of Persia adjoining, or in the neighborhood of, the Russian frontier on the one hand, and the frontiers of Afghanistan and Baluchistan on the other hand; and being desirous of avoiding all cause of conflict between their respective interests in the above-mentioned provinces of Persia;

Have agreed on the following terms:—

I. Great Britain engages not to seek for herself, and not to support in favour of British subjects, or in favour of the subjects of third Powers, any Concessions of a political or commercial nature—such as Concessions for railways, banks, telegraphs, roads, transport, insurance, etc.—beyond a line starting from Kasr-i-Shirin, passing through Isfahan, Yezd, Kakhk, and ending at a point on the Persian frontier at the intersection of the Russian and Afghan frontiers, and not to oppose, directly or indirectly, demands for similar Concessions in this region which are supported by the Russian Government. It is understood that the above-mentioned places are included in the region in which Great Britain engages not to seek the Concessions referred to.

II. Russia, on her part, engages not to seek for herself and not to support, in favour of Russian subjects, or in favour of the subjects of third Powers, any Concessions of a political or commercial nature—such as Concessions for railways, banks, telegraphs, roads, transport, insurance, etc.—beyond a line going from the Afghan frontier by way of Gazik, Birjand, Kerman, and ending at Bunder Abbas, and not to oppose, directly or indirectly, demands for similar Concessions in this region which are supported by the British Government. It is understood that the above-mentioned places are included in the region in which Russia engages not to seek the Concessions referred to.

III. Russia, on her part, engages not to oppose, without previous arrangement with Great Britain, the grant of any Concessions whatever to British subjects in the regions of Persia situated between the lines mentioned in Articles I and II.

Great Britain undertakes a similar engagement as regards the grant of Concessions to Russian subjects in the same regions of Persia.

All Concessions existing at present in the regions indicated in Articles I and II are maintained.

IV. It is understood that the revenues of all the Persian customs, with the exception of those of Farsistan and of the Persian Gulf, revenues guaranteeing the amortization and the interest of the loans concluded by the Government of the Shah with the "Banque d'Escompte et des Prêts de Perse" up to the date of the signature of the present Agreement, shall be devoted to the same purpose as in the past.

It is equally understood that the revenues of the Persian customs of Farsistan and of the Persian Gulf, as well as those of the fisheries on the Persian shore of the Caspian Sea and those of the Posts and Telegraphs, shall be devoted, as in the past, to the service of the loans concluded by the Government of the Shah with the Imperial Bank of Persia up to the date of the signature of the present Agreement.

V. In the event of irregularities occurring in the amortization or the payment of the interest of the Persian loans concluded with the "Banque d'Escompte et des Prets de Perse" and with the Imperial Bank of Persia up to the date of the signature of the present Agreement, and in the event of the necessity arising for Russia to establish control over the sources of revenue guaranteeing the regular service of the loans concluded with the first-named bank, and situated in the region mentioned in Article II of the present Agreement, or for Great Britain to establish control over the sources of revenue guaranteeing the regular service of the loans concluded with the second-named bank, and situated in the region mentioned in Article I of the present Agreement, the British and Russian Governments undertake to enter beforehand into a friendly exchange of ideas with a view to determine, in agreement with each other, the measures of control in question and to avoid all interference which would not be in conformity with the principles governing the present Agreement. . . .

Source: Great Britain, *Parliamentary Papers.* Volume CXXV. London: 1908.

Sykes-Picot Agreement (May 9, 1916)

The Sykes-Picot Treaty, named after its negotiators, Mark Sykes of Britain and Georges Picot of France, was a secret agreement reached by the two countries, with the assent of ally Russia, during World War I. The purpose of the agreement was to divide up the Middle Eastern holdings of the enemy Ottoman Empire after the war. This agreement completely contravened an understanding reached between Hashemite ruler Husain ibn Ali, the sharif of Mecca, and British High Commissioner for Egypt Henry McMahon, promising independence for Arab peoples after the war. Following the Russian Revolu-

tion of 1917, Bolshevik leaders released the details of the agreement, causing a deep sense of betrayal among many Arab leaders.

It is accordingly understood between the French and British governments:

That France and Great Britain are prepared to recognize and protect an independent Arab states or a confederation of Arab states (a) and (b) marked on the annexed map, under the suzerainty of an Arab chief. That in area (a) France, and in area (b) great Britain, shall have priority of right of enterprise and local loans. That in area (a) France, and in area (b) great Britain, shall alone supply advisers or foreign functionaries at the request of the Arab state or confederation of Arab states.

That in the blue area France, and in the red area great Britain, shall be allowed to establish such direct or indirect administration or control as they desire and as they may think fit to arrange with the Arab state or confederation of Arab states.

That in the brown area there shall be established an international administration, the form of which is to be decided upon after consultation with Russia, and subsequently in consultation with the other allies, and the representatives of the sheriff of Mecca.

That great Britain be accorded (1) the ports of Haifa and acre, (2) guarantee of a given supply of water from the Tigres and Euphrates in area (a) for area (b). His majesty's government, on their part, undertake that they will at no time enter into negotiations for the cession of Cyprus to any third power without the previous consent of the French government.

That Alexandretta shall be a free port as regards the trade of the British empire, and that there shall be no discrimination in port charges or facilities as regards British shipping and British goods; that there shall be freedom of transit for British goods through Alexandretta and by railway through the blue area, or (b) area, or area (a); and there shall be no discrimination, direct or indirect, against British goods on any railway or against British goods or ships at any port serving the areas mentioned.

That Haifa shall be a free port as regards the trade of France, her dominions and protectorates, and there shall be no discrimination in port charges or facilities as regards French shipping and

French goods. There shall be freedom of transit for French goods through Haifa and by the British railway through the brown area, whether those goods are intended for or originate in the blue area, area (a), or area (b), and there shall be no discrimination, direct or indirect, against French goods on any railway, or against French goods or ships at any port serving the areas mentioned.

That in area (a) the Baghdad railway shall not be extended southwards beyond Mosul, and in area (b) northwards beyond Samarra, until a railway connecting Baghdad and Aleppo via the Euphrates valley has been completed, and then only with the concurrence of the two governments.

That great Britain has the right to build, administer, and be sole owner of a railway connecting Haifa with area (b), and shall have a perpetual right to transport troops along such a line at all times. It is to be understood by both governments that this railway is to facilitate the connection of Baghdad with Haifa by rail, and it is further understood that, if the engineering difficulties and expense entailed by keeping this connecting line in the brown area only make the project unfeasible, that the French government shall be prepared to consider that the line in question may also traverse the Polgon Banias Keis Marib Salkhad tell Otsda Mesmie before reaching area (b).

For a period of twenty years the existing Turkish customs tariff shall remain in force throughout the whole of the blue and red areas, as well as in areas (a) and (b), and no increase in the rates of duty or conversions from *ad valorem* to specific rates shall be made except by agreement between the two powers.

There shall be no interior customs barriers between any of the above mentioned areas. The customs duties leviable on goods destined for the interior shall be collected at the port of entry and handed over to the administration of the area of destination.

It shall be agreed that the French government will at no time enter into any negotiations for the cession of their rights and will not cede such rights in the blue area to any third power, except the Arab state or confederation of Arab states, without the previous agreement of his majesty's government, who, on their part, will give a similar undertaking to the French government regarding the red area.

The British and French government, as the protectors of the Arab state, shall agree that they will not themselves acquire and will not consent to a third power acquiring territorial possessions in the Arabian peninsula, nor consent to a third power installing a naval base either on the east coast, or on the islands, of the red sea. This, however, shall not prevent such adjustment of the Aden frontier as may be necessary in consequence of recent Turkish aggression.

The negotiations with the Arabs as to the boundaries of the Arab states shall be continued through the same channel as heretofore on behalf of the two powers.

It is agreed that measures to control the importation of arms into the Arab territories will be considered by the two governments.

I have further the honor to state that, in order to make the agreement complete, his majesty's government are proposing to the Russian government to exchange notes analogous to those exchanged by the latter and your excellency's government on the 26th April last. Copies of these notes will be communicated to your excellency as soon as exchanged. I would also venture to remind your excellency that the conclusion of the present agreement raises, for practical consideration, the question of claims of Italy to a share in any partition or rearrangement of turkey in Asia, as formulated in article 9 of the agreement of the 26th April, 1915, between Italy and the allies.

His Majesty's government further consider that the Japanese government should be informed of the arrangements now concluded.

Source: Winer, Joel H. *Great Britain: Foreign Policy and the Span of Empire, 1689–1971, A Documentary History*, vol. 3. New York: Chelsea House, 1972.

Vladimir Lenin: *Imperialism, the Highest Stage of Capitalism* (1917)

With his Imperialism, the Highest Stage of Capitalism, *Russian Bolshevik leader Vladimir Lenin attempted to apply Marxist theory to the phenomenon of empire. In the lengthy pamphlet, originally published in 1917, Lenin emphasized the importance of monopoly capitalism as a motivating factor for the acquisition of empire, as well as the need for markets for surplus investment capital in metro-*

poles. In much of this theorizing, Lenin was borrowing from the path-breaking work of British economist John A. Hobson and his work Imperialism: A Study. [See above, p. 168]

During the last fifteen to twenty years, especially since the Spanish-American War (1898), and the Anglo-Boer War (1899–1902), the economic and also the political literature of the two hemispheres has more and more often adopted the term "imperialism" in order to describe the present era. In 1902, a book by the English economist J. A. Hobson, *Imperialism,* was published in London and New York. This author, whose point of view is that of bourgeois social reformism and pacifism which, in essence, is identical with the present point of view of the ex-Marxist, K. Kautsky, gives a very good and comprehensive description of the principal specific economic and political features of imperialism. . . .

I. CONCENTRATION OF PRODUCTION AND MONOPOLIES

The enormous growth of industry and the remarkably rapid process of concentration of production in ever-larger enterprises are one of the most characteristic features of capitalism. Modern censuses of production give most complete and most exact data on this process. . . .

And concentration goes on further and further. Individual enterprises are becoming larger and larger. An ever-increasing number of enterprises in one, or in several different industries, join together in giant enterprises, backed up and directed by half a dozen big Berlin banks. In relation to the German mining industry, the truth of the teachings of Karl Marx on concentration is definitely proved, true, this applies to a country where industry is protected by tariffs and freight rates. The German mining industry is ripe for expropriation

Such is the conclusion which a conscientious bourgeois economist, and such are the exception, had to arrive at. It must be noted that he seems to place Germany in a special category because her industries are protected by high tariffs. But this circumstance could only accelerate concentration and the formation of monopolist manufacturers' combines, cartels, syndicates, etc. It is extremely important to note that in free-trade England, con-

centration also leads to monopoly, although somewhat later and perhaps in another form. . . .

Half a century ago, when Marx was writing Capital, free competition appeared to the overwhelming majority of economists to be a "natural law." Official science tried, by a conspiracy of silence, to kill the works of Marx, who by a theoretical and historical analysis of capitalism proved that free competition gives rise to the concentration of production, which, in turn, at a certain stage of development, leads to monopoly. Today, monopoly has become a fact.

The economists are writing mountains of books in which they describe the diverse manifestations of monopoly, and continue to declare in chorus that "Marxism is refuted." But facts are stubborn things, as the English proverb says, and they have to be reckoned with, whether we like it or not. The facts show that differences between capitalist countries, e.g., in the matter of protection or free trade, only give rise to insignificant variations in the form of monopolies or in the moment of their appearance; and that the rise of monopolies, as the result of the concentration of production, is a general and fundamental law of the present stage of development of capitalism.

For Europe, the time when the new capitalism definitely superseded the old can be established with fair precision: it was the beginning of the twentieth century. . . .

Competition becomes transformed into monopoly. The result is immense progress in the socialization of production. In particular, the process of technical invention and improvement becomes socialized.

This is something quite different from the old free competition between manufacturers, scattered and out of touch with one another, and producing for an unknown market. Concentration has reached the point at which it is possible to make an approximate estimate of all sources of raw materials (for example, the iron ore deposits) of a country and even, as we shall see, of several countries, or of the whole world. Not only are such estimates made, but these sources are captured by gigantic monopolist combines. An approximate estimate of the capacity of markets is also made, and the combines "divide" them up amongst themselves by agreement. Skilled labor is monopolized, the best engineers are engaged; the means of transport are captured: railways in America, shipping companies in Europe and America. Capitalism in its imperialist stage leads right up to the most comprehensive socialization of production; it, so to speak, drags the capitalists, against their will and consciousness, into some sort of a new social order, a transitional one from complete free competition to complete socialization.

Production becomes social, but appropriation remains private. The social means of production remain the private property of a few. The general framework of formally recognized free competition remains, but the yoke of a few monopolists on the rest of the population becomes a hundred times heavier, more burdensome and intolerable. . . .

Crises of every kind—economic crises most frequently, but not only these—in their turn increase very considerably the tendency towards concentration and towards monopoly.

In other words, the old capitalism, the capitalism of free competition with its indispensable regulator, the Stock Exchange, is passing away. A new capitalism has come to take its place, bearing obvious features of something transient, a mixture of free competition and monopoly. The question naturally arises: to what is this new capitalism "passing"? But the bourgeois scholars are afraid to raise this question.

"Thirty years ago, businessmen, freely competing against one another, performed nine-tenths of the work connected with their business other than manual labor. At the present time, nine-tenths of this 'brain work' is performed by officials. Banking is in the forefront of this evolution. . . ." This admission by Schulze-Gaevernitz brings us once again to the question: to what is this new capitalism, capitalism in its imperialist stage, passing?

Among the few banks which remain at the head of all capitalist economy as a result of the process of concentration, there is naturally to be observed an increasingly marked tendency towards monopolist agreements, towards a bank trust. In America, not nine, but two very big banks, those of the billionaires Rockefeller and Morgan, control a capital of eleven billion marks.

The old capitalism has had its day. The new capitalism represents a transition towards something. It is hopeless, of course, to seek for "firm principles and a concrete aim" for the purpose of "reconciling" monopoly with free competition. . . .

At precisely what period were the "new activities" of the big banks finally established? Jeidels gives us a fairly exact answer to this important question:

"The connections between the banks and industrial enterprises, with their new content, their new forms and their new organs, namely, the big banks which are organized on both a centralized and a decentralized basis, were scarcely a characteristic economic phenomenon before the nineties; in one sense, indeed this initial date may be advanced to the year 1897, when the important 'mergers' took place and when, for the first time, the new form of decentralized organization was introduced to suit the industrial policy of the banks. This starting point could perhaps be placed at an even later date, for it was the crisis of 1900 that enormously accelerated and intensified the process of concentration of industry and of banking, consolidated that process, for the first time transformed the connection with industry into the actual monopoly of the big banks, and made this connection much closer and more active."

Thus, the twentieth century marks the turning point from the old capitalism to the new, from the domination of capital in general to the domination of finance capital. . . .

III. FINANCE CAPITAL AND THE FINANCIAL OLIGARCHY

. . . . We now have to describe how, under the general conditions of commodity production and private property, the "business operations" of capitalist monopolies inevitably become the domination of a financial oligarchy. It should be noted that the representatives of bourgeois German—and not only German—science, like Riesser, Schulze-Gaevernitz, Liefmann and others, are all apologists of imperialism and of finance capital. . . .

But the monstrous facts concerning the monstrous rule of the financial oligarchy are so glaring that in all capitalist countries, in America, France and Germany, a whole literature has sprung up, written from the bourgeois point of view, but which, nevertheless, gives a fairly truthful picture and criticism—petty-bourgeois, naturally—of this oligarchy.

The "holding system," to which we have already briefly referred above, should be made the cornerstone. The German economist, Heymann, probably the first to call attention to this matter, describes the essence of it in this way:

"The head of the concern controls the principal company" (literally: the "mother company"); "the latter reigns over the subsidiary companies" ("daughter companies") "which in their turn control still other subsidiaries" ["grandchild companies"], "etc. In this way, it is possible with a comparatively small capital to dominate immense spheres of production. Indeed, if holding 50 per cent of the capital is always sufficient to control a company, the head of the concern needs only one million to control eight million in the second subsidiaries. And if this 'interlocking' is extended, it is possible with one million to control sixteen million, thirty-two million, etc."

. . . It is characteristic of capitalism in general that the ownership of capital is separated from the application of capital to production, that money capital is separated from industrial or productive capital, and that the rentier who lives entirely on income obtained from money capital is separated from the entrepreneur and from all who are directly concerned in the management of capital. Imperialism, or the domination of finance capital, is that highest stage of capitalism at which this separation reaches vast proportions. The supremacy of finance capital over all other forms of capital means the predominance of the rentier and of the financial oligarchy; it means the singling out of a small number of financially "powerful" states from among all the rest. . . .

IV. THE EXPORT OF CAPITAL

Typical of the old capitalism, when free competition had undivided sway, was the export of goods. Typical of the latest stage of capitalism, when monopolies rule, is the export of capital.

Capitalism is commodity production at its highest stage of development, when labor power itself becomes a commodity. The growth of internal exchange, and particularly of international exchange, is the characteristic distinguishing feature of capitalism. Uneven and spasmodic development of individual enterprises, of individual branches of industry and individual countries, is inevitable under the capitalist system. England became a capitalist country before any other, and by the middle of the nineteenth century, having adopted free trade, claimed to be the "workshop of the world," the purveyor of manufactured goods to all countries, which in exchange were to keep her supplied with raw materials. But in the last quarter of the nineteenth century, this monopoly was already undermined; for other countries, sheltering themselves by "protective" tariffs, developed into independent capitalist states. On the threshold of the twentieth century we see the formation of a new type of monopoly: firstly, monopolist capitalist combines in all capitalistically developed countries; secondly, the monopolist position of a few very rich countries, in which the accumulation of capital has reached gigantic proportions. An enormous "superabundance of capital" has arisen in the advanced countries.

It goes without saying that if capitalism could develop agriculture, which today frightfully lags behind industry everywhere, if it could raise the standard of living of the masses, who are everywhere still half-starved and poverty-stricken, in spite of the amazing technical progress, there could be no talk of a superabundance of capital. This "argument" is very often advanced by the petty-bourgeois critics of capitalism. But if capitalism did these things it would not be capitalism; for both uneven development and a semi-starvation level of existence of the masses are fundamental and inevitable conditions and premises of this mode of production. As long as capitalism remains what it is, surplus capital will be utilized not for the purpose of raising the standard of living of the masses in a given country, for this would mean a decline in profits for the capitalists, but for the purpose of increasing profits by exporting capital abroad to the backward countries. In these backward countries profits are usually high, for capital is scarce, the price of land is relatively low, wages are low, raw materials are cheap. The possibility of exporting capital is created by the fact that a number of backward countries have already been drawn into world capitalist intercourse; main railways have either been or are being built there, the elementary conditions for industrial development have been created, etc. The necessity for exporting capital arises from the fact that in a few countries capitalism has become "overripe" and (owing to the backward stage of agriculture and the impoverished state of the masses) capital cannot find a field for "profitable" investment. . . .

The capital exporting countries have divided the world among themselves in the figurative sense of the term. But finance capital has led to the actual division of the world.

V. THE DIVISION OF THE WORLD AMONG CAPITALIST COMBINES

Monopolist capitalist combines, cartels, syndicates and trusts divide among themselves, first of all, the home market, seize more or less complete possession of the industry of a country. But under capitalism the home market is inevitably bound up with the foreign market. Capitalism long ago created a world market. As the export of capital increased, and as the foreign and colonial connections and "spheres of influence" of the big monopolist combines expanded in all ways, things "naturally" gravitated towards an international agreement among these combines, and towards the formation of international cartels.

This is a new stage of world concentration of capital and production, incomparably higher than the preceding stages. . . .

The capitalists divide the world, not out of any particular malice, but because the degree of concentration which has been reached forces them to adopt this method in order to obtain profits. And they divide it "in proportion to capital," "in proportion to strength," because there cannot be any other method of division under commodity production and capitalism. But strength varies with the degree of economic and political development. In order to understand what is taking place, it is necessary to know what questions are settled by the changes in strength. The question as to whether these changes are "purely" economic or non-economic (e.g., military) is a secondary one, which cannot in the least affect the fundamental views on the latest epoch of capitalism. To substitute the question of the form of the struggle and agreements (today peaceful, tomorrow warlike, the next day warlike again) for the question of the substance of the struggle and agreements between capitalist combines is to sink to the role of a sophist.

The epoch of the latest stage of capitalism shows us that certain relations between capitalist combines grow up, based on the economic division of the world, while parallel and in connection with it, certain relations grow up between political combines, between states, on the basis of the territorial division of the world, of the struggle for colonies, of the "struggle for economic territory."

VI. THE DIVISION OF THE WORLD AMONG THE GREAT POWERS

. . . The characteristic feature of the period under review is the final partition of the globe—final, not in the sense that a repartition is impossible; on the contrary, repartitions are possible and inevitable—but in the sense that the colonial policy of the capitalist countries has completed the seizure of the unoccupied territories on our planet. For the first time the world is completely divided up, so that in the future only redivision is possible, i.e., territories can only pass from one "owner" to another, instead of passing as ownerless territory to an "owner."

Hence, we are passing through a peculiar epoch of world colonial policy, which is most closely connected with the "latest stage in the development of capitalism," with finance capital. For this reason, it is essential first of all to deal in greater detail with the facts, in order to ascertain as exactly as possible what distinguishes this epoch from those preceding it, and what the present situation is. In the first place, two questions of fact arise here: is an intensification of colonial policy, a sharpening of the struggle for colonies, observed precisely in this epoch of finance capital? And how, in this respect, is the world divided at the present time?

The American writer, Morris, in his book on the history of colonization, has made an attempt to sum up the data on the colonial possessions of Great Britain, France and Germany during different periods of the nineteenth century. . . . We clearly see how "complete" was the partition of the world on the border line between the nineteenth and the twentieth centuries. After 1876 colonial possessions increased to enormous dimensions, more than fifty per cent, from 40,000,000 to 25,000,000 square kilometers in area for the six biggest powers; the increase amounts to 25,000,000 square kilometers, fifty per cent larger than the area of the metropolitan countries (16,500,000 square kilometers). In 1876 three powers had no colonies, and a fourth, France, had scarcely any. By 1914 these four powers had acquired colonies of an area of 14,100,000 square kilometers, i.e., about kitty per cent larger than that of Europe, with a population of nearly 100,000,000. The unevenness in the rate of expansion of colonial possessions is very great. If, for instance, we compare France, Germany and Japan, which do not differ very much in area and population, we will see that the first has acquired almost three times as much colonial territory as the other two combined. In regard to finance capital, France, at the beginning of the period we are considering, was also, perhaps, several times richer than Germany and Japan put together. In addition to, and on the basis of, purely economic conditions, geographical and other conditions also affect the dimensions of colonial possessions. However strong the process of leveling the world, of leveling the economic and living conditions in different countries, may have been in the past decades as a result of the pressure of large-scale industry, exchange and finance capital, considerable differences still remain; and among the six powers mentioned we see, firstly, young capitalist countries (America, Germany, Japan) whose progress has been extraordinarily rapid; secondly, countries with an old capitalist development (France and Great Britain), whose progress lately has been much slower than that of the previously mentioned countries, and thirdly, a country which is economically most backward (Russia), where modern capitalist imperialism is enmeshed, so to speak, in a particularly close network of precapitalist relations.

Alongside the colonial possessions of the Great Powers, we have placed the small colonies of the small states, which are, so to speak, the next objects of a possible and probable "redivision" of colonies. Most of these small states are able to retain their colonies only because of the conflicting interests, friction, etc., among the big powers, which prevent them from coming to an agreement in regard to the division of the spoils. The "semicolonial" states provide an example of the transitional forms which are to be found in all spheres of nature and society. Finance capital is such a great, it may be said, such a decisive force in all economic and in all international relations, that it is capable of subjecting, and actually does subject to itself even states enjoying the fullest political independence; we shall shortly see examples of this. Of course, finance capital finds most "convenient," and is able to extract the greatest profit from such

a subjection as involves the loss of the political independence of the subjected countries and peoples. In this connection, the semicolonial countries provide a typical example of the "middle stage." It is natural that the struggle for these semidependent countries should have become particularly bitter in the epoch of finance capital, when the rest of the world has already been divided up.

Colonial policy and imperialism existed before this latest stage of capitalism, and even before capitalism. Rome, founded on slavery, pursued a colonial policy and practiced imperialism. But "general" disquisitions on imperialism, which ignore, or put into the background, the fundamental difference between social-economic systems, inevitably degenerate into the most vapid banality or bragging, like the comparison: "Greater Rome and Greater Britain." Even the capitalist colonial policy of previous stages of capitalism is essentially different from the colonial policy of finance capital.

The principal feature of the latest stage of capitalism is the domination of monopolist combines of the big capitalists. These monopolies are most firmly established when all the sources of raw materials are captured by one group, and we have seen with what zeal the international capitalist combines exert every effort to make it impossible for their rivals to compete with them by buying up, for example, iron ore fields, oil fields, etc. Colonial possession alone gives the monopolies complete guarantee against all contingencies in the struggle with competitors, including the contingency that the latter will defend themselves by means of a law establishing a state monopoly. The more capitalism is developed, the more strongly the shortage of raw materials is felt, the more intense the competition and the hunt for sources of raw materials throughout the whole world, the more desperate is the struggle for the acquisition of colonies.

. . . . Since we are speaking of colonial policy in the epoch of capitalist imperialism, it must be observed that finance capital and its corresponding foreign policy, which reduces itself to the struggle of the Great Powers for the economic and political division of the world, give rise to a number of transitional forms of state dependence. Typical of this epoch is not only the two main groups of countries: those owning colonies, and colonies, but also the diverse forms of dependent countries which, officially, are politically independent, but in fact, are enmeshed in the net of financial and diplomatic dependence. We have already referred to one form of dependence—the semicolony. An example of another is provided by Argentina.

"South America, and especially Argentina," writes Schulze-Gaevernitz in his work on British imperialism, "is so dependent financially on London that it ought to be described as almost a British commercial colony." Basing himself on the report of the Austro-Hungarian consul at Buenos Aires for 1909, Schilder estimates the amount of British capital invested in Argentina at 8,750,000 francs. It is not difficult to imagine what strong connections British finance capital (and its faithful "friend," diplomacy) thereby acquires with the Argentine bourgeoisie, with the circles that control the whole of that country's economic and political life. . . .

VII. IMPERIALISM, AS A SPECIAL
STAGE OF CAPITALISM

We must now try to sum up, put together, what has been said above on the subject of imperialism. Imperialism emerged as the development and direct continuation of the fundamental characteristics of capitalism in general. But capitalism only became capitalist imperialism at a definite and very high stage of its development, when certain of its fundamental characteristics began to change into their opposites, when the features of the epoch of transition from capitalism to a higher social and economic system had taken shape and revealed themselves all along the line. Economically, the main thing in this process is the displacement of capitalist free competition by capitalist monopoly. Free competition is the fundamental characteristic of capitalism, and of commodity production generally; monopoly is the exact opposite of free competition, but we have seen the latter being transformed into monopoly before our eyes, creating large-scale industry and forcing out small industry, replacing large-scale by still larger-scale industry, and carrying concentration of production and capital to the point where out of it has grown and is growing monopoly: cartels, syndicates and trusts, and merging with them, the capital of a dozen or so banks, which manipulate thousands of millions. At the same time the monopolies, which have grown out of free competi-

tition, do not eliminate the latter, but exist over it and alongside of it, and thereby give rise to a number of very acute, intense antagonisms, frictions and conflicts. Monopoly is the transition from capitalism to a higher system.

If it were necessary to give the briefest possible definition of imperialism we should have to say that imperialism is the monopoly stage of capitalism. Such a definition would include what is most important, for, on the one hand, finance capital is the bank capital of a few very big monopolist banks, merged with the capital of the monopolist combines of industrialists; and, on the other hand, the division of the world is the transition from a colonial policy which has extended without hindrance to territories unseized by any capitalist power, to a colonial policy of monopolistic possession of the territory of the world which has been completely divided up.

But very brief definitions, although convenient, for they sum up the main points, are nevertheless inadequate, since very important features of the phenomenon that has to be defined have to be especially deduced. And so, without forgetting the conditional and relative value of all definitions in general, which can never embrace all the concatenations of a phenomenon in its complete development, we must give a definition of imperialism that will include the following five of its basic features: 1) the concentration of production and capital has developed to such a high stage that it has created monopolies which play a decisive role in economic life; 2) the merging of bank capital with industrial capital, and the creation, on the basis of this "finance capital," of a financial oligarchy; 3) the export of capital as distinguished from the export of commodities acquires exceptional importance; 4) the formation of international monopolist capitalist combines which share the world among themselves, and 5) the territorial division of the whole world among the biggest capitalist powers is completed. Imperialism is capitalism in that stage of development in which the dominance of monopolies and finance capital has established itself; in which the export of capital has acquired pronounced importance; in which the division of the world among the international trusts has begun; in which the division of all territories of the globe among the biggest capitalist powers has been completed.

We shall see later that imperialism can and must be defined differently if we bear in mind, not only the basic, purely economic concepts—to which the above definition is limited—but also the historical place of this stage of capitalism in relation to capitalism in general, or the relation between imperialism and the two main trends in the working-class movement. The point to be noted just now is that imperialism, as interpreted above, undoubtedly represents a special stage in the development of capitalism. To enable the reader to obtain the most well-grounded idea of imperialism possible, we deliberately tried to quote as largely as possible bourgeois economists who are obliged to admit the particularly incontrovertible facts concerning the latest stage of capitalist economy. With the same object in view, we have quoted detailed statistics which enable one to see to what degree bank capital, etc., has grown, in what precisely the transformation of quantity into quality, of developed capitalism into imperialism, was expressed. Needless to say, of course, all boundaries in nature and in society are conditional and changeable, that it would be absurd to argue, for example, about the particular year or decade in which imperialism "definitely" became established. . . .

One of the special features of imperialism connected with the facts we are describing, is the decline in emigration from imperialist countries and the increase in immigration into these countries from the more backward countries where lower wages are paid. As Hobson observes, emigration from Great Britain has been declining since 1884. In that year the number of emigrants was 242,000, while in 1900, the number was 169,000.

. . . Imperialism has the tendency to create privileged sections also among the workers, and to detach them from the broad masses of the proletariat.

It must be observed that in Great Britain the tendency of imperialism to divide the workers, to strengthen opportunism among them and to cause temporary decay in the working-class movement, revealed itself much earlier than the end of the nineteenth and the beginning of the twentieth centuries. . . .

This clearly shows the causes and effects. The causes are: 1) exploitation of the whole world by this country; 2) its monopolistic position in the world market; 3) its colonial monopoly. The effects

are: 1) a section of the British proletariat becomes bourgeois; 2) a section of the proletariat permits itself to be led by men bought by, or at least paid by, the bourgeoisie. The imperialism of the beginning of the twentieth century completed the division of the world among a handful of states, each of which today exploits (i.e., draws superprofits from) a part of the "whole world" only a little smaller than that which England exploited in 1858; each of them occupies a monopoly position in the world market thanks to trusts, cartels, finance capital and creditor and debtor relations; each of them enjoys to some degree a colonial monopoly. . . .

The distinctive feature of the present situation is the prevalence of such economic and political conditions as could not but increase the irreconcilability between opportunism and the general and vital interests of the working-class movement: imperialism has grown from the embryo into the predominant system; capitalist monopolies occupy first place in economics and politics; the division of the world has been completed; on the other hand, instead of the undivided monopoly of Great Britain, we see a few imperialist powers contending for the right to share in this monopoly, and this struggle is characteristic of the whole period of the beginning of the twentieth century. Opportunism cannot now be completely triumphant in the working-class movement of one country for decades as it was in England in the second half of the nineteenth century; but in a number of countries it has grown ripe, overripe, and rotten, and has become completely merged with bourgeois policy in the form of "social chauvinism." . . .

IX. THE CRITIQUE OF IMPERIALISM

By the critique of imperialism, in the broad sense of the term, we mean the attitude towards imperialist policy of the different classes of society in connection with their general ideology.

The enormous dimensions of finance capital concentrated in a few hands and creating an extraordinarily far-flung and close network of relationships and connections which subordinates not only the small and medium, but also even the very small capitalists and small masters, on the one hand, and the increasingly intense struggle waged against other national state groups of financiers for the division of the world and domination over other countries, on the other hand, cause the possessing classes to go over entirely to the side of imperialism. "General" enthusiasm over the prospects of imperialism, furious defense of it and painting it in the brightest colors—such are the signs of the times. The imperialist ideology also penetrates the working class. No Chinese Wall separates it from the other classes. The leaders of the present-day, so-called, "Social-Democratic" Party of Germany are justly called "social-imperialists," that is, Socialists in words and imperialists in deeds; but as early as 1902, Hobson noted the existence in England of "Fabian imperialists" who belonged to the opportunist Fabian Society.

Bourgeois scholars and publicists usually come out in defense of imperialism in a somewhat veiled form; they obscure its complete domination and its profound roots, strive to push into the forefront particular and secondary details and do their very best to distract attention from essentials by means of absolutely ridiculous schemes for "reform," such as police supervision of the trusts or banks, etc. Less frequently, cynical and frank imperialists come forward who are bold enough to admit the absurdity of the idea of reforming the fundamental characteristics of imperialism.

X. THE PLACE OF IMPERIALISM IN HISTORY

. . . The extent to which monopolist capital has intensified all the contradictions of capitalism is generally known. It is sufficient to mention the high cost of living and the tyranny of the cartels. This intensification of contradictions constitutes the most powerful driving force of the transitional period of history, which began from the time of the final victory of world finance capital.

Monopolies, oligarchy, the striving for domination instead of striving for liberty, the exploitation of an increasing number of small or weak nations by a handful of the richest or most powerful nations—all these have given birth to those distinctive characteristics of imperialism which compel us to define it as parasitic or decaying capitalism. More and more prominently there emerges, as one of the tendencies of imperialism, the creation of the "rentier state," the usurer state, in which the bourgeoisie to an ever increasing degree lives on the proceeds of capital exports and by "clipping coupons." It would be a mistake to believe that this tendency to decay precludes the rapid growth of capitalism. It does not. In the epoch of imperial-

ism, certain branches of industry, certain strata of the bourgeoisie and certain countries betray, to a greater or lesser degree, now one and now another of these tendencies. On the whole, capitalism is growing far more rapidly than before; but this growth is not only becoming more and more uneven in general, its unevenness also manifests itself, in particular, in the decay of the countries which are richest in capital (England).

In regard to the rapidity of Germany's economic development, Riesser, the author of the book on the big German banks, states: "The progress of the preceding period (1848–70), which had not been exactly slow, stood in about the same ratio to the rapidity with which the whole of Germany's national economy, and with it German banking, progressed during this period (1870–1905) as the speed of the mail coach in the good old days stood to the speed of the present-day automobile . . . which is whizzing past so fast that it endangers not only innocent pedestrians in its path, but also the occupants of the car." In its turn, this finance capital which has grown with such extraordinary rapidity is not unwilling, precisely because it has grown so quickly, to pass on to a more "tranquil" possession of colonies which have to be seized—and not only by peaceful methods—from richer nations. In the United States, economic development in the last decades has been even more rapid than in Germany, and for this very reason, the parasitic features of modern American capitalism have stood out with particular prominence. On the other hand, a comparison of, say, the republican American bourgeoisie with the monarchist Japanese or German bourgeoisie shows that the most pronounced political distinction diminishes to an extreme degree in the epoch of imperialism—not because it is unimportant in general, but because in all these cases we are discussing a bourgeoisie which has definite features of parasitism.

The receipt of high monopoly profits by the capitalists in one of the numerous branches of industry, in one of the numerous countries, etc., makes it economically possible for them to bribe certain sections of the workers, and for a time a fairly considerable minority of them, and win them to the side of the bourgeoisie of a given industry or given nation against all the others. The intensification of antagonisms between imperialist nations for the division of the world increases this striving. And so there is created that bond between imperialism and opportunism, which revealed itself first and most clearly in England, owing to the fact that certain features of imperialist development were observable there much earlier than in other countries. Some writers, L. Martov, for example, are prone to wave aside the connection between imperialism and opportunism in the working-class movement—a particularly glaring fact at the present time—by resorting to "official optimism" (à la Kautsky and Huysmans) like the following: the cause of the opponents of capitalism would be hopeless if it were precisely progressive capitalism that led to the increase of opportunism, or, if it were precisely the best paid workers who were inclined towards opportunism, etc. We must have no illusions about "optimism" of this kind. It is optimism in regard to opportunism; it is optimism which serves to conceal opportunism. As a matter of fact the extraordinary rapidity and the particularly revolting character of the development of opportunism is by no means a guarantee that its victory will be durable: the rapid growth of a malignant abscess on a healthy body can only cause it to burst more quickly and thus relieve the body of it. The most dangerous of all in this respect are those who do not wish to understand that the fight against imperialism is a sham and humbug unless it is inseparably bound up with the fight against opportunism.

From all that has been said in this book on the economic essence of imperialism, it follows that we must define it as capitalism in transition, or, more precisely, as moribund capitalism.

Written January–June 1916

Published in pamphlet form in Petrograd, April 1917

Source: Lenin, Vladimir. *Imperialism, the Highest Stage of Capitalism.* New York: International Publishers, 1939.

Joseph A. Schumpeter: "The Sociology of Imperialism" (1918)

Joseph Schumpeter, a German economist, differed with British economist John Hobson and Bolshevik leader Vladimir Lenin about the causes of imperialism. It was not essentially an outgrowth of the capitalist economy, as the British liberal and Russian Marxist argued, but an atavistic impulse of colonizer nations' warrior classes, a carry-over from the time of absolute monarchies, argued Schumpeter in this excerpt from Imperialism and Social Classes, *originally published in 1918. Indeed, he said, by rational capitalist decision-making, imperialism made no sense whatsoever.*

Imperialism is objectless expansion, a pattern simply learned from the behavior of other nations and institutionalized into the domestic political processes of a state by a "warrior" class. This warrior class is created because of the need for defense, but, over time, the class will manufacture reasons to perpetuate its existence, usually through manipulation of crises.

For it is always a question, when one speaks of imperialism, of the assertion of an aggressiveness whose real basis does not lie in the aims followed at the moment but an aggressiveness in itself. And actually history shows us people and classes who desire expansion for the sake of expanding, war for the sake of fighting, domination for the sake of dominating. It values conquest not so much because of the advantages it brings, which are often more than doubtful, as because it is conquest, success, activity. Although expansion as self-purpose always needs concrete objects to activate it and support it, its meaning is not included therein. Hence its tendency toward the infinite unto the exhaustion of its forces, and its motto: *plus ultra.* Thus we define: *Imperialism is the object-less disposition of a state to expansion by force without assigned limits.*

Our analysis of historical material show: First, the undoubted fact that object-less tendencies toward forceful expansion without definite limits of purpose, non-rational and irrational, purely instinctive inclinations to war and conquest, play a very great role in the history of humanity. As paradoxical as it sounds, innumerable wars, perhaps the majority of all wars, have been waged without sufficient reason. Secondly, the explanation of the martial, functional need, this will to war, lies in the necessities of a situation, in which peoples and classes must become fighters or go under, and in the fact that the physical dispositions and social structure acquired in the past, once existent and consolidated, maintain themselves and continue to work after they have lost their meaning and their function of preserving life. Thirdly, the existence of supporting elements which ease the continued life of these dispositions and structures can be divided into groups. Martial dispositions are especially furthered by the groups ruling the internal relationships of interests. And with martial dispositions are allied the influences of all those who individually stand to gain, either economically or socially, by martial policy. Both groups of motives are in general overgrown by another kind of foliage which is not merely political propaganda but also individual psychological motivation. Imperialism is an atavism. It falls in the great group of those things that live on from earlier epochs, things which play so great a role in every concrete situation and which are to be explained not from the conditions of the present but from the conditions of the past. It is an atavism of social structure and an atavism of individual emotional habits. Since the necessities which created it have gone forever, it must—though ever martial development tends to revitalize it—disappear in time.

Modern Imperialism is one of the heirlooms of the absolute monarchical state. The "inner logic" of capitalism would have never evolved it. Its sources come from the policy of the princes and the customs of a pre-capitalist milieu. But even export monopoly is not imperialism and it would never have developed to imperialism in the hands of the pacific bourgeoisie. This happened only because the war machine, its social atmosphere, and the martial will were inherited and because a martially-oriented class (*i.e.*, the nobility) maintained itself in a ruling position with which of all the varied interests of the bourgeoisie the martial ones could ally themselves. This alliance keeps alive fighting instincts and ideas of domination. It led to social relations which perhaps ultimately are to be explained by relations of production but not by the productive relations of capitalism alone.

Source: Schumpeter, Joseph Alois. *Imperialism and Social Classes.* Trans. Heinz Norden; ed. and with an introduction by Paul M. Sweezy. New York: A. M. Kelly, 1951.

E. D. Morel: *Black Man's Burden* (1920)

Born in Paris in 1873, but raised in England, E. D. Morel was a Liverpool-based journalist and one of the most articulate and forceful spokespersons for colonized Africa in the age of high imperialism. In the early 1900s, Morel led an international human rights campaign that helped liberate the Congo River basin from the brutal regime established by King Leopold II of Belgium. Although couched in what now seems like condescending language, Morel's Black Man's Burden *of 1920 remains one of the great anti-imperialist books of the era, as it argued powerfully against the common notion that the white man's rule in Africa was largely benevolent, helping to "civilize" a benighted continent.*

It is [the peoples of Africa] who carry the "Black man's burden." They have not withered away before the white man's occupation. Indeed . . . Africa has ultimately absorbed within itself every Caucasian and, for that matter, every Semitic invader, too. In hewing out for himself a fixed abode in Africa, the white man has massacred the African in heaps. The African has survived, and it is well for the white settlers that he has. . . .

What the partial occupation of his soil by the white man has failed to do; what the mapping out of European political "spheres of influence" has failed to do; what the maxim and the rifle, the slave gang, labor in the bowels of the earth and the lash, have failed to do; what imported measles, smallpox and syphilis have failed to do; what ever the overseas slave trade failed to do, the power of modern capitalistic exploitation, assisted by modern engines of destruction, may yet succeed in accomplishing.

For from the evils of the latter, scientifically applied and enforced, there is no escape for the African. Its destructive effects are not spasmodic: they are permanent. In its permanence resides its fatal consequences. It kills not the body merely, but the soul. It breaks the spirit. It attacks the African at every turn, from every point of vantage. It wrecks his polity, uproots him from the land, invades his family life, destroys his natural pursuits and occupations, claims his whole time, enslaves him in his own home.

Economic bondage and wage slavery, the grinding pressure of a life of toil, the incessant demands of an industrial capitalism—these things a landless European proletariat physically endures, though hardly. . . . The recuperative forces of a temperate climate are there to arrest the ravages, which alleviating influences in the shape of prophylactic and curative remedies will still further circumscribe. But in Africa, especially in tropical Africa, which a capitalistic imperialism threatens and has, in part, already devastated, man is incapable of reacting against unnatural conditions. In those regions man is engaged in a perpetual struggle against disease and an exhausting climate, which tells heavily upon child-bearing; and there is no scientific machinery for salving the weaker members of the community. The African of the tropics is capable of tremendous physical labors. But he cannot accommodate himself to the European system of monotonous, uninterrupted labor, with its long and regular hours, involving, moreover, as it frequently does, severance from natural surroundings . . .[resulting in] melancholy resulting from separation from home, a malady to which the African is specially prone. Climatic conditions forbid it. When the system is forced upon him, the tropical African droops and dies.

Nor is violent physical opposition to abuse and injustice henceforth possible for the African in any part of Africa. His chances of effective resistance have been steadily dwindling with the increasing perfectibility in the killing power of modern armament . . . Against the latest intentions, physical bravery, though associated with a perfect knowledge of the country, can do nothing. . . .

Thus the African is really helpless against the material gods of the white man, as embodied in the trinity of imperialism, capitalistic-exploitation, and militarism. . . .

To reduce all the varied and picturesque, and stimulating episodes in savage life to a dull routine of endless toil for uncomprehended ends; to dislocate social ties and disrupt social institutions; to stifle nascent desires and crush mental development; to graft upon primitive passions the annihilating evils of scientific slavery, and the bestial imaginings of civilized man, unrestrained by convention or law; in fine, to kill the soul in a people—this is a crime which transcends physical murder.

Source: Morel, E. D. *The Black Man's Burden.* London, 1920.

League of Nations Charter, Article 22 (Mandates) (1924)

Among the issues that the League of Nations had to deal with in the wake of World War I was what to do

with the colonies belonging to the defeated central powers of Germany and the former Ottoman Empire. The League came up with the system of mandates, whereby the colonies were turned over to the victorious Allies—most notably Britain and France—for administration. The mandatory powers were expected to prepare most of these territories for self-government, although no schedule for this process was laid out.

To those colonies and territories which as a consequence of the late war have ceased to be under the sovereignty of the States which formerly governed them and which are inhabited by peoples not yet able to stand by themselves under the strenuous conditions of the modern world, there should be applied the principle that the well-being and development of such peoples form a sacred trust of civilisation and that securities for the performance of this trust should be embodied in this Covenant.

The best method of giving practical effect to this principle is that the tutelage of such peoples should be entrusted to advanced nations who by reason of their resources, their experience or their geographical position can best undertake this responsibility, and who are willing to accept it, and that this tutelage should be exercised by them as Mandatories on behalf of the League.

The character of the mandate must differ according to the stage of the development of the people, the geographical situation of the territory, its economic conditions and other similar circumstances.

Certain communities formerly belonging to the Turkish Empire have reached a stage of development where their existence as independent nations can be provisionally recognized subject to the rendering of administrative advice and assistance by a Mandatory until such time as they are able to stand alone. The wishes of these communities must be a principal consideration in the selection of the Mandatory.

Other peoples, especially those of Central Africa, are at such a stage that the Mandatory must be responsible for the administration of the territory under conditions which will guarantee freedom of conscience and religion, subject only to the maintenance of public order and morals, the prohibition of abuses such as the slave trade, the arms traffic and the liquor traffic, and the prevention of the establishment of fortifications or military and naval bases and of military training of the natives for other than police purposes and the defence of territory, and will also secure equal opportunities for the trade and commerce of other Members of the League.

There are territories, such as South-West Africa and certain of the South Pacific Islands, which, owing to the sparseness of their population, or their small size, or their remoteness from the centres of civilisation, or their geographical contiguity to the territory of the Mandatory, and other circumstances, can be best administered under the laws of the Mandatory as integral portions of its territory, subject to the safeguards above mentioned in the interests of the indigenous population.

In every case of mandate, the Mandatory shall render to the Council an annual report in reference to the territory committed to its charge.

The degree of authority, control, or administration to be exercised by the Mandatory shall, if not previously agreed upon by the Members of the League, be explicitly defined in each case by the Council.

A permanent Commission shall be constituted to receive and examine the annual reports of the Mandatories and to advise the Council on all matters relating to the observance of the mandates.

Source: www.rmc.ca/academic/gradrech/UNCharter-LeagueCov.doc.

United Nations Monetary and Financial Conference at Bretton Woods. Summary of Agreements (July 22, 1944)

*The Allied political and business leaders who met at Bretton Woods, New Hampshire, in 1944 created a number of institutions that have dominated the international finances of the postwar era, including the International Monetary Fund (IMF) and the World Bank. While these leaders believed that the institutions they were creating would avoid the kind of nationalist economics that many saw as the cause of the Great Depression and hence World War II, critics have come to see the IMF and the World Bank as pillars of a neocolonial order, whereby large donors to the bank—most notably the United States—can con-*trol the economic destinies of the underdeveloped nations of the world.*

This Conference at Bretton Woods, representing nearly all the peoples of the world, has considered matters of international money and finance which are important for peace and prosperity. The Conference has agreed on the problems needing attention, the measures which should be taken, and the forms of international cooperation or organization which are required. The agreements reached on these large and complex matters are without precedent in the history of international economic relations.

I. THE INTERNATIONAL MONETARY FUND

Since foreign trade affects the standard of life of every people, all countries have a vital interest in the system of exchange of national currencies and the regulations and conditions which govern its working. Because these monetary transactions are international exchanges, the nations must agree on the basic rules which govern the exchanges if the system is to work smoothly. When they do not agree, and when single nations and small groups of nations attempt by special and different regulations of the foreign exchanges to gain trade advantages, the result is instability, a reduced volume of foreign trade, and damage to national economies. This course of action is likely to lead to economic warfare and to endanger the world's peace.

The Conference has therefore agreed that broad international action is necessary to maintain an international monetary system which will promote foreign trade. The nations should consult and agree on international monetary changes which affect each other. They should outlaw practices which are agreed to be harmful to world prosperity, and they should assist each other to overcome short-term exchange difficulties.

The Conference has agreed that the nations here represented should establish for these purposes a permanent international body, *The International Monetary Fund,* with powers and resources adequate to perform the tasks assigned to it. Agreement has been reached concerning these powers and resources and the additional obligations which the member countries should undertake. Draft Articles of Agreement on these points have been prepared.

II. THE INTERNATIONAL BANK FOR RECONSTRUCTION AND DEVELOPMENT [WORLD BANK]

It is in the interest of all nations that post-war reconstruction should be rapid. Likewise, the development of the resources of particular regions is in the general economic interest. Programs of reconstruction and development will speed economic progress everywhere, will aid political stability and foster peace.

The Conference has agreed that expanded international investment is essential to provide a portion of the capital necessary for reconstruction and development.

The Conference has further agreed that the nations should cooperate to increase the volume of foreign investment for these purposes, made through normal business channels. It is especially important that the nations should cooperate to share the risks of such foreign investment, since the benefits are general.

The Conference has agreed that the nations should establish a permanent international body to perform these functions, to be called The International Bank for Reconstruction and Development. It has been agreed that the Bank should assist in providing capital through normal channels at reasonable rates of interest and for long periods for projects which will raise the productivity of the borrowing country. There is agreement that the Bank should guarantee loans made by others and that through their subscriptions of capital in all countries should share with the borrowing country in guaranteeing such loans. The Conference has agreed on the powers and resources which the Bank must have and on the obligations which the member countries must assume, and has prepared draft Articles of Agreement accordingly.

The Conference has recommended that in carrying out the policies of the institutions here proposed special consideration should be given to the needs of countries which have suffered from enemy occupation and hostilities.

The proposals formulated at the Conference for the establishment of the Fund and the Bank are now submitted, in accordance with the terms of the invitation, for consideration of the governments and people of the countries represented.

Source: Pillars of Peace, Documents Pertaining to American Interest in Establishing a Lasting World

Peace: January 1941–February 1946. Pamphlet No. 4. Carlisle Barracks, PA: Book Department, Army Information School, 1946.

United Nations Charter (1945)

The Charter of the United Nations was signed on June 26, 1945, in San Francisco, at the conclusion of the United Nations Conference on International Organization, and came into force on October 24, 1945. Like the League of Nations charter, which it replaced, the UN charter included provisions on non-self-governing territories. But in place of the old League mandate system, the UN established trusteeships. As in the case of the League's mandates, many of the trusteeships were for territories seized from the enemies of the Allies, specifically Japan, during the world war just concluded.

Chapter XI: Declaration Regarding Non-Self-Governing Territories
Article 73

Members of the United Nations which have or assume responsibilities for the administration of territories whose peoples have not yet attained a full measure of self-government recognize the principle that the interests of the inhabitants of these territories are paramount, and accept as a sacred trust the obligation to promote to the utmost, within the system of international peace and security established by the present Charter, the well-being of the inhabitants of these territories, and, to this end:

a. to ensure, with due respect for the culture of the peoples concerned, their political, economic, social, and educational advancement, their just treatment, and their protection against abuses;

b. to develop self-government, to take due account of the political aspirations of the peoples, and to assist them in the progressive development of their free political institutions, according to the particular circumstances of each territory and its peoples and their varying stages of advancement;

c. to further international peace and security;

d. to promote constructive measures of development, to encourage research, and to co-operate with one another and, when and where appropriate, with specialized international bodies with a view to the practical achievement of the social, economic, and scientific purposes set forth in this Article; and

e. to transmit regularly to the Secretary-General for information purposes, subject to such limitation as security and constitutional considerations may require, statistical and other information of a technical nature relating to economic, social, and educational conditions in the territories for which they are respectively responsible other than those territories to which Chapters XII and XIII apply.

Article 74

Members of the United Nations also agree that their policy in respect of the territories to which this Chapter applies, no less than in respect of their metropolitan areas, must be based on the general principle of good-neighbourliness, due account being taken of the interests and well-being of the rest of the world, in social, economic, and commercial matters.

Chapter XII: International Trusteeship System
Article 75

The United Nations shall establish under its authority an international trusteeship system for the administration and supervision of such territories as may be placed thereunder by subsequent individual agreements. These territories are hereinafter referred to as trust territories.

Article 76

The basic objectives of the trusteeship system, in accordance with the Purposes of the United Nations laid down in Article 1 of the present Charter, shall be:

a. to further international peace and security;

b. to promote the political, economic, social, and educational advancement of the inhabitants of the trust territories, and their progressive development towards self-government or independence as may be appropriate to the particular circumstances of each territory and its peoples and the freely expressed wishes of the peoples concerned, and as may be provided by the terms of each trusteeship agreement;

c. to encourage respect for human rights and for fundamental freedoms for all without distinction as to race, sex, language, or religion, and to encourage recognition of the interdependence of the peoples of the world; and

d. to ensure equal treatment in social, economic, and commercial matters for all Members of the United Nations and their nationals, and also equal treatment for the latter in the administration of justice, without prejudice to the attainment of the foregoing objectives and subject to the provisions of Article 80.

Article 77

1. The trusteeship system shall apply to such territories in the following categories as may be placed thereunder by means of trusteeship agreements:

a. territories now held under mandate;

b. territories which may be detached from enemy states as a result of the Second World War; and

c. territories voluntarily placed under the system by states responsible for their administration.

2. It will be a matter for subsequent agreement as to which territories in the foregoing categories will be brought under the trusteeship system and upon what terms.

Article 78

The trusteeship system shall not apply to territories which have become Members of the United Nations, relationship among which shall be based on respect for the principle of sovereign equality.

Article 79

The terms of trusteeship for each territory to be placed under the trusteeship system, including any alteration or amendment, shall be agreed upon by the states directly concerned, including the mandatory power in the case of territories held under mandate by a Member of the United Nations, and shall be approved as provided for in Articles 83 and 85.

Article 80

1. Except as may be agreed upon in individual trusteeship agreements, made under Articles 77, 79, and 81, placing each territory under the trusteeship system, and until such agreements have been concluded, nothing in this Chapter shall be construed in or of itself to alter in any manner the rights whatsoever of any states or any peoples or the terms of existing international instruments to which Members of the United Nations may respectively be parties.

2. Paragraph 1 of this Article shall not be interpreted as giving grounds for delay or postponement of the negotiation and conclusion of agreements for placing mandated and other territories

under the trusteeship system as provided for in Article 77.

Article 81

The trusteeship agreement shall in each case include the terms under which the trust territory will be administered and designate the authority which will exercise the administration of the trust territory. Such authority, hereinafter called the administering authority, may be one or more states or the Organization itself.

Article 82

There may be designated, in any trusteeship agreement, a strategic area or areas which may include part or all of the trust territory to which the agreement applies, without prejudice to any special agreement or agreements made under Article 43.

Article 83

1. All functions of the United Nations relating to strategic areas, including the approval of the terms of the trusteeship agreements and of their alteration or amendment shall be exercised by the Security Council.

2. The basic objectives set forth in Article 76 shall be applicable to the people of each strategic area.

3. The Security Council shall, subject to the provisions of the trusteeship agreements and without prejudice to security considerations, avail itself of the assistance of the Trusteeship Council to perform those functions of the United Nations under the trusteeship system relating to political, economic, social, and educational matters in the strategic areas.

Article 84

It shall be the duty of the administering authority to ensure that the trust territory shall play its part in the maintenance of international peace and security. To this end the administering authority may make use of volunteer forces, facilities, and assistance from the trust territory in carrying out the obligations towards the Security Council undertaken in this regard by the administering authority, as well as for local defence and the maintenance of law and order within the trust territory.

Article 85

1. The functions of the United Nations with regard to trusteeship agreements for all areas not designated as strategic, including the approval of the terms of the trusteeship agreements and of

their alteration or amendment, shall be exercised by the General Assembly.

2. The Trusteeship Council, operating under the authority of the General Assembly shall assist the General Assembly in carrying out these functions.

Chapter XIII. The Trusteeship Council

COMPOSITION

Article 86

3. The Trusteeship Council shall consist of the following Members of the United Nations:

a. those Members administering trust territories;

b. such of those Members mentioned by name in Article 23 as are not administering trust territories; and

c. as many other Members elected for three-year terms by the General Assembly as may be necessary to ensure that the total number of members of the Trusteeship Council is equally divided between those Members of the United Nations which administer trust territories and those which do not.

4. Each member of the Trusteeship Council shall designate one specially qualified person to represent it therein.

FUNCTIONS and POWERS

Article 87

The General Assembly and, under its authority, the Trusteeship Council, in carrying out their functions, may:

a. consider reports submitted by the administering authority;

b. accept petitions and examine them in consultation with the administering authority;

c. provide for periodic visits to the respective trust territories at times agreed upon with the administering authority; and

d. take these and other actions in conformity with the terms of the trusteeship agreements.

Article 88

The Trusteeship Council shall formulate a questionnaire on the political, economic, social, and educational advancement of the inhabitants of each trust territory, and the administering authority for each trust territory within the competence of the

General Assembly shall make an annual report to the General Assembly upon the basis of such questionnaire.

VOTING

Article 89

3. Each member of the Trusteeship Council shall have one vote.

4. Decisions of the Trusteeship Council shall be made by a majority of the members present and voting.

PROCEDURE

Article 90

1. The Trusteeship Council shall adopt its own rules of procedure, including the method of selecting its President.

2. The Trusteeship Council shall meet as required in accordance with its rules, which shall include provision for the convening of meetings on the request of a majority of its members.

Article 91

The Trusteeship Council shall, when appropriate, avail itself of the assistance of the Economic and Social Council and of the specialized agencies in regard to matters with which they are respectively concerned.

Source: United Nations. United Nations Charter, 1945. www.un.org/aboutun/charter/.

UN General Assembly Resolution 181 (Partition Plan for Palestine) (November 29, 1947)

From just after World War I until shortly after World War II, Britain had a mandate to govern Palestine, formerly a province of the Ottoman Empire. During that nearly thirty-year mandate, Jewish settlers emigrated to Palestine in large numbers, alienating the native Arab population. Britain tried to placate the two groups by making them both promises of an independent state in the territory. Despairing of ever reconciling the two antagonistic populations, Britain turned the problem over to the newly formed United Nations, which drew up the following partition plan for two states—one Jewish and one Arab—in the mandate. Ultimately, the Arabs, angry that over 50 percent of the territory was being given to the Jews, who represented about 10 percent of the population, rejected the plan and went to war with the Jews, resulting in the formation of the Jewish state of Israel, which occupied roughly 75 percent of the former Palestine mandate.

The General Assembly,

Having met in special session at the request of the mandatory Power to constitute and instruct a Special Committee to prepare for the consideration of the question of the future Government of Palestine at the second regular session;

Having constituted a Special Committee and instructed it to investigate all questions and issues relevant to the problem of Palestine, and to prepare proposals for the solution of the problem, and

Having received and examined the report of the Special Committee (document A/364)(1) including a number of unanimous recommendations and a plan of partition with economic union approved by the majority of the Special Committee,

Considers that the present situation in Palestine is one which is likely to impair the general welfare and friendly relations among nations;

Takes note of the declaration by the mandatory Power that it plans to complete its evacuation of Palestine by 1 August 1948;

Recommends to the United Kingdom, as the mandatory Power for Palestine, and to all other Members of the United Nations the adoption and implementation, with regard to the future Government of Palestine, of the Plan of Partition with Economic Union set out below;

Requests that

a. The Security Council take the necessary measures as provided for in the plan for its implementation;

b. The Security Council consider, if circumstances during the transitional period require such consideration, whether the situation in Palestine constitutes a threat to the peace. If it decides that such a threat exists, and in order to maintain international peace and security, the Security Council should supplement the authorization of the General Assembly by taking measures, under Articles 39 and 41 of the Charter, to empower the United Nations Commission, as provided in this resolution, to exercise in Palestine the functions which are assigned to it by this resolution;

c. The Security Council determine as a threat to the peace, breach of the peace or act of aggression, in accordance with Article 39 of the Charter, any attempt to alter by force the settlement envisaged by this resolution;

d. The Trusteeship Council be informed of the responsibilities envisaged for it in this plan;

Calls upon the inhabitants of Palestine to take such steps as may be necessary on their part to put this plan into effect;

Appeals to all Governments and all peoples to refrain from taking any action which might hamper or delay the carrying out of these recommendations, and

Authorizes the Secretary-General to reimburse travel and subsistence expenses of the members of the Commission referred to in Part 1, Section B, Paragraph I below, on such basis and in such form as he may determine most appropriate in the circumstances, and to provide the Commission with the necessary staff to assist in carrying out the functions assigned to the Commission by the General Assembly.*

The General Assembly,

Authorizes the Secretary-General to draw from the Working Capital Fund a sum not to exceed 2,000,000 dollars for the purposes set forth in the last paragraph of the resolution on the future government of Palestine.

PLAN OF PARTITION WITH ECONOMIC UNION

Part I.—Future Constitution and Government of Palestine

A. TERMINATION OF MANDATE, PARTITION AND INDEPENDENCE

1. The Mandate for Palestine shall terminate as soon as possible but in any case not later than 1 August 1948.

2. The armed forces of the mandatory Power shall be progressively withdrawn from Palestine, the withdrawal to be completed as soon as possible but in any case not later than 1 August 1948. The mandatory Power shall advise the Commission, as far in advance as possible, of its intention to terminate the mandate and to evacuate each area. The mandatory Power shall use its best endeavours to ensure that an area situated in the territory of the Jewish State, including a seaport and hinterland adequate to provide facilities for a sub-stantial immigration, shall be evacuated at the earliest possible date and in any event not later than 1 February 1948.

3. Independent Arab and Jewish States and the Special International Regime for the City of Jerusalem, set forth in Part III of this Plan, shall come into existence in Palestine two months after the evacuation of the armed forces of the mandatory Power has been completed but in any case not later than 1 October 1948. The boundaries of the Arab State, the Jewish State, and the City of Jerusalem shall be as described in Parts II and III below.

4. The period between the adoption by the General Assembly of its recommendation on the question of Palestine and the establishment of the independence of the Arab and Jewish States shall be a transitional period.

B. STEPS PREPARATORY TO INDEPENDENCE

1. A Commission shall be set up consisting of one representative of each of five Member States. The Members represented on the Commission shall be elected by the General Assembly on as broad a basis, geographically and otherwise, as possible.

2. The administration of Palestine shall, as the mandatory Power withdraws its armed forces, be progressively turned over to the Commission, which shall act in conformity with the recommendations of the General Assembly, under the guidance of the Security Council. The mandatory Power shall to the fullest possible extent coordinate its plans for withdrawal with the plans of the Commission to take over and administer areas which have been evacuated. In the discharge of this administrative responsibility the Commission shall have authority to issue necessary regulations and take other measures as required. The mandatory Power shall not take any action to prevent, obstruct or delay the implementation by the Commission of the measures recommended by the General Assembly.

3. On its arrival in Palestine the Commission shall proceed to carry out measures for the establishment of the frontiers of the Arab and Jewish States and the City of Jerusalem in accordance with the general lines of the recommendations of the General Assembly on the partition of Palestine. Nevertheless, the boundaries as described in Part II of this Plan are to be modified in such a way

that village areas as a rule will not be divided by state boundaries unless pressing reasons make that necessary.

4. The Commission, after consultation with the democratic parties and other public organizations of the Arab and Jewish States, shall select and establish in each State as rapidly as possible a Provisional Council of Government. The activities of both the Arab and Jewish Provisional Councils of Government shall be carried out under the general direction of the Commission. If by 1 April 1948 a Provisional Council of Government cannot be selected for either of the States, or, if selected, cannot carry out its functions, the Commission shall communicate that fact to the Security Council for such action with respect to that State as the Security Council may deem proper, and to the Secretary-General for communication to the Members of the United Nations.

5. Subject to the provisions of these recommendations, during the transitional period the Provisional Councils of Government, acting under the Commission, shall have full authority in the areas under their control including authority over matters of immigration and land regulation.

6. The Provisional Council of Government of each State, acting under the Commission, shall progressively receive from the Commission full responsibility for the administration of that State in the period between the termination of the Mandate and the establishment of the State's independence.

7. The Commission shall instruct the Provisional Councils of Government of both the Arab and Jewish States, after their formation, to proceed to the establishment of administrative organs of government, central and local.

8. The Provisional Council of Government of each State shall, within the shortest time possible, recruit an armed militia from the residents of that State, sufficient in number to maintain internal order and to prevent frontier clashes. This armed militia in each State shall, for operational purposes, be under the command of Jewish or Arab officers resident in that State, but general political and military control, including the choice of the militia's High Command, shall be exercised by the Commission.

9. The Provisional Council of Government of each State shall, not later than two months after the withdrawal of the armed forces of the mandatory Power, hold elections to the Constituent Assembly which shall be conducted on democratic lines. The election regulations in each State shall be drawn up by the Provisional Council of Government and approved by the Commission. Qualified voters for each State for this election shall be persons over eighteen years of age who are (a) Palestinian citizens residing in that State; and (b) Arabs and Jews residing in the State, although not Palestinian citizens, who, before voting, have signed a notice of intention to become citizens of such State. Arabs and Jews residing in the City of Jerusalem who have signed a notice of intention to become citizens, the Arabs of the Arab State and the Jews of the Jewish State, shall be entitled to vote in the Arab and Jewish States respectively. Women may vote and be elected to the Constituent Assemblies. During the transitional period no Jew shall be permitted to establish residence in the area of the proposed Arab State, and no Arab shall be permitted to establish residence in the area of the proposed Jewish State, except by special leave of the Commission.

10. The Constituent Assembly of each State shall draft a democratic constitution for its State and choose a provisional government to succeed the Provisional Council of Government appointed by the Commission. The Constitutions of the States shall embody Chapters 1 and 2 of the Declaration provided for in section C below and include, inter alia, provisions for:

a. Establishing in each State a legislative body elected by universal suffrage and by secret ballot on the basis of proportional representation, and an executive body responsible to the legislature;

b. Settling all international disputes in which the State may be involved by peaceful means in such a manner that international peace and security, and justice, are not endangered;

c. Accepting the obligation of the State to refrain in its international relations from the threat or use of force against the territorial integrity or political independence of any State, or in any other manner inconsistent with the purpose of the United Nations;

d. Guaranteeing to all persons equal and non-discriminatory rights in civil, political, economic and religious matters and the enjoyment of human rights and fundamental freedoms, including freedom of religion, language, speech and publication, education, assembly and association;

e. Preserving freedom of transit and visit for all residents and citizens of the other State in Palestine and the City of Jerusalem, subject to considerations of national security, provided that each State shall control residence within its borders.

11. The Commission shall appoint a preparatory economic commission of three members to make whatever arrangements are possible for economic co-operation, with a view to establishing, as soon as practicable, the Economic Union and the Joint Economic Board, as provided in section D below.

12. During the period between the adoption of the recommendations on the question of Palestine by the General Assembly and the termination of the Mandate, the mandatory Power in Palestine shall maintain full responsibility for administration in areas from which it has not withdrawn its armed forces. The Commission shall assist the mandatory Power in the carrying out of these functions. Similarly the mandatory Power shall co-operate with the Commission in the execution of its functions.

13. With a view to ensuring that there shall be continuity in the functioning of administrative services and that, on the withdrawal of the armed forces of the mandatory Power, the whole administration shall be in the charge of the Provisional Councils and the Joint Economic Board, respectively, acting under the Commission, there shall be a progressive transfer, from the mandatory Power to the Commission, of responsibility for all the functions of government, including that of maintaining law and order in the areas from which the forces of the mandatory Power have been withdrawn.

14. The Commission shall be guided in its activities by the recommendations of the General Assembly and by such instructions as the Security Council may consider necessary to issue. The measures taken by the Commission, within the recommendations of the General Assembly, shall become immediately effective unless the Commission has previously received contrary instructions from the Security Council. The Commission shall render periodic monthly progress reports, or more frequently if desirable, to the Security Council.

15. The Commission shall make its final report to the next regular session of the General Assembly and to the Security Council simultaneously.

C. DECLARATION

A declaration shall be made to the United Nations by the Provisional Government of each proposed State before independence. It shall contain, inter alia, the following clauses:

General Provision

The stipulations contained in the Declaration are recognized as fundamental laws of the State and no law, regulation or official action shall conflict or interfere with these stipulations, nor shall any law, regulation or official action prevail over them.

Chapter 1: Holy Places, Religious Buildings and Sites

1. Existing rights in respect of Holy Places and religious buildings or sites shall not be denied or impaired.

2. In so far as Holy Places are concerned, the liberty of access, visit, and transit shall be guaranteed, in conformity with existing rights, to all residents and citizens of the other State and of the City of Jerusalem, as well as to aliens, without distinction as to nationality, subject to requirements of national security, public order and decorum. Similarly, freedom of worship shall be guaranteed in conformity with existing rights, subject to maintenance of public order and decorum.

3. Holy Places and religious buildings or sites shall be preserved. No act shall be permitted which may in any way impair their sacred character. If at any time it appears to the Government that any particular Holy Place, religious building or site is in need of urgent repair, the Government may call upon the community or communities concerned to carry out such repair. The Government may carry it out itself at the expense of the community or community concerned if no action is taken within a reasonable time.

4. No taxation shall be levied in respect of any Holy Place, religious building or site which was exempt from taxation on the date of the creation of the State. No change in the incidence of such taxation shall be made which would either discriminate

between the owners or occupiers of Holy Places, religious buildings or sites, or would place such owners or occupiers in a position less favourable in relation to the general incidence of taxation than existed at the time of the adoption of the Assembly's recommendations.

5. The Governor of the City of Jerusalem shall have the right to determine whether the provisions of the Constitution of the State in relation to Holy Places, religious buildings and sites within the borders of the State and the religious rights appertaining thereto, are being properly applied and respected, and to make decisions on the basis of existing rights in cases of disputes which may arise between the different religious communities or the rites of a religious community with respect to such places, buildings and sites. He shall receive full co-operation and such privileges and immunities as are necessary for the exercise of his functions in the State.

Chapter 2: Religious and Minority Rights

1. Freedom of conscience and the free exercise of all forms of worship, subject only to the maintenance of public order and morals, shall be ensured to all.

2. No discrimination of any kind shall be made between the inhabitants on the ground of race, religion, language or sex.

3. All persons within the jurisdiction of the State shall be entitled to equal protection of the laws.

4. The family law and personal status of the various minorities and their religious interests, including endowments, shall be respected.

5. Except as may be required for the maintenance of public order and good government, no measure shall be taken to obstruct or interfere with the enterprise of religious or charitable bodies of all faiths or to discriminate against any representative or member of these bodies on the ground of his religion or nationality.

6. The State shall ensure adequate primary and secondary education for the Arab and Jewish minority, respectively, in its own language and its cultural traditions. The right of each community to maintain its own schools for the education of its own members in its own language, while conforming to such educational requirements of a general nature as the State may impose, shall not be denied or impaired. Foreign educational estab-

lishments shall continue their activity on the basis of their existing rights.

7. No restriction shall be imposed on the free use by any citizen of the State of any language in private intercourse, in commerce, in religion, in the Press or in publications of any kind, or at public meetings.(3)

8. No expropriation of land owned by an Arab in the Jewish State (by a Jew in the Arab State)(4) shall be allowed except for public purposes. In all cases of expropriation full compensation as fixed by the Supreme Court shall be said previous to dispossession.

Chapter 3: Citizenship, International Conventions and Financial Obligations

1. Citizenship

Palestinian citizens residing in Palestine outside the City of Jerusalem, as well as Arabs and Jews who, not holding Palestinian citizenship, reside in Palestine outside the City of Jerusalem shall, upon the recognition of independence, become citizens of the State in which they are resident and enjoy full civil and political rights. Persons over the age of eighteen years may opt, within one year from the date of recognition of independence of the State in which they reside, for citizenship of the other State, providing that no Arab residing in the area of the proposed Arab State shall have the right to opt for citizenship in the proposed Jewish State and no Jew residing in the proposed Jewish State shall have the right to opt for citizenship in the proposed Arab State. The exercise of this right of option will be taken to include the wives and children under eighteen years of age of persons so opting.

Arabs residing in the area of the proposed Jewish State and Jews residing in the area of the proposed Arab State who have signed a notice of intention to opt for citizenship of the other State shall be eligible to vote in the elections to the Constituent Assembly of that State, but not in the elections to the Constituent Assembly of the State in which they reside.

2. International conventions

a. The State shall be bound by all the international agreements and conventions, both general and special, to which Palestine has become a party. Subject to any right of denunciation provided for therein, such agreements and conventions shall be respected by the State throughout the period for which they were concluded.

b. Any dispute about the applicability and continued validity of international conventions or treaties signed or adhered to by the mandatory Power on behalf of Palestine shall be referred to the International Court of Justice in accordance with the provisions of the Statute of the Court.

3. Financial obligations

a. The State shall respect and fulfil all financial obligations of whatever nature assumed on behalf of Palestine by the mandatory Power during the exercise of the Mandate and recognized by the State. This provision includes the right of public servants to pensions, compensation or gratuities.

b. These obligations shall be fulfilled through participation in the Joint Economic Board in respect of those obligations applicable to Palestine as a whole, and individually in respect of those applicable to, and fairly apportionable between, the States.

c. A Court of Claims, affiliated with the Joint Economic Board, and composed of one member appointed by the United Nations, one representative of the United Kingdom and one representative of the State concerned, should be established. Any dispute between the United Kingdom and the State respecting claims not recognized by the latter should be referred to that Court.

d. Commercial concessions granted in respect of any part of Palestine prior to the adoption of the resolution by the General Assembly shall continue to be valid according to their terms, unless modified by agreement between the concession-holders and the State.

Chapter 4: Miscellaneous Provisions

1. The provisions of chapters 1 and 2 of the declaration shall be under the guarantee of the United Nations, and no modifications shall be made in them without the assent of the General Assembly of the United Nations. Any Member of the United Nations shall have the right to bring to the atten-

tion of the General Assembly any infraction or danger of infraction of any of these stipulations, and the General Assembly may thereupon make such recommendations as it may deem proper in the circumstances.

2. Any dispute relating to the application or interpretation of this declaration shall be referred, at the request of either party, to the International Court of Justice, unless the parties agree to another mode of settlement.

D. ECONOMIC UNION AND TRANSIT

1. The Provisional Council of Government of each State shall enter into an undertaking with respect to Economic Union and Transit. This undertaking shall be drafted by the Commission provided for in section B, paragraph 1, utilizing to the greatest possible extent the advice and cooperation of representative organizations and bodies from each of the proposed States. It shall contain provisions to establish the Economic Union of Palestine and provide for other matters of common interest. If by 1 April 1948 the Provisional Councils of Government have not entered into the undertaking, the undertaking shall be put into force by the Commission.

The Economic Union of Palestine

2. The objectives of the Economic Union of Palestine shall be:

a. A customs union;

b. A joint currency system providing for a single foreign exchange rate;

c. Operation in the common interest on a non-discriminatory basis of railways inter-State highways; postal, telephone and telegraphic services and ports and airports involved in international trade and commerce;

d. Joint economic development, especially in respect of irrigation, land reclamation and soil conservation;

e. Access for both States and for the City of Jerusalem on a non-discriminatory basis to water and power facilities.

3. There shall be established a Joint Economic Board, which shall consist of three representatives of each of the two States and three foreign members appointed by the Economic and Social Council of the United Nations. The foreign members shall be appointed in the first instance for a term

of three years; they shall serve as individuals and not as representatives of States.

4. The functions of the Joint Economic Board shall be to implement either directly or by delegation the measures necessary to realize the objectives of the Economic Union. It shall have all powers of organization and administration necessary to fulfil its functions.

5. The States shall bind themselves to put into effect the decisions of the Joint Economic Board. The Board's decisions shall be taken by a majority vote.

6. In the event of failure of a State to take the necessary action the Board may, by a vote of six members, decide to withhold an appropriate portion of the part of the customs revenue to which the State in question is entitled under the Economic Union. Should the State persist in its failure to cooperate, the Board may decide by a simple majority vote upon such further sanctions, including disposition of funds which it has withheld, as it may deem appropriate.

7. In relation to economic development, the functions of the Board shall be planning, investigation and encouragement of joint development projects, but it shall not undertake such projects except with the assent of both States and the City of Jerusalem, in the event that Jerusalem is directly involved in the development project.

8. In regard to the joint currency system, the currencies circulating in the two States and the City of Jerusalem shall be issued under the authority of the Joint Economic Board, which shall be the sole issuing authority and which shall determine the reserves to be held against such currencies.

9. So far as is consistent with paragraph 2(b) above, each State may operate its own central bank, control its own fiscal and credit policy, its foreign exchange receipts and expenditures, the grant of import licences, and may conduct international financial operations on its own faith and credit. During the first two years after the termination of the Mandate, the Joint Economic Board shall have the authority to take such measures as may be necessary to ensure that—to the extent that the total foreign exchange revenues of the two States from the export of goods and services permit, and provided that each State takes appropriate measures to conserve its own foreign exchange resources—each State shall have avail-

able, in any twelve months' period, foreign exchange sufficient to assure the supply of quantities of imported goods and services for consumption in its territory equivalent to the quantities of such goods and services consumed in that territory in the twelve months' period ending 31 December 1947.

10. All economic authority not specifically vested in the Joint Economic Board is reserved to each State.

11. There shall be a common customs tariff with complete freedom of trade between the States, and between the States and the City of Jerusalem.

12. The tariff schedules shall be drawn up by a Tariff Commission, consisting of representatives of each of the States in equal numbers, and shall be submitted to the Joint Economic Board for approval by a majority vote. In case of disagreement in the Tariff Commission, the Joint Economic Board shall arbitrate the points of difference. In the event that the Tariff Commission fails to draw up any schedule by a date to be fixed, the Joint Economic Board shall determine the tariff schedule.

13. The following items shall be a first charge on the customs and other common revenue of the Joint Economic Board:

a. The expenses of the customs service and of the operation of the joint services;
b. The administrative expenses of the Joint Economic Board;
c. The financial obligations of the Administration of Palestine, consisting of:
i. The service of the outstanding public debt;
ii. The cost of superannuation benefits, now being paid or falling due in the future, in accordance with the rules and to the extent established by paragraph 3 of chapter 3 above.

14. After these obligations have been met in full, the surplus revenue from the customs and other common services shall be divided in the following manner: not less than 5 per cent and not more than 10 per cent to the City of Jerusalem; the residue shall be allocated to each State by the Joint Economic Board equitably, with the objective of maintaining a sufficient and suitable level of government and social services in each State, except

that the share of either State shall not exceed the amount of that State's contribution to the revenues of the Economic Union by more than approximately four million pounds in any year. The amount granted may be adjusted by the Board according to the price level in relation to the prices prevailing at the time of the establishment of the Union. After five years, the principles of the distribution of the joint revenue may be revised by the Joint Economic Board on a basis of equity.

15. All international conventions and treaties affecting customs tariff rates, and those communications services under the jurisdiction of the Joint Economic Board, shall be entered into by both States. In these matters, the two States shall be bound to act in accordance with the majority of the Joint Economic Board.

16. The Joint Economic Board shall endeavour to secure for Palestine's exports fair and equal access to world markets.

17. All enterprises operated by the Joint Economic Board shall pay fair wages on a uniform basis.

Freedom of Transit and Visit

18. The undertaking shall contain provisions preserving freedom of transit and visit for all residents or citizens of both States and of the City of Jerusalem, subject to security considerations; provided that each State and the City shall control residence within its borders.

Termination, Modification and Interpretation of the Undertaking

19. The undertaking and any treaty issuing therefrom shall remain in force for a period of ten years. It shall continue in force until notice of termination, to take effect two years thereafter, is given by either of the parties.

20. During the initial ten-year period, the undertaking and any treaty issuing therefrom may not be modified except by consent of both parties and with the approval of the General Assembly.

21. Any dispute relating to the application or the interpretation of the undertaking and any treaty issuing therefrom shall be referred, at the request of either party, to the International Court Of Justice, unless the parties agree to another mode of settlement.

E. ASSETS

1. The movable assets of the Administration of Palestine shall be allocated to the Arab and Jewish States and the City of Jerusalem on an equitable basis. Allocations should be made by the United Nations Commission referred to in section B, paragraph 1, above. Immovable assets shall become the property of the government of the territory in which they are situated.

2. During the period between the appointment of the United Nations Commission and the termination of the Mandate, the mandatory Power shall, except in respect of ordinary operations, consult with the Commission on any measure which it may contemplate involving the liquidation, disposal or encumbering of the assets of the Palestine Government, such as the accumulated treasury surplus, the proceeds of Government bond issues, State lands or any other asset.

F. ADMISSION TO MEMBERSHIP IN THE UNITED NATIONS

When the independence of either the Arab or the Jewish State as envisaged in this plan has become effective and the declaration and undertaking, as envisaged in this plan, have been signed by either of them, sympathetic consideration should be given to its application for admission to membership in the United Nations in accordance with article 4 of the Charter of the United Nations.

Part II.—Boundaries

A. THE ARAB STATE

The area of the Arab State in Western Galilee is bounded on the west by the Mediterranean and on the north by the frontier of the Lebanon from Ras en Naqura to a point north of Saliha. From there the boundary proceeds southwards, leaving the built-up area of Saliha in the Arab State, to join the southernmost point of this village. There it follows the western boundary line of the villages of 'Alma, Rihaniya and Teitaba, thence following the northern boundary line of Meirun village to join the Acre-Safad Sub-District boundary line. It follows this line to a point west of Es Sammu'i village and joins it again at the northernmost point of Farradiya. Thence it follows the sub-district boundary line to the Acre-Safad main road. From here it follows the western boundary of Kafr-I'nan village until it reaches the Tiberias-Acre Sub-District boundary line, passing to the west of the junction of the Acre-Safad and Lubiya-Kafr-I'nan roads. From the south-west corner of Kafr-I'nan village the boundary line follows the western boundary of the Tiberias Sub-District to a point close to the boundary line between the villages of Maghar and 'Eilabun, thence bulging out to the west to include as much of the eastern part of the plain of Battuf as is necessary for the reservoir proposed by the Jewish Agency for the irrigation of lands to the south and east.

The boundary rejoins the Tiberias Sub-District boundary at a point on the Nazareth-Tiberias road south-east of the built-up area of Tur'an; thence it runs southwards, at first following the sub-district boundary and then passing between the Kadoorie Agricultural School and Mount Tabor, to a point due south at the base of Mount Tabor. From here it runs due west, parallel to the horizontal grid line 230, to the north-east corner of the village lands of Tel Adashim. It then runs to the northwest corner of these lands, whence it turns south and west so as to include in the Arab State the sources of the Nazareth water supply in Yafa village. On reaching Ginneiger it follows the eastern, northern and western boundaries of the lands of this village to their south-west corner, whence it proceeds in a straight line to a point on the Haifa-Afula railway on the boundary between the villages of Sarid and El-Mujeidil. This is the point of intersection. The south-western boundary of the area of the Arab State in Galilee takes a line from this point, passing northwards along the eastern boundaries of Sarid and Gevat to the north-eastern corner of Nahalal, proceeding thence across the land of Kefar ha Horesh to a central point on the southern boundary of the village of 'Ilut, thence westwards along that village boundary to the eastern boundary of Beit Lahm, thence northwards and north-eastwards along its western boundary to the north-eastern corner of Waldheim and thence north-westwards across the village lands of Shafa 'Amr to the southeastern corner of Ramat Yohanan. From here it runs due north-north-east to a point on the Shafa 'Amr-Haifa road, west of its junction with the road of I'billin. From there it proceeds north-east to a point on the southern boundary of I'billin situated to the west of the I'billin-Birwa road. Thence along that boundary to its westernmost point, whence it turns to the north, follows across the village land of Tamra to the north-western-most corner and along the western boundary of Julis until it reaches the Acre-Safad road. It then runs westwards along the southern side of the

Safad-Acre road to the Galilee-Haifa District boundary, from which point it follows that boundary to the sea.

The boundary of the hill country of Samaria and Judea starts on the Jordan River at the Wadi Malih south-east of Beisan and runs due west to meet the Beisan-Jericho road and then follows the western side of that road in a north-westerly direction to the junction of the boundaries of the Sub-Districts of Beisan, Nablus, and Jenin. From that point it follows the Nablus-Jenin sub-District boundary westwards for a distance of about three kilometres and then turns north-westwards, passing to the east of the built-up areas of the villages of Jalbun and Faqqu'a, to the boundary of the Sub-Districts of Jenin and Beisan at a point northeast of Nuris. Thence it proceeds first northwestwards to a point due north of the built-up area of Zie'in and then westwards to the Afula-Jenin railway, thence north-westwards along the District boundary line to the point of intersection on the Hejaz railway. From here the boundary runs southwestwards, including the built-up area and some of the land of the village of Kh. Lid in the Arab State to cross the Haifa-Jenin road at a point on the district boundary between Haifa and Samaria west of El- Mansi. It follows this boundary to the southernmost point of the village of El-Buteimat. From here it follows the northern and eastern boundaries of the village of Ar'ara rejoining the Haifa-Samaria district boundary at Wadi 'Ara, and thence proceeding south-south-westwards in an approximately straight line joining up with the western boundary of Qaqun to a point east of the railway line on the eastern boundary of Qaqun village. From here it runs along the railway line some distance to the east of it to a point just east of the Tulkarm railway station. Thence the boundary follows a line half-way between the railway and the Tulkarm-Qalqiliya-Jaljuliya and Ras El-Ein road to a point just east of Ras El-Ein station, whence it proceeds along the railway some distance to the east of it to the point on the railway line south of the junction of the Haifa-Lydda and Beit Nabala lines, whence it proceeds along the southern border of Lydda airport to its south-west corner, thence in a south-westerly direction to a point just west of the built-up area of Sarafand El 'Amar, whence it turns south, passing just to the west of the built-up area of Abu El-Fadil to the north-east corner of the lands of Beer Ya'aqov. (The boundary line should be so demarcated as to allow direct access from the Arab State to the airport.) Thence the boundary line follows the western and southern boundaries of Ramle village, to the north-east corner of El Na'ana village, thence in a straight line to the southernmost point of El Barriya, along the eastern boundary of that village and the southern boundary of 'Innaba village. Thence it turns north to follow the southern side of the Jaffa-Jerusalem road until El-Qubab, whence it follows the road to the boundary of Abu-Shusha. It runs along the eastern boundaries of Abu Shusha, Seidun, Hulda to the southernmost point of Hulda, thence westwards in a straight line to the north-eastern corner of Umm Kalkha, thence following the northern boundaries of Umm Kalkha, Qazaza and the northern and western boundaries of Mukhezin to the Gaza District boundary and thence runs across the village lands of El-Mismiya El-Kabira, and Yasur to the southern point of intersection, which is midway between the built-up areas of Yasur and Batani Sharqi.

From the southern point of intersection the boundary lines run north-westwards between the villages of Gan Yavne and Barqa to the sea at a point half way between Nabi Yunis and Minat El-Qila, and south-eastwards to a point west of Qastina, whence it turns in a south-westerly direction, passing to the east of the built-up areas of Es Sawafir Esh Sharqiya and 'Ibdis. From the south-east corner of 'Ibdis village it runs to a point southwest of the built-up area of Beit 'Affa, crossing the Hebron–El-Majdal road just to the west of the built-up area of 'Iraq Suweidan. Thence it proceeds southward along the western village boundary of El-Faluja to the Beersheba Sub-District boundary. It then runs across the tribal lands of 'Arab El-Jubarat to a point on the boundary between the Sub-Districts of Beersheba and Hebron north of Kh. Khuweilifa, whence it proceeds in a south-westerly direction to a point on the Beersheba-Gaza main road two kilometres to the north-west of the town. It then turns south-eastwards to reach Wadi Sab' at a point situated one kilometer to the west of it. From here it turns north-eastwards and proceeds along Wadi Sab' and along the Beersheba-Hebron road for a dis-

tance of one kilometer, whence it turns eastwards and runs in a straight line to Kh. Kuseifa to join the Beersheba-Hebron Sub-District boundary. It then follows the Beersheba-Hebron boundary eastwards to a point north of Ras Ez-Zuweira, only departing from it so as to cut across the base of the indentation between vertical grid lines 150 and 160.

About five kilometres north-east of Ras Ez-Zuweira it turns north, excluding from the Arab State a strip along the coast of the Dead Sea not more than seven kilometres in depth, as far as 'Ein Geddi, whence it turns due east to join the Trans-jordan frontier in the Dead Sea.

The northern boundary of the Arab section of the coastal plain runs from a point between Minat El-Qila and Nabi Yunis, passing between the built-up areas of Gan Yavne and Barqa to the point of intersection. From here it turns south-westwards, running across the lands of Batani Sharqi, along the eastern boundary of the lands of Beit Daras and across the lands of Julis, leaving the built-up areas of Batani Sharqi and Julis to the westwards, as far as the north-west corner of the lands of Beit-Tima. Thence it runs east of El-Jiya across the village lands of El-Barbara along the eastern boundaries of the villages of Beit Jirja, Deir Suneid and Dimra. From the south-east corner of Dimra the boundary passes across the lands of Beit Hanun, leaving the Jewish lands of Nir-Am to the eastwards. From the south-east corner of Beit Hanun the line runs south-west to a point south of the parallel grid line 100, then turns north-west for two kilometres, turning again in a southwesterly direction and continuing in an almost straight line to the north-west corner of the village lands of Kirbet Ikhza'a. From there it follows the boundary line of this village to its southernmost point. It then runs in a southerly direction along the vertical grid line 90 to its junction with the horizontal grid line 70. It then turns south-eastwards to Kh. El-Ruheiba and then proceeds in a southerly direction to a point known as El-Baha, beyond which it crosses the Beersheba-EI 'Auja main road to the west of Kh. El-Mushrifa. From there it joins Wadi El-Zaiyatin just to the west of El-Subeita. From there it turns to the north-east and then to the south-east following this Wadi and passes to the east of 'Abda to join Wadi Nafkh. It then bulges to the south-west along Wadi Nafkh, Wadi 'Ajrim and Wadi Lassan to the point where Wadi Lassan crosses the Egyptian frontier.

The area of the Arab enclave of Jaffa consists of that part of the town-planning area of Jaffa which lies to the west of the Jewish quarters lying south of Tel-Aviv, to the west of the continuation of Herzl street up to its junction with the Jaffa-Jerusalem road, to the south-west of the section of the Jaffa-Jerusalem road lying south-east of that junction, to the west of Miqve Yisrael lands, to the northwest of Holon local council area, to the north of the line linking up the north-west corner of Holon with the northeast corner of Bat Yam local council area and to the north of Bat Yam local council area. The question of Karton quarter will be decided by the Boundary Commission, bearing in mind among other considerations the desirability of including the smallest possible number of its Arab inhabitants and the largest possible number of its Jewish inhabitants in the Jewish State.

B. THE JEWISH STATE

The north-eastern sector of the Jewish State (Eastern Galilee) is bounded on the north and west by the Lebanese frontier and on the east by the frontiers of Syria and Trans-jordan. It includes the whole of the Huleh Basin, Lake Tiberias, the whole of the Beisan Sub-District, the boundary line being extended to the crest of the Gilboa mountains and the Wadi Malih. From there the Jewish State extends north-west, following the boundary described in respect of the Arab State. The Jewish section of the coastal plain extends from a point between Minat El-Qila and Nabi Yunis in the Gaza Sub-District and includes the towns of Haifa and Tel-Aviv, leaving Jaffa as an enclave of the Arab State. The eastern frontier of the Jewish State follows the boundary described in respect of the Arab State.

The Beersheba area comprises the whole of the Beersheba Sub-District, including the Negeb and the eastern part of the Gaza Sub-District, but excluding the town of Beersheba and those areas described in respect of the Arab State. It includes also a strip of land along the Dead Sea stretching from the Beersheba-Hebron Sub-District boundary line to 'Ein Geddi, as described in respect of the Arab State.

C. THE CITY OF JERUSALEM

The boundaries of the City of Jerusalem are as defined in the recommendations on the City of Jerusalem. (See Part III, section B, below).

Part III.—City of Jerusalem(5)

A. SPECIAL REGIME

The City of Jerusalem shall be established as a corpus separatum under a special international regime and shall be administered by the United Nations. The Trusteeship Council shall be designated to discharge the responsibilities of the Administering Authority on behalf of the United Nations.

B. BOUNDARIES OF THE CITY

The City of Jerusalem shall include the present municipality of Jerusalem plus the surrounding villages and towns, the most eastern of which shall be Abu Dis; the most southern, Bethlehem; the most western, 'Ein Karim (including also the built-up area of Motsa); and the most northern Shu'fat, as indicated on the attached sketch-map (annex B).

C. STATUTE OF THE CITY

The Trusteeship Council shall, within five months of the approval of the present plan, elaborate and approve a detailed statute of the City which shall contain, inter alia, the substance of the following provisions:

1. Government machinery; special objectives. The Administering Authority in discharging its administrative obligations shall pursue the following special objectives:

a. To protect and to preserve the unique spiritual and religious interests located in the city of the three great monotheistic faiths throughout the world, Christian, Jewish and Moslem; to this end to ensure that order and peace, and especially religious peace, reign in Jerusalem;

b. To foster cooperation among all the inhabitants of the city in their own interests as well as in order to encourage and support the peaceful development of the mutual relations between the two Palestinian peoples throughout the Holy Land; to promote the security, well-being and any constructive measures of development of the residents having regard to the special circumstances and customs of the various peoples and communities.

2. Governor and Administrative staff. A Governor of the City of Jerusalem shall be appointed by the Trusteeship Council and shall be responsible to it. He shall be selected on the basis of special

qualifications and without regard to nationality. He shall not, however, be a citizen of either State in Palestine. The Governor shall represent the United Nations in the City and shall exercise on their behalf all powers of administration, including the conduct of external affairs. He shall be assisted by an administrative staff classed as international officers in the meaning of Article 100 of the Charter and chosen whenever practicable from the residents of the city and of the rest of Palestine on a non-discriminatory basis. A detailed plan for the organization of the administration of the city shall be submitted by the Governor to the Trusteeship Council and duly approved by it.

3. Local autonomy

a. The existing local autonomous units in the territory of the city (villages, townships and municipalities) shall enjoy wide powers of local government and administration.
b. The Governor shall study and submit for the consideration and decision of the Trusteeship Council a plan for the establishment of special town units consisting, respectively, of the Jewish and Arab sections of new Jerusalem. The new town units shall continue to form part the present municipality of Jerusalem.

4. Security measures

a. The City of Jerusalem shall be demilitarized; neutrality shall be declared and preserved, and no para-military formations, exercises or activities shall be permitted within its borders.
b. Should the administration of the City of Jerusalem be seriously obstructed or prevented by the non-cooperation or interference of one or more sections of the population the Governor shall have authority to take such measures as may be necessary to restore the effective functioning of administration.
c. To assist in the maintenance of internal law and order, especially for the protection of the Holy Places and religious buildings and sites in the city, the Governor shall organize a special police force of adequate strength, the members of which shall be recruited outside of Palestine. The Governor shall be empowered to direct such budgetary provision as may be necessary for the maintenance of this force.

5. Legislative Organization.

A Legislative Council, elected by adult residents of the city irrespective of nationality on the basis of universal and secret suffrage and proportional representation, shall have powers of legislation and taxation. No legislative measures shall, however, conflict or interfere with the provisions which will be set forth in the Statute of the City, nor shall any law, regulation, or official action prevail over them. The Statute shall grant to the Governor a right of vetoing bills inconsistent with the provisions referred to in the preceding sentence. It shall also empower him to promulgate temporary ordinances in case the Council fails to adopt in time a bill deemed essential to the normal functioning of the administration.

6. Administration of Justice.

The Statute shall provide for the establishment of an independent judiciary system, including a court of appeal. All the inhabitants of the city shall be subject to it.

7. Economic Union and Economic Regime.

The City of Jerusalem shall be included in the Economic Union of Palestine and be bound by all stipulations of the undertaking and of any treaties issued therefrom, as well as by the decisions of the Joint Economic Board. The headquarters of the Economic Board shall be established in the territory City. The Statute shall provide for the regulation of economic matters not falling within the regime of the Economic Union, on the basis of equal treatment and non-discrimination for all members of the United Nations and their nationals.

8. Freedom of Transit and Visit.

Control of residents. Subject to considerations of security, and of economic welfare as determined by the Governor under the directions of the Trusteeship Council, freedom of entry into, and residence within the borders of the City shall be guaranteed for the residents or citizens of the Arab and Jewish States. Immigration into, and residence within, the borders of the city for nationals of other States shall be controlled by the Governor under the directions of the Trusteeship Council.

9. Relations with Arab and Jewish States.

Representatives of the Arab and Jewish States shall be accredited to the Governor of the City and charged with the protection of the interests of their States and nationals in connection with the international administration of the City.

10. Official languages.

Arabic and Hebrew shall be the official languages of the city. This will not preclude the adoption of one or more additional working languages, as may be required.

11. Citizenship.

All the residents shall become ipso facto citizens of the City of Jerusalem unless they opt for citizenship of the State of which they have been citizens or, if Arabs or Jews, have filed notice of intention to become citizens of the Arab or Jewish State respectively, according to Part 1, section B, paragraph 9, of this Plan. The Trusteeship Council shall make arrangements for consular protection of the citizens of the City outside its territory.

12. Freedoms of citizens

a. Subject only to the requirements of public order and morals, the inhabitants of the City shall be ensured the enjoyment of human rights and fundamental freedoms, including freedom of conscience, religion and worship, language, education, speech and press, assembly and association, and petition.
b. No discrimination of any kind shall be made between the inhabitants on the grounds of race, religion, language or sex.
c. All persons within the City shall be entitled to equal protection of the laws.
d. The family law and personal status of the various persons and communities and their religious interests, including endowments, shall be respected.
e. Except as may be required for the maintenance of public order and good government, no measure shall be taken to obstruct or interfere with the enterprise of religious or charitable bodies of all faiths or to discriminate against any representative or member of these bodies on the ground of his religion or nationality.
f. The City shall ensure adequate primary and secondary education for the Arab and Jewish communities respectively, in their own languages and in accordance with their cultural traditions. The right of each community to maintain its own schools for the education of its own members in its own language, while

conforming to such educational requirements of a general nature as the City may impose, shall not be denied or impaired. Foreign educational establishments shall continue their activity on the basis of their existing rights.
g. No restriction shall be imposed on the free use by any inhabitant of the City of any language in private intercourse, in commerce, in religion, in the Press or in publications of any kind, or at public meetings.

13. Holy Places

a. Existing rights in respect of Holy Places and religious buildings or sites shall not be denied or impaired.
b. Free access to the Holy Places and religious buildings or sites and the free exercise of worship shall be secured in conformity with existing rights and subject to the requirements of public order and decorum.
c. Holy Places and religious buildings or sites shall be preserved. No act shall be permitted which may in any way impair their sacred character. If at any time it appears to the Governor that any particular Holy Place, religious building or site is in need of urgent repair, the Governor may call upon the community or communities concerned to carry out such repair. The Governor may carry it out himself at the expense of the community or communities concerned if no action is taken within a reasonable time.
d. No taxation shall be levied in respect of any Holy Place, religious building or site which was exempt from taxation on the date of the creation of the City. No change in the incidence of such taxation shall be made which would either discriminate between the owners or occupiers of Holy Places, religious buildings or sites or would place such owners or occupiers in a position less favourable in relation to the general incidence of taxation than existed at the time of the adoption of the Assembly's recommendations.

14. Special powers of the Governor in respect of the Holy Places, religious buildings and sites in the City and in any part of Palestine.

a. The protection of the Holy Places, religious buildings and sites located in the City of Jerusalem shall be a special concern of the Governor.

b. With relation to such places, buildings and sites in Palestine outside the city, the Governor shall determine, on the ground of powers granted to him by the Constitution of both States, whether the provisions of the Constitution of the Arab and Jewish States in Palestine dealing therewith and the religious rights appertaining thereto are being properly applied and respected.

c. The Governor shall also be empowered to make decisions on the basis of existing rights in cases of disputes which may arise between the different religious communities or the rites of a religious community in respect of the Holy Places, religious buildings and sites in any part of Palestine. In this task he may be assisted by a consultative council of representatives of different denominations acting in an advisory capacity.

D. DURATION OF THE SPECIAL REGIME

The Statute elaborated by the Trusteeship Council the aforementioned principles shall come into force not later than 1 October 1948. It shall remain in force in the first instance for a period of ten years, unless the Trusteeship Council finds it necessary to undertake a re-examination of these provisions at an earlier date. After the expiration of this period the whole scheme shall be subject to examination by the Trusteeship Council in the light of experience acquired with its functioning. The residents the City shall be then free to express by means of a referendum their wishes as to possible modifications of regime of the City.

Part IV. Capitulations

States whose nationals have in the past enjoyed in Palestine the privileges and immunities of foreigners, including the benefits of consular jurisdiction and protection, as formerly enjoyed by capitulation or usage in the Ottoman Empire, are invited to renounce any right pertaining to them to the re-establishment of such privileges and immunities in the proposed Arab and Jewish States and the City of Jerusalem.

Adopted at the 128th plenary meeting:
In favour: 33
Australia, Belgium, Bolivia, Brazil, Byelorussian S.S.R., Canada, Costa Rica, Czechoslovakia, Denmark, Dominican Republic, Ecuador, France, Guatemala, Haiti, Iceland, Liberia, Luxemburg, Netherlands, New Zealand, Nicaragua, Norway, Panama, Paraguay, Peru, Philippines, Poland, Sweden, Ukrainian S.S.R., Union of South Africa, U.S.A., U.S.S.R., Uruguay, Venezuela.

Against: 13
Afghanistan, Cuba, Egypt, Greece, India, Iran, Iraq, Lebanon, Pakistan, Saudi Arabia, Syria, Turkey, Yemen.

Abstained: 10
Argentina, Chile, China, Colombia, El Salvador, Ethiopia, Honduras, Mexico, United Kingdom, Yugoslavia.

(1) See Official Records of the General Assembly, Second Session Supplement No. 11, Volumes I-IV.

*At its hundred and twenty-eighth plenary meeting on 29 November 1947 the General Assembly, in accordance with the terms of the above resolution, elected the following members of the United Nations Commission on Palestine: Bolivia, Czechoslovakia, Denmark, Panama, and Philippines.

(2) This resolution was adopted without reference to a Committee.

(3) The following stipulation shall be added to the declaration concerning the Jewish State: "In the Jewish State adequate facilities shall be given to Arabic-speaking citizens for the use of their language, either orally or in writing, in the legislature, before the Courts and in the administration."

(4) In the declaration concerning the Arab State, the words "by an Arab in the Jewish State" should be replaced by the words "by a Jew in the Arab State."

(5) On the question of the internationalization of Jerusalem, see also General Assembly resolutions 185 (S-2) of 26 April 1948; 187 (S-2) of 6 May 1948, 303 (IV) of 9 December 1949, and resolutions of the Trusteeship Council (Section IV).

Source: Israeli Ministry of Foreign Affairs website.
http://www.mfa.gov.il/mfa/go.asp?MFAH00ps0.

Jawaharlal Nehru: Speech to Bandung Conference Political Committee (1955)

As leader of the largest noncommunist state in the world, Jawaharlal Nehru of India was a natural spokesperson for the group of developing nations meeting at Bandung, Indonesia, in 1955. In his speech, Nehru laid out one of the main principles of the new Non-Aligned Movement of nations established at Bandung: the need for neutrality in the Cold War between the United States and the Soviet Union. But this neutrality was distrusted by both superpowers, who continued to try to manipulate the governments of the underdeveloped world throughout the decades of the Cold War.

We do not agree with the communist teachings, we do not agree with the anti-communist teachings, because they are both based on wrong principles. I never challenged the right of my country to defend itself; it has to. We will defend ourselves with whatever arms and strength we have, and if we have no arms we will defend ourselves without arms. I am dead certain that no country can conquer India. Even the two great power blocs together cannot conquer India; not even the atom or the hydrogen bomb. I know what my people are. But I know also that if we rely on others, whatever great powers they might be if we look to them for sustenance, then we are weak indeed. . . .

My country has made mistakes. Every country makes mistakes. I have no doubt we will make mistakes; we will stumble and fall and get up. The mistakes of my country and perhaps the mistakes of other countries here do not make a difference; but the mistakes the Great Powers make do make a difference to the world and may well bring about a terrible catastrophe. I speak with the greatest respect of these Great Powers because they are not only great in military might but in development, in culture, in civilization. But I do submit that greatness sometimes brings quite false values, false standards. When they begin to think in terms of military strength—whether it be the United Kingdom, the Soviet Union or the U.S.A.—then they are going away from the right track and the result of that will be that the overwhelming might of one country will conquer the world. Thus far the world has succeeded in preventing that; I cannot speak for the future. . . .

. . . So far as I am concerned, it does not matter what war takes place; we will not take part in it unless we have to defend ourselves. If I join any of these big groups I lose my identity. . . . If all the world were to be divided up between these two big blocs what would be the result? The inevitable result would be war. Therefore every step that takes place in reducing that area in the world which may be called the *unaligned area* is a dangerous step and leads to war. It reduces that objective, that balance, that outlook which other countries without military might can perhaps exercise.

Honorable Members laid great stress on moral force. It is with military force that we are dealing now, but I submit that moral force counts and the moral force of Asia and Africa must, in spite of the atomic and hydrogen bombs of Russia, the U.S.A. or another country, count. . . .

. . . Many members present here do not obviously accept the communist ideology, while some of them do. For my part I do not. I am a positive person, not an 'anti' person. I want positive good for my country and the world. Therefore, are we, the countries of Asia and Africa, devoid of any positive position except being pro-communist or anti-communist? Has it come to this, that the leaders of thought who have given religions and all kinds of things to the world have to tag on to this kind of group or that and be hangers-on of this party or the other carrying out their wishes and occasionally giving an idea? It is most degrading and humiliating to any self-respecting people or nation. It is an intolerable thought to me that the great countries of Asia and Africa should come out of bondage into freedom only to degrade themselves or humiliate themselves in this way. . . .

I submit to you, every pact has brought insecurity and not security to the countries which have entered into them. They have brought the danger of atomic bombs and the rest of it nearer to them than would have been the case otherwise. They have not added to the strength of any country, I submit, which it had singly. It may have produced some idea of security, but it is a false security. It is a bad thing for any country thus to be lulled into security. . . .

. . . Today in the world, I do submit, not only because of the presence of these two colossuses but also because of the coming of the atomic and hydrogen-bomb age, the whole concept of war, of peace, of politics, has changed. We are thinking and acting in terms of a past age. No matter what generals and soldiers learned in the past, it is useless in this atomic age. They do not understand its implications or its use. As an eminent military critic said: 'The whole conception of War is changed. There is no precedent.' It may be so. Now it does not matter if one country is more powerful than the other in the use of the atomic bomb and the hydrogen bomb. One is more powerful in its ruin than the other. That is what is meant by saying that the point of saturation has been reached. However powerful one country is, the other is also powerful. To hit the nail on the head, the world suffers; there can be no victory. It may be said perhaps rightly that owing to this very terrible danger, people refrain from going to war. I hope so. The difficulty is that while Governments want to refrain from war, something suddenly happens and there is war and utter ruin. There is another thing: because of the present position in the world there can be aggression. If there is aggression anywhere in the world, it is bound to result in world war. It does not matter where the aggression is. If one commits the aggression there is world war.

I want the countries here to realise it and not to think in terms of any limitation. Today, a war however limited it may be is bound to lead to a big war. Even if tactical atomic weapons, as they are called, are used, the next step would be the use of the big atomic bomb. You cannot stop these things. In a country's life and death struggle, it is not going to stop short of this. It is not going to decide on our or anybody else's resolutions but it would engage in war, ruin and annihilation of others before it annihilates itself completely. Annihilation will result not only in the countries engaged in war, but owing to the radioactive waves which go thousands and thousands of miles it will destroy everything. That is the position. It is not an academic position; it is not a position of discussing ideologies; nor is it a position of discussing past history. It is looking at the world as it is today.

Source: Kahin, G. M. *The Asian-African Conference.* Ithaca, NY: Cornell University Press, 1956.

President Gamel Abdel Nasser: Denouncement of the Proposal for a Canal Users' Association (September 15, 1956)

In 1956, newly elected President Gamel Abdel Nasser of the United Arab Republic—a temporary state comprising Syria and Egypt—nationalized the Suez Canal, seizing control of the waterway from Britain and France. In response, the French and British threatened punitive action against the canal. In this speech, Nasser—a staunch Arab nationalist—denounces this attempt to reassert western control over the canal. Within six weeks, Britain and France, along with ally Israel, would go to war with Egypt. While successful on the battlefield, Egypt's attackers were forced to back down when the United States objected to their actions. Historians often consider the Suez War of 1956 the last hurrah for old-style European imperialism in the Middle East.

In these decisive days in the history of mankind, these days in which truth struggles to have itself recognized in international chaos where powers of evil domination and imperialism have prevailed, Egypt stands firmly to preserve her sovereignty. Your country stands solidly and staunchly to preserve her dignity against imperialistic schemes of a number of nations who have uncovered their desires for domination and supremacy.

In these days and in such circumstances Egypt has resolved to show the world that when small nations decide to preserve their sovereignty, they will do that all right and that when these small nations are fully determined to defend their rights and maintain their dignity, they will undoubtedly succeed in achieving their ends. . . .

I am speaking in the name of every Egyptian Arab and in the name of all free countries and of all those who believe in liberty and are ready to defend it. I am speaking in the name of principles proclaimed by these countries in the Atlantic Charter. But they are now violating these principles and it has become our lot to shoulder the responsibility of reaffirming and establishing them anew. . . .

We have tried by all possible means to cooperate with those countries which claim to assist smaller nations and which promised to collaborate with us but they demanded their fees in advance. This we refused so they started to fight with us. They said they will pay toward building the High Dam and then they withdrew their offer and cast doubts on the Egyptian economy. Are we to [disclaim] our sovereign right? Egypt insists her sovereignty must remain intact and refuses to give up any part of that sovereignty for the sake of money.

Egypt nationalized the Egyptian Suez Canal company. When Egypt granted the concession to de Lesseps it was stated in the concession between the Egyptian Government and the Egyptian company that the company of the Suez Canal is an Egyptian company subject to Egyptian authority. Egypt nationalized this Egyptian company and declared freedom of navigation will be preserved.

But the imperialists became angry. Britain and France said Egypt grabbed the Suez Canal as if it were part of France or Britain. The British Foreign Secretary forgot that only two years ago he signed an agreement stating the Suez Canal is an integral part of Egypt.

Egypt declared she was ready to negotiate. But as soon as negotiations began threats and intimidations started. . . .

Eden stated in the House of Commons there shall be no discrimination between states using the canal. We on our part reaffirm that and declare there is no discrimination between canal users. He also said Egypt shall not be allowed to succeed because that would spell success for Arab nationalism and would be against their policy, which aims at the protection of Israel.

Today they are speaking of a new association whose main objective would be to rob Egypt of the canal and deprive her of rightful canal dues. Suggestions made by Eden in the House of Commons which have been backed by France and the United States are a clear violation of the 1888 convention, since it is impossible to have two bodies organizing navigation in the canal. . . .

By stating that by succeeding, Abdel Nasser would weaken Britain's stand against Arab nationalism, Eden is in fact admitting his real objective is not Abdel Nasser as such but rather to defeat Arab nationalism and crush its cause. Eden speaks and finds his own answer. A month ago he let out the cry that he was after Abdel Nasser. Today the Egyptian people are fully conscious of their sovereign rights and Arab nationalism is fully awakened to its new destiny. . . .

Those who attack Egypt will never leave Egypt alive. We shall fight a regular war, a total war, a guerrilla war. Those who attack Egypt will soon realize they brought disaster upon themselves. He who attacks Egypt attacks the whole Arab world. They say in their papers the whole thing will be over in forty-eight hours. They do not know how strong we really are.

We believe in international law. But we will never submit. We shall show the world how a small country can stand in the face of great powers threatening with armed might. Egypt might be a small power but she is great inasmuch as she has faith in her power and convictions. I feel quite certain every Egyptian shares the same convictions as I do and believes in everything I am stressing now.

We shall defend our freedom and independence to the last drop of our blood. This is the stanch feeling of every Egyptian. The whole Arab nation will stand by us in our common fight against aggression and domination. Free peoples, too, people who are really free will stand by us and support us against the forces of tyranny. . . .

Source: U.S. Department of State. *The Suez Canal Problem, 26 July–22 September 1956, U.S. Department of State Publication No. 6392.* Washington, DC: Government Printing Office, 1956.

All-African People's Conference: Resolution on Imperialism and Colonialism (December 5–13, 1958)

In 1957, the British Gold Coast (renamed Ghana) became the first black-controlled colony in sub-Saharan Africa to win its independence from European colonists. Under the leadership of African nationalist Kwame Nkrumah, Ghana became a leader in pushing for the decolonization of Africa. In late 1958, Nkrumah called together a conference of African independence leaders in Accra, Ghana's capital. The Ghanaian leader's desire for independence for Africa was achieved within the next half dozen years, as most of the continent became sovereign states. But Nkrumah's vision for a unified Africa was never truly realized, although conferences like this one eventually resulted in the formation of the Organization of African Unity in 1963.

CONFERENCE RESOLUTION ON IMPERIALISM
AND COLONIALISM

(1) Whereas the great bulk of the African continent has been carved out arbitrarily to the detriment of the indigenous African peoples by European Imperialists, namely: Britain, France, Belgium, Spain, Italy and Portugal.

(2) Whereas in this process of colonisation two groups of colonial territories have emerged, to wit:

(a) Those territories where indigenous Africans are dominated by foreigners who have their seats of authority in foreign lands, for example, French West Africa, French Equatorial Africa, Nigeria, Sierra Leone, Gambia, Belgian Congo, Portuguese Guinea, Basutoland, Swaziland and Bechuanaland.

(b) Those where indigenous Africans are dominated and oppressed by foreigners who have settled permanently in Africa and who regard the position of Africa under their sway as belonging more to them than to the Africa, e.g., Kenya, Union of South Africa, Algeria, Rhodesia, Angola and Mozambique.

(3) Whereas world opinion unequivocally condemns oppression and subjugation of one race by another in whatever shape or form.

(4) Whereas all African peoples everywhere strongly deplore the economic exploitation of African peoples by imperialist countries thus reducing Africans to poverty in the midst of plenty.

(5) Whereas all African peoples vehemently resent the militarisation of Africans and the use of African soldiers in a nefarious global game against their brethren as in Algeria, Kenya, South Africa, Cameroons, Ivory Coast, Rhodesia and in the Suez Canal invasion.

(6) Whereas fundamental human rights, freedom of speech, freedom of association, freedom of movement, freedom of worship, freedom to live a full and abundant life, as approved by the All-African People's Conference on 13th December, 1958, are denied to Africans through the activities of imperialists.

(7) Whereas denial of the franchise to Africans on the basis of race or sex has been one of the principal instruments of colonial policy by imperialists and their agents, thus making it feasible for a few white settlers to lord it over mil-

lions of indigenous Africans as in the proposed Central African Federation, Kenya, Union of South Africa, Algeria, Angola, Mozambique and the Cameroons.

(8) Whereas imperialists are now coordinating their activities by forming military and economic pacts such as NATO, European Common Market, Free Trade Area, Organisation for European Economic Co-operation, Common Organisation in Sahara for the purpose of strengthening their imperialist activities in Africa and elsewhere,

Be it resolved and it is hereby resolved by; the All-African People's Conference meeting in Accra 5th to 13th December, 1958, and comprising over 300 delegates representing over 200 million Africans from all parts of Africa as follows:

1. That the All-African People's Conference vehemently condemns colonialism and imperialism in whatever shape or form these evils are perpetuated.

2. That the political and economic exploitation of Africans by imperialist Europeans should cease forthwith.

3. That the use of African manpower in the nefarious game of power politics by imperialists should be a thing of the past.

4. That independent African States should pursue in their international policy principles which will expedite and accelerate the independence and sovereignty of all dependent and colonial African territories.

5. That fundamental human rights be extended to all men and women in Africa and that the rights of indigenous Africans to the fullest use of their lands be respected and preserved.

6. That universal adult franchise be extended to all persons in Africa regardless of race or sex.

7. That independent African states ensure that fundamental human rights and universal adult franchise are fully extended to everyone within their states as an example to imperial nations who abuse and ignore the extension of those rights to Africans.

8. That a permanent secretariat of the All-African People's Conference be set up to organise the All-African Conference on a firm basis.

9. That a human rights committee of the Conference be formed to examine complaints of abuse of human rights in every part of Africa and to take appropriate steps to ensure the enjoyment of the rights by everyone.

10. That the All-African People's Conference in Accra declares its full support to all fighters for freedom in Africa, to all those who resort to peaceful means of non-violence and civil disobedience, as well as to all those who are compelled to retaliate against violence to attain national independence and freedom for the people. Where such retaliation becomes necessary, the Conference condemns all legislations which consider those who fight for their independence and freedom as ordinary criminals.

Source: All-African People's Conference News Bulletin (Accra, Ghana) 1, 4 (1959).

Castro Denounces Imperialism and Colonialism at the United Nations (September 1960)

In September 1960, Fidel Castro—who had recently taken power in Cuba after a lengthy armed struggle against the dictatorship of Fulgencio Batista—came to the United Nations to address the General Assembly. In a lengthy speech, he lambasted the United States for its hostility to the Cuban revolution. More significant for the subject of this encyclopedia, he laid out his vision of how neocolonialism worked. According to Castro, industrial countries—most notably, the United States—were able to exploit formerly colonized regions without actually annexing them politically through the support of repressive regimes and the control of local economies by Western corporate interests.

Mr. President,

Fellow Delegates

...How did our country become a colony of the United States? It was not because of its origins; the same men did not colonize the United States and Cuba. Cuba has a very different ethnical and cultural origin, and the difference was widened over the centuries. Cuba was the last country in America to free itself from Spanish colonial rule, to cast off, with due respect to the representative of Spain, the Spanish colonial yoke; and because it was the last, it also had to fight more fiercely.

Spain had only one small possession left in America and it defended it with tooth and nail. Our people, small in numbers, scarcely a million inhabitants at that time, had to face alone, for almost thirty years, an army considered one of the strongest in Europe. Against our small national population the Spanish Government mobilized an army as big as the total forces that had fought against South American independence. Half a million Spanish soldiers fought against the historic and unbreakable will of our people to be free.

For thirty years the Cubans fought alone for their independence; thirty years of struggle that strengthened our love for freedom and independence. But Cuba was a fruit—according to the opinion of a President of the United States at the beginning of the past century, John Adams—, it was an apple hanging from the Spanish tree, destined to fall, as soon as it was ripe enough, into the hands of the United States. Spanish power had worn itself out in our country. Spain had neither the men nor the economic resources to continue the war in Cuba; Spain had been defeated. Apparently the apple was ripe, and the United States Government held out its open hands.

Not one but several apples fell in to the hands of the United States. Puerto Rico fell—heroic Puerto Rico, which had begun its struggle for independence at the same time as Cuba. The Philippine Islands fell, and several other possessions. However, the method of dominating our country could not be the same. Our country had struggled fiercely, and thus had gained the favor of world public opinion. Therefore the method of taking our country had to be different.

The Cubans who fought for our independence and at that very moment were giving their blood and their lives believed in good faith in the joint resolution of the Congress of the United States of April 20, 1898, which declared that "Cuba is, and by right ought to be, free and independent."

The people of the United States were sympathetic to the Cuban struggle for liberty. That joint declaration was a law adopted by the Congress of the United States through which war was declared on Spain. But that illusion was followed by a rude awakening. After two years of military occupation of our country, the unexpected happened: at the very moment that the people of Cuba, through their Constituent Assembly, were drafting the Constitution of the Republic, a new law was passed by the United States Congress, a law proposed by Senator Platt, bearing such unhappy memories for the Cubans. That law stated that the constitution of the Cuba must have an appendix under which the United States would be granted the right to intervene in Cuba's political affairs and, furthermore, to lease certain parts of Cuba for naval bases or coal supply station.

In other words, under a law passed by the legislative body of a foreign country, Cuban's Constitution had to contain an appendix with those provisions. Our legislators were clearly told that if they did not accept the amendment, the occupation forces would not be withdrawn. In other words, an agreement to grant another country the right to intervene and to lease naval bases was imposed by force upon my country by the legislative body of a foreign country.

It is well, I think, for countries just entering this Organization, countries just beginning their independent life, to bear in mind our history and to note any similar conditions which they may find waiting for them along their own road. And if it is not they, then those who came after them, or their children, or grandchildren, although it seems to us that we will not have to wait that long.

Then began the new colonization of our country, the acquisition of the best agricultural lands by United States firms, concessions of Cuban natural resources and mines, concessions of public utilities for exploitation purposes, commercial concessions of all types. These concessions, when linked with the constitutional right—constitutional by force—of intervention in our country, turned it from a Spanish colony into an American colony.

Colonies do not speak. Colonies are not known until they have the opportunity to express themselves. That is why our colony and its problems were unknown to the rest of the world. In geography books reference was made to a flag and a coat of arms. There was an island with another color on the maps, but it was not an independent republic. Let us not deceive ourselves, since by doing so we only make ourselves ridiculous. Let no one be mistaken. There was no independent republic; there was only a colony where orders were given by the Ambassador of the United States.

We are not ashamed to have to declare this. On the contrary: we are proud to say that today no embassy rules our country; our country is ruled by its people!

Once again the Cuban people had to resort to fighting in order to achieve independence, and

that independence was finally attained after seven bloody years of tyranny, who forced this tyranny upon us? Those who in our country were nothing more than tools of the interests which dominated our country economically . . .

How can an unpopular regime, inimical to the interests of the people, stay in power unless it is by force? Will we have to explain to the representatives of our sister republics of Latin America what military tyrannies are? Will we have to outline to them how these tyrannies have kept themselves in power? Will we have to explain the history of several of those tyrannies which are already classical? Will we have to say what forces, what national and international interests support them?

The military group which tyrannized our country was supported by the most reactionary elements of the nation, and, above all, by the foreign interests that dominated the economy of our country. Everybody knows, and we understand that even the Government of the United States admits it, that that was the type of government favored by the monopolies. Why? Because by the use of force it was possible to check the demands of the people; by the use of force it was possible to suppress strikes for improvement of living standards; by the use of force it was possible to crush all movements on the part of the peasants to own the land they worked; by the use of force it was possible to curb the greatest and most deeply felt aspirations of the nation.

That is why governments of force were favored by the ruling circles of the United States. That is why governments of force stayed in power for so long, and why there are governments of force still in power in America.

Naturally, it all depends on whether it is possible to secure the support of the United States.

For instance, now they say they oppose one of these governments of force; the Government of Trujillo. But they do not say they are against other governments of force—that of Nicaragua, or Paraguay, for example.

The Nicaraguan one is no longer government of force; it is a monarchy that is almost as constitutional as that of the United Kingdom, where the reins of power are handed down from father to son. The same would have occurred in my own country. It was the type of government of force—that of Fulgencio Batista—which suited the American monopolies in Cuba, but it was not, of course, the type of government which suited the Cuban people, and the Cuban people, at a great cost in lives and sacrifices, over threw the government.

What did the Revolution find when it came to power in Cuba? What marvels did the Revolution find when it came to power in Cuba? First of all the Revolution found that 600,000 able Cubans were unemployed—as many, proportionately, as were unemployed in the United States at the time of the great depression which shook this country and which almost created a catastrophe in the United States. That was our permanent unemployment.

Three million out of a population of somewhat over 6,000,000 did not have electric lights and did not enjoy the advantages and comforts of electricity. Three and a half million out of a total of slightly more than 6,000,000 lived in huts, shacks and slums, without the slightest sanitary facilities. In the cities, rents took almost one third of family incomes.

Electricity rates and rents were among the highest in the world.

Thirty-seven and one half percent of our population were illiterate; 70 per cent of the rural children had no teachers; 2 per cent of population, that is, 100,000 persons out of a total of more than 6,000,000 suffered from tuberculosis. Ninety-five per cent of the children in rural areas were affected by parasites, and the infant mortality rate was therefore very high, just the opposite of the average life span.

On the other hand, 85 per cent of the small farmers were paying rents for the use of land to the tune of almost 30 per cent of their income, while 1 1/2 percent of the landowners controlled 46 per cent of the total area of the nation. Of course, the proportion of hospital beds to the number of inhabitants of the country was ridiculous, when compared with countries that only have halfway decent medical services.

Public utilities, electricity and telephone services all belonged to the United States monopolies. A major portion of the banking business, of the importing business and the oil refineries, the greater part of the sugar production, the best land in Cuba, and the most important industries in all fields belonged to American companies. The balance of payments in the last ten years, from 1950 to 1960, had been favorable to the United States with regard to Cuba to the extent of one thousand million dollars.

This is without taking in to account the hundreds of millions of dollars that were extracted from the treasury of the country by the corrupt officials of the tyranny and were later deposited in United States or European Banks.

One thousand million dollars in ten years. This poor and underdeveloped Caribbean country, with 600,000 unemployed, was contributing greatly to the economic development of the most highly industrialized country in the world.

That was the situation we found, and it is probably not foreign to many of the countries represented in this Assembly, because, when all is said and done, what we have said about Cuba is like a diagnostic x-ray applicable to many of the countries represented here.

What alternative was there for the Revolutionary Government? To betray the people? Of course, as far as the President of the United States is concerned, we have betrayed our people, but it would certainly not have been considered so, if, instead of the Revolutionary Government being true to its people, it had been loyal to the big American monopolies that exploited the economy of our country. At least, let note be taken here of the wonders the Revolution found when it came to power. They were no more and no less than the usual wonder of imperialism, which are in themselves the wonders of the free world as far as we, the colonies, are concerned!.

...And so the Revolutionary Government began to take the first steps . . .

Then another law was passed, a law canceling the concessions which had been granted by the tyranny of Batista to the Telephone Company, an American monopoly. Taking advantage of the fact our people were defenseless, they had obtained valuable concessions. The Revolutionary Government then cancelled these concessions and re-established normal prices for telephone services. Thus began the first conflict with the American monopolies.

The third measure was the reduction of electricity rates, which were the highest in the world. Then followed the second conflict with the American monopolies. We were beginning to appear communist; they were beginning to daub us in red because we had clashed head on with the interests of the United States monopolies.

Then followed the next law, an essential and inevitable law for our country, and a law which sooner or later will have to be adopted by all countries of the world, at least by those which have not yet adopted it: the Agrarian Reform Law. Of course, in theory everybody agrees with the Agrarian Reform Law. Nobody will deny the need for it unless he is a fool.

No one can deny that agrarian reform is one of the essential conditions for the economic development of the country. In Cuba, even the big landowners agreed about the agrarian reform— only they wanted their own kind of reform, such as the one defended by many theoreticians; a reform which would not harm their interests, and above all, one which would not be put into effect as long as it could be avoided. This is something that is well known to the economic bodies of the United Nations, something nobody even cares to discuss any more. In my country it was absolutely necessary: more than 200,000 peasant families lived in the countryside without land on which to grow essential food crops.

Without an agrarian reform, our country would have been unable to take that step; we made an agrarian reform. Was it a radical agrarian reform?

We think not. It was a reform adjusted to the needs of our development, and in keeping with our own possibilities of agricultural development. In other words, was an agrarian reform which was to solve the problems of the landless peasants, the problem of supplying basic foodstuffs, the problem of rural unemployment, and which was to end, once and for all, the ghastly poverty which existed in the countryside of our native land.

And that is where the first major difficulty arose. In the neighboring Republic of Guatemala a similar case had occurred. And I honestly warn my colleagues of Latin America, Africa and Asia; whenever you set out to make a just agrarian reform, you must be ready to face a similar situation, especially if the best and largest tracts of land are owned by American monopolies, as was the case in Cuba . . .

But the truth is that in our country it was not only the land that was the property of the agrarian monopolies. The largest and most important mines were also owned by those monopolies. Cuba produces, for example, a great deal of nickel. All of the nickel was exploited by American interests, and under the tyranny of Batista, an American company, the Moa Bay, had obtained such a juicy concession that in a mere five years—mark my words, in a mere five years—it intended amortizing an investment of $120,000,000. A $120,000,000 investment amortized in five years!

And who had given the Moa Bay company this concession through the intervention of the Government of the United States? Quite simply, the tyrannical government of Fulgencio Batista, which was there to defend the interests of the monopolies. And this is an absolutely true fact. Exempt from all taxes what were those companies going to leave for the Cubans?

The empty, worked out mines, the impoverished land, and not the slightest contribution to the economic development of our country.

And so the Revolutionary Government passed a mining law which forced those monopolies to pay a 25 per cent tax on the exportation of minerals.

The attitude of the Revolutionary Government already had been too bold. It had clashed with the interests of the international electric trusts; it had clashed with the interests of the international telephone trusts; it had clashed with the interests of the mining trusts; it had clashed with the interests of the United Fruit Co; and it had in effect, clashed with the most powerful interests of the United States, which, as you know, are very closely linked with each other. And that was more than the Government of the United States—or rather, the representatives of the United States monopolies— could possibly tolerate.

Then began a new period of harassment of the Revolution . . .

The attitude of the Cuban Revolution therefore had to be punished.

Punitive actions of all sorts—even the destruction of those insolent people—had to follow the audacity of the Revolutionary Government.

On our honor, we swear that up to that moment we had not had the opportunity even to exchange letters with the distinguished Prime Minister of the Soviet Union, Nikita Khrushchev. That is to say that when, for the North American press and the international news agencies that supply information to the world, Cuba was already a Communist Government, a red peril ninety miles from the

United States with a Government dominated by Communists, the Revolutionary Government had not even had the opportunity of establishing diplomatic and commercial relations with the Soviet Union . . .

Then came the threats against our sugar quota, imperialism's cheap philosophy of showing generosity, egotistical and exploiting generosity; and they began showing kindness towards Cuba, declaring that they were paying us a preferential price for sugar, which amounted to a subsidy to Cuban sugar—a sugar which was not so sweet for Cubans, since we were not the owners of the best sugar-producing land, nor the owners of the largest sugar mills. Furthermore, in that affirmation lay hidden the true history of Cuban sugar, of the sacrifices which had been imposed upon my country during the periods when it was economically attacked.

However when quotas were established, our participation was reduced to 28 per cent, and the advantages which that law had granted us, the very few advantages which that law had granted us, were gradually taken away in successive laws, and, of course the colony depended on the colonial power.

The economy of the colony had been organized by the colonial power.

The colony had to be subjected to the colonial power, and if the colony took measures to free itself from the colonial powers that country would take measures to crush the colony. Conscious of the subordination of our economy to their market, the Government of the United States began to issue a series of warnings that our quota would be reduced further, and at the same time, other activities were taking place in the United States of America: the activities of counterrevolutionaries . . .

Did they sincerely believe in what they said when they stated that the agrarian reform would cause a drop in production? Perhaps they did.

Surely it is logical for each one to believe what his mind has been conditioned to believe. It is quite possible they may have felt that without the all-powerful monopolist companies, we Cubans would be unable to produce sugar; perhaps they were even sure we would ruin the country. And of course, if the Revolution had ruined the country, then the United States would not have had to attack us; it would have left us alone, and the United States Government would have appeared as a good and honorable government, and we as people who ruined our own Nation, and as a great example that Revolutions should not be made because they ruin countries.

Fortunately, that was not the case. There is proof that revolutions do not ruin countries, and that proof has just been furnished by the Government of the United States. Among other things, it has been proved that revolutions do not ruin countries, and that imperialist governments do try to ruin countries.

Cuba had not been ruined; she therefore had to be ruined. Cuba needed new markets for its products, and we would honestly ask any delegation present if it does not want its country to sell what it produces and its export to increase. We wanted our exports to increase, and this is what all countries wish; this must be a universal law. Only egotistical interests can oppose the universal interest in trade and commercial exchange, which surely is one of the most ancient aspirations and needs of mankind.

We wanted to sell our products and went in search of new markets. We signed a trade treaty with the Soviet Union, according to which we would sell one million tons of sugar and would purchase a certain amount of Soviet products or articles. Surely no one can say that this is an incorrect procedure. There may be some who would not do such a thing because it might displease certain interests. We really did not have to ask permission from the State Department in order to sign a trade treaty with the Soviet Union, because we considered ourselves, and we continue to consider ourselves and we will always consider ourselves, a truly independent and free country . . .

Cuba was not the first victim of aggression; Cuba was not the first country to be in danger of aggression. In this hemisphere everyone knows that the Government of the United States has always imposed its own law—the law of the strongest, in virtue of which they have destroyed Puerto Rican nationhood and have imposed their domination on that friendly country law in accordance with which they seized and held the Panama Canal . . .

That is why we, the small countries, do not yet feel too sure that our rights will be preserved; that is why we, the small countries, whenever we decide to become free, know that we become free at our own risk. In truth, when people are united and are defending a just right, they can trust their own energies. We are not, as we have been pictured, a mere group of men governing the country. We are a whole people governing a country—a whole people firmly united, with a great revolutionary consciousness, defending its rights. And this should be known by the enemies of the revolution and of Cuba, because if they ignore this fact, they will be making a regrettable error . . .

Thus far, the monopolies have certainly not cared very much, except about exploiting the underdeveloped countries. But comes the Cuban Revolution and suddenly the monopolists are worrying, and while they attack us economically trying to crush us, they offer aims to the countries of Latin America. The countries of Latin America are offered, not the resources for development that Latin America needs, but resources for social development—houses for men who have no work, schools where children will not go, and hospitals that would not be necessary if there were enough food to eat (APPLAUSE).

After all, although some of my Latin American colleagues may feel it their duty to be discreet at the United Nations, they should all welcome a revolution such as the Cuban Revolution which at any rate has forced the monopolists to return at least a small part of what they have been extracting from the natural resources and the sweat of the Latin American peoples . . .

Why is the United States Government unwilling to talk of development?

It is very simple: because the Government of the United States does not want to oppose the monopolies, and the monopolies require natural resources and markets for the investment of their capital. That is where the great contradiction lies. That is why the real solution to this problem is not sought. That is why planning for the development of underdeveloped countries with public funds is not done . . .

But there are even more alarming circumstances for our people. It is well known that, in virtue of the Platt Amendment, imposed by force upon our people, the Government of the United States assumed the right to establish naval bases on our territory, a right forcefully imposed and

maintained. A naval base in the territory of any country is surely a cause for concern. First of all, there is concern over the fact that a country which follows an aggressive and warlike international policy has a base in the heart of our country, which brings us the risk of being involved in any international conflict, in any atomic conflict, without our having anything to do with the problem, because we have absolutely nothing to do with the problems of the United States and the crises provoked by the Government of the United States. Yet, there is a base in the heart of our Island which entails danger for us in case of war.

But is that only danger? No. There is another danger that concerns us even more, since it is closer to home. The Revolutionary Government of Cuba has repeatedly expressed its concern over the fact that the imperialist government of the United States may use that base, located in the heart of our national territory, as an excuse to promote a self-aggression, in order to justify an attack on our country. I repeat: the Revolutionary Government of Cuba is seriously concerned—and makes known this concern—over the fact that the imperialist government of the United States of America may use a self-aggression in order to justify an attack on our country. And this concern on our part is becoming increasingly greater because of the intensified aggressiveness that the United States is displaying . . .

What does all this mean? There are many countries that have American bases in their territory, but they are not directed against the governments that made these concessions—at least not as far as we know. Yet ours is the most tragic case. There is a base on our island territory directed against Cuba and the Revolutionary Government of Cuba, in the hands of those who declare themselves enemies of our country, enemies of our revolution, and enemies of our people. In the entire history of the world's present-day bases, the most tragic case is that of Cuba; a base imposed upon us by force, well within our territory, which is a good many miles away from the coast of the United States, an instrument used against Cuba and the Cuban people imposed by the use of force, and a constant threat and a cause for concern for our people.

That is why we must state here that all these rumors of attacks are intended to create hysteria and prepare the conditions for an aggression against our country, that we have never spoken a single word implying the thought of any type of attack on the Guantanamo base, because we are the first in not wanting to give imperialism an excuse to attack us, and we state this categorically. But we also declare that from the very moment that base was turned into a threat to the security and peace of our country, a danger to our country, the Revolutionary Government of Cuba has been considering very seriously the requesting, within the framework of international law, of the withdrawal of the naval and military forces of the United States from that portion of our National territory.

But it is imperative that this Assembly be kept well informed regarding the problems of Cuba, because we have to be on the alert against deceit and confusion. We have to explain these problems very clearly because with them go the security and the fate of our country. And that is why we want exact note to be taken of the words I have spoken, particularly when one takes into consideration the fact that the opinions or erroneous ideas of the politicians of this country as regards Cuban problems do not show any signs of improving. I have here some declarations by Mr. Kennedy that would surprise anybody. On Cuba he says. "We must use all the power of the Organization of American States to prevent Castro from interfering in other Latin American countries, and we must use all that power to return freedom to Cuba." They are going to give freedom back to Cuba!

"We must state our intention," he says, "of not allowing the Soviet Union to turn Cuba into its Caribbean base, and of applying the Monroe Doctrine." Half-way or more into the twentieth century, this gentleman speaks of the Monroe doctrine!

"We must make Prime Minister Castro understand that we intend to defend our right to the Naval Base of Guantanamo." He is the third who speaks of the problem. "And we must make the Cuban people know that we sympathize with their legitimate economic aspirations. . . ." Why did they not feel sympathetic before? ". . . . that we know their love of freedom, and that we shall never be happy until democracy is restored in Cuba. . . ." What democracy? The democracy "made" by the imperialist monopolies of the Government of the United States?

"The forces in exile that are struggling for freedom," he says—note this very carefully so that you will understand why there are planes flying from American territory over Cuba: pay close attention to what this gentleman has to say. "The forces that struggle for liberty in exile and in the mountains of Cuba should be supported and assisted, and in other countries of Latin America communism must be confined and not allowed to expand."

If Kennedy were not an illiterate and ignorant millionaire (APPLAUSE) . . . he would understand that it is not possible to carry out a revolution supported by landowners against the peasant in the mountains, and that every time imperialism has tried to encourage counterrevolutionary groups, the peasant militia has captured them in the course of a few days.

But he seems to have read a novel, or seen a Hollywood film, about guerrillas, and he thinks it is possible to carry on guerrilla warfare in a country where the relations of the social forces are what they are in Cuba.

In any case, this is discouraging. Let no one think, however, that these opinions as regards Kennedy's statements indicate that we feel any sympathy towards the other one, Mr. Nixon . . . (LAUGHTER) who has made similar statements. As far as we are concerned, both lack political brains.

Up to this point we have been dealing with the problem of our country, a fundamental duty of ours when coming before the United Nations, but we understand that it would be a little egotistical on our part if our concern were to be limited to our specific case alone. It is also true that we have used up the greater part of our time informing this Assembly about the Cuban case, and that there is not much time left for us to deal with the remaining questions, to which we wish to refer briefly.

The case of Cuba is not isolated case. It would be an error to think of it only as the case of Cuba. The case of Cuba is the case of all underdeveloped countries. The case of Cuba is like that of the Congo, Egypt, Algeria, Iran . . . (APPLAUSE) . . . like that of Panama, which wishes to have its canal; it is like that of Puerto Rico, whose national spirit they are destroying; like that of Honduras, a portion of whose territory has been alienated. In short, although we have not make specific reference to other countries, the case of Cuba is the case of all underdeveloped, colonized countries.

The problems which we have been describing in relation to Cuba can be applied just as well to all of Latin America. The control of Latin American economic resources by the monopolies, which, when they do not own the mines directly and are in charge of extraction, as the case with the copper of Chile, Peru, or Mexico, and with the oil of Venezuela—when this control is not exercised directly it is because they are the owners of the public utility companies, as is the case in Argentina, Brazil, Chile, Peru, Ecuador and Colombia, or the owners of telephone services, which is the case in Chile, Brazil, Peru, Venezuela, Paraguay and Bolivia, or they commercialize our products, as is the case with coffee in Brazil, Colombia, El Salvador, Costa Rica, and Guatemala, or with the cultivation, marketing and transportation of bananas by the United Fruit Co. in Guatemala, Costa Rica, and Honduras, or with the cotton in Mexico and Brazil. In other words, the monopolies control the most important industries. Woe to those countries, the day they try to make an agrarian reform! They will be asked for immediate, efficient, and just payment. And if, in spite of everything they make an agrarian reform, the representative of the friendly country who comes to the United Nations will be confined to Manhattan; they will not rent hotel space to him; insult will he heaped upon him, and it is even possible that he may be physically mistreated by the police.

The problem of Cuba is just an example of the situation in Latin America. And how long will Latin America wait for its development? It will have to wait, according to the point of view of the monopolies, until there are two Fridays in a week.

Who is going to industrialize Latin America? The monopolies?

Certainly not. There is a report by the economic Commission of the United Nations which explains how private capital, instead of going to the countries that need it most for the establishment of basic industries to contribute to their development, is being channeled referentially to the more industrialized countries, because there, according to their beliefs, private capital finds greater security. And, of course, even the Economic Secretariat of the United Nations has had to admit there is no possible chance for development through the investment of private capital—that is, through the monopolies.

The development of Latin America will have to be achieved through public investment, planned and granted unconditionally without any political strings attached, because, naturally, we all like to be representatives of free countries. None of us like to represent a country that does not feel itself in full possession of its freedom . . .

The problems of Latin America are similar to those of the rest of the world: to those of Africa and Asia. The world is divided up among the monopolies; the same monopolies that we find in Latin America are also found in the Middle East. There the oil is in the hands of monopolistic companies that are controlled by France, the United States, the United Kingdom, the Netherlands. . . . in Iran, Iraq, Saudi Arabia, Kuwait, in short, in all corners of the world. The same thing is true, for instance, in the Philippines, and in Africa. The world has been divided among the monopolistic interests. Who would dare deny this historic truth? The monopolistic interests do not want to see the development of countries and the people themselves. And the sooner they recover or amortize the capital invested, the better.

The problems the Cuban people have had to face with the imperialistic government of the United States are the same which Saudi Arabia would face if it nationalized its oil, and this also applies to Iran or Iraq; the same problems that Egypt had when it quite justifiably nationalized the Suez Canal; the very same problems that Indonesia had when it wanted to become independent; the same surprise attacks as against Egypt and the Congo.

Have colonialists or imperialists ever lacked a pretext when they wanted to invade a country? Never! Somehow they have always found a pretext. And which are the colonialist and imperialist countries? Four or five countries—no, four or five groups of monopolies are the owners of the wealth of the world.

If a being from another planet were to come to this Assembly, one who had read neither the *Communist Manifesto* of Karl Marx nor the cables of the United Press or the Associated Press or other monopolist publications, if he were to ask how the world had been divided, and he saw on a map that the wealth of the world was divided among the monopolies of four or five countries, he would say, without further consideration; "The wealth of this world has been badly distributed, the world is being exploited . . ."

We have spoken here of the Cuban case. Our case has taught us because of the problems we have had with our own imperialism, that is, the particular imperialism that is ranged against us. But, since all imperialism are alike, they are all allies. A country that exploits the people of Latin America, or any other parts of the world, is an ally of the exploiters of the rest of the world . . .

The colonialists, therefore, are against disarmament. Using the weapon of world public opinion, we must fight to force disarmament on them as we must force them to respect the right of peoples to economic and political liberation.

The monopolies are against disarmament, because, besides being able to defend those interests with arms, the arms race has always been good business for them. For example, it is well known that the great monopolies in this country doubled their capital shortly after the Second World War.

Like vultures, the monopolies feed on the corpses which are the harvest of war.

And war is a business. Those who trade in war, those who enrich themselves by war, must be unmasked. We must open the eyes of the world and expose those who trade in the destiny of mankind, in the danger of war, particularly when the war may be so frightful that it leaves no hope of salvation.

We, the small and underdeveloped countries, urge the whole Assembly and especially the other small and underdeveloped nations to devote themselves to this task and to have this problem discussed here, because afterwards we will never forgive ourselves if, through our neglect or lack of firmness and energy on this basic issue, the world becomes involved once again in the perils of war . . .

That is to say, it is for Franco, for the colonization of Algeria, for the colonization of the Congo; it is for the maintenance of its privileges and interests in the Panama Canal, for colonialism through the world. It is for the German militarism and for the resurgence of German militarism. It is for Japanese militarism and for the resurgence of Japanese militarism . . .

That is why it has to be against the sovereignty of nations, because it must constantly limit sovereignty in order to maintain its policy of encircling the Soviet Union with bases. We believe that these problems are not properly explained to the American people. But the American people need only imagine how uneasy they would feel if the Soviet Union began to establish a ring of atomic bases in Cuba, Mexico, or Canada. The population would not feel secure or calm. World opinion, including American opinion, must be taught to see the other person's point of view.

The underdeveloped peoples should not always be represented as aggressors; revolutionaries should not be presented as aggressors, as enemies of the American people, because we have seen Americans like Carleton Beals, Waldo Frank, and others, famous and distinguished intellectuals, shed tears at the thought of the mistakes that are being made, at the breach of hospitality towards us; there are many Americans, the most humane, the most progressive, and the most esteemed writers, in whom I see the nobility of this country's early leaders, the Washingtons, the Jeffersons, and the Lincolns. I say this in no spirit of demagogy, but with the sincere admiration that we feel for those who once succeeded in freeing their people from colonial status and who did not fight in order that their country might today be the ally of all the reactionaries, the gangsters, the big landowners, the monopolists, the exploiters, the militarists, the fascists in the world, that is to say, the ally of the most reactionary forces, but rather in order that their country might always be the champion of noble and just ideals.

We know well what will be said about us, today, tomorrow, every day, to deceive the American people. But is does not matter. We are doing our duty by stating our views in this historic Assembly.

We proclaim the right of people to freedom, the right of people to nationhood; those who know that nationalism means the desire of the people to regain what is rightly theirs, their wealth, their natural resources, conspire against nationalism.

We are, in short, for all the noble aspirations of all the peoples.

That is our position. We are, and always shall be for everything that is just: against colonialism, exploitation, monopolies, militarism, the armaments race, and warmongering. We shall always be against such things.

That will be our position . . .

Some people wanted to know what the policy of the Revolutionary Government of Cuba was. Very well, then, this is our policy.

Source: Embassy of Cuba.

UN Declaration on Granting Independence to Colonial Countries and Peoples (December 14, 1960)

Conscious of the wave of decolonization sweeping Africa in the late 1950s and early 1960s, the UN General Assembly went on record supporting an end to all colonial empires (Resolution 1514 [XV]). While Britain generally accepted the idea of decolonization, other colonizing nations in Europe—notably France and Portugal—resisted. However, like most General Assembly resolutions, number 1514 on independence had nothing in the way of enforcement power. The real power at the UN lay in the Security Council, where colonial powers like Britain and France had permanent seats and a permanent power of veto.

The General Assembly,

Mindful of the determination proclaimed by the peoples of the world in the Charter of the United Nations to reaffirm faith in fundamental human rights, in the dignity and worth of the human person, in the equal rights of men and women and of nations large and small and to promote social progress and better standards of life in larger freedom,

Conscious of the need for the creation of conditions of stability and well-being and peaceful and friendly relations based on respect for the principles of equal rights and self-determination of all peoples, and of universal respect for, and observance of, human rights and fundamental freedoms for all without distinction as to race, sex, language or religion,

Recognizing the passionate yearning for freedom in all dependent peoples and the decisive role of such peoples in the attainment of their independence,

Aware of the increasing conflicts resulting from the denial of or impediments in the way of freedom of such peoples, which constitute a serious threat to world peace,

Considering the important role of the United Nations in assisting the movement for independence in Trust and Non-Self-Governing Territories,

Recognizing that the peoples of the world ardently desire the end of colonialism in all its manifestations,

Convinced that the continued existence of colonialism prevents the development of international economic co-operation, impedes the social, cultural and economic development of dependent peoples and militates against the United Nations ideal of universal peace,

Affirming that peoples may, for their own ends, freely dispose of their natural wealth and resources without prejudice to any obligations arising out of international economic co-operation, based upon the principle of mutual benefit, and international law,

Believing that the process of liberation is irresistible and irreversible and that, in order to avoid serious crises, an end must be put to colonialism and all practices of segregation and discrimination associated therewith,

Welcoming the emergence in recent years of a large number of dependent territories into freedom and independence, and recognizing the increasingly powerful trends towards freedom in such territories which have not yet attained independence,

Convinced that all peoples have an inalienable right to complete freedom, the exercise of their sovereignty and the integrity of their national territory,

Solemnly proclaims the necessity of bringing to a speedy and unconditional end colonialism in all its forms and manifestations;

And to this end Declares that:

1. The subjection of peoples to alien subjugation, domination and exploitation constitutes a denial of fundamental human rights, is contrary to the Charter of the United Nations and is an impediment to the promotion of world peace and co-operation.

2. All peoples have the right to self-determination; by virtue of that right they freely determine their political status and freely pursue their economic, social and cultural development.

3. Inadequacy of political, economic, social or educational preparedness should never serve as a pretext for delaying independence.

4. All armed action or repressive measures of all kinds directed against dependent peoples shall cease in order to enable them to exercise peacefully and freely their right to complete independence, and the integrity of their national territory shall be respected.

5. Immediate steps shall be taken, in Trust and Non-Self-Governing Territories or all other territories which have not yet attained independence, to transfer all powers to the peoples of those territories, without any conditions or reservations, in

accordance with their freely expressed will and desire, without any distinction as to race, creed or colour, in order to enable them to enjoy complete independence and freedom.

6. Any attempt aimed at the partial or total disruption of the national unity and the territorial integrity of a country is incompatible with the purposes and principles of the Charter of the United Nations.

7. All States shall observe faithfully and strictly the provisions of the Charter of the United Nations, the Universal Declaration of Human Rights and the present Declaration on the basis of equality, non-interference in the internal affairs of all States, and respect for the sovereign rights of all peoples and their territorial integrity.

Source: United Nations, General Assembly, *Official Records, Fifteenth Session, Supplement No. 16, 1960.*

Organization of African Unity Charter (May 25, 1963)

The Organization of African Unity was founded in Addis Ababa in 1963, during a period in which much of sub-Saharan Africa was gaining its independence from European colonizers. The name the organization adopted reflected the hopes of a new generation of African leaders that the continent might overcome its colonial legacy. But Article III reflected a deeper reality. In its defense of state sovereignty and territorial integrity, it recognized the dangers of disputing existing borders, even though these latter were based on the whims of the colonizers rather than on the realities of African human and natural geography.

We, the Heads of African States and Governments assembled in the City of Addis Ababa, Ethiopia,

Convinced that it is the inalienable right of all people to control their own destiny,

Conscious of the fact that freedom, equality, justice and dignity are essential objectives for the achievement of the legitimate aspirations of the African peoples,

Conscious of our responsibility to harness the natural and human resources of our continent for the total advancement of our peoples in all spheres of human endeavour,

Inspired by a common determination to promote understanding among our peoples and co-operation among our states in response to the aspirations of our peoples for brother-hood and solidarity, in a larger unity transcending ethnic and national differences,

Convinced that, in order to translate this determination into a dynamic force in the cause of human progress, conditions for peace and security must be established and maintained,

Determined to safeguard and consolidate the hard-won independence as well as the sovereignty and territorial integrity of our states, and to fight against neo-colonialism in all its forms,

Dedicated to the general progress of Africa,

Persuaded that the Charter of the United Nations and the Universal Declaration of Human Rights, to the Principles of which we reaffirm our adherence, provide a solid foundation for peaceful and positive cooperation among States,

Desirous that all African States should henceforth unite so that the welfare and well-being of their peoples can be assured,

Resolved to reinforce the links between our states by establishing and strengthening common institutions,

Have agreed to the present Charter.

ESTABLISHMENT

Article I

1. The High Contracting Parties do by the present Charter establish Organisation to be known as the ORGANIZATION OF AFRICAN UNITY.

2. The Organization shall include the Continental African States, Madagascar and other Islands surrounding Africa.

PURPOSES

Article II

1. The Organization shall have the following purposes:

(a) To promote the unity and solidarity of the African States;
(b) To coordinate and intensify their cooperation and efforts to achieve a better life for the peoples of Africa;
(c) To defend their sovereigns, their territorial integrity and independence;
(d) To eradicate all forms of colonialism from Africa; and

(e) To promote international cooperation, having due regard to the Charter of the United Nations and the Universal Declaration of Human Rights....

3. To these ends, the Member States shall coordinate and harmonize their general policies, especially in the following fields:

(a) Political and diplomatic cooperation;
(b) Economic cooperation, including transport end communications;
(c) Educational and cultural cooperation;
(d) Health, sanitation and nutritional cooperation;
(e) Scientific and technical cooperation; and
(f) Cooperation for defence and security.

PRINCIPLES
Article III
The Member States, in pursuit of the purposes stated in Article II solemnly affirm and declare their adherence to the following principles:
1. The sovereign equality of all Member States.
2. Non-interference in the internal affairs of States.
3. Respect for the sovereignty and territorial integrity of each State and for its inalienable right to independent existence.

4. Peaceful settlement of disputes by negotiation, mediator conciliation or arbitration.
5. Unreserved condemnation, in all its forms, of political assassination as well as of subversive activities on the part of neighbouring States or any other States.
6. Absolute dedication to the total emancipation of the African territories, which are still dependent.
7. Affirmation of a policy of non-alignment with regard to all blocs....

COMMISSION OF MEDIATION, CONCILIATION AND ARBITRATION
Article XIX
Member States pledge to settle all disputes among themselves by peaceful means and, to this end decide to establish a Commission of Mediation, Conciliation and Arbitration, the composition of which and condition of service shall be defined by a separate Protocol to be approved by the Assembly of Heads of State and Government. Said Protocol shall be regarded as forming an integral part of the present Charter . . .

IN FAITH WHEREOF, We, the Heads of African State Governments have signed this Charter.

Done in the City of Addis Ababa, Ethiopia, 25th day of May, 1963

Source: Organization of African Unity. *Charter of the Organization of African Unity.* Addis Ababa, Ethiopia: General Secretariat of the Organization of African Unity, 1965.

ITALIAN EMPIRE

Ferdinando Martini: "Imperialism of the Have-Nots" (1897)

In the late nineteenth century, Europeans divided their continent into the imperial "haves"—old nation-states like Britain, France, the Netherlands, and Portugal—with vast colonial holdings and "have-nots"—newer nations, most notably, Germany and Italy, with few colonies. In this excerpt from his book Concerning Africa, *Ferdinando Martini, a liberal politician from Tuscany, argues that Italy should have an empire of its own. It was needed, he argued, not so much as a market for manufactured goods or a source of raw materials—Italy was still largely an agricultural nation—but as a repository for excess population, which was emigrating instead to the United States and Latin America, and thus draining Italy of human resources.*

Italy has 108 inhabitants per square kilometer; France has only 73. In proportion to the territory, only these states in Europe surpass Italy in density of population: Belgium, Holland, and Great Britain. If we go on like this, soon there will be no state that surpasses Italy: in the ten years 1871–1881 the births surpassed the deaths by seven per cent, and in the ten following years by eleven per cent. Every year 100,000 farmers and agricultural laborers emigrate from Italy. In spite of this immense exodus, the country witnesses the fact that, to the greatest danger of her political and economic future, her place in the family of civilized peoples is growing smaller and smaller. In fact, during the last eighty years the English-speaking peoples have risen from 22 to 90 mil-

lions; the Russian-speaking peoples from 50 to 70; and so forth, down to the Spanish-speaking peoples who were 18 millions and are now 39. On the other hand, the Italian-speaking peoples have increased only from 20 to 31, and most of the increase has taken place within Italy's own geographical borders. And this is not surprising. Even though our emigrants at first seem to be spreading in foreign lands the name, the language, and the prestige of Italy, since all or nearly all of them go to areas very advanced in civilization, their sons or their grandsons, being attracted and encircled by the vigorous peoples giving them hospitality, end up by forgetting the language of their fathers and ancestors. They merely increase the number of other nations, like branches grafted on a different plant. . . .

. . .Since our stubbornness and our mistakes have cost all that they cost and are costing, even if one wants to leave aside all other considerations and to take into account only the expenditure and the chances of success, I believe that it is less safe and more expensive to endeavor to bring under culture three million hectares in Italy, than to insure the prosperity of a large agricultural colony in Eritrea. . . .

It is easy to make jokes about Abyssinian huts. But, once one has made jokes and laughed, one has good reason to cry when comparing those huts—where our colonial officers yet are living without discomfort—with the sandstone caves where the plowmen and the reapers of the Roman Campagna are sleeping; or with the crumbling slums of Basilicata, where men, women and children are heaped together, and where, according to medical descriptions, it is possible to breathe only because air filters through the cracks of the rotten walls.

Source: Martini, Ferdinando. *Concerning Africa.* Milan: Treves, 1897.

King Victor Emmanuel III of Italy Assumes the Imperial Title (May 9, 1936)

Fascist dictator Benito Mussolini took power in Italy in 1922. Bent on recreating the Roman Empire, he sent his troops into Africa to conquer Ethiopia in the 1930s. After several setbacks, Italy was triumphant, vanquishing the last independent kingdom on the African continent. As part of Italy's glorification, Mussolini decreed that King Victor Emmanuel III—the titular head of Italy—be crowned Emperor of Ethiopia in an elaborate ceremony in Rome in 1936.

Victor Emmanuel III, by the Grace of God and by the Will of The Nation, King of Italy

In consideration of Article 5 of the Fundamental Statute of the Kingdom; in consideration of Article 3, No. 2, of the law of January 31, 1926, in the fourth year of Fascism, No. 100; in consideration of the law of December 9, 1928, in the seventh year of Fascism, No. 2693; having recognized the urgency and absolute necessity of passing this provision; the Grand Council of Fascism having considered it; the Council of Ministers having heard it; on proposal of the Head of the Government, the Prime Minister Secretary of State;

We have decreed and we now decree:

Article I. The territory and peoples which belong to the Empire of Ethiopia are hereby placed under the full and complete sovereignty of the Kingdom of Italy.

The title of Emperor of Ethiopia is assumed for himself and for his successors by the King of Italy.

Article II. Ethiopia is ruled and represented by a Governor-General who has the title of Viceroy and on whom are dependent also the Governors of Eritrea and Somaliland.

All the civil and military authorities of the territory placed under his jurisdiction are dependent upon the Governor-General, Viceroy of Ethiopia.

The Governor-General, Viceroy of Ethiopia, is nominated by Royal Decree on proposal of the Head of the Government, the Prime Minister Secretary of State, and the Minister Secretary of State for the Colonies.

Article III. Regulations for Ethiopia will be provided by Royal Decree, to be issued on the proposal of the Head of the Government, the Prime Minister Secretary of State, and the Minister Secretary of State for the Colonies.

Article IV. The present Decree, which becomes elective on the day of its date, will be presented to Parliament for conversion into law. The Head of the Government, Prime Minister Secretary of State, on his proposal, is authorized to present the draft law.

We order the present Decree stamped with the seal of the State and inserted in the official collection of laws and decrees of the Kingdom of Italy, making its observation and enforcement obligatory.

Done at Rome, 9th May 1936—Year XIV

Victor Emmanuel

Benito Mussolini

Source: *Gazetta Ufficiale del Regno d'Italia* (Ministry of Grace and Justice, Rome), no. 108 (May 9, 1936).

JAPANESE EMPIRE

The Emperor's Charter Oath (1868)

From the sixteenth century through the mid-nine-teenth century, Japan was able to keep westerners at bay. But the arrival of U.S. naval commander Matthew Perry in 1853 ended that isolation. In-deed, following Perry's arrival, Japan was forced—like China—to sign unequal treaties by western powers. In response, the Japanese reor-ganized their government from a feudal regime dominated by daimyo, *or lords, and their warrior retainers, known as* samurai, *to a centralized regime around the figure of the emperor. This re-organization, first promulgated in the Emperor's Charter Oath of 1868, helped Japan avoid being subjected to western domination in the way that nearby China was.*

. . . II. All power and authority in the empire shall be vested in a Council of State, and thus the grievances of divided government shall be done away with. The power and authority of the Council of State shall be threefold, legislative, executive and judicial. Thus the imbalance of authority among the different branches of the government shall be avoided.

III. The legislative organ shall not be permitted to perform executive functions, nor shall the exec-utive organ be permitted to perform legislative functions. However, on extraordinary occasions the legislative organ may still perform such func-tions as tours of inspection of cities and the con-duct of foreign affairs.

IV. Attainment to offices of the first rank shall be limited to princes of the blood, court nobles

and territorial lords, and shall be by virtue of [the sovereign's] intimate trust in the great ministers of state. . . .

V. Each great city, clan, and imperial prefecture shall furnish qualified men to be members of the Assembly. A deliberative body shall be instituted so that the views of the people may be discussed openly.

VI. A system of official ranks shall be instituted so that each official may know the importance of his office and dare not hold it in contempt.

VII. Princes of the blood, court nobles, and ter-ritorial lords shall be accompanied by six two-sworded and three commoners, and persons of lower rank by two two-sworded men and one commoner, so that the appearance of pomp and grandeur may be done away with and the evils of class barriers may be avoided.

VIII. Officers shall not discuss the affairs of the government in their own houses with unofficial persons. If any persons desire interviews with them for the purpose of giving expression to their own opinions, they shall be sent to the office of the appropriate department and the matter shall be discussed openly.

IX. All officials shall be changed after four years' service. They shall be selected by means of public balloting. However, at the first expiration of terms hereafter, half of the officials shall retain of-fice for two additional years, after which their terms shall expire, so that the government may be caused to continue without interruption. Those whose relief is undesirable because they enjoy the approval of the people may be retained for an ad-ditional period of years.

X. A system shall be established for levying taxes on territorial lords, farmers, artisans, and merchants, so that the government revenue may be supplemented, military installations strengthened, and public security maintained. For this purpose, even persons of rank or office shall have taxes levied upon them . . .

XI. Each large city, clan, and imperial prefecture shall promulgate regulations, and these shall comply with the Charter Oath. The laws peculiar to one locality shall not be generalized to apply to other localities. There shall be no private conferral of titles or rank, no private coinage, no private employment of foreigners, and no conclusion of alliances with neighboring clans or with foreign countries, lest inferior authorities be confounded with superior and government be thrown into confusion.

Source: http://web.jjay.cuny.edu/~jobrien/reference/ob65.html.

Tanaka Memorial: Japan's Blueprint for Colonization of the Far East (1927)

The Tanaka Memorial, a summary of a conference held in 1927 on Japan's role in Far Eastern affairs and headed by Prime Minister Baron Gi-ichi Tanaka, has been denounced by some historians as a Chinese forgery. While its crude explicitness lends credence to the forgery theory, the document nonetheless anticipates many of Tokyo's moves in the Far East over the following decade.

Since the European War, Japan's political as well as economic interests have been in an unsettled condition. This is due to the fact that we have failed to take advantage of our special privileges in Manchuria and Mongolia and fully to realize our acquired rights. But upon my appointment as premier, I was instructed to guard our interests in this region and watch for opportunities for further expansion. Such injunctions one cannot take lightly. Ever since I advocated a positive policy towards Manchuria and Mongolia as a common citizen, I have longed for its realization. So in order that we may lay plans for the colonization of the Far East and the development of our new continental empire, a special conference was held from June 27th to July 7th lasting in all eleven days. It was attended by all the civil and military officers connected with Manchuria and Mongolia, whose discussions resulted in the following resolutions. These we respectfully submit to Your Majesty for consideration.

General Considerations

The term Manchuria and Mongolia includes the provinces Fengtien, Kirin, Heilung-kiang and Outer and Inner Mongolia. It extends an area of 74,000 square miles, having a population of 28,000,000 people. The territory is more than three times as large as our own empire not counting Korea and Formosa, but it is inhabited by only one-third as many people. The attractiveness of the land does not arise from the scarcity of population alone; its wealth of forestry, minerals and agricultural products is also unrivalled elsewhere in the world. In order to exploit these resources for the perpetuation of our national glory, we created especially the South Manchuria Railway Company. The total investment involved in our undertakings in railway, shipping, mining, forestry, steel, manufacture, agriculture, and in cattle raising, as schemes pretending to be mutually beneficial to China and Japan, amount to no less than Yen 440,000,000. It is veritably the largest single investment and the strongest organization of our country. Although nominally the enterprise is under the joint ownership of the government and the people, in reality the government has complete power and authority. In so far as the South Manchuria Railway is empowered to undertake diplomatic, police, and ordinary administrative functions so that it may carry out our imperialistic policies, the Company forms a peculiar organization which has exactly the same powers as the Governor-General of Korea. This fact alone is sufficient to indicate the immense interests we have in Manchuria and Mongolia. Consequently the policies towards this country of successive administrations since Meiji are all based on his injunctions, elaborating and continuously completing the development of the new continental empire in order to further the advance of our national glory and prosperity for countless generations to come.

Unfortunately, since the European War there have been constant changes in diplomatic as well as domestic affairs. The authorities of the Three Eastern Provinces [Manchuria] are also awakened and gradually work toward reconstruction and industrial development following our example. Their progress is astonishing. It has affected the spread of our influence in a most serious way, and has put us to so many disadvantages that the dealings with Manchuria and Mongolia of successive governments have resulted in failure. Furthermore, the restrictions of the Nine-Power Treaty signed at the Washington Conference have reduced our special rights and privileges in Manchuria and Mongolia to such an extent that there is no freedom left for us. The very existence of our country is endangered. Unless these obstacles are removed, our national existence will be insecure and our national strength will not develop. Moreover, the resources of wealth are congregated in North Manchuria. If we do not have the right of way here, it is obvious that we shall not be able to tap the riches of this country. Even the resources of South Manchuria which we won by the Russo-Japanese War will also be greatly restricted by the Nine-Power Treaty. The result is that while our people cannot migrate into Manchuria as they please, the Chinese are flowing in as a flood. Hordes of them move into the Three Eastern Provinces every year, numbering in the neighborhood of several millions. They have jeopardized our acquired rights in Manchuria and Mongolia to such an extent that our annual surplus population of eight hundred thousand has no place to seek refuge. In view of this we have to admit our failure in trying to effect a balance between our population and food supply. If we do not devise plans to check the influx of Chinese immigrants immediately, in five years' time the number of Chinese will exceed 6,000,000. Then we shall be confronted with greater difficulties in Manchuria and Mongolia.

It will be recalled that when the Nine-Power Treaty was signed which restricted our movements in Manchuria and Mongolia, public opinion was greatly aroused. The late Emperor Taisho called a conference of Yamagata and other high officers of the army and navy to find a way to counteract this new engagement. I was sent to Europe and America to ascertain secretly the attitude of the important statesmen towards it. They were all agreed that the Nine-Power Treaty was initiated by the United States. The other Powers which signed it were willing to see our influence increase in Manchuria and Mongolia in order that

we may protect the interests of international trade and investments. This attitude I found out personally from the political leaders of England, France and Italy. The sincerity of these expressions could be depended upon. Unfortunately, just as we were ready to carry out our policy and declare void the Nine-Power Treaty with the approval of those whom I met on my trip, the Seiyukai cabinet suddenly fell and our policy failed of fruition. It was indeed a great pity. After I had secretly exchanged views with the Powers regarding the development of Manchuria and Mongolia, I returned by way of Shanghai. At the wharf there a Chinese attempted to take my life. An American woman was hurt, but I escaped by the divine protection of my emperors of the past. It seems that it was by divine will that I should assist Your Majesty to open a new era in the Far East and to develop the new continental empire.

The Three Eastern Provinces are politically the imperfect spot in the Far East. For the sake of self-protection as well as the protection of others, Japan cannot remove the difficulties in Eastern Asia unless she adopts the policy of "Blood and Iron." But in carrying out this policy we have to face the United States which has been turned against us by China's policy of fighting poison with poison. In the future if we want to control China, we must first crush the United States just as in the past we had to fight in the Russo-Japanese War. But in order to conquer China we must first conquer Manchuria and Mongolia. In order to conquer the world, we must first conquer China. If we succeed in conquering China the rest of the Asiatic countries and the South Sea countries will fear us and surrender to us. Then the world will realize that Eastern Asia is ours and will not dare to violate our rights. This is the plan left to us by Emperor Meiji, the success of which is essential to our national existence.

The Nine-Power Treaty is entirely an expression of the spirit of commercial rivalry. It was the intention of England and America to crush our influence in China with their power of wealth. The proposed reduction of armaments is nothing but a means to limit our military strength, making it impossible for us to conquer the vast territory of China. On the other hand, China's sources of wealth will be entirely at their disposal. It is merely a scheme by which England and America may defeat our plans. And yet the Minseito made the Nine-Power Treaty the important thing and emphasized our TRADE rather than our RIGHTS in China. This is a mistaken policy—a policy of national suicide. England can afford to talk about trade relations only because she has India and Australia to supply her with foodstuffs and other materials. So can America because South America and Canada are there to supply her needs. Their spare energy could be entirely devoted to developing trade in China to enrich themselves.

But in Japan her food supply and raw materials decrease in proportion to her population. If we merely hope to develop trade, we shall eventually be defeated by England and America, who possess unsurpassable capitalistic power. In the end, we shall get nothing. A more dangerous factor is the fact that the people of China might some day wake up. Even during these years of internal strife, they can still toil patiently, and try to imitate and displace our goods so as to impair the development of our trade. When we remember that the Chinese are our sole customers, we must beware lest one day China becomes unified and her industries become prosperous. Americans and Europeans will compete with us; our trade in China will be wrecked. Minseito's proposal to uphold the Nine-Power Treaty and to adopt the policy of trade towards Manchuria is nothing less than a suicide policy.

After studying the present conditions and possibilities of our country, our best policy lies in the direction of taking positive steps to secure rights and privileges in Manchuria and Mongolia. These will enable us to develop our trade. This will not only forestall China's own industrial development, but also prevent the penetration of European Powers. This is the best policy possible!

The way to gain actual rights in Manchuria and Mongolia is to use this region as a base and under the pretence of trade and commerce penetrate the rest of China. Armed by the rights already secured we shall seize the resources all over the country. Having China's entire resources at our disposal we shall proceed to conquer India, the Archipelago, Asia Minor, Central Asia, and even Europe. But to get control of Manchuria and Mongolia is the first step if the Yamato race wishes to distinguish itself on Continental Asia. Final success belongs to the country having raw materials;

the full growth of national strength belongs to the country having extensive territory. If we pursue a positive policy to enlarge our rights in Manchuria and China, all these prerequisites of a powerful nation will constitute no problem. Furthermore our surplus population of 700,000 each year will also be taken care of.

If we want to inaugurate a new policy and secure the permanent prosperity of our empire, a positive policy towards Manchuria and Mongolia is the only way.

Source: Crow, Carl, ed. *The Tanaka Memorial.* London: Allen and Unwin, 1943.

Mao Zedong: On Tactics against Japanese Imperialism (December 27, 1935)

Beginning with its invasion of Manchuria in 1931, the Japanese Empire moved to acquire vast tracts of Chinese territory for the purposes of exploiting resources and labor and providing lands for the settlement of Japanese colonists. In 1937, Japan invaded the rest of China but was met with fierce resistance by Chinese nationalists, one contingent of whom were the Communists under the leadership of Mao Zedong. In this report to the Conference of Party Activists, Mao emphasizes the need for politicizing and mobilizing the masses in order to drive the Japanese out of China.

The Characteristics of the Present Political Situation

Comrades! A great change has now taken place in the political situation. Our Party has defined its tasks in the light of this changed situation.

What is the present situation?

Its main characteristic is that Japanese imperialism wants to turn China into a colony.

As we all know, for nearly a hundred years China has been a semi-colonial country jointly dominated by several imperialist powers. Owing to the Chinese people's struggle against imperialism and to conflicts among the imperialist powers, China has been able to retain a semi-independent status. For a time World War I gave Japanese imperialism the opportunity of dominating China exclusively. But the treaty surrendering China to

Japan, the Twenty-one Demands signed by Yuan Shih-kai, the arch-traitor of that time, was inevitably rendered null and void as a result of the Chinese people's fight against Japanese imperialism and of the intervention by other imperialist powers. In 1922 at the Washington Nine-Power Conference called by the United States, a treaty was signed which once again placed China under the joint domination of several imperialist powers. But before long the situation changed again. The Incident of September 18, 1931, began the present stage of Japan's colonization of China. As Japanese aggression was temporarily limited to the four northeastern provinces, some people felt that the Japanese imperialists would probably advance no farther. Today things are different. The Japanese imperialists have already shown their intention of penetrating south of the Great Wall and occupying all China. Now they want to convert the whole of China from a semi-colony shared by several imperialist powers into a colony monopolized by Japan. The recent Eastern Hopei Incident and diplomatic talks are clear indications of this trend of events which threatens the survival of the whole Chinese people. This faces all classes and political groups in China with the question of what to do. Resist? Surrender? Or vacillate between the two?

Now let us see how the different classes in China answer this question.

The workers and the peasants are all demanding resistance. The revolution of 1924–27, the agrarian revolution from 1927 to the present day, and the anti-Japanese tide since the Incident of September 18, 1931, have all proved that the working class and peasantry are the most resolute forces in the Chinese revolution.

The petty bourgeoisie is also demanding resistance. Have not the student youth and the urban petty bourgeoisie already started a broad anti-Japanese movement? This section of the Chinese petty bourgeoisie took part in the revolution of 1924–27. Like the peasants, they are small producers in their economic status, and their interests are irreconcilable with those of imperialism. Imperialism and the Chinese counter-revolutionary forces have done them great harm, driving many into unemployment, bankruptcy or semi-bankruptcy. Now, faced with the immediate danger of becoming slaves to a foreign nation, they have no alternative but to resist.

But how do the national bourgeoisie, the comprador and landlord classes, and the Kuomintang face up to this question?

The big local tyrants and evil gentry, the big warlords and the big bureaucrats and compradors have long made up their minds. They maintain, as they have done all along, that revolution of whatever kind is worse than imperialism. They have formed a camp of traitors, for whom the question of whether to become slaves of a foreign nation simply does not exist because they have already lost all sense of nationality and their interests are inseparably linked with imperialism. Their chieftain is Chiang Kai-shek. This camp of traitors are deadly enemies of the Chinese people. Japanese imperialism could not have become so blatant in its aggression were it not for this pack of traitors. They are the running dogs of imperialism.

The national bourgeoisie presents a complicated problem. This class took part in the revolution of 1924–27, but terrified by the flames of revolution, it later deserted to the enemy of the people, the Chiang Kai-shek clique. The question is whether there is any possibility that this class will undergo a change in the present circumstances. We think there is. For the national bourgeoisie is not the same as either the landlord or the comprador class; there is a difference between them. The national bourgeoisie is less feudal than the landlord class and not so comprador as the comprador class. The section having more ties with foreign capital and the Chinese landed interests form the right-wing of the national bourgeoisie; and we shall not, for the moment, consider whether it can change or not. The problem lies with those sections which have few or no such ties. We believe that in the new situation in which China is threatened with being reduced to a colony these sections may change their attitude. The change will be marked by vacillation. On the one hand they dislike imperialism, and on the other they fear thorough revolution, and they vacillate between the two. This explains why they took part in the revolution of 1924–27 and why, in the end, they went over to Chiang Kai-shek's side. In what respect does the present period differ from 1927 when Chiang Kai-shek betrayed the revolution? China was then still a semi-colony, but now she is on the way to becoming a colony. Over the past nine years the national bourgeoisie has deserted its ally, the working class, and made friends with the landlord and comprador classes, but has it gained anything? Nothing, except the bankruptcy or semi-bankruptcy of its industrial and commercial enterprises. Hence we believe that in the present situation the attitude of the national bourgeoisie can change. What will be the extent of the change? The general characteristic of the national bourgeoisie is to vacillate. But at a certain stage of the struggle, one section (the left-wing) may join in, while another section may vacillate towards neutrality.

Whose class interests does the 19th Route Army led by Tsai Ting-kai and others represent? Those of the national bourgeoisie, the upper petty bourgeoisie, and the rich peasants and small landlords in the countryside. Did not Tsai Ting-kai and his associates once fight bitterly against the Red Army? Yes, but they subsequently concluded an anti-Japanese and anti-Chiang alliance with the Red Army. In Kiangsi they had attacked the Red Army, but later in Shanghai they fought the Japanese imperialists; later still, in Fukien they came to terms with the Red Army and turned their guns against Chiang Kai-shek. Whatever course Tsai Ting-kai and his associates may take in the future, and despite their Fukien People's Government's adherence to old practice in failing to arouse the people to struggle, it must be considered beneficial to the revolution that they turned their guns, originally trained on the Red Army, against Japanese imperialism and Chiang Kai-shek. It marked a split within the Kuomintang camp. If the circumstances following the September 18th Incident could cause this group to split away, why cannot the present circumstances give rise to other splits in the Kuomintang? Those Party members who hold that the whole landlord and bourgeois camp is united and permanent and will not change under any circumstances are wrong. They not only fail to appreciate the present grave situation, they have even forgotten history.

Let me speak a little more about the past. In 1926 and 1927, during the time when the revolutionary army advanced on Wuhan, captured it and marched into Honan, Tang Sheng-chih and Feng Yu-hsiang took part in the revolution. In 1933, Feng Yu-hsiang co-operated for a time with the Communist Party in forming the Anti-Japanese Allied Army in Chahar Province.

Take another striking example. Did not the 26th Route Army, which, together with the 19th Route Army, had attacked the Red Army in Kiangsi, stage the Ningtu Uprising in December 1931 and become part of the Red Army? The leaders of the Ningtu Uprising, Chao Po-sheng, Tung Chen-tang and others, have become steadfast comrades in the revolution.

The anti-Japanese operations of Ma Chan-shan in the three northeastern provinces represented another split in the ruling class camp.

All these instances indicate that splits will occur in the enemy camp when all China comes within the range of Japanese bombs, and when the struggle changes its normal pace and suddenly surges forward.

Now, comrades, let us turn to another aspect of the question.

Is it correct to object to our view on the ground that China's national bourgeoisie is politically and economically flabby, and to argue that it cannot possibly change its attitude in spite of the new circumstances? I think not. If weakness is the reason for its inability to change its attitude, why did the national bourgeoisie behave differently in 1924–27 when it did not merely vacillate towards the revolution but actually joined it? Can one say that the weakness of the national bourgeoisie is a new disease, and not one that accompanies it from the very womb? Can one say that the national bourgeoisie is weak today, but was not weak in 1924–27? One of the chief political and economic characteristics of a semi-colonial country is the weakness of its national bourgeoisie. That is exactly why the imperialists dare to bully them, and it follows that one of their characteristics is dislike of imperialism. Of course, so far from denying it, we fully recognize that it is the very weakness of the national bourgeoisie that may make it easy for the imperialists, landlords and compradors to entice them with the bait of some temporary advantage; hence their lack of revolutionary thoroughness. Nevertheless, it cannot be said that in the present circumstances there is no difference between the national bourgeoisie and the landlord and comprador classes.

Therefore, we emphatically assert that when the national crisis reaches a crucial point, splits will occur in the Kuomintang camp. Such splits have revealed themselves in the vacillation of the national bourgeoisie and the emergence of such anti-Japanese figures as Feng Yu-hsiang, Tsai Ting-kai and Ma Chan-shan, who have become popular for a time. Basically, these splits are unfavourable to the counterrevolution and favourable to the revolution. Their possibility is increased by China's uneven political and economic development, and the consequent uneven development of the revolution.

Comrades, so much for the positive side of the question. Now let me take up the negative side, namely, the fact that certain elements among the national bourgeoisie are often past masters at deceiving the people. Why? Because apart from the genuine supporters of the people's revolutionary cause, this class includes many who temporarily appear as revolutionaries or semi-revolutionaries, and who thus acquire a deceptive status which makes it difficult for the people to see through their lack of revolutionary thoroughness and their false trappings. This increases the responsibility devolving on the Communist Party to criticize its allies, unmask the fake revolutionaries, and gain the leadership. To deny the possibility that the national bourgeoisie may vacillate and join the revolution during great upheavals amounts to abandoning, or at any rate to minimizing, our Party's task of contending for leadership. For if the national bourgeoisie were exactly the same as the landlords and compradors and had the same vile and traitorous visage, there would be little or no problem of contending with it for leadership.

In making a general analysis of the attitude of the Chinese landlord class and the bourgeoisie in times of great upheaval, we should also point to another aspect, namely, that even the landlord and comprador camp is not completely united. The reason is that China is a semicolonial country for which many imperialist powers are contending. When the struggle is directed against Japanese imperialism, then the running dogs of the United States or Britain, obeying the varying tones of their masters' commands, may engage in veiled or even open strife with the Japanese imperialists and their running dogs. There have been many instances of such dog-fights and we shall not dwell on them. We will only mention the fact that Hu Han-min, a Kuomintang politician once detained by Chiang Kai-shek, has recently added his signature to the Six-Point Programme for Resisting Japan and Saving the Nation which we have advanced. The warlords of the Kwangtung and Kwangsi cliques who back Hu Han-min are also opposing Chiang Kai-shek, under the deceitful slogans of "Recover our lost territory," and "Resist Japan and at the same time suppress the bandits" (as against Chiang Kai-shek's slogan of "First suppress the bandits, then resist Japan"). Is this not rather strange? No, it is not strange at all, but merely a particularly interesting example of a fight between large and small dogs, between well-fed and ill-fed dogs. It is not a big rift, but neither is it small; it is at once an irritating and painful contradiction. But such fights, such rifts, such contradictions are of use to the revolutionary people. We must turn to good account all such fights, rifts and contradictions in the enemy camp and turn them against our present main enemy.

Summing up the question of class relations, we may say that the basic change in the situation, namely, the Japanese invasion of China south of the Great Wall, has changed the relationship among the various classes in China, strengthening the camp of national revolution and weakening that of counter-revolution.

Now let us discuss the situation in the camp of China's national revolution.

First, the Red Army. As you know, comrades, for almost a year and a half the three main contingents of the Chinese Red Army have carried out great shifts of position. The Sixth Army Group led by Jen Pi-shih and other comrades began to shift to Comrade Ho Lung's area in August last year, and in October we ourselves started to shift position. In March this year the Red Army in the Szechuan-Shensi border area began its shift. All three Red Army contingents have abandoned their old positions and moved to new regions. These great shifts have turned the old areas into guerrilla zones. The Red Army has been considerably weakened in the process. From this aspect of the over-all situation, we can see that the enemy has won a temporary and partial victory, while we have suffered a temporary and partial defeat. Is this statement correct? I think it is. For it is a statement of fact. However, some people (Chang Kuo-tao for instance) say that the Central Red Army has failed. Is that correct? No. For it is not a statement of fact. In approaching a problem a Marxist should see the whole as well as the parts. A frog in a well says, "The sky is no bigger than the mouth of the well."

That is untrue, for the sky is not just the size of the mouth of the well. If it said, "A part of the sky is the size of the mouth of a well," that would be true, for it tallies with the facts. What we say is that in one respect the Red Army has failed (i.e., failed to maintain its original positions), but in another respect it has won a victory (i.e., in executing the plan of the Long March). In one respect the enemy won a victory (i.e., in occupying our original positions), but in another respect he has failed (i.e., failed to execute his plan of "encirclement and suppression" and of "pursuit and suppression"). That is the only appropriate formulation, for we have completed the Long March.

Speaking of the Long March, one may ask, "What is its significance?" We answer that the Long March is the first of its kind in the annals of history, that it is a manifesto, a propaganda force, a seeding-machine. Since Pan Ku divided the heavens from the earth and the Three Sovereigns and Five Emperors reigned, has history ever witnessed a long march such as ours? For twelve months we were under daily reconnaissance and bombing from the skies by scores of planes, while on land we were encircled and pursued, obstructed and intercepted by a huge force of several hundred thousand men, and we encountered untold difficulties and dangers on the way; yet by using our two legs we swept across a distance of more than twenty thousand *li* through the length and breadth of eleven provinces. Let us ask, has history ever known a long march to equal ours? No, never. The Long March is a manifesto. It has proclaimed to the world that the Red Army is an army of heroes, while the imperialists and their running dogs, Chiang Kai-shek and his like, are impotent. It has proclaimed their utter failure to encircle, pursue, obstruct and intercept us. The Long March is also a propaganda force. It has announced to some 200 million people in eleven provinces that the road of the Red Army is their only road to liberation. Without the Long March, how could the broad masses have learned so quickly about the existence of the great truth which the Red Army embodies? The Long March is also a seeding-machine. In the eleven provinces it has sown many seeds which will sprout, leaf, blossom, and bear fruit, and will yield a harvest in the future. In a word, the Long March has ended with victory for us and defeat for the enemy. Who brought the Long March to victory? The Communist Party. Without the Communist Party, a long march of this kind would have been inconceivable. The Chinese Communist Party, its leadership, its cadres and its members fear no difficulties or hardships. Whoever questions our ability to lead the revolutionary war will fall into the morass of opportunism. A new situation arose as soon as the Long March was over. In the battle of Chihlochen the Central Red Army and the Northwestern Red Army, fighting in fraternal solidarity, shattered the traitor Chiang Kai-shek's campaign of "encirclement and suppression" against the Shensi-Kansu border area and thus laid the cornerstone for the task undertaken by the Central Committee of the Party, the task of setting up the national headquarters of the revolution in northwestern China.

This being the situation with regard to the main body of the Red Army, what about the guerrilla warfare in the southern provinces? Our guerrilla forces there have suffered some setbacks but have not been wiped out. In many places, they are reasserting themselves, growing and expanding.

In the Kuomintang areas, the workers' struggle is now moving beyond the factory walls, and from being an economic struggle is becoming a political struggle. A heroic working-class struggle against the Japanese and the traitors is now in intense ferment and, judging by the situation, it will erupt before long.

The peasants' struggle has never ceased. Harassed by aggression from abroad, by difficulties at home and by natural disasters, the peasants have unleashed widespread struggles in the form of guerrilla warfare, mass uprisings and famine riots. The anti-Japanese guerrilla warfare now going on in the northeastern provinces and eastern Hopei is their reply to the attacks of Japanese imperialism.

The student movement has already grown considerably and will certainly go on doing so. But this movement can sustain itself and break through the martial law imposed by the traitors and the policy of disruption and massacre practised by the police, the secret service agents, the scoundrels in the educational world and the fascists only if it is co-ordinated with the struggles of the workers, peasants and soldiers.

We have already dealt with the vacillation of the national bourgeoisie, the rich peasants and small landlords and the possibility that they may actually participate in the anti-Japanese struggle.

The minority nationalities, and especially the people of Inner Mongolia who are directly menaced by Japanese imperialism, are now rising up in struggle. As time goes on, their struggle will merge with that of the people in northern China and with the operations of the Red Army in the Northwest.

All this indicates that the revolutionary situation is now changing from a localized into a nation-wide one and that it is gradually changing from a state of unevenness to a certain degree of evenness. We are on the eve of a great change. The task of the Party is to form a revolutionary national united front by combining the activities of the Red Army with all the activities of the workers, the peasants, the students, the petty bourgeoisie and the national bourgeoisie throughout the country.

The National United Front

Having surveyed the situation with regard to both the counterrevolution and the revolution, we shall find it easy to define the Party's tactical tasks.

What is the basic tactical task of the Party? It is none other than to form a broad revolutionary national united front.

When the revolutionary situation changes, revolutionary tactics and methods of leadership must change accordingly. The task of the Japanese imperialists, the collaborators and the traitors is to turn China into a colony, while our task is to turn China into a free and independent country with full territorial integrity.

To win independence and freedom for China is a great task. It demands that we fight against foreign imperialism and the domestic counter-revolutionary forces. Japanese imperialism is determined to bludgeon its way deep into China. As yet the domestic counter-revolutionary forces of the big landlord and comprador classes are stronger than the people's revolutionary forces. The overthrow of Japanese imperialism and the counter-revolutionary forces in China cannot be accomplished in a day, and we must be prepared to devote a long time to it; it cannot be accomplished by small forces, and we must therefore accumulate great forces. In China, as in the world as a whole, the counter-revolutionary forces are weaker than before and the revolutionary forces stronger. This

estimate is correct, representing one aspect of the matter. At the same time, it must be pointed out that the counter-revolutionary forces in China and in the world as a whole are stronger than the revolutionary forces for the time being. This estimate is also correct, representing another aspect of the matter. The uneven political and economic development of China gives rise to the uneven development of her revolution. As a rule, revolution starts, grows and triumphs first in those places in which the counterrevolutionary forces are comparatively weak, while it has yet to start or grows very slowly in those places in which they are strong. Such has long been the situation for the Chinese revolution. It can be predicted that the general revolutionary situation will grow further at certain stages in the future but that the unevenness will remain. The transformation of this unevenness into a general evenness will require a very long time, very great efforts, and the Party's application of a correct line. Seeing that the revolutionary war led by the Communist Party of the Soviet Union took three years to conclude, we must be prepared to devote to the already protracted revolutionary war led by the Chinese Communist Party the longer time necessary to dispose of the domestic and foreign counter-revolutionary forces finally and thoroughly. The kind of impatience that was formerly displayed will never do. Moreover, sound revolutionary tactics must be worked out; we will never achieve great things if we keep on milling around within narrow confines. This does not mean that in China things have to be done slowly; no, they must be done boldly, because the danger of national subjugation does not allow us to slacken for a moment. From now on the revolution will certainly develop much faster than before, for both China and the world are approaching a new period of war and revolution. For all that, China's revolutionary war will remain a protracted one; this follows from the strength of imperialism and the uneven development of the revolution. We say that the present situation is one in which a new high tide in the national revolution is imminent and in which China is on the eve of a great new nation-wide revolution; this is one characteristic of the present revolutionary situation. This is a fact, and it represents one aspect of the matter. But we must also say that imperialism is still a force to be earnestly reckoned with, that the unevenness in the development of the revolutionary forces is a serious weakness, and that to defeat our enemies we must be prepared to fight a protracted war; this is another characteristic of the present revolutionary situation. This, too, is a fact, and represents another aspect of the matter. Both characteristics, both facts, teach and urge us to revise our tactics and change our ways of disposing our forces and carrying on the struggle to suit the situation. The present situation demands that we boldly discard all closed-doorism, form a broad united front and guard against adventurism. We must not plunge into decisive battles until the time is ripe and unless we have the necessary strength.

Here I shall not discuss the relation of adventurism to closed-doorism, or the possible dangers of adventurism as events unfold on a larger scale; that can be left for later. For the moment I shall confine myself to explaining that united front tactics and closed-door tactics are diametrically opposed.

The former requires the recruiting of large forces for the purpose of surrounding and annihilating the enemy.

The latter means fighting single-handed in desperate combat against a formidable enemy.

The advocates of united front tactics say, if we are to make a proper estimate of the possibility of forming a broad revolutionary national united front, a proper estimate must be made of the changes that may occur in the alignment of revolutionary and counter-revolutionary forces in China resulting from the attempt of Japanese imperialism to turn China into a colony. Without a proper estimate of the strong and weak points of the Japanese and Chinese counter-revolutionary forces and of the Chinese revolutionary forces, we shall be unable fully to understand the necessity of organizing a broad revolutionary national united front, or to take firm measures to break down closed-doorism, or to use the united front as a means of organizing and rallying millions of people and all the armies that are potentially friendly to the revolution for the purpose of advancing to strike at our main target, namely, Japanese imperialism and its running dogs, the Chinese traitors, or to use this tactical weapon of ours to strike at the main target before us, but instead we shall aim at a variety of targets so that our bullets will hit not the principal enemy but our lesser enemies or even

our allies. This would mean failure to single out the principal enemy and waste of ammunition. It would mean inability to close in and isolate him. It would mean inability to draw to our side all those in the enemy camp and on the enemy front who have joined them under compulsion, and those who were our enemies yesterday but may become our friends today. It would in fact mean helping the enemy, holding back, isolating and constricting the revolution, and bringing it to a low ebb and even to defeat.

The advocates of closed-door tactics say the above arguments are all wrong. The forces of the revolution must be pure, absolutely pure, and the road of the revolution must be straight, absolutely straight. Nothing is correct except what is literally recorded in Holy Writ. The national bourgeoisie is entirely and eternally counter-revolutionary. Not an inch must be conceded to the rich peasants. The yellow trade unions must be fought tooth and nail. If we shake hands with Tsai Ting-kai, we must call him a counter-revolutionary at the same moment. Was there ever a cat that did not love fish or a warlord who was not a counter-revolutionary? Intellectuals are three-day revolutionaries whom it is dangerous to recruit. It follows therefore that closed-doorism is the sole wonder-working magic, while the united front is an opportunist tactic.

Comrades, which is right, the united front or closed-doorism? Which indeed is approved by Marxism-Leninism? I answer without the slightest hesitation the united front and not closed-doorism. Three-year-olds have many ideas which are right, but they cannot be entrusted with serious national or world affairs because they do not understand them yet. Marxism-Leninism is opposed to the "infantile disorder" found in the revolutionary ranks. This infantile disorder is just what the confirmed exponents of closed-doorism advocate. Like every other activity in the world, revolution always follows a tortuous road and never a straight one. The alignment of forces in the revolutionary and counter-revolutionary camps can change, just as everything else in the world changes. The Party's new tactics of a broad united front start from the two fundamental facts that Japanese imperialism is bent on reducing all China to a colony and that China's revolutionary forces still have serious weaknesses. In order to attack the forces of the counter-revolution, what the revolutionary forces need today is to organize millions upon millions of the masses and move a mighty revolutionary army into action. The plain truth is that only a force of such magnitude can crush the Japanese imperialists and the traitors and collaborators. Therefore, united front tactics are the only Marxist-Leninist tactics. The tactics of closed-doorism are, on the contrary, the tactics of the regal isolationist. Closed-doorism just "drives the fish into deep waters and the sparrows into the thickets," and it will drive the millions upon millions of the masses, this mighty army, over to the enemy's side, which will certainly win his acclaim. In practice, closed-doorism is the faithful servant of the Japanese imperialists and the traitors and collaborators. Its adherents' talk of the "pure" and the "straight" will be condemned by Marxist-Leninists and commended by the Japanese imperialists. We definitely want no closed-doorism; what we want is the revolutionary national united front, which will spell death to the Japanese imperialists and the traitors and collaborators.

The People's Republic

If our government has hitherto been based on the alliance of the workers, the peasants and the urban petty bourgeoisie, from now on it must be so transformed as to include also the members of all other classes who are willing to take part in the national revolution.

At the present time, the basic task of such a government should be to oppose the annexation of China by Japanese imperialism. It will have a broader representation so that it may include those who are interested only in the national revolution and not in the agrarian revolution, and even, if they so desire, those who may oppose Japanese imperialism and its running dogs, though they are not opposed to the European and U.S. imperialists because of their close ties with the latter. Therefore, as a matter of principle, the program of such a government should be in keeping with the basic task of fighting Japanese imperialism and its lackeys, and we should modify our past policies accordingly.

The special feature on the revolutionary side at present is the existence of a well-steeled Communist Party and Red Army. This is of crucial importance. Great difficulties would arise if they did not exist. Why? Because the traitors and collaborators in China are numerous and powerful and are sure to devise every possible means to wreck the united front; they will sow dissension by means of intimidation and bribery and by maneuvering among various groupings, and will employ their armies to oppress and crush, one by one, all those weaker than themselves who want to part company with them and join us in fighting Japan. All this would hardly be avoidable if the anti-Japanese government and army were to lack this vital factor, *i.e.*, the Communist Party and the Red Army. The revolution failed in 1927 chiefly because, with the opportunist line then prevailing in the Communist Party, no effort was made to expand our own ranks (the workers' and peasants' movement and the armed forces led by the Communist Party), and exclusive reliance was placed on a temporary ally, the Kuomintang. The result was that when imperialism ordered its lackeys, the landlord and comprador classes, to spread their numerous tentacles and draw over first Chiang Kai-shek and then Wang Ching-wei, the revolution suffered defeat. In those days the revolutionary united front had no mainstay, no strong revolutionary armed forces, and so when the defections came thick and fast, the Communist Party was forced to fight single-handed and was powerless to foil the tactics of crushing their opponents one by one which were adopted by the imperialists and the Chinese counter-revolutionaries. True, we had the troops under Ho Lung and Yeh Ting, but they were not yet politically consolidated, and the Party was not very skilled in leading them, so that they were finally defeated. The lesson we paid for with our blood was that the lack of a hard core of revolutionary forces brings the revolution to defeat. Today things are quite different. Now we have a strong Communist Party and a strong Red Army, and we also have the base areas of the Red Army. Not only are the Communist Party and the Red Army serving as the initiator of a national united front against Japan today, but in the future too they will inevitably become the powerful mainstay of China's anti-Japanese government and army, capable of preventing the Japanese imperialists and Chiang Kai-shek from carrying through their policy of disrupting this united front. However, we must be very vigilant because the Japanese imperialists and Chiang

Kai-shek will undoubtedly resort to every possible form of intimidation and bribery and of manoeuvering among the various groupings.

Naturally we cannot expect every section of the broad national united front against Japan to be as firm as the Communist Party and the Red Army. In the course of their activities some bad elements may withdraw from the united front under the influence of the enemy. However, we need not fear the loss of such people. While bad elements may drop out under the enemy's influence, good people will come in under ours. The national united front will live and grow as long as the Communist Party and the Red Army live and grow. Such is the leading role of the Communist Party and the Red Army in the national united front. The Communists are no longer political infants and are able to take care of themselves and to handle relations with their allies. If the Japanese imperialists and Chiang Kai-shek can manoeuvre in relation to the revolutionary forces, the Communist Party can do the same in relation to the counter-revolutionary forces. If they can draw bad elements in our ranks over to their side, we can equally well draw their "bad elements" (good ones from our point of view) over to our side. If we can draw a larger number over to our side, this will deplete the enemy's ranks and strengthen ours. In short, two basic forces are now locked in struggle, and in the nature of things all the forces in between will have to line up on one side or the other. The Japanese imperialists' policy of subjugating China and Chiang Kai-shek's policy of betraying China will inevitably drive many people over to our side—either directly into joining the ranks of the Communist Party and the Red Army or into forming a united front with us. This will come about unless we pursue closed door tactics.

Why change the "workers' and peasants' republic" into a "people's republic"?

Our government represents not only the workers and peasants but the whole nation. This has been implicit in our slogan of a workers' and peasants' democratic republic, because the workers and peasants constitute 80 to 90 per cent of the population. The Ten-Point Program adopted by the Sixth National Congress of our Party embodies the interests of the whole nation and not of the workers and peasants alone. But the present situation requires us to change our slogan, to change it into one of a people's republic. The reason is that Japanese invasion has altered class relations in China, and it is now possible not only for the petty bourgeoisie but even for the national bourgeoisie to join the anti-Japanese struggle.

The people's republic will definitely not represent the interests of the enemy classes. On the contrary, it will stand in direct opposition to the landlord and comprador classes, the lackeys of imperialism, and will not count them among the people. In the same way, Chiang Kai-shek's "National Government of the Republic of China" represents only the wealthiest, but not the common people whom it does not count as part of the nation. As 80 to 90 per cent of China's population is made up of workers and peasants, the people's republic ought to represent their interests first and foremost. However, by throwing off imperialist oppression to make China free and independent and by throwing off landlord oppression to free China from semi-feudalism, the people's republic will benefit not only the workers and peasants but other sections of the people too. The sum total of the interests of the workers, peasants and the rest of the people constitutes the interests of the whole Chinese nation. The comprador and the landlord classes also live on Chinese soil, but as they have no regard for the national interests, their interests clash with those of the majority. This small minority are the only ones that we break with and are clashing with, and we therefore have the right to call ourselves the representatives of the whole nation.

There is, of course, a clash of interests between the working class and the national bourgeoisie. We shall not be able to extend the national revolution successfully unless the working class, the vanguard of the national revolution, is accorded political and economic rights and is enabled to direct its strength against imperialism and its running dogs, the traitors. However if the national bourgeoisie joins the anti-imperialist united front, the working class and the national bourgeoisie will have interests in common. In the period of the bourgeois-democratic revolution, the people's republic will not expropriate private property other than imperialist and feudal private property, and so far from confiscating the national bourgeoisie's industrial and commercial enterprises, it will encourage their development. We shall protect every national capitalist who does not support the imperialists or the Chinese traitors. In the stage of democratic revolution there are limits to the struggle between labour and capital. The labour laws of the people's republic will protect the interests of the workers, but will not prevent the national bourgeoisie from making profits or developing their industrial and commercial enterprises, because such development is bad for imperialism and good for the Chinese people. Thus it is clear that the people's republic will represent the interests of all strata opposed to imperialism and the feudal forces. The government of the people's republic will be based primarily on the workers and peasants, but will also include representatives of the other classes which are opposed to imperialism and the feudal forces.

But is it not dangerous to let the representatives of such classes join the government of the people's republic? No. The workers and peasants are the basic masses of the republic. In giving the urban petty bourgeoisie, the intellectuals and other sections of the population who support the anti-imperialist and anti-feudal programme the right to have a voice in the government of the people's republic and to work in it, the right to vote and stand for election, we must not allow the interests of the workers and peasants, the basic masses, to be violated. The essential part of our programme must be the protection of their interests. With their representatives comprising the majority in this government and with the Communist Party exercising leadership and working within it, there is a guarantee that the participation of other classes will present no danger. It is perfectly obvious that the Chinese revolution at the present stage is still a bourgeois-democratic and not a proletarian socialist revolution in nature. Only the counter-revolutionary Trotskyites talk such nonsense as that China has already completed her bourgeois-democratic revolution and that any further revolution can only be socialist. The revolution of 1924–27 was a bourgeois-democratic revolution, which was not carried to completion but failed. The agrarian revolution which we have led since 1927 is also a bourgeois-democratic revolution, because it is directed not against capitalism, but against imperialism and feudalism. This will remain true of our revolution for quite a long time to come.

Basically, the workers, the peasants and the urban petty bourgeoisie arc still the motive forces of the revolution, but now there may be the national bourgeoisie as well.

The change in the revolution will come later. In the future the democratic revolution will inevitably be transformed into a socialist revolution. As to when the transition will take place, that will depend on the presence of the necessary conditions, and it may take quite a long time. We should not hold forth about transition until all the necessary political and economic conditions are present and until it is advantageous and not detrimental to the overwhelming majority of the people throughout China. It is wrong to have any doubts on this matter and expect the transition to take place soon, as some of our comrades did when they maintained that the transition in the revolution would begin the moment the democratic revolution began to triumph in key provinces. They did so because they failed to understand what kind of country China is politically and economically and to realize that, compared with Russia, China will find it more difficult, and require much more time and effort, to complete her democratic revolution politically and economically.

International Support

Finally, a word is necessary about the relation between the Chinese and the world revolution.

Ever since the monster of imperialism came into being, the affairs of the world have become so closely interwoven that it is impossible to separate them. We Chinese have the spirit to fight the enemy to the last drop of our blood, the determination to recover our lost territory by our own efforts, and the ability to stand on our own feet in the family of nations. But this does not mean that we can dispense with international support; no, today international support is necessary for the revolutionary struggle of any nation or country. There is the old adage, "In the Spring and Autumn Era there were no righteous wars." This is even truer of imperialism today, for it is only the oppressed nations and the oppressed classes that can wage just wars. All wars anywhere in the world in which the people rise up to fight their oppressors are just struggles. The February and October Revolutions in Russia were just wars. The revolutions of the people in various European countries after World War I were just struggles. In China, the

Anti-Opium War, the War of the Taiping Heavenly Kingdom, the Yi Ho Tuan War, the Revolutionary War of 1911, the Northern Expedition of 1926–27, the Agrarian Revolutionary War from 1927 to the present, and the present resistance to Japan and punitive actions against traitors—these are all just wars. Now, in the mounting tide of nation-wide struggle against Japan and of world-wide struggle against fascism, just wars will spread all over China and the globe. All just wars support each other, while all unjust wars should be turned into just wars— this is the Leninist line. Our war against Japan needs the support of the people of the whole world and, above all, the support of the people of the Soviet Union, which they will certainly give us because they and we are bound together in a common cause. In the past, the Chinese revolutionary forces were temporarily cut off from the world revolutionary forces by Chiang Kai-shek, and in this sense we were isolated. Now the situation has changed, and changed to our advantage. Henceforth it will continue to change to our advantage. We can no longer be isolated. This provides a necessary condition for China's victory in the war against Japan and for victory in the Chinese revolution.

Source: Marxists org. Internet Archive website: www.marxists.org/reference/archive/mao/works/1935/12_27.htm.

Hachiro Arita: "The Greater East Asia Co-Prosperity Sphere" (1940)

The only Asian country to effectively resist European imperialists in the nineteenth century and the only one to create an empire of its own, Japan became increasingly aggressive under military rule in the 1930s. While its rule in the Asian lands it conquered was harsh, the Japanese couched their imperialistic mission in the language of anticolonialism, that is, freeing Asians from European overlords. Japan's so-called Greater East Asia Co-Prosperity Sphere, despite its name and in imitation of the European imperialism it was meant to replace, was aimed at empowering and enriching Japan at the expense of its Asian neighbors; excerpts from the foreign minister's speech on the subject follow.

It seems to be a most natural step that peoples who are closely related with each other geographically, racially, culturally, and economically should first form a sphere of their own for co-existence and co-prosperity and establish peace and order within that sphere, and at the same time secure a relationship of common existence and prosperity with other spheres. The cause of strife which mankind has hitherto experienced lies generally in the failure to give due consideration to the necessity of some such natural and constructive world order and to remedy old irrationalities and injustices. . . .

It is in this spirit that Japan is now engaged in the task of establishing a new order in East Asia. It is extremely regrettable, therefore, that there should be those who not only fail to understand Japan's great undertaking based upon this fundamental principle, but on the contrary, obstruct establishment of peace in East Asia by supporting the regime of Chiang Kai-shek. We have urged them to reconsider such an attitude in the past, and now we intend further to urge their serious reflection. We are determined to leave no stone unturned in order to eradicate all activities for assisting Chiang Kai-shek. Sometimes there are those who would disapprove a change in the status quo by force of arms regardless of the reasons therefor. It is for the purpose of bringing about a just and permanent peace that Japan has been fighting in China for the past 3 years. Her employment of armed force is an act looking beyond the immediate present. The sword she has drawn is intended to be nothing other than a life-giving sword that destroys evil and makes justice manifest. Countries of East Asia and regions of the South Seas are geographically, historically, racially, and economically very closely related to each other. They are destined to help each other and minister to one another's needs for their common well-being and prosperity, and to promote peace and progress in their regions. Uniting of all these regions under a single sphere on the basis of common existence and insuring thereby the stability of that sphere is, I think, a natural conclusion. The idea to establish first a righteous peace in each of the various regions and then establish collectively a just peace for the whole world has long existed also in Europe and America.

This system presupposes the existence of a stabilizing force in each region, with which as a center the peoples within that region are to secure their co-existence and co-prosperity and as well the stability of their sphere. It also presupposes that these groups will respect [one] another's individual characteristics, political, cultural, and economic, and they will cooperate and fulfill one another's needs for their common good. . . .

Japan, while carrying on vigorously her task of constructing a new order in East Asia, is paying serious attention to developments in the European war and to its repercussions in the various quarters of East Asia, including the South Seas region. I desire to declare that the destiny of these regions in any development therein, and any disposal thereof, is a matter for grave concern to Japan in view of her mission and responsibility as the stabilizing force in East Asia.

Source: Foreign Relations: Japan: 1931–1941. Washington, DC: Government Printing Office, 1943.

OTTOMAN EMPIRE

Firman of Appointment of Muhammad Ali as Pasha of Egypt Issued by Ottoman Sultan (1840)

Born in Albania, Muhammad Ali rose through the ranks of the Ottoman imperial army in the late eighteenth and early nineteenth centuries. Appointed pasha, or governor, of Egypt in this firman (edict), he modernized the political and economic structures of this province of the empire and became virtually independent of the sultan. To entice him to fight against Greek separatists, Sultan Mahmud II promised him the governorship of Syria. When the sultan reneged on the promise, Ali revolted, challenging the sultan's rule. Unable to win European allies, however, Ali was forced to accept an offer by the sultan making the position of pasha of Egypt a hereditary post of Ali's lineage. Despite this ultimate triumph of the sultan, Ali's rebellion understated the growing forces of disintegration within the weakening Ottoman Empire of the nineteenth century.

The act of submission which thou hast just made, the assurances of fidelity and devotion which thou hast given, and the upright and sincere intentions which thou hast manifested, as well with regard to myself as in the interests of my Sublime Porte, have come to my sovereign knowledge, and have been very agreeable to me.

In consequence, and as the zeal and sagacity by which thou art characterized, as likewise the experience and knowledge which thou hast acquired in the affairs of Egypt during the long space of time that thou hast held the post of Governor of Egypt, give reason to believe that thou hast acquired a title to the favor and to the confidence which I may grant to thee, that is to say, that thou wilt be sensible of their full extent, and all the gratitude which thou shouldst have for them, that thou wilt apply thyself to cause these feelings to descend to thy sons and thy nephews, I grant unto thee the Government of Egypt within its ancient boundaries, such as they are to be found in the map which is sent unto thee by my Grand Vizier now in office, with a seal affixed to it, together with the additional privilege of hereditary succession, and with the following conditions:-

Henceforth, when the post shall be vacant, the Government of Egypt shall descend in a direct line, from the elder to the elder, in the male race among the sons and grandsons. As regards their nomination, that shall be made by my Sublime Porte.

If at any time fate should decide that the male line should become extinct, as in that case it will devolve upon my Sublime Porte to confer the Government of Egypt on another person, the male children, issue of the daughters of the Governors of Egypt, shall possess no right to, no legal capacity for, the succession of the Government.

Although the Pashas of Egypt have obtained the privilege of hereditary succession, they still must be considered, as far as precedency is concerned, to be on a footing of equality with the other Viziers, they shall be treated like the other Viziers of my Sublime Porte, and they shall receive the same titles as are given to the other Viziers when they are written to.

The principles founded on the laws of security of life, of the security of property, and the preservation of honor, principles recorded in the salutary ordinances of my Hatti Sherif of Gulhane; all the Treaties concluded and to be concluded between my Sublime Porte and the friendly Powers, shall be completely executed in the Province of Egypt likewise.

In Egypt, all the taxes, all the revenues, shall be levied and collected in my sovereign name; and all the regulations made and to be made by my Sublime Porte shall also be put in practice in Egypt, reconciling them in the best way possible with the local circumstances and with the principles of justice and of equity, Nevertheless, as the Egyptians are likewise the subjects of my Sublime Porte, and in order that they may not one day be oppressed, the tithe, the duties, and the other taxes which are levied there, shall be so, in conformity with the equitable system adopted by my Sublime Porte; and care shall be taken to pay, when the period for payment shall arrive, out of the customs duties, the capitation tax, the tithe, the revenues, and other produce of the Province of Egypt, the annual tribute of which the amount is inserted and defined in another Imperial firman.

It being customary to send every year from Egypt provisions in kind to the two Holy Cities, the provisions and other articles, whatever they may be, which have up to this time been sent thither, shall continue to be sent to each place separately.

As my Sublime Porte has taken the resolution of improving the coin, which is the soul of the operations of society, and of effecting this in such manner that henceforth there can be no variation either in the alloy, or in the value, I grant permission for money to be coined in Egypt; but the gold and silver monies which I permit thee to coin shall bear my name, and shall resemble in all respects, as regards their determination, value, and form, the monies which are coined here.

In time of peace, 18,000 men will suffice for the internal service of the province of Egypt; it shall not be allowed to increase their numbers. But as the land and sea forces of Egypt are raised for the service of my Sublime Porte, it shall be allowable, in time of war, to increase them to the number which shall be deemed suitable by my Sublime Porte.

The principle has been adopted that the soldiers employed in the other parts of my dominions shall serve for five years, at the end of which term they shall be exchanged for recruits.

That being the case, it would be requisite that the same system should also be observed in Egypt in that respect. But with regard to the duration of the service, the dispositions of the people shall be attended to, observing what is required by equity with regard to them.

Four hundred men shall be sent every year to Constantinople to replace others.

There shall be no difference between the distinguishing marks and the flags of the other troops which shall be employed there, and the distinguishing marks and the flags of the other troops of my Sublime Porte. The officers of the Egyptian vessels shall have the same flags as the officers and vessels of this place.

The Governor of Egypt shall appoint the officers of the land and sea forces up to the rank of Colonel. With regard to the appointments to ranks higher than that of Colonel, that is to say, of Pashas Mirliva (Brigadier-Generals), and of Pashas Ferik (Generals of Division), it will be absolutely necessary to apply for permission for them, and to take my orders thereupon.

Henceforth the Pashas of Egypt shall not be at liberty to build vessels of war without having first applied for the permission of my Sublime Porte, and having obtained from it a clear and positive authority.

As each of the conditions settles as above is annexed to the privilege of hereditary succession, if a single one of them is not executed, that privilege of hereditary succession shall forthwith be abolished and annulled.

Such being my supreme pleasure on all the points above specified, thou, thy children, and thy descendants, grateful for this exalted sovereign favour, ye shall always be diligent in scrupulously executing the conditions laid down, ye shall take need not to infringe them, ye shall be careful to ensure the repose and the tranquility of the Egyptians by protecting them from all injury and from all oppressions, ye shall report to this place, and ye shall apply for orders on all matters of importance which concern those countries, it being for these purposes that the present Imperial FIRMAN, which is decorated with my sovereign signature, has been written, and is sent to you.

Source: Historical Text Archive: historicaltextarchive.com/ sections.php?op=viewarticle&artid=15.

Imperial Ottoman Government: Circular on the End of Capitulations (September 9, 1914)

In the vocabulary of the imperial Ottoman government, "capitulations" refers to the immunity granted under various treaties to citizens of powerful western states. Negotiated out of weakness, capitulation treaties often allowed these westerners to engage in smuggling and various forms of corruption without fear of prosecution. With the beginning of World War I, the Ottoman government sought to end such capitulations.

The Imperial Ottoman Government, in its sentiments of hospitality and sympathy towards the subjects of the friendly Powers, had in former times determined in a special manner the rules to which foreigners coming to the Orient to trade there should be subject, and had communicated those rules to the Powers. Subsequently those rules, which the Sublime Porte had decreed entirely of its own accord, were interpreted as privileges, corroborated and extended by certain practices, and were maintained down to our days under the name of ancient treaties (or Capitulations). Meanwhile these privileges, which on the one hand were found to be in complete opposition to the juridical rules of the century and to the principle of national sovereignty, constituted on the other hand an impediment to the progress and the development of the Ottoman Empire, just as they gave birth to certain misunderstandings in its relations with the foreign Powers; and thus they form an obstacle to the attainment of the desired degree of cordiality and sincerity in those relations.

The Ottoman Empire, surmounting all resistance, continues to march in the path of renaissance and reform which it entered upon in 1855 by the Hatti-Humayoun of Gul Hané, and, in order to assure for itself the place which was due it in the family of the civilized peoples of Europe, it accepted the most modern juridical principles and did not deviate from the program of supporting the edifice of the State on these foundations. The establishment of the constitutional regime demonstrates with what happy success the efforts of the Ottoman Government in the way of progress were crowned.

However, as consequences deduced from the Capitulations, the intervention of foreigners in the exercise of judiciary power, which constitutes the most important basis of the sovereignty of the State; the limitation of the legislative power, by the claim put forth that many laws could not be applied to foreigners; the fact that a criminal who has committed an offense against public security is screened from the application of the laws on the sole ground of his being of foreign nationality; or again the fact that public action is compromised by the necessity of respecting in regard to the foreign delinquent all sorts of restrictions and conditions; the fact finally that, according to the nationality of the contracting parties, a difference arising from a single contract admits of a different forum and mode of procedure—all these facts and other similar restrictive privileges constitute an insurmountable barrier to all organization of tribunals begun with a view to assuring in the country the perfect working of justice.

Likewise, that consequence of the Capitulations which renders foreigners exempt and free from taxes in the Ottoman Empire renders the Sublime Porte powerless not only to procure the necessary means for providing for the carrying out of reforms, but even for satisfying current administrative needs, without having recourse to a loan. In the same order of ideas, the obstacles raised to the increase of indirect taxes result in raising the quota of direct taxes and in overburdening the Ottoman taxpayers. The fact that foreigners trading in the Ottoman Empire and enjoying there all sorts of immunities and privileges are less heavily taxed than Ottomans constitutes at the same time a manifest injustice and an infringement of the independence and dignity of the State. The Imperial Government, in spite of all these obstacles, was zealously pursuing its efforts at reform when the unforeseen outbreak of the general war brought the financial difficulties in the country to the last degree of acuteness, endangering the accomplishment of all the work which had been begun or the undertaking of which had been decided upon. Now the Sublime Porte is convinced that the only means of salvation for Turkey is to bring into being this work of reform and of development as soon as possible, and it is likewise convinced that all the steps that it takes in this direction will meet with the encouragement of all the friendly Powers.

It is on the basis of this conviction that the decision has been taken to abrogate, reckoning from October 1, 1914, the Capitulations, which up to the present have constituted a hindrance to all progress in the Empire, as well as all privileges and toleration accessory to these Capitulations or resulting from them, and to adopt as the basis of relations with all States the general principles of international law.

While having the honor of communicating the present decision, which as it is to open an era of happiness for the Ottoman Empire will for this reason, I have no doubt, be received with satisfaction by the American Government, I consider it my duty to add that the Sublime Porte, inspired exclusively in its decision by the higher interests of the Ottoman land, does not nourish, in abrogating the Capitulations, any unfriendly thought in regard to any Power and that it is quite disposed to enter upon negotiations with a view to concluding with the American Government treaties of commerce on the basis of the general principles of public international law.

Source: *Papers Relating to the Foreign Relations of the United States, 1914.* Washington, DC: Government Printing Office, 1922.

Treaty of Sèvres (August 10, 1920)

The 1920 Treaty of Sèvres between the Allied and Associated Powers and Turkey dismantled the five-hundred-year-old Ottoman Empire after the latter's defeat in World War I. Vast Ottoman territories in the Middle East were handed over to British and French control under the treaty, and significant territories within the Anatolian peninsula were to be administered by the Greeks, who were widely distrusted by Turks. Indeed, the treaty practically eliminated the Turkish state altogether. The vindictive terms of the treaty would spark a revival of Turkish nationalism under military commander Mustafa Kemal, later Ataturk or "Father of the Turks," whose victories over the Greeks in the early 1920s would force the Allies to negotiate a new treaty, giving Turkey unconditional control over the entire Anatolian peninsula, although former Ottoman territories in the Middle East were never returned.

THE BRITISH EMPIRE, FRANCE, ITALY AND JAPAN,

These Powers being described in the present Treaty as the Principal Allied Powers;

ARMENIA, BELGIUM, GREECE, THE HEDJAZ, POLAND, PORTUGAL, ROUMANIA, THE SERB-CROAT-SLOVENE STATE AND CZECHO-SLOVAKIA,

These Powers constituting, with the Principal Powers mentioned above, the Allied Powers, of the one part;

AND TURKEY, on the other part;

Whereas on the request of the Imperial Ottoman Government an Armistice was granted to Turkey on October 30, 1918, by the Principal Allied Powers in order that a Treaty of Peace might be concluded, and

Whereas the Allied Powers are equally desirous that the war in which certain among them were successively involved, directly or indirectly, against Turkey, and which originated in the declaration of war against Serbia on July 28, 1914, by the former Imperial and Royal Austro-Hungarian Government, and in the hostilities opened by Turkey against the Allied Powers on October 29, 1914, and conducted by Germany in alliance with Turkey, should be replaced by a firm, just and durable Peace,

For this purpose the HIGH CONTRACTING PARTIES have appointed as their Plenipotentiaries:

HIS MAJESTY THE KING OF THE UNITED KINGDOM OF GREAT BRITAIN AND IRELAND AND OF THE BRITISH DOMINIONS BEYOND THE SEAS, EMPEROR OF INDIA: Sir George Dixon GRAHAME, K. C. V. O., Minister Plenipotentiary of His Britannic Majesty at Paris; for the DOMINION OF CANADA: The Honourable Sir George Halsey PERLEY, K. C. M. High Commissioner for Canada in the United Kingdom; for the COMMONWEALTH of AUSTRALIA: The Right Honourable Andrew FISHER, High Commissioner for Australia in the United Kingdom; for the DOMINION of NEW ZEALAND: Sir George Dixon GRAHAME, K. C. V. O., Minister Plenipotentiary of His Britannic Majesty at Paris; for the UNION of SOUTH AFRICA: Mr. Reginald Andrew BLANKENBERG, O. B. E., Acting High Commissioner for the Union of South Africa in the United Kingdom; for INDIA: Sir Arthur HIRTZEL, K. C. B., Assistant Under Secretary of State for India;

THE PRESIDENT OF THE FRENCH REPUBLIC: Mr. Alexandre MILLERAND, President of the Council, Minister for Foreign Affairs Mr. Frederic FRANÇOIS-MARSAL, Minister of Finance Mr. Auguste Paul-Louis ISAAC, Minister of Commerce and Industry; Mr. Jules CAMBON, Ambassador of France Mr. Georges Maurice PALÉOLOGUE, Ambassador of France, Secretary-General of the Ministry of Foreign Affairs;

His MAJESTY THE KING OF ITALY: Count LELIO BONIN LONGARE, Senator of the Kingdom;

Ambassador Extraordinary and Plenipotentiary of H.M. the King of Italy at Paris General Giovanni MARIETTI, Italian Military Representative on the Supreme War Council;

His MAJESTY THE EMPEROR OF JAPAN: Viscount CHINDA, Ambassador Extraordinary and Plenipotentiary of H.M. the Emperor of Japan at London; Mr. K. MATSUI, Ambassador Extraordinary and Plenipotentiary of H.M. the Emperor of Japan at Paris;

ARMENIA: Mr. Avetis AHARONIAN, President of the Delegation of the Armenian Republic;

HIS MAJESTY THE KING OF THE BELGIANS: Mr. Jules VAN DEN HEUVEL, Envoy Extraordinary and Minister Plenipotentiary, Minister of State; Mr. ROLIN JAEQUEMYNS, Member of the Institute of Private International Law, Secretary-General of the Belgian Delegation;

HIS MAJESTY THE KING OF THE HELLENES: Mr. Eleftherios K. VENIZELOS, President of the Council of Ministers; Mr. Athos ROMANOS, Envoy Extraordinary and Minister Plenipotentiary of H.M. the King of the Hellenes at Paris;

HIS MAJESTY THE KING OF THE HEDJAZ:

THE PRESIDENT OF THE POLISH REPUBLIC: Count Maurice ZAMOYSKI, Envoy Extraordinary and Minister Plenipotentiary of the Polish Republic at Paris; Mr. Erasme PILTZ;

THE PRESIDENT OF THE PORTUGUESE REPUBLIC: Dr. Affonso da COSTA, formerly President of the Council of Ministers;

His MAJESTY THE KING OF ROUMANIA: Mr. Nicolae TITULESCU, Minister of Finance;

Prince DIMITRIE GHIKA, Envoy Extraordinary and Minister Plenipotentiary of H.M. the King of Roumania at Paris;

His MAJESTY THE KING OF THE SERBS, THE CROATS AND THE SLOVENES:

Mr. Nicolas P. PACHITCH, formerly President of the Council of Ministers; Mr. Ante TRUMBIC, Minister for Foreign Affairs;

THE PRESIDENT OF THE CZECHO-SLOVAK REPUBLIC: Mr. Edward BENES, Minister for Foreign Affairs; Mr. Stephen OSUSKY, Envoy Extraordinary and Minister Plenipotentiary of the Czecho-Slovak Republic at London;

TURKEY: General HAADI Pasha, Senator; RIZA TEVFIK Bey, Senator; RECHAD HALISS Bey, Envoy Extraordinary and Minister Plenipotentiary of Turkey at Berne; WHO, having communicated their full powers, found in good and due form, have AGREED AS FOLLOWS:

From the coming into force of the present Treaty the state of war will terminate.

From that moment and subject to the provisions of the present Treaty, official relations will exist between the Allied Powers and Turkey . . .

PART II. FRONTIERS OF TURKEY.
ARTICLE 27.

I. In Europe, the frontiers of Turkey will be laid down as follows: 1. The Black Sea: from the entrance of the Bosphorus to the point described below.

2. With Greece: From a point to be chosen on the Black Sea near the mouth of the Biyuk Dere, situated about 7 kilometres north-west of Podima, south-westwards to the most north-westerly point of the limit of the basin of the Istranja Dere (about 8 kilometres northwest of Istranja), a line to be fixed on the ground passing through Kapilja Dagh and Uchbunar Tepe; thence south-south-eastwards to a point to be chosen on the railway from Chorlu to Chatalja about 1 kilometre west of the railway station of Sinekli, a line following as far as possible the western limit of the basin of the Istranja Dere; thence south-eastwards to a point to be chosen between Fener and Kurfali on the watershed between the basins of those rivers which flow into Biyuk Chekmeje Geul, on the north-east, and the basin of those rivers which flow direct into the Sea of Marmora on the south-west, a line to be fixed on the ground passing south of Sinekli; thence south-eastwards to a point to be chosen on the Sea of Marmora about 1 kilometre south-west of Kalikratia, a line following as far as possible this watershed.

3. The Sea of Marmora: from the point defined above to the entrance of the Bosphorus.

II. In Asia, the frontiers of Turkey will be laid down as follows: 1. On the West and South: From the entrance of the Bosphorus into the Sea of Marmora to a point described below, situated in the eastern Mediterranean Sea in the neighbourhood of the Gulf of Alexandretta near Karatash Burun the Sea of Marmora, the Dardanelles, and the Eastern Mediterranean Sea; the islands of the Sea of Marmora, and those which are situated within a distance of 3 miles from the coast, remaining Turkish, subject to the provisions of Section IV and Articles 84 and 122, Part III (Political Clauses).

2. With Syria: From a point to be chosen on the eastern bank of the outlet of the Hassan Dede, about 3 kilometres north-west of Karatash Burun, north-eastwards to a point to be chosen on the Djaihun Irmak about 1 kilometre north of Babeli, a line to be fixed on the ground passing north of Karatash; thence to Kesik Kale, the course of the Djaihun Irmak upstream; thence north-eastwards to a point to be chosen on the Djaihun Irmak about 15 kilometres east-southeast of Karsbazar, a line to be fixed on the ground passing north of Kara Tepe; thence to the bend in the Djaihun Irmak situated west of Duldul Dagh, the course of the Djaihun Irmak upstream; thence in a general south-easterly direction to a point to be chosen on Emir Musi Dagh about 15 kilometres south-south-west of Giaour Geul a line to be fixed on the ground at a distance of about 18 kilometres from the railway, and leaving Duldul Dagh to Syria; thence eastwards to a point to be chosen about 5 kilometres north of Urfa a generally straight line from west to east to be fixed on the ground passing north of the roads connecting the towns of Baghche, Aintab, Biridjik, and Urfa and leaving the last three named towns to Syria; thence eastwards to the south-western extremity of the bend in the Tigris about 6 kilometres north of Azekh (27 kilometres west of Djezire-ibn-Omar), a generally straight line from west to east to be fixed on the ground leaving the town of Mardin to Syria; thence to a point to be chosen on the Tigris between the point of confluence of the Khabur Su with the Tigris and the bend in the Tigris situated about 10 kilometres north of this point, the course of the Tigris downstream, leaving the island on which is situated the town of Djezire-ibn-Omar to Syria.

3. With Mesopotamia: Thence in a general easterly direction to a point to be chosen on the northern boundary of the vilayet of Mosul, a line to be fixed on the ground; thence eastwards to the point where it meets the frontier between Turkey and Persia, the northern boundary of the vilayet of Mosul, modified, however, so as to pass south of Amadia.

4. On the East and the North East: From the point above defined to the Black Sea, the existing frontier between Turkey and Persia, then the former frontier between Turkey and Russia, subject to the provisions of Article 89.

5. The Black Sea.

ARTICLE 28.

The frontiers described by the present Treaty are traced on the one in a million maps attached to the present Treaty. In case of differences between the text and the map, the text will prevail. [See Introduction.]

ARTICLE 29.

Boundary Commissions, whose composition is or will be fixed in the present Treaty or in Treaties supplementary thereto, will have to trace these frontiers on the ground.

They shall have the power, not only of fixing those portions which are defined as "a line to be fixed on the ground," but also, if the Commission considers it necessary, of revising in matters of detail portions defined by administrative boundaries or otherwise. They shall endeavour in all cases to follow as nearly as possible the descriptions given in the Treaties, taking into account, as far as possible, administrative boundaries and local economic interests.

The decisions of the Commissions will be taken by a majority, and shall be binding on the parties concerned.

The expenses of the Boundary Commissions will be borne in equal shares by the parties concerned.

ARTICLE 30.

In so far as frontiers defined by a waterway are concerned, the phrases "course" or "channel" used in the descriptions of the present Treaty signify, as regards non-navigable rivers, the median line of the waterway or of its principal branch, and, as regards navigable rivers, the median line of the principal channel of navigation. It will rest with the Boundary Commissions provided for by the present Treaty to specify whether the frontier line shall follow any changes of the course or channel which may take place, or whether it shall be definitely fixed by the position of the course or channel at the time when the present Treaty comes into force.

In the absence of provisions to the contrary in the present Treaty, islands and islets lying within three miles of the coast are included within the frontier of the coastal State.

ARTICLE 31.

The various States concerned undertake to furnish to the Commissions all documents necessary for their tasks, especially authentic copies of agreements fixing existing or old frontiers, all large scale maps in existence, geodetic data, surveys completed but unpublished, and information concerning the changes of frontier watercourses. The maps, geodetic data, and surveys, even if unpublished, which are in the possession of the Turkish authorities must be delivered at Constantinople, within thirty days from the coming into force of the present Treaty, to such representative of the Commissions concerned as may be appointed by the principal Allied Powers.

The States concerned also undertake to instruct the local authorities to communicate to the Commissions all documents, especially plans, cadastral and land books, and to furnish on demand all details regarding property, existing economic conditions, and other necessary information.

ARTICLE 32.

The various States interested undertake to give every assistance to the Boundary Commissions, whether directly or through local authorities, in everything that concerns transport, accommodation, labour, materials (sign-posts, boundary pillars) necessary for the accomplishment of their mission.

In particular the Turkish Government undertakes to furnish to the Principal Allied Powers such technical personnel as they may consider necessary to assist the Boundary Commissions in the accomplishment of their mission.

ARTICLE 33.

The various States interested undertake to safeguard the trigonometrical points, signals, posts or frontier marks erected by the Commissions.

ARTICLE 34.

The pillars will be placed so as to be intervisible; they will be numbered, and their position and their number will be noted on a cartographic document.

ARTICLE 35.

The protocols defining the boundary and the maps and documents attached thereto will be made out in triplicate, of which two copies will be forwarded to the Governments of the limitrophe States, and the third to the Government of the French Republic, which will deliver authentic copies to the Powers who sign the present Treaty.

PART III.

POLITICAL CLAUSES. SECTION I. CONSTANTINOPLE. ARTICLE 36.

Subject to the provisions of the present Treaty, the High Contracting Parties agree that the rights and title of the Turkish Government over Constantinople shall not be affected, and that the said Government and His Majesty the Sultan shall be entitled to reside there and to maintain there the capital of the Turkish State.

Nevertheless, in the event of Turkey failing to observe faithfully the provisions of the present Treaty, or of any treaties or conventions supplementary thereto, particularly as regards the protection of the rights of racial, religious or linguistic minorities, the Allied Powers expressly reserve the right to modify the above provisions, and Turkey hereby agrees to accept any dispositions which may be taken in this connection.

SECTION II.

STRAITS.

ARTICLE 37.

The navigation of the Straits, including the Dardanelles, the Sea of Marmora and the Bosphorus, shall in future be open, both in peace and war, to every vessel of commerce or of war and to military and commercial aircraft, without distinction of flag.

These waters shall not be subject to blockade, nor shall any belligerent right be exercised nor any act of hostility be committed within them, unless in pursuance of a decision of the Council of the League of Nations.

ARTICLE 38.

The Turkish Government recognises that it is necessary to take further measures to ensure the freedom of navigation provided for in Article 37, and accordingly delegates, so far as it is concerned, to a Commission to be called the "Commission of the Straits," and hereinafter referred to as 'the Commission," the control of the waters specified in Article 39.

The Greek Government, so far as it is concerned, delegates to the Commission the same powers and undertakes to give it in all respects the same facilities.

Such control shall be exercised in the name of the Turkish and Greek Governments respectively, and in the manner provided in this Section.

ARTICLE 39.

The authority of the Commission will extend to all the waters between the Mediterranean mouth of the Dardanelles and the Black Sea mouth of the Bosphorus, and to the waters within three miles of each of these mouths.

This authority may be exercised on shore to such extent as may be necessary for the execution of the provisions of this Section.

ARTICLE 40.

The Commission shall be composed of representatives appointed respectively by the United States of America (if and when that Government is willing to participate), the British Empire, France, Italy, Japan, Russia (if and when Russia becomes a member of the League of Nations), Greece, Roumania, and Bulgaria and Turkey (if and when the two latter States become members of the League of Nations). Each Power shall appoint one representative. The representatives of the United States of America, the British Empire, France, Italy, Japan and Russia shall each have two votes. The representatives of Greece, Roumania, and Bulgaria and Turkey shall each have one vote. Each Commissioner shall be removable only by the Government which appointed him.

ARTICLE 41.

The Commissioners shall enjoy, within the limits specified in Article 39, diplomatic privileges and immunities.

ARTICLE 42.

The Commission will exercise the powers conferred on it by the present Treaty in complete independence of the local authority. It will have its own flag, its own budget and its separate organisation.

ARTICLE 43.

Within the limits of its jurisdiction as laid down in Article 39 the Commission will be charged with the following duties:

(a) the execution of any works considered necessary for the improvement of the channels or the approaches to harbours; (b) the lighting and buoying of the channels; (c) the control of pilotage and towage; (d) the control of anchorages; (e) the control necessary to assure the application in the ports of Constantinople and Haidar Pasha of the regime prescribed in Articles 335 to 344, Part XI (Ports, Waterways and Railways) of the present Treaty; (f) the control of all matters relating to wrecks and salvage; (g) the control of lighterage;

ARTICLE 44.

In the event of the Commission finding that the liberty of passage is being interfered with, it will inform the representatives at Constantinople of the Allied Powers providing the occupying forces provided for in Article 178. These representatives will thereupon concert with the naval and military commanders of the said forces such measures as may be deemed necessary to preserve the freedom of the Straits. Similar action shall be taken by the said representatives in the event of any external action threatening the liberty of passage of the Straits.

ARTICLE 45.

For the purpose of the acquisition of any property or the execution of any permanent works which may be required, the Commission shall be entitled to raise such loans as it may consider necessary. These loans will be secured, so far as possible, on the dues to be levied on the shipping using the Straits, as provided in Article 53.

ARTICLE 46.

The functions previously exercised by the Constantinople Superior Council of Health and the Turkish Sanitary Administration which was directed by the said Council, and the functions exercised by the National Life-boat Service of the Bosphorus will within the limits specified in Article 39 be discharged under the control of the Commission and in such manner as it may direct.

The Commission will co-operate in the execution of any common policy adopted by the League of Nations for preventing and combating disease.

ARTICLE 47.

Subject to the general powers of control conferred upon the Commission, the rights of any persons or companies now holding concessions relating to lighthouses, docks, quays or similar matters shall be maintained; but the Commission shall be entitled if it thinks it necessary in the general interest to buy out or modify such rights upon the conditions laid down in Article 311 Part IX (Economic Clauses) of the present Treaty, or itself to take up a new concession.

ARTICLE 48.

In order to facilitate the execution of the duties with which it is entrusted by this Section, the Commission shall have power to organise such a force of special police as may be necessary. This force shall be drawn so far as possible from the native population of the zone of the Straits and islands referred to in Article 178, Part V (Military, Naval and Air Clauses), excluding the islands of Lemnos, Imbros, Samothrace, Tenedos and Mitylene. The said force shall be commanded by foreign police officers appointed by the Commission.

ARTICLE 49.

In the portion of the zone of the Straits, including the islands of the Sea of Marmora, which remains Turkish, and pending the coming into force of the reform of the Turkish judicial system provided for in Article I36, all infringements of the regulations and by-laws made by the Commission, committed by nationals of capitulatory Powers, shall be dealt with by the Consular Courts of the said Powers. The Allied Powers agree to make such infringements justiciable before their Consular Courts or authorities. Infringements committed by Turkish nationals or nationals of non-capitulatory Powers shall be dealt with by the competent Turkish judicial authorities.

In the portion of the said zone placed under Greek sovereignty such infringements will be dealt with by the competent Greek judicial authorities.

ARTICLE 50.

The officers or members of the crew of any merchant vessel within the limits of the jurisdiction of the Commission who may be arrested on shore for any offence committed either ashore or afloat within the limits of the said jurisdiction shall be brought before the competent judicial authority by the Commission's police. If the accused was arrested otherwise than by the Commission's police he shall immediately be handed over to them.

ARTICLE 51.

The Commission shall appoint such subordinate officers or officials as may be found indispensable to assist it in carrying out the duties with which it is charged.

ARTICLE 52.

In all matters relating to the navigation of the waters within the limits of the jurisdiction of the Commission all the ships referred to in Article 37 shall be treated upon a footing of absolute equality.

ARTICLE 53.

Subject to the provisions of Article 47 the existing rights under which dues and charges can be levied for various purposes, whether direct by the Turkish Government or by international bodies or private companies, on ships or cargoes within the limits of the jurisdiction of the Commission shall be transferred to the Commission. The Commission shall fix these dues and charges at such amounts only as may be reasonably necessary to cover the cost of the works executed and the services rendered to shipping, including the general costs and expenses of the administration of the Commission, and the salaries and pay provided for in paragraph 3 of the Annex to this Section.

For these purposes only and with the prior consent of the Council of the League of Nations the Commission may also establish dues and charges other than those now existing and fix their amounts.

ARTICLE 54.

All dues and charges imposed by the Commission shall be levied without any discrimination and on a footing of absolute equality between all vessels, whatever their port of origin, destination or departure, their flag or ownership, or the nationality or ownership of their cargoes.

This disposition does not affect the right of the Commission to fix in accordance with tonnage the dues provided for by this Section.

ARTICLE 55.

The Turkish and Greek Governments respectively undertake to facilitate the acquisition by the Commission of such land and buildings as the Commission shall consider it necessary to acquire in order to carry out effectively the duties with which it is entrusted.

ARTICLE 56.

Ships of war in transit through the waters specified in Article 39 shall conform in all respects to the regulations issued by the Commission for the observance of the ordinary rules of navigation and of sanitary requirements.

ARTICLE 57.

(1) Belligerent warships shall not re-victual nor take in stores except so far as may be strictly necessary to enable them to complete the passage of the Straits and to reach the nearest port where

they can call, nor shall they replenish or increase their supplies of war material or their armament or complete their crews, within the waters under the control of the Commission. Only such repairs as are absolutely necessary to render them seaworthy shall be carried out, and they shall not add in any manner whatever to their fighting force. The Commission shall decide what repairs are necessary, and these must be carried out with the least possible delay.

(2) The passage of belligerent warships through the waters under the control of the Commission shall be effected with the least possible delay, and without any other interruption than that resulting from the necessities of the service.

(3) The stay of such warships at ports within the jurisdiction of the Commission shall not exceed twenty-four hours except in case of distress. In such case they shall be bound to leave as soon as possible. An interval of at least twenty-four hours shall always elapse between the sailing of a belligerent ship from the waters under the control of the Commission and the departure of a ship belonging to an opposing belligerent.

(4) Any further regulations affecting in time of war the waters under the control of the Commission, and relating in particular to the passage of war material and contraband destined for the enemies of Turkey, or re-victualling, taking in stores or carrying out repairs in the said waters, will be laid down by the League of Nations.

ARTICLE 58.

Prizes shall in all respects be subjected to the same conditions as belligerent vessels of war.

ARTICLE 59.

No belligerent shall embark or disembark troops, munitions of war or warlike materials in the waters under the control of the Commission, except in case of accidental hindrance of the passage, and in such cases the passage shall be resumed with all possible dispatch.

ARTICLE 60.

Nothing in Articles 57, 58 or 59 shall be deemed to limit the powers of a belligerent or belligerents acting in pursuance of a decision by the Council of the League of Nations.

ARTICLE 61.

Any differences which may arise between the Powers as to the interpretation or execution of the provisions of this Section, and as regards Constan-

tinople and Haidar Pasha of the provisions of Articles 335 to 344, Part Xl (Ports, Waterways, and Railways) shall be referred to the Commission. In the event of the decision of the Commission not being accepted by any Power, the question shall, on the demand of any Power concerned, be settled as provided by the League of Nations, pending whose decision the ruling of the Commission will be carried out.

ANNEX

1. The Chairmanship of the Commission of the Straits shall be rotatory for the period of two years among the members of the Commission entitled to two votes.

The Commission shall take decisions by a majority vote and the Chairman shall have a casting vote. Abstention shall be regarded as a vote against the proposal under discussion.

Each of the Commissioners will have the right to designate a deputy Commissioner to replace him in his absence.

2. The salary of each member of the Commission will be paid by the Government which appointed him; these salaries will be fixed at reasonable amounts agreed upon from time to time between the Governments represented on the Commission.

3. The salaries of the police officers referred to in Article 48, of such other officials and officers as may be appointed under Article 51, and the pay of the local police referred to in Article 48, shall be paid out of the receipts from the dues and charges levied on shipping.

The Commission shall frame regulations as to the terms and conditions of employment of all officers and officials appointed

4. The Commission shall have at its disposal such vessels as may be necessary to enable it to carry out its functions as laid down in this Section and Annex.

5. In order to carry out all the duties with which it is charged by the provisions of this Section and Annex and within the limits therein laid down the Commission will have the power to prepare, issue and enforce the necessary regulations; this power will include the right of amending so far as may be necessary or repealing the existing regulations.

6. The Commission shall frame regulations as to the manner in which the accounts of all rev-

enues and expenditure of the funds under its control shall be kept, the auditing of such accounts and the publication every year of a full and accurate report thereof.

SECTION III. KURDISTAN. ARTICLE 62.

A Commission sitting at Constantinople and composed of three members appointed by the British, French and Italian Governments respectively shall draft within six months from the coming into force of the present Treaty a scheme of local autonomy for the predominantly Kurdish areas lying east of the Euphrates, south of the southern boundary of Armenia as it may be hereafter determined, and north of the frontier of Turkey with Syria and Mesopotamia, as defined in Article 27, II (2) and (3). If unanimity cannot be secured on any question, it will be referred by the members of the Commission to their respective Governments. The scheme shall contain full safeguards for the protection of the Assyro-Chaldeans and other racial or religious minorities within these areas, and with this object a Commission composed of British, French, Italian, Persian and Kurdish representatives shall visit the spot to examine and decide what rectifications, if any, should be made in the Turkish frontier where, under the provisions of the present Treaty, that frontier coincides with that of Persia.

ARTICLE 63.

The Turkish Government hereby agrees to accept and execute the decisions of both the Commissions mentioned in Article 62 within three months from their communication to the said Government.

ARTICLE 64.

If within one year from the coming into force of the present Treaty the Kurdish peoples within the areas defined in Article 62 shall address themselves to the Council of the League of Nations in such a manner as to show that a majority of the population of these areas desires independence from Turkey, and if the Council then considers that these peoples are capable of such independence and recommends that it should be granted to them, Turkey hereby agrees to execute such a recommendation, and to renounce all rights and title over these areas.

The detailed provisions for such renunciation will form the subject of a separate agreement between the Principal Allied Powers and Turkey.

If and when such renunciation takes place, no objection will be raised by the Principal Allied Powers to the voluntary adhesion to such an independent Kurdish State of the Kurds inhabiting that part of Kurdistan which has hitherto been included in the Mosul vilayet.

SECTION IV. SMYRNA. ARTICLE 65.

The provisions of this Section will apply to the city of Smyrna and the adjacent territory defined in Article 66, until the determination of their final status in accordance with Article 83.

ARTICLE 66.

The geographical limits of the territory adjacent to the city of Smyrna will be laid down as follows:

From the mouth of the river which flows into the Aegean Sea about 5 kilometres north of Skalanova, eastwards, the course of this river upstream; then south-eastwards, the course of the southern branch of this river; then south-eastwards, to the western point of the crest of the Gumush Dagh; a line to be fixed on the ground passing west of Chinar K, and east of Akche Ova; thence north-eastwards, this crest line; thence northwards to a point to be chosen on the railway from Ayasoluk to Deirmendik about 1 kilometre west of Balachik station, a line to be fixed on the ground leaving the road and railway from Sokia to Balachik station entirely in Turkish territory; thence northwards to a point to be chosen on the southern boundary of the Sandjak of Smyrna, a line to be fixed on the ground; thence to a point to be chosen in the neighbourhood of Bos Dagh situated about 15 kilometres north-east of Odemish, the southern and eastern boundary of the Sandjak of Smyrna; thence northwards to a point to be chosen on the railway from Manisa to Alashehr about 6 kilometres west of Salihli, a line to be fixed on the ground; thence northwards to Geurenez Dagh, a line to be fixed on the ground passing east of Mermer Geul west of Kemer, crossing the Kum Chai approximately south of Akshalan, and then following the watershed west of Kavakalan; thence north-westwards to a point to be chosen on the boundary between the Cazas of Kirkagach and Ak Hissar about 18 kilometres east of Kirkagach and 20 kilometres north of Ak Hissar, a line to be fixed on the ground; thence westwards to its junction with the boundary of the Caza of Soma, the southern boundary of the Caza of Kirkagach, thence westwards to its junction with the boundary of the Sandjak of Smyrna, the southern boundary of the Caza of Soma; thence northwards to its junction with the boundary of the vilayet of Smyrna, the north-eastern boundary of the Sandjak of Smyrna; thence westwards to a point to be chosen in the neighbourhood of Charpajik (Tepe). the northern boundary of the vilayet of Smyrna; thence northwards to a point to be chosen on the ground about 4 kilometres southwest of Keuiluje, a line to be fixed on the ground; thence westwards to a point to be selected on the ground between Cape Dahlina and Kemer Iskele, a line to be fixed on the ground passing south of Kemer and Kemer Iskele together with the road joining these places.

ARTICLE 67.

A Commission shall be constituted within fifteen days from the coming into force of the present Treaty to trace on the spot the boundaries of the territories described in Article 66. This Commission shall be composed of three members nominated by the British, French and Italian Governments respectively, one member nominated by the Greek Government, and one nominated by the Turkish Government.

ARTICLE 68.

Subject to the provisions of this Section, the city of Smyrna and the territory defined in Article 66 will be assimilated, in the application of the present Treaty, to territory detached from Turkey.

ARTICLE 69.

The city of Smyrna and the territory defined in Article 66 remain under Turkish sovereignty. Turkey, however, transfers to the Greek Government the exercise of her rights of sovereignty over the city of Smyrna and the said territory. In witness of such sovereignty the Turkish flag shall remain permanently hoisted over an outer fort in the town of Smyrna. The fort will be designated by the Principal Allied Powers.

ARTICLE 70.

The Greek Government will be responsible for the administration of the city of Smyrna and the territory defined in Article 66, and will effect this administration by means of a body of officials which it will appoint specially for the purpose.

ARTICLE 71.

The Greek Government shall be entitled to maintain in the city of Smyrna and the territory defined in Article 66 the military forces required for the maintenance of order and public security.

ARTICLE 72.

A local parliament shall be set up with an electoral system calculated to ensure proportional representation of all sections of the population, including racial, linguistic and religious minorities. Within six months from the coming into force of the present Treaty the Greek Government shall submit to the Council of the League of Nations a scheme for an electoral system complying with the above requirements; this scheme shall not come into force until approved by a majority of the Council.

The Greek Government shall be entitled to postpone the elections for so long as may be required for the return of the inhabitants who have been banished or deported by the Turkish authorities, but such postponement shall not exceed a period of one year from the coming into force of the present Treaty.

ARTICLE 73.

The relations between the Greek administration and the local parliament shall be determined by the said administration in accordance with the principles of the Greek Constitution.

ARTICLE 74.

Compulsory military service shall not be enforced in the city of Smyrna and the territory defined in Article 66 pending the final determination of their status in accordance with Article 83.

ARTICLE 75.

The provisions of the separate Treaty referred to in Article 86 relating to the protection of racial, linguistic and religious minorities, and to freedom of commerce and transit, shall be applicable to the city of Smyrna and the territory defined in Article 66.

ARTICLE 76.

The Greek Government may establish a Customs boundary along the frontier line defined in Article 66, and may incorporate the city of Smyrna and the territory defined in the said Article in the Greek customs system.

ARTICLE 77.

The Greek Government engages to take no measures which would have the effect of depreciating the existing Turkish currency, which shall retain its character as legal tender pending the determination, in accordance with the provisions of Article 83, of the final status of the territory.

ARTICLE 78.

The provisions of Part XI (Ports, Waterways and Railways) relating to the regime of ports of international interest, free ports and transit shall be applicable to the city of Smyrna and the territory defined in Article 66.

ARTICLE 79.

As regards nationality, such inhabitants of the city of Smyrna and the territory defined in Article 66 as are of Turkish nationality and cannot claim any other nationality under the terms of the present Treaty shall be treated on exactly the same footing as Greek nationals. Greece shall provide for their diplomatic and consular protection abroad.

ARTICLE 80.

The provisions of Article 24I, Part VIII (Financial Clauses) will apply in the case of the city of Smyrna and the territory defined in Article 66.

The provisions of Article 293, Part IX (Economic Clauses) will not be applicable in the case of the said city and territory.

ARTICLE 81.

Until the determination, in accordance with the provisions of Article 83, of the final status of Smyrna and the territory defined in Article 66, the rights to exploit the salt marshes of Phocea belonging to the Administration of the Ottoman Public Debt, including all plant and machinery and materials for transport by land or sea, shall not be altered or interfered with. No tax or charge shall be imposed during this period on the manufacture, exportation or transport of salt produced from these marshes. The Greek administration will have the right to regulate and tax the consumption of salt at Smyrna and within the territory defined in Article 66.

If after the expiration of the period referred to in the preceding paragraph Greece considers it opportune to effect changes in the provisions above set forth, the salt marshes of Phocea will be treated as a concession and the guarantees provided by Article 312, Part IX (Economic Clauses) will apply, subject, however, to the provisions of Article 246, Part VIII (Financial Clauses) of the present Treaty.

ARTICLE 82.

Subsequent agreements will decide all questions which are not decided by the present Treaty and which may arise from the execution of the provisions of this Section.

ARTICLE 83.

When a period of five years shall have elapsed after the coming into force of the present Treaty the local parliament referred to in Article 72 may, by a majority of votes, ask the Council of the League of Nations for the definitive incorporation in the Kingdom of Greece of the city of Smyrna and the territory defined in Article 66. The Council may require, as a preliminary, a plebiscite under conditions which it will lay down.

In the event of such incorporation as a result of the application of the foregoing paragraph, the Turkish sovereignty referred to in Article 69 shall cease. Turkey hereby renounces in that event in favour of Greece all rights and title over the city of Smyrna and the territory defined in Article 66.

SECTION V. GREECE. ARTICLE 84.

Without prejudice to the frontiers of Bulgaria laid down by the Treaty of Peace signed at Neuilly-sur-Seine on November 27, 1919, Turkey renounces in favour of Greece all rights and title over the territories of the former Turkish Empire in Europe situated outside the frontiers of Turkey as laid down by the present Treaty.

The islands of the Sea of Marmora are not included in the transfer of sovereignty effected by the above paragraph.

Turkey further renounces in favour of Greece all her rights and title over the islands of Imbros and Tenedos. The decision taken by the Conference of Ambassadors at London in execution of Articles 5 of the Treaty of London of May 17–30, 1913, and 15 of the Treaty of Athens of November 1–14, 1913, and notified to the Greek Government on February 13, 1914, relating to the sovereignty of Greece over the other islands of the Eastern Mediterranean, particularly Lemnos, Samothrace, Mytilene, Chios, Samos and Nikaria, is confirmed, without prejudice to the provisions of the present Treaty relating to the islands placed under the sovereignty of Italy and referred to in Article 122, and to the islands lying less than three miles from the coast of Asia.

Nevertheless, in the portion of the zone of the Straits and the islands, referred to in Article 178, which under the present Treaty are placed under Greek sovereignty, Greece accepts and undertakes to observe, failing any contrary stipulation in the present Treaty, all the obligations which, in order to assure the freedom of the Straits, are imposed by the present Treaty on Turkey in that portion of the said zone, including the islands of the Sea of Marmora, which remains under Turkish sovereignty.

ARTICLE 85.

A Commission shall be constituted within fifteen days from the coming into force of the present Treaty to trace on the spot the frontier line described in Article 27, 1 (2). This Commission shall be composed of four members nominated by the Principal Allied Powers, one member nominated by Greece, and one member nominated by Turkey.

ARTICLE 86.

Greece accepts and agrees to embody in a separate Treaty such provisions as may be deemed necessary, particularly as regards Adrianople, to protect the interests of inhabitants of that State who differ from the majority of the population in race, language or religion.

Greece further accepts and agrees to embody in a separate Treaty such provisions as may be deemed necessary to protect freedom of transit and equitable treatment for the commerce of other nations.

ARTICLE 87.

The proportion and nature of the financial obligations of Turkey which Greece will have to assume on account of the territory placed under her sovereignty will be determined in accordance with Articles 241 to 244, Part VIII (Financial Clauses) of the present Treaty.

Subsequent agreements will decide all questions which are not decided by the present Treaty and which may arise in consequence of the transfer of the said territories.

SECTION VI. ARMENIA. ARTICLE 88.

Turkey, in accordance with the action already taken by the Allied Powers, hereby recognises Armenia as a free and independent State.

ARTICLE 89.

Turkey and Armenia as well as the other High Contracting Parties agree to submit to the arbitration of the President of the United States of America the question of the frontier to be fixed between Turkey and Armenia in the vilayets of Erzerum, Trebizond, Van and Bitlis, and to accept his decision thereupon, as well as any stipulations he may prescribe as to access for Armenia to the sea, and as to the demilitarisation of any portion of Turkish territory adjacent to the said frontier.

ARTICLE 90.

In the event of the determination of the frontier under Article 89 involving the transfer of the whole or any part of the territory of the said Vilayets to Armenia, Turkey hereby renounces as from the date of such decision all rights and title over the territory so transferred. The provisions of the present Treaty applicable to territory detached from Turkey shall thereupon become applicable to the said territory.

The proportion and nature of the financial obligations of Turkey which Armenia will have to assume, or of the rights which will pass to her, on account of the transfer of the said territory will be determined in accordance with Articles 241 to 244, Part VIII (Financial Clauses) of the present Treaty.

Subsequent agreements will, if necessary, decide all questions which are not decided by the present Treaty and which may arise in consequence of the transfer of the said territory.

ARTICLE 91.

In the event of any portion of the territory referred to in Article 89 being transferred to Armenia, a Boundary Commission, whose composition will be determined subsequently, will be constituted within three months from the delivery of the decision referred to in the said Article to trace on the spot the frontier between Armenia and Turkey as established by such decision.

ARTICLE 92.

The frontiers between Armenia and Azerbaijan and Georgia respectively will be determined by direct agreement between the States concerned.

If in either case the States concerned have failed to determine the frontier by agreement at the date of the decision referred to in Article 89, the frontier line in question will be determined by the Principal Allied Powers, who will also provide for its being traced on the spot.

ARTICLE 93.

Armenia accepts and agrees to embody in a Treaty with the Principal Allied Powers such provisions as may be deemed necessary by these Powers to protect the interests of inhabitants of that State who differ from the majority of the population in race, language, or religion.

Armenia further accepts and agrees to embody in a Treaty with the Principal Allied Powers such provisions as these Powers may deem necessary to protect freedom of transit and equitable treatment for the commerce of other nations.

SECTION VII. SYRIA, MESOPOTAMIA, PALESTINE. ARTICLE 94.

The High Contracting Parties agree that Syria and Mesopotamia shall, in accordance with the fourth paragraph of Article 22, Part I (Covenant of the League of Nations), be provisionally recognised as independent States subject to the rendering of administrative advice and assistance by a Mandatory until such time as they are able to stand alone.

A Commission shall be constituted within fifteen days from the coming into force of the present Treaty to trace on the spot the frontier line described in Article 27, II (2) and (3). This Commission will be composed of three members nominated by France, Great Britain and Italy respectively, and one member nominated by Turkey; it will be assisted by a representative of Syria for the Syrian frontier, and by a representative of Mesopotamia for the Mesopotamian frontier.

The determination of the other frontiers of the said States, and the selection of the Mandatories, will be made by the Principal Allied Powers.

ARTICLE 95.

The High Contracting Parties agree to entrust, by application of the provisions of Article 22, the administration of Palestine, within such boundaries as may be determined by the Principal Allied Powers, to a Mandatory to be selected by the said Powers. The Mandatory will be responsible for putting into effect the declaration originally made on November 2, 1917, by the British Government, and adopted by the other Allied Powers, in favour of the establishment in Palestine of a national home for the Jewish people, it being clearly understood that nothing shall be done which may prejudice the civil and religious rights of existing non-Jewish communities in Palestine, or the rights and political status enjoyed by Jews in any other country.

The Mandatory undertakes to appoint as soon as possible a special Commission to study and regulate all questions and claims relating to the different religious communities. In the composition of this Commission the religious interests concerned will be taken into account. The Chairman of the Commission will be appointed by the Council of the League of Nations.

ARTICLE 96.

The terms of the mandates in respect of the above territories will be formulated by the Principal Allied Powers and submitted to the Council of the League of Nations for approval.

ARTICLE 97.

Turkey hereby undertakes, in accordance with the provisions of Article 132, to accept any decisions which may be taken in relation to the questions dealt with in this Section.

SECTION VIII. HEDJAZ. ARTICLE 98.

Turkey, in accordance with the action already taken by the Allied Powers, hereby recognises the Hedjaz as a free and independent State, and renounces in favour of the Hedjaz all rights and titles over the territories of the former Turkish Empire situated outside the frontiers of Turkey as laid down by the present Treaty, and comprised within the boundaries which may ultimately be fixed.

ARTICLE 99.

In view of the sacred character attributed by Moslems of all countries to the cities and the Holy Places of Mecca and Medina His Majesty the King of the Hedjaz undertakes to assure free and easy access thereto to Moslems of every country who desire to go there on pilgrimage or for any other religious object, and to respect and ensure respect for the pious foundations which are or may be established there by Moslems of any countries in accordance with the precepts of the law of the Koran.

ARTICLE 100.

His Majesty the King of the Hedjaz undertakes that in commercial matters the most complete equality of treatment shall be assured in the territory of the Hedjaz to the persons, ships and goods of nationals of any of the Allied Powers, or of any of the new States set up in the territories of the former Turkish Empire, as well as to the persons, ships and goods of nationals of States, Members of the League of Nations.

SECTION IX. EGYPT, SOUDAN, CYPRUS.

1. EGYPT. ARTICLE 101.

Turkey renounces all rights and title in or over Egypt. This renunciation shall take effect as from November 5, 1914. Turkey declares that in conformity with the action taken by the Allied Powers she recognises the Protectorate proclaimed over Egypt by Great Britain on December 18, 1914.

ARTICLE 102.

Turkish subjects habitually resident in Egypt on December 18, 1914, will acquire Egyptian nationality ipso facto and will lose their Turkish nationality, except that if at that date such persons were temporarily absent from, and have not since returned to, Egypt they will not acquire Egyptian nationality without a special authorisation from the Egyptian Government.

ARTICLE 103.

Turkish subjects who became resident in Egypt after December 18, 1914, and are habitually resident there at the date of the coming into force of the present Treaty may, subject to the conditions prescribed in Article 105 for the right of option, claim Egyptian nationality, but such claim may in individual cases be refused by the competent Egyptian authority.

ARTICLE 104.

For all purposes connected with the present Treaty, Egypt and Egyptian nationals, their goods and vessels, shall be treated on the same footing, as from August I, 1914, as the Allied Powers, their nationals, goods and vessels, and provisions in respect of territory under Turkish sovereignty, or of territory detached from Turkey in accordance with the present Treaty, shall not apply to EGYPT.

ARTICLE 105.

Within a period of one year after the coming into force of the present Treaty persons over eighteen years of age acquiring Egyptian nationality under the provisions of Article 102 will be entitled to opt for Turkish nationality. In case such persons, or those who under Article 103 are entitled to claim Egyptian nationality, differ in race from the majority of the population of Egypt, they will within the same period be entitled to opt for the nationality of any State in favour of which territory is detached from Turkey, if the majority of the population of that State is of the same race as the person exercising the right to opt.

Option by a husband covers a wife and option by parents covers their children under eighteen years of age.

Persons who have exercised the above right to opt must, except where authorised to continue to reside in Egypt, transfer within the ensuing twelve months their place of residence to the State for which they have opted. They will be entitled to retain their immovable property in Egypt, and may carry with them their movable property of every description. No export or import duties or charges may be imposed upon them in connection with the removal of such property.

ARTICLE 106.

The Egyptian Government shall have complete liberty of action in regulating the status of Turkish subjects in Egypt and the conditions under which they may establish themselves in the territory.

ARTICLE 107.

Egyptian nationals shall be entitled, when abroad, to British diplomatic and consular protection.

ARTICLE 108.

Egyptian goods entering Turkey shall enjoy the treatment accorded to British goods.

ARTICLE 109.

Turkey renounces in favour of Great Britain the powers conferred upon His Imperial Majesty the Sultan by the Convention signed at Constantinople on October 29, 1888, relating to the free navigation of the Suez Canal.

ARTICLE 110.

All property and possessions in Egypt belonging to the Turkish Government pass to the Egyptian Government without payment.

ARTICLE 111.

All movable and immovable property in Egypt belonging to Turkish nationals (who do not acquire Egyptian nationality) shall be dealt with in accordance with the provisions of Part IX (Economy Clauses) of the present Treaty.

ARTICLE 112.

Turkey renounces all claim to the tribute formerly paid by Egypt.

Great Britain undertakes to relieve Turkey of all liability in respect of the Turkish loans secured on the Egyptian tribute.

These loans are:

The guaranteed loan of 1855; The loan of 1894 representing the converted loans of 1854 and 1871; The loan of 1891 representing the converted loan of 1877.

The sums which the Khedives of Egypt have from time to time undertaken to pay over to the houses by which these loans were issued will be applied as heretofore to the interest and the sinking funds of the loans of 1894 and 1891 until the final extinction of those loans. The Government of Egypt will also continue to apply the sum hitherto paid towards the interest on the guaranteed loan of 1855.

Upon the extinction of these loans of 1894, 1891 and 1855, all liability on the part of the Egyptian Government arising out of the tribute formerly paid by Egypt to Turkey will cease.

2. SOUDAN.

ARTICLE 113.

The High Contracting Parties declare and place on record that they have taken note of the Convention between the British Government and the Egyptian Government defining the status and regulating the administration of the Soudan, signed on January 19, 1899, as amended by the supplementary Convention relating to the town of Suakin signed on July 10, 1899.

ARTICLE 114.

Soudanese shall be entitled when in foreign countries to British diplomatic and consular protection.

3. CYPRUS

ARTICLE 115.

The High Contracting Parties recognise the annexation of Cyprus proclaimed by the British Government on November 5, 1914.

ARTICLE 116.

Turkey renounces all rights and title over or relating to Cyprus, including the right to the tribute formerly paid by that island to the Sultan.

ARTICLE 117.

Turkish nationals born or habitually resident in Cyprus will acquire British nationality and lose their Turkish nationality, subject to the conditions laid down in the local law.

SECTION X. MOROCCO, TUNIS. ARTICLE 118.

Turkey recognises the French Protectorate in Morocco, and accepts all the consequences thereof. This recognition shall take effect as from March 30, 1912.

ARTICLE 119.

Moroccan goods entering Turkey shall be subject to the same treatment as French goods.

ARTICLE 120.

Turkey recognises the French Protectorate over Tunis and accepts all the consequences thereof. This recognition shall take effect as from May 12, 1881.

Tunisian goods entering Turkey shall be subject to the same treatment as French goods.

SECTION XI. LIBYA, AEGEAN ISLANDS. ARTICLE 121.

Turkey definitely renounces all rights and privileges which under the Treaty of Lausanne of October 18, 1912, were left to the Sultan in Libya.

ARTICLE 122.

Turkey renounces in favour of Italy all rights and title over the following islands of the Aegean Sea: Stampalia (Astropalia), Rhodes (Rhodos), Calki (Kharki), Scarpanto, Casos (Casso), Pscopis (Tilos), Misiros (Nisyros), Calymnos (Kalymnos), Leros, Patmos, Lipsos (Lipso), Sini (Symi), and Cos (Kos), which are now occupied by Italy, and the islets dependent thereon, and also over the island of Castellorizzo.

SECTION XII. NATIONALITY. ARTICLE 123.

Turkish subjects habitually resident in territory which in accordance with the provisions of the present Treaty is detached from Turkey will become ipso facto, in the conditions laid down by the local law, nationals of the State to which such territory is transferred.

ARTICLE 124.

Persons over eighteen years of age losing their Turkish nationality and obtaining ipso facto a new nationality under Article 123 shall be entitled within a period of one year from the coming into force of the present Treaty to opt for Turkish nationality.

ARTICLE 125.

Persons over eighteen years of age habitually resident in territory detached from Turkey in accordance with the present Treaty and differing in race from the majority of the population of such territory shall within one year from the coming into force of the present Treaty be entitled to opt for Armenia, Azerbaijan, Georgia, Greece, the Hedjaz, Mesopotamia, Syria, Bulgaria or Turkey, if the majority of the population of the State selected is of the same race as the person exercising the right to opt.

ARTICLE 126.

Persons who have exercised the right to opt in accordance with the provisions of Articles 124 or 125 must within the succeeding twelve months transfer their place of residence to the State for which they have opted.

They will be entitled to retain their immovable property in the territory of the other State where they had their place of residence before exercising their right to opt.

They may carry with them their movable property of every description. No export or import duties may be imposed upon them in connection with the removal of such property.

ARTICLE 127.

The High Contracting Parties undertake to put no hindrance in the way of the exercise of the right which the persons concerned have under the present Treaty, or under the Treaties of Peace concluded with Germany, Austria, Bulgaria or Hungary or under any treaty concluded by the Allied Powers, or any of them, with Russia, or between any of the Allied Powers themselves, to choose any other nationality which may be open to them.

In particular, Turkey undertakes to facilitate by every means in her power the voluntary emigration of persons desiring to avail themselves of the right to opt provided by Article 125, and to carry out any measures which may be prescribed with this object by the Council of the League of Nations.

ARTICLE 128.

Turkey undertakes to recognise any new nationality which has been or may be acquired by her nationals under the laws of the Allied Powers or new States and in accordance with the decisions of the competent authorities of these Powers pursuant to naturalisation laws or under Treaty stipulations, and to regard such persons as having, in consequence of the acquisition of such new nationality, in all respects severed their allegiance to their country of origin.

In particular, persons who before the coming into force of the present Treaty have acquired the nationality of one of the Allied Powers in accordance with the law of such Power shall be recognised by the Turkish Government as nationals of such Power and as having lost their Turkish nationality, notwithstanding any provisions of Turkish law to the contrary. No confiscation of property or other penalty provided by Turkish law shall be incurred on account of the acquisition of any such nationality.

ARTICLE 129.

Jews of other than Turkish nationality who are habitually resident, on the coming into force of the present Treaty, within the boundaries of Palestine, as determined in accordance with Article 95 will ipso facto become citizens of Palestine to the exclusion of any other nationality.

ARTICLE 130.

For the purposes of the provisions of this Section, the status of a married woman will be governed by that of her husband and the status of children under eighteen years of age by that of their parents.

ARTICLE 131.

The provisions of this Section will apply to the city of Smyrna and the territory defined in Article 66 as from the establishment of the final status of the territory in accordance with Article 83.

SECTION XIII. GENERAL PROVISIONS. ARTICLE 132.

Outside her frontiers as fixed by the present Treaty Turkey hereby renounces in favour of the Principal Allied Powers all rights and title which she could claim on any ground over or concerning any territories outside Europe which are not otherwise disposed of by the present Treaty.

Turkey undertakes to recognise and conform to the measures which may be taken now or in the future by the Principal Allied Powers, in agreement where necessary with third Powers, in order to carry the above stipulation into effect.

ARTICLE 133.

Turkey undertakes to recognise the full force of the Treaties of Peace and Additional Conventions concluded by the Allied Powers with the Powers who fought on the side of Turkey, and to recognise whatever dispositions have been or may be made concerning the territories of the former German Empire, of Austria, of Hungary and of Bulgaria, and to recognise the new States within their frontiers as there laid down.

ARTICLE 134.

Turkey hereby recognises and accepts the frontiers of Germany, Austria, Bulgaria, Greece, Hungary, Poland, Roumania, the Serb-Croat-Slovene State and the Czecho-Slovak State as these frontiers may be determined by the Treaties referred to in Article 133 or by any supplementary conventions.

ARTICLE 135.

Turkey undertakes to recognise the full force of all treaties or agreements which may be entered into by the Allied Powers with States now existing or coming into existence in future in the whole or part of the former Empire of Russia as it existed on August 1, 1914, and to recognise the frontiers of any such States as determined therein.

Turkey acknowledges and agrees to respect as permanent and inalienable the independence of the said States.

In accordance with the provisions of Article 259, Part VIII (Financial Clauses), and Article 277, Part IX (Economic Clauses), of the present Treaty, Turkey accepts definitely the abrogation of the Brest-Litovsk Treaties and of all treaties conventions and agreements entered into by her with the Maximalist Government in Russia.

ARTICLE 136.

A Commission composed of four members, appointed by the British Empire, France, Italy and Japan respectively, shall be set up within three months from the coming into force of the present Treaty, to prepare, with the assistance of technical experts representing the other capitulatory Powers, Allied or neutral, who with this object will each be invited to appoint an expert, a scheme of judicial reform to replace the present capitulatory system in judicial matters in Turkey. This Commission may recommend, after consultation with the Turkish Government, the adoption of either a mixed or an unified judicial system.

The scheme prepared by the Commission will be submitted to the Governments of the Allied and neutral Powers concerned. As soon as the Principal Allied Powers have approved the scheme they will inform the Turkish Government, which hereby agrees to accept the new system.

The Principal Allied Powers reserve the right to agree among themselves, and if necessary with the other Allied or neutral Powers concerned, as to the date on which the new system is to come into force.

ARTICLE 137.

Without prejudice to the provisions of Part VII (Penalties), no inhabitant of Turkey shall be disturbed or molested, under any pretext whatever, on account of any political or military action taken by him, or any assistance of any kind given by him to the Allied Powers, or their nationals, between August 1, 1914, and the coming into force of the present Treaty; all sentences pronounced against any inhabitant of Turkey for the above reasons shall be completely annulled, and any proceedings already instituted shall be arrested.

ARTICLE 138.

No inhabitant of territory detached from Turkey in accordance with the present Treaty shall be disturbed or molested on account of his political attitude after August 1, 1914, or of the determination of his nationality effected in accordance with the present Treaty.

ARTICLE 139.

Turkey renounces formally all rights of suzerainty or jurisdiction of any kind over Moslems who are subject to the sovereignty or protectorate of any other State.

No power shall be exercised directly or indirectly by any Turkish authority whatever in any territory detached from Turkey or of which the existing status under the present Treaty is recognised by Turkey.

PART IV.

PROTECTION OF MINORITIES.

ARTICLE 140.

Turkey undertakes that the stipulations contained in Articles 141, 145 and 147 shall be recognised as fundamental laws, and that no civil or military law or regulation, no Imperial Iradeh nor official action shall conflict or interfere with these stipulations, nor shall any law, regulation, Imperial Iradeh nor official action prevail over them.

ARTICLE 141.

Turkey undertakes to assure full and complete protection of life and liberty to all inhabitants of Turkey without distinction of birth, nationality, language, race or religion. All inhabitants of Turkey shall be entitled to the free exercise, whether public or private, of any creed, religion or belief.

The penalties for any interference with the free exercise of the right referred to in the preceding paragraph shall be the same whatever may be the creed concerned.

ARTICLE 142.

Whereas, in view of the terrorist regime which has existed in Turkey since November 1, 1914, conversions to Islam could not take place under normal conditions, no conversions since that date are recognised and all persons who were non-Moslems before November 1, 1914, will be considered as still remaining such, unless, after regaining their liberty, they voluntarily perform the necessary formalities for embracing the Islamic faith.

In order to repair so far as possible the wrongs inflicted on individuals in the course of the massacres perpetrated in Turkey during the war, the Turkish Government undertakes to afford all the assistance in its power or in that of the Turkish authorities in the search for and deliverance of all persons, of whatever race or religion, who have disappeared, been carried off, interned or placed in captivity since November 1, 1914.

The Turkish Government undertakes to facilitate the operations of mixed commissions appointed by the Council of the League of Nations to receive the complaints of the victims themselves, their families or their relations, to make the necessary enquiries, and to order the liberation of the persons in question.

The Turkish Government undertakes to ensure the execution of the decisions of these commissions, and to assure the security and the liberty of the persons thus restored to the full enjoyment of their rights.

ARTICLE 143.

Turkey undertakes to recognise such provisions as the Allied Powers may consider opportune with respect to the reciprocal and voluntary emigration of persons belonging to racial minorities.

Turkey renounces any right to avail herself of the provisions of Article I6 of the Convention between Greece and Bulgaria relating to reciprocal emigration, signed at Neuilly-sur-Seine on November 27, 1919. Within six months from the coming into force of the present Treaty, Greece and Turkey will enter into a special arrangement relating to the reciprocal and voluntary emigration of the populations of Turkish and Greek race in the territories transferred to Greece and remaining Turkish respectively.

In case agreement cannot be reached as to such arrangement, Greece and Turkey will be entitled to apply to the Council of the League of Nations, which will fix the terms of such arrangement.

ARTICLE 144.

The Turkish Government recognises the injustice of the law of 1915 relating to Abandoned Properties (Emval-i-Metroukeh), and of the supplementary provisions thereof, and declares them to be null and void, in the past as in the future.

The Turkish Government solemnly undertakes to facilitate to the greatest possible extent the return to their homes and re-establishment in their businesses of the Turkish subjects of non-Turkish race who have been forcibly driven from their homes by fear of massacre or any other form of pressure since January 1, 1914. It recognises that any immovable or movable property of the said Turkish subjects or of the communities to which they belong, which

can be recovered, must be restored to them as soon as possible, in whatever hands it may be found. Such property shall be restored free of all charges or servitudes with which it may have been burdened and without compensation of any kind to the present owners or occupiers, subject to any action which they may be able to bring against the persons from whom they derived title.

The Turkish Government agrees that arbitral commissions shall be appointed by the Council of the League of Nations wherever found necessary. These commissions shall each be composed of one representative of the Turkish Government, one representative of the community which claims that it or one of its members has been injured, and a chairman appointed by the Council of the League of Nations. These arbitral commissions shall hear all claims covered by this Article and decide them by summary procedure.

The arbitral commissions will have power to order:

(1) The provision by the Turkish Government of labour for any work of reconstruction or restoration deemed necessary. This labour shall be recruited from the races inhabiting the territory where the arbitral commission considers the execution of the said works to be necessary;

(2) The removal of any person who, after enquiry, shall be recognised as having taken an active part in massacres or deportations or as having provoked them; the measures to be taken with regard to such person's possessions will be indicated by the commission;

(3) The disposal of property belonging to members of a community who have died or disappeared since January 1, 1914, without leaving heirs; such property may be handed over to the community instead of to the State;

(4) The cancellation of all acts of sale or any acts creating rights over immovable property concluded after January 1, 1914. The indemnification of the holders will be a charge upon the Turkish Government, but must not serve as a pretext for delaying the restitution. The arbitral commission will, however have the power to impose equitable arrangements between the interested parties, if any sum has been paid by the present holder of such property.

The Turkish Government undertakes to facilitate in the fullest possible measure the work of the commissions and to ensure the execution of their decisions, which will be final. No decision of the Turkish judicial or administrative authorities shall prevail over such decisions.

ARTICLE 145.

All Turkish nationals shall be equal before the law and shall enjoy the same civil and political rights without distinction as to race, language or religion.

Difference of religion, creed or confession shall not prejudice any Turkish national in matters relating to the enjoyment of civil or political rights, as for instance admission to public employments, functions and honours, or the exercise of professions and industries.

Within a period of two years from the coming into force of the present Treaty the Turkish Government will submit to the Allied Powers a scheme for the organisation of an electoral system based on the principle of proportional representation of racial minorities.

No restriction shall be imposed on the free use by any Turkish national of any language in private intercourse, in commerce, religion, in the press or in publications of any kind, or at public meetings. Adequate facilities shall be given to Turkish nationals of non-Turkish speech for the use of their language, either orally or in writing, before the courts.

ARTICLE 146.

The Turkish Government undertakes to recognize the validity of diplomas granted by recognised foreign universities and schools, and to admit the holders thereof to the free exercise of the professions and industries for which such diplomas qualify.

This provision will apply equally to nationals of Allied powers who are resident in Turkey.

ARTICLE 147.

Turkish nationals who belong to racial, religious or linguistic minorities shall enjoy the same treatment and security in law and in fact as other Turkish nationals. In particular they shall have an equal right to establish, manage and control at their own expense, and independently of and without interference by the Turkish authorities, any charitable, religious and social institutions, schools for primary, secondary and higher instruction and other educational establishments, with the right to use their own language and to exercise their own religion freely therein.

ARTICLE 148.

In towns and districts where there is a considerable proportion of Turkish nationals belonging to racial, linguistic or religious minorities, these minorities shall be assured an equitable share in the enjoyment and application of the sums which may be provided out of public funds under the State, municipal or other budgets for educational or charitable purposes.

The sums in question shall be paid to the qualified representatives of the communities concerned.

ARTICLE 149.

The Turkish Government undertakes to recognise and respect the ecclesiastical and scholastic autonomy of all racial minorities in Turkey. For this purpose, and subject to any provisions to the contrary in the present Treaty, the Turkish Government confirms and will uphold in their entirety the prerogatives and immunities of an ecclesiastical, scholastic or judicial nature granted by the Sultans to non-Moslem races in virtue of special orders or imperial decrees (firmans, hattis, berats, etc.) as well as by ministerial orders or orders of the Grand Vizier.

All laws, decrees, regulations and circulars issued by the Turkish Government and containing abrogations, restrictions or amendments of such prerogatives and immunities shall be considered to such extent null and void.

Any modification of the Turkish judicial system which may be introduced in accordance with the provisions of the present Treaty shall be held to override this Article, in so far as such modification may affect individuals belonging to racial minorities.

ARTICLE 150.

In towns and districts where there is resident a considerable proportion of Turkish nationals of the Christian or Jewish religions the Turkish Government undertakes that such Turkish nationals shall not be compelled to perform any act which constitutes a violation of their faith or religious observances, and shall not be placed under any disability by reason of their refusal to attend courts of law or to perform any legal business on their weekly day of rest. This provision, however, shall not exempt such Turkish nationals (Christians or Jews) from such obligations as shall be imposed upon all other Turkish nationals for the preservation of public order.

ARTICLE 151.

The Principal Allied Powers, in consultation with the Council of the League of Nations, will decide what measures are necessary to guarantee the execution of the provisions of this Part. The Turkish Government hereby accepts all decisions which may be taken on this subject.

PART V.

MILITARY, NAVAL AND AIR CLAUSES.

In order to render possible the initiation of a general limitation of the armaments of all nations, Turkey undertakes strictly to observe the military, naval and air clauses which follow.

SECTION I.

MILITARY CLAUSES.

CHAPTER I. GENERAL CLAUSES. ARTICLE 152.

The armed force at the disposal of Turkey shall only consist of:

(1) The Sultan's bodyguard; (2) Troops of gendarmerie, intended to maintain order and security in the interior and to ensure the protection of minorities; (3) Special elements intended for the reinforcement of the troops of gendarmerie in case of serious trouble, and eventually to ensure the control of the frontiers.

ARTICLE 153.

Within six months from the coming into force of the present Treaty, the military forces other than that provided for in Article 152 shall be demobilised and disbanded.

CHAPTER II.

EFFECTIVES, ORGANISATION AND CADRES OF THE TURKISH ARMED FORCE.

ARTICLE 154.

The Sultan's bodyguard shall consist of a staff and infantry and cavalry units, the strength of which shall not exceed 700 officers and men. This strength is not included in the total force provided for in Article 155.

The composition of this guard is given in Table 1 annexed to this Section.

ARTICLE 155.

The total strength of the forces enumerated in paragraphs (2) and (3) of Article 152 shall not exceed 50,000 men, including staffs, officers, training personnel and depot troops.

ARTICLE 156.

The troops of gendarmerie shall be distributed over the territory of Turkey, which for this purpose will be divided into territorial areas to be delimited as provided in Article 200.

A legion of gendarmerie, composed of mounted and unmounted troops, provided with machine guns and with administrative and medical services will be organised in each territorial region, it will supply in the vilayets, sandjaks, cazas, etc., the detachments necessary for the organisation of a fixed protective service, mobile reserves being at its disposal at one or more points within the region.

On account of their special duties, the legions shall not include either artillery or technical services.

The total strength of the legions shall not exceed 35,000 men, to be included in the total strength of the armed force provided for in Article 155.

The maximum strength of any one legion shall not exceed one quarter of the total strength of the legions.

The elements of any one legion shall not be employed outside the territory of their region, except by special authorisation from the Inter-Allied Commission provided for in Article 200.

ARTICLE 157.

The special elements for reinforcements may include details of infantry, cavalry, mountain artillery, pioneers and the corresponding technical and general services; their total strength shall not exceed 15,000 men, to be included in the total strength provided for in Article 155.

The number of such reinforcements for any one legion shall not exceed one third of the whole strength of these elements without the special authority of the Inter-Allied Commission provided for in Article 200.

The proportion of the various arms and services entering into the composition of these special elements is laid down in Table II annexed to this Section.

Their quartering will be fixed as provided in Article 200.

ARTICLE 158.

In the formations referred to in Articles 156 and 157, the proportion of officers, including the personnel of staffs and special services, shall not exceed one twentieth of the total effectives with the colours, and that of non-commissioned officers shall not exceed one twelfth of the total effectives with the colours.

ARTICLE 159.

Officers supplied by the various Allied or neutral Powers shall collaborate, under the direction of the Turkish Government, in the command, the organisation and the training of the gendarmerie officers authorised by Article 158, but their number shall not exceed fifteen per cent. of that strength. Special agreements to be drawn up by the Inter-Allied Commission mentioned in Article 200 shall fix the proportion of these officers according to nationality, and shall determine the conditions of their participation in the various missions assigned to them by this Article.

ARTICLE 160.

In any one territorial region all officers placed at the disposal of the Turkish Government under the conditions laid down in Article 159 shall in principle be of the same nationality.

ARTICLE 161.

In the zone of the Straits and islands referred to in Article 178, excluding the islands of Lemnos, Imbros, Samothrace Tenedos and Mitylene, the forces (of Turkey), will be under the Inter-Allied Command of the forces in occupation of that zone.

ARTICLE 162.

All measures of mobilisation, or appertaining to mobilisation or tending to an increase of the strength or of the means of transport of any of the forces provided for in this Chapter are forbidden.

The various formations, staffs and administrative services shall not, in any case, include supplementary cadres.

ARTICLE 163.

Within the period fixed by Article 153, all existing forces of gendarmerie shall be amalgamated with the legions provided for in Article 156.

ARTICLE 164.

The formation of any body of troops not provided for in this Section is forbidden.

The suppression of existing formations which are in excess of the authorised strength of 50,000 men (not including the Sultan's bodyguard) shall be effected progressively from the date of the signature of the present Treaty, in such manner as to be completed within six months at the latest after the coming into force of the Treaty, in accordance with the provisions of Article 158.

The number of officers, or persons in the position of officers, in the War Ministry and the Turkish General Staff, as well as in the administrations attached to them, shall, within the same period, be reduced to the establishment considered by the Commission referred to in Article 200 as strictly necessary for the good working of the general services of the armed Turkish force, this establishment being included in the maximum figure laid down in Article 158.

CHAPTER III.
RECRUITING.
ARTICLE 165.

The Turkish armed force shall in future be constituted and recruited by voluntary enlistment only.

Enlistment shall be open to all subjects of the Turkish State equally, without distinction of race or religion.

As regards the legions referred to in Article 156, their system of recruiting shall be in principle regional, and so regulated that the Moslem and non-Moslem elements of the population of each region may be, so far as possible, represented on the strength of the corresponding legion.

The provisions of the preceding paragraphs apply to officers as well as to men.

ARTICLE 166.

The length of engagement of non-commissioned officers and men shall be twelve consecutive years.

The annual replacement of men released from service for any reason whatever before the expiration of their term of engagement shall not exceed five per cent. of the total effectives fixed by Article 155.

ARTICLE 167.

All officers must be regulars (officers de carrière).

Officers at present serving in the army or the gendarmerie who are retained in the new armed force must undertake to serve at least up to the age of forty-five.

Officers at present serving in the army or the gendarmerie who are not admitted to the new armed force shall be definitely released from all military obligations, and must not take part in any military exercises, theoretical or practical.

Officers newly-appointed must undertake to serve on the active list for at least twenty-five consecutive years.

The annual replacement of officers leaving the service for any cause before the expiration of their term of engagement shall not exceed five per cent. of the total effectives of officers provided by Article 158.

CHAPTER IV.

SCHOOLS, EDUCATIONAL ESTABLISHMENTS, MILITARY CLASS AND SOCIETIES

ARTICLE 168.

On the expiration of three months from the coming into force of the present Treaty there must only exist in Turkey the number of military schools which is absolutely indispensable for the recruitment of officers and non-commissioned officers of the units allowed, i. e.: school for officers;

1 school per territorial region for non-commissioned officers.

The number of students admitted to instruction in these schools shall be strictly in proportion to the vacancies to be filled in the cadres of officers and non-commissioned officers.

ARTICLE 169.

Educational establishments, other than those referred to in Article 168, as well as all sporting or other societies, must not occupy themselves with any military matters.

CHAPTER V.

CUSTOMS OFFICIALS, LOCAL URBAN AND RURAL POLICE, FOREST GUARDS.

ARTICLE 170.

Without prejudice to the provisions of Article 48, Part III (Political Clauses), the number of customs officials, local urban or rural police, forest guards or other like officials shall not exceed the number of men employed in a similar capacity in 1913 within the territorial limits of Turkey as fixed by the present Treaty.

The number of these officials may only be increased in the future in proportion to the increase of population in the localities or municipalities which employ them.

These employees and officials, as well as those employed in the railway service, must not be assembled for the purpose of taking part in any military exercises.

In each administrative district the local urban and rural police and forest guards shall be recruited and officered according to the principles laid down in the case of the gendarmerie by Article 165.

In the Turkish police, which, as forming part of the civil administration of Turkey, will remain distinct from the Turkish armed force, officers or officials supplied by the various Allied or neutral Powers shall collaborate, under the direction of the Turkish Government, in the organisation, the command and the training of the said police. The number of these officers or officials shall not exceed fifteen per cent. of the strength of similar Turkish officers or officials.

CHAPTER VI.

ARMAMENT, MUNITIONS AND MATERIAL

ARTICLE 171.

On the expiration of six months from the coming into force of the present Treaty, the armament which may be in use or held in reserve for replacement in the various formations of the Turkish armed force shall not exceed the figures fixed per thousand men in Table III annexed to this Section.

ARTICLE 172.

The stock of munitions at the disposal of Turkey shall not exceed the amounts fixed in Table III annexed to this Section.

ARTICLE 173.

Within six months from the coming into force of the present Treaty all existing arms, munitions of the various categories and war material in excess of the quantities authorised shall be handed over to the Military Inter-Allied Commission of Control provided for in Article 200 in such places as shall be appointed by this Commission.

The Principal Allied Powers will decide what is to be done with this material.

ARTICLE 174.

The manufacture of arms, munitions and war material, including aircraft and parts of aircraft of every description, shall take place only in the factories or establishments authorised by the Inter-Allied Commission referred to in Article 200.

Within six months from the coming into force of the present Treaty all other establishments for the manufacture, preparation, storage or design of arms, munitions or any war material shall be abolished or converted to purely commercial uses.

The same will apply to all arsenals other than those utilised as depots for the authorised stocks of munitions.

The plant of establishments or arsenals in excess of that required for the authorised manufacture shall be rendered useless or converted to purely commercial uses, in accordance with the decisions of the Military Inter-Allied Commission of Control referred to in Article 200.

ARTICLE 175.

The importation into Turkey of arms, munitions and war materials, including aircraft and parts of aircraft of every description, is strictly forbidden, except with the special authority of the Inter-Allied Commission referred to in Article 200.

The manufacture for foreign countries and the exportation of arms, munitions and war material of any description is also forbidden.

ARTICLE 176.

The use of flame-throwers, asphyxiating, poisonous or other gases and all similar liquids, materials or processes being forbidden, their manufacture and importation are strictly forbidden in Turkey.

Material specially intended for the manufacture, storage or use of the said products or processes is equally forbidden.

The manufacture and importation into Turkey of armoured cars, tanks or any other similar machines suitable for use in war are equally forbidden.

CHAPTER VII.

FORTIFICATIONS

ARTICLE 177.

In the zone of the Straits and islands referred to in Article 178 the fortifications will be disarmed and demolished as provided in that Article.

Outside this zone, and subject to the provisions of Article 89, the existing fortified works may be preserved in their present condition, but will be disarmed within the same period of three months.

CHAPTER VIII.

MAINTENANCE OF THE FREEDOM OF THE STRAITS

ARTICLE 178.

For the purpose of guaranteeing the freedom of the Straits, the High Contracting Parties agree to the following provisions:

(1) Within three months from the coming into force of the present Treaty, all works, fortifications and batteries within the zone defined in Article 179 and comprising the coast and islands of the Sea of Marmora and the coast of the Straits, also those in the Islands of Lemnos, Imbros, Samothrace, Tenedos and Mitylene, shall be disarmed and demolished.

The reconstruction of these works and the construction of similar works are forbidden in the above zone and islands. France, Great Britain and Italy shall have the right to prepare for demolition any existing roads and railways in the said zone and in the islands of Lemnos, Imbros, Samothrace, and Tenedos which allow of the rapid transport of mobile batteries, the construction there of such roads and railways remaining forbidden.

In the islands of Lemnos, Imbros, Samothrace and Tenedos the construction of new roads or railways must not be undertaken except with the authority of the three Powers mentioned above.

(2) The measures prescribed in the first paragraph of (1) shall be executed by and at the expense of Greece and Turkey as regards their respective territories, and under control as provided in Article 203.

(3) The territories of the zone and the islands of Lemnos, Imbros, Samothrace, Tenedos, and Mitylene shall not be used for military purposes, except by the three Allied Powers referred to above, acting in concert. This provision does not exclude the employment in the said zone and islands of forces of Greek and Turkish gendarmerie, who will be under the Inter-Allied command of the forces of occupation, in accordance with the provisions of Article 161, nor the maintenance of a garrison of Greek troops in the island of Mitylene, nor the presence of the Sultan's bodyguard referred to in Article 152.

(4) The said Powers, acting in concert, shall have the right to maintain in the said territories and islands such military and air forces as they may consider necessary to prevent any action being taken or prepared which might directly or indirectly prejudice the freedom of the Straits.

This supervision will be carried out in naval matters by a guard-ship belonging to each of the said Allied Powers.

The forces of occupation referred to above may, in case of necessity, exercise on land the right of requisition, subject to the same conditions as those laid down in the Regulations annexed to the Fourth Hague Convention, 1907, or any other Convention replacing it to which all the said Powers are parties. Requisitions shall, however, only be made against payment on the spot.

Source: Carnegie Endowment for International Peace. *The Treaties of Peace 1919–1923*, vol. 2. New York: Carnegie Endowment for International Peace, 1924.

Mustafa Kemal Ataturk to the National Convention of the People's Party of the Republic (1927)

During World War I, the decaying Ottoman Empire sided with the losing Central Powers of Germany and the Austro-Hungarian Empire. With that loss came the dismantling of the Ottoman Empire. Indeed, the very Turkish homeland on the Anatolian peninsula was threatened with dismemberment into its component nationalities. Kemal Mustafa, a Turkish commander, was able to save the integrity of the Turkish homeland, earning him the name Ataturk, "Father of the Turks." In this speech, Ataturk discusses how he saved the integrity of the Turkish nation during the collapse of the Ottoman Empire after World War I.

The General State of Affairs When I Disembarked at Samsun

Gentlemen,

I landed at Samsun on the nineteenth day of May of year 1919. This was the general state of affairs:

The group of Powers which included the Ottoman Government had been defeated in the Great War. The Ottoman Army had been crushed on every front. An armistice had been signed under severe conditions. The prolongation of the Great War had left the people exhausted and impoverished. Those who had driven the people and the country into the World War had fled and now cared for nothing but their own safety. Vahdettin, the degenerate occupant of the throne and the Caliphate, was seeking for some despicable way to save his person and his throne, the only objects of his anxiety. The Cabinet, of which Damat Ferit Pasha was the head, was weak and lacked dignity and courage. It was subservient to the will of the Sultan alone and agreed to every proposal that could protect its members and their sovereign.

The Army had been deprived of their arms and ammunition, and this state of affairs continued.

The Entente Powers did not consider it necessary to respect the terms of the armistice. On various pretexts, their men-of-war and troops remained at Istanbul. The Vilayet of Adana was occupied by the French; Urfa, Maras, Antep by the English. In Antalya and Konya were the Italians, whilst at Merzifon and Samsun were English troops. Foreign officers and officials and their special agents were very active everywhere. At last, on the 15th May, that is to say, four days before the following account of events begins, the Greek Army, with the consent of the Entente Powers, had landed at Izmir.

Christian elements were also at work all over the country, either openly or in secret, trying to realize their own particular ambitions and thereby hasten the breakdown of the State.

Certain information and authentic documents that fell into our hands later on prove that the Greek organisation "Mavri Mira," established by the patriarchate in Istanbul, was forming bands, organizing meetings and making propaganda in the vilayets. The Greek Red Cross and the Official Emigrants Commission supported the work of the "Mavri Mira." The formation of Boy Scouts in the Greek schools directed by the "Mavri Mira" were reinforced by the admission even of young men over twenty years of age.

The Armenian Patriarch, Zaven Efendi, also worked in connection with the "Mavri Mira." The preparations made by the Armenians progressed side by side with those made by the Greeks.

A society called the "Pontus" at Trabzon, Samsun and other places along the entire Black Sea coast, having their headquarters in Istanbul, worked openly and successfully.

Considered Means for Salvation

On account of the appalling seriousness of the situation which was apparent everywhere, particularly in all the vilayets, certain prominent personalities had begun to develop countermeasures to improve the situation. This resulted in new organisations being started. Thus, for instance, there were unions or societies at Edirne and surrounding districts called "Trakya-Pasaeli." In the east, at Erzurum and Elazig, the "Union of Defence of the National Rights of the Eastern Provinces" had been formed, also with their headquarters in Istanbul. Again, in Trabzon there was a society called the "Defence of Rights" and in Istanbul a "League for the Separation of Trabzon and its District." Through the exertions of the members of this league, sub-committees had been established at Of and in the district of Lazistan.

Some of the young patriots at Izmir, who since the 13th May had noticed distinct indications of the approaching occupation of the town, had held meetings about the distressing condition of affairs during the night of the 14th, and in principle had agreed to oppose the occupation by the Greeks, which at that time was considered to be practically an accomplished fact, designed to end in annexation, and resisted it on the principle of "No Annexation." During the same night, those of the inhabitants who were able to meet at the Jewish cemetery at Izmir drew up a protest and spread it broadcast. But as the Greek troops actually landed on the following morning this attempt failed to achieve the desired result.

National Organisations and their Political Aims

I would like to give you a short account of the object and political aims of these organisations.

I had already had a conversation in Istanbul with some of the leaders of the "Trakya-Pasaeli" Society. They considered that the breakdown of the Ottoman Empire was extremely probable. In face of the threatened danger of the dismemberment of their country, their first thought was to save Eastern Trakya and later on if possible, to form a Turco-Islamic community that would include Western Trakya. The only way by which they thought they could realize this aim was to put their trust in England or, if this was not possible, in France. With this object they tried to get in touch with certain political personalities belonging to foreign countries. It was believed that their intention was to establish a Trakya Republic.

The object of the "Defence of the National Rights of the Eastern Provinces Union," on the other hand (Article 2 of their regulations), was to use all lawful means to ensure the free exercise and development of their religious and political rights for all elements inhabiting these provinces; to defend, if it should become necessary, the historical and national rights of the Muslim population of these provinces; to institute an impartial inquiry for the purpose of discovering the motives, the instigators and agitators implicated in the extortions and cruelties committed in the Eastern Provinces, so that the guilty ones might be punished without delay; to do their utmost to remove the misunderstandings that existed between the different elements in the country, and to restore the good relations that had formerly existed between them; and, finally, to appeal to the Government to alleviate as far as it lay in their power the misery resulting from the war.

Acting on these principles that emanated from the Central Committee in Istanbul, the Erzurum Branch decided to undertake, in defence of the rights of the Turks, to inform the civilised world by means of convincing documents that since the deportation the people had been taking no part whatever in the excesses. Further, that the property of the Armenians had been protected up to the time when the country was invaded by the Russians. On the other hand that the muslims had been compelled to suffer from the cruelest acts of violence and that some Armenians who had been saved from deportation had, in disobedience of orders, attacked their own protectors. The Branch were doing their very best to resist any attempt to annex the Eastern Provinces. (Proclamation by the Erzurum Branch.)

The members of the Erzurum Branch of the "Defence of the National Rights of the Eastern Provinces" resolved, as stated in their printed report, after having studied the propaganda circulated in these provinces as well the Turkish, Kurdish and Armenian questions, from the scientific and historical point of view, to concentrate their further efforts on the following points:

1. On no account to emigrate;

2. Forthwith to form scientific, economic and religious organisations;

3. To unite in the defence of even the smallest part of the Eastern Provinces that might be attacked.

It can be seen that the headquarters of the "Defence of the National Rights of the Eastern Provinces" were far too optimistic in their expectation to succeed through civil and scientific means. They continued to exert themselves indefatigably in this direction. For the purpose of defending the rights of muslims dwelling in the Eastern Provinces they published a French journal, which they called "Le Pays." They acquired the right to publish a magazine called "Hadisat." They also presented memorials to the representatives of the Entente Powers in Istanbul and tried to send a delegation to Europe.

From the foregoing statements, it appears to me to be clearly evident that the possible cession of the Eastern Provinces to Armenia was the most important reason for this Society having been formed. They anticipated that this possibility might become a reality if those who tried to prove that the Armenians were in the majority in these provinces, claiming the oldest historical rights, were to succeed in misleading the public opinion of the world by alleged scientific and historic documents and by perpetuating the calumny that the muslim population was composed of savages whose chief occupation was to massacre the Armenians. Consequently, the Society aimed at the defence of the national and historic rights by corresponding methods and arguments.

The fear also existed that a Greek Pontic State might be founded on the shores of the Black Sea. At Trabzon several persons had formed another society with the object of protecting the rights of the muslim population, to safeguard their existence and prevent them from falling under the yoke of the Greeks.

Their political aim and programme is already sufficiently obvious from its name: "The Society for the Cession of the Territory of Trabzon," whose head office was in Istanbul. In any case, they set out with the idea of separating this district from the Central Government.

Organisations, in the Country and in Istanbul, Hostile to the National Existence

Besides these organisations, which were being formed in the manner I have described, other societies and enterprises began to make their appearance. In the provinces of Diyarbakir, Bitlis and Elazig, among others, there was a "League for the Resuscitation of the Kurds" with its head offices also in Istanbul. Their aim was to erect a Kurdish State under foreign protection.

Work was going on at Konya and the surrounding district for the formation of a league having for its object the revival of Islam—also with its offices in Istanbul. There were organisations named "Unity and Freedom" and "Peace and Salvation" throughout almost the whole country.

Society of the Friends of England

In Istanbul, there were numerous public and secret organizations calling themselves parties or societies and pursuing various aims.

One of the most important of these, the "Society of the Friends of England" is worthy of special mention. It does not follow from its name that its members were necessarily friends of England. In my opinion, the founders of this society were people who thought, before anything else, of their own safety and their own particular interests, and who tried to secure both by inducing Lloyd George's Government to afford them English protection. I wonder whether these misguided persons really imagined for a moment that the English Government had any idea at all of maintaining and preserving the Ottoman State in its integrity?

At the head of this Society were Vahdettin, who bore the title of Ottoman Sultan and Caliph, Damat Ferit Pasha, Ali Kemal, Minister of the Interior, Adil Bey, Mehmet Ali Bey, and Sait Molla. Certain English adventurers, for instance a clergyman named Frew, also belonged to this Society. Their correspondence and operation make it clear that clergyman Frew was their chairman.

The Society had a double face and a twofold character. On the one hand, it openly sought the protection of England by methods inspired by civilization. On the other, it worked in secret and showed that its real aim was to incite the people to revolt by forming organisations in the interior, to paralyse the national conscience and encourage foreign countries to interfere. These were the treacherous designs underlying the work of the secret section of the Society. We shall see later how Sait Molla played just as active a part, or even a still more important one, in this secret work as in the public enterprises of the Society. What I have just said about this Society will become much clearer to you when I enter into further particulars later on and lay before you certain documents which will astonish you.

Sympathizers for American Mandate

Certain prominent personalities—amongst them some women—in Istanbul were convinced that the real salvation of the country lay in securing an American protectorate over it. They stubbornly persisted in this idea and tried to prove that acceptance of their point of view was the only thing possible. About this I shall also have a great deal more to say at the proper time.

Condition of the Military Units

So that you may clearly appreciate the general situation, I would like to point out exactly where and in what condition the military units were at the time of which I am speaking. Two Army Inspections had been established on principle in Anatolia. Immediately after the conclusion of the armistice the regular soldiers at the front were disbanded. Deprived of their arms and ammunition, the Army consisted of units having no fighting value.

The distribution of the troops under the second Army Inspection, with its headquarters at Konya, was as follows: The XIIth Army Corps, with its Staff at Konya, consisted of one division—the 41st—at Konya and another—the 23rd—at Afyonkarahisar. To this Army Corps was attached the 57th Division, stationed at Denizli, belonging to the XVIIth Army Corps, which had been captured at Izmir.

The XXth Corps and its Staff was stationed at Ankara—one of its divisions, the 24th, in Ankara itself and the other, the 11th, at Nigde.

The 1st Division stationed at Izmit was attached to the XXVth Army Corps, which also included the Caucasian Division.

The 61st and 56th Divisions were quartered in the district of Balikesir and Bursa and formed the XIVth Army Corps, with headquarters at Bandirma and directly under the command of Istanbul. The late Yusuf Izzet Pasha commanded this Army Corps until the National Assembly was opened.

I was myself at the head of the third Inspection when I landed with my Staff at Samsun. I was to have had two Army Corps under my personal command: One of them, the IIIrd, had its base at Sivas and was commanded by Colonel Refet Bey, who came with me to Samsun. One division of this Corps, the 5th Caucasian, was at Amasya; the other, the 15th, was at Samsun. The second Army Corps under my command was the XVth, stationed at Erzurum and commanded by Kazim Karabekir Pasha. One of his divisions, commanded by Rustu Bey, was in garrison at Erzurum; the other, the 3rd, under the command of Lt. Colonel Halit Bey, was at Trabzon. After Halit Bey had been called to Istanbul, he abandoned his command and hid himself at Bayburt. Another man took command temporarily of the division.

One of the two remaining divisions of the Army Corps, the 12th, was near Hasankale, on the eastern frontier, and the 11th was at Bayazit.

The XIIIth Army Corps consisted of two divisions stationed in the district of Diyarbakir and was independent, as it was directly under Istanbul. One of its divisions, the 2nd, was at Siirt, while the other, the 5th, was at Mardin.

Broad Powers of My Inspection Duty

These two Army Corps were directly under my command and I was also authorized to give orders to other troops lying within the district of my Inspection, in all the Vilayets comprised within it and in the neighbouring provinces.

In virtue of the authority vested in me, I had the right to enter into communication and correspondence with the XXth Army Corps at Ankara, with its superior Army Inspection, as well as with the Army Corps at Diyarbakir and the heads of the Civil Administration in nearly the whole of Anadolu.

You might, perhaps, be inclined to ask why those who sent me to Anadolu with the idea of banishing me from Istanbul entrusted me with such wide powers. The answer is, that they did not know themselves what they were doing. They invented the pretext that it was necessary for me to go to Samsun to report on the spot on the unsettled condition of the district and to take the necessary measures to deal with it. I had pointed out that in order to do this I should be given special authority and special powers. There did not seem to be any objection to this. I discussed the question with men who were on the General Staff at that time and who to a certain extent guessed my intentions. These were the persons who conceived the idea of my taking up the position, and I dictated the order giving me full powers. Apparently Sakir Pasha, the Minister of War, after reading them, hesitated to sign them and his seal that was attached to the document was scarcely recognizable.

Closer Examination of the State of Affairs

Let us return to a closer examination of the facts, so that we may rapidly review them as a whole.

Morally and materially, the enemy Powers were openly attacking the Ottoman Empire and the country itself. They were determined to disintegrate and annihilate both. The Padisah-Caliph had one sole anxiety—namely, to save his own life and comfort. The members of the government had the same feeling. Without being aware of it, the nation had no longer anyone to lead it, but lived in darkness and uncertainty, waiting to see what would happen. Those who began to understand clearly the terrors and the extent of the catastrophe were seeking some means whereby to save the country, each guided by the circumstances that surrounded him and the sentiments that inspired him. The Army existed merely in name. The commanders and other officers were still suffering from the exhaustion resulting from the war. Their hearts were bleeding on account of the threatened dismemberment of their country. Standing on the brink of the dark abyss which yawned before their eyes, they racked their brains to discover a way out of the danger . . .

Here I must add and explain a very important point. The Nation and the Army had no suspicion at all of the Padisah-Caliph's treachery. On the contrary, on account of religious and traditional ties handed down for centuries, they remained loyal to the throne and its occupant. Seeking for means of salvation under the influence of this tradition, the security of the Caliphate and the Sultanate concerned them far more than their own safety. That the country could possibly be saved without a Caliph and without a Padisah was an idea too impossible for them to comprehend. And woe to those who ventured to think otherwise! They would immediately have been looked down upon as men without faith and without patriotism and as such would have been scorned.

I must mention another point here. In seeking ways to save the situation, it was considered to be specially important to avoid irritating the Great Powers—England, France and Italy. The idea that it was impossible to fight even one of these Powers had taken root in the mind of nearly everybody. Consequently, to think of doing so and thus bring on another war after the Ottoman Empire, all-powerful Germany and Austria-Hungary together had been defeated and crushed would have been looked upon as sheer madness.

Not only the mass of the people thought in this strain, but those also who must be regarded as their chosen leaders shared the same opinion.

Therefore, in seeking a way out of the difficulty, two questions had to be eliminated from discussion. First of all, no hostility was to be shown towards the Entente Powers; secondly, the most important thing of all was to remain, heart and soul, loyal to the Padisah-Caliph.

Considered Means for Salvation

Now, Gentlemen, I will ask you what decision could have been arrived at under such circumstances for salvation?

As I have already explained, there were three propositions that had been put forward:

1. To demand protection from England;

2. To accept the United States of America as a mandatory Power.

The originators of these two proposals had as their aim the preservation of the Ottoman Empire in its complete integrity and preferred to place it as a whole under the protection of a single Power, rather than allow it to be divided among several States.

3. The third proposal was to deliver the country by allowing each district to act in its own way and according to its own capability. Thus, for instance, certain districts, in opposition to the theory of separation, endeavoured to remain an integral part of the Empire. Others holding a different opinion already appeared to regard the dismemberment of the Empire as an accomplished fact and sought only their own safety.

My above explanations are inclusive of the leading motives of these three kinds of propositions.

My Decision

I did not think any of these three proposals could be accepted as sagacious, because the arguments and considerations on which they were based were groundless. In reality, the foundations of the Ottoman Empire were themselves shattered at that time. Its existence was threatened with extermination. All the Ottoman districts were practically dismembered. Only the fatherland, affording protection to a mere handful of Turks, still remained, and it was now suggested also to divide this. Such expressions as: the Ottoman Empire, Independence, Padisah-Caliph, Government—all of them were mere meaningless words.

Whose existence was it essential to save? And with whose help? And how?

Therefore, what could be a serious and correct resolution?

In these circumstances, one resolution alone was possible, namely, to create a New Turkish State, the sovereignty and independence of which would be unreservedly recognized.

This was the resolution we adopted before we left Istanbul and which we began to put into execution immediately after we set foot on Anadolu soil at Samsun.

Independence or Death

These were the most logical and most powerful arguments in support of this resolution:

The foundational principle is that the Turkish nation should live in honour and dignity. Such a condition can only be attained by complete independence. No matter how wealthy and prosperous a nation is, if it is deprived of its independence it no longer deserves to be regarded otherwise than as a slave in the eyes of civilised world.

To accept the protectorate of a foreign Power is to admit lack of all human qualities, weakness and incapacity. It is not at all thinkable that those who have never been in such a humiliating state, will appoint a foreign master out of their own desire.

But the Turk is both dignified and proud; he is also capable and talented. Such a nation will prefer to perish rather than subject itself to the life of a slave.

Therefore, Independence or Death!

This was the rallying cry of all those who honestly desired to save their country.

Let us suppose for a moment that in trying to accomplish this we had failed. What would have been the result?—Why slavery!

In that case, would not the consequence have been the same if we had submitted to the other proposals?

Undoubtedly, it would; but with this difference, that a nation that defies death in its struggle for independence drives comfort from the thought that it had resolved to make every sacrifice compatible with human dignity. There is no doubt whatever that in the eyes of both friend and foe throughout the world its position is more respected than would be that of a craven and degraded nation capable of surrendering itself to the yoke of slavery.

Moreover, to labour for the maintenance of the Ottoman dynasty and its sovereign would have

been to inflict the greatest harm upon the Turkish nation; for, if its independence could have been secured at the price of every possible sacrifice, it could not have been regarded as secure so long as the Sultanate existed. How could it be deemed permissable that a crowd of madmen, united by neither a moral nor a spiritual bond to the country or the nation as a whole, could still be trusted to protect the independence and the dignity of the nation and the State?

As for the Caliphate, it would only have been the laughing-stock in the eyes of the civilised world, enjoying the blessings of science and technology.

As you see, in order to carry out our resolution, questions had to be dealt with about which the nation had hitherto known practically nothing. It was imperative that questions which were considered dangerous to discuss publicly be discussed openly.

We were compelled to rebel against the Ottoman Government, against the Padisah, against the Caliph of all muslims, and we had to bring the whole nation and the army into a state of rebellion.

Dividing the Implementation into Stages and Reaching the Aim by Degrees

It was essential that the entire nation take up arms against whoever would venture to attack the fatherland of Turks and Turkish independence. It would undoubtedly have been of little advantage if we had made clear to the public at the very beginning all the implications of a resolution of such far-reaching importance. On the contrary, it was necessary to proceed by stages, utilizing all opportunities to prepare the feeling and the spirit of the nation and to try to reach our aim by degrees. This is actually what happened. If our attitude and our actions during nine years are examined in their logical sequence, however, it becomes evident that our general behaviour has never deviated from the lines laid down in our original resolution, nor from the purpose we had set out to achieve.

In order to dispel any doubts which might be entertained, one fact is urged upon us for mutual examination.

As the national struggle, carried on for the sole purpose of delivering the country from foreign invasion, developed and was crowned with success, it was natural and inevitable that it would gradually, step by step to the present day, have established all the principles and forms essential in government founded on national sovereignty. The sovereign of the dynasty who, thanks to his traditional instincts, foresaw this fatal course of historical events, declared himself from the very beginning the most embittered enemy of the national struggle. I, also from the first moment on, anticipated this historical progress. But I did not disclose all of my views although I have maintained them all the time. If I had spoken too much about future prospects our realistic endeavours would have been looked upon as dreams; and consequently from the outset it would have caused the alienation of those who—discouraged by the closeness of dangers that threatened from without—were fearful of possible changes which would be contrary to their tradition, their way of thinking and their psychology. The only practical and safe road to success lay in dealing with each problem at the right time. This was the way to ensure the development and restoration of the nation. This was how I acted. This practical and safe way to success, however, caused certain differences of opinion between me and some individuals reputed to be my most intimate co-workers sometimes in regard to principles, at other times as to the method and the execution of our programme and it even caused friction between us that led to discouragement, and dissension. Some of my companions who had entered into the national fight with me went over to the opposition, according as the limitation of their own mental appreciation led them and their moral courage succumbed in the effort to develop national life, to proclaim the Republic and enact its laws. So that you may be informed, so that the public opinion be enlightened, I shall refer to these cases individually as I proceed with my statement.

National Secret

To summarize what I have been saying, I may add that it was incumbent upon me to develop our entire social organisation, step by step, until it corresponded to the great capability of progress which I perceived in the soul and future of the nation and which I kept to myself in my own consciousness as a national secret.

Contact with the Army

My first object now, Gentlemen, was to get into touch with the whole Army.

In a telegram in cipher, on the 21st May, 1919, I told the commander of the XVth Army Corps at Erzurum that I was greatly distressed at the seriousness of our general situation; that I had accepted my present position in the certainty that it would be possible to fulfil our highest duty towards the nation and the country if we worked together with all our strength; that although I had wanted to go to Erzurum before this, I was obliged to remain for a few days longer at Samsun, because serious events were threatening the position there, which was very uncertain. I further asked him, if he thought it necessary, to keep me well informed about anything I ought to know.

In fact, the position had been made considerably worse by attacks that had been made by Greek bands against the Muslims at Samsun and its surroundings, as well as many difficulties that had been placed in the way of the local government by foreign interference, the former being incapable of rendering any resistance.

Whilst I was undertaking steps to secure the appointment of a person well known to us and from whom we expected a great deal as Mutasarrif of Samsun, I was provisionally appointed the commander of the XIIIth Army Corps Governor of Canik. Besides this, we took all steps that were possible on the spot itself: that is to say, we enlightened the population as to the real state of affairs and told them that they need not be alarmed about foreign bodies of troops or their officers being among them, and to do nothing to resist them. The formation of national organisations was immediately undertaken in this district.

On the 23rd May, 1919, I informed the commander of the XXth Army Corps at Ankara that I had arrived at Samsun and would keep in close touch with him. I requested him to inform me about everything he could ascertain concerning the district of Izmir.

Before I had left Istanbul I had turned my attention to the position of this Army Corps. It had been suggested that it should be transported by rail from the south to the district of Ankara, but being well aware of the resistance attending this, I asked Cevat Pasha, the Chief of the General Staff, during the days preceding my departure from Istanbul to lead the Army Corps to Ankara on foot, in case the transport by rail would involve any delay. For this purpose, I inquired in the telegram in cipher I have already mentioned, whether all the units belonging to the XXth Army Corps would succeed in reaching Ankara. After having added certain information about the district of Canik, I announced that in a few days I would be going with my Staff from Samsun to Havza for some time and that I hoped, in any case, to receive the required information before my departure.

In his reply, which arrived three days later, on the 26th May, the commander of the XXth Army Corps reported that he had not received any regular communication from Izmir; that the occupation of Manisa had been reported by telegraph office employees, that the detachments belonging to the Army Corps stationed at Eregli had already left on foot as it was impossible to transport them by rail, but that, because of the great distance they had to march, it was uncertain when they would arrive.

In the same telegram the commander of the Corps remarked that the actual strength of the 23rd Division at Afyonkarahisar was low and that for this reason all the men that could be mustered had been ordered to join this division. He added that news had recently been received about local unrest in the districts of Kastamonu and Kayseri, and that he would keep me well informed.

In a dispatch dated the 27th May, 1919, from Havza, I ordered the commander of the XXth Army Corps and the Army Inspection at Konya, under whose command this Corps was, to inform me from what sources the reinforcements destined for the division at Afyonkarahisar were being drawn; whether there was any practical possibility of reinforcing them and what in the present circumstances their duty would be.

On the 28th May the commander of the Corps gave me the information. I had been awaiting: "In case of any attempt at occupation by the enemy, the 23rd Division will not surrender its position, but if it is attacked it will defend it, recruiting reinforcements from among the inhabitants."

On the 30th May the Inspector of the Army replied: "While maintaining order and security at Karahisar at the same time, the 23rd Division will resist any attempt at occupation with all the means at their disposition." He reported that he was making all preparations and that he was trying to collect reinforcements at Konya, but that it had no name or title.

In my telegram to the Army Inspector, I had said: "Rumours are in circulation about the raising of an army at Konya which is called the 'Patriotic Army'. What is its composition and how is it organised?" I asked this question, because I wanted to encourage it and hasten it on. I received the reply I have already mentioned in response to this question.

The commander of the Corps had replied to the same question, saying that he knew nothing about the formation of a "Patriotic Army" at Konya.

On the 1st of June I informed the commanders of the XVth Army Corps at Erzurum, of the IIIrd at Samsun and of the XIIIth at Diyarbakir of the intelligence that had reached me through my communication with the XXth Army Corps and the Inspection at Konya, as far as it concerned them.

I had received no information about the troops in Trakya or their commander and had, therefore, applied to Cevat Pasha, Chief of the General Staff in Istanbul, in a telegram in cipher on the 16th June, 1919, (I had arranged a private cipher personally with Cevat Pasha before I left), asking him to tell me who was in command of the Army Corps at Edirne and where Cafer Tayyar Bey was. On the 17th June, Cevat Pasha replied: "I have been informed that Cafer Tayyar is at Edirne in command of the 1st Army Corps."

The report I sent in cipher on the 18th June, 1919, to Cafer Tayyar Bey, commanding the 1st Army Corps at Edirne, mainly contained the following: "You are aware of the actions the Entente Powers, which strangle our national independence and the way for the disintegration of our country; you have also heard of the servile and apathetic attitude of the Government."

"To confide the fate of the nation to the hands of a Government of this type means to abandon it to ruin."

"It has been decided to set up an energetic assembly at Sivas—which is a safe place—for the purpose of bringing together the national organisation of Trakya and Anadolu, so that they can boldly proclaim the voice of the nation before the whole world."

"The League of Trakya-Pasaeli may have a representative corporation in Istanbul, but they are not provided with full powers."

"When I was in Istanbul I spoke to several members of the Trakya League. Now is the time for us to begin. After you have spoken in confidence to these people you will immediately begin to form the necessary organisations. Send one or two competent men to me as delegates. Before they arrive send me a telegram in cipher, signed by yourself, giving me authority to uphold the rights of the Vilayet of Edirne."

"I have sworn by everything I hold sacred that I shall work loyally and devotedly with the nation until we have gained our complete independence. I have firmly resolved not to leave Anadolu."

In order to raise the spirits of the inhabitants of Trakya, I added the following: "From one end to the other of Anadolu the population is united. All decisions are taken jointly by all the commanders and our comrades. Nearly all the Valis and Mutasarrifs are on our side. The national organisation in Anadolu comprises every district and community. The propaganda aiming at the erection of an independent Kurdistan under English protectorate has been successfully countered and the followers of this movement have been dispersed. The Kurds have joined the Turks."

Source: Internet Ataturk Library, Ministry of Education, Ankara, Turkey. http://ataturk.turkiye.org/soylev/spchtm/spcsh-1.htm.

RUSSIAN EMPIRE

Lease of Port Arthur (1898)

Manchuria, a vast and resource-rich province in northeastern China, was coveted by both Russia and Japan. As the only year-round, ice-free harbor in the province, Port Arthur (now Lüshun) was of especial interest to both expanding empires. Through bullying a weakened Chinese government and bribing the right officials, Russia was able to win a twenty-five-year lease on the harbor and the rights to build a railroad that would connect it to the trans-Siberian railway. In 1904, the Japanese would launch a surprise naval attack against the port, eventually winning it in the Treaty of Portsmouth that ended the Russo-Japanese war in 1905.

Article I. It being necessary for the due protection of her navy in the waters of North China that Russia should possess a station she can defend, the Emperor of China agrees to lease to Russia Port Arthur and Ta-lien-wan, together with the adjacent seas, but on the understanding that such lease shall not prejudice China's sovereignty over this territory. . . .

Article III. The duration of the lease shall be twenty-five years from the day this treaty is signed, but may be extended by mutual agreement between Russia and China.

Article IV. The control of all military forces in the territory leased by Russia, and of all naval forces in the adjacent seas, as well as of the civil officials in it, shall be vested in one high Russian official, who shall, however, be designated by some title other than Governor-General (Tsungtu) or Governor (Hsün-fu). All Chinese military forces shall, without exception, be withdrawn from the territory, but it shall remain optional with the ordinary Chinese inhabitants either to remain or to go; and no coercion shall be used towards them in this matter. . . .

Article VI. The two nations agree that Port Arthur shall be a naval port for the sole use of Russian and Chinese men-of-war, and be considered as an unopened port so far as the naval and mercantile vessels of other nations are concerned. As regards Ta-lien-wan, one portion of the harbour shall be reserved exclusively for Russian and Chinese men-of-war, just like Port Arthur, but the remainder shall be a commercial port freely open to the merchant vessels of all countries.

Article VII. Port Arthur and Ta-lien-wan are the points in the territory leased most important for Russian military purposes. Russia shall, therefore, be at liberty to erect, at her own expense, forts, and build barracks and provide defences at such places as she desires.

Article VIII. China agrees that the procedure sanctioned in 1896 regarding the construction of railroads by the Board of the Eastern China Railway shall, from the date of the signature of this treaty, be extended so as to include the construction of a branch line to Ta-lien-wan, or, if necessary, in view of the interests involved, of a branch line to the most suitable point on the coast between Newchang and the Yalu River. Further, the agreement entered into in September 1896 between the Chinese Government and the Russo-Chinese Bank shall also apply with equal strength to this branch line. The direction of this branch and the places it shall touch shall be arranged between Hsu Ta-jen and the Board of the Eastern Railroads. The construction of this line shall never, however, be made a ground for encroaching on the sovereignty or integrity of China.

Source: "Vladimir." *Russia on the Pacific and the Siberian Railway.* London, 1899.

SPANISH EMPIRE

Privileges and Prerogatives Granted by Their Catholic Majesties to Christopher Columbus (1492)

To finance his costly expeditions westward across the ocean to East Asia in 1492, Christopher Columbus won the backing of the king and queen of Spain. In this letter, the twin monarchs offer Columbus the post of admiral. More notable, they describe his mission as one of discovery and conquest, a rather remarkable chore given the fact that his destination was China, one of the wealthiest and most powerful nations on Earth at the time.

FERDINAND and ISABELLA, by the Grace of God, King and Queen of *Castile*, of *Leon*, of *Arragon*, of *Sicily*, of *Granada*, of *Toledo*, of *Valencia*, of *Galicia*, of *Majorca*, of *Minorca*, of *Sevil*, of *Sardinia*, of *Jaen*, of *Algarve*, of *Algezira*, of *Gibraltar*, of the *Canary Islands*, Count and Countess of *Barcelona*, Lord and Lady of *Biscay* and *Molina*, Duke and Duchess of *Athens* and *Neopatria*. Count and Countess of *Rousillion* and *Cerdaigne*, Marquess and Marchioness of *Oristan* and *Gociano*, &c.

For as much as you, *Christopher Columbus,* are going by our command, with some of our vessels and men, to discover and subdue some Islands and Continent in the ocean, and it is hoped that by God's assistance, some of the said Islands and Continent in the ocean will be discovered and conquered by your means and conduct, therefore it is but just and reasonable, that since you expose yourself to such danger to serve us, you should be rewarded for it. And we being willing to honour and favour You for the reasons aforesaid: Our will

is, That you, *Christopher Columbus,* after discovering and conquering the said Islands and Continent in the said ocean, or any of them, shall be our Admiral of the said Islands and Continent you shall so discover and conquer; and that you be our Admiral, Vice-Roy, and Governour in them, and that for the future, you may call and stile yourself, D. *Christopher Columbus,* and that your sons and successors in the said employment, may call themselves Dons, Admirals, Vice-Roys, and Governours of them; and that you may exercise the office of Admiral, with the charge of Vice-Roy and Governour of the said Islands and Continent, which you and your Lieutenants shall conquer, and freely decide all causes, civil and criminal, appertaining to the said employment of Admiral, Vice-Roy, and Governour, as you shall think fit in justice, and as the Admirals of our kingdoms use to do; and that you have power to punish offenders; and you and your Lieutenants exercise the employments of Admiral, Vice-Roy, and Governour, in all things belonging to the said offices, or any of them; and that you enjoy the perquisites and salaries belonging to the said employments, and to each of them, in the same manner as the High Admiral of our kingdoms does. And by this our letter, or a copy of it signed by a *Public Notary:* We command Prince *John,* our most dearly beloved Son, the Infants, Dukes, Prelates, Marquesses, Great Masters and Military Orders, Priors, Commendaries, our Counsellors, Judges, and other Officers of Justice whatsoever, belonging Courts, and Chancery, and Constables of Castles, Strong Houses, and others; and all Corporations, Bayliffs, Governours, Judges, Commanders, Sea Officers; and the Aldermen,

Common Council, Officers, and Good People of all Cities, Lands, and Places in our Kingdoms and Dominions, and in those you shall conquer and subdue, and the captains masters, mates, and other officers and sailors, our natural subjects now being, or that shall be for the time to come, and any of them that when you shall have discovered the said Islands and Continent in the ocean; and you, or any that shall have your commission, shall have taken the usual oath in such cases, that they for the future, look upon you as long as you live, and after you, your son and heir, and so from one heir to another forever, as our Admiral on our said Ocean, and as Vice-Roy and Governour of the said Islands and Continent, by you, *Christopher Columbus,* discovered and conquered; and that they treat you and your Lieutenants, by you appointed, for executing the employments of Admiral, Vice-Roy, and Governour, as such in all respects, and give you all the perquisites and other things belonging and appertaining to the said offices; and allow, and cause to be allowed you, all the honours, graces, concessions, prehaminences, prerogatives, immunities, and other things, or any of them which are due to you, by virtue of your commands of Admiral, Vice-Roy, and Governour, and to be observed completely, so that nothing be diminished; and that they make no objection to this, or any part of it, nor suffer it to be made; forasmuch as we from this time forward, by this our letter, bestow on you the employments of Admiral, Vice-Roy, and perpetual Governour forever; and we put you into possession of the said offices, and of every of them, and full power to use and exercise them, and to receive the perquisites and salaries belonging to them, or any of them, as was said above. Concerning all which things, if it be requisite, and you shall desire it, We command our Chancellour, Notaries, and other Officers, to pass, seal, and deliver to you, our Letter of Privilege, in such form and legal manner, as you shall require or stand in need of. And that none of them presume to do any thing to the contrary, upon pain of our displeasure, and forfeiture of 30 ducats for each offence. And we command him, who shall show them this our Letter, that he summon them to appear before us at our Court, where we shall then be, within fifteen days after such summons, under the said penalty. Under which same, we also command any Public Notary whatsoever, that he give to him that shows

it him, a certificate under his seal, that we may know how our command is obeyed.

GIVEN at *Granada,* on the 30th of April, in the year of our Lord, 1492.

I, THE KING, I, THE QUEEN.
By their Majesties Command,
John Coloma
Secretary to the King and Queen.
Entered according to order.
RODERICK. Doctor.
SEBASTIAN DOLONA,
FRANCIS DE MADRID,
Councellors.
Registered

Source: Thorpe, Francis Newton. *The Federal and State Constitutions, Colonial Charters, and Other Organic Laws of the States, Territories, and Colonies Now or Heretofore Forming the United States of America.* Washington, DC: Government Printing Office, 1909.

Columbus's Letter to the King and Queen of Spain (1494)

As this letter from Christopher Columbus to King Ferdinand and Queen Isabella of Spain indicates, the primary concern behind the settlement of the island of Hispaniola (spelled Espanola in the letter) was the discovery and processing of the gold that Columbus believed to be abundant on the island. In fact, Hispaniola had very little gold, and many of the native people were worked to death over the coming decade by the Spanish in the latter's futile quest to find deposits. Eventually, almost the entire native population of Hispaniola would die out, most from European disease and overwork.

Most High and Mighty Sovereigns,

In obedience to your Highnesses' commands, and with submission to superior judgment, I will say whatever occurs to me in reference to the colonization and commerce of the Island of Espanola, and of the other islands, both those already discovered and those that may be discovered hereafter.

In the first place, as regards the Island of Espanola: Inasmuch as the number of colonists who desire to go thither amounts to two thousand, owing to the land being safer and better for farming and trading, and because it will serve as a place to which they can return and from which they can carry on trade with the neighboring islands:

1. That in the said island there shall be founded three or four towns, situated in the most convenient places, and that the settlers who are there be assigned to the aforesaid places and towns.

2. That for the better and more speedy colonization of the said island, no one shall have liberty to collect gold in it except those who have taken out colonists' papers, and have built houses for their abode, in the town in which they are, that they may live united and in greater safety.

3. That each town shall have its alcalde [Mayor] . . . and its notary public, as is the use and custom in Castile.

4. That there shall be a church, and parish priests or friars to administer the sacraments, to perform divine worship, and for the conversion of the Indians.

5. That none of the colonists shall go to seek gold without a license from the governor or alcalde of the town where he lives; and that he must first take oath to return to the place whence he sets out, for the purpose of registering faithfully all the gold he may have found, and to return once a month, or once a week, as the time may have been set for him, to render account and show the quantity of said gold; and that this shall be written down by the notary before the alcalde, or, if it seems better, that a friar or priest, deputed for the purpose, shall be also present

6. That all the gold thus brought in shall be smelted immediately, and stamped with some mark that shall distinguish each town; and that the portion which belongs to your Highnesses shall be weighed, and given and consigned to each alcalde in his own town, and registered by the above-mentioned priest or friar, so that it shall not pass through the hands of only one person, and there shall be no opportunity to conceal the truth.

7. That all gold that may be found without the mark of one of the said towns in the possession of any one who has once registered in accordance with the above order shall be taken as forfeited, and that the accuser shall have one portion of it and your Highnesses the other.

8. That one per centum of all the gold that may be found shall be set aside for building churches and adorning the same, and for the support of the priests or friars belonging to them; and, if it should be thought proper to pay any thing to the alcaldes or notaries for their services, or for ensuring the faithful perforce of their duties, that this amount shall be sent to the governor or treasurer who may be appointed there by your Highnesses.

9. As regards the division of the gold, and the share that ought to be reserved for your Highnesses, this, in my opinion, must be left to the aforesaid governor and treasurer, because it will have to be greater or less according to the quantity of gold that may be found. Or, should it seem preferable, your Highnesses might, for the space of one year, take one half, and the collector the other, and a better arrangement for the division be made afterward.

10. That if the said alcaldes or notaries shall commit or be privy to any fraud, punishment shall be provided, and the same for the colonists who shall not have declared all the gold they have.

11. That in the said island there shall be a treasurer, with a clerk to assist him, who shall receive all the gold belonging to your Highnesses, and the alcaldes and notaries of the towns shall each keep a record of what they deliver to the said treasurer.

12. As, in the eagerness to get gold, every one will wish, naturally, to engage in its search in preference to any other employment, it seems to me that the privilege of going to look for gold ought to be withheld during some portion of each year, that there may be opportunity to have the other business necessary for the island performed.

13. In regard to the discovery of new countries, I think permission should be granted to all that wish to go, and more liberality used in the matter of the fifth, making the tax easier, in some fair way, in order that many may be disposed to go on voyages.

I will now give my opinion about ships going to the said Island of Espanola, and the order that should be maintained; and that is, that the said ships should only be allowed to discharge in one or two ports designated for the purpose, and should register there whatever cargo they bring or unload; and when the time for their departure comes, that they should sail from these same ports, and register all the cargo they take in, that nothing may be concealed.

- In reference to the transportation of gold from the island to Castile, that all of it should be taken on board the ship, both that belonging to your Highnesses and the property of every one else; that it should all be placed in one chest with two locks, with their keys, and that the master of the vessel keep one key and some person selected by the governor and treasurer the other; that there should come with the gold, for a testimony, a list of all that has been put into the said chest, properly marked, so that each owner may receive his own; and that, for the faithful performance of this duty, if any gold whatsoever is found outside of the said chest in any way, be it little or much, it shall be forfeited to your Highnesses.

- That all the ships that come from the said island shall be obliged to make their proper discharge in the port of Cadiz, and that no person shall disembark or other person be permitted to go on board until the ship has been visited by the person or persons deputed for that purpose, in the said city, by your Highnesses, to whom the master shall show all that he carries, and exhibit the manifest of all the cargo, it may be seen and examined if the said ship brings any thing hidden and not known at the time of lading.
- That the chest in which the said gold has been carried shall be opened in the presence of the magistrates of the said city of Cadiz, and of the person deputed for that purpose by your Highnesses, and his own property be given to each owner.

I beg your Highnesses to hold me in your protection; and I remain, praying our Lord God for your Highnesses' lives and the increase of much greater States.

Source: Florida A & M University website: www.famu. edu/acad/colleges/cas/histpol/eidahl/Spring/ WOH1022/Columbus2.html.

Hernan Cortés: Letter to Charles V (1520)

The Aztec city of Tenochtitlan (Cortés calls it Temixtitlan) was the largest city in the Americas, and among the largest in the world, when first encountered by Hernan Cortés in 1520. While Cortés was impressed with the technology and architecture of the city, it is also clear that he considered the Aztec religion a form of idolatry. Within several years, Cortés would return to the great Aztec capital as a conqueror. Justifying his conquest as spreading the true faith, he destroyed many of the temples and subjected the native inhabitants of Mexico to Spanish rule for nearly 300 years.

In order, most potent Sire, to convey to your Majesty a just conception of the great extent of this noble city of Temixtitlan, and of the many rare and wonderful objects it contains; of the government and dominions of Moctezuma, the sovereign; of the religious rights and customs that prevail, and the order that exists in this as well as the other cities appertaining to his realm; it would require the labor of many accomplished writers, and much time for the completion of the task. I shall not be able to relate an hundredth part of what could be told respecting these matters; but I will endeavor to describe, in the best manner in my power, what I have myself seen; and imperfectly as I may succeed in the attempt, I am fully aware that the account will appear so wonderful as to be deemed scarcely worthy of credit; since even we who have seen these things with our own eyes, are yet so amazed as to be unable to comprehend their reality. But your Majesty may be assured that if there is any fault in my relation, either in regard to the present subject, or to any other matters of which I shall give your Majesty an account, it will arise from too great brevity rather than extravagance or prolixity in the details; and it seems to me but just to my Prince and Sovereign to declare the truth in the clearest manner, without saying anything that would detract from it, or add to it.

Before I begin to describe this great city and the others already mentioned, it may be well for the better understanding of the subject to say something of the configuration of Mexico, in which they are situated, it being the principal seat of Moctezuma's power. This Province is in the form of a circle, surrounded on all sides by lofty and rugged mountains; its level surface comprises an area of about seventy leagues in circumference, including two lakes, that overspread nearly the whole valley, being navigated by boats more than fifty leagues round. One of these lakes contains fresh and the other, which is the larger of the two, salt water. On one side of the lakes, in the middle of the valley, a range of highlands divides them from one another, with the exception of a narrow strait which lies between the highlands and the lofty sierras. This strait is a bow-shot wide, and connects the two lakes; and by this means a trade is carried on between the cities and other settlements on the lakes in canoes without the necessity of traveling by land. As the salt lake rises and falls with its tides like the sea, during the time of high water it pours into the other lake with the rapidity of a powerful stream; and on the other hand, when the tide has ebbed, the water runs from the fresh into the salt lake.

This great city of Temixtitlan is situated in this salt lake, and from the main land to the denser parts of it, by whichever route one chooses to enter, the distance is two leagues. There are four avenues or entrances to the city, all of which are formed by artificial causeways, two spears' length in width. The city is as large as Seville or Cordoba; its streets, I speak of the principal ones, are very wide and straight; some of these, and all the inferior ones, are half land and half water, and are navigated by canoes. All the streets at intervals have openings, through which the water flows, crossing from one street to another; and at these openings, some of which are very wide, there are also very wide bridges, composed of large pieces of timber, of great strength and well put together; on many of these bridges ten horses can go abreast. Foreseeing that if the inhabitants of the city should prove treacherous, they would possess great advantages from the manner in which the city is constructed, since by removing the bridges at the entrances, and abandoning the place, they could leave us to perish by famine without our being able to reach the main land, as soon as I had entered it, I made great haste to build four brigantines, which were soon finished, and were large enough to take ashore three hundred men and the horses, whenever it should become necessary.

This city has many public squares, in which are situated the markets and other places for buying and selling. There is one square twice as large as that of the city of Salamanca, surrounded by porticoes, where are daily assembled more than sixty thousand souls, engaged in buying and selling; and where are found all kinds of merchandise that the world affords, embracing the necessaries of

life, as for instance articles of food, as well as jewels of gold and silver, lead, brass, copper, tin, precious stones, bones, shells, snails, and feathers. There are also exposed for sale wrought and unwrought stone, bricks burnt and unburnt, timber hewn and unhewn, of different sorts. There is a street for game, where every variety of birds in the country are sold, as fowls, partridges, quails, wild ducks, fly-catchers, widgeons, turtledoves, pigeons, reed-birds, parrots, sparrows, eagles, hawks, owls, and kestrels; they sell likewise the skins of some birds of prey, with their feathers, head, beak, and claws. There are also sold rabbits, hares, deer, and little dogs, which are raised for eating. There is also an herb street, where may be obtained all sorts of roots and medicinal herbs that the country affords. There are apothecaries' shops, where prepared medicines, liquids, ointments, and plasters are sold; barbers' shops, where they wash and shave the head; and restaurateurs, that furnish food and drink at a certain price. There is also a class of men like those called in Castile porters, for carrying burdens. Wood and coal are seen in abundance, and braziers of earthenware for burning coals; mats of various kinds for beds, others of a lighter sort for seats, and for halls and bedrooms.

There are all kinds of green vegetables, especially onions, leeks, garlic, watercress, nasturtium, borage, sorrel, artichokes, and golden thistle; fruits also of numerous descriptions, amongst which are cherries and plums, similar to those in Spain; honey and wax from bees, and from the stalks of maize, which are as sweet as the sugarcane; honey is also extracted from the plant called maguey, which is superior to sweet or new wine; from the same plant they extract sugar and wine, which they also sell. Different kinds of cotton thread of all colors in skeins are exposed for sale in one quarter of the market, which has the appearance of the silk-market at Granada, although the former is supplied more abundantly. Painters' colors, as numerous as can be found in Spain, and as fine shades; deerskins dressed and undressed, dyed different colors; earthen-ware of a large size and excellent quality; large and small jars, jugs, pots, bricks, and endless variety of vessels, all made of fine clay, and all or most of them glazed and painted; maize or Indian corn, in the grain and in the form of bread, preferred in the grain for its flavor to that of the other islands and terra-firma; patés of birds and fish; great quantities of fish—fresh, salt, cooked and uncooked; the eggs of hens, geese, and of all the other birds I have mentioned, in great abundance, and cakes made of eggs; finally, everything that can be found throughout the whole country is sold in the markets, comprising articles so numerous that to avoid prolixity, and because their names are not retained in my memory, or are unknown to me, I shall not attempt to enumerate them.

Every kind of merchandise is sold in a particular street or quarter assigned to it exclusively, and thus the best order is preserved. They sell everything by number or measure; at least so far we have not observed them to sell anything by weight. There is a building in the great square that is used as an audience house, where ten or twelve persons, who are magistrates, sit and decide all controversies that arise in the market, and order delinquents to be punished. In the same square there are other persons who go constantly about among the people observing what is sold, and the measures used in selling; and they have been seen to break measures that were not true.

This great city contains a large number of temples, or houses, for their idols, very handsome edifices, which are situated in the different districts and the suburbs; in the principal ones religious persons of each particular sect are constantly residing, for whose use, besides the houses containing the idols, there are other convenient habitations. All these persons dress in black, and never cut or comb their hair from the time they enter the priesthood until they leave it; and all the sons of the principal inhabitants, both nobles and respectable citizens, are placed in the temples and wear the same dress from the age of seven or eight years until they are taken out to be married; which occurs more frequently with the first-born who inherit estates than with the others. The priests are debarred from female society, nor is any woman permitted to enter the religious houses. They also abstain from eating certain kinds of food, more at some seasons of the year than others.

Among these temples there is one which far surpasses all the rest, whose grandeur of architectural details no human tongue is able to describe; for within its precincts, surrounded by a lofty wall, there is room enough for a town of five hundred families. Around the interior of the enclosure there are handsome edifices, containing large halls and corridors, in which the religious persons attached to the temple reside. There are fully forty towers, which are lofty and well built, the largest of which has fifty steps leading to its main body, and is higher than the tower of the principal tower of the church at Seville. The stone and wood of which they are constructed are so well wrought in every part, that nothing could be better done, for the interior of the chapels containing the idols consists of curious imagery, wrought in stone, with plaster ceilings, and wood-work carved in relief, and painted with figures of monsters and other objects. All these towers are the burial places of the nobles, and every chapel in them is dedicated to a particular idol, to which they pay their devotions.

Three halls are in this grand temple, which contain the principal idols; these are of wonderful extent and height, and admirable workmanship, adorned with figures sculptured in stone and wood; leading from the halls are chapels with very small doors, to which the light is not admitted, nor are any persons except the priests, and not all of them. In these chapels are the images of idols, although, as I have before said, many of them are also found on the outside; the principal ones, in which the people have greatest faith and confidence, I precipitated from their pedestals, and cast them down the steps of the temple, purifying the chapels in which they had stood, as they were all polluted with human blood, shed ill the sacrifices. In the place of these I put images of Our Lady and the Saints, which excited not a little feeling in Moctezuma and the inhabitants, who at first remonstrated, declaring that if my proceedings were known throughout the country, the people would rise against me; for they believed that their idols bestowed on them all temporal good, and if they permitted them to be ill-treated, they would be angry and without their gifts, and by this means the people would be deprived of the fruits of the earth and perish with famine. I answered, through the interpreters, that they were deceived in expecting any favors from idols, the work of their own hands, formed of unclean things; and that they must learn there was but one God, the universal Lord of all, who had created the heavens and earth, and all things else, and had made them and us; that He was without beginning and immortal, and they were bound to adore and believe Him, and no other creature or thing.

I said everything to them I could to divert them from their idolatries, and draw them to a knowledge of God our Lord. Moctezuma replied, the others assenting to what he said, "That they had already informed me they were not the aborigines of the country, but that their ancestors had emigrated to it many years ago; and they fully believed that after so long an absence from their native land, they might have fallen into some errors; that I having more recently arrived must know better than themselves what they ought to believe; and that if I would instruct them in these matters, and make them understand the true faith, they would follow my directions, as being for the best."

Afterwards, Moctezuma and many of the principal citizens remained with me until I had removed the idols, purified the chapels, and placed the images in them, manifesting apparent pleasure; and I forbade them sacrificing human beings to their idols as they had been accustomed to do; because, besides being abhorrent in the sight of God, your sacred Majesty had prohibited it by law, and commanded to put to death whoever should take the life of another. Thus, from that time, they refrained from the practice, and during the whole period of my abode in that city, they were never seen to kill or sacrifice a human being.

The figures of the idols in which these people believe surpass in stature a person of more than ordinary size; some of them are composed of a mass of seeds and leguminous plants, such as are used for food, ground and mixed together, and kneaded with the blood of human hearts taken from the breasts of living persons, from which a paste is formed in a sufficient quantity to form large statues. When these are completed they make them offerings of the hearts of other victims, which they sacrifice to them, and besmear their faces with the blood. For everything they have an idol, consecrated by the use of the nations that in ancient times honored the same gods. Thus they have an idol that they petition for victory in war; another for success in their labors; and so for everything in which they seek or desire prosperity, they have their idols, which they honor and serve.

This noble city contains many fine and magnificent houses; which may be accounted for from the fact, that all the nobility of the country, who are the vassals of Moctezuma, have houses in the city, in which they reside a certain part of the year; and besides, there are numerous wealthy citizens who also possess fine houses. All these persons, in addition to the large and spacious apartments for ordinary purposes, have others, both upper and lower, that contain conservatories of flowers. Along one of these causeways that lead into the city are laid two pipes, constructed of masonry, each of which is two paces in width, and about five feet in height. An abundant supply of excellent water, forming a volume equal in bulk to the human body, is conveyed by one of these pipes, and distributed about the city, where it is used by the inhabitants for drink and other purposes. The other pipe, in the meantime, is kept empty until the former requires to be cleansed, when the water is let into it and continues to be used till the cleaning is finished. As the water is necessarily carried over bridges on account of the salt water crossing its route, reservoirs resembling canals are constructed on the bridges, through which the fresh water is conveyed. These reservoirs are of the breadth of the body of an ox, and of the same length as the bridges. The whole city is thus served with water, which they carry in canoes through all the streets for sale, taking it from the aqueduct in the following manner: the canoes pass under the bridges on which the reservoirs are placed, when men stationed above fill them with water, for which service they are paid. At all the entrances of the city, and in those parts where the canoes are discharged, that is, where the greatest quantity of provisions is brought in, huts are erected, and persons stationed as guards, who receive a certain sum of everything that enters. I know not whether the sovereign receives this duty or the city, as I have not yet been informed; but I believe that it appertains to the sovereign, as in the markets of other provinces a tax is collected for the benefit of the cacique.

In all the markets and public places of this city are seen daily many laborers waiting for some one to hire them. The inhabitants of this city pay a greater regard to style in their mode of dress and politeness of manners than those of the other provinces and cities; since, as the Cacique Moctezuma has his residence in the capital, and all the nobility, his vassals, are in constant habit of meeting there, a general courtesy of demeanor necessarily prevails. But not to be prolix in describing what relates to the affairs of this great city, although it is with difficulty I refrain from proceeding, I will say no more than that the manners of the people, as shown in their intercourse with one another, are marked by as great an attention to the proprieties of life as in Spain, and good order is equally well observed; and considering that they are barbarous people, without the knowledge of God, having no intercourse with civilized nations, these traits of character are worthy of admiration.

In regard to the domestic appointments of Moctezuma, and the wonderful grandeur and state that he maintains, there is so much to be told, that I assure your Highness I know not where to begin my relation, so as to be able to finish any part of it. For, as I have already stated, what can be more wonderful than a barbarous monarch, as he is, should have every object found in his dominions imitated in gold, silver, precious stones, and feathers; the gold and silver being wrought so naturally as not to be surpassed by any smith in the world; the stone work executed with such perfection that it is difficult to conceive what instruments could have been used; and the feather work superior to the finest productions in wax or embroidery. The extent of Moctezuma's dominions has not been ascertained, since to whatever point he dispatched his messengers, even two hundred leagues from his capital, his commands were obeyed, although some of his provinces were in the midst of countries with which he was at war. But as nearly as I have been able to learn, his territories are equal in extent to Spain itself, for he sent messengers to the inhabitants of a city called Cumatan (requiring them to become subjects of your Majesty), which is sixty leagues beyond that part of Putunchan watered by the river Grijalva, and two hundred and thirty leagues distant from the great city; and I sent some of our people a distance of one hundred and fifty leagues in the same direction.

All the principle chiefs of these provinces, especially those in the vicinity of the capital, reside, as I have already stated, the greater part of the year in that great city, and all or most of them have their oldest sons in the service of Moctezuma. There are fortified places in all the provinces, garrisoned with his own men, where are also stationed his governors and collectors of the rents and tribute, rendered him by every province; and an account is kept of what each is obliged to pay, as they have characters and figures made on paper that are used for this purpose. Each province renders a tribute of its own peculiar productions, so that the sovereign receives a great variety of articles from different quarters. No prince was ever more feared by his subjects, both in his presence and absence. He possessed out of the city as well as within numerous villas, each of which had its peculiar sources of amusement, and all were constructed in the best possible manner for the use of a great prince and lord. Within the city his palaces were so wonderful that it is hardly possible to describe their beauty and extent; I can only say that in Spain there is nothing equal to them.

There was one palace somewhat inferior to the rest, attached to which was a beautiful garden with balconies extending over it, supported by marble columns, and having a floor formed of jasper elegantly inlaid. There were apartments in this palace sufficient to lodge two princes of the highest rank with their retinues. There were likewise belonging to it ten pools of water, in which were kept the different species of water birds found in this country, of which there is a great variety, all of which are domesticated; for the sea birds there were pools of salt water, and for the river birds, of fresh water. The water is let off at certain times to keep it pure, and is replenished by means of pipes. Each specie of bird is supplied with the food natural to it, which it feeds upon when wild. Thus fish is given to the birds that usually eat it; worms, maize, and the finer seeds, to such as prefer them. And I assure your Highness, that to the birds accustomed to eat fish there is given the enormous quantity of ten arrobas every day, taken in the salt lake. The emperor has three hundred men whose sole employment is to take care of these birds; and there are others whose only business is to attend to the birds that are in bad health.

Over the polls for the birds there are corridors and galleries, to which Moctezuma resorts, and from which he can look out and amuse himself with the sight of them. There is an apartment in the same palace in which are men, women and children, whose faces, bodies, hair, eyebrows, and eyelashes are white from their birth. The emperor has another very beautiful palace, with a large court-yard, paved with handsome flags, in the style of a chess-board. There are also cages, about nine feet in height and six paces square, each of which was half covered with a roof of tiles, and the other half had over it a wooden grate, skillfully made. Every cage contained a bird of prey, of all the species found in Spain, from the kestrel to the eagle, and many unknown there. There was a great number of each kind; and in the covered part of the cages there was a perch, and another on the outside of the grating, the former of which the birds used in the night time, and when it rained; and the other enabled them to enjoy the sun and air. To all these birds fowls were daily given for food, and nothing else. There were in the same palace several large halls on the ground floor, filled with immense cages built of heavy pieces of timber, well put together, in all or most of which were kept lions, tigers, wolves, foxes, and a variety of animals of the cat kind, in great numbers, which were fed also on fowls. The care of these animals and birds was assigned to three hundred men. There was another palace that contained a number of men and women of monstrous size, and also dwarfs, and crooked and ill-formed persons, each of which had their separate apartments. These also had their respective keepers. As to the other remarkable things that the emperor had in his city for his amusement, I can only say that they were numerous and of various kinds.

He was served in the following manner: Every day as soon as it was light, six hundred nobles and men of rank were in attendance at the palace, who either sat, or walked about the halls and galleries, and passed their time in conversation, but without entering the apartment where his person was. The servants and attendants of these nobles remained in the court-yards, of which there were two or three of great extent, and in the adjoining street, which was also very spacious. They all remained in attendance from morning until night; and when his meals were served, the nobles were likewise served with equal profusion, and their servants and secretaries also had their allowance. Daily his larder and wine-cellar were open to all who wished to eat or drink. The meals were served by three or four hundred youths, who brought on an infinite variety of dishes; indeed, whenever he dined or supped, the table was loaded with every kind of flesh, fish, fruits, and vegetables that the country produced. As the climate is cold, they put a chafing-dish with live coals under every plate and dish, to keep them warm. The meals were served in a large hall, in which Moctezuma was accustomed to eat, and the dishes quite filled the room, which was covered with mats and kept very clean. He sat on a small cushion curiously wrought of leather. During the meals there were present, at a little distance from him, five or six elderly caciques, to whom he presented some of the food. And there was constantly in attendance one of the servants, who arranged and handed the dishes, and who received from others whatever was wanted for the supply of the table.

Both at the beginning and end of every meal, they furnished water for the hands; and the napkins used on these occasions were never used a second time; this was the case also with the plates and dishes, which were not brought again, but new ones in place of them; it was the same also with the chafing-dishes. He is also dressed every day in four different suits, entirely new, which he never wears a second time. None of the caciques who enter his palace have their feet covered, and when those for whom he sends enters his presence, they incline their heads and look down, bending their bodies; and when they address him, they do not look him in the face; this arises from excessive modesty and reverence. I am satisfied that it proceeds from respect, since certain caciques reproved the Spaniards for their boldness in addressing me, saying that it showed a want of becoming deference. Whenever Moctezuma appeared in public, which is seldom the case, all those who accompanied him, or whom he accidentally met in the streets, turned away without looking towards him, and others prostrated themselves until he had passed. One of the nobles always preceded him on these occasions, carrying three slender rods erect, which I suppose was to give notice of the approach of his person. And when they descended from the litters, he took one of them in his hand, and held it until he reached the place where he was going. So many and various were the ceremonies and customs observed by those in the service of Moctezuma, that more space than I can spare would be required for the details, as well as a better memory than I have to recollect them; since no sultan or other infidel lord, of whom any knowledge now exists; ever had so much ceremonial in his court.

Source: Thatcher, Oliver J., ed., *The Library of Original Sources: Volume V: 9th to 16th Centuries.* Milwaukee: University Research Extension Co., 1907, 317–326.

Hernan Cortés: Letter to Charles V (1521)

In these excerpts from a letter to the Emperor Charles V of Spain, the conquistador Hernan Cortés describes his meeting with the Aztec Emperor Moctezuma. As Cortés quotes Moctezuma, the Aztec leader believed that Cortés's coming to Mexico was a fulfillment of Aztec prophecy, whereby an emissary from the god Quetzalcoatl would arrive in the Aztec capital from the east. This mistaken belief in Cortés as a god weakened Aztec resolve and helped lead to the quick downfall of the vast military empire to a handful of Spanish soldiers and their native allies.

I followed the said causeway for about half a league before I came to the city proper of Temixtitlan. I found at the junction of another causeway, which joins this one from the mainland, another strong fortification, with two towers, surrounded by walls, twelve feet high with castellated tops. This commands the two roads, and has only two gates, by one of which they enter, and from the other they come out. About one thousand of the principal citizens came out to meet me, and speak to me, all richly dressed alike according to their fashion; and when they had come, each one in approaching me, and before speaking, would use a ceremony which is very common amongst them, putting his hand on the ground, and afterward kissing it, so that I was kept waiting almost an hour, until each had performed his ceremony. There is a wooden bridge, ten paces broad, in the very outskirts of the city, across an opening in the causeway, where the water may flow in and out as it rises and falls. This bridge is also for defense, for they remove and replace the long broad wooden beams, of which the bridge is made, whenever they wish; and there are many of these bridges in the city, as Your Highness will see in the account which I shall make of its affairs.

Having passed this bridge, we were received by that lord, Moctezuma, with about two hundred chiefs, all barefooted and dressed in a kind of livery, very rich, according to their custom, and some more so than others. They approached in two processions near the walls of the street, which is very broad, and straight, and beautiful, and very uniform from one end to the other, being about two thirds of a league long, and having, on both sides, very large houses, both dwelling places, and mosques. Moctezuma came in the middle of the street, with two lords, one on the right side, and the other on the left, one of whom was the same great lord, who, as I said, came in that litter to speak with me, and the other was the brother of Moctezuma, lord of that city Iztapalapan, whence I had come that day. All were dressed in the same manner, except that Moctezuma was shod, and the other lords were barefooted. Each supported him below his arms, and as we approached each other, I descended from my horse, and was about to embrace him, but the two lords in attendance prevented me, with their hands, that I might not touch him, and they, and he also, made the ceremony of kissing the ground. This done, he ordered his brother who came with him, to remain with me, and take me by the arm, and the other attendant walked a little ahead of us. After he had spoken to me, all the other lords, who formed the two processions, also saluted me, one after the other, and then returned to the procession. When I approached to speak to Moctezuma, I took off a collar of pearls and glass diamonds, that I wore, and put it on his neck, and, after we had gone through some of the streets, one of his servants came with two collars, wrapped in a cloth, which were made of colored shells. These they esteem very much; and from each of the collars hung eight golden shrimps executed with great perfection and a span long. When he received them, he turned towards me, and put them on my neck, and again went on through the streets, as I have already indicated, until we came to a large and handsome house, which he had prepared for our reception. There he took me by the hand, and led me into a spacious room, in front of the court where we had entered, where he made me sit on a very rich platform, which had been ordered to be made for him, and told me to wait there; and then he went away.

After a little while, when all the people of my company were distributed to their quarter, he returned with many valuables of gold and silver work, and five or six thousand pieces of rich cotton stuffs, woven, and embroidered in divers ways. After he had given them to me, he sat down on another platform, which they immediately prepared near the one where I was seated, and being seated he spoke in the following manner:

"We have known for a long time, from the chronicles of our forefathers, that neither I, nor those who inhabit this country, are descendants from the aborigines of it, but from strangers who came to it from very distant parts; and we also hold, that our race was brought to these parts by a lord, whose vassals they all were, and who returned to his native country, and had many descendants, and had built towns where they were living; when, therefore, he wished to take them away with him they would not go, nor still less receive him as their ruler, so he departed. And we have always held that those who descended from his would come to subjugate this country and us, as his vassals; and according to the direction from which you say you come, which is where the sun rises, and from what you tell us of your great lord, or king, who has sent you here, we believe, and hold for certain, that he is our rightful sovereign, especially as you tell us that since many days he has had news of us. Hence you may be sure, that we shall obey you, and hold you as the representative of this great lord of whom you speak, and that in this there will be no lack or deception; and throughout the whole country you may command at your will (I speak of what I possess in my dominions), because you will be obeyed, and recognized, and all we possess is at your disposal. Since you are in your rightful place, and in your own homes, rejoice and rest, free from all the trouble of the journey, and wars which you have had, for I am well aware of all that has happened to you, between Puntunchan and here, and I know very well, that the people of Cempoal, and Tascaltecal, have told you many evil things respecting me. Do not believe more than you see with your own eyes, especially from those who are my enemies, and were my vassals, yet rebelled against me on your coming (as they say), in order to help you. I know they have told you also that I have houses, with walls of gold, and that the furniture of my halls, and other things of my service, were also of gold, and that I am, or make myself, a god, and many other things. The houses you have seen are of lime and stone

and earth." And then he held up his robes, and showing me his body he said to me, "Look at me, and see that I am flesh and bones, the same as you, and everybody, and that I am mortal, and tangible." And touching his arms and body with his hands, "Look how they have lied to you! It is true indeed that I have some things of gold, which have been left to me by my forefathers. All that I possess, you may have whenever you wish. I shall now go to other houses where I live; but you will be provided here with everything necessary for you and your people, and you shall suffer no annoyance, for you are in your own house and country."

I answered to all he said, certifying that which seemed to be suitable, especially in confirming his belief that it was Your Majesty whom they were expecting. After this, he took his leave, and, when he had gone, we were well provided with chickens, and bread, and fruits, and other necessities, especially such as were required for the service of our quarters. Thus I passed six days well provided with everything necessary, and visited by many of the lords.

Source: Thatcher, Oliver J., ed., *The Library of Original Sources, Volume V: 9th to 16th Centuries.* Milwaukee: University Research Extension Co., 1907, 317–326.

An Aztec Account of the Conquest of Mexico (circa 1528)

In 1519 Hernan Cortés sailed from Cuba, landed in Mexico, and made his way to the Aztec capital. Miguel Leon-Portilla, a Mexican anthropologist, gathered accounts by the Aztecs, some of which were written shortly after the conquest.

Speeches of Motecuhzoma and Cortés

When Motecuhzoma [Montezuma] had given necklaces to each one, Cortés asked him: "Are you Motecuhzoma? Are you the king? Is it true that you are the king Motecuhzoma?"

And the king said: "Yes, I am Motecuhzoma." Then he stood up to welcome Cortés; he came forward, bowed his head low and addressed him in these words: "Our lord, you are weary. The journey has tired you, but now you have arrived on the earth. You have come to your city, Mexico. You have come here to sit on your throne, to sit under its canopy.

"The kings who have gone before, your representatives, guarded it and preserved it for your coming. The kings Itzcoatl, Motecuhzoma the Elder, Axayacatl, Tizoc and Ahuitzol ruled for you in the City of Mexico. The people were protected by their swords and sheltered by their shields.

"Do the kings know the destiny of those they left behind, their posterity? If only they are watching! If only they can see what I see!

"No, it is not a dream. I am not walking in my sleep. I am not seeing you in my dreams. . . . I have seen you at last! I have met you face to face! I was in agony for five days, for ten days, with my eyes fixed on the Region of the Mystery. And now you have come out of the clouds and mists to sit on your throne again.

"This was foretold by the kings who governed your city, and now it has taken place. You have come back to us; you have come down from the sky. Rest now, and take possession of your royal houses. Welcome to your land, my lords!"

When Motecuhzoma had finished, La Malinche translated his address into Spanish so that the Captain could understand it. Cortés replied in his strange and savage tongue, speaking first to La Malinche: "Tell Motecuhzoma that we are his friends. There is nothing to fear. We have wanted to see him for a long time, and now we have seen his face and heard his words. Tell him that we love him well and that our hearts are contented."

Then he said to Motecuhzoma: "We have come to your house in Mexico as friends. There is nothing to fear."

La Malinche translated this speech and the Spaniards grasped Motecuhzoma's hands and patted his back to show their affection for him. . . .

Massacre in the Main Temple

During this time, the people asked Motecuhzoma how they should celebrate their god's fiesta. He said: "Dress him in all his finery, in all his sacred ornaments."

During this same time, The Sun commanded that Motecuhzoma and Itzcohuatzin, the military chief of Tlatelolco, be made prisoners. The Spaniards hanged a chief from Acolhuacan named Nezahualquentzin. They also murdered the king of Nauhtla, Cohualpopocatzin, by wounding him with arrows and then burning him alive.

For this reason, our warriors were on guard at the Eagle Gate. The sentries from Tenochtitlan stood at one side of the gate, and the sentries from Tlatelolco at the other. But messengers came to tell them to dress the figure of Huitzilopochtli. They left their posts and went to dress him in his sacred finery: his ornaments and his paper clothing.

When this had been done, the celebrants began to sing their songs. That is how they celebrated the first day of the fiesta. On the second day they began to sing again, but without warning they were all put to death. The dancers and singers were completely unarmed. They brought only their embroidered cloaks, their turquoises, their lip plugs, their necklaces, their clusters of heron feathers, their trinkets made of deer hooves. Those who played the drums, the old men, had brought their gourds of snuff and their timbrels.

The Spaniards attacked the musicians first, slashing at their hands and faces until they had killed all of them. The singers—and even the spectators—were also killed. This slaughter in the Sacred Patio went on for three hours. Then the Spaniards burst into the rooms of the temple to kill the others: those who were carrying water, or bringing fodder for the horses, or grinding meal, or sweeping, or standing watch over this work.

The king Motecuhzoma, who was accompanied by Itzcohuatzin and by those who had brought food for the Spaniards, protested: "Our lords, that is enough! What are you doing? These people are not carrying shields or macanas. Our lords, they are completely unarmed!"

The Sun had treacherously murdered our people on the twentieth day after the captain left for the coast. We allowed the Captain to return to the city in peace. But on the following day we attacked him with all our might, and that was the beginning of the war.

Source: From Leon-Portilla, Miguel, ed. *The Broken Spears: The Aztec Account of the Conquest of Mexico.* Boston: Beacon Press. 1962, pp. 64–66, 129–131.

New Laws of the Indies (1542)

Following years of abuse and exploitation of the indigenous peoples living within the Spanish Empire in the Americas, the Spanish government issued a new law for their treatment. The laws guaranteed royal protection and justice for the Native Americans. Indeed, the new laws, excerpted here, were considered overly indulgent by the colonial settlers and administrators of Spain's empire in the Americas, leading to protests. The viceroy of Peru was murdered by settlers when he tried to enforce the new laws too rigorously.

Charles by the divine clemency Emperor ever august ... To the Most Illustrious Prince Don Philip our very dear and very beloved grandson and son, and to the Infantes our grandsons and sons, and to the President, and those of our Council of the Indies, and to our Viceroys, Presidents and Auditors of our Audiencias and royal Chanceries of our said Indies, Islands and Continent of the Ocean Sea; to our Governors, Alcaldes mayores and our other Authorities thereof, and to all the Councils, magistrates, regidores, knights, esquires, officers, and commoners of all the cities, towns, and villages of our said Indies, Islands, and Tierra-firme of the Ocean Sea, discovered and to be discovered; and to any other persons, captains, discoverers, settlers, and inhabitants dwelling in and being natives thereof, of whatever state, quality, condition and pre-eminence ...

Know ye, That having for many years had will and intention as leisure to occupy ourselves with the affairs of the Indies, on account of their great importance, as well in that touching the service of God our Lord and increase of his holy Catholic faith, as in the preservation of the natives of those parts, and the good government and preservation of their persons; and although we have endeavoured to disengage ourselves to this effect, it has not been possible through the many and continual affairs that have occurred from which we were not able to excuse ourselves, and through the absences from these kingdoms which the King have made for most necessary causes, as is known to all: and although this incessant occupation has not ceased this present year, nevertheless we commanded persons to assemble of all ranks, both prelates and knights and the clergy with some of our Council to discuss and treat of the things of most importance, of which we had information that they ought to be provided for: the which having been maturely debated and consulted upon, and in presence of me the King divers times argued and discussed: and finally having taken the opinion of all, we resolved on commanding to enact and ordain the things contained below: which besides the other Ordinances and Provisions that at different times we have commanded to be made, as by them shall appear, we command to be from henceforwards kept inviolably as laws. ...

Whereas one of the most important things in which the Audiencias are to serve us is in taking very especial care of the good treatment of the Indians and preservation of them, We command that the said Audiencias enquire continually into the excesses or ill treatment which are or shall be done to them by governors or private persons; and how the ordinances and instructions which have been given to them, and are made for the good treatment of the said Indians have been observed. And if there had been any excesses, on the part of the said Governors, or should any be committed hereafter, to take care that such excesses are properly corrected, chastizing the guilty parties with all rigour conformably to justice. The Audiencias must not allow that in the suits between Indians, or with them, there be ordinary proceedings at law, nor dilatory expedients, as is wont to happen through the malice of some advocates and solicitors, but that they be determined summarily, observing their usages and customs, unless they be manifestly unjust; and that the said Audiencias take care that this be so observed by the other, inferior judges.

Item, We ordain and command that from henceforward for no cause of war nor any other whatsoever, though it be under title of rebellion, nor by ransom nor in other manner can an Indian be made a slave, and we will that they be treated as our vassals of the Crown of Castile since such they are.

No person can make use of the Indians by way of Naboria or Tapia or in any other manner against their will.

As We have ordered provision to be made that from henceforward the Indians in no way be made slaves, including those who until now have been enslaved against all reason and right and contrary to the provisions and instructions thereupon, We ordain and command that the Audiencias having first summoned the parties to their presence, without any further judicial form, but in a summary way, so that the truth may be ascertained, speedily set the said Indians at liberty unless the persons who hold them for slaves show title why they should hold and possess them legitimately. And in order that in default of persons to solicit the aforesaid, the Indians may not remain in slavery unjustly, We command that the Audiencias appoint persons who may pursue this cause for the Indians and be paid out of the Exchequer fines, provided they be men of trust and diligence.

Also, We command that with regard to the lading of the said Indians the Audiencias take especial care that they be not laden, or in case that in some parts this cannot be avoided that it be in such a manner that no risk of life, health and preservation of the said Indians may ensue from an immoderate burthen; and that against their own will and without their being paid, in no case be it permitted that they be laden, punishing very severely him who shall act contrary to this. In this there is to be no remission out of respect to any person.

Because report has been made to us that owing to the pearl fisheries not having been conducted in a proper manner deaths of many Indians and Negroes have ensued, We command that no free Indian be taken to the said fishery under pain of death, and that the bishop and the judge who shall be at Veneçuela direct what shall seem to them most fit for the preservation of the slaves working in the said fishery, both Indians and Negroes, and that the deaths may cease. If, however, it should appear to them that the risk of death cannot be avoided by the said Indians and Negroes, let the fishery of the said pearls cease, since we value much more highly (as is right) the preservation of their lives than the gain which may come to us from the pearls.

Whereas in consequence of the allotments of Indians made to the Viceroys, Governors, and their lieutenants, to our officials, and prelates, monasteries, hospitals, houses of religion and mints, offices of our Hazienda and treasury thereof, and other persons favoured by reason of their offices, disorders have occurred in the treatment of the said Indians, it is our will, and we command that forthwith there be placed under our Royal Crown all the Indians whom they hold and possess by any title and cause whatever, whoever the said parties are, or may be, whether Viceroys, Governors, or their lieutenants, or any of our officers, as well of Justice as of our Hazienda, prelates, houses of religion, or of our Hazienda, hospitals, confraternities, or other similar institutions, although the Indians may not have been allotted to them by reason of the said offices; and although such functionaries or governors may say that they wish to resign the offices or governments and keep the Indians, let this not avail them nor be an excuse for them not to fulfill what we command.

Moreover, We command that from all those persons who hold Indians without proper title, having entered into possession of them by their own authority, such Indians be taken away and be placed under our Royal Crown.

And because we are informed that other persons, although possessing a sufficient title, have had an excessive number of Indians allotted to them, We order that the Audiencias, each in its jurisdiction diligently inform themselves of this, and with all speed, and reduce the allotments made to the said persons to a fair and moderate quantity, and then place the rest under our Royal Crown notwithstanding any appeal or application which may be interposed by such persons: and send us a report with all speed of what the said Audiencias have thus done, that we may know how our command is fulfilled. And in New Spain let it be especially provided as to the Indians held by Joan Infante, Diego de Ordas, the Maestro Roa, Francisco Vasquez de Coronado, Francisco Maldonado, Bernardino Vazquez de Tapia, Joan Xaramillo, Martin Vazquez, Gil Gongales de Venavides, and many other persons who are said to hold Indians in very excessive quantity, according to the report made to us. And, whereas we are informed that there are some persons in the said New Spain who are of the original Conquistadores and have no repartimiento of Indians, We ordain that the President and Auditors of the said New Spain do inform themselves if there be any persons of this kind, and if any, to give them out of the tribute which the Indians thus taken away have to pay, what to them may seem fit for the moderate support and honourable maintenance of the said original Conquistadores who had no Indians allotted to them.

So also, The said Audiencias are to inform themselves how the Indians have been treated by the persons who have held them in encomienda, and if it be clear that in justice they ought to be deprived of the said Indians for their excesses and the ill-usage to which they have subjected them, We ordain that they take away and place such Indians under our Royal Crown. And in Peru, besides the aforesaid, let the Viceroy and Audiencia inform themselves of the excesses committed during the occurrences between Governors Pizarro and Almagro in order to report to us thereon, and from the principal persons whom they find notoriously blameable in those feuds they then take away the Indians they have, and place them under our Royal Crown.

Moreover, We ordain and command that from henceforward no Viceroy, Governor, Audiencia, discoverer, or any other person have power to allot Indians in encomienda by new provision, or by means of resignation, donation, sale, or any other form or manner, neither by vacancy nor inheritance, but that the person dying who held the said Indians, they revert to our Royal Crown. And let the Audiencias take care to inform themselves then particularly of the person who died, of his quality, his merits and services, of how he treated the said Indians whom he held, if he left wife and children or what other heirs, and send us a report thereof with the condition of the Indians and of the land, in order that we may give directions to provide what may be best for our service, and may do such favour as may seem suitable to the wife and children of the defunct. If in the meantime it should appear to the Audiencia that there is a necessity to provide some support for such wife and children, they can do it out of the tribute which the said Indians will have to pay, or allowing them a moderate pension, if the said Indians are under our Crown, as aforesaid.

Item, We ordain and command that our said Presidents and Auditors take great care that the Indians who in any of the ways above mentioned are taken away, and those who may become vacant be very well treated and instructed in the matters of our holy Catholic faith, and as our free vassals. This is to be their chief care, that on which we principally desire them to report, and in which they can best serve us. They are also to provide that they be governed with justice in the way and manner that the Indians who are under our Royal Crown are at present governed in New Spain.

Source: Stevens, Henry, ed. *The New Laws* of *the Indies.* London: Chiswick Press, 1893.

Simón Bolívar: Proclamation to the People of Venezuela (June 15, 1813)

Simón Bolívar, Liberator of Venezuela, Brigadier of the Union, General in Chief of the Northern Army, issued this proclamation to the people of his native Venezuela, asking their support in the independence struggle against Spain. Still, it would take eight more years, until the decisive battle of Carabobo, for Bolívar to completely rid the country of its Spanish rulers.

An army of our brothers, sent by the Sovereign Congress of New Granada, has come to liberate you. Having expelled the oppressors from the provinces of Mérida and Trujillo, it is now among you.

We are sent to destroy the Spaniards, to protect the Americans, and to reestablish the republican governments that once formed the Confederation of Venezuela. The states defended by our arms are again governed by their former constitutions and tribunals, in full enjoyment of their liberty and independence, for our mission is designed only to break the chains of servitude which still shackle some of our towns, and not to impose laws or exercise acts of dominion to which the rules of war might entitle us.

Moved by your misfortunes, we have been unable to observe with indifference the afflictions you were forced to experience by the barbarous Spaniards, who have ravished you, plundered you, and brought you death and destruction. They have violated the sacred rights of nations. They have broken the most solemn agreements and treaties. In fact, they have committed every manner of crime, reducing the Republic of Venezuela to the most frightful desolation. Justice therefore demands vengeance, and necessity compels us to exact it. Let the monsters who infest Colombian soil, who have drenched it in blood, be cast out forever; may their punishment be equal to the enormity of their perfidy, so that we may eradicate the stain of our ignominy and demonstrate to the nations of the world that the sons of America cannot be offended with impunity.

Despite our just resentment toward the iniquitous Spaniards, our magnanimous heart still commands us to open to them for the last time a path to reconciliation and friendship; they are invited to live peacefully among us, if they will abjure their crimes, honestly change their ways, and cooperate with us in destroying the intruding Spanish government and the reestablishment of the Republic of Venezuela.

Any Spaniard who does not, by every active and effective means, work against tyranny in behalf of this just cause, will be considered an enemy and punished; as a traitor to the nation, he will inevitably be shot by a firing squad. On the other hand, a general and absolute amnesty is granted to those who come over to our army with or without their arms, as well as to those who render aid to the good citizens who are endeavoring to throw off the yoke of tyranny. Army officers and civil magistrates who proclaim the government of Venezuela and join us shall retain their posts and positions; in a word, those Spaniards who render outstanding service to the State shall be regarded and treated as Americans.

And you Americans who, by error or treachery, have been lured from the paths of justice, are informed that your brothers, deeply regretting the error of your ways, have pardoned you as we are profoundly convinced that you cannot be truly to blame, for only the blindness and ignorance in which you have been kept up to now by those responsible for your crimes could have induced you to commit them. Fear not the sword that comes to avenge you and to sever the ignoble ties with which your executioners have bound you to their own fate. You are hereby assured, with absolute impunity, of your honor, lives, and property. The single title, "Americans," shall be your safeguard and guarantee. Our arms have come to protect you, and they shall never be raised against a single one of you, our brothers.

This amnesty is extended even to the very traitors who most recently have committed felonious acts, and it shall be so religiously applied that no reason, cause, or pretext will be sufficient to oblige us to violate our offer, however extraordinary and extreme the occasion you may give to provoke our wrath.

Spaniards and Canary Islanders, you will die, though you be neutral, unless you actively espouse the cause of America's liberation. Americans, you will live, even if you have trespassed.

General Headquarters, Trujillo, June 15, 1813.

Source: Biblioteca Virtual de Simon Bolivar website: www.geocities.com/Athens/Acropolis/7609/eng/bolivar/venezuela1813.html.

Simón Bolívar: Message to the Congress of Angostura (1819)

Like many other elites of South America in the early nineteenth century, Simón Bolívar, one of the liberators of the continent from Spanish rule, was heavily influenced by the revolutions in the United States and France and by the long-standing parliamentary institutions of Great Britain. At the same time, he recognized that the new South American republics required political institutions appropriate to their culture and history. At the Congress of Angostura, held to discuss the future of the political system of greater Colombia (today the republics of Colombia, Ecuador, Panama, and Venezuela), Bolívar suggested borrowing different elements from European and North American governments and creating a uniquely South American form of republican governance.

Gentlemen!

Let us review the past to discover the base upon which the Republic of Venezuela is founded.

America, in separating from the Spanish monarchy, found herself in a situation similar to that of the Roman Empire when its enormous framework fell to pieces in the midst of the ancient world. Each Roman division then formed an independent nation in keeping with its location or interests; but this situation differed from America's in that those members proceeded to re-establish their former associations. We, on the contrary, do not even retain the vestiges of our original being.

We are not Europeans; we are not Indians; we are but a mixed species of aborigines and Spaniards. Americans by birth and Europeans by law, we find ourselves engaged in a dual conflict: we are disputing with the natives for titles of ownership, and at the same time we are struggling to maintain ourselves in the country that gave us birth against the opposition of the invaders. Thus our position is most extraordinary and complicated. But there is more. As our role has always been strictly passive and political existence nil, we find that our quest for liberty is now even more difficult of accomplishment; for we, having been placed in a state lower than slavery, had been robbed not only of our freedom but also of the right to exercise an active domestic tyranny. Permit me to explain this paradox.

In absolute systems, the central power is unlimited. The will of the despot is the supreme law, arbitrarily enforced by subordinates who take part in the organized oppression in proportion to the authority that they wield. They are charged with civil, political, military, and religious functions; but, in the final analysis, the satraps of Persia are Persian, the pashas of the Grand Turk are Turks, and the sultans of Tartary are Tartars. China does not seek her mandarins in the homeland of Genghis Khan, her conqueror. America, on the contrary, received everything from Spain, who, in effect, deprived her of the experience that she would have gained from the exercise of an active tyranny by not allowing her to take part in her own domestic affairs and administration. This exclusion made it impossible for us to acquaint ourselves with the management of public affairs; nor did we enjoy that personal consideration, of such great value in major revolutions, that the brilliance of power inspires in the eyes of the multitude. In brief, Gentlemen, we were deliberately kept in ignorance and cut off from the world in all matters relating to the science of government.

Subject to the three-fold yoke of ignorance, tyranny, and vice, the American people have been unable to acquire knowledge, power, or [civic] virtue. The lessons we received and the models we studied, as pupils of such pernicious teachers, were most destructive. We have been ruled more by deceit than by force, and we have been degraded more by vice than by superstition. Slavery is the daughter of darkness: an ignorant people is a blind instrument of its own destruction. Ambition and intrigue abuse the credulity and experience of men lacking all political, economic, and civic knowledge; they adopt pure illusion as reality; they take license for liberty, treachery for patriotism, and vengeance for justice. This situation is similar to that of the robust blind man who, beguiled by his strength, strides forward with all the assurance of one who can see, but, upon hitting every variety of obstacle, finds himself unable to retrace his steps.

If a people, perverted by their training, succeed in achieving their liberty, they will soon lose it, for it would be of no avail to endeavor to explain to them that happiness consists in the practice of virtue; that the rule of law is more powerful than the rule of tyrants, because, as the laws are more inflexible, every one should submit to their beneficent austerity; that proper morals, and not force, are the bases of law; and that to practice justice is to practice liberty. Therefore, Legislators, your work is so much the more arduous, inas-

much as you have to re-educate men who have been corrupted by erroneous illusions and false incentives. Liberty, says Rousseau, is a succulent morsel, but one difficult to digest. Our weak fellow-citizens will have to strengthen their spirit greatly before they can digest the wholesome nutriment of freedom. Their limbs benumbed by chains, their sight dimmed by the darkness of dungeons, and their strength sapped by the pestilence of servitude, are they capable of marching toward the august temple of Liberty without faltering? Can they come near enough to bask in its brilliant rays and to breathe freely the pure air which reigns therein? . . .

The more I admire the excellence of the federal Constitution of Venezuela, the more I am convinced of the impossibility of its application to our state. And to my way of thinking, it is a marvel that its prototype in North America endures so successfully and has not been overthrown at the first sign of adversity or danger. Although the people of North America are a singular model of political virtue and moral rectitude; although that nation was cradled in liberty, reared on freedom, and maintained by liberty alone; and—I must reveal everything—although those people, so lacking in many respects, are unique in the history of mankind, it is a marvel, I repeat, that so weak and complicated a government as the federal system has managed to govern them in the difficult and trying circumstances of their past. But, regardless of the effectiveness of this form of government with respect to North America, I must say that it has never for a moment entered my mind to compare the position and character of two states as dissimilar as the English-American and Spanish-American. Would it not be most difficult to apply to Spain the English system of political, civil, and religious liberty: Hence, it would be even more difficult to adapt to Venezuela the laws of North America . . .

Venezuela had, has, and should have a republican government. Its principles should be the sovereignty of the people, division of powers, civil liberty, proscription of slavery, and the abolition of monarchy and privileges. We need equality to recast, so to speak, into a unified nation, the classes of men, political opinions, and public customs . . .

The creation of a hereditary senate would in no way be a violation of political equality. I do not solicit the establishment of a nobility, for as a celebrated republican has said, that would simultaneously destroy equality and liberty. What I propose is an office for which the candidates must prepare themselves, an office that demands great knowledge and the ability to acquire such knowledge. All should not be left to chance and the outcome of elections. The people are more easily deceived than is Nature perfected by art; and, although these senators, it is true, would not be bred in an environment that is all virtue, it is equally true that they would be raised in an atmosphere of enlightened education. Furthermore, the liberators of Venezuela are entitled to occupy forever a high rank in the Republic that they have brought into existence. I believe that posterity would view with regret the effacement of the illustrious names of its first benefactors. I say, moreover, that it is a matter of public interest and national honor, of gratitude on Venezuela's part, to honor gloriously, until the end of time, a race of virtuous, prudent, and persevering men who, overcoming every obstacle, have founded the Republic at the price of the most heroic sacrifices. And if the people of Venezuela do not applaud the elevation of their benefactors, then they are unworthy to be free, and they will never be free.

A hereditary senate, I repeat, will be the fundamental basis of the legislative power, and therefore the foundation of the entire government. It will also serve as a counterweight to both government and people; and as a neutral power it will weaken the mutual attacks of these two eternally rival powers. In all conflicts the calm reasoning of a third party will serve as the means of reconciliation. Thus the Venezuelan senate will give strength to this delicate political structure, so sensitive to violent repercussions; it will be the mediator that will lull the storms and it will maintain harmony between the head and the other parts of the political body.

No matter what citizen occupies the office of the Chief Executive, he will be aided by the Constitution, and therein being authorized to do good, he can do no harm, because his ministers will cooperate with him only insofar as he abides by the law. If he attempts to infringe upon the law, his own ministers will desert him, thereby isolating him

from the Republic, and they will even bring charges against him in the Senate. The ministers, being responsible for any transgressions committed, will actually govern, since they must account for their actions. The obligation which this system places upon the officials closest to the executive power, that is to take a most interested and active part in governmental deliberations and to regard this department as their own, is not the smallest advantage of the system. Should the president be a man of no great talent or virtue, yet, notwithstanding his lack of these essential qualities, he will be able to discharge his duties satisfactorily, for in such a case the ministry, managing everything by itself, will carry the burdens of the state . . .

[T]he balance of power between the branches of government must be distributed in two ways. In republics the executive should be the stronger, for everything conspires against it; while in monarchies the legislative power should be superior, as everything works in the monarch's favor. The people's veneration of royal power results in a self-fascination that tends greatly to increase the superstitious respect paid to such authority. The splendor inherent in the throne, the crown, and the purple; the formidable support that it receives from the nobility; the immense wealth that a dynasty accumulates from generation to generation; and the fraternal protection that kings grant to one another are the significant advantages that work in favor of royal authority, thereby rendering it almost unlimited. Consequently, the significance of these same advantages should serve to justify the necessity of investing the chief magistrate of a republic with a greater measure of authority than that possessed by a constitutional prince.

Let the balance of power be drawn up in such a manner that it will be permanent and incapable of decay because of its own tenuity. Precisely because no form of government is so weak as the democratic, its framework must be firmer, and its institutions must be studied to determine their degree of stability. Unless this is done, we must plan on the establishment of an experimental rather than a permanent system of government; and we will have to reckon with an ungovernable, tumultuous, and anarchic society, not with a social order where happiness, peace, and justice prevail.

The people of Venezuela already enjoy the rights that they may legitimately and easily exercise. Let us now, therefore, restrain the growth of immoderate pretensions which, perhaps, a form of government unsuited to our people might excite. Let us abandon the federal forms of government unsuited to us; let us put aside the triumvirate which holds the executive power and center it in a president. We must grant him sufficient authority to enable him to continue the struggle against the obstacles inherent in our recent situation, our present state of war, and every variety of foe, foreign and domestic, when we must battle for some time to come. Let the legislature relinquish the powers that rightly belong to the executive; let it acquire, however, a new consistency, a new influence in the balance of authority. Let the courts be strengthened by increasing the stability and independence of the judges and by the establishment of juries and civil and criminal codes dictated, not by antiquity nor by conquering kings, but by the voice of Nature, the cry of Justice, and the genius of Wisdom.

My desire is for every branch of government and administration to attain that degree of vigor which alone can insure equilibrium, not only among the members of the government, but also among the different factions of which our society is composed. It would matter little if the springs of a political system were to relax because of its weakness, so long as this relaxation itself did not contribute to the dissolution of the body social and the ruination of its membership. The shouts of humanity, on the battlefields or in tumultuous crowds denounce to the world the blind, unthinking legislators who imagined that experiments with chimerical institutions could be made with impurity. All the peoples of the world have sought freedom, some by force of arms, others by force of law, passing alternately from anarchy to despotism, or from despotism to anarchy. Few peoples have been content with moderate aims, establishing their institutions according to their means, their character, and their circumstances. We must not aspire to the impossible, lest, in trying to rise above the realm of liberty, we again descend into the realm of tyranny. Absolute liberty invariably lapses into absolute power, and the mean between these two extremes is supreme social liberty. Abstract theories create the pernicious idea of unlimited freedom.

Let us see to it that the strength of the public is kept within the limits prescribed by reason and interest; that the national will is confined within the bonds set by a just power; that the judiciary is rigorously controlled by civil and criminal laws, analogous to those in our present Constitution—then an equilibrium between the powers of government will exist, the conflicts that hamper the progress of the state will disappear, and those complications which tend to hinder rather than unite society will be eliminated.

Source: Bolívar, Simón. *An Address of Bolívar at the Congress of Angostura (February 15, 1819),* reprint ed. Washington, DC: B. S. Adams, 1919.

U.S. EMPIRE

Monroe Doctrine (December 2, 1823)

In 1823, the United States was still in its infancy, a republic of fewer than 10 million people situated largely east of the Mississippi River and equipped with the tiniest of militaries. But that didn't stop President James Monroe from issuing his very broad proclamation aimed at European powers with an eye on territory in the Americas. Responding to the successful independence struggle of the new republics of Latin America in the first two decades of the nineteenth century, Monroe warned European powers to resist recolonizing that region or acquiring new territories in North America.

...At the proposal of the Russian Imperial Government, made through the minister of the Emperor residing here, a full power and instructions have been transmitted to the minister of the United States at St. Petersburg to arrange by amicable negotiation the respective rights and interests of the two nations on the northwest coast of this continent. A similar proposal has been made by His Imperial Majesty to the Government of Great Britain, which has likewise been acceded to. The Government of the United States has been desirous by this friendly proceeding of manifesting the great value which they have invariably attached to the friendship of the Emperor and their solicitude to cultivate the best understanding with his Government. In the discussions to which this interest has given rise and in the arrangements by which they may terminate the occasion has been judged proper for asserting, as a principle in which the rights and interests of the United States are involved, that the American continents, by the free and independent condition which they have assumed and maintain, are henceforth not to be considered as subjects for future colonization by any European powers . . .

It was stated at the commencement of the last session that a great effort was then making in Spain and Portugal to improve the condition of the people of those countries, and that it appeared to be conducted with extraordinary moderation. It need scarcely be remarked that the results have been so far very different from what was then anticipated. Of events in that quarter of the globe, with which we have so much intercourse and from which we derive our origin, we have always been anxious and interested spectators. The citizens of the United States cherish sentiments the most friendly in favor of the liberty and happiness of their fellow-men on that side of the Atlantic. In the wars of the European powers in matters relating to themselves we have never taken any part, nor does it comport with our policy to do so. It is only when our rights are invaded or seriously menaced that we resent injuries or make preparation for our defense. With the movements in this hemisphere we are of necessity more immediately connected, and by causes which must be obvious to all enlightened and impartial observers. The political system of the allied powers is essentially different in this respect from that of America. This difference proceeds from that which exists in their respective Governments; and to the defense of our own, which has been achieved by the loss of so much blood and treasure, and matured by the wisdom of their most enlightened citizens, and under which we have enjoyed unexampled felicity, this whole nation is devoted. We owe it, therefore, to candor and to the amicable relations existing between the United States and those powers to declare that we should consider any attempt on their part to extend their system to any portion of this hemisphere as dangerous to our peace and safety. With the existing colonies or dependencies of any European power we have not interfered and shall not interfere. But with the Governments who have declared their independence and maintain it, and whose independence we have, on great consideration and on just principles, acknowledged, we could not view any interposition for the purpose of oppressing them, or controlling in any other manner their destiny, by any European power in any other light than as the manifestation of an unfriendly disposition toward the United States. In the war between those new Governments and Spain we declared our neutrality at the time of their recognition, and to this we have adhered, and shall continue to adhere, provided no change shall occur which, in the judgement of the competent authorities of this Government, shall make a corresponding change on the part of the United States indispensable to their security.

The late events in Spain and Portugal shew that Europe is still unsettled. Of this important fact no stronger proof can be adduced than that the allied powers should have thought it proper, on any principle satisfactory to themselves, to have interposed by force in the internal concerns of Spain. To what extent such interposition may be carried, on the same principle, is a question in which all independent powers whose governments differ from theirs are interested, even those most remote, and surely none of them more so than the United States. Our policy in regard to Europe, which was adopted at an early stage of the wars which have so long agitated that quarter of the globe, nevertheless remains the same, which is, not to interfere in the internal concerns of any of its powers; to consider the government de facto as the legitimate government for us; to cultivate friendly relations with it, and to preserve those relations by a frank, firm, and manly policy, meeting in all instances the just claims of every power, submitting to injuries from none. But in regard to those continents circumstances are eminently and conspicuously different.

It is impossible that the allied powers should extend their political system to any portion of either continent without endangering our peace and happiness; nor can anyone believe that our southern brethren, if left to themselves, would adopt it of their own accord. It is equally impossible, therefore, that we should behold such interposition in any form with indifference. If we look to the comparative strength and resources of Spain and those new Governments, and their distance from each other, it must be obvious that she can never subdue them. It is still the true policy of the United States to leave the parties to themselves, in hope that other powers will pursue the same course . . .

Source: Richardson, J. D., ed. *Compilations of the Messages and Papers of the Presidents.* Washington, DC: Government Printing Office, 1896–1899.

Alfred T. Mahan: *The Influence of Sea Power upon History, 1660–1783* (1890)

In 1890, Alfred Mahan, a navy officer and professor of history at the Naval War College, published The Influence of Sea Power upon History, 1660–1783. *In this and several other books, Mahan argued that a large navy was the key to international power and influence and sine qua non of empire. The book had an enormous impact on a number of young policymakers in the United States, including Theodore Roosevelt, assistant secretary of the navy in the first McKinley administration. Indeed, within the decade, the United States would acquire an ocean-borne empire, served by a newly expanded navy.*

To turn now from the particular lessons drawn from the history of the past to the general question of the influence of government upon the sea career of its people, it is seen that that influence can work in two distinct but closely related ways.

First, in peace: The government by its policy can favor the natural growth of a people's industries and its tendencies to seek adventure and gain by way of the sea; or it can try to develop such industries and such sea-going bent, when they do not naturally exist; or, on the other hand, the government may, by mistaken action check and fetter the progress which the people left to themselves would make. In any one of these ways the influence of the government will be felt, making or marring the sea power of the country in the matter of peaceful commerce; upon which alone, it cannot be too often insisted, a thoroughly strong navy can be based.

Secondly, for war: The influence of the government will be felt in its most legitimate manner in maintaining an armed navy, of a size commensurate with the growth of its shipping and the importance of the interests connected with it. More important even than the size of the navy is the question of its institutions, favoring a healthful spirit and activity, and providing for rapid development in time of war by an adequate reserve of men and of ships and by measures for drawing out that general reserve power which has before been pointed to, when considering the character and pursuits of the people. Undoubtedly under this second head of warlike preparation must come the maintenance of suitable naval stations, in those distant parts of the world to which the armed shipping must follow the peaceful vessels of commerce. The protection of such stations must depend either upon direct military force, as do Gibraltar and Malta, or upon a surrounding friendly population, such as the American colonists once were to England, and, it may be presumed, the Australian colonists now are. Such friendly surroundings and backing, joined to a reasonable military provision, are the best of defences, and when combined with decided preponderance at sea, make a scattered and extensive empire, like that of England, secure; for while it is true that an unexpected attack may cause disaster in some one quarter, the actual superiority of naval power prevents such disaster from being general or irremediable. History has sufficiently proved this. England's naval bases have been in all parts of the world; and her fleets have at once protected them, kept open the communications between them, and relied upon them for shelter.

Colonies attached to the mother-country afford, therefore, the surest means of supporting abroad the sea power of a country. In peace, the influence of the government should be felt in promoting by all means a warmth of attachment and a unity of interest which will make the welfare of one the welfare of all, and the quarrel of one the quarrel of all; and in war, or rather for war, by inducing such measures of organization and defence

as shall be felt by all to be a fair distribution of a burden of which each reaps the benefit.

Such colonies the United States has not and is not likely to have. As regards purely military naval stations, the feeling of her people was probably accurately expressed by an historian of the English navy a hundred years ago, speaking then of Gibraltar and Port Mahon. "Military governments," said he, "agree so little with the industry of a trading people, and are in themselves so repugnant to the genius of the British people, that I do not wonder that men of good sense and of all parties have inclined to give up these, as Tangiers was given up." Having therefore no foreign establishments, either colonial or military, the ships of war of the United States, in war, will be like land birds, unable to fly far from their own shores. To provide resting-places for them, where they can coal and repair, would be one of the first duties of a government proposing to itself the development of the power of the nation at sea. . . .

The question is eminently one in which the influence of the government should make itself felt, to build up for the nation a navy which, if not capable of reaching distant countries, shall at least be able to keep clear the chief approaches to its own. The eyes of the country have for a quarter of a century been turned from the sea; the results of such a policy and of its opposite will be shown in the instance of France and of England. Without asserting a narrow parallelism between the case of the United States and either of these, it may safely be said that it is essential to the welfare of the whole country that the conditions of trade and commerce should remain, as far as possible, unaffected by an external war. In order to do this, the enemy must be kept not only out of our ports, but far away from our coasts.

Source: Mahan, A. T. *The Influence of Sea Power upon History, 1660–1783.* Boston: Little, Brown and Company, 1890.

Official Report of the Naval Court of Inquiry into the Loss of the Battleship *Maine* (1898)

On January 25, 1898, the battleship USS Maine *sailed into Havana Harbor. Tensions were running high between Spain—which then controlled Cuba—and the*

United States. Many Americans were angry about Spain's harsh treatment of Cuban rebels fighting to liberate their island. When the Maine *mysteriously blew up on the evening of February 15, with the loss of over 260 American sailors, the American public was quick to blame the Spanish. The official U.S. Navy inquiry, known as the Sampson Board, conducted the following month led to a similar conclusion. The destruction of the* Maine *was the single most important incident leading to the Spanish-American War and the subsequent acquisition of an American empire in the Caribbean and the Pacific. In 1976, Admiral Hyman Rickover conducted his own investigation and decided the cause of the explosion was an accident, specifically, fumes in the ship's coal bunkers.*

U.S.S. *Iowa,* First Rate, Key West, Fla., Monday, March 21, 1898.

After full and mature consideration of all the testimony before it, the court finds as follows:

First—That the United States *battleship Maine* arrived in the harbor of Havana, Cuba, on January 25, 1898, and was taken to buoy 4, in from five and a-half to six fathoms of water by the regular government pilot. The United States consul-general at Havana had notified the authorities at that place the previous evening of the intended arrival of the Maine.

Second—The state of discipline on board the Maine was excellent, and all orders and regulations in regard to the care and safety of the ship were strictly carried out. All ammunition was stowed in accordance with prescribed instructions, and proper care was taken whenever ammunition was handled. Nothing was stowed in any one of the magazines or shell-rooms which was not permitted to be stowed there.

The magazines and shell-rooms were always locked after having been opened; and after the destruction of the Maine the keys were found in their proper place in the Captain's cabinet, everything having been reported secure that evening at 8 P.M. The temperature of the magazines and shellrooms was taken daily and reported. The only magazine which had an undue amount of heat was the after ten-inch magazine, and that did not explode at the time the Maine was destroyed. The torpedo war heads were all stowed in the after part of the ship, under the wardroom, and neither caused nor participated in the destruction of the Maine.

The dry gun cotton primers and detonators were stowed in the cabin aft, and remote from the scene of the explosion. Waste was carefully looked after on board the Maine to obviate danger. Special orders in regard to this had been given by the commanding officer. Varnishes, dryers, alcohol and other combustibles of this nature were stowed on or above the main deck, and could not have had anything to do with the destruction of the Maine. The medical stores were stowed aft, under the wardroom, and remote from the scene of the explosion. No dangerous stores of any kind were stowed below in any of the other staterooms.

The coal bunkers were inspected daily. Of those bunkers adjacent to the forward magazines and shell-rooms, four were empty, namely, "B3, B4, B5, B6." "A 15" had been in use that day, and "A16" was full of New River coal. This coal had been carefully inspected before receiving on board. The bunker in which it had been stowed was accessible on three sides at all times, and the fourth side at this time, on account of bunkers "B4" and "B6" being empty. This bunker, "A16," had been inspected that day by the engineer officer on duty. The fire-alarms in the bunkers were in working order, and there had never been a case of spontaneous combustion of coal on board the Maine.

The two after boilers of the ship were in use at the time of the disaster, but for auxiliary purposes only, with a comparatively low pressure of steam, and being tended by a reliable watch. These boilers could not have caused the explosion of the ship. The four forward boilers have since been found by the divers and are in fair condition.

The finding of the court of inquiry was reached after twenty-three days of continuous labor, on the 21st of March instant, and having been approved on the 22d by the commander-in-chief of the United States naval force on the North Atlantic station was transmitted to the Executive.

On the night of the destruction of the Maine everything had been reported secure for the night at 8 P.M. by reliable persons, through the proper authorities, to the commanding officer. At the time the MAINE was destroyed the ship was quiet, and therefore least liable to accident caused by movements from those on board.

Third—The destruction of the MAINE occurred at 9:40 P.M. on February 15, 1898, in the harbor of Havana, Cuba, she being at the time moored to the same buoy to which she had been taken upon her arrival. There were two explosions of a distinctly different character, with a very short but distinct interval between them, and the forward part of the ship was lifted to a marked degree at the time of the first explosion. The first explosion was more in the nature of a report, like that of a gun, while the second explosion was more open, prolonged and of greater volume. The second explosion was, in the opinion of the court, caused by the partial explosion of two or more of the forward magazines of the MAINE.

Fourth—The evidence bearing upon this, being principally obtained from divers, did not enable the court to form a definite conclusion as to the condition of the wreck, although it was established that the after part of the ship was practically intact and sank in that condition a very few minutes after the destruction of the forward part. The following facts in regard to the forward part of the ship are, however, established by the testimony:

That portion of the port side of the protective deck which extends from about frame 30 to about frame 41 was blown up aft and over to port. The main deck, from about frame 30 to about frame 41, was blown up aft and slightly over to starboard, folding the frame forward part of the middle superstructure over and on top of the after part.

This was, in the opinion of the court, caused by the partial explosion of two or more of the forward magazines of the Maine.

Fifth—At frame 17 the outer shell of the ship, from a point eleven and one half feet from the middle line of the ship and six feet above the keel when in its normal position, has been forced up so as to be now about four feet above the surface of the water; therefore, about thirty-four feet above where it would be had the ship been uninjured. The outside bottom-plating is bent into a reversed V shape, the after wing of which, about fifteen feet broad and thirty-two feet in length (from frame 17 to frame 25), is doubled back upon itself against the continuation of the same plating extending forward.

At frame 18 the vertical keel is broken in two and the flat keel is bent at an angle similar to the angle formed by the outside bottom plating. This break is now about six feet below the surface of the water, and about thirty feet above its normal position.

In the opinion of the court, this effect could have been produced only by the explosion of a mine situated under the bottom of the ship at about frame 18, and somewhat on the port side of the ship.

Above and to the right of the small boat, plating at frames 17, 18 and 19 protrudes above the water surface.

Sixth—The court finds that the loss of the Maine on the occasion named was not in any respect due to fault or negligence on the part of any of the officers or members of the crew of said vessel.

Seventh—In the opinion of the court, the Maine was destroyed by the explosion of a submarine mine, which caused the partial explosion of two or more of her forward magazines.

Eighth—The court has been unable to obtain evidence fixing the responsibility for the destruction of the Maine upon any person or persons.

W. T. SAMPSON, Captain U.S.N., President.

A. MARIX, Lieut.-Commander U.S.N., Judge Advocate.

The court, having finished the inquiry it was ordered to make, adjourned at 11 A.M. to await the action of the convening authority.

W. T. SAMPSON, Captain U.S.N., President.

A. MARIX, Lieut.-Commander U.S.N. Judge Advocate.

U.S. Flagship *New York,* March 22, 1898 Off Key West, Fla.

The proceedings and findings of the court of inquiry in the above case are approved.

M. SICARD, Rear-Admiral, Commander-in-chief of the United Naval Force on the North Atlantic Station.

Source: U.S. Congress, House. *Report of the Naval Court of Inquiry upon the Destruction of the United States Battleship Maine in Havana Harbor, February 15, 1898, Together with the Testimony Taken Before the Court.* 55th Cong., 2d Sess. 1898. H. Doc. 207.

Admiral Dewey's Report on the Battle of Manila Bay (1898)

The war between the United States and Spain originally broke out over Cuba, but soon became a two-ocean conflict when Admiral George Dewey, in charge of the U.S. Navy in the Pacific, sailed into

Manila Harbor, Philippines, and defeated the Span-
ish fleet. In this dispatch to the secretary of the navy,
Dewey describes the naval battle, most notably the
ease with which the antiquated Spanish vessels were
dispatched by the modern American warships.

U.S. Naval Force on Asiatic Station, Flagship
"Olympia," Cavite, Philippine Islands, May 4, 1898
Sir:

I have the honor to submit the following report
of operations of the squadron under my command: The squadron left Mirs Bay on April 27, immediately on the arrival of Mr. O. F. Williams,
United States consul at Manila, who brought important information and who accompanies the
squadron. Arrived off Bolinao on the morning of
April 30 and, finding no vessels there, proceeded
down the coast and arrived off the entrance to
Manila Bay on the same afternoon.

The *Boston* and *Concord* were sent to reconnoi-
ter Port Subic, I having been informed that the
enemy intended to take position there. A thorough
search of the port was made by *Boston* and *Concord,* but the Spanish fleet was not found, although
from a letter afterwards found in the arsenal (inclosed with translation), it appears that it had been
their intention to go there.

Entered the Boca Grande, or south channel, at
11.30 P.M., steaming in column at distance at 8
knots. After half the squadron had passed, a battery on the south side of the channel opened fire,
none of the shots taking effect, The *Boston* and
McCullough returned the fire. The squadron proceeded across the bay at slow speed, and arrived
off Manila at daybreak, and was fired upon at 5.15
A.M. by three batteries at Manila and two at Cavite
and by the Spanish fleet anchored in an approximately east and west line across the mouth of
Bakor Bay, with their left in shoal water in Canacao
Bay. The squadron then proceeded to the attack,
the flagship *Olympia,* under my personal direction, leading, followed at distance by the *Baltimore, Raleigh, Petrel, Concord,* and *Boston,* in the
order named, which formation was maintained
throughout the action. The squadron opened fire
at 5.41 A.M. While advancing to the attack, two
mines were exploded ahead of the flagship, too far
to be effective.

The squadron maintained a continuous and
precise fire at ranges varying from 5,000 to 2,000

yards, countermarching in a line approximately
parallel to the Spanish fleet. The enemy's fire was
vigorous, but generally ineffective. Early in the
engagement two launches put out toward the
Olympia with the apparent intention of using
torpedoes. One was sunk and the other disabled
by our fire and beached before an opportunity
occurred to fire torpedoes. At 7 A.M. the Spanish
flagship *Reina Cristina* made a desperate attempt to leave the line and come out to engage at
short range, but was received with such galling
fire, the entire battery of the *Olympia* being concentrated upon her, that she was barely able to
return to the shelter of the point. The fires
started in her by our shell at this time were not
extinguished until she sank. At 7.35 A.M., it having been erroneously reported to me that only 15
rounds per gun remained for the 5-inch rapid
fire battery, I ceased firing and withdrew the
squadron for consultation and a redistribution
of ammunition, if necessary.

The three batteries at Manila had kept up a
continuous fire from the beginning of the engagement, which fire was not returned by this
squadron. The first of these batteries was situated
on the south mole head at the entrance to the Pasig
River, the second on the south bastion of the
walled city of Manila, and the third Malate, about
one-half mile farther south. At this point a message to the Governor-General to the effect that if
the batteries did not cease firing the city would be
shelled. This had the effect of silencing them.

At 11.16 A.M., finding that the report of scarcity
of ammunition was incorrect, I returned with the
squadron to the attack. By this time the flagship
and almost the entire Spanish fleet were in flames,
and at 12:30 P.M. the squadron ceased firing, the
batteries being silenced and the ships sunk, burnt,
and deserted. At 12.40 P.M. the squadron returned
and anchored off Manila, the *Petrel* being left behind to complete the destruction of the smaller
gunboats, which were behind the point of Cavite.
This duty was performed by Commander E. P.
Wood in the most expeditious and complete manner possible.

The Spanish fleet lost the following vessels:
Sunk—*Reina Cristina, Castilla, Don Antonio de
Ulloa.* Burnt—*Don Juan de Austria, Isla de Luzon,
Isla de Cuba, General Lezo, Marques Del Duero, El
Correo, Velasco,* and *Isla de Mindanao* (Transport).

Captured—*Rapido* and *Hercules* (tugs) and several small launches.

I am unable to obtain complete accounts of the enemy's killed and wounded, but believe their loss to be very heavy. The *Reina Cristina* alone had 150 killed, including her captain, and 90 wounded. I am happy to report that damage done to the squadron under my command was inconsiderable. There were none killed, and only seven men in the squadron very slightly wounded. As will be seen by the reports of the commanding officers which are herewith inclosed, several of the vessels were struck and even penetrated, but the damage was of the slightest, and the squadron is in as good condition now as before the battle. I beg to state to the Department that I doubt if any commander-in-chief, under similar circumstances, was ever served by more loyal, efficient, and gallant captains than those of the squadron now under my command. Captain Frank Wildes, commanding the *Boston,* volunteered to remain in command of his vessel, although his relief arrived before leaving Hongkong. Assistant Surgeon C. P. Kindleberger, of the *Olympia,* and Gunner J. C. Evans, of the *Boston* also volunteered to remain after orders detaching them had arrived. The conduct of my personal staff was excellent. Commander B. P. Lamberton, chief of staff, was a volunteer for that position, and gave me most efficient aid. Lieutenant T. M. Brumby, flag lieutenant, and Ensign W. P. Scott, aid, performed their duties as signal officers in a highly creditable manner. The *Olympia* being short of officers for the battery, Ensign H. H. Caldwell, flag secretary volunteered for and was assigned to a subdivision of the 5-inch battery. Mr. J. L. Stickney, formerly an officer in the United States Navy, and now correspondent for the New York Herald, volunteered for duty as my aid, and rendered valuable service.

While leaving to the commanding officers to comment on the conduct of the officers and men under their commands, I desire especially to mention the coolness of Lieutenant C. G. Calkins, the navigator of the *Olympia,* who came under my personal observation, being on the bridge with me throughout the entire action, and giving the ranges to the guns with an accuracy that was proven by the excellence of the firing. On May 2, the day following the engagement, the squadron again went to Cavite, where it remains. A landing party was sent to destroy the guns and magazines of the batteries there. The first battery, near the end of Sangley Point, was composed of two modern Trubia B. L. rifles of 15 centimeters caliber. The second was one mile farther down the beach, and consisted of a modern Canet 12-centimeter B. L. rifle behind improvised earthworks.

On the 3d the military forces evacuated the Cavite arsenal, which was taken possession of by a landing party. On the same day that *Raleigh* and *Baltimore* secured the surrender of the batteries on Corregidor Island, paroling the garrison and destroying the guns. On the morning of May 4 the transport MANILA, which had been aground in Bakor Bay, was towed off and made a prize.

Very respectfully, your obedient servant,

George Dewey Commodore, U.S. Navy Commanding U.S. Naval Force on Asiatic Station.

Source: Spanish American War Centennial website: www.spanamwar.com/dyreport.htm.

Treaty of Peace between the United States and Spain (December 10, 1898)

In April 1898, the United States went to war with Spain. Initially, the conflict concerned Cuba, specifically, Spanish atrocities against Cuban rebels fighting for national independence and threats to extensive U.S. property interests on the island caused by the ongoing liberation struggle. Soon, however, the war spread to all parts of the Spanish Empire. In the end, the decrepit Spanish military was no match for the modern navy and economic might of the United States, and the war ended in just four months. The terms of the peace treaty, by which Spain surrendered all of its remaining colonies in the Caribbean and the Pacific, reflected the uneven struggle.

The United States of America and Her Majesty the Queen Regent of Spain, in the name of her august son Don Alfonso XIII, desiring to end the state of war now existing between the two countries, have for that purpose appointed as plenipotentiaries:

The President of the United States, William R. Day, Cushman K. Davis, William P. Frye, George Gray, and Whitelaw Reid, citizens of the United States;

And Her Majesty the Queen Regent of Spain,

Don Eugenio Montero Rios, president of the senate, Don Buenaventura de Abarzuza, senator of the Kingdom and ex-minister of the Crown; Don Jose de Garnica, deputy of the Cortes and associate justice of the supreme court; Don Wenceslao Ramirez de Villa-Urrutia, envoy extraordinary and minister plenipotentiary at Brussels, and Don Rafael Cerero, general of division;

Who, having assembled in Paris, and having exchanged their full powers, which were found to be in due and proper form, have, after discussion of the matters before them, agreed upon the following articles:

Article I.

Spain relinquishes all claim of sovereignty over and title to Cuba. And as the island is, upon its evacuation by Spain, to be occupied by the United States, the United States will, so long as such occupation shall last, assume and discharge the obligations that may under international law result from the fact of its occupation, for the protection of life and property.

Article II.

Spain cedes to the United States the island of Porto Rico and other islands now under Spanish sovereignty in the West Indies, and the island of Guam in the Marianas or Ladrones.

Article III.

Spain cedes to the United States the archipelago known as the Philippine Islands . . . The United States will pay to Spain the sum of twenty million dollars ($20,000,000) within three months after the exchange of the ratifications of the present treaty.

Article IV.

The United States will, for the term of ten years from the date of the exchange of the ratifications of the present treaty, admit Spanish ships and merchandise to the ports of the Philippine Islands on the same terms as ships and merchandise of the United States.

Article V.

The United States will, upon the signature of the present treaty, send back to Spain, at its own cost, the Spanish soldiers taken as prisoners of war on the capture of Manila by the American forces. The arms of the soldiers in question shall be restored to them.

Spain will, upon the exchange of the ratifications of the present treaty, proceed to evacuate the Philippines, as well as the island of Guam, on terms similar to those agreed upon by the Commissioners appointed to arrange for the evacuation of Porto Rico and other islands in the West Indies, under the Protocol of August 12, 1898, which is to continue in force till its provisions are completely executed . . .

Article VI.

Spain will, upon the signature of the present treaty, release all prisoners of war, and all persons detained or imprisoned for political offences, in connection with the insurrections in Cuba and the Philippines and the war with the United States.

Reciprocally, the United States will release all persons made prisoners of war by the American forces, and will undertake to obtain the release of all Spanish prisoners in the hands of the insurgents in Cuba and the Philippines.

The Government of the United States will at its own cost return to Spain and the Government of Spain will at its own cost return to the United States, Cuba, Porto Rico, and the Philippines, according to the situation of their respective homes, prisoners released or caused to be released by them, respectively, under this article.

Article VII.

The United States and Spain mutually relinquish all claims for indemnity, national and individual, of every kind, of either Government, or of its citizens or subjects, against the other Government, that may have arisen since the beginning of the late insurrection in Cuba and prior to the exchange of ratifications of the present treaty, including all claims for indemnity for the cost of the war.

The United States will adjudicate and settle the claims of its citizens against Spain relinquished in this article.

Article VIII.

In conformity with the provisions of Articles I, II, and III of this treaty, Spain relinquishes in Cuba, and cedes in Porto Rico and other islands in the West Indies, in the island of Guam, and in the Philippine Archipelago, all the buildings, wharves, barracks, forts, structures, public highways and other immovable property which, in conformity with law, belong to the public domain, and as such belong to the Crown of Spain . . .

Article IX.

Spanish subjects, natives of the Peninsula, residing in the territory over which Spain by the present treaty relinquishes or cedes her sovereignty, may remain in such territory or may remove therefrom, retaining in either event all their rights of property, including the right to sell or dispose of such property or of its proceeds; and they shall also have the right to carry on their industry, commerce and professions, being subject in respect thereof to such laws as are applicable to other foreigners. In case they remain in the territory they may preserve their allegiance to the Crown of Spain by making, before a court of record, within a year from the date of the exchange of ratifications of this treaty, a declaration of their decision to preserve such allegiance; in default of which declaration they shall be held to have renounced it and to have adopted the nationality of the territory in which they may reside.

The civil rights and political status of the native inhabitants of the territories hereby ceded to the United States shall be determined by the Congress.

Article X.

The inhabitants of the territories over which Spain relinquishes or cedes her sovereignty shall be secured in the free exercise of their religion.

Article XI.

The Spaniards residing in the territories over which Spain by this treaty cedes or relinquishes her sovereignty shall be subject in matters civil as well as criminal to the jurisdiction of the courts of the country wherein they reside, pursuant to the ordinary laws governing the same; and they shall have the right to appear before such courts, and to pursue the same course as citizens of the country to which the courts belong.

Article XII.

Judicial proceedings pending at the time of the exchange of ratifications of this treaty in the territories over which Spain relinquishes or cedes her sovereignty shall be determined according to the following rules:

1. Judgments rendered either in civil suits between private individuals, or in criminal matters, before the date mentioned, and with respect to which there is no recourse or right of review under the Spanish law, shall be deemed to be final, and shall be executed in due form by competent authority in the territory within which such judgments should be carried out.

2. Civil suits between private individuals which may on the date mentioned be undetermined shall

be prosecuted to judgment before the court in which they may then be pending or in the court that may be substituted therefor.

3. Criminal actions pending on the date mentioned before the Supreme Court of Spain against citizens of the territory which by this treaty ceases to be Spanish shall continue under its jurisdiction until final judgment; but, such judgment having been rendered, the execution thereof shall be committed to the competent authority of the place in which the case arose.

Article XIII.

The rights of property secured by copyrights and patents acquired by Spaniards in the Island of Cuba and in Porto Rico, the Philippines and other ceded territories, at the time of the exchange of the ratifications of this treaty, shall continue to be respected. Spanish scientific, literary and artistic works, not subversive of public order in the territories in question, shall continue to be admitted free of duty into such territories, for the period of ten years, to be reckoned from the date of the exchange of the ratifications of this treaty.

Article XIV.

Spain will have the power to establish consular officers in the ports and places of the territories, the sovereignty over which has been either relinquished or ceded by the present treaty.

Article XV.

The Government of each country will, for the term of ten years, accord to the merchant vessels of the other country the same treatment in respect of all port charges, including entrance and clearance dues, light dues, and tonnage duties, as it accords to its own merchant vessels, not engaged in the coastwise trade.

Article XVI.

It is understood that any obligations assumed in this treaty by the United States with respect to Cuba are limited to the time of its occupancy thereof; but it will upon termination of such occupancy, advise any Government established in the island to assume the same obligations.

Article XVII.

The present treaty shall be ratified by the President of the United States, by and with the advice and consent of the Senate thereof, and by Her Majesty the Queen Regent of Spain; and the ratifications shall be exchanged at Washington within six months from the date hereof, or earlier if possible. In faith whereof, we, the respective Plenipotentiaries, have signed this treaty and have hereunto affixed our seals. Done in duplicate at Paris, the tenth day of December, in the year of Our Lord one thousand eight hundred and ninety-eight.

[Seal] William R. Day [Seal] Cushman K. Davis [Seal] William P. Frye [Seal] Geo. Gray[Seal] Whitelaw Reid [Seal] Eugenio Montero Rios [Seal] B. de Abarzuza[Seal] J. de Garnica [Seal] W. R. de Villa Urrutia [Seal] Rafael Cerero

Source: A Treaty of Peace between the United States and Spain, U.S. Congress, 55th Cong., 3d sess., Senate Doc. No. 62, Part 1. Washington, DC: Government Printing Office, 1899, 5–11.

Emilio Aguinaldo: Manifesto Protesting U.S. Claim of Sovereignty over the Philippines (January 5, 1899)

Beginning in the mid-1890s, a Filipino named Emilio Aguinaldo had been leading a rebellion against Spanish colonial rule. When the United States went to war with Spain in 1898, Aguinaldo welcomed the news, believing that the anticolonial United States would help him liberate his island nation. But when it refused to do so, Aguinaldo began a guerrilla campaign against the new occupier. In the two-year war that followed, Americans employed tactics—including search-and-destroy missions and the internment of civilians who could potentially aid the guerrillas—that would be used later in Vietnam. After the death of several thousand Americans and tens of thousands of Filipinos, Aguinaldo was forced to surrender.

Manifesto Protesting US Claim of Sovereignty over the Philippines, January, 5, 1899

General Otis styles himself Military Governor of these Islands, and I protest one and a thousand times and with all the energy of my soul against such authority. I proclaim solemnly that I have not recognized either Singapore or in Hong Kong or in the Philippines, by word or in writing, the sovereignty of America over this beloved soil. On the contrary, I say that I returned to these Islands on an American warship on the 19th of May last for the express purpose of making war on the Spaniards to regain our liberty and independen-

dence. I stated this in my proclamation of the 24th of May last, and I publish it in my Manifesto addressed to the Philippine people on the 12th of June. Lastly, all this was confirmed by the American General Merritt himself, predecessor of General Otis, in his Manifesto to the Philippine people some days before he demanded the surrender of Manila from the Spanish General Jaudenes. In that Manifesto it is distinctly stated that the naval and field forces of the United States had come to give us our liberty, by subverting the bad Spanish Government, And I hereby protest against this unexpected act of the United States claiming sovereignty over these Islands. My relations with the United States did not bring me over here from Hong Kong to make war on the Spaniards for their benefit, but for the purpose of our own liberty and independence . . .

Source: The Statutes at Large of the United States of America from March 1897 to March 1899 and Recent Treaties, Conventions, Executive Proclamations, and The Concurrent Resolutions of the Two Houses of Congress, Vol. 30. Washington, DC: Government Printing Office, 1899.

First "Open Door Note" (September 6, 1899)

Unlike most of Asia, China was never formally colonized by any of the European powers or Japan. Still, during the late nineteenth century, the Chinese Empire was carved into "spheres of influence" where foreign powers controlled commerce. The United States opposed such a system, not only because it lacked a sphere of its own, but also because it believed that all nations should have free trade access to all parts of China. In a series of diplomatic communiqués, known as the "open door notes," Secretary of State John Hay laid out the U.S. position to France, German, Italy, Japan, Russia, and the United Kingdom, the six powers seeking to control trade in China.

United States Department of State Washington, September 6, 1899

At the time when the Government of the United States was informed by that of Germany that it had leased from His Majesty the Emperor of China the port of Kiao-chao and the adjacent territory in the province of Shantung, assurances were given to the ambassador of the United States at Berlin by the Imperial German minister for foreign affairs that the rights and privileges insured by treaties with China to citizens of the United States would not thereby suffer or be in anywise impaired within the area over which Germany had thus obtained control.

More recently, however, the British Government recognized by a formal agreement with Germany the exclusive right of the latter country to enjoy in said leased area and the contiguous "sphere of influence or interest" certain privileges, more especially those relating to railroads and mining enterprises; but as the exact nature and extent of the rights thus recognized have not been clearly defined, it is possible that serious conflicts of interest may at any time arise not only between British and German subjects within said area, but that the interests of our citizens may also be jeopardized thereby.

Earnestly desirous to remove any cause of irritation and to insure at the same time to the commerce of all nations in China the undoubted benefits which should accrue from a formal recognition by the various powers claiming "spheres of interest" that they shall enjoy perfect equality of treatment for their commerce and navigation within such "spheres," the Government of the United States would be pleased to see His German Majesty's Government give formal assurances, and lend its cooperation in securing like assurances from the other interested powers, that each, within its respective sphere of whatever influence—

First. Will in no way interfere with any treaty port or any vested interest within any so-called "sphere of interest" or leased territory it may have in China.

Second. That the Chinese treaty tariff of the time being shall apply to all merchandise landed or shipped to all such ports as are within said "sphere of interest" (unless they be "free ports"), no matter to what nationality it may belong, and that duties so leviable shall be collected by the Chinese Government.

Third. That it will levy no higher harbor dues on vessels of another nationality frequenting any port in such "sphere" than shall be levied on vessels of its own nationality, and no higher railroad charges over lines built, controlled, or operated within its "sphere" on merchandise belonging to citizens or subjects of other nationalities transported through such "sphere" than shall be levied on similar merchandise belonging to its own nationals transported over equal distances.

The liberal policy pursued by His Imperial German Majesty in declaring Kiao-chao a free port and in aiding the Chinese Government in the establishment there of a customhouse are so clearly in line with the proposition which this Government is anxious to see recognized that it entertains the strongest hope that Germany will give its acceptance and hearty support. The recent ukase of His Majesty the Emperor of Russia declaring the port of Ta-lien-wan open during the whole of the lease under which it is held from China to the merchant ships of all nations, coupled with the categorical assurances made to this Government by His Imperial Majesty's representative at this capital at the time and since repeated to me by the present Russian ambassador, seem to insure the support of the Emperor to the proposed measure. Our ambassador at the Court of St. Petersburg has in consequence, been instructed to submit it to the Russian Government and to request their early consideration of it. A copy of my instruction on the subject to Mr. Tower is herewith inclosed for your confidential information.

The commercial interests of Great Britain and Japan will be so clearly observed by the desired declaration of intentions, and the views of the Governments of these countries as to the desirability of the adoption of measures insuring the benefits of equality of treatment of all foreign trade throughout China are so similar to those entertained by the United States, that their acceptance of the propositions herein outlined and their cooperation in advocating their adoption by the other powers can be confidently expected. I inclose herewith copy of the instruction which I have sent to Mr. Choate on the subject.

In view of the present favorable conditions, you are instructed to submit the above considerations to His Imperial German Majesty's Minister for Foreign Affairs, and to request his early consideration of the subject.

Source: Papers Relating to the Foreign Relations of the United States, 1899. Washington, DC: Government Printing Office, 1899.

American Anti-Imperialist League Platform (1899)

In October 1899, a group of prominent Americans—including steel magnate Andrew Carnegie, author Mark Twain, and American Federation of Labor leader Samuel Gompers—came together to form the American Anti-Imperialist League. The organization was founded even as the U.S. Senate was considering annexation of the Philippines, a former colony of Spain seized by the United States in the Spanish-American War a year earlier. As U.S. troops stayed on to fight Filipino rebels fighting for their national independence, the Anti-Imperialist League argued that imperial acquisition was inappropriate for a country founded in an anticolonial struggle and that the governance of subject peoples was incompatible with democracy. In the end, however, the rebellion was crushed, the Philippines annexed, and the Anti-Imperialist League dissolved.

We hold that the policy known as imperialism is hostile to liberty and tends toward militarism, an evil from which it has been our glory to be free. We regret that it has become necessary in the land of Washington and Lincoln to reaffirm that all men, of whatever race or color, are entitled to life, liberty and the pursuit of happiness. We maintain that governments derive their just powers from the consent of the governed. We insist that the subjugation of any people is "criminal aggression" and open disloyalty to the distinctive principles of our Government.

We earnestly condemn the policy of the present National Administration in the Philippines. It seeks to extinguish the spirit of 1776 in those islands. We deplore the sacrifice of our soldiers and sailors, whose bravery deserves admiration even in an unjust war. We denounce the slaughter of the Filipinos as a needless horror. We protest against the extension of American sovereignty by Spanish methods.

We demand the immediate cessation of the war against liberty, begun by Spain and continued by us. We urge that Congress be promptly convened to announce to the Filipinos our purpose to concede to them the independence for which they have so long fought and which of right is theirs.

The United States have always protested against the doctrine of international law which permits the subjugation of the weak by the strong. A self-governing state cannot accept sovereignty over an unwilling people. The United States cannot act upon the ancient heresy that might makes right.

Imperialists assume that with the destruction of self-government in the Philippines by American hands, all opposition here will cease. This is a grievous error. Much as we abhor the war of "criminal aggression" in the Philippines, greatly as we regret that the blood of the Filipinos is on American hands, we more deeply resent the betrayal of American institutions at home. The real firing line is not in the suburbs of Manila. The foe is of our own household. The attempt of 1861 was to divide the country. That of 1899 is to destroy its fundamental principles and noblest ideals.

Whether the ruthless slaughter of the Filipinos shall end next month or next year is but an incident in a contest that must go on until the Declaration of Independence and the Constitution of the United States are rescued from the hands of their betrayers. Those who dispute about standards of value while the foundation of the Republic is undermined will be listened to as little as those who would wrangle about the small economies of the household while the house is on fire. The training of a great people for a century, the aspiration for liberty of a vast immigration are forces that will hurl aside those who in the delirium of conquest seek to destroy the character of our institutions.

We deny that the obligation of all citizens to support their Government in times of grave National peril applies to the present situation. If an Administration may with impunity ignore the issues upon which it was chosen, deliberately create a condition of war anywhere on the face of the globe, debauch the civil service for spoils to promote the adventure, organize a truth-suppressing censorship and demand of all citizens a suspension of judgment and their unanimous support while it chooses to continue the fighting, representative government itself is imperiled.

We propose to contribute to the defeat of any person or party that stands for the forcible subjugation of any people. We shall oppose for reelection all who in the White House or in Congress betray American liberty in pursuit of un-American ends. We still hope that both of our great political parties will support and defend the Declaration of Independence in the closing campaign of the century.

We hold, with Abraham Lincoln, that "no man is good enough to govern another man without that other's consent. When the white man governs himself, that is self-government, but when he governs himself and also governs another man, that is more than self-government-that is despotism." "Our reliance is in the love of liberty which God has planted in us. Our defense is in the spirit which prizes liberty as the heritage of all men in all lands. Those who deny freedom to others deserve it not for themselves, and under a just God cannot long retain it."

We cordially invite the cooperation of all men and women who remain loyal to the Declaration of Independence and the Constitution of the United States.

Bancroft, Frederick, ed. *Speeches, Correspondence, and Political Papers of Carl Schurz.* New York: G. P. Putnam's Sons, 1913.

William Jennings Bryan: "The Paralyzing Influence of Imperialism" (1900)

In this his second run for the presidency on the Democratic ticket, populist William Jennings Bryan was faced with a new issue: America's acquisition of a colonial empire in the Caribbean and the Pacific. In this anti-imperialist speech at the Democratic National Convention, Bryan counters the arguments presented by the Republican administration that the United States needed an empire for glory and commerce.

If it is right for the United States to hold the Philippine Islands permanently and imitate European empires in the government of colonies, the Republican Party ought to state its position and defend it, but it must expect the subject races to protest against such a policy and to resist to the extent of their ability.

The Filipinos do not need any encouragement from Americans now living. Our whole history has been an encouragement, not only to the Filipinos but to all who are denied a voice in their own government. If the Republicans are prepared to censure all who have used language calculated to make the Filipinos hate foreign domination, let them condemn the speech of Patrick Henry. When he uttered that passionate appeal, "Give me liberty or give me death," he expressed a sentiment which still echoes in the hearts of men.

Let them censure Jefferson; of all the statesmen of history none have used words so offensive to those who would hold their fellows in political bondage. Let them censure Washington, who declared that the colonists must choose between liberty and slavery. Or, if the statute of limitations has run against the sins of Henry and Jefferson and Washington, let them censure Lincoln, whose Gettysburg speech will be quoted in defense of popular government when the present advocates of force and conquest are forgotten.

Someone has said that a truth once spoken can never be recalled. It goes on and on, and no one can set a limit to its ever widening influence. But if it were possible to obliterate every word written or spoken in defense of the principles set forth in the Declaration of Independence, a war of conquest would still leave its legacy of perpetual hatred, for it was God Himself who placed in every human heart the love of liberty. He never made a race of people so low in the scale of civilization or intelligence that it would welcome a foreign master.

Those who would have this nation enter upon a career of empire must consider not only the effect of imperialism on the Filipinos but they must also calculate its effects upon our own nation. We cannot repudiate the principle of self-government in the Philippines without weakening that principle here.

Lincoln said that the safety of this nation was not in its fleets, its armies, its forts, but in the spirit which prizes liberty as the heritage of all men, in all lands, everywhere, and he warned his countrymen that they could not destroy this spirit without planting the seeds of despotism at their own doors.

Even now we are beginning to see the paralyzing influence of imperialism. Heretofore this nation has been prompt to express its sympathy with those who were fighting for civil liberty. While our sphere of activity has been limited to the Western Hemisphere, our sympathies have not been bounded by the seas. We have felt it due to ourselves and to the world, as well as to those who were struggling for the right to govern themselves, to proclaim the interest which our people have, from the date of their own independence, felt in every contest between human rights and arbitrary power. . . .

A colonial policy means that we shall send to the Philippine Islands a few traders, a few taskmasters, and a few officeholders, and an army large enough to support the authority of a small fraction of the people while they rule the natives.

If we have an imperial policy we must have a great standing army as its natural and necessary complement. The spirit which will justify the forcible annexation of the Philippine Islands will justify the seizure of other islands and the domination of other people, and with wars of conquest we can expect a certain, if not rapid, growth of our military establishment.

That a large permanent increase in our regular army is intended by Republican leaders is not a matter of conjecture but a matter of fact. In his message of Dec. 5, 1898, the President asked for authority to increase the standing army to 100,000. In 1896 the army contained about 25,000. Within two years the President asked for four times that many, and a Republican House of Representatives complied with the request after the Spanish treaty had been signed, and when no country was at war with the United States.

If such an army is demanded when an imperial policy is contemplated but not openly avowed, what may be expected if the people encourage the Republican Party by endorsing its policy at the polls?

A large standing army is not only a pecuniary burden to the people and, if accompanied by compulsory service, a constant source of irritation but it is even a menace to a republican form of government. The army is the personification of force, and militarism will inevitably change the ideals of the people and turn the thoughts of our young men from the arts of peace to the science of war. The government which relies for its defense upon its citizens is more likely to be just than one which has at call a large body of professional soldiers.

A small standing army and a well-equipped and well-disciplined state militia are sufficient at ordinary times, and in an emergency the nation should in the future as in the past place its dependence upon the volunteers who come from all occupations at their country's call and return to productive labor when their services are no longer required—men who fight when the country needs fighters and work when the country needs workers. . . .

The Republican platform promises that some measure of self-government is to be given the Filipinos by law; but even this pledge is not fulfilled. Nearly sixteen months elapsed after the ratification of the treaty before the adjournment of Congress last June and yet no law was passed dealing with the Philippine situation. The will of the President has been the only law in the Philippine Islands wherever the American authority extends.

Why does the Republican Party hesitate to legislate upon the Philippine question? Because a law would disclose the radical departure from history and precedent contemplated by those who control the Republican Party. The storm of protest which greeted the Puerto Rican bill was an indication of what may be expected when the American people are brought face to face with legislation upon this subject.

If the Puerto Ricans, who welcomed annexation, are to be denied the guarantees of our Constitution, what is to be the lot of the Filipinos, who resisted our authority? If secret influences could compel a disregard of our plain duty toward friendly people living near our shores, what treatment will those same influences provide for unfriendly people 7,000 miles away? If, in this country where the people have a right to vote, Republican leaders dare not take the side of the people against the great monopolies which have grown up within the last few years, how can they be trusted to protect the Filipinos from the corporations which are waiting to exploit the islands?

Is the sunlight of full citizenship to be enjoyed by the people of the United States and the twilight of semi-citizenship endured by the people of Puerto Rico, while the thick darkness of perpetual vassalage covers the Philippines? The Puerto Rico tariff law asserts the doctrine that the operation of the Constitution is confined to the forty-five states.

The Democratic Party disputes this doctrine and denounces it as repugnant to both the letter and spirit of our organic law. There is no place in our system of government for the deposit of arbitrary and irresistible power. That the leaders of a great party should claim for any President or Congress the right to treat millions of people as mere "possessions" and deal with them unrestrained by the Constitution or the Bill of Rights shows how far we have already departed from the ancient landmarks and indicates what may be expected if this nation deliberately enters upon a career of empire.

The territorial form of government is temporary and preparatory, and the chief security a citizen of a territory has is found in the fact that he enjoys the same constitutional guarantees and is subject to the same general laws as the citizen of a state. Take away this security and his rights will be violated and his interests sacrificed at the demand of those who have political influence. This is the evil of the colonial system, no matter by what nation it is applied.

What is our title to the Philippine Islands? Do we hold them by treaty or by conquest? Did we buy them or did we take them? Did we purchase the people? If not, how did we secure title to them? Were they thrown in with the land? Will the Republicans say that inanimate earth has value but that when that earth is molded by the Divine Hand and stamped with the likeness of the Creator it becomes a fixture and passes with the soil? If governments derive their just powers from the consent of the governed, it is impossible to secure title to people, either by force or by purchase.

We could extinguish Spain's title by treaty, but if we hold title we must hold it by some method consistent with our ideas of government. When we made allies of the Filipinos and armed them to fight against Spain, we disputed Spain's title. If we buy Spain's title, we are not innocent purchasers. There can be no doubt that we accepted and utilized the services of the Filipinos and that when we did so we had full knowledge that they were fighting for their own independence; and I submit that history furnishes no example of turpitude baser than ours if we now substitute our yoke for the Spanish yoke. . . .

Some argue that American rule in the Philippine Islands will result in the better education of the Filipinos. Be not deceived. If we expect to maintain a colonial policy, we shall not find it to our advantage to educate the people. The educated Filipinos are now in revolt against us, and the most ignorant ones have made the least resistance to our domination. If we are to govern them without their consent and give them no voice in determining the taxes which they must pay, we dare not educate them lest they learn to read the Declaration of Independence and the Constitution of the United States and mock us for our inconsistency.

The principal arguments, however, advanced by those who enter upon a defense of imperialism are:

First, that we must improve the present opportunity to become a world power and enter into international politics.

Second, that our commercial interests in the Philippine Islands and in the Orient make it necessary for us to hold the islands permanently.

Third, that the spread of the Christian religion will be facilitated by a colonial policy.

Fourth, that there is no honorable retreat from the position which the nation has taken.

The first argument is addressed to the nation's pride and the second to the nation's pocketbook. The third is intended for the church member and the fourth for the partisan.

It is sufficient answer to the first argument to say that for more than a century this nation has been a world power. For ten decades it has been the most potent influence in the world. Not only has it been a world power but it has done more to affect the policies of the human race than all the other nations of the world combined. Because our Declaration of Independence was promulgated, others have been promulgated. Because the patriots of 1776 fought for liberty, others have fought for it. Because our Constitution was adopted, other constitutions have been adopted.

The growth of the principle of self-government, planted on American soil, has been the overshadowing political fact of the 19th century. It has made this nation conspicuous among the nations and given it a place in history, such as no other nation has ever enjoyed. Nothing has been able to check the onward march of this idea. I am not willing that this nation shall cast aside the omnipotent weapon of truth to seize again the weapons of physical warfare. I would not exchange the glory of this republic for the glory of all the empires that have risen and fallen since time began.

The permanent chairman of the last Republican National Convention presented the pecuniary argument in all its baldness when he said:

We make no hypocritical pretense of being interested in the Philippines solely on account of others. While we regard the welfare of those people as a sacred trust, we regard the welfare of the American people first. We see our duty to ourselves as well as to others. We believe in trade expansion. By every legitimate means within the province of government and constitution we mean to stimulate the expansion of our trade and open new markets.

This is the commercial argument. It is based upon the theory that war can be rightly waged for pecuniary advantage and that it is profitable to purchase trade by force and violence. Franklin denied both of these propositions. When Lord Howe asserted that the acts of Parliament which brought on the Revolution were necessary to prevent American trade from passing into foreign channels, Franklin replied:

To me it seems that neither the obtaining nor retaining of any trade, howsoever valuable, is an object for which men may justly spill each other's blood; that the true and sure means of extending and securing commerce are the goodness and cheapness of commodities, and that the profits of no trade can ever be equal to the expense of compelling it and holding it by fleets and armies. I consider this war against us, therefore, as both unjust and unwise.

I place the philosophy of Franklin against the sordid doctrine of those who would put a price upon the head of an American soldier and justify a war of conquest upon the ground that it will pay. The Democratic Party is in favor of the expansion of trade. It would extend our trade by every legitimate and peaceful means; but it is not willing to make merchandise of human blood.

But a war of conquest is as unwise as it is unrighteous. A harbor and coaling station in the Philippines would answer every trade and military necessity and such a concession could have been secured at any time without difficulty. It is not necessary to own people in order to trade with them. We carry on trade today with every part of the world, and our commerce has expanded more rapidly than the commerce of any European empire. We do not own Japan or China, but we trade with their people. We have not absorbed the republics of Central and South America, but we trade with them. Trade cannot be permanently profitable unless it is voluntary.

When trade is secured by force, the cost of securing it and retaining it must be taken out of the profits, and the profits are never large enough to cover the expense. Such a system would never be defended but for the fact that the expense is borne by all the people while the profits are enjoyed by a few.

Imperialism would be profitable to the Army contractors; it would be profitable to the shipowners, who would carry live soldiers to the Philippines and bring dead soldiers back; it would be profitable to those who would seize upon the franchises, and it would be profitable to the officials whose salaries would be fixed here and paid over there; but to the farmer, to the laboring man, and to the vast majority of those engaged in other occupations, it would bring expenditure without return and risk without reward.

Farmers and laboring men have, as a rule, small incomes, and, under systems which place the tax upon consumption, pay much more than their fair share of the expenses of government. Thus the very people who receive least benefit from imperialism will be injured most by the military burdens which accompany it. In addition to the evils which he and the former share in common, the laboring man will be the first to suffer if Oriental subjects seek work in the United States; the first to suffer if American capital leaves our shores to employ Oriental labor in the Philippines to supply the trade of China and Japan; the first to suffer from the violence which the military spirit arouses, and the first to suffer when the methods of imperialism are applied to our own government. It is not strange, therefore, that the labor organizations have been quick to note the approach of these dangers and prompt to protest against both militarism and imperialism.

The pecuniary argument, though more effective with certain classes, is not likely to be used so often or presented with so much enthusiasm as the religious argument. If what has been termed the "gunpowder gospel" were urged against the Filipinos only, it would be a sufficient answer to say that a majority of the Filipinos are now members of one branch of the Christian Church; but the principle involved is one of much wider application and challenges serious consideration.

The religious argument varies in positiveness from a passive belief that Providence delivered the Filipinos into our hands for their good and our glory to the exultation of the minister who said that we ought to "thrash the natives (Filipinos) until they understand who we are," and that "every bullet sent, every cannon shot, and every flag waved means righteousness."

We cannot approve of this doctrine in one place unless we are willing to apply it everywhere. If there is poison in the blood of the hand, it will ultimately reach the heart. It is equally true that forcible Christianity, if planted under the American flag in the far-away Orient, will sooner or later be transplanted upon American soil. . . .

The argument made by some that it was unfortunate for the nation that it had anything to do with the Philippine Islands, but that the naval victory at Manila made the permanent acquisition of those islands necessary, is also unsound. We won a naval victory at Santiago, but that did not compel us to hold Cuba.

The shedding of American blood in the Philippine Islands does not make it imperative that we should retain possession forever; American blood was shed at San Juan Hill and El Caney, and yet the President has promised the Cubans independence. The fact that the American flag floats over Manila does not compel us to exercise perpetual sovereignty over the islands; the American flag waves over Havana today, but the President has promised to haul it down when the flag of the Cuban republic is ready to rise in its place. Better a thousand times that our flag in the Orient give way to a flag representing the idea of self-government than that the flag of this republic should become the flag of an empire.

There is an easy, honest, honorable solution of the Philippine question. It is set forth in the Democratic platform and it is submitted with confidence to the American people. This plan I unreservedly endorse. If elected, I will convene Congress in extraordinary session as soon as inaugurated and recommend an immediate declaration of the nation's purpose: first, to establish a stable form of government in the Philippine Islands, just as we are now establishing a stable form of government in Cuba; second, to give independence to the Cubans; third, to protect the Filipinos from outside interference while they work out their destiny, just as we have protected the republics of Central and South America, and are, by the Monroe Doctrine, pledged to protect Cuba.

A European protectorate often results in the plundering of the ward by the guardian. An American protectorate gives to the nation protected the advantage of our strength without making it the victim of our greed. For three-quarters of a century the Monroe Doctrine has been a shield to neighboring republics and yet it has imposed no pecuniary burden upon us. After the Filipinos had aided us in the war against Spain, we could not honorably turn them over to their former masters; we could not leave them to be the victims of the ambitious designs of European nations, and since we do not desire to make them a part of us or to hold them as subjects, we propose the only alternative, namely, to give them independence and guard them against molestation from without.

When our opponents are unable to defend their position by argument, they fall back upon the assertion that it is destiny and insist that we must submit to it no matter how much it violates our moral precepts and our principles of government. This is a complacent philosophy. It obliterates the distinction between right and wrong and makes individuals and nations the helpless victims of circumstances. Destiny is the subterfuge of the invertebrate, who, lacking the courage to oppose error, seeks some plausible excuse for supporting it. Washington said that the destiny of the republican form of government was deeply, if not finally, staked on the experiment entrusted to the American people.

How different Washington's definition of destiny from the Republican definition! The Republicans say that this nation is in the hands of destiny; Washington believed that not only the destiny of our own nation but the destiny of the republican form of government throughout the world was entrusted to American hands. Immeasurable responsibility!

The destiny of this republic is in the hands of its own people, and upon the success of the experiment here rests the hope of humanity. No exterior force can disturb this republic, and no foreign influence should be permitted to change its course. What the future has in store for this nation no one has authority to declare, but each individual has his own idea of the nation's mission, and he owes it to his country as well as to himself to contribute as best he may to the fulfillment of that mission.

Mr. Chairman and Gentlemen of the Committee, I can never fully discharge the debt of gratitude which I owe to my countrymen for the honors which they have so generously bestowed upon me; but, sirs, whether it be my lot to occupy the high office for which the convention has named me or to spend the remainder of my days in private life, it shall be my constant ambition and my controlling purpose to aid in realizing the high ideals of those whose wisdom and courage and sacrifices brought this republic into existence.

I can conceive of a national destiny surpassing the glories of the present and the past—a destiny which meets the responsibilities of today and measures up to the possibilities of the future. Behold a republic, resting securely upon the foundation stones quarried by revolutionary patriots from the mountain of eternal truth—a republic applying in practice and proclaiming to the world the self-evident proposition that all men are created equal; that they are endowed with inalienable rights; that governments are instituted among men to secure these rights, and that governments derive their just powers from the consent of the governed.

Behold a republic in which civil and religious liberty stimulate all to earnest endeavor and in which the law restrains every hand uplifted for a neighbor's injury—a republic in which every citizen is a sovereign, but in which no one cares to wear a crown. Behold a republic standing erect while empires all around are bowed beneath the weight of their own armaments—a republic whose flag is loved while other flags are only feared. Behold a republic increasing in population, in wealth, in strength, and in influence, solving the problems of civilization and hastening the coming of an universal brotherhood—a republic which shakes thrones and dissolves aristocracies by its silent example and gives light and inspiration to those who sit in darkness. Behold a republic gradually but surely becoming a supreme moral factor in the world's progress and the accepted arbiter of the world's disputes—a republic whose history, like the path of the just, "is as the shining light that shineth more and more unto the perfect day."

Source: Official Proceedings of the Democratic National Convention Held in Kansas City, Missouri, July 4, 5 and 6, 1900. Chicago, 1900.

President William McKinley: Inaugural Speech (1901)

First elected to the presidency in 1896, William McKinley declared war on Spain in April 1898, urged on by a public outraged by Spanish atrocities against Cuban rebels and American business interests on the island hurt by the fighting there. The "splendid little war" left America with territories stretching from Puerto Rico to the Philippines and an important question: should a country that arose in a struggle out of colonialism take on colonies itself? In this excerpt from his inaugural speech in 1901, McKinley answered in the affirmative, saying it was America's duty to govern the inhabitants of those territories, as they were incapable of self-government yet.

We face at this moment a most important question that of the future relations of the United States and Cuba. With our near neighbors we must remain close friends. The declaration of the purposes of this Government in the resolution of April 20, 1898, must be made good. Ever since the evacuation of the island by the army of Spain, the Executive, with all practicable speed, has been assisting its people in the successive steps necessary to the establishment of a free and independent government prepared to assume and perform the obligations of international law which now rest upon the United States under the treaty of Paris. The convention elected by the people to frame a constitution is approaching the completion of its labors. The transfer of American control to the new government is of such great importance, involving an obligation resulting from our intervention and the treaty of peace, that I am glad to be advised by the recent act of Congress of the policy which the legislative branch of the Government deems essential to the best interests of Cuba and the United States. The principles which led to our intervention require that the fundamental law upon which the new government rests should be adapted to secure a government capable of performing the duties and discharging the functions of a separate nation, of observing its international obligations of protecting life and property, insuring order, safety, and liberty, and conforming to the established and historical policy of the United States in its relation to Cuba.

The peace which we are pledged to leave to the Cuban people must carry with it the guaranties of permanence. We became sponsors for the pacification of the island, and we remain accountable to the Cubans, no less than to our own country and people, for the reconstruction of Cuba as a free commonwealth on abiding foundations of right, justice, liberty, and assured order. Our enfranchisement of the people will not be completed until free Cuba shall "be a reality, not a name; a perfect entity, not a hasty experiment bearing within itself the elements of failure."

While the treaty of peace with Spain was ratified on the 6th of February, 1899, and ratifications were exchanged nearly two years ago, the Congress has indicated no form of government for the Philippine Islands. It has, however, provided an army to enable the Executive to suppress insurrection, restore peace, give security to the inhabitants, and establish the authority of the United States throughout the archipelago. It has authorized the organization of native troops as auxiliary to the regular force. It has been advised from time to time of the acts of the military and naval officers in the islands, of my action in appointing civil commissions, of the instructions with which they were charged, of their duties and powers, of their recommendations, and of their several acts under executive commission, together with the very complete general information they have submitted. These reports fully set forth the conditions, past and present, in the islands, and the instructions clearly show the principles which will guide the Executive until the Congress shall, as it is required to do by the treaty, determine "the civil rights and political status of the native inhabitants." The Congress having added the sanction of its authority to the powers already possessed and exercised by the Executive under the Constitution, thereby leaving with the Executive the responsibility for the government of the Philippines, I shall continue the efforts already begun until order shall be restored throughout the islands, and as fast as conditions permit will establish local governments, in the formation of which the full co-operation of the people has been already invited, and when established will encourage the people to administer them. The settled purpose, long ago proclaimed, to afford the inhabitants of the islands self-government as fast as they were ready for it will be pursued with earnestness and fidelity. Already something has been accomplished in this direction. The Government's representatives, civil and military, are doing faithful and noble work in their mission of emancipation and merit the approval and support of their countrymen. The most liberal terms of amnesty have already been communicated to the insurgents, and the way is still open for those who have raised their arms against the Government for honorable submission to its authority. Our countrymen should not be deceived. We are not waging war against the inhabitants of the Philippine Islands. A portion of them are making war against the United States. By far the greater part of the inhabitants recognize American sovereignty and welcome it as a guaranty of order and of security for life, property, liberty, freedom of conscience, and the pursuit of happiness. To them full protection will be given. They shall not be abandoned. We will not leave the destiny of the loyal millions the islands to the disloyal thousands who are in rebellion against the United States. Order under civil institutions will come as soon as those who now break the peace shall keep it. Force will not be needed or used when those who make war against us shall make it no more. May it end without further bloodshed, and there be ushered in the reign of peace to be made permanent by a government of liberty under law!

Source: http://www.bartleby.com/124/pres41.html.

Emilio Aguinaldo: Proclamation of Formal Surrender to the United States (April 19, 1901)

Following the Spanish-American War of 1898, the United States occupied the former Spanish colony of the Philippines, annexing them formally the following year. Many Filipinos, however, had other ideas. A rebellion, led by revolutionary Emilio Aguinaldo, arose to confront U.S. occupation. For three years, the U.S. Army fought a brutal guerrilla-style war against Aguinaldo's forces, leading to the deaths of over 4,000 American soldiers and countless thousands of Filipino rebels and civilians. Finally, facing defeat and eager to end the bloodshed, Aguinaldo issued this formal surrender and pledged allegiance to U.S. authority.

To the Filipino People:

I believe that I am not in error in presuming that the unhappy fate to which my adverse fortune has led me is not a surprise to those who have been familiar day to day with the progress of the war. The lessons thus taught, the full meaning of which has recently come to my knowledge, suggested to me with irresistible force that the complete termination of hostilities and a lasting peace are not only desirable but absolutely essential to the welfare of the Philippines.

The Filipinos have never been dismayed by their weakness, nor have they faltered in following the path pointed out by their fortitude and courage. The time has come, however, in which they find their advance along the path impeded by an irresistible force—a force which, while it restrains them, yet enlightens the mind and opens another course by presenting to them the cause of peace. This cause has been joyfully embraced around glorious and sovereign banner of the United States. In this manner they repose their trust in the belief that under its protection our people will attain all the promised liberties which they are even now beginning to enjoy.

The country has declared unmistakably in favor of peace; so be it. Enough of blood; enough of tears and desolation. This wish cannot be ignored by the men still in arms if they are animated by no other desire than to serve this noble people which has clearly manifested its will.

So also do I respect this will now that it is known to me, and after mature deliberation resolutely proclaim to the world that I cannot refuse to heed the voice of a people longing for peace, nor the lamentations of thousands of families yearning to see their dear ones in the enjoyment of the liberty promised by the generosity of the great American nation.

By acknowledging and accepting the sovereignty of the United States throughout the entire Archipelago, as I now do without any reservations whatsoever, I believe that I am serving thee, my beloved country. May happiness be thine!

Source: The Statutes at Large of the United States of America from March 1897 to March 1899 and Recent Treaties, Conventions, Executive Proclamations, and The Concurrent Resolutions of the Two Houses of Congress, Volume 30. Washington, DC: Government Printing Office, 1899.

Platt Amendment (1901)

One of the small ironies of the Spanish-American War was that Cuba, the territory over which the United States went to war with Spain in 1898, was the first territory to be given independence by the United States, in 1902. However, to ensure protection of U.S. interests in the new country, Congress passed the Platt Amendment, sponsored by Connecticut Senator Orville Platt. The amendment gave the United States the right to intervene in island affairs, even to the point of sending troops, to maintain pro-U.S. governments. U.S. officials also insisted that similar language be incorporated into the first Cuban constitution of 1902, despite much resistance. The Platt Amendment was abrogated in 1934, although the United States maintained its base at Guantánamo Bay.

Whereas the Congress of the United States of America, by an Act approved March 2, 1901, provided as follows:

Provided further, That in fulfillment of the declaration contained in the joint resolution approved April twentieth, eighteen hundred and ninety-eight, entitled "For the recognition of the independence of the people of Cuba, demanding that the Government of Spain relinquish its authority and government in the island of Cuba, and withdraw its land and naval forces from Cuba and Cuban waters, and directing the President of the United States to use the land and naval forces of the United States to carry these resolutions into effect," the President is hereby authorized to "leave the government and control of the island of Cuba to its people" so soon as a government shall have been established in said island under a constitution which, either as a part thereof or in an ordinance appended thereto, shall define the future relations of the United States with Cuba, substantially as follows:

"I. That the government of Cuba shall never enter into any treaty or other compact with any foreign power or powers which will impair or tend to impair the independence of Cuba, nor in any manner authorize or permit any foreign power or powers to obtain by colonization or for military or naval purposes or otherwise, lodgement in or control over any portion of said island."

"II. That said government shall not assume or contract any public debt, to pay the interest upon which, and to make reasonable sinking fund provision for the ultimate discharge of which, the ordinary revenues of the island, after defraying the current expenses of government shall be inadequate."

"III. That the government of Cuba consents that the United States may exercise the right to intervene for the preservation of Cuban independence, the maintenance of a government adequate for the protection of life, property, and individual liberty, and for discharging the obligations with respect to Cuba imposed by the treaty of Paris on the United States, now to be assumed and undertaken by the government of Cuba."

"IV. That all Acts of the United States in Cuba during its military occupancy thereof are ratified and validated, and all lawful rights acquired thereunder shall be maintained and protected."

"V. That the government of Cuba will execute, and as far as necessary extend, the plans already devised or other plans to be mutually agreed upon, for the sanitation of the cities of the island, to the end that a recurrence of epidemic and infectious diseases may be prevented, thereby assuring protection to the people and commerce of Cuba, as well as to the commerce of the southern ports of the United States and the people residing therein."

"VI. That the Isle of Pines shall be omitted from the proposed constitutional boundaries of Cuba, the title thereto being left to future adjustment by treaty."

"VII. That to enable the United States to maintain the independence of Cuba, and to protect the people thereof, as well as for its own defense, the government of Cuba will sell or lease to the United States lands necessary for coaling or naval stations at certain specified points to be agreed upon with the President of the United States."

"VIII. That by way of further assurance the government of Cuba will embody the foregoing provisions in a permanent treaty with the United States."

Source: "The Platt Amendment," in *Treaties and Other International Agreements of the United States of America, 1776–1949*, vol. 8. Washington, DC: Government Printing Office, 1971.

President Theodore Roosevelt: Proclamation, Formally Ending the Philippine "Insurrection" and Granting of Pardon and Amnesty (July 4, 1902)

During the last years of Spanish rule in the Philippines in the 1890s, liberation leader Emilio Aguinaldo led a struggle for national independence. At first welcoming the American war against Spain in 1898, Aguinaldo turned against the United States when he realized that the Americans intended to take the Spaniards' place as the colonial rulers of the Philippines. A bitter three-year guerrilla struggle ensued between American troops and Aguinaldo's rebels that resulted in tens of thousands of lives lost, mostly among rebels and Filipino civilians. Attempting to heal the wounds and cement loyalty to the American colonial government, President Theodore Roosevelt issued the following amnesty to all those who took up arms against the United States.

Whereas, many of the inhabitants of the Philippine Archipelago were in insurrection against the authority and sovereignty of the Kingdom of Spain at divers times from August, eighteen hundred and ninety-six, until the cession of the archipelago by that Kingdom to the United States of America, and since such cession many of the persons so engaged in insurrection have until recently resisted the authority and sovereignty of the United States; and

Whereas, the insurrection against the authority and sovereignty of the United States is now at an end, and peace has been established in all parts of the archipelago except in the country inhabited by the Moro tribes, to which this proclamation does not apply; and

Whereas, during the course of the insurrection against the Kingdom of Spain and against the Government of the United States, persons engaged therein, or those in sympathy with and abetting them, committed many acts in violation of the laws of civilized warfare, but it is believed that such acts were generally committed in ignorance of those laws, and under orders issued by the civil or insurrectionary leaders; and

Whereas, it is deemed to be wise and humane, in accordance with the beneficent purposes of the Government of the United States towards the Filipino people, and conducive to peace, order, and loyalty among them, that the doers of such acts who have not already suffered punishment shall not be held criminally responsible, but shall be relieved from punishment for participation in these insurrections, and for unlawful acts committed during the course thereof, by a general amnesty and pardon:

Now, therefore, be it known that I, Theodore Roosevelt, President of the United States of America, by virtue of the power and authority vested in me by the Constitution, do hereby proclaim and declare, without reservation or condition, except as hereinafter provided, a full and complete pardon and amnesty to all persons in the Philippine Archipelago who have participated in the insurrections aforesaid, or who have given aid and comfort to persons participating in said insurrections, for the offenses of treason or sedition and for all offenses political in their character committed in the course of such insurrections pursuant to orders issued by the civil or military insurrectionary authorities, or which grew out of internal political feuds or dissension between Filipinos and Spaniards or the Spanish authorities, or which resulted from internal political feuds or dissension among the Filipinos themselves, during either of said insurrections:

Provided, however, That the pardon and amnesty hereby granted shall not include such persons committing crimes since May first, nineteen hundred and two, in any province of the archipelago in which at the time civil government was established, nor shall it include such persons as have been heretofore finally convicted of the crimes of murder, rape, arson, or robbery by any military or civil tribunal organized under the authority of Spain, or of the United States of America, but special application may be made to the proper authority for pardon by any person belonging to the exempted classes, and such clemency as is consistent with humanity and justice will be liberally extended; and

Further provided, That this amnesty and pardon shall not affect the title or right of the Government of the United States, or that of the Philippine Islands, to any property or property rights heretofore used or appropriated by the military or civil authorities of the Government of the United States, or that of the Philippine Islands, organized under authority of the United States, by way of confiscation or otherwise;

Provided further, That every person who shall seek to avail himself of this proclamation shall take and subscribe the following oath before any authority in the Philippine Archipelago authorized to administer oaths, namely:

"I, _____, solemnly swear (or affirm) that I recognize and accept the supreme authority of the United States of America in the Philippine Islands and will maintain true faith and allegiance thereto; that I impose upon myself this obligation voluntarily, without mental reservation or purpose of evasion. So help me God."

Given under my hand at the City of Washington this fourth day of July in the year of our Lord one thousand nine hundred and two, and in the one hundred and twenty-seventh year of the Independence of the United States.

Source: The Statutes at Large of the United States of America from March 1897 to March 1899 and Recent Treaties, Conventions, Executive Proclamations, and The Concurrent Resolutions of the Two Houses of Congress, vol. 30. Washington, DC: Government Printing Office, 1899.

Convention for the Construction of a Ship Canal (Hay–Bunau-Varilla Treaty) (November 18, 1903)

For several years around the turn of the twentieth century, the United States had tried to get Colombia—which then controlled the isthmus of Panama—to allow it to build and operate an interocean canal on terms favorable to Washington. Recognizing the value of such a canal, Colombia insisted on a very high price. Rather than accepting such terms, the United States fomented a rebellion in the isthmus in 1903, and the province of Panama broke away from Colombia. Very shortly after, the United States negotiated with the new Republic of Panama a treaty whose terms Colombia had largely rejected. The treaty was ratified by the Senate and signed by President Theodore Roosevelt in February 1904; the canal was completed a decade later.

The United States of America and the Republic of Panama being desirous to insure the construction of a ship canal across the Isthmus of Panama to connect the Atlantic and Pacific oceans, and the Congress of the United States of America having passed an act approved June 28, 1902, in furtherance of that object, by which the President of the United States is authorized to acquire within a reasonable time the control of the necessary territory of the Republic of Colombia, and the sovereignty of such territory being actually vested in the Republic of Panama, the high contracting parties have resolved for that purpose to conclude a convention and have accordingly appointed as their plenipotentiaries,-

The President of the United States of America, John Hay, Secretary of State, and

The Government of the Republic of Panama, Philippe Bunau-Varilla, Envoy Extraordinary and Minister Plenipotentiary of the Republic of Panama, thereunto specially empowered by said government, who after communicating with each other their respective full powers, found to be in good and due form, have agreed upon and concluded the following articles:

ARTICLE I

The United States guarantees and will maintain the independence of the Republic of Panama.

ARTICLE II

The Republic of Panama grants to the United States in perpetuity the use, occupation and control of a zone of land and land under water for the construction maintenance, operation, sanitation and protection of said Canal of the width of ten miles extending to the distance of five miles on each side of the center line of the route of the Canal to be constructed; the said zone beginning in the Caribbean Sea three marine miles from mean low water mark and extending to and across the Isthmus of Panama into the Pacific ocean to a distance of three marine miles from mean low water mark with the proviso that the cities of Panama and Colon and the harbors adjacent to said cities, which are included within the boundaries of the zone above described, shall not be included within this grant. The Republic of Panama further grants to the United States in perpetuity the use, occupation and control of any other lands and waters outside of the zone above described which may be necessary and convenient for the construction, maintenance, operation, sanitation and protection of the said Canal or of any auxiliary canals or other works necessary and convenient for the construction, maintenance, operation, sanitation and protection of the said enterprise . . .

ARTICLE III

The Republic of Panama grants to the United States all the rights, power and authority within the zone mentioned and described in Article II of this agreement and within the limits of all auxiliary lands and waters mentioned and described in said Article II which the United States would pos-

sess and exercise if it were the sovereign of the territory within which said lands and waters are located to the entire exclusion of the exercise by the Republic of Panama of any such sovereign rights, power or authority.

ARTICLE IV

As rights subsidiary to the above grants the Republic of Panama grants in perpetuity to the United States the right to use the rivers, streams, lakes and other bodies of water within its limits for navigation, the supply of water or water-power or other purposes, so far as the use of said rivers, streams, lakes and bodies of water and the waters thereof may be necessary and convenient for the construction, maintenance, operation, sanitation and protection of the said Canal.

ARTICLE V

The Republic of Panama grants to the United States in perpetuity a monopoly for the construction, maintenance and operation of any system of communication by means of canal or railroad across its territory between the Caribbean Sea and the Pacific ocean.

ARTICLE VI

The grants herein contained shall in no manner invalidate the titles or rights of private land holders or owners of private property in the said zone or in or to any of the lands or waters granted to the United States by the provisions of any Article of this treaty, nor shall they interfere with the rights of way over the public roads passing through the said zone or over any of the said lands or waters unless said rights of way or private rights shall conflict with rights herein granted to the United States in which case. the rights of the United States shall be superior . . .

ARTICLE VIII

The Republic of Panama grants to the United States all rights which it now has or hereafter may acquire to the property of the New Panama Canal Company and the Panama Railroad Company as a result of the transfer of sovereignty from the Republic of Colombia to the Republic of Panama over the Isthmus of Panama and authorizes the New Panama Canal Company to sell and transfer to the United States its rights, privileges, properties and concessions as well as the Panama Railroad and all the shares or part of the shares of that company; but the public lands situated outside of the zone described in Article II of this treaty now included in the concessions to both said enterprises and not required in the construction or operation of the Canal shall revert to the Republic of Panama except any property now owned by or in the possession of said companies within Panama or Colon or the ports or terminals thereof.

ARTICLE IX

The United States agrees that the ports at either entrance of the Canal and the waters thereof, and the Republic of Panama agrees that the towns of Panama and Colon shall be free for all time so that there shall not be imposed or collected custom house tolls, tonnage, anchorage, lighthouse, wharf, pilot, or quarantine dues or any other charges or taxes of any kind upon any vessel using or passing through the Canal or belonging to or employed by the United States, directly or indirectly, in connection with the construction, maintenance, operation, sanitation and protection of the main Canal, or auxiliary works, or upon the cargo, officers, crew, or passengers of any such vessels, except such tolls and charges as may be imposed by the United States for the use of the Canal and other works, and except tolls and charges imposed by the Republic of Panama upon merchandise destined to be introduced for the consumption of the rest of the Republic of Panama, and upon vessels touching at the ports of Colon and Panama and which do not cross the Canal . . .

ARTICLE X

The Republic of Panama agrees that there shall not be imposed any taxes, national, municipal, departmental, or of any other class, upon the Canal, the railways and auxiliary works, tugs and other vessels employed in bye service of the Canal, store houses, work shops, offices, quarters for laborers, factories of all kinds, warehouses, wharves, machinery and other works, property, and effects appertaining to the Canal or railroad and auxiliary works, or their officers or employees, situated within the cities of Panama and Colon, and that there shall not be imposed contributions or charges of a personal character of any kind upon officers, employees, laborers, and other individuals in the service of the Canal and railroad and auxiliary works . . .

ARTICLE XII

The Government of the Republic of Panama shall permit the immigration and free access to the lands and workshops of the Canal and its aux-iliary works of all employees and workmen of Whatever nationality under contract to work upon or seeking employment upon or in any wise connected with the said Canal and its auxiliary works, with their respective families, and all such persons shall be free and exempt from the military service of the Republic of Panama . . .

ARTICLE XIV

As the price or compensation for the rights, powers and privileges granted in this convention by the Republic of Panama to the United States, the Government of the United States agrees to pay to the Republic of Panama the sum of ten million dollars ($10,000,000) in gold coin of the United States on the exchange of the ratification of this convention and also an annual payment during the life of this convention of two hundred and fifty thousand dollars ($250,000) in like gold coin, beginning nine years after the date aforesaid.

The provisions of this Article shall be in addition to all other benefits assured to the Republic of Panama under this convention.

But no delay or difference of opinion under this Article or any other provisions of this treaty shall affect or interrupt the full operation and effect of this convention in all other respects.

ARTICLE XV

The joint commission referred to in Article VI shall be established as follows:

The President of the United States shall nominate two persons and the President of the Republic of Panama shall nominate two persons and they shall proceed to a decision; but in case of disagreement of the Commission (by reason of their being equally divided in conclusion) an umpire shall be appointed by the two Governments who shall render the decision. In the event of the death, absence, or incapacity of a Commissioner or Umpire, or of his omitting, declining or ceasing to act, his place shall be filled by the appointment of another person in the manner above indicated. All decisions by a majority of the Commission or by the Umpire shall be final.

ARTICLE XVI

The two Governments shall make adequate provision by future agreement for the pursuit, capture, imprisonment, detention and delivery within said zone and auxiliary lands to the authorities of the Republic of Panama of persons charged with the commitment of crimes, felonies or misdemeanors without said zone and for the pursuit, capture, imprisonment, detention and delivery without said zone to the authorities of the United States of persons charged with the commitment of crimes, felonies and misdemeanors within said zone and auxiliary lands . . .

ARTICLE XVIII

The Canal, when constructed, and the entrances thereto shall be neutral in perpetuity, and shall be opened upon the terms provided for by Section I of Article three of, and in conformity with all the stipulations of, the treaty entered into by the Governments of the United States and Great Britain on November 18, 1901.

ARTICLE XIX

The Government of the Republic of Panama shall have the right to transport over the Canal its vessels and its troops and munitions of war in such vessels at all times without paying charges of any kind. The exemption is to be extended to the auxiliary railway for the transportation of persons in the service of the Republic of Panama, or of the police force charged with the preservation of public order outside of said zone, as well as to their baggage, munitions of war and supplies.

ARTICLE XX

If by virtue of any existing treaty in relation to the territory of the Isthmus of Panama, whereof the obligations shall descend or be assumed by the Republic of Panama, there may be any privilege or concession in favor of the Government or the citizens and subjects of a third power relative to an interoceanic means of communication which in any of its terms may be incompatible with the terms of the present convention, the Republic of Panama agrees to cancel or modify such treaty in due form, for which purpose it shall give to the said third power the requisite notification within the term of four months from the date of the present convention, and in case the existing treaty contains no clause permitting its modification or annulment, the Republic of Panama agrees to procure its modification or annulment in such form that there shall not exist any conflict with the stipulations of the present convention.

ARTICLE XXI

The rights and privileges granted by the Republic of Panama to the United States in the preceding Articles are understood to be free of all anterior debts, liens, trusts, or liabilities, or concessions or privileges to other Governments, corporations, syndicates or individuals, and consequently, if there should arise any claims on account of the present concessions and privileges or otherwise, the claimants shall resort to the Government of the Republic of Panama and not to the United States for any indemnity or compromise which may be required.

ARTICLE XXII

The Republic of Panama renounces and grants to the United States the participation to which it might be entitled in the future earnings of the Canal under Article XV of the concessionary contract with Lucien N. B. Wyse now owned by the New Panama Canal Company and any and all other rights or claims of a pecuniary nature arising under or relating to said concession, or arising under or relating to the concessions to the Panama Railroad Company or any extension or modification thereof; and it likewise renounces, confirms and grants to the United States, now and hereafter, all the rights and property reserved in the said concessions which otherwise would belong to Panama at or before the expiration of the terms of ninety-nine years of the concessions granted to or held by the above mentioned party and companies, and all right, title and interest which it now has or many hereafter have, in and to the lands, canal, works, property and rights held by the said companies under said concessions or otherwise, and acquired or to be acquired by the United States from or through the New Panama Canal Company, including any property and rights which might or may in the future either by lapse of time, forfeiture or otherwise, revert to the Republic of Panama, under any contracts or concessions, with said Wyse, the Universal Panama Canal Company, the Panama Railroad Company and the New Panama Canal Company.

The aforesaid rights and property shall be and are free and released from any present or reversionary interest in or claims of Panama and the title of the United States thereto upon consummation of the contemplated purchase by the United States from the New Panama Canal Company, shall be absolute, so far as concerns the Republic of Panama, excepting always the rights of the Republic specifically secured under this treaty.

ARTICLE XXIII

If it should become necessary at any time to employ armed forces for the safety or protection of the Canal, or of the ships that make use of the same, or the railways and auxiliary works, the United States shall have the right, at all times and in its discretion, to use its police and its land and naval forces or to establish fortifications for these purposes.

ARTICLE XXIV

No change either in the Government or in the laws and treaties of the Republic of Panama shall, without the consent of the United States, affect any right of the United States under the present convention, or under any treaty stipulation between the two countries that now exists or may hereafter exist touching the subject matter of this convention.

If the Republic of Panama shall hereafter enter as a constituent into any other Government or into any union or confederation of states, so as to merge her sovereignty or independence in such Government, union or confederation, the rights of the United States under this convention shall not be in any respect lessened or impaired.

ARTICLE XXV

For the better performance of the engagements of this convention and to the end of the efficient protection of the Canal and the preservation of its neutrality, the Government of the Republic of Panama will sell or lease to the United States lands adequate and necessary for naval or coaling stations on the Pacific coast and on the western Caribbean coast of the Republic at certain points to be agreed upon with the President of the United States.

ARTICLE XXVI

This convention when signed by the Plenipotentiaries of the Contracting Parties shall be ratified by the respective Governments and the ratifications shall be exchanged at Washington at the earliest date possible.

In faith whereof the respective Plenipotentiaries have signed the present convention in duplicate and have hereunto affixed their respective seals.

Done at the City of Washington the 18th day of November in the year of our Lord nineteen hundred and three.

John Hay [Seal]

P. Bunau-Varilla [Seal]

Source: U.S. Stats., vol. 33, in Sklar, Barry, and Virginia M. Hagen, compilers, *Inter-American Relations:*

Collection of Documents, Legislation, Descriptions of Inter-American Organizations, and Other Material Pertaining to Inter-American Affairs. Washington, DC: Government Printing Office, 1972.

U.S. Apology for the Overthrow of the Kingdom of Hawaii (November 23, 1993)

During the late nineteenth century, wealthy American settlers established large sugar, cattle, and other plantations in the Hawaiian Islands (then known as the Sandwich Islands). When native Hawaiian supporters of Queen Liliuokalani attempted to confirm their independence through a new constitution in 1893, the settlers responded with a coup, supported by the United States, which quickly annexed the islands. One hundred years later, a resolution of Congress, which laid out some of the details of this coup and annexation, apologized for these events. The resolution was written to commemorate the hundredth anniversary of the January 17, 1893, overthrow of the Kingdom of Hawaii and to apologize to the Native Hawaiians on behalf of the government of the United States. However, the resolution made clear that the apology did not affect land claims and certainly not Hawaii's status as the fiftieth state, despite the remarks of U.S. Senator Slade Gorton, an opponent of the bill, that "the logical consequences of this resolution would be independence."

Whereas, prior to the arrival of the first Europeans in 1778, the Native Hawaiian people lived in a highly organized, self-sufficient, subsistent social system based on communal land tenure with a sophisticated language, culture, and religion;

Whereas, a unified monarchical government of the Hawaiian Islands was established in 1810 under Kamehameha I, the first King of Hawaii;

Whereas, from 1826 until 1893, the United States recognized the independence of the Kingdom of Hawaii, extended full and complete diplomatic recognition to the Hawaiian Government, and entered into treaties and conventions with the Hawaiian monarchs to govern commerce and navigation in 1826, 1842, 1849, 1875, and 1887;

Whereas, the Congregational Church (now known as the United Church of Christ), through its American Board of Commissioners for Foreign

Missions, sponsored and sent more than 100 missionaries to the Kingdom of Hawaii between 1820 and 1850;

Whereas, on January 14, 1893, John L. Stevens (hereafter referred to in this Resolution as the "United States Minister"), the United States Minister assigned to the sovereign and independent Kingdom of Hawaii, conspired with a small group of non-Hawaiian residents of the Kingdom of Hawaii, including citizens of the United States, to overthrow the indigenous and lawful Government of Hawaii;

Whereas, in pursuance of the conspiracy to overthrow the Government of Hawaii, the United States Minister and the naval representatives of the United States caused armed naval forces of the United States to invade the sovereign Hawaiian nation on January 16, 1893, and to position themselves near the Hawaiian Government buildings and the Iolani Palace to intimidate Queen Liliuokalani and her Government;

Whereas, on the afternoon of January 17,1893, a Committee of Safety that represented the American and European sugar planters, descendants of missionaries, and financiers deposed the Hawaiian monarchy and proclaimed the establishment of a Provisional Government;

Whereas, the United States Minister thereupon extended diplomatic recognition to the Provisional Government that was formed by the conspirators without the consent of the Native Hawaiian people or the lawful Government of Hawaii and in violation of treaties between the two nations and of international law;

Whereas, soon thereafter, when informed of the risk of bloodshed with resistance, Queen Liliuokalani issued the following statement yielding her authority to the United States Government rather than to the Provisional Government:

"I Liliuokalani, by the Grace of God and under the Constitution of the Hawaiian Kingdom, Queen, do hereby solemnly protest against any and all acts done against myself and the Constitutional Government of the Hawaiian Kingdom by certain persons claiming to have established a Provisional Government of and for this Kingdom.

"That I yield to the superior force of the United States of America whose Minister Plenipotentiary, His Excellency John L. Stevens, has caused United States troops to be landed at Honolulu and declared that he would support the Provisional Government.

"Now to avoid any collision of armed forces, and perhaps the loss of life, I do this under protest and impelled by said force yield my authority until such time as the Government of the United States shall, upon facts being presented to it, undo the action of its representatives and reinstate me in the authority which I claim as the Constitutional Sovereign of the Hawaiian Islands."

Done at Honolulu this 17th day of January, A.D. 1893.

Whereas, without the active support and intervention by the United States diplomatic and military representatives, the insurrection against the Government of Queen Liliuokalani would have failed for lack of popular support and insufficient arms;

Whereas, on February 1, 1893, the United States Minister raised the American flag and proclaimed Hawaii to be a protectorate of the United States;

Whereas, the report of a Presidentially established investigation conducted by former Congressman James Blount into the events surrounding the insurrection and overthrow of January 17, 1893, concluded that the United States diplomatic and military representatives had abused their authority and were responsible for the change in government;

Whereas, as a result of this investigation, the United States Minister to Hawaii was recalled from his diplomatic post and the military commander of the United States armed forces stationed in Hawaii was disciplined and forced to resign his commission;

Whereas, in a message to Congress on December 18, 1893, President Grover Cleveland reported fully and accurately on the illegal acts of the conspirators, described such acts as an "act of war, committed with the participation of a diplomatic representative of the United States and without authority of Congress," and acknowledged that by such acts the government of a peaceful and friendly people was overthrown;

Whereas, President Cleveland further concluded that a "substantial wrong has thus been done which a due regard for our national character as well as the rights of the injured people requires we should endeavor to repair" and called for the restoration of the Hawaiian monarchy;

Whereas, the Provisional Government protested President Cleveland's call for the restoration of the monarchy and continued to hold state power and pursue annexation to the United States;

Whereas, the Provisional Government successfully lobbied the Committee on Foreign Relations of the Senate (hereafter referred to in this Resolution as the "Committee") to conduct a new investigation into the events surrounding the overthrow of the monarchy;

Whereas, the Committee and its chairman, Senator John Morgan, conducted hearings in Washington, D.C., from December 27, 1893, through February 26, 1894, in which members of the Provisional Government justified and condoned the actions of the United States Minister and recommended annexation of Hawaii;

Whereas, although the Provisional Government was able to obscure the role of the United States in the illegal overthrow of the Hawaiian monarchy, it was unable to rally the support from two-thirds of the Senate needed to ratify a treaty of annexation;

Whereas, on July 4, 1894, the Provisional Government declared itself to be the Republic of Hawaii;

Whereas, on January 24, 1895, while imprisoned in Iolani Palace, Queen Liliuokalani was forced by representatives of the Republic of Hawaii to officially abdicate her throne;

Whereas, in the 1896 United States Presidential election, William McKinley replaced Grover Cleveland;

Whereas, on July 7, 1898, as a consequence of the Spanish-American War, President McKinley signed the Newlands Joint Resolution that provided for the annexation of Hawaii;

Whereas, through the Newlands Resolution, the self-declared Republic of Hawaii ceded sovereignty over the Hawaiian Islands to the United States;

Whereas, the Republic of Hawaii also ceded 1,800,000 acres of crown, government and public lands of the Kingdom of Hawaii, without the consent of or compensation to the Native Hawaiian people of Hawaii or their sovereign government;

Whereas, the Congress, through the Newlands Resolution, ratified the cession, annexed Hawaii as part of the United States, and vested title to the lands in Hawaii in the United States;

Whereas, the Newlands Resolution also specified that treaties existing between Hawaii and foreign nations were to immediately cease and be replaced by United States treaties with such nations;

Whereas, the Newlands Resolution effected the transaction between the Republic of Hawaii and the United States Government;

Whereas, the indigenous Hawaiian people never directly relinquished their claims to their inherent sovereignty as a people or over their national lands to the United States, either through their monarchy or through a plebiscite or referendum;

Whereas, on April 30, 1900, President McKinley signed the Organic Act that provided a government for the territory of Hawaii and defined the political structure and powers of the newly established Territorial Government and its relationship to the United States;

Whereas, on August 21, 1959, Hawaii became the 50th State of the United States;

Whereas, the health and well-being of the Native Hawaiian people is intrinsically tied to their deep feelings and attachment to the land;

Whereas, the long-range economic and social changes in Hawaii over the nineteenth and early twentieth centuries have been devastating to the population and to the health and well-being of the Hawaiian people;

Whereas, the Native Hawaiian people are determined to preserve, develop and transmit to future generations their ancestral territory, and their cultural identity in accordance with their own spiritual and traditional beliefs, customs, practices, language, and social institutions;

Whereas, in order to promote racial harmony and cultural understanding, the Legislature of the State of Hawaii has determined that the year 1993, should serve Hawaii as a year of special reflection on the rights and dignities of the Native Hawaiians in the Hawaiian and the American societies;

Whereas, the Eighteenth General Synod of the United Church of Christ in recognition of the denomination's historical complicity in the illegal overthrow of the Kingdom of Hawaii in 1893 directed the Office of the President of the United Church of Christ to offer a public apology to the Native Hawaiian people and to initiate the process of reconciliation between the United Church of Christ and the Native Hawaiians; and

Whereas, it is proper and timely for the Congress on the occasion of the impending one hundredth anniversary of the event, to acknowledge the historic significance of the illegal overthrow of the Kingdom of Hawaii, to express its deep regret to the Native Hawaiian people, and to support the reconciliation efforts of the State of Hawaii and the United Church of Christ with Native Hawaiians;

Now, therefore, be it

Resolved by the Senate and House of Representatives of the United States of America in Congress assembled,

SECTION 1. Acknowledgment and Apology.

The Congress—

(1) on the occasion of the 100th anniversary of the illegal overthrow of the Kingdom of Hawaii on January 17, 1893, acknowledges the historical significance of this event which resulted in the suppression of the inherent sovereignty of the Native Hawaiian people;

(2) recognizes and commends efforts of reconciliation initiated by the State of Hawaii and the United Church of Christ with Native Hawaiians;

(3) apologizes to Native Hawaiians on behalf of the people of the United States for the overthrow of the Kingdom of Hawaii on January 17, 1893 with the participation of agents and citizens of the United States, and the deprivation of the rights of Native Hawaiians to self-determination;

(4) expresses its commitment to acknowledge the ramifications of the overthrow of the Kingdom of Hawaii, in order to provide a proper foundation for reconciliation between the United States and the Native Hawaiian people; and

(5) urges the President of the United States to also acknowledge the ramifications of the overthrow of the Kingdom of Hawaii and to support reconciliation efforts between the United States and the Native Hawaiian people.

SEC. 2. Definitions.

As used in this Joint Resolution, the term "Native Hawaiians" means any individual who is a descendent of the aboriginal people who, prior to 1778, occupied and exercised sovereignty in the area that now constitutes the State of Hawaii.

SEC. 3. Disclaimer.

Nothing in this Joint Resolution is intended to serve as a settlement of any claims against the United States.

Approved November 23, 1993.

Source: U.S. Public Law 103–150, November 23, 1993.
Legislative History—S.J. Res. 19: Senate Reports: No. 103–125 (Select Committee on Indian Affairs), *Congressional Record* 139 (1993).

INDEX